LEGAL ESSAYS IN TRIBUTE TO ORRIN KIP McMURRAY

ORRIN KIP McMURRAY

LEGAL ESSAYS

In Tribute to

ORRIN KIP McMURRAY

EDITED BY

MAX RADIN AND A. M. KIDD

Published for
University of California
Law School Association

UNIVERSITY OF CALIFORNIA PRESS
BERKELEY, CALIFORNIA
1935

UNIVERSITY OF CALIFORNIA PRESS
BERKELEY, CALIFORNIA

CAMBRIDGE UNIVERSITY PRESS
LONDON, ENGLAND

BY SAMUEL T. FARQUHAR, UNIVERSITY PRINTER

CONTENTS

CONTENTS

CONTENTS

CONTENTS

CONTENTS

CONTENTS

FOREWORD

There are those to whom a teacher's work consists in testing by questions the student's memory of the contents of a book; others, who have had the good fortune to know a real teacher, appreciate that his success lies not in his ability to expound the isolated facts of a subject, but rather in his ability to reveal the relations of the subject to the past and present life of man and to penetrate deeper and deeper into the conflicts and mysteries of life in the field of its development that is his special province. The ways in which a man does these things are often intangible and elusive; but they are begotten of a substantial background of history and experience, combined with a rich imagination. As Dean McMurray has observed: "With all its faults, the college of letters opens to sentient beings with the intelligence to receive it some vision of science and civilization. As Sir Walter Scott says: 'A lawyer without history and literature is a mechanic, a mere working mason; if he possesses some knowledge of these, he may venture to call himself an architect.' If the law of the more or less static society in which Scott lived, demanded for its true comprehension studies beyond the technique of practice, what of a legal system in a dynamic state of society like ours?"

That Orrin Kip McMurray possesses in full measure these tectonic qualities, no one can question. Born in San Francisco in 1869, he attended the Urban School, where the emphasis was on the humanistic side of Latin and English literature. In 1890 he received from the University of California the degree of bachelor of philosophy, with honors as the most distinguished student of his class. For him the academic training in Latin, literature, history and the other social sciences, was both a foundation on which to build and a treasure house from which to draw at need. Almost any of his writings is enriched with apposite quotations from Burke, De Quincey, Macaulay, Bagehot, De Tocqueville, Montesquieu, Savigny, Hegel, Hooker, Browning, Matthew Arnold, Dicey, Shaw, Chesterton, and others; and their use is no empty display of erudition; they come spontaneously to suggest an idea or give the felicitous turn to a sentence.

After obtaining the degree of bachelor of laws from the Hastings College of the Law in 1893, he practiced for ten uninterrupted years in San Francisco—a fruitful experience. In those years he gained familiarity with the personnel and traditions of the bar and an encyclopedic knowledge of California law; he gained also his distinctive keen appreciation of the practical considerations that influence legal rules and judicial opinions. General practice reveals to the receptive mind the complexity of the world of legal relations, the impossibility of solving them by the application of academic formulae, the effects upon the law's administration of business customs, personality of judges, habit patterns, and a perplexing complex of influences that cannot be defined. It might be said of the Dean as he has said of Justice Field: "One of the elements of his strength as a jurist lay in the fact that he made life into law; that he would never have been so great a judge had he not been a man with a mind sensitive to experience.... The jurist, no less than the poet or the painter or the sculptor, though subject of course to different limitations, embodies forth his own experience. The mere closet philosopher, the arid compiler of precedent, the mechanical repeater of legal formulae, never creates law, never embodies in legal institutions the needs of mankind struggling for utterance."

In 1903 the practicing lawyer was called to the School of Jurisprudence of the University of California. His own formal training he had received in the early nineties, when law-school training in California was not good; when one instructor, with the book before him, would require the student to name the incorporeal hereditaments in the order in which Blackstone enumerated them. Paradoxical as it may seem, however, the poverty of his formal instruction had proved for him a blessing. For he had approached the law with the originality and freshness of a mind that was free from the bias of premature exposure to the partial views persuasively developed by brilliant theorists. As he remarked in his introductory note to the *California Law Review* (in 1912): "The trouble with great thinkers, John Bright once said, is that they usually think wrong."

The greater number of legal scholars specialize in a particular field and build up within it a system. Such a system, however, is an artificial creation, not the living body of the law which continually bursts through the forms in which jurists attempt to confine it. The McMurray method can be compared to the projection of pictures from a sensitive film which shows us the image of a reality that we cannot, unaided, see. By this method is exhibited the living law, not dead rules.

One is as much amazed at the variety of subjects that are dealt with in Dean McMurray's articles, addresses, notes, and book reviews, as at the originality of the ideas, together with the lucidity and felicity of their expression. If there is one note more dominant than others, it is the relation of law to life. This note is heard in the brilliant study of seventy-five years of California Jurisprudence read to the State Bar, in the presidential address read to the Association of American Law Schools, and in the study, "Liberty of Testation and Some Modern Limitations Thereon." It is sounded conspicuously in the analyses of the defects of procedure, also in the exposition of needed improvements therein. Some of these, moreover, in the capacity of a member of governmental charter and constitutional commissions, he has been able to put into the law. He is no apologist for laws that cannot be justified by their effect on human relations. One could multiply indefinitely from his writings quotations such as the following, in which a particular decision or statute is related to the life of the past or present.

Conceding the truth of the subtle connection between institutions and external forms, it may well be doubted whether the twentieth century man is much affected by the "mysterious dignity" of the courts. He has no particular reverence for the wig and gown, which he regards rather as anachronisms than as solemn symbols. Respect for law must find a wider basis upon which to rest than is afforded by a reverence for mere external incidents or even for the abstract conception of a set of forms absolutely moulding and determining human conduct.

Now that the theory of sovereignty exemplified in Prussian political philosophy has been so thoroughly discredited, is it not desirable that the whole question of the liability of the State and its political sub-divisions for wrongs done to individuals should be re-examined? It is indeed strange that England and America, the homes of political liberty, should harbor the doctrine of non-liability of the sovereign—a theory long discarded in the legislation of continental Europe.

Children may not, under the terms of the act, be taught at home by a tutor, or other person (in which term presumably would be included mothers and fathers), in lieu of attendance on a public school or a private day time school, unless the "tutor or other person" holds a valid state credential for the grade taught.... No future John Stuart Mill, Herbert Spencer, or John Ruskin will be taught by "uncertified" parents in California, if the act is to be literally interpreted.

"When, in the judgment of the state board of education, there exists sufficient evidence that a text book listed by said board contains sectarian or denominational doctrine contrary to law or contains propaganda injurious to the welfare of the public schools, said board shall cause the book to be investigated by a committee of impartial experts...." Of course, it has always been true that text books have been selected by some one responsible for the task, and all of us carry with us almost ineradicable opinions gathered from early reading and teaching. But when such matters are left more or less to accident, the prejudices thus acquired are likely to be balanced or possibly tempered by contact with others who have acquired a different set of likes and dislikes. The idea of putting into statutory form such a provision as that just cited seems to give much force to Henry Adams' cynical remark that education is the organization of prejudice.

If we contrast the opening of the twentieth century with the opening of the nineteenth, the difference is amazing. Water supply, sanitation, police protection, fire protection, elementary education, these commonest necessities of our daily life, in 1800 either did not exist at all, even in our largest cities, or if they existed were of the most primitive and elemental sort. The individual was free to go through life without the constant interference of organized society. He was also free to live in ignorance and to die from preventable epidemics.

An interesting clause, retained in our present constitution, is the provision disqualifying parties and seconds in a duel from holding office or enjoying the suffrage, which seems to have been borrowed from the Texas constitution. It is by no means clear that this clause ever produced any effect; the early history of the state was characterized by an enormous number of duels in proportion to the population. The practice died out because it became the fashion not to issue or accept challenges to duels, not because of the written law. The fate of duelling provokes the thought that fashion may produce deeper effects in the evolution of jurisprudence and the alteration of society than the most Draconian code, unsupported by opinion.

Yet there is never lost to sight the importance of clear legal thinking, and the social value of adherence to the complex rules which must necessarily govern a complex civilization. When a court ignorantly confuses fundamental legal relations, the comment in the Dean's inimitable reviews of current decisions shows a trace of exasperation. "The dictum to the effect that a highway may be gained either 'by prescription' or by 'implied dedication' is of a sort further to darken judgment in the whole field of prescriptive rights."

For thirty years Orrin Kip McMurray has been a living part of the School of Jurisprudence of the University of California as a teacher and, in addition, since 1923 as the School's beloved Dean. From him his students have indeed learned technical law; but they have learned much more. Many of them have found in the Dean's offhand remarks, his obiter dicta, richer wisdom than in all the formal legal doctrine expounded by others. This volume is a gift from students and colleagues, in this and other countries, in commemoration and in grateful appreciation of the scholar and in love and affection for the man.

SOME SUGGESTIONS CONCERNING THE CALIFORNIA LAW OF RIPARIAN RIGHTS

BY JOSEPH W. BINGHAM

IN THE DEVELOPMENT of the law of water rights, the Supreme Court of California has a record of constructive juridical accomplishment unexcelled by that of any other court in the United States. It is a long and honorable record, including many controversies with important interests and eminent counsel arrayed on each side, and many determinations which precedents had not made obvious and which required a measure of judicial statesmanship. A reference only to three of these cases, *Lux v. Haggin*,[1*] *Katz v. Walkinshaw*,[2] and *Antioch v. Williams Irrig. Dist.*,[3] will suffice to illustrate and emphasize this statement. In the course of solution of problems of riparian rights, of appropriation, and of underground waters, the court has not only evolved a coherent system for California, but also has produced precedents that have had great influence on the law of other states.

Neither perfection nor permanence is attainable in social institutions, and therefore it is not surprising, even in view of the great labor, logical thought, and ingenuity spent in developing the water law of California, that it now is under bitter attack at many points. If there were no other reason for adverse criticism, the great changes in social and economic conditions in the state since the turn of the century would have brought a demand for a corresponding change in the law. As the state has increased in population and industry the uses of the water resources have increased until there has arisen a pressing need for measures of economy and coördinated adjustment of uses. Likewise there has been a shifting of the relative importance to the state of various sorts of competing demands on some of the sources of supply. Consequently we have in near prospect the adoption of a scheme or schemes for works designed to permit more efficient use of some of our streams and to serve at once meritorious competing claims. The

* Superior figures refer to notes following the text of each essay.

hope of engineers—a comprehensive, scientific plan of development and conservation, with an adjustment of uses in some order of economic merit unhampered by technical vested rights of little public advantage—is still a pious hope only; but at least a beginning of the passage from the chaos of casual individual initiative and insistent competing claims will soon be made. In this period of dissatisfaction and discussion, some comment on certain undesirable uses of our present water law and some suggestions of remedies may be of interest.

Elementary knowledge of the common law of riparian rights is part of the professional equipment of all well trained lawyers. It is generally known also that riparian rights are recognized by the law of California and that it supports another large and even more important class of water rights called appropriation rights. In the opinion of most engineers the system of appropriation of water is better adapted to satisfy the needs of the people of our western states than is the riparian right system. Indeed they believe that the California courts have caused much economic loss and much confusion in the law by adopting the system of riparian rights, instead of discarding it as the courts of Colorado, Nevada, Utah, Wyoming, Montana, Idaho, New Mexico, and Arizona have done. However, there are strong advocates of riparian rights, among whom may be mentioned for his zeal, Mr. Samuel C. Wiel, author of the well-known textbook *Water Rights in the Western States*. It does not lie within the purposes of this essay to enter the debate over this point of legal history. The essay takes the water law as it finds it, with the riparian system established beyond controversy, and will attempt to show some detrimental effects of the system upon development of the uses of our streams and to suggest how, to some degree, these effects may be avoided.

It will aid my purpose to direct attention to the salient differences between a riparian right and an appropriation right. Independently of legislation an appropriation right is initiated by an expression of intention to put water from a certain source of supply to a definite use. The use must be made within a reasonable time, or the priority of the right will not date from the initiation of the project, but only from use of the water. The right does not depend on possession of land. It is a right to use for the appropriation purpose at any place, near the stream or far from it. Diversions or uses of the stream which do not actually interfere with a prior appropriation use will not violate the prior appropriation right.[4]

In all these respects a riparian right differs from an appropriation right. The title to a riparian right does not include use of the water or intention to use, but is simply the possession of riparian land—that is, land in contact with the stream or other source of supply. Independently of prescription or other special acquisition, an upper or lower diverter or user obtains no priority over a riparian because of priority of use.[5] This is a defect in our water law, in the opinion of most irrigation engineers, since it denies to an early developer of an irrigation project protection against a much later riparian use.[6] The law of prescription mitigates this hardship for prior upstream diverters, and the period of prescription in California is short—five years—but prior diverters downstream generally cannot gain a prescriptive title against an upper riparian, since their use will not be adverse—*i.e.*, wrongful—as against the upper riparian, and prescription in California law is founded on adverse use.[7] However, a riparian right pertains only to uses on riparian land. Uses elsewhere than on the particular riparian land to which the right throughout its duration is inseparably attached, cannot be protected or justified under it.[8] This is a point of considerable weight in appraising the value of a riparian right in eminent domain proceedings or in computing damages for violation of such a right. It has importance also in other phases of controversies between riparian and non-riparian users.

In estimating the effect of California water law upon the use of streams it is convenient to start with the premise that, except so far as their natural rights have been postponed or extinguished by prescription, condemnation, release, reservation, contract, or other specific adverse titular fact, the riparian possessors have the first priorities of private use of these water resources. But it is also important for the purposes of this article to emphasize the limitations of these prior riparian rights. The natural rights of the riparians extend to as much of the flow of the stream as can be beneficially used on the riparian lands, but no farther. This limitation is implicit in any sensible apprehension of the riparian doctrine and I believe is well established by

California decisions, but it has not always been clearly perceived and there are many loose statements in judicial opinions and in textbooks which may seem opposed to it. One of the chief objectives of this article is to demonstrate the validity of the limitation and its value for obviating some of the uneconomic riparian opposition to development of uses of the water resources of the state.

One of the most frequent expressions concerning riparian rights is that the riparian is entitled to the flow of the water by his land as it was wont to flow without material (sometimes the word "sensible" or "perceptible" is used) diminution or alteration. *"Aqua currit et debet currere ut currere solebat"* is the Latin maxim which is quoted to add the dignity of antique learning to this dogma. There is truth behind the dogma, of course, else it would not be so often repeated, but it expresses only a fragment or phase of that truth. It is not a definition of the riparian right, but a preliminary observation on it which needs much elaboration and qualification before a correct statement of the law will be completed. A riparian is entitled to the stream as it was wont to flow, but his right so casually indicated is subject to various limitations, qualifications, and exceptions of which this dogma gives no hint. Nevertheless we find it repeated even in the opinions of cases between two riparians, and sometimes given the credit of being an accurate expression of the law of England and the eastern states.[9] Yet the law of the eastern states and England does not differ in general on this point from the law of California, and it is as easy to find cases in those jurisdictions as in California in which one riparian is permitted to alter materially the flow of a stream for riparian use as against another riparian without liability.[10] Indeed the riparian doctrine does not concede to the lowest riparian a fuller right of use against the upper riparian than the upper riparian may claim against him, as seems to be implied in the dogma. The rights of riparians *inter se* are correlative and entitle them to proportional shares in the uses of the stream. The upper possessor's use may thus quite materially diminish the flow of the stream and yet he will have a valid defense against the lower riparian if he can establish that his use is no more than his proper share.[11] Furthermore, so far as one of the riparian possessors is not using or benefiting from the stream to the maximum permitted him under his correlative right, the uses of the other riparians on their riparian lands may be extended without liability.[12] These well established points should suffice to dissipate entirely the hasty apprehension that a riparian, regardless of present use on or benefit to his riparian land or possibility of such use or benefit in the future, is entitled to have the stream flow as it was wont to flow. This is not, and never has been, the law of England or of any American state, so far as I know. In support of an opinion contrary to mine can be cited only such loose, general statements as I have indicated above; against a contrary opinion there are numerous well decided cases from many jurisdictions.[13]

If there were a general definite realization and acknowledgment that at common law the principle of beneficial use applies to all water rights and therefore to riparian rights as well as appropriation rights, the lawyer's, the judge's, and the legislator's task of determining and developing the water law of the state would be much simplified. It is true that commonly riparian possessors have prior rights in the streams of the state, but these rights are only rights of use on or for the benefit of the riparian lands to which the rights pertain.[14] They are not rights of arbitrary monopoly and do not support an insistence on economic waste. Therefore the extent of the priority of the riparian possessors as against competing subsequent non-riparian rights of use is properly determinable by reference to the possibility of use on or benefit to the riparian lands.

In the light of this fundamental idea, the decisions of our state supreme court in cases involving conflicting riparian and non-riparian claims to flood waters are easily understood and reconciled, and in turn these cases admirably illustrate and support the principle which I have emphasized.[15] Nevertheless they have puzzled many lawyers. In conversation with experts in water law and in the arguments of cases, and even in some judicial opinions, I encounter a confused impression of the purport of these precedents. Generally the confusion seems to proceed from an assumption that essentially the decisions turn on some occult distinction between flood waters and the "ordinary flow of the stream." Some of the language in the opinions may inspire or encourage the assumption, but a careful comparison of decisions and distinguishing of issues should dissipate it entirely.

It is true that the riparian right does not extend to water which is not considered part of the flow of the watercourse, but is "surface water," although that surface water may contribute to the flow of the stream.[16] Accordingly, if floods overflow the banks of the stream and spread over the surrounding country, such parts of this flood water as become stagnant or do not move along with the stream in its general course, are "surface waters" as distinguished from stream waters, and therefore are not subject to riparian rights. Nevertheless riparian rights do extend to overflow waters which still move with the stream in its course.[17] The reason that in some cases diversion of such flood waters has been held not to infringe a riparian priority, is that the diversion left enough water in the stream to satisfy all possible uses of the riparians. Indeed the opinions commonly emphasize that the flood waters were a detriment and not a benefit to the riparians and that the diversion therefore was a benefit as far as the scope of riparian use was concerned.[18] In the leading case of *Miller & Lux v. Madera Canal & Irrig. Co.*,[19] on the contrary, the riparian claim was supported on the ground that the floods benefited the riparian lands.

On principle it should make no difference that the flood contributing to a water course was unusual or casual, instead of "ordinary," or "natural," or "recurring," and it is submitted that any such distinction in the law would be very difficult of application under the climatic conditions of California. It would tend to become vague and illusive and would merely furnish an additional constant ground for litigation. Yet generally the opinions, in cases in which a riparian's claim to flood waters against an appropriator is upheld, emphasize not only the fact that the waters were useful to the riparian, but also that the floods were "natural," "ordinary," and "recurring." The causes of this, I think, are the fact that the principle of possible use or benefit has not often been firmly stated as the foundation of the determination of the extent of riparian rights, and a passing confusion of the two distinct questions in cases like *Miller & Lux v. Madera Canal & Irrig. Co.* Those two distinct questions are: (1) Are the flood waters part of the flow of the stream or are they vagrant surface waters to which riparian rights do not extend? (2) Granted that the flood waters are a part of the stream, will diversion of them be a detriment to the riparians? If the flood waters are not part of the stream but are segregated from it, rights do not extend to them, and frequently there are such waters in casual or "unusual" floods. If the waters are part of the flow of the stream, their being flood water besides has a bearing only so far as it supports the argument that they are not a benefit, but perhaps rather a detriment to riparians.

Applying the fundamental principle of beneficial use, we may outline the priority of riparians against subsequent appropriators by the following formula. First, determine all uses and benefits on or to the riparian lands which might be derived from the stream (without improper waste). This includes prospective possible as well as actual present uses and benefits. So much of the flow of the stream as would be necessary to supply these uses and benefits if they were all presently required is given over to the priority of the riparians as against appropriators. As a matter of convenience let us now adopt a phrase to which we attach a technical meaning that should be remembered carefully throughout our subsequent discussion. The phrase is "material alteration of the stream." Any artificial change in the stream which renders it less usable or beneficial to the riparians, that is, which leaves it insufficient to afford all the riparian uses and benefits which might be derived from it if the fullest possible uses were being demanded presently on all the riparian lands, is a "material alteration of the stream." Any change which leaves the stream as sufficient as before in this sense is an immaterial alteration. If the immaterial alteration is a permanent diversion of part of the water of the stream, we may say that it is a diversion of surplus water, which can be taken by an appropriator without an infringement of riparian rights. It is, then, only a *material* alteration of the stream in this sense which raises a cause of action in favor of a riparian.[20]

If there is a material artificial alteration of a stream as it flows by riparian land, the riparian possessor has *prima facie* a cause of action against the person responsible although the change has not resulted in present detriment to a riparian use.[21] Against the *prima facie* cause of action, however, there may exist any of various nullifications. The person responsible may have a superiority of title and priority covering the alteration by prescription, release, contract, estoppel, or condemnation under eminent domain, or he may be a co-riparian who has caused the alteration as a necessary incident of his fair share of riparian use of the stream. Indeed, if he has caused the alteration by use on riparian lands only and claims under the riparian right pertaining to those lands, he has a complete defense no matter how much he alters the stream without present damage to the opposing riparian interest, for a riparian, so far as his co-riparian would have no present use or benefit from the stream, may increase his riparian use accordingly without liability.[22] Correlatively, as other riparian uses increase, the particular riparian may have to diminish his prior use to avoid liability, for co-riparians originally have equal priorities.[23] Similarly, as between two appropriators, the prior cannot maintain a claim to continued flow of the stream if he does not need it for his appropriation use.[24] Damage to his appropriation use is an element of a cause of action in his favor. Beneficial use is the foundation, measure, and limit of the appropriation right. But if the stream is materially altered at riparian land by an appropriation use which is subsequent in priority to the riparian right, the riparian at common law has a cause of action against the person responsible although there is no present damage to the riparian interest.[25] This rule that present damage is not an element in a riparian's cause of action against a non-riparian is a troublesome feature of California water law on which I proceed to offer some suggestions.

If as between co-riparians and as between two appropriators of different priorities an alteration of the stream will not be actionable unless the plaintiff suffers actual damage, why should a riparian have a cause of action against a non-riparian (appropriator) although the non-riparian diversion has not caused damage to the plaintiff? Would it not be better policy for the law to permit an appropriator to use the stream so long as the riparians are not actually damaged? What possible justification is there for assessing liability against an appropriator for putting to use water which otherwise would run to waste? The answer to these questions lies partly in knowledge of the origin of this rule of liability and partly in appreciation of its purpose and limitations.

The origin of the rule was not a desire to give a monopoly of the stream to riparians against non-riparians regardless of present needs.

It is part of the history of the English law of prescription. In the greater number of American states today one element of a good prescriptive title is adverse use for the prescriptive period—and an adverse use in this sense generally is a wrongful use.[26] But this was not so in the early English law of prescription. Under that law, a prescriptive right was founded on use "for time out of mind" and the use needed not to be adverse in the sense mentioned above. In the latter part of the eighteenth century the well-known "lost grant" fiction was devised to broaden the law of prescription by shortening its period to that of the provision of the statute of limitations applying to actions of ejectment. After the adoption of this fiction the courts developed gradually the modern English law of prescription, and concomitantly our American doctrine was developed under which adverse use is generally an element of title. In the first half of the nineteenth century the English law of prescription was still in the flux of development and it was not clear just what qualities a use must have to suffice for a short-term prescriptive title. The great leading case of *Angus v. Dalton*,[27] which played a decisive part in settling the modern English doctrine, had not yet arisen. Therefore, when in this transitory period the leading English cases on the law of riparian rights were decided, in which the question was raised whether damage was an essential element of a riparian's cause of action against a non-riparian, the courts denied that damage was essential and the judges gave as their reason that otherwise the non riparian use might ripen into a prescriptive title before the riparian had legal ground to maintain an action in assertion of his right.[28] Of course, today in most American jurisdictions this argument is of no logical force, because if the use is not adverse prescription will not run, and the use will not be adverse unless it gives a ground of action to the other party. Therefore to say that an action must be given the riparian to prevent prescription running against him, under the American law of prescription, is to put the cart before the horse. If the cause of action is not given, prescription will not run. Nevertheless the decisions in these leading English water right cases have been followed universally in American states, and when a justifying reason is given, it is that of the English opinions, *i.e.*, if an action is not given, prescription may run against the riparian right without a preventive legal remedy.[29] A similar argument, similarly unsound today, might have been advanced to give a prior lower appropriator a right of action against a subsequent upper appropriator diverting from the stream during periods of non-use by the prior appropriator; but here the courts were deciding a new question not covered by precedent exactly in point and they were clear on their law of prescription. No cause of action exists without damage in this situation; and consequently prescription does not run in favor of the upper use since it is not adverse (wrongful).[30]

It should be clear, then, that the legal right of action of a riparian who has suffered no damage is an anachronism. At least judges should cease to justify it by the traditional formula which is nonsense in our modern American law of prescription. The rule may be too well established by precedent to be subject to obliteration, but if its origin, purpose, and proper limitation are clearly perceived, certain pernicious effects can easily be avoided.

There is one argument that might be advanced for maintaining the rule, limited as I shall explain that it is. It is an argument the reverse of the traditional one. In our law of water rights, and in property law in general, the sound old principle applies that what has been done for long without objection should, for that reason, be permitted to continue unless some stronger countervailing argument applies. This is the basic idea of prescription and of many other legal institutions. Now an upper appropriation use may have continued many years before a riparian is damaged and raises an objection. The riparian may not have been using, or other riparian uses may not have been sufficient in the past to bring about a condition in which the added appropriation use causes damage.[31] If after all these years of untroubled use the appropriator suddenly can be enjoined from a continuance, it may be that a great hardship will be visited on him quite contrary to the fundamental principle of law with which I began the argument of this paragraph. Indeed the public interest may be involved because the appropriation use may be a great power project the promoters of which would have to purchase releases from all riparians below, including those who may never have any use for the stream, or face the possibility of successful suits at remote times. This would tend, of course, to increase the cost of the project and therefore the rates of service. To cut down these possibilities of suits in the indefinite future, if releases are not obtained from unobjecting lower riparians, it is arguable that prescription should be caused to run against these riparian claims from the time the appropriation alteration of the stream begins. To accomplish this result, it is necessary to give the riparian a cause of action without the element of present damage, thus making the appropriation use adverse. The same argument is not so strong in respect of the rights of lower appropriators prior to the power project appropriation, because generally an appropriator uses frequently and if the power appropriation is a detriment to this use, the damage will occur soon. Indeed, under our present California law, if an appropriator's non-use continues for a period of three years without reasonable justification, he loses his right by non-use.[32] A riparian, on the contrary, independently of legislation, may hold his riparian right without use for a century or longer and no extinguishment results.[33]

I am not sure, therefore, that the traditional rule giving a riparian a cause of action without present damage is not sound policy, although the traditional reason for it does not fit sensibly into our law. I am sure, however, that the rule should be closely limited to its purpose. How may this limitation be accomplished?

Uniformly the riparian has been given a cause of action against an appropriator of inferior priority whose use materially altered the stream at the plaintiff's land, irrespective of present damage. Uniformly on the representation that such a remedy was necessary to avoid multiplicity of suits and afford adequate relief, the California courts have enjoined the appropriator to cease to cause a material alteration of the stream,[34] unless the appropriator paid the full value of a release of the infringed riparian rights to the plaintiff, in cases in which it was shown that the appropriator possessed eminent domain rights and asserted them by proper procedure or had erected permanent works under circumstances justifying an estoppel against the demand for a permanent unconditional injunction.[35] Clearly if the riparian is entitled to this relief he can force a cessation of the appropriation use above although it has not caused him damage and may never interfere with any use of the stream on his riparian land. This would run counter to the fundamental idea underlying all water law. A stream is a natural resource available for uses. Rights to use should be recognized and protected; but no right should be conceded to a private claimant to prevent a use of the stream which in no way interferes with his use or affects detrimentally his right to use.[36] Rights to demand that the stream flow to waste, when appropriators wish to use it, should not be upheld by the courts. So evidently against public policy are such rights where water is scarce as compared with needs, that law declarers who maintained such absurd claims would be defenseless against the charge of incompetence.[37] It is my belief that our California judges have not established such rights by their decisions and that proper defense by counsel will establish that no riparian is entitled to an injunction merely to prevent defendant from using stream water which otherwise would run to waste. If I am right in this, an appropriator who purposes to alter materially the flow of a natural stream, need not obtain a release from riparians who may never be damaged. He may at his option await the time when damage to the riparian is imminent and then purchase a release. This course obviously will reduce the condemnation charges of a large power project considerably, for many of the riparians will never use water from the stream although they may be quite ready to demand a fancy price from the power company in return for yielding their claim of right to a presently operative injunction. The juridical policy which I advocate would also enable appropriators, who have not eminent domain rights and who cannot force a sale and release of the riparian plaintiff's right, to use for irrigation or other purposes water which otherwise would run unused past riparian lands to waste. The point therefore is of great practical importance and I proceed to establish it by precedent and reason.

What is the purport of the precedents which give to a riparian, who has not been damaged by an appropriator's diversion and who may never have a use for the water, a cause of action at law for nominal damages and also an injunction in equity against a continuance of the diversion? It is clear on the authorities that the purpose of both remedies is to establish and quiet the riparian's priority against the appropriator, and only this.[38] There is no purpose to establish in the riparian an arbitrary, royal prerogative to let the stream run to waste as against attempts to use it on non-riparian land. The right of action at law was given to prevent postponement of the riparian right to the appropriation by prescription before the riparian might have occasion to use the stream. The injunctive relief was conceded in order to quiet the title of the riparian so that he would not have to sue at law periodically. Now it is evident that all this can be accomplished under California procedure by a declaratory decree establishing the priority of the riparian's right to use whenever he shall have occasion to use and enjoining an interference with the riparian use whenever that use arises.[39] This decree will not prevent a continuance of the appropriation use except at times when an infringement of the declared riparian priority of use would result. Thus the purpose of protecting the riparian priority is accomplished without violating the fundamental principle of our water law, *i.e.*, no waste of our water resources is included in private water rights. This is the solution of the problem adopted in the leading case of *Ulbricht v. Eufaula Water Co.*[40] Strangely enough a clear-cut contest over the principle of this case has never arisen in California litigation and therefore that principle has never been formally announced by judicial opinion as part of our non-statutory riparian right law. That it would not have been adopted and followed if counsel on occasion had argued for it is almost unbelievable. The fact that, in all California riparian right cases in which an injunction has been asked, a presently operative injunction has been granted, should not have weight against adoption of the principle of the *Ulbricht* case, because (1) in many of these cases present damage to the riparian was an element, and (2) apparently in none of them was the argument made for a declaratory decree only. The contest was always over the bare question—injunction or no injunction.

It is true also that in many American states the *Ulbricht* decision cannot be duplicated independently of legislation. This is because in those jurisdictions traditional procedure does not include the remedy of a declaratory decree in such cases.[41] California procedure permits of such a decree and it is peculiarly adapted to the sort of case which we are now discussing. Here then is one important constructive aid which our courts could give to the solution of our water law puzzles without the assistance of legislation.

But, the practitioner in this field may say, this does not go far in dissolving difficulties, for quite generally the riparian proves that the stream as it was wont to flow afforded a present use or a benefit to his riparian land and that the defendant's material alteration has deprived him of this use or benefit. In short, he proves present damage, however slight, as an element of his case and then demands and obtains an injunction, and if the defendant has power of eminent domain or has the advantage of an estoppel to force a sale or a release of the riparian right, the riparian proceeds to prove all possible uses and advantages of the stream to his land including uses never made, as a basis for determining the price of a release. There is truth in this reply to my suggestion and it opens a further, though related, field for comment. If the fundamental idea which I have emphasized is firmly apprehended and applied, a reasonable solution of these irritating cases also should be possible. No water right should entitle the holder to insist on a waste of the water of a natural stream or to speculate or racketeer at the expense of another claimant of a right to use. A riparian is entitled to remedies to maintain and protect his riparian right, but the primary riparian right covers only *bona fide* uses of the stream.[42] It does not include prevention of another's use or increase in the cost of another's use except so far as this is a consequence of the riparian's use. Prevention of another's use through legal remedies is a secondary right which the law gives to the riparian only in order to maintain and protect his primary right to use within his priority. Therefore, in affording remedies, it is incumbent on the courts, if they are to prove themselves efficient, to see that these remedies are limited to their proper purposes and not misused to force an expense on appropriators which tends to hamper the development of the fullest and most economical uses of the water resources of the state, and sometimes to increase the capital cost of public service undertakings and therefore the rates to consumers or the taxes which are levied to meet the cost. To clarify these statements let us consider in succession two variants:

P, a riparian, is making no use of his land or, if he is using his land, that use is not affected by the alteration of the stream and therefore is irrelevant. The stream irrigates part of the riparian tract near it and causes grasses to grow which conceivably might be used to graze cattle.

P has no cattle and makes no use of the grass. It does not serve any useful purpose. *D,* an appropriator, diverts water from the stream above *P's* land and thus materially alters the stream at *P's* land. *D* uses the water for irrigating non-riparian land, or stores it in a pond in furtherance of a non-riparian power use, or supplies customers at a distance who use it for irrigation or domestic purposes. *P* sues *D* for infringing his riparian rights and asks damages and an injunction against a continuance of the material alteration of the stream.

The ordinary result is that *P* is granted the relief demanded, unless *D* has eminent domain powers and asserts them by proper procedure or *P* by his conduct has raised an estoppel against his demand for an unconditional injunction. In these cases the injunctive relief is subject to a condition that *P* accept from *D* the value of a release of his riparian priority against *D's* use in satisfaction of this phase of his claim. The injunction is issued merely to secure payment of these damages and is terminated upon payment. The measurement of the damages allowed is not merely the value of the grasses destroyed, nor the value of raising such grasses indefinitely into the future; *P* is permitted to recover much more than this. Having established his right to a conditional injunction, he is permitted to recover the full value of his riparian priority and this value will be estimated by comparing the values of the riparian land with and without the riparian priority. Evidence of all possible uses that might be made of the stream on the riparian land within the riparian right is admissible, whether or not the uses have ever been made or dreamed of by the riparian.[43]

What objection can be offered to such a disposal of such a case as a matter of sound justice or as a matter of the law?

First, an objection in the interest of sound justice. The premises of justice should include not only an appraisal of the individual interests of the adversaries in the case, but also the larger element of social and public economic advantage. It should be clear that the demands of such a justice are not efficiently met by the usual disposal of the kind of case which I have outlined above. If *D's* case does not entitle him to force a sale of a release of *P's* prority against *D, D* is prevented by injunction from using the stream to the economic advantage of himself and the public in order that *P* may derive the hypothetical satisfaction of growing unused grasses. *P* has no actual desire that the grasses grow. He only desires to force *D* to pay him what he demands for a release of his priority. In essence it is what the man in the street calls a racket. *P's* legitimate interests would be protected adequately by a judgment for such reasonable damages, assessed by the judge, as result from the loss of the grass and a declaratory decree establishing his riparian priority to use for other purposes whenever in the future he may desire to use. Since in many cases a *bona fide* future use by the riparian is highly improbable, a denial of a presently operative injunction in such suits will tend greatly to discourage them, for it nullifies the racket motive.

If the case is one in which the injunction is issued in order to secure a sale of the riparian priority at the option of the defendant, appropriator, the comment of the last paragraph applies with the following addition. Practically, the purchase is forced by the terms of the injunction and often increases the expense of a public service. Furthermore, the estimate of the price is generally made by a jury and often is affected by a natural prejudice in favor of the individual landowner and against a power company or distant municipality which is putting a great burden of use on the stream to the detriment of development of possible future local irrigation uses.

How about the law of such cases? I believe that independently of specific legislation our courts have sufficient powers to dispose of these cases efficiently. Courts of equity always have been free to grant or deny injunctive relief in accordance with the demands of justice. If the injunction will cause injustice to the defendant and detriment to the public interest and if the plaintiff's rights can be sustained and protected adequately without an injunction, it is well within the powers of a court of equity to deny an injunction.[44] In the cases under consideration, the plaintiff's claim to damages for the loss actually suffered can be satisfied easily, and a presently operative permanent injunction is not necessary to quiet his right, since a declaratory decree will have that effect.[45] The cases differ materially from those in which the plaintiff sues to prevent occupation or use of his land, *e.g.*, by a railroad or highway, unless he is paid the full value of the permanent use of the land. In such cases the plaintiff has been deprived of possession of his land or his possession has been infringed by an adverse use and occupation which practically is exclusive. That he has never used this land himself and may never do so is no detriment to his case, because the legal premise is well established that a land possessor is entitled to full protection of his rightful possession regardless of whether the land is used or unused by him. On the contrary, a riparian right is only a right to use the stream on or for the benefit of the riparian land. The riparian has no possession of the water of the stream before it reaches his land.[46] His riparian uses should be protected, but this does not mean that he is entitled to play dog in the manger against appropriators as a land possessor is entitled to do against adverse claimants. In giving damages in the land case, the full value of the land taken must be given as a logical consequence of the land possessor's exclusive right; in a riparian right case, there is no legal necessity for giving damages for more than the value of uses with which the defendant has already interfered. To allow possible interferences with possible future riparian uses never yet contemplated by the plaintiff to enter into the estimate of damages, is to give the plaintiff more than justice and to invite racketeering litigation. Of course, if the right to interfere with such possible future riparian uses is not purchased by the defendant, the plaintiff is entitled to a declaratory decree quieting his priority to them; but the defendant should be permitted at his option to await the course of events and thus avoid the necessity of paying for releases of rights which never may be used. It is a fallacy to treat the riparian right as a unit; it really is a bundle made up of a multitude of particular rights of use, and a release of each of these multitudinous rights may be sold and purchased separately. Thus, if I am a riparian, I may release to an upper manufacturer my right to restrain the pollution of the stream by him in a certain way which interferes with some of my riparian uses but not others, or I may release to him my right against him to have the stream flow to me, excepting certain times and certain of my present or possible future uses. Furthermore, my releases to him will not affect my rights against other appropriation users except in certain incidental respects in some matters of adjustment of relative priorities.[47] This should suffice to illustrate the truth of my dictum that the riparian "right" is not single and indivisible, but is a bundle of multitudinous particular rights of use against multitudinous possible adversaries, and that each of those particular rights may be released or retained separately. A similar statement would be true, of course, of a land possessor's rights, but in the event of adverse possession or occupation of land the land possessor is at once ousted of his possession or occupation completely, while a riparian's water right is not adversely taken by an appropriator, nor is it infringed except with reference to the particular uses adversely affected by the defendant's use, and the plaintiff's possible future uses properly come into the suit only for the purpose of protection against prescription and to prevent multiplicity of suits. Prevention of multiplicity of suits is not a universal dominating consideration and yields always to the counter arguments of injustice and public disadvantage.

Whether I am right or wrong in my opinion of the adequacy of the inherent powers of a court of equity to dispose efficiently and justly of these cases without specific authorization by legislation, there should be little doubt that our California courts now have power to do so as a result of the amendment to article 14 of the state constitution, adopted November 6, 1928. This amendment added a new section, 3, to the article, which reads as follows:

> Section 3. It is hereby declared that because of the conditions prevailing in this state the general welfare requires that the water resources of the state be put to beneficial use to the fullest extent of which they are capable, and that the waste or unreasonable use or unreasonable method of use of water be prevented, and that the conservation of such waters is to be exercised with a view to the reasonable and beneficial use thereof in the interest of the people and for the public welfare. The right to water or to the use or flow of water in or from any natural stream or watercourse in this state is and shall be limited to such water as shall be reasonably required for the beneficial use to be served, and such right does not and shall not extend to the waste or unreasonable use or unreasonable method of use or unreasonable method of diversion of water. Riparian rights in a stream or watercourse attach to, but to no more than so much of the flow thereof as may be required or used consistently with this section, for the purposes for which such lands are, or may be made adaptable, in view of such reasonable and beneficial uses; provided, however, that nothing herein contained shall be construed as depriving any riparian owner of the reasonable use of water of the stream to which his land is riparian under reasonable methods of

diversion and use, or of depriving any appropriator of water to which he is lawfully entitled. This section shall be self-executing, and the legislature may also enact laws in the furtherance of the policy in this section contained.

In the recent case of *Gin S. Chow v. City of Santa Barbara,*[48] the opinion of the supreme court, *per* Shenk, J., declares a policy of so construing this constitutional amendment as to justify a disposal of riparian right cases which runs in the direction of my suggestions. The opinion affirms the validity of the amendment, assuming that it abolishes existing rights of riparians to insist on the flow of the stream to waste against appropriators who wish to divert and use the water. Such a modification of riparian rights, the opinion says, could be justified under federal constitutional law as an exercise of the state's police power. That the opinion of the court is sound on this point should be beyond controversy in view of the citation of authorities in the opinion. It is quite clear that the United States Supreme Court would consider the matter one of local water law on which, following a consistent, long established policy, it would not overturn the determinations of the state courts.[49] It would have been more in accordance with the traditions of a strong, efficient court, however, if the opinion had added that the dicta on which the plaintiffs relied, if literally and broadly interpreted to support their claims, were not good law, that the decisions in their cited cases were distinguishable, and that the constitutional amendment was merely a safety device (*sotto voce*) insuring what would be the law anyway against a possible timorous and fumbling use of precedents.

The second sort of case which I propose for discussion is like the first in all respects except that *P* is using the stream for certain valuable purposes and these uses are interfered with by *D's* use. This difference strengthens *P's* case from the social and ethical viewpoint. Certainly it greatly diminishes the suspicion of a racketeering motive for the suit. *P* should obtain, of course, damages for the past interference with his uses, a declaration of his priority, and an injunction against continuance of the interference, for in this case the damage is quite material and not merely a technical basis for compelling a purchase of a release. If, however, the case is one in which *D* can force a sale of a release because of an estoppel against *P's* claim for an unconditional injunction or because *D* has eminent domain power, *P's* relief should be directed by the principles which I have advocated in discussing my first hypothetical case. *P* should not be given damages based on hypothetical possible future uses other than a continuance of those which he has made in the past, unless *D* elects to purchase a release of the right against *D* to make these other uses, for these other uses may never be desired by *P* or his successors in interest and to permit *P* to recover their value will increase the cost of *D's* use unjustly on a speculative basis which encourages a racketeering motive in *P*. If *D* chooses to exclude releases of the rights to these other uses from his purchase, of course these rights of *P* to future uses should be protected by a declaration of his surviving priority in the decree. For this suggested solution of my second case also, I believe the inherent traditional powers of a court of equity are sufficient; but if my opinion on this point is deemed wrong as a matter of law because of the current of disposition of such cases in California in the past, then I offer as a base for a change in method of disposition, the recent constitutional amendment discussed above. There will be involved no taking of property without due process of law or without compensation in so applying the legislation, for none of *P's* substantive rights are taken without compensation. Those not paid for under the terms of the decree are maintained in unimpaired priority by the terms of the decree. Indeed the legislature has police power to readjust competing private claims to uses of land to quite an extent without compensation; and the case for such legislative power over the adjustment of competing claims to uses of water from natural sources of supply is at least as strong, for the right to take and use water from a natural source of supply does not include possession of the water before it is taken. Possession is not invaded or modified therefore in changing the details of remedies in support of rights to use of water in the interests of a better adjustment of competing uses.

Two or three further suggestions remain for brief statement before I conclude.

Often it will be possible to satisfy *P's* requirements for present use by some adjustment or substitution without a discontinuance of *D's* use.

Such adjustments have been ordered by the courts and adequate substitutions of supply at expense of *D* have been permitted in satisfaction of *P's* priority, as between contesting riparians and as between contesting appropriators.[50] It seems clear that similar adjustments should be made between an appropriator and a riparian.[51] They serve the fundamental policy of promoting the fullest use of our natural water resources with economy, and especially without waste, and they discourage unjust assertions of claims by a riparian which increase the expense of the appropriator.

In spite of a dictum in the opinion in a leading case, it also seems clear that the principle of economy of uses should apply against a riparian and in favor of an appropriator. Should a riparian be permitted to make or demand a use of water on his land for irrigation by a method which is very wasteful of water, when appropriators of subsequent priorities need the water for their uses? One riparian is not entitled to do so against the present needs of another riparian; nor is an appropriator entitled to do so against the present needs of a subsequent appropriator or riparian.[52] Why should a riparian have a special privilege to waste water against the present need of a subsequent appropriator? A riparian does not possess the stream or any part of it. His right, like an appropriator's, is a right of use only. It differs from an appropriation right in the circumstances of its title and in a related confinement of scope of uses under it to the riparian land, but in general it is the same sort of right as an appropriation right. With confidence the opinion may be ventured that the inference which may be drawn from the dictum in the opinion on rehearing of *Miller & Lux v. Madera Canal & Irrig. Co.*[53] is not the law. The courts cannot draw and apply that inference as a matter of decision without violating common sense and a very important public and social interest, and competent courts are not wont to do this. Therefore, even had section 3 not been added to article 14 of our state constitution, one could have predicted with some confidence that the easy broad interpretation of Judge Sloss's dictum would not have been supported by decisions of our supreme court.[54] Indeed the broad interpretation of Judge Sloss's dictum is not, I think, the proper one. In spite of the sweeping terms of his statement I doubt that he meant that a riparian could waste water which an appropriator needed for use or demand water for a wasteful use against an appropriator in all occurrences in which the riparian priority is superior. In the *Madera Co.* case the riparian was demanding a valuable use—the natural deposit of silt on its riparian land by the overflowing stream, as against the defendant's diversion for non-riparian use above. The argument was not directed against the plaintiff's method of taking this use as wasteful, for it was the only method by which the particular benefit could be obtained, but against his taking it at the expense of depriving appropriators above of all uses of the stream however useful to him the benefit might be. The problem was a different one from that which I am now considering, although a broad general argument of economy in use of our natural water resources can be applied to both problems. The problem to which Judge Sloss's dictum refers is this: Among the uses made of a stream, by methods which involve no undue waste to obtain the use in question, some will be found to place a burden on other users disproportionate to the benefit resulting from the particular use. Should not an indefeasible right to some such uses be denied on the ground that they burden unduly the fullest development of uses of the stream against the principle of economy of use in the general social interest? This is the problem which was solved in the affirmative as between appropriators in the leading case of *Schodde v. Twin Falls Land & Water Co.*[55] and in the later California case of *Antioch v. Williams Irrig. Dist.*[56] It is to this problem that Judge Sloss perhaps intended his dictum to be limited; and this problem is the subject-matter for my next suggestions.

Let me interpret by restatement Judge Sloss's dictum as a starting point for my suggestions concerning the applicability of the principle of the last two decisions to riparian rights.

It is contended that the plaintiff's claim to have the water flow over its land in times of flood so that its land may be fertilized by the deposits of sediment and moistened sufficiently to bear crops without further irrigation, is unreasonable as against claims of appropriators above who desire to divert otherwise unused flood waters for non-riparian use, and that the maintenance of the plaintiff's claim will tend to obstruct the fullest development of the water resources of the state and, by preventing uses far more beneficial in their totality than the plaintiff's use, will result in waste of these resources. This argument is unsound as a matter of law, since the principles of reasonable adjustment of uses and of relative economy of uses is not applicable to a controversy between a riparian and a subsequent appropriator.

> The doctrine that a riparian owner is limited to a reasonable use of the water applies only as between different riparian proprietors. As against an appropriator who seeks to divert water to non-riparian lands, the riparian owner is entitled to restrain any diversion which will deprive him of the customary flow of water which is or may be beneficial to his land. He is not limited by any measure of reasonableness. . . . But the riparian owners have a right to have the stream flow past their land in its usual course, and this right, so far as it is of regular occurrence and beneficial to their land, is, as we have frequently said, a right of property, "a parcel of the land itself." Neither a court nor the legislature has the right to say that because such water may be more beneficially used by others it may be freely taken by them. Public policy is at best a vague and uncertain guide, and no consideration of policy can justify the taking of private property without compensation.[57]

There is much in this dictum as a statement of existing law with which it is impossible to disagree. Of course, the mere fact that the defendant's non-riparian use is more beneficial or more important to the public than the plaintiff's use should not lead to a denial of the plaintiff's right to priority for his use over the defendant's use, and in general, assuming the plaintiff's right of priority, he should not be deprived of it to the profit of the defendant without compensation. But this does not hit the target of the problem. Consider the decisions in *Schodde v. Twin Falls Land & Water Co.* and *Antioch v. Williams Irrig. Dist.* In the first of these two cases a prior appropriator had placed water wheels in the stream to lift a small amount of water to a ditch for irrigating his land. The defendant, a subsequent appropriator, diverted a larger volume from the stream for supplying distant landholders with water for irrigation. After this diversion, the current was no longer sufficient to turn the plaintiff's water wheels, although there was sufficient water left in the stream to supply the plaintiff's irrigation needs. He sued to enjoin the defendant's diversion. The court denied him relief on the ground that to support the plaintiff's demand of a priority to use the full natural current to turn the water wheels as against the defendant's appropriation use would be wasteful of the stream as a natural resource for uses. It would prevent the development of large possible uses above the plaintiff's wheels to supply the plaintiff's relatively unimportant use of turning the wheels. The plaintiff's appropriation was held not valid to an extent justifying his suit.

Similarly in *Antioch v. Williams Irrig. Dist.,* the plaintiff city was a prior appropriator which diverted water from the Sacramento River near its mouth for purposes of a city water supply. Large diversions by the defendants, subsequent appropriators above, for irrigating rice fields so diminished the current of the river that its opposition to the tides was no longer sufficient to keep the salt water out of the plaintiff's pipes. The court held, however, that the plaintiff's claim of a right to have the current unimpaired to keep the tides from salting the water at the plaintiff's pump was a claim to a use of the stream which so much diminished the possibility of development of uses above that it should not be supported against such upper subsequent uses.

Unquestionably these decisions are sound as a matter of economic policy and therefore they are sound law. Why should not a similar disposition be made of similar cases in which the plaintiff has a prior riparian right instead of a prior appropriation right? Why should not a riparian's legal priority of right be limited in respect to uses as against appropriators as well as co-riparians by the principle of these cases? A prior appropriator has as firmly vested a right as a riparian. The problem, either way, is a primary one of determining how far the right extends. Is it absolute in respect to uses and their effects regardless of consequences to the public interest or is it subject, as all other legal rights are, to controlling considerations of the public or general economic and social interest? Should a single riparian be able to prevent all private extensive non-riparian uses of a large river, with a flow ample for satisfaction of all reasonable demands of riparians and others, merely to secure some relatively trivial and perhaps bizarre and wasteful use on his riparian lands? Judge Sloss's dictum seems to answer this question in the affirmative; but if it does and he is right, then our courts have proved inefficient in this particular in developing our common law, for there can be no question that such private rights of obstruction of beneficial development of our natural resources are highly pernicious and do not appeal to common sense.[58]

At any rate section 3 of article 14 of the state constitution, added in 1928, should furnish a sufficient basis for decisions in accord with sound policy on this point, in spite of Judge Sloss's dictum against the state legislative power thus to ameliorate the law. Since this legislation is a state constitutional provision it settles the law except so far as the federal constitution may nullify the provision; and it is highly improbable that the United States Supreme Court would hold the provision invalid in any respect. It has been a consistent policy of that court to leave private water right questions which do not involve federal or interstate interests, such as may arise with respect to navigable or interstate streams, to the control of local law policies of the individual states. Cases of the sort with which I am now concerned are not happily receptive of the contention that a federal question is involved; for (1) no federal legislation except the constitution is involved, (2) legislation was really not necessary except to encourage the California judges to adopt policies which they had power before to develop as part of the common law, and (3) federal constitutional law recognizes in the several states a wide and flexible legislative police power to readjust the conflicting claims of use of opposing property owners as governmental policy dictates without providing compensation.[59]

My conclusions then are:

1. Riparian rights do not offer such an insurmountable or expensive obstacle to a satisfactory development of economical uses and conservation of our water resources as is sometimes thought by pessimistic observers.

2. For the purposes of this development no legislative changes of the fundamental principles of our water law are necessary. In the main, legislation should be directed to making more efficient the procedure for determining and quieting water right priorities and keeping an adequate record of these priorities and to authorizing the organization and equipment of needed development and conservation projects in the public interest.

3. Essential to a satisfactory solution of our water problems is a policy of intelligent, progressive, and constructive judicial statesmanship

on the part of our judges. If they take a narrowly biased view of the law, the expense of a just and adequate development will be increased tremendously to the profit of racketeering litigants and certain members of the legal profession, but to the detriment of the public interest. That a liberal and constructive spirit will influence their decisions seems almost certain, not only in view of the policies of all the other western courts in that direction, but also from the opinion of the supreme court, *per* Shenk, J., in the recent case, *Gin S. Chow v. City of Santa Barbara.* Apparently Justice Shenk and the majority of the justices of the supreme court believe that article 14, section 3, of the state constitution is valid and forms a sufficient basis for accomplishing the legal results for which this essay argues. There should be no doubt that the burden of progress or frustration is on the legal profession and principally on the judges, because if they have the ability and courage for sound decisions, there is no barrier to them. Certainly they have the power, as all judges have, to develop the law in accord with sound social and economic policy except so far as they are hampered by legislation, and there is no legislation which hampers them in solving the problems within the scope of this essay. On the contrary, legislation has been drafted with great care and circumspection to urge them to proper decisions without in any way impairing the legitimate interests of any holder of a water right. The opinion in *Gin S. Chow v. City of Santa Barbara* is a welcome announcement that the supreme court purposes to do its part.

NOTES TO BINGHAM ESSAY

[1] (1884) 69 Cal. 255, 4 Pac. 919.

[2] (1903) 141 Cal. 138, 70 Pac. 663.

[3] (1922) 188 Cal. 451, 205 Pac. 688.

[4] Basey v. Gallagher (1875) 20 Wall. (87 U. S.) 670; Maeris v. Bicknell (1857) 7 Cal. 262; White v. Todd's Valley Water Co. (1857) 8 Cal. 443; The Bear River & Auburn Water & Mining Co. v. Boles (1864) 24 Cal. 359; Smith v. O'Hara (1872) 43 Cal. 371; Seaward v. Pacific Live Stock Co. (1907) 49 Ore. 157, 88 Pac. 963.

[5] Pabst v. Finmand (1922) 190 Cal. 124, 211 Pac. 11; Mason v. Hill (1832) 3 Barn. & Adol. 304.

[6] Reno Smelting, Milling & Reduction Works v. Stevenson (1889) 20 Nev. 269, 21 Pac. 317; Grunsky, *The Riparian Doctrine in California* (1930) 4 Calif. State Bar J. nos. 8, 9, pp. 178, 204.

[7] Hargrave v. Cook (1895) 108 Cal. 72, 41 Pac. 18; Pabst v. Finmand, *supra* note 5; Oliver v. Robnett (1922) 190 Cal. 51, 210 Pac. 408; Scott v. Fruit Growers' Supply Co. (1927) 202 Cal. 47, 258 Pac. 1095.

[8] Heinlen v. Fresno Canal & Irrig. Co. (1885) 68 Cal. 35, 8 Pac. 513; Gould v. Stafford (1888) 77 Cal. 66, 18 Pac. 879; Bathgate v. Irvine (1899) 126 Cal. 135, 58 Pac. 422, 77 Am. St. Rep. 158; Duckworth v. Watsonville Water & Light Co. (1907) 150 Cal. 520, 89 Pac. 338; Stockport Water-Works Co. v. Potter (1864) 3 H. & C. 300.

[9] McFarland, J., in Harris v. Harrison (1892) 93 Cal. 676, 29 Pac. 325; Lord Tenterden, C. J., in Mason v. Hill, *supra* note 5; Roberts v. Gwyrfai Dist. Council [1899] 1 Ch. 583.

[10] Wiggins v. Muscupiabe Land & Water Co. (1896) 113 Cal. 182, 45 Pac. 160, 32 L. R. A. 667; Weston v. Alden (1811) 8 Mass. 135; Pitts v. The Lancaster Mills (Mass. 1847) 13 Metc. 156; Dumont v. Kellogg (1847) 29 Mich. 420; Hayes v. Waldron (1863) 44 N. H. 580, 84 Am. Dec. 105; Bullard v. The Saratoga Victory Co. (1879) 77 N. Y. 525.

[11] *Ibid.*

[12] Half Moon Bay Land Co. v. Cowell (1916) 173 Cal. 543, 160 Pac. 675; Pabst v. Finmand, *supra* note 5; *cf.* Seneca Cons. Gold Mines Co. v. Great Western Power Co. (1930) 209 Cal. 206, 287 Pac. 93.

[13] But see Miller v. Miller (1848) 9 Pa. 74, 49 Am. Dec. 545.

[14] Heinlen v. Fresno Canal & Irrig. Co.; Duckworth v. Watsonville Water & Light Co.; Stockport Water-Works Co. v. Potter, all *supra* note 8.

[15] Modoc Land & Live Stock Co. v. Booth (1894) 102 Cal. 151, 36 Pac. 431; Fifield v. Spring Valley Water Works (1900) 130 Cal. 552, 62 Pac. 1054; Miller & Lux v. Madera Canal & Irrig. Co. (1907) 155 Cal. 59, 99 Pac. 502, 22 L. R. A. (n.s.) 391; San Joaquin & Kings River Canal & Irrig. Co. v. Fresno Flume & Irrig. Co. (1910) 158 Cal. 626, 112 Pac. 182, 35 L. R. A. (n.s.) 832; Gallatin v. Corning Irrig. Co. (1912) 163 Cal. 405, 126 Pac. 864; San Joaquin & Kings River Canal & Irrig. Co. v. Stevinson (1912) 164 Cal. 221, 128 Pac. 924; E. Clemens Horst Co. v. Tarr Mining Co. (1917) 174 Cal. 430, 163 Pac. 492.

[16] Broadbent v. Ramsbotham (1856) 11 Ex. 602.

[17] Miller & Lux v. Madera Canal & Irrig. Co., *supra* note 15.

[18] Modoc Land & Live Stock Co. v. Booth, *supra* note 15.

[19] *Supra* note 15.

[20] Modoc Land & Live Stock Co. v. Booth; San Joaquin etc. Co. v. Fresno Flume Co., both *supra* note 15; Gin S. Chow v. City of Santa Barbara (1933) 217 Cal. 673, 22 P. (2d) 5; Elliot v. The Fitchburg R. R. (Mass. 1852) 10 Cush. 191; Stratton v. Mount Hermon Boys' School (1913) 216 Mass. 83, 103 N. E. 87, 49 L. R. A. (n.s.) 57.

[21] Anaheim Union Water Co. v. Fuller (1907) 150 Cal. 327, 88 Pac. 978, 11 L. R. A. (n.s.) 1062.

[22] Half Moon Bay Land Co. v. Cowell, *supra* note 12; Pabst v. Finmand, *supra* note 5.

[23] Dumont v. Kellogg, *supra* note 10; Mason v. Hall, *supra* note 5.

[24] The Bear River & Auburn Water & Mining Co. v. Boles, *supra* note 4.

[25] Huffner v. Sawday (1908) 153 Cal. 86, 94 Pac. 424.

[26] Hanson v. McCue (1871) 42 Cal. 303; Hargrave v. Cook (1895) 108 Cal. 72, 41 Pac. 18; Pabst v. Finmand, *supra* note 5; Oliver v. Robnett, *supra* note 7.

[27] (1881) 6 App. Cas. 740.

[28] Wood v. Waud (1849) 3 Ex. 748; Lord Cairns, L. C., in Swindon Water Works Co. v. Wilts & Berks Canal Navig. Co. (1785) L. R. 7 H. L., 697 at 705; *cf.* Williams v. Morland (1824) 2 B. & C. 910; Mason v. Hill (1833) 5 Barn. & Adol. 1.

[29] Stanford v. Felt (1886) 71 Cal. 249, 16 Pac. 900; Ulbricht v. Eufaula Water Co. (1888) 86 Ala. 587, 6 So. 78, 4 L. R. A. 572.

[30] The Bear River & Auburn Water & Mining Co. v. Boles, *supra* note 4; Smith v. Duff (1909) 39 Mont. 374, 102 Pac. 981; Boehler v. Boyer (1925) 72 Mont. 472, 234 Pac. 1086; Masterson v. Kennard (1932) 140 Ore. 288, 12 P. (2d) 560; Spring Creek Co. v. Zollinger (1921) 58 Utah 90, 197 Pac. 737; Mally v. Weidensteiner (1915) 88 Wash. 398, 153 Pac. 342.

[31] Anaheim Union Water Co. v. Fuller, *supra* note 21.

[32] Smith v. Hawkins (1895) 110 Cal. 122, 42 Pac. 453; Cal. Stats. 1917, p. 746, Cal. Gen. Laws (1923), art. 9091, § 20a.

[33] Hargrave v. Cook, *supra* note 7; Mason v. Hill, *supra* note 5.

[34] Stanford v. Felt, *supra* note 29; Gould v. Eaton (1897) 117 Cal. 539, 49 Pac. 577; Southern California Invest. Co. v. Wilshire (1904) 144 Cal. 68, 77 Pac. 767; Anaheim Union Water Co. v. Fuller, *supra* note 21; Roberts v. Gwyrfai Dist. Council, *supra* note 9.

[35] Newport v. Temescal Water Co. (1906) 149 Cal. 531, 87 Pac. 372, 6 L. R. A. (n.s.) 1098; Conaway v. Yolo Water & Power Co. (1928) 204 Cal. 125, 266 Pac. 944, 58 A. L. R. 674; Collier v. Merced Irrig. Dist. (1931) 213 Cal. 554, 2 P. (2d) 790; Peabody v. City of Vallejo (1933) 86 Cal. Dec. 371, 25 P. (2d) 454.

[36] Modoc Land & Live Stock Co. v. Booth, *supra* note 15; Elliot v. The Fitchburg R. R., *supra* note 20.

[37] A practitioner of any other learned profession, or even a mechanic, who uses his tools clumsily with unhappy results is commonly denounced as a bungler. Is there any sound reason why judges who by their decisions seriously affect not only private fortunes, but also great public interests, should be free from similar just criticism when they use inefficiently their tools of precedents (which they are free even to overrule if they see fit) and remedial and procedural devices? Honesty and a good intent in our judges are essential to a sound administration of justice, but courage and efficient intelligence also are very important. It is high time that attention was turned by vigorous thoughtful criticism to the racketeering within the law which inefficient and timorous judges en-

courage by their decisions. These judges and lawyers who advocate such socially unsound but successful causes contribute to justification of a growing sense of disgust with our present social order.

"I have known judges," once said Chief Justice Erle, "bred in the world of legal studies, who delighted in nothing so much as in a strong decision. Now a strong decision is a decision opposed to common-sense and to common convenience."—Senior, *Conversations with Distinguished Persons* (1880) 314. Compare the following excerpt from the opinion of Lord Nottingham, C., in Duke of Norfolk's Case (1682) 2 Cas. Ch. 1: "Pray let us so resolve cases here, that they may stand with the reason of mankind, when they are debated abroad. Shall that be reason here that is not reason in any part of the world besides?"

[38] Stanford v. Felt, *supra* note 29; Modoc Land & Live Stock Co. v. Booth, *supra* note 15; Anaheim Union Water Co. v. Fuller, *supra* note 21; Newhall v. Ireson (Mass. 1852) 8 Cush. 595; Wood v. Waud, *supra* note 28; Roberts v. Gwyrfai Dist. Council, *supra* note 9.

[39] This is the usual practice in the analogous matter of conflicting appropriation and *quasi*-riparian claims to percolating waters. The possessors of lands overlying a mass of percolating water have rights in the water similar to riparian rights. These rights do not depend on prior use, but simply on possession of the overlying land. Appropriations of the water may be made and the relative priorities of such appropriations and the rights of the possessors of overlying lands are determined analogously to the determination of the relative priorities of riparian rights and appropriation rights in surface streams. Nevertheless a non-using possessor of overlying lands who sues to confirm his priority against an appropriator for use at a distance will not be given an injunction against the defendant's appropriation use which is causing no present damage. The plaintiff will be given only a declaratory decree establishing his priority of right to use whenever he chooses in the future and any further protection to that right of future use which the circumstances justify. Katz v. Walkinshaw, *supra* note 2, *reh'g* (1903) 141 Cal. 116, 74 Pac. 766; Burr v. Maclay Rancho Water Co. (1908) 154 Cal. 428, 98 Pac. 260.

[40] *Supra* note 29.

[41] Borchard, *The Declaratory Judgment—A Needed Procedural Reform* (1918) 28 Yale L. J. 1; Harrison, *California Legislation of 1921 Providing for Declaratory Relief* (1921) 9 Calif. L. Rev. 359; Sunderland, *A Modern Evolution in Remedial Rights—The Declaratory Judgment* (1917) 16 Mich. L. Rev. 69; Notes (1921) 12 A. L. R. 52; (1927) 50 *ibid.* 42; (1930) 68 *ibid.* 110.

[42] Heinlen v. Fresno Canal & Irrig. Co.; Duckworth v. Watsonville Water & Light Co., both *supra* note 8.

[43] City of Santa Ana v. Harlin (1893) 99 Cal. 538, 34 Pac. 224; Seneca Cons. Gold Mines Co. v. Great Western Power Co., *supra* note 12; San Joaquin & Kings River Canal & Irrig. Co. v. Stevinson, *supra* note 15.

[44] Lord Cairns, L. C., in Swindon Water Works Co. v. Wilts & Berks Canal Navig. Co., *supra* note 28; Pomeroy, *Equity Jurisprudence* (ed. 4; 1918) § 1338.

[45] Burr v. Maclay Rancho Water Co., *supra* note 39. Indeed such uses (and some other sorts of uses which have been protected by past decisions) should not be supported any longer as within the riparian priority in view of the increased necessity of conserving the uses of our water resources. The general principle against economic waste should be applied to vitiate them. This principle is now reënforced by art. 14, sec. 3 of the state constitution. See my comments on this principle *supra*, pp. 24–25, and especially note 58 at p. 36 *post.*

[46] Heinlen v. Fresno Canal & Irrig. Co.; Duckworth v. Watsonville Water & Light Co., both *supra* note 8.

[47] Such a release of a riparian priority is not a conveyance of the riparian rights. Indeed a conveyance of riparian rights is impossible except as an incident of transfer of possession of the riparian land. Stockport Water-Works Co. v. Potter; Duckworth v. Watsonville Water & Light Co., both *supra* note 8. Therefore the releaser still holds the riparian rights, subject, however, to a postponement of priority to the releasee's appropriation right because of the release. Similarly there is no transfer of riparian rights but only a relative postponement of priority effected by the running of prescription in favor of an appropriator, Southern California Invest. Co. v. Wilshire, *supra* note 34; or by release of the riparian priority enforced through condemnation by a public service company. Failure to perceive clearly this distinction between a conveyance of a riparian right or its utter extinction on the one hand and a mere postponement of its relative priority in favor of a certain appropriation on the other, is a fertile source of confused thinking and muddled opinions.

[48] *Supra* note 20.

[49] See opinion of Holmes, J., in Hudson County Water Co. v. McCarter (1908) 209 U. S. 349; Fox River Paper Co. v. Railroad Comm. of Wisconsin (1927) 274 U. S. 651.

[50] Wiggins v. Muscupiabe Land & Water Co., *supra* note 10; Hufford v. Dye (1912) 162 Cal. 147, 121 Pac. 400; Comstock v. Larimer & Weld Co. (1914) 58 Colo. 186, 145 Pac. 700; United States v. Caldwell (1924) 64 Utah 490, 231 Pac. 434.

[51] Colorado Power Co. v. Pacific Gas & Elec. Co. (1933) 86 Cal. Dec. 116, 24 P. (2d) 495; Crum v. Mt. Shasta Power Corp. (1933) 86 Cal. Dec. 235, 24 P. (2d) 801, *reh'g* granted, Sept. 25, 1933.

[52] Gould v. Stafford, *supra* note 8; Barrows v. Fox (1893) 98 Cal. 63, 32 Pac. 811.

[53] *Supra* note 15.

[54] An appropriator who has acquired a prescriptive priority of use against all lower riparians may enjoin a damaging diversion by an upper riparian of superior priority to that of the plaintiff's appropriation, so far as the diversion exceeds the riparian's needs measured economically. Arroyo Ditch & Water Co. v. Baldwin (1909) 155 Cal. 280, 100 Pac. 874. This decision would seem directly opposed to the loose broad interpretations often made of dicta like that of Sloss, J., in Miller & Lux v. Madera Canal & Irrig. Co., *supra* note 15. See also comment of Wiel, *Water Rights in Western States* (ed. 3; 1911) § 822, 876, n. 1.

[55] (1911) 224 U. S. 107.

[56] *Supra* note 3.

[57] *Supra* note 15, at 64, 99 Pac. at 511.

[58] This argument does not necessitate disapproval of decisions such as Huffner v. Sawday, *supra* note 25, and Peabody v. City of Vallejo, *supra* note 35, for on balancing considerations of justice and policy including those potent ones of common prejudices and usages it may reasonably be decided that, on the one hand, riparians at present have against subsequent appropriators a prior right (1) to saturation of the bed of a stream so as to carry enough of the surface flow to their lands to satisfy their riparian needs and (2) to the full pressure of the flow to cause sub-irrigation of their lands. On the other hand, as the need for economy of uses increases, the time may come when the waste involved in such uses will cause common sense to adjudge that the expense of a proper conservation and economical adjustment of uses so as to save the losses inherent in the "natural" method of using water downstream—*e.g.*, saving by piping in one of the cases, *supra*, and by surface irrigation in the other—should be shared by all the holders of water rights interested and not wholly by the holder of the subsequent priority as the price of his desired use. *Cf. Re* Water Rights Ahtarum Creek-State v. Achepal *et al.* (Wash. 1926) 245 Pac. 758; Hufford v. Dye, 162 Cal. 147.

The present point is that each type of case presenting this problem is to be carefully considered on its merits in the light of the prejudices of common sense affecting it. Decidedly the cases should not all be settled one way by an abstract sweeping formula. Nevertheless several sorts of wasteful uses which past decisions of the Supreme Court of California have permitted riparians to make as against subsequent appropriators will bear careful reconsideration in view of greatly changed conditions and especially in the light of art. 14, sec. 3, of the state constitution. Why should the raising of unused grasses be any longer held a proper riparian use at the expense of important desired uses above, especially when the claim includes insistence on the full flow of the stream for flooding or natural sub-irrigation? Even if the grasses are used, it is possible in some circumstances that the use should be adjudged too wasteful for legal support under the riparian priority in view of all the competing possibilities of valuable uses above, because of the heavy burden on the stream which it imposes in comparison to the slight economic gain.

[59] See the cases cited in the opinion of Shenk, J., in Gin S. Chow v. City of Santa Barbara, *supra* note 20; *Ex parte* Maas (1933) 86 Cal. Dec. 602, 27 P. (2d) 373.

THE REALITY OF WHAT THE COURTS ARE DOING

BY FRANCIS H. BOHLEN

LAW REVIEWS, in the last few years, have been filled with articles which purport to deal with law realistically or functionally and which attack what, to paraphrase Jerome Frank, may be called "Bealeistic" conceptualism. Many of these articles have gone to what appears to the writer to be extravagant extremes. However, they all show a healthy tendency to urge judges, lawyers, and law teachers to look rather to what the law does than to what the courts say. After all, it is a comparatively easy matter to construct a beautifully consistent and symmetrical system of supposed law if it is phrased in terms so vague as, without more elucidation, to be inapplicable to the facts of any situation which has not, in the past, constantly come before the courts in the course of litigation. The present article is intended to deal with two particulars only, in which an intensive investigation may be valuable not only in shedding light upon the nature of the judicial process but also in aiding courts themselves to realize the precise nature and effect of the function which they exercise.

The first of these is the exact function exercised by courts and juries in those fields of law in which the principles and rules are couched in terms which require human judgment for their definition before they can be applied to the facts of any particular case. Many years ago, Professor James Bradley Thayer demonstrated to the satisfaction of the entire profession the fact that judges are often not only permitted but indeed required to decide pure and simple questions of fact in passing upon the admissibility of testimony. This shattered the old idea that anything which courts decided was, therefore, matter of law. Unfortunately, Professor Thayer was almost exclusively preoccupied with the admission of evidence. He accordingly paid scant, if any, attention to the function of court and jury in dealing with evidence once it was admitted. No one of equal authority has attempted to demonstrate the corollary of his proposition—namely, that juries do, under the guise of passing on matters of fact, often lay down the law as it is applicable to the actual facts of the case before them. This is most obvious in negligence cases and in dealing with a somewhat similar situation, namely, whether there is a privilege which justifies intentional aggression. In both of these situations, not only the general principles but also the rules applicable to the particular types of situation are so phrased that someone must determine whether the plaintiff or defendant acted reasonably in view of the circumstances which existed at the time of his action.

Whatever else it is, this question is not one of fact in any true sense of that word.[1] It might be so if the standard of so-called "reasonable" conduct was what the ordinary man did. It might be so if it meant what the particular jurymen customarily did; but both of these tests have been rejected. To describe negligence as the failure to use that care which a reasonable man would use under the circumstances is merely a convenient way of leaving it to the judgment of someone, either court or jury, to say whether the defendant (or the plaintiff in a case of contributory negligence) acted as the court or jury think he ought to have acted. To speak of this as what a reasonable man should do, has certain advantages. The very fact that the social judgment of court or jury is personified in a reasonable *man* emphasizes the fact that account must be taken of the fact that the defendant or plaintiff is a man with certain unescapable frailties. But, after all, this technique is nothing more nor less than a convenient method of leaving it to someone to pass an *ex post facto* judgment upon the conduct of the particular party litigant.

If this is kept constantly in mind the task of ascertaining the proper function of court and jury in forming such judgments is greatly simplified. It may be possible to segregate those matters upon which a court has, or under our concept of justice is assumed to have, a peculiar competence to pass a proper judgment from those upon which the judgment of the ordinary man is likely to be satisfactory. It is possible to recognize certain conflicts between the popular and the legal concept of what is just. There is an immense field in which intelligent

[1] See Bohlen, *Mixed Questions of Law and Fact* (1924) 72 U. of Pa. L. R. 111, reprinted in Bohlen, *Studies in the Law of Torts*, p. 601.

investigation might show extremely interesting and probably exceedingly valuable results.

The control which courts exercise over juries, under the guise of their power to rule that the evidence is not sufficient to justify reasonable men in finding that the defendant's conduct was negligent, varies enormously in different jurisdictions. Indeed, there are many state constitutions the words of which, at least, prohibit the court from exercising anything approaching a true control over the jury. What are the causes of these variations? It is more than possible that they may arise from deep-rooted differences in social values. It is entirely natural, on the one hand, that courts in highly industrialized states, in which the whole tone of public opinion is favorable to the removal of every bar to effective production, should tend to regard it as unreasonable to demand of industry any precautions which might check intensive production by making it unprofitable. On the other hand, in agricultural states it is quite natural that no such regard should be paid to the supposedly harmful economic effect of requiring decent consideration for the interest of the individual's life, limb, and property. The statutes in the various states show some such difference in attitude on the part of the legislatures. It would be extraordinary if the attitude of the judiciary were not similarly influenced.

Another matter may safely be said to have led courts which have been given or have assumed a fairly effective power of control over the juries, to exercise their power in a manner which to the ordinary man may appear to infringe unduly upon the proper functions of the jury. For good or evil, judges feel that the mine run of juries entertain a prejudice in favor of the injured man which, if the decision is left to them, will lead them to find in his favor, irrespective of whether they believe that either he or the defendant has acted properly or improperly. After all, the concept that tort liability is based on fault is legal rather than popular. The supposedly archaic idea that he who breaks must pay still has a very large following in the class from which jurymen are drawn.

Furthermore, courts feel an intense and probably well warranted distrust of partisan expert testimony. They are naturally reluctant to permit actions to be brought in which recovery depends upon the jury's estimate of the truthfulness and reliability of the testimony of the plaintiff and the conflicting testimony of partisan medical witnesses. If there be any justification for the attitude of the great majority of the industrial states of this country in refusing to allow recovery for illness or miscarriage caused by negligent conduct of the defendant (negligent, that is, as likely to cause more direct physical harm), it lies in this distrust by the courts of the jury's competence to handle such testimony intelligently and fairly.

In addition, it is a regrettable fact that, taken by and large, though with many honorable exceptions, of course, courts do not implicitly, to say the least, trust the accident bar. The scent of perjury and fabrication clings to cases in which it would be puerile for any court to expect the jury to detect it. In their effort to prevent disreputable practitioners from winning verdicts by improper practices, courts have been forced to decisions which have subsequently, in more meritorious cases, been effectively cited as precedents.

The field of investigation is immense. If honestly cultivated by investigators who have no theory to sustain, no thesis to demonstrate, but the single desire to establish the truth, the effort of cultivating it will, I feel sure, bear a harvest which will amply repay the labor which must be expended.

Too little attention has been paid to the fact that a very large part of our law consists of rules for the creation of machinery and instrumentalities to accomplish certain purposes of those who use them. There may be many cases in which there are two separate and distinct questions: first, the propriety of the purpose for which the legal instrumentality is to be used; secondly, and equally important, the effectiveness of the steps taken to create an instrument effective to accomplish that purpose. The first involves what may not improperly be called social judgment; the second involves merely a knowledge of the technique of creating a tool capable of doing the job desired.

It is in the latter field that the so-called functional approach may be most valuably employed. There is no doubt that much of the legal machinery by which the business of life is accomplished is archaic in the sense that it was designed to meet social needs far more simple and, in the main, quite different from those of the present day. The old machinery has been patched from time to time. It has been in part rebuilt, but too often by legislatures and courts which have been more concerned with preserving the integrity of the original design than in adapting the machinery to its new uses. After all, what is a contract? It is a device by which the future can be made measurably secure. What is a corporation? It is a "method" by which business may be done collectively without individual responsibility. From time to time these pieces of legal machinery should be reëxamined, not to see whether they conform to their original design but to see whether under modern conditions they are effective to accomplish the ends which they were designed to serve.

But the inquiry must not stop at this point, and here the so-called functional approach is exceedingly valuable, if not essential. If it be recognized that the corporate structure is merely a method, a device, a piece of machinery, to accomplish socially desirable ends, we have the basis for ascertaining intelligently whether it is being properly used or improperly abused. Mere efficiency alone is not enough. The value of a machine is gauged not by the quantity but by the quality of its product. The ingenuity of our profession has led to the use of the corporate device for ends which are quite outside those for which it was originally designed. If these ends are socially desirable, the adaptation of the old machine to accomplish them is itself desirable and all that remains is to make the machinery ideally effective for that purpose. If the ends be undesirable, it is well to recognize the point at which courts have been led to permit the abuse of the corporate mechanism. It is the task of statesmanship, using that word in its broadest sense, to determine what is socially desirable. This task the inertia of our legislatures often forces the judiciary to perform. Perhaps they are best fitted to perform it. Cases involving corporation law come before them daily. They have material for understanding the manner in which the corporate structure is used and abused. Investigations of corporate finance, such as those made by Professor Berle and others, are immensely helpful. If our courts can be persuaded to rid themselves of the idea that a corporation is an end or object in itself, and recognize that it is merely a method or means to an end, it is safe to predict that these investigations will produce a rich harvest.

Luckily, in the forty years which have passed since the writer came to the bar, the attitude of law teachers, law students, and even of judges toward the law has fundamentally changed. In 1892, it would have been considered well-nigh impious to look beyond the words used by judges and to try to find out what they were doing by the use of their words and why they wished to do it. The teaching of law was an exegesis on sacred texts culled from judicial opinions. Many of us may have gone too far in our efforts to psychoanalyze, as it were, the judiciary, who not only do not desire such treatment but indeed often do not realize that they need it. None-the-less, the change in approach seems to the writer altogether healthful.

The law student today recognizes that many of the most beautifully intricate and subtle of legal theories are merely a particular form of legal rationalization or fiction designed to make the circle of the assumption of an immutable body of law square with the necessity that the administration of law must accomplish what are recognized as desirable social ends. Theories are now recognized as often a means of justifying decisions rather than as reasons for making them. Many situations can be pointed out where like results have been reached upon entirely unlike theories. The introduction of the automobile, with the realization of the danger which is inseparable from its use, has led to a wide extension of the ambit of vicarious responsibility of those who permit others to drive their cars. There is perceptible a very definite feeling that the automobile is so dangerous a means of locomotion that the owner of it should answer not only for the manner in which he drives it, or in which it is driven by those who, as his servants, are engaged in forwarding his business or affairs, but also by anyone whom he permits to drive. In some jurisdictions, statutes provide specifically that the registered owner of the car shall be liable for the negligence of anyone whom he permits to drive it for any purpose. In others, insurance is required which, by the terms of the statute or in practice, covers a similar liability. In others, the family-purpose doctrine extends the owner's liability beyond that which the law of agency would impose. In others, the owner is required to control his licensee's driving when he has the opportunity to do so. In an English case the licensee was called the agent of the owner, although the owner was not present and therefore had no opportunity to exercise the power of control which his ownership was held to give him. In some jurisdictions, the liability is frankly put on the ground that the automobile is a dangerous instrument. Thus the same result is in whole or in part reached by quite different routes.

So, too, the very prevalent feeling that one who has negligently put himself in peril should not thereby be barred from recovery against a defendant who, with knowledge of plaintiff's dangerous position, fails thereafter to exercise carefully his then existing ability to avert the accident, is given expression in various jurisdictions in various ways. In many, it is expressed by holding that the defendant had the last clear chance of averting the accident and that, therefore, the contributory negligence of the plaintiff does not bar him from recovery; in others, by treating the defendant's failure to take reasonable care after knowledge of the plaintiff's peril as wanton, willful, or reckless misconduct. The same result has been reached in a few jurisdictions by the application of the so-called comparative negligence doctrine. Here again, the theories differ but the result is the same. Obviously, the theories do not require the result but are merely justifications of it. These are only two of a large number of examples which every judge, lawyer, and law teacher, conversant not only with the law of his own jurisdiction but with that of others as well, will immediately recognize as of like kind.

If, however, we are to look at the law realistically, if we accept Justice Holmes's view that the law consists of a prophecy in respect to how the majority of seven or nine men will decide in a given case, we must not overemphasize the importance of decisions rendered under similar states of fact. What the practitioner called upon to advise his client must consider is, as Justice Holmes has indicated, how a particular court will react to the facts which he believes his client's testimony is sufficient to establish. It is the effect of those facts upon court and jury which is all important. Whether courts should attach as much importance as they do to the language, particularly if it be striking, of some highly respected brother or previous member of the bench, may be doubtful: that they are apt to do so is clear. The desire for symmetry, for consistency, whether adult or infant as one disagrees or agrees with

Jerome Frank, is likely to be decisive except where the application of a previously announced principle shocks the judge or court. There is wide room in the very broad formulæ in which much of our law is couched for the exercise of the judicial judgment or, to use a less formal word, "hunch"; but it is the reverse of "realism" to exaggerate the field in which this judgment or "hunch" operates.

Modern students, who will be the *corps d'élite* of the practicing bar of the near future and from whom it is to be hoped and perhaps expected that ultimately the bench will be recruited, are beginning to recognize what may be termed the "invocatory" word. By this is meant a word which has customarily been used to describe a situation that has habitually been recognized as requiring a particular legal result. Students are being taught to realize that, where this result is desired, courts often justify it by using an "invocatory" word to describe a situation to which the word is entirely inappropriate if it be taken in its traditional sense and not so extended as to be valueless as a word of definition or even of description.

It is interesting to find this survival of the primitive instinct of word magic. There is an obvious similarity between the action of a court, on the one hand, which, for one reason or another wishing to hold one man responsible for the action of another, calls the one the agent of the other, although many of the most essential requirements for agency are absent, and, on the other hand, the keeping secret the name of the tribal god so that its enemies may not invoke him to destroy the tribe of which he is the deity. Little harm is done by this if exactly what the court is doing is recognized and why the invocatory word is being used. Unfortunately, this understanding is not always present. Cases in which, for a reason quite different from that professed, a customary term is used in an entirely new sense, are too often used by analogy to extend unduly the meaning of the original term in fields in which it is appropriate. A more serious example of archaic recrudescence, in the writer's opinion, is the doctrine, to which the authority of a very great name has given immense vogue, that the court's construction of the words of a contract determines its scope and effect, even though neither of the parties so understood them. This is interesting to music lovers in that it calls to mind the runes on Wotan's spear; but it is unfortunate that such currency should have been given to a concept of so important a legal tool as a contract, which is not only archaic but also differs radically from the understanding of it that is held by substantially everyone who uses it. This is particularly so since every end which this technique serves could have been reached by other methods more in conformity with modern legal thought.

The failure to recognize that many of our legal principles and rules deal with the creation of instrumentalities or tools to accomplish a desired result, has had what appears to the writer to be a highly undesirable consequence. A tool has no value as a thing in itself: it is a means to accomplish an end. In order to attain its proper efficiency a tool must be designed for the particular purpose for which it is to be used. The mere fact that a certain type of tool is called by a common name does not, in ordinary life, imply that each tool shall be in every particular the same. There are many forms of spanners, the diameter of which depends on that of the nut which is to be tightened or loosened. Thus, while certain characteristics are common to all spanners, certain other characteristics vary with the use to which they are to be put. Is not this equally true of such devices as "contracts" or "corporations"? Should it not be recognized that, while certain characteristics are common to all contracts, the contract for insurance, or the contract for the issuing of share certificates, may have other characteristics peculiar to the subject-matter with which it deals, that may differ very radically from the characteristics of the ordinary mercantile or commercial contract?

The idea that a single word carried with it always a unitary connotation has made immense trouble in other fields. Throughout the law, the problem of causation continually arises. When the writer came to the bar it was accepted that there was such a thing as legal "causation," a body of rules and principles by which the causation requisite to responsibility in every field could be ascertained. Today there is a growing recognition that this is not so. To condense what Lord Haldane said in *Upton v. Great Central Ry. Co.*, 1924 AC 302, 307, it is now recognized that causation is relative to the problem under discussion. After all, the rules of causation are rules which limit responsibility at some point short of answering for all the events of which the actor's conduct is a necessary antecedent. The problem is one of determining the ambit of responsibility. There is no reason why the same rules should apply in criminal prosecutions, in which the purpose is purely punitive, and in tort actions, in which the purpose is in the main compensatory. There is even less reason why the same rules should apply where the responsibility is based, in theory at least, and still too largely also in fact, on the wrongdoing of the defendant and where, as in workmen's compensation cases and insurance cases, culpability, real or legalistically assumed, has no part in determining the existence or extent of responsibility.

It is perhaps too much to ask that courts should abandon the use of words and phrases which in fact are valueless as affording a yardstick by which to measure the legal effects of a situation or even as giving to a jury any aid in determining the matter in controversy. To regard such vague, unmeaning phrases as expressing the law is extremely convenient. It enables courts to leave at large to the jury the determination of many matters which are essential to the decision of the case in hand while at the same time not appearing to abrogate any of their own functions. "Power of control" is the traditional test of agency. Yet, without the ability to exercise it, "power of control" is merely a metaphysical abstraction. It exists when the circumstances are such as to make it just to hold the alleged principal vicariously responsible for the acts of the alleged agent. Indeed, the arrangement between the two may be such that an attempt to exercise the power would be a breach of the contract between them. None-the-less, it is convenient and may be valuable to leave the whole question of vicarious responsibility under novel circumstances to a jury. The circumstances of the cases presented for adjudication are infinitely various. If courts were themselves to decide whether agency exists under a particular state of facts, their rulings would arise to trouble them in the future when a case before them was similar but not identical. This is so because, unfortunately, any ruling of a court, being an application of a legal principle, is assumed to partake of the immutability which it flatters the legal profession to ascribe to the common law. The decision of the jury, on the contrary, is merely ephemeral, "good for the day and trip only." Their decision in no way binds the future. It does not preclude a contrary finding in a case in which the circumstances may be only slightly different. It may therefore be well that courts should leave the matter to the control of the jury. If so, the phrase "power of control" is as convenient a device as can be imagined.

It is futile to believe that anything any one man could write, certainly anything which the present writer can say, can change court practices so traditional and in many respects so convenient. However, and here, unlike a sermon, the text is at the end, there is great gain in the fact that in many of our principal law schools the reality of what the courts are doing is being brought to the attention of students. It is possible that, if students are taught to see that many of the methods adopted by courts are mere devices, they will, if and when they come to the bench, remember some little of their teaching. Perhaps indeed, like a growing number of eminent and conspicuous judges, they will, when the need arises, tell the real reasons for their decisions and not conceal them beneath legalistic and often meaningless phrases.

LA «PROPRIÉTÉ COMMERCIALE»

PAR HENRI CAPITANT

I

L'EXPRESSION DE «PROPRIÉTÉ COMMERCIALE», appliquée à la loi française du 30 juin 1926, qui règle les rapports entre locataires et bailleurs pour le renouvellement des baux d'immeubles ou de locaux à usage commercial ou industriel, ne doit pas faire illusion. Si elle traduit, d'ailleurs imparfaitement, les aspirations encore assez confuses et sans homogénéité des petits commerçants d'avant-guerre, à l'époque où ils commencèrent à réclamer une réglementation législative du renouvellement de leurs baux, elle donne une idée non seulement excessive, mais fausse de la portée de cette loi. Entre le moment où elles ont été formulées et celui où le législateur français les a examinées, les revendications des commerçants ont été en effet très vivement combattues, non seulement par les propriétaires aux droits desquels elles s'attaquaient, mais aussi par les milieux juridiques, à cause des atteintes qu'elles risquaient de porter aux principes généraux du Droit, et, par contre-coup, à l'ordre social. Au Parlement même, si elles ont reçu de la Chambre cartelliste, élue en 1924, un accueil assez complaisant, le Sénat, de tendance plus modérée et plus conservatrice, leur a retiré leurs traits les plus avancés et les plus insolites. La loi du 30 juin 1926 est le point de convergence de ces divers mouvements d'opinions et d'idées; elle est le fruit d'une transaction; et son contenu n'a plus grand chose de commun avec celui que ses promoteurs avaient mis sous le mot d'ordre de «propriété commerciale.» Mais l'expression est commode; elle a fait fortune, et c'est sous le bénéfice des observations qui précèdent que nous pourrons être amené à l'employer dans cette étude.

Une autre confusion doit encore être évitée. La date récente de la réforme ne doit pas faire illusion. Bien que contemporaine de la réglementation qui a dû être édictée après la guerre en matière de loyers, la loi du 30 juin 1926 n'est pas une loi de circonstance; il ne faut pas la comprendre dans les lois sur les loyers, qualifiées à juste titre de «spéciales,» qui ont, avant ou depuis, autorisé les moratoires, prorogé les baux, limité leurs prix, permis leur revision. Celles-ci étaient ou sont encore essentiellement provisoires. Nécessitées par l'état de choses qu'ont créé la guerre et ses suites,—mobilisation des locataires, pénurie des locaux, baisse du franc, crise économique,—elles ne peuvent être invoquées que pendant un temps déterminé, limitent elles-mêmes leur durée d'application et disparaissent avec les circonstances qui les ont provoquées. La réglementation législative du renouvellement des baux commerciaux ne présente aucun de ces caractères. C'est une loi définitive, et non provisoire comme les précédentes; seule une autre loi pourrait l'abroger; et si, comme nous le verrons, la question de la propriété commerciale n'a pris de l'acuité qu'après la guerre, elle était posée dès avant et avait provoqué, à partir de 1911, le dépôt au Parlement de plusieurs propositions de lois.

Il est même assez curieux de suivre les vicissitudes par lesquelles ont passé les revendications des commerçants avant et depuis la guerre. Lorsqu'elles ont commencé de s'exprimer, elles semblaient vouées à l'échec: la situation économique n'en soulignait nullement l'urgence et, par ailleurs, les principes généraux du Droit s'opposaient à ce qu'elles fussent prises en considération. Puis, la guerre et les bouleversements de tout ordre qu'elle entraîna leur apportèrent une justification au moins temporaire, tandis que, de leur côté, les principes juridiques perdaient, au contact des événements, de leur rigidité première. Sous cette double poussée, les propriétaires durent céder du terrain: après avoir opposé aux prétentions des commerçants une fin de non-recevoir pure et simple, ils s'en tinrent à soutenir que ces prétentions n'étaient justifiées que par quelques abus exceptionnels consécutifs à une situation anormale, auxquels le droit commun suffisait à remédier; c'était là affaire de juge, non de législateur. Enfin, quand cette position de repli eût elle-même été jugée insuffisante et l'intervention du Parlement inévitable, tout leur effort et celui du Sénat, hostile à la réforme, tendirent à en circonscrire le plus possible la portée et les effets. C'est cette évolution des événements et des idées qui, en dehors de contingences plus étroites et passagères, paraît expliquer la nouvelle institution, que nous voudrions retracer brièvement dans les lignes qui suivent.

II

Au début du xixe siècle, époque à laquelle fut rédigé notre Code civil, la vie économique est calme et facile; les produits satisfont à peu près aux besoins; l'homme est modeste; pour s'enrichir, il sait qu'il n'est pas trop d'une vie; ni la concurrence, ni les conflits sociaux n'ont encore empoisonné l'atmosphère. On peut croire, avec Bastiat, aux harmonies universelles.

Les rapports entre bailleurs et locataires s'en ressentent heureusement. Il y a des locaux disponibles; le propriétaire est heureux de leur trouver preneur; il consent un long bail à un prix courant; le commerçant a le temps de récupérer son prix d'achat; la clientèle n'exige encore ni luxe ni renouveau; elle est fidèle à son fournisseur. Des relations courtoises s'établissent entre les parties; à l'échéance, la situation se dénoue sans heurt; la plupart du temps le propriétaire renouvelle au commerçant son bail; si, pour une raison quelconque, il ne le peut pas, le locataire trouve aisément à proximité un local à des conditions comparables; ni l'un ni l'autre ne s'estime lésé.

Mais bientôt les choses commencent à se gâter. D'une part l'intensification des échanges, due à l'essor de la production, exige un accroissement parallèle des locaux. La transformation des locaux d'habitation en locaux commerciaux, si fréquente depuis la guerre, n'y suffit pas. Et la multiplication des constructions ne suit pas la cadence. Il en résulte que chaque local disponible est guetté par une pluralité de commerçants. D'où une première cause de surenchère dans l'offre des loyers.

D'autre part, dès cette époque, on peut constater comme aujourd'hui, quoique sur une moindre échelle, que l'accroissement de l'offre des marchandises ne s'accompagne pas sur le marché d'un accroissement parallèle du pouvoir d'achat des consommateurs. Une âpre concurrence s'instaure entre commerçants pour la conquête de la clientèle, où les plus forts s'efforcent d'absorber les plus faibles. Selon une formule bien connue des économistes, la concurrence tue la concurrence et engendre le monopole. Et si cette concentration des capitaux ne nous importe pas dans toute la mesure où les grandes firmes sont propriétaires de leurs locaux, elle intéresse les rapports entre bailleurs et locataires en tant que ce grand commerce tend à prendre la place du moyen et du petit commerce, notamment sous la forme de maisons à succursales multiples, car il peut faire au bailleur des offres de loyers bien supérieures à celles de ses concurrents. Ceux-ci, il est vrai, opposent à ce mouvement une résistance qui, en France, a été efficace. Le petit commerce n'a été qu'en partie atteint par l'essor du grand; mais il n'a pu se défendre qu'au prix de lourds sacrifices qui ont constitué par incidence une nouvelle source de profit pour les propriétaires. Pour retenir en effet sa clientèle, le petit commerçant se met en frais: l'aménagement est modernisé, adapté tant bien que mal à l'exigence du public qui s'est habitué et complu au luxe du grand magasin. La valeur vénale du local s'en accroît, et donc aussi sa valeur locative. D'autant plus qu'avec la vie moderne, le temps est devenu plus précieux; le public est pressé; il va au plus près; ce n'est plus la personnalité du patron qui attire, mais la proximité du local; l'achalandage remplace la clientèle. L'emplacement, et par suite le droit au bail, deviennent, avec l'aménagement, les éléments primordiaux de la valeur du fonds. Et ce sont précisément ceux-là qui, par la force des choses, profitent en fin de bail au propriétaire. Car, à ce moment, celui-ci ne consent tout naturellement à renouveler le bail que moyennant un loyer supérieur, puisque, comme nous l'avons vu, la valeur du local s'est accrue. Pour ne pas perdre le bénéfice futur de ses dépenses d'amélioration, le locataire sortant accepte presque toujours l'augmentation. Et, comme le vent est à la hausse, le propriétaire, qui espère pouvoir renouveler bientôt cette fructueuse opération, ne consent qu'un bail relativement court. Le commerçant se voit tenu d'amortir des frais lourds dans un laps de temps bref et, pour cela, d'augmenter son prix de vente. C'est en ce sens qu'on a pu dire que la précarité du droit du commerçant sur son bail était génératrice de vie chère. Si le locataire sortant ne peut accepter le nouveau loyer, c'est un rival plus puissant qui prend sa place, ou bien le propriétaire lui-même, pour y exercer un commerce similaire. Dans tous les cas, le bailleur profite gratuitement de l'aménagement fait par le prédécesseur et de la plus-value que les circonstances économiques ont donnée à l'emplacement du local.

III

Cet état de choses avait à la longue aigri les rapports entre bailleurs et locataires commerçants et motivé dès avant la guerre le dépôt au Parlement de propositions de lois. Cependant l'abus n'était pas si caractérisé qu'il méritât une intervention législative et surtout l'opportunité de cette intervention était condamnée par les principes généraux du Droit. Non seulement les propriétaires, mais les juristes n'ont pas eu de mal à démontrer qu'en portant atteinte à ces principes, c'était l'ordre social lui-même que le législateur risquerait d'ébranler.

Le sort de deux notions fondamentales, de deux assises de la civilisation moderne est en effet engagé dans le débat: la propriété individuelle et la liberté des conventions.

La propriété d'abord. Depuis l'antiquité sa notion n'a pas changé. Les rédacteurs du Code civil n'ont eu, pour la définir, qu'à traduire en français les attributs que lui reconnaissaient déjà les jurisconsultes romains: *usus, fructus, abusus.* «La propriété», dit l'article 544, «est le droit de jouir et disposer des choses de la manière la plus absolue, pourvu—ajoute, il est vrai, l'article—qu'on n'en fasse pas un usage prohibé par les lois ou par les règlements»; mais aucune loi ni aucun règlement ne déclare illicite le profit tiré par le propriétaire de l'état de choses d'alors. Personne n'est en faute, dit un adage, qui ne fait qu'user de son droit. La propriété immobilière, en particulier, a conservé la prééminence que lui reconnaissait déjà le Droit romain, qui la classait parmi les biens les plus précieux, les *res mancipi,* et l'ancien Droit attache peu de prix à la propriété mobilière: «*res mobilis, res vilis.*»

Le Code civil n'a pas rompu avec cette tradition: on en cite souvent comme exemple-type le privilège reconnu au bailleur pour le recouvrement de ses loyers, que beaucoup s'accordent à juger encore excessif, malgré les limitations que lui ont apportées des lois postérieures. Le locataire, lui, est tout simplement créancier du bailleur de la jouissance des lieux loués, moyennant le payement périodique d'une somme d'argent. Le contrat intervenu entre les parties est le seul soutien de leurs droits. A aucun moment durant le contrat, la propriété ne se trouve démembrée entre bailleur et locataire, comme entre nu propriétaire et usufruitier. A son expiration, le droit du preneur s'évanouit comme s'évanouissent tous rapports entre créancier et débiteur, une fois que chacun d'eux a accompli la prestation que le contrat lui imposait. Etant donné une telle situation, quel argument le locataire pourrait-il trouver dans la législation pour défendre sa conception?

Ce n'est pas seulement la propriété individuelle dont la stabilité est en jeu, c'est la liberté des conventions ou ce qu'on a appelé encore l'autonomie de la volonté. Ce principe est l'expression juridique du libre arbitre philosophique et du laissez faire économique. Les rédacteurs du Code civil l'ont consacré en termes énergiques dans l'art. 1134, aux termes duquel «les conventions légalement formées tiennent lieu de loi à ceux qui les ont faites.» Ce principe doit être respecté dans le louage comme ailleurs. Le contrat expiré, bailleur et preneur se retrouvent face à face comme des tiers; le même processus qu'à la conclusion du bail originaire doit se reproduire, c'est-à-dire que la loi de l'offre et de la demande doit jouer librement; les volontés sont souveraines et indépendantes; aucune ne peut s'imposer à l'autre; encore moins une volonté tierce peut-elle s'immiscer et dicter sa loi pour régler leur conflit d'intérêts.

Pour traduire l'appréhension que l'atteinte à de tels principes inspirait au législateur lui-même, il n'est que de rappeler les mots dont le rapporteur à la Chambre des Députés qualifiait, dès 1911, la réforme projetée: «un saut dans le collectivisme.»

IV

Cependant des années passèrent, au cours desquelles survint la guerre. Ce n'est pas elle, nous l'avons dit, qui a mis à l'ordre du jour la question de la propriété commerciale, mais c'est elle qui lui a donné de l'acuité. L'esprit inventif, le progrès technique, le besoin de luxe, un moment réfrénés, ont repris leur essor à un rythme accéléré. L'industrie s'est équipée à nouveau, le commerce intensifié, les locaux disponibles sont raréfiés; la surenchère aux loyers s'est faite plus âpre, la résistance du petit commerce plus difficile. Le conflit est passé à l'état aigu.

Par ailleurs, si l'évolution économique rend l'intervention du législateur plus impérieuse, l'évolution juridique la rend moins anormale. Les concepts classiques n'ont pas échappé à l'universel désarroi des hommes et des choses. Il ne faut pas trop s'étonner qu'une ou deux décades aient suffi pour ébranler une orthodoxie millénaire, si l'on songe à la rapidité, à l'amplitude, à la profondeur des transformations économiques modernes. Les notions de propriété et de liberté des conventions en particulier n'avaient pu se maintenir dans leur pureté et leur rigidité premières.

L'*abusus* du propriétaire, le droit de disposer de sa chose selon son bon plaisir, a été attaqué à la fois dans son fondement et dans ses conséquences. Dans son fondement d'abord. En France même, des théoriciens comme Duguit, remontant aux sources mêmes du Droit, condamnaient comme antiscientifique, parcequ'à base métaphysique, le subjectivisme juridique. Le droit, disaient-ils, n'est pas une qualité inhérente à la personne humaine; il est un cadeau fait par le législateur à l'individu, en apparence dans son intérêt, auquel il donne ainsi une sanction légale, en réalité dans l'intérêt général, parcequ'il juge que le meilleur moyen de satisfaire ce dernier est d'accorder un droit à l'individu. La conséquence est rigoureuse: si le droit n'est accordé à l'individu qu'en vue de la satisfaction de l'intérêt général, le jour où ce droit se révèle incompatible avec cet intérêt, le législateur a non seulement le pouvoir, mais aussi le devoir de le retirer à son bénéficiaire, *a fortiori* de le réglementer. La propriété n'échappe pas à cette analyse: de «droit réel par excellence», elle tombe, dans la langue des tenants de cette doctrine, au rang de «fonction sociale.» D'ailleurs, la doctrine est bientôt confirmée par les faits. De plus en plus, la jurisprudence est obligée de limiter, dans toute la mesure où son rôle le lui permet, les conséquences de la toute-puissance du propriétaire, notamment dans ses rapports avec ses voisins. L'écoulement des eaux à la campagne, l'émanation des fumées dans les villes sont les sujets les plus fréquents de disputes. Des décisions innombrables qui ont été rendues en cette matière, la doctrine a peu à peu dégagé cette règle que le propriétaire qui dispose de sa chose en vue soit de nuire à autrui, soit sans utilité personnelle, soit en excédant les inconvénients ordinaires du voisinage, commet une faute et en doit réparation en vertu de l'art. 1382 du Code civil. Par un curieux retour de la terminologie, qui traduit bien le renversement des positions doctrinales, le droit d'abuser dégénère en abus de droit. L'omnipotence et l'impunité du propriétaire sont mises en échec au nom de l'intérêt général.

Le principe de la liberté des conventions subit une atteinte parallèle. D'après le Code civil, les conventions sont obligatoires pour les parties, quelque dures qu'en soient les conditions, quelques bouleversements que les circonstances ultérieures lui apportent. La lésion n'est une cause de rescision que dans des cas exceptionnels: seule la force majeure peut relever les parties de leurs obligations, c'est-à-dire un événement indépendant de la volonté du débiteur, imprévisible et qui rend impossible l'exécution de l'obligation. Les bouleversements économiques ne remplissent pas ces conditions: ils peuvent et doivent être prévus des parties en contractant, et la plupart du temps, ils ne rendent pas l'exécution de l'obligation impossible, mais seulement plus onéreuse. Aussi la Cour de cassation, approuvée par la grande majorité des auteurs, a-t-elle maintenu très ferme, malgré les circonstances actuelles, le caractère obligatoire, sacré des conventions. L'évolution a été l'œuvre, ici, non pas du juge, mais du législateur. Celui-ci a admis à diverses reprises que les parties devaient être relevées de leurs obligations ou que les conditions devaient en être modifiées lorsque les circonstances étaient devenues telles que, si les contractants avaient pu les prévoir, ils n'auraient pas traité dans les mêmes termes. D'où l'expression de «théorie de l'imprévision» sous laquelle a triomphé ce point de vue. Ainsi une loi de 1918, appelée du nom de son promoteur «loi Failliot», a autorisé la revision des conditions de certains marchés passés par des particuliers avec l'Administration. Toute la législation spéciale sur les loyers, à laquelle nous faisons allusion au début de cette étude, a modifié les conventions entre bailleurs et locataires au point de vue des délais de payement, de la durée du bail et de son prix. Il faut rapprocher aussi de ce mouvement législatif la jurisprudence du Conseil d'Etat qui, en raison de la nécessité d'assurer la continuité des services publics, a autorisé la revision, au profit du concessionnaire d'un service public ou d'un marché de fournitures, du contrat qu'il avait passé avec l'Administration à une date où l'on ne pouvait prévoir la hausse énorme qui s'est produite dans le prix des matières premières.

V

Le jour où il fut certain que la majorité parlementaire était disposée à donner satisfaction aux réclamations des commerçants, on se contenta de discuter désormais sur la forme et les limites que son intervention devait comporter.

Les milieux commerciaux se partageaient eux-mêmes, selon leur tendance, entre deux prétentions. Les plus exigeants réclamaient un droit pur et simple, sans exception ni réserve, au renouvellement du bail. Si les parties ne tombent pas d'accord sur les nouvelles conditions, les arbitres statueront. Le locataire a ainsi sur le local loué un véritable droit de priorité. Nul ne pourrait exercer dans l'immeuble devenu vacant un commerce similaire sans avoir préalablement acquis le fonds. Les plus modérés demandaient seulement que fût interdite au propriétaire, pendant un temps à déterminer, la faculté de relouer le local où s'exploitait le fonds ou de le reprendre pour lui-même ou l'un des siens en vue d'y exercer un commerce similaire. En privant ainsi le propriétaire du bénéfice qu'il aurait pu faire gratuitement aux dépens du locataire, soit en exigeant un loyer supérieur du nouveau locataire, soit en profitant personnellement de l'aménagement et de l'achalandage, les partisans de ce système pensaient écarter ainsi toute raison au refus de renouveler.

En face de chacune de ces prétentions, les propriétaires prirent une position particulière. De la première—droit au renouvellement—ils ne voulaient à aucun prix. Elle était attentatoire, disaient-ils, au droit de propriété comme à la liberté des conventions qu'ils défendaient dans leur pureté première. La Société d'Etudes législatives se prononça pour les mêmes raisons dans le même sens, mais, devant l'inutilité de la résistance, la Chambre paraissant décidée à passer outre, elle présenta, pour faire œuvre utile, un texte qui consacrait le droit au renouvellement.[1]

De la seconde prétention—interdiction temporaire de l'exercice d'un commerce similaire—les propriétaires admettaient le principe. Mais, selon eux, il n'était pas besoin, pour donner satisfaction aux commerçants, d'une intervention législative. Ceux-ci trouvaient dans l'arsenal juridique deux armes à leur disposition : contre le préjudice causé par le non-renouvellement, la théorie jurisprudentielle de l'abus du droit; contre le profit tiré par le propriétaire de l'exercice par un nouveau locataire ou par lui-même d'un commerce similaire, les prescriptions

[1] *Bulletin de la Société d'études législatives,* 1923, 1924, *passim.*

légales sur l'enrichissement sans cause. Le propriétaire, disaient-ils, lorsqu'il refuse de renouveler le bail, abuse de son droit, car il l'exerce contrairement à sa fonction normale et cause une lésion excessive au locataire sortant. Et s'il aggrave son cas en reprenant le local ou en le relouant en vue de l'exercice d'un commerce similaire, il profite gratuitement de la plus-value que le locataire sortant a donnée au fonds; il s'enrichit injustement, c'est-à-dire sans cause. Suivant le cas, le locataire obtiendra une indemnité soit d'éviction, soit d'enrichissement.

Mais cette application à notre matière des notions d'abus de droit et d'enrichissement sans cause ne laisse pas d'être tendancieuse; elle en déforme les contours et les détourne de leur rôle. L'abus de droit, même dans sa conception la plus large, ne punit jamais qu'un acte *positif* du propriétaire. Une omission peut bien entraîner la responsabilité de son auteur, mais cette responsabilité n'a pas pour fondement un abus. Un abus, c'est un excès, et un excès ne se résout jamais dans une omission, mais dans le dépassement d'une limite normale. Le propriétaire serait mis encore en état d'infériorité sous le rapport de la *preuve*. D'ordinaire c'est à celui qui se plaint d'avoir été victime d'un abus de droit à en prouver l'existence. Ici le législateur impose au propriétaire de prouver qu'il a un motif légitime de refuser le renouvellement, sous peine d'être condamné à des dommages-intérêts. Enfin et surtout—et l'on ne comprend pas très bien comment les propriétaires n'ont pas vu le danger de leur proposition—si l'on considère comme un abus du droit de propriété le fait de vouloir en tirer un meilleur rendement, c'est la condamnation de ce droit dans son attribut essentiel: le profit.

On pourrait faire une démonstration similaire pour l'enrichissement sans cause. Il est vrai que la jurisprudence en fait de nos jours des applications de plus en plus nombreuses, qu'on retrouve en notre matière l'enrichissement du patrimoine du bailleur corrélatif à l'appauvrissement de celui du locataire et qu'à cet égard il n'y aura pas de faute à prouver, mais seulement un fait—le déplacement de valeur d'un patrimoine à l'autre. Mais il faut en outre que cet enrichissement ne soit fondé sur aucune cause légitime. Or ici le nouveau locataire ne s'enrichit pas sans cause. La cause c'est le bail et les loyers qu'il s'est engagé à verser. Que si le propriétaire reprend les locaux pour lui-même, la cause de son enrichissement c'est encore sa propriété. Et décider qu'il pourrait devoir une indemnité au locataire sortant pour avoir tiré profit de sa chose, c'est encore découronner la propriété d'un de ses attributs essentiels.

Ni l'abus du droit, ni l'enrichissement sans cause ne suffisent donc à remédier au mal. Il faut faire du neuf. Mais le temps a singulièrement limité la portée du débat. Il n'est plus question de laisser les choses en l'état ni de trouver un remède à la situation dans la législation existante; des deux indemnités réclamées par les commerçants—indemnité d'éviction, indemnité d'enrichissement—la seconde est reconnue légitime par les propriétaires. Il ne reste plus qu'un point de friction: le droit au renouvellement. L'heure est aux transactions.

VI

Le Parlement se trouve alors saisi de deux sortes de propositions de lois: tandis que les plus modérés s'en tiennent à l'indemnité d'enrichissement, les plus exigeants réclament en outre l'indemnité d'éviction au cas de refus illégitime de renouvellement. Toute la discussion parlementaire qui s'ouvre alors se résume en un conflit entre le Sénat, plus modéré, et la Chambre, plus avancée et plus sensible aux réclamations électorales. La Chambre, où avaient été déposées les propositions de lois, vota en 1919 un texte qui consacrait en principe les revendications des commerçants aux deux indemnités. Le Sénat admit bien l'indemnité d'enrichissement mais repoussa l'indemnité d'éviction, comme attentatoire au droit de propriété et à la liberté des conventions, et pour bien marquer le sens qu'il donnait à ce rejet, il renvoya à la Chambre le texte modifié en substituant au titre de «Protection de la propriété commerciale,» sous lequel la proposition lui avait été transmise, celui moins compromettant de «Modification de l'article 1737 du Code civil, en ce qui concerne le renouvellement des baux à loyers d'immeubles à usage commercial ou industriel.»

Entre temps la France procède à des élections législatives. La Chambre «bleue horizon» arrive au pouvoir. Elle est plus modérée que la précédente et se rapproche du point de vue sénatorial. Trois traits marquent cette évolution: 1° le locataire n'a plus un droit de *priorité,* mais seulement un droit de *préférence,* c'est-à-dire qu'à offres égales le propriétaire est obligé de lui renouveler son bail, au lieu de le consentir à un nouveau venu; 2° la reprise par le propriétaire est toujours ***légitime,*** donc n'entraîne pas à sa charge de dommages-intérêts, à moins qu'il n'y exerce un commerce similaire; 3° chacune des parties conserve le ***droit de se rétracter*** après le jugement réglant leur litige: le propriétaire, en renouvelant le bail, s'il estime trop élevée l'indemnité mise à sa charge pour défaut de renouvellement; le locataire, en abandonnant le local, s'il estime trop élevé le nouveau loyer fixé par les arbitres. Pendant plusieurs années ce texte fit la «navette» entre les deux assemblées que séparaient encore des points de détail. Mais une échéance approchait, qui les obligeait à se mettre d'accord: le 1er juillet 1926, expiraient toutes les prorogations de guerre et d'après guerre consenties aux locataires commerçants qui allaient se trouver désormais occupants sans droit de leurs locaux. La loi fut votée la veille, le 30 juin. L'accord s'était fait dans les termes suivants:

Peuvent invoquer le bénéfice de la loi les locataires de locaux commerciaux ou industriels, les artisans et façonniers, les établissements d'enseignement qui occupent les lieux depuis au moins deux ans, s'il y a bail écrit, et depuis six ans, si la location est verbale.[2]

Le locataire doit toujours demander le renouvellement de son bail; il n'y a pas droit *de plano*.

Si le propriétaire consent au renouvellement mais que les parties ne soient pas d'accord sur les conditions, celles-ci sont fixées par des arbitres choisis par les parties ou, à défaut d'accord, par le Président du Tribunal civil, et dont les pouvoirs sont limités en ce qui concerne la fixation de la durée du nouveau bail et du loyer: si le locataire était titulaire d'un bail écrit, la durée du nouveau bail est égale à celle de l'ancien, sans pouvoir dépasser neuf ans; si la location était verbale, la durée du nouveau bail est de trois ans. Les arbitres doivent, pour apprécier la valeur locative, «tenir compte de toutes les considérations de

[2] Les locataires étrangers sont en principe exclus du bénéfice de la loi. Les propriétaires étrangers sont exclus du droit de reprise personnelle. Cette exclusion des étrangers est limitée par l'idée de *réciprocité législative,* c'est-à-dire que ceux dont la loi nationale reconnaît la propriété commerciale et en concède le bénéfice aux Français dans leur pays d'origine, jouiront à leur tour du bénéfice de la législation française. Mais cette concession est toute théorique, puisque, jusqu'à présent, le législateur français est le seul, à notre connaissance, à avoir consacré le droit du locataire commerçant au renouvellement de son bail. La jurisprudence a, il est vrai, assimilé la réciprocité diplomatique à la réciprocité législative.

fait, et notamment de la situation économique.» Toutefois, si le propriétaire peut faire état d'une offre supérieure émanée d'un tiers, le nouveau loyer, si cette offre est reconnue sincère et réelle, sera porté à ce chiffre.

Le prix ainsi déterminé est susceptible de revision tous les trois ans, si la valeur locative des locaux a varié de plus du quart par suite des circonstances économiques, soit au profit du bailleur, soit au profit du preneur. Les autres conditions du bail sont fixées librement sous cette seule réserve qu'il ne peut être fait échec au droit du locataire d'obtenir dans l'avenir un nouveau renouvellement. Enfin le nouveau bail ne peut, sauf motif légitime, être cédé avant trois ans.

Quand le propriétaire refuse le renouvellement, ce qui est toujours son droit, il encourt une condamnation à des dommages-intérêts envers le locataire évincé: 1° s'il n'avait pas de motif grave et légitime de ne pas renouveler: il doit lui payer une *indemnité d'éviction* (art. 4 et 5); 2° s'il installe pour son propre compte dans les locaux un commerce ou une industrie différente, mais qui profitent des améliorations et travaux effectués par l'ancien locataire: c'est l'*indemnité de plus-value* (art. 7), ou, s'il y exerce dans les cinq ans qui suivent l'expiration du bail non renouvelé, un commerce ou une industrie similaire et profite ainsi de la clientèle de l'ancien locataire: il est tenu de verser une *indemnité d'enrichissement* (art. 8). Lorsque le propriétaire donne à bail les locaux à un autre commerçant, celui-ci doit personnellement l'indemnité de plus-value ou celle d'enrichissement.

Cet exposé sommaire des principales dispositions de la loi indique suffisamment que, dans cet irritant et long conflit, le dernier mot est resté aux locataires. Ils ont vu en effet consacrer, sinon leur droit absolu de priorité, du moins les indemnités d'éviction et d'enrichissement—cette dernière, on l'a vu, scindée en indemnité de plus-value et en indemnité d'enrichissement proprement dite, selon que le propriétaire ou le nouveau locataire profite de l'aménagement des locaux ou de la clientèle.

Les lois postérieures qui ont modifié la loi primitive n'ont fait que confirmer cette tendance: les locataires ont obtenu des délais de grâce, des garanties pour le maintien provisoire dans les lieux, tant que l'indemnité à laquelle ils ont droit n'a pas été liquidée et réglée. Toutes ces propositions tendent à élargir le droit accordé au commerçant et à le rapprocher d'un véritable droit de propriété commerciale. Tout récemment encore, une discussion était en cours devant les Chambres, provoquée par le dépôt de nombreux amendements à cette législation qui, selon le mot d'un sénateur, est devenu le «cauchemar du Parlement.»[8]

VII

Il est encore trop tôt pour pouvoir juger des effets bons ou mauvais que produira cette législation. On peut affirmer toutefois qu'elle a eu pour résultat de fixer le commerçant dans le local où il exploite son commerce et par là d'accroître la valeur de son fonds. Il le vend donc plus cher lorsqu'il se retire, parce que le droit au bail qui en est un de principaux éléments comporte également le droit au renouvellement ou à une indemnité compensatrice. Il n'est pas douteux que le prix des fonds de commerce se soit sensiblement élevé au cours de ces dernières années, et cela malgré la terrible crise économique qui paralyse les affaires.

Cette hausse de la valeur des fonds de commerce contribue certainement au maintien de la vie chère. Le commerçant ayant payé un prix élevé le fonds qu'il a acheté, est obligé de vendre ses marchandises plus cher. Toutes les enquêtes qui ont été faites, notamment en ce qui concerne la différence énorme qui existe entre le prix du bétail sur pied et le prix de la viande chez le boucher détaillant, font ressortir l'importance des charges qui grèvent ce dernier et, parmi elles, le prix qu'il a dû débourser pour acquérir son fonds.

Il faut ajouter que le fait de la stabilisation du commerçant dans le local où il exploite son fonds rend plus difficile la création de nouveaux fonds pour les débutants et diminue par conséquent la concurrence qui pourrait faire baisser les prix.

On peut encore constater que l'application de cette loi a donné lieu à un nombre considérable de procès à tel point qu'il a fallu créer au tribunal civil de la Seine une chambre spéciale pour les juger. Cela tient non seulement à ce qu'elle est, comme toutes les lois modernes, fort mal rédigée, mais encore aux conflits qu'elle suscite entre propriétaires

[8] Depuis la rédaction de ces pages, une loi du 13 juillet 1933 a modifié dans le sens général que nous indiquons la loi du 30 juin 1926.

et locataires. Tout cela ne permet pas de bien augurer de l'avenir de cette loi. Notre avis est que le Parlement a cédé imprudemment aux réclamations des associations syndicales de commerçants qui ont su user de la force électorale qu'elle représentent pour faire pression sur les candidats aux élections législatives, et qu'en votant ces mesures sans en pouvoir calculer la portée, le Parlement a non seulement porté atteinte sans raison décisive aux grands principes ci-dessus rappelés, mais provoqué des conflits qui ne paraissent pas en voie de s'apaiser. A notre avis les nations étrangères ont eu raison de ne pas imiter en cette matière l'exemple de notre pays.

THE FREEDOM OF THE MINER AND ITS INFLUENCE ON WATER LAW

BY WILLIAM E. COLBY

MINING HAS HAD A PROFOUND INFLUENCE on the laws and social usages of the communities throughout the world where mining has flourished. The available record of the mining laws of different countries throughout the ages establishes the fact that there is a remarkable uniformity of underlying principle in these usages and customs. In very ancient times mining was carried on as a sovereign venture or concession and as a consequence laws governing mining in those days were practically non-existent. It was only with the advent of the autocratic democracy created by the Athenians that individual mining assumed any considerable importance. The silver mines of Laurium were divided into small tracts and leased to individuals or groups of citizen adventurers.[1]

Under Roman rule there was a partial emergence of the right of the individual to mine on his own account. The Romans were not as a rule skilled in the art of mining. They therefore found it more expedient to allow the peoples whom they had conquered to continue mining operations in accordance with local customs and to exact a tribute or royalty from them. Certain Roman emperors, in order to increase this flow of wealth into Roman coffers, distinctly encouraged the leasing of mining claims by individual adventurers.

> In the title "De Metallariis" of the Code of Justinian was found the constitution of Valentinian, by which any one was permitted, and invited, to become an *aurilegulus,* and to work for his own profit, on the condition of rendering a certain metallic canon, and of selling the produce to the *fisc* in preference to others.[2]

GERMANY: Out of the darkness and welter of the Middle Ages, important institutions, social and governmental, were born and many of their essential principles can be traced down to the present day. During these medieval times mining became of increasing importance, particularly in the Germanic states. The German miners were exceptionally proficient in the art of mining and their services were in demand in many parts of the civilized world. The first edition of Agricola's comprehensive treatise, *De Re Metallica,* was published in Germany in 1555 and is a veritable encyclopedia of the then existing phases of the mining industry.[3]

In this same medieval period the miner acquired a considerable measure of freedom (*Bergbaufreiheit,* to use the German expression). This is all the more remarkable when we remember the bondage which the feudal system at that time imposed upon the farmer and ordinary laborer, who were serfs in every sense of the word. Writers differ as to just how this mining freedom came about. Some contend that the miners themselves threw off the shackles of serfdom,[4] but the more conservative view is that the miners constituted a skilled class with special knowledge of an art, the practice of which brought large royalties to the overlords and feudal rulers. In order to attract and encourage miners to work in a particular area that they might thus receive the royalties paid on the metals mined, these overlords vied with one another in issuing liberal charters under which the miners operated.

> The princes of Germany imitated the policy of the Roman emperors, and invited adventure by indefinite liberty of search on terms which gave to the adventurers a strong interest in their success. This liberty (the *Freierklärung* of the German mines) is indicated obscurely in the Iglavian mine laws of the thirteenth century; more distinctly in those of Wenceslaus the Second; and the system received its full development in the fifteenth and sixteenth centuries. By the general practice of that country, every one is entitled to a provisional right of search within certain limits.[5]

Medieval mining was largely carried on in uncultivated and mountainous districts, on lands claimed by the overlords.

While the miners' right to enter upon this waste land and stake out and work mining claims was, in the Middle Ages, largely controlled by charters issued by the local rulers, it is also true that the provisions of these charters were based upon and chiefly reflected the customs and usages of the miners themselves.[6] This is true also of mining in other parts of the world. The miner, having developed a special art, the successful exercise of which he alone could carry on, was able to impose customs and usages of his own making upon his superiors in power, who accepted this measure of dictation because of the financial benefits accruing to them through payment of royalties.

One of the conspicuous rights asserted by these early miners in the Middle Ages was freedom to go upon "common" or "wastrel" lands and to stake out claims, the right to work which was recognized both by charter and by custom as the miners' individual property.[7] The free miners in Germany, France, and Great Britain not only had a right to mine on these lands, but also were entitled to the use of rights of way, timber, fuel, and water, space for buildings, and refineries. They were exempted from various tolls, taxes, and duties, from military service, from obligations of a servile tenure or condition, and from disability and forfeiture by reason of alienage. They were also provided with local officers and courts for the administration of justice. There was special protection of person and property.[8] As long as the miner complied with the usages and customs of the district, he had the right to mine his own claim to the exclusion of all other persons and the right to the product of his industry subject only to payment of the royalty.

> Upon the discovery of a vein or other mineral deposit, he is entitled, as of right, to a grant of a certain measured space of ground for the purpose of pursuing his discovery; and the ceremony of bounding this area is announced by three consecutive proclamations. The demand made upon the Bergmeister, or other local officer of the sovereign, cannot be refused unless there be conflicting claims, in which case the first finder, and not the first claimant, is entitled to preference. The interest of the concessionary is permanent, assignable, and transmissible; but is subject to the obligation of continual working, of payment of the tenth or other proportion, and of a small fixed quarterly rent.[9]

Ordinarily, it is true, he exercised this right under the general terms of a charter or other proclamation issued by the ruler in control of the land in question, and the important point to bear in mind is that the overlord, by granting this free right to go upon waste lands and stake out claims, had yielded up the ordinary privilege of an owner of real property to select and designate the particular person who might acquire such rights; in other words, the right of personal selection of the individual grantee was waived. The overlord no longer dictated and determined who the particular individual should be who might mine a specific parcel of his land. This right of free mining subsequently spread into other parts of the world and eventually was exercised on our own federal public domain in the mining regions of the West following the discovery of gold.[10]

As soon as the door was thrown open so that qualified miners could freely locate individual claims on waste lands, it became essential to determine their respective rights as among themselves in order to prevent inevitable conflict. Virtually all systems of mining law in which the individual or claim system of location prevails, early recognized as a cardinal principle the superior right of the first locator or appropriator in time. This is variously referred to as the "Doctrine of Priority" or "Law of the First Finder."[11] *Qui prior est in tempore, potior est in jure,* was the Roman wording of this equitable doctrine.

The same principle of "prior appropriation" was quite naturally applied by the Germanic miners in their customs governing the acquisition of water for use in the mines. Most mining operations require a considerable use of water and the greater number of mines are not so situated that the use of this water can be enjoyed through the ordinary exercise of a riparian right. The water, in order to be beneficially enjoyed, must of necessity be diverted from the stream and conducted to the nonriparian mining land where it is needed.

The early German mining law, which in the majority of its main principles resembles the original German general law, from the beginning guaranteed to the mine operator free use of the flowing water.[12]

The necessity of the use of water for mining purposes, and the fact that mining first occurred in uncultivated and undivided districts *(Marks)* and in royal and feudal forests, explain two later facts: (1) that the free use of water and pasturage was given to the mine operators as well as to the members of the Mark Association and (2) that the right to the free use of water continued in special recognition of the economic importance of mining when mining entered upon ground which had already become private property and when the general law enacted into statute no longer recognized a free use of flowing water. The older mining rules *(Bergfreiheiten)* permit no doubt. Thus we read in the *Bergfreiheit* for the silver mine at Fischbach of the year 1426 (Lori, p. 27):

All our forests and waters, wherever situate and suitable for mining purposes, shall at all times be free and open....

The *Bergfreiheit* for Fischbachau for the year 1446 (Lori, p. 32) granted the miners "dwelling and pasturage," for their cattle, also wood, water, roads, and pathways "if the same are of use and convenience."

In the *Bergfreiheit for Kutzbuchel, Ratenberg,* etc. 1459, Section 8, it was provided:

We allow, grant and confirm the mines and minerals wherever the same may be found and worked, in the herein mentioned dominions and assizes, together with forests, mining claims [*Hüttslegen*], pathways, roads, water and stone and all other things as are usually appurtenant to mines.

Compare Section 8 of the *Bergfreiheit* for Lam (Lori, p. 65). *Bergfreiheit of The Duchy of Braunschweig* for Gittelde, Grund, and Zellerfeld of 1532 (Calvor, p. 218):

From the beginning to all our subjects throughout our domain and duchy all our mining roads, ways, and footpaths shall be free and open, together with water for smelters and stamp mills and all other works, according to the mining law and custom from time immemorial.

Bergfreiheit of the Mark Brandenburg of the year 1539 (Wagner, p. 421):

We give and grant to them herewith the right and privilege to enjoy, have and use our forests and water. We concede and grant for ourselves, our heirs and our sovereignty to each and all of them, our lands and estate and the right to go upon the mines, mills, forests and waters, to ride or drive upon now and forever more.

Bergfreiheit of Nassau-Katzenemb of the year 1559 (Brassert, p. 9):

Those who come to dwell among us for mining purposes shall hold freely and unhindered in common, water, pasturage, streets, footpaths and roads (excepting fisheries and hunting grounds), according to the mining custom.

Bergfreiheit of Kurtrier of the year 1564 (Brassert, p. 101):

We grant to the miners in the designated district the right to use the water, pasturage, to hunt rabbits, to shoot and fish, and therefore that all roads, water, pasturage and foot paths shall be free, except that we reserve to ourselves certain hunting grounds and fishing waters.

These examples show that, as a part of the *Bergfreiheiten* (free mining privileges), the free use of flowing water was maintained for mining, or at least that in the common *Mark* (district) and in the manors the right to the free use of water, which had existed from time immemorial in favor of mining, was recognized and declared applicable.

Just as the right to mine minerals found in open land was acquired by the individual miner by priority of location, so the custom similarly arose of acquiring the use of water for mining purposes by prior appropriation. Neither the lord of the manor nor the owner of the ground had any right to dispute the acquiring of such right to the use of water by the miner. This right of the miner to appropriate water establishes the fact that the owner of land riparian to the flowing water did not have an exclusive use of such water but had to yield to the miner.

The one who received a grant of the right to use water had either to dam up the water or divert it within a period of one half-year. If this was not done, or if the water conduits were allowed to deteriorate for a half-year, then, after such fact had been established, other persons might be granted the water. These provisions were not applicable to a proprietor of a mine which produced its own water, for he did not need to obtain a grant of a water right: they applied only to such users of water as required a grant.

All those waters which were discovered by means of tunnels, shafts, prospect works, or ditches, were to be granted by the *Bergmeister* to those who had appropriated them or taken possession of them, but always with the restriction, namely, that such grant of such water should not interfere with the mine or the mine workings of the district, and that the miners might at all times use the same for the dressing of ores, if the necessity arose.[13]

Wells and springs as a general rule were not objects of grant by the Bergmeister. The right to the use of water in creeks and rivers for mining purposes, on the contrary, was acquired by appropriation and grant. If the use of the water had already been granted to a third person, and the latter had constructed special works for the use of the same, nevertheless, mining took precedence. If no appropriation and grant of the water in streams and rivers had occurred, either according to law or to custom, nevertheless, according to the *Bergfreiheiten* and the common mining laws, mining had the preferential right to the use of such water. Water in streams and rivers, in contrast to mine waters, could only be acquired for mining purposes by appropriation and grant of the *Bergmeister*.[14]

The other mines and newly discovered claims, of whatever sort they may be, whether old workings or newly discovered, which are situated within the boundaries of our *Niederoester* lands and therein opened up, together with rivers, coal lands, and forests, are to be granted by our mining authorities, representing us, and by no one else.[15]

The flowing brooks and waters are not to be granted or given as exclusive property to anyone, but such waters are always to be used for those purposes which chiefly promote and maintain mining, such as *Heintzen* (bucket pumps) and *Künsten* (Hertwig, *Bergbuch*, p. 249, defines these as machines for raising or pumping water out of mines), regardless of stamp mills, lumber mills, hydraulic machines, etc.[16]

If a water power is still open to appropriation and we have no right ourselves to build a stamp mill upon it, and such water power does not interfere with other stamp mills, then our *Oberbergmeister* may grant such water power to the next one who makes application therefor, etc.[17] (This coincides in the main with the Schlackenwalder Tinn ordinance.)

In conformity with the tradition of his office *(Oberbergmeister)* and that which we permit him to do, the *Oberbergmeister* shall grant and confirm to those who desire to develop them, mines, tunnels, water powers, stamp mills, smelter works, forges *(Hammer)*, saw mills, and the like.[18]

The provisions of the Prussian *Allgemeines Landrecht*, although somewhat obscure, reflect the foregoing provisions and customs concerning the use of water in brooks and rivers for mining purposes. The material portions of the *Landrecht*[19] entitle one to conclude that the old law was intended to be retained, as is evidenced by the following provisions (Part II, Tit. 16, Sec. 80):

Washworks (dressing works) and stamp mills, as well as ditches and water conduits on the surface, are not included in the location of a mine, but must be separately appropriated and granted. (Waters of operating mines [mine waters], for the use of which, according to the German mining law, the mine proprietor does not require a grant, constitute an exception.)

Even Section 110: "Ponds and mills must also give way to mining, if it is necessary for the further prosecution thereof," accords with the former law, since the latter law prescribed the compensation to be paid to the one who was formerly entitled to the water. Section 109, according to which the owner of the soil is obliged to surrender to mine proprietors, "the water necessary for the operation of mine engines, stamp mills, dressing works and smelters," does not follow the old law since, under the new law, according to Section 112, there must be compensation for every surrender of a water right.

The *Austrian* Mining Law of May 23, 1854, Section 105, provides:

> Surface waters which are necessary for carrying on mining must even against the will of the owner be surrendered to the *Revierstöllner* even by other mine owners, so far as water police regulations and other public considerations do not stand in the way and the desired surrender of the water results in greater national economic advantages....

In respect to mine waters, the same law in Section 128 materially follows the older law. Such waters are reserved to the mine owner for mining and smelting purposes, but may, however, under certain provisions be granted to third persons "for any purpose whatever." The mine owner is not responsible for any changes in the quantity of the mine water flowing out of the mine.

The mining law of the *Kingdom of Saxony* dated May 22, 1850, similarly prescribes, in Section 216, that rights to the use of water may be acquired for mining purposes by dispossession proceedings. A special chapter (IX) contains very explicit provisions concerning the use of mine water. If the mine owner does not use the waters discovered in the course of his mining operations, the *Bergamt* must grant the same to other mine proprietors for mining purposes. If the mine proprietor in whose workings the waters were discovered does not make use of his right of priority, the law then looks upon these mine waters as being the common property of all mine proprietors. In the event of a grant to one of the latter, the former cannot thereafter enforce his right of priority. This is a variation from the older law. In the event of a conflict among various miners, the greatest politico-economic value decides, where conditions are equal, but the priority of the application must also be considered. For other than mining purposes only a temporary use may be permitted, with the provision that the waters must again be surrendered for mining purposes without compensation (Sec. 252).

The foregoing mining laws cited clearly reflect the older German law. The Prussian *Allgemeines Berggesetz* of June 24, 1865, has entirely broken away from this precedent for it recognizes no appropriation and grant of flowing water, nor a compulsory surrender of the use of the water for mining purposes.

FRANCE: The impress of these Germanic usages upon the mining law of France is quite apparent.

Smirke[20] comments on the fact that Charles the Sixth and Louis the Eleventh, in the fifteenth century promulgated a system for the government of the mines of France, "evidently founded on the practice in Germany." He further states that these edicts emphasize "general liberty of search for minerals in all uncultivated places" and "rights of way and water." With some modifications in later reigns, these edicts formed the groundwork of the general mining law of France. Still later Napoleon's Mining Code of 1810 was adopted, which provided that:

> Streams of water which are found within reach or which can be brought to these establishments without detriment to their use by the inhabitants etc., may be granted to those having mining concessions.[21]

ENGLAND: As already noted, the English mining law received its impress from the Germanic. At the same time it must be recognized that the mining usages and customs in certain of the mining districts of England are of great antiquity.[22] The great mass of English mining law in the Middle Ages represents usage pure and simple.[23]

The following authorities establish the fact that the law of prior appropriation which prevailed in the mining districts in Germany also prevailed in the mining districts of the British Isles.

In *Derbyshire,* the miners were "entitled to rights of way . . . from the mine to the nearest running stream, spring, or natural pond; and to use the water from such stream, spring or pond for mining purposes."[24] They had the right to "running water to wash their ore withal" "and also shall have the next water to their several uses" and "all Miners within the King's Field ought to have the next Wood and Waters of the King's Land."[25]

In *Cornwall,*

Bounders (claim stakers) are entitled by custom to the free use of the water over the whole of the district within their bounds; and to the right of diverting that water into other streams. Indeed "streaming for tin," which is a process for obtaining grain tin by means of washing, is almost always a necessary part of their operations; and for this purpose, "streamers for tin" usually secure a conduit of water from the nearest stream. Bounders may, moreover, carry an adit for the passage of water through other men's bounds in waste lands without leave.[26]

. . . the right of every tinner to divert water for the use of his tin bound is affirmed in the charters of Edw. 1, . . . "divertere aquas—*sicut consueverunt. . . .*"[27]

The right to the use of, and to divert and foul water and water courses for the purposes of mining is affirmed in the charters of John and Edward. . . .[28]

In the tinner's charters this right is merely confirmed as having already existed time out of mind. It appears as the right of "diverting streams."[29] *"Et divertere aquas ad operationem eorum."*[30]

These customs were later enacted into statutes:

The course of streams may be altered for mining purposes under the Incl. Act, 22 and 23 Vict. c. 43. So the Duke of Cornwall, and persons acting under his authority, may take, use, and divert water for mining purposes under the Act, 7 and 8 Vict. c. 105. So streams may be diverted and used for mining purposes under the Irish Act, 46 Geo. 3 c. 71. And streams may be employed for mining purposes under the Irish Act, 23 and 24 Vict. c. 154.[31]

British Colonies: In more recent times, in other parts of the British Empire, similar rights have been recognized. The mining laws of the *Malay Peninsula* provided as follows:

58. (i) It shall be lawful for the Warden to issue to any person who is working or is about to work any land for mining by virtue of any legal title, a license to divert, make use of and deliver such water as is therein mentioned, in such places, by such means, in such manner, in such quantities and on such conditions as he may think fit.[32]

Natal had similar provisions:

70. Water rights shall be granted to the registered holder of a prospecting or mining claim, or machine stand.[33]

The mining laws of the *Orange Free State of South Africa* similarly provided for "mining water rights" to be used by the holder of a "mynpacht" or mining claim.[34]

The mining laws of the *Transvaal Colony* contained the following provision:

115. It shall be lawful for every holder of a mynpacht or claim or parts thereof to obtain on application to the Resident Magistrate a certificate of special registration of his mynpacht or claim or parts thereof, together with any mining water rights, rights of way, rights of leading water, etc.[35]

In all the *Australian States* the holder of a "miner's right" has the privilege of entering upon any Crown lands for the purpose of prospecting and may secure in his own right certain claims and the use of water therefor.[36]

The mining laws of *Queensland*, Australia, provided that the holder of a miner's right shall be entitled:

(3) To take or divert water from any natural spring, lake, pool, or stream situate in or flowing through Crown lands, and to use such water for mining purposes and for his own domestic purposes....[37]

Similarly, the laws of *Tasmania* provided that a mining lessee might take and divert water

...from any spring, lake, pool or stream situate or flowing upon or through, or bounded by, any Crown lands in such manner as shall be prescribed by such water right and Regulations, in order to supply water for mining and domestic purposes to such person.[38]

Under the Gold Mining Ordinance of 1867 (Part X), the Water Clauses Consolidation Act, and the Placer Mining Act of 1891 (Sec. 64) of *British Columbia*, the right to divert and use water for mining was granted to the first appropriator.[39]

SPAIN: King Charles the Third of Spain ordered a study to be made of the mining laws of the world, and Gamboa's famous *Comentarios a las Ordenanzos de Minas*, published in the year 1759, sets forth the result of this research. Gamboa states that the mining laws of Germany formed the basis of the new Spanish ordinances.

The "Royal Ordinances for the Miners of New Spain" promulgated by the King of Spain in 1783 provided that water might be "taken from the river, brook or pool" for washing ores (XLVII) and that owners of mines might establish their refining plants near and "freely make use" of the waters of a river or brook (LII).[40]

These ordinances of Spain became the mining law of the Spanish possessions in South and Central America, and in Mexico. We find that either these ordinances, with modifications, are still in force in the South and Central American Republics or that new codes patterned upon these have been adopted.

The *Argentine Republic* has the following:

Mines, by reason of the benefits which the public derives from their proper operation, are privileged property. ... Under the same principle a number of easements are created in favor of the mines. ... These easements are substantially governed by the same rules which are observed in all countries since the days of the Roman law. The owner of a mine has always, for instance, the right of way through the lands of his neighbor, or the right to use the water which he needs for his works.[41]

In the *Mining Laws of the Republic of Colombia,* Chapter XIV, entitled "Waters for Mines," these provisions are given:

Art. 205. *The discoverer of the first mine* found in any locality *has a preferential right,* over all other subsequent discoverers, to take the water necessary in the judgment of experts for an ordinary installation, and for the persons thereof; and he can enforce this right at any time whatsoever, even though he has not worked the mine and even though, to make such right effective, it may be necessary to suspend work in an establishment installed on a mine discovered subsequently (to the first mine).

Art. 206. *Other discoverers acquire a like right, subordinated to that of prior, and preferential to that of subsequent discoverers, in strict order in point of time.* (Italicized by the author.)[42]

In the *Honduras Republic* we find the following:

The mining industry shall have "the right to use the woods and waters extant in public or vacant lands."[43]

In *Mexico* the law reads:

Art. 93. Should there occur the denouncement [location or appropriation] of some current of water for power or for the washing of metals, said denouncement shall be admitted and substantiated with the same procedure employed in the denouncement of mines both in the case in which the same water may have been previously utilized for said purpose, if it be denounced as abandoned or deserted and when it has no known owner....

The ownership of a current of water or water fall shall be lost and may be adjudged to the party denouncing, whenever it shall not have been utilized during twenty-six consecutive or interrupted weeks inside of one year previous to the denouncement. The water which may have been utilized in reduction works cannot be denounced unless the works themselves are abandoned.[44]

...Whatever may have been the general law throughout the Republic of Mexico on the subject of water, it is reasonably certain that in the *State of Sonora* [Mexico] the doctrine of appropriation, as now recognized, was to some extent in force by custom.[45]

In *Nicaragua* the law states:

Sec. 20. Authorization can be given to the owners either of a mine or of a reducing or smelting establishment, to take advantage ... of the waters of some river or water course running in the neighborhood of their property.[46]

Title XIII of the *Mining Ordinances of Peru* provides for acquisition of water rights for mines.[47]

In *Uruguay,*

Art. 19 of the Code of Mining Laws authorizes "the use of the natural water running" in the vicinity of the mine.[48]

UNITED STATES: The mining regions of the western United States have been no exception to the general rule that has been here developed. In the very early days of mining in California, the miners adopted as a part of their rules and customs the right of prior appropriation of water for use in operating the mines. The conditions which surrounded these pioneer adventurers were virtually the same as the conditions confronting the miners of the Middle Ages. The mining regions were unoccupied, uncultivated, waste lands constituting the "Public Domain." There were no mining laws applicable. The miners were technically trespassers. The federal government remained inactive, so that the miners were compelled to make their own laws. Their rules, usages, and customs bear a striking resemblance to those which arose centuries earlier in Germany, England, and other parts of the world. The right of the discoverer or first finder of the mineral was everywhere recognized. The same necessities resulted in giving a superior right to the first appropriator of water from a flowing stream. *Qui prior est in tempore, potior est in jure,*[49] was made applicable to water rights as well as to mining claims. Pomeroy has made in *The Law of Riparian Rights* (1887) an excellent statement of

> . . . the origin of the peculiar doctrines concerning water rights as settled in the Pacific communities. Water was an indispensable requisite for carrying on mining operations; a permanent right to use certain amounts of water was as essential as the permanent right to occupy a certain parcel of mineral land. The streams and lakes were all on the public domain. For their advantageous employment it was often necessary to divert water from its natural bed, and to carry it through artificial channels,—"ditches" or "flumes,"—sometimes of great length and constructed at an enormous cost. There were no riparian owners or occupants except the miners, and the streams could be put to no beneficial use except for purposes of mining. From all these circumstances, and from the very necessities of the situation, it universally became one of the mining customs or regulations that the right to use a definite quantity of water, and to divert it if necessary from these streams and lakes, could be acquired by prior appropriation (Sec. 15).[50]

As with the customs and usages which had developed in Europe in the Middle Ages, a failure to use the water for periods of time that varied in different mining districts resulted in a forfeiture of the appropriation right just as a failure to work the mining claim resulted in its forfeiture. The right to mine the claim rather than ownership of the fee simple was of outstanding importance in the early days, and the right to use the water in connection with such mining was what counted. The Supreme Court of California recognized these "customs of the diggings" at a very early date. The fact of priority controlled "the right to divert the streams from their natural channels" as well as "the privilege to work the mines."[51]

The Supreme Court of the United States also gave its sanction to this principle of priority, and we find set forth in Justice Fields' inimitable style a picture of the conditions which confronted the miner on the public domain in the early days.[52] He directs attention to the fact that this doctrine of prior appropriation was, after eighteen years, during which the miners occupied the public domain under sufferance, finally recognized by Act of Congress. This Act of 1866 provided that

> Whenever, by priority of possession, rights to the use of water for min-

ing . . . have vested and accrued, and the same are recognized and acknowledged by the local customs, laws and decisions of the courts, the possessors and owners of such vested rights shall be maintained and protected in the same.[53]

The doctrine of prior appropriation as applied to water rights was codified in Sections 1410–1422 of the Civil Code of California. The doctrine spread all over the West wherever mining was carried on. It obtained such a firm foothold in many of the states and was so well suited to the semi-arid conditions of those states, as well as to the necessities of the mining industry, that the riparian doctrine was repudiated, and today the doctrine of prior appropriation created by the miners controls exclusively the acquisition and tenure of water rights in those states. The history of the origin and development of this prior appropriation doctrine has received such adequate and comprehensive treatment by text writers that it would be out of place to present the subject here.[54] In other western states, notably California, Oregon, and Washington, a dual system has grown up, the law of these states recognizing both the riparian and appropriation doctrines. In California the riparian doctrine has the ascendancy in spite of the fact that it was in California that the miners originated the appropriation idea as applicable to water; in Oregon, by judicial interpretation, the riparian doctrine has been relegated to a subordinate position. In California, the conflict between these two doctrines and the supremacy given the riparian doctrine in the famous case of *Lux v. Haggin* 69 Cal. 255 furnishes one of the most picturesque and stirring incidents in the annals of California litigation.[55]

The authorities cited herein were collected in a research which was by no means exhaustive; there are doubtless many other authorities for the free right of the prior appropriator to use water for mining purposes, that might be added to this formidable list. These examples, however, at least serve to establish the main thesis of this article, namely: that the doctrine of prior appropriation of water has been almost universally in force in the important mining regions of the world, and that it even antedates the extant records.

NOTES TO COLBY ESSAY

[1] Demosthenes in some of his orations describes in great detail the laws governing these operations. *Man and Metals,* by T. A. Rickard (1932), contains an excellent and authoritative chapter on "The Athenians and Their Silver Mines."

[2] Smirke, *Stannaries of Cornwall* (1843), p. 81 Appendix. See also Hoover's translation of Agricola's *De Re Metallica,* fn., pp. 83–84, and *Man and Metals,* Chap. XI, on "The Law of the Mines and the Freedom of the Miner."

[3] A splendid English translation was published by Herbert C. Hoover in 1912. In a footnote to Agricola's Book IV dealing with the Germanic mining laws, pp. 82–86, Mr. Hoover has given a comprehensive and valuable comment on comparative mining law.

[4] Chas. H. Shinn, *Mining Camps* (1885).

[5] Smirke, *op. cit.,* 83 Appendix. Also see Arundel Rogers, *The Laws of Mines, Minerals, and Quarries* (ed. 2), p. 53.

[6] "The mining laws of the Middle Ages do not create, but rather recognize and establish, the customs of miners previously existing. . . ."—*Ibid.,* 52.

[7] See Rickard, *op. cit.* Chap. XI; Alford, *Mining Law of the British Empire.*

[8] Smirke, *op. cit.* 84, 85, 88.

[9] *Ibid.,* 83 Appendix. It was not the land so much as the necessary privilege of working the mine that was granted.—Mander's *Derbyshire Mining Glossary* (1834), p. 57.

[10] That the Germanic mining laws founded on custom were adopted by other countries, notably England, France, Spain, Russia, etc., see Smirke, *op. cit.* 85–95 and note "g" p. 94; Alford, *op. cit.* 12; Walmesley, *Guide to the Mining Laws of the World,* p. 22. The last-named concludes that the American mining law, which originated in the miners' customs of California, "is probably Germanic in origin."—p. 163.

[11] The rights of "der erste Finder" are mentioned in a decision made in the mining district of Joachimsthal, December, 1606, being the thirty-sixth decision in a digest of six hundred Germanic mining decisions, published in 1636 A.D. (*Sechs Hundert Bergt Urthel,* pp. 4, 10).

[12] Probably the most comprehensive and authoritative exposition of the Germanic law of waters used for mining purposes is to be found in an article the title to which as translated is "The Right of a Mine Owner to the Use of Flowing Water, etc.," by Dr. H. Achenbach, in the *Zeitschrift für Bergrecht* for the year 1870, p. 76. Dr. Achenbach was for many years co-editor of this Journal of Mining Law and published several treatises on mining law. He was also Privy Counselor of Mining at Berlin. Most of the material on Germanic law in this essay is derived from this source and from Hertwig's *Bergbuch* and the *Sechs Hundert Bergt Urthel* published in Germany in 1636. The writer takes this opportunity of expressing his profound appreciation of the masterly work of the late Walter J. Aschenbrenner in translating the old Germanic material which forms the basis of this portion of this essay. He would also express his great debt to his wife, Rachel Vrooman Colby, for unfailing assistance in translations and similar matters.

[13] Joachimsthaler Bergordnung, 1548, Part II, Art. 104.

[14] *Kursächsische Bergwerkeverfassung,* pp. 97, 101, LXXIII.

[15] Nieder-Oesterreichische Bergordnung, 1553, Art. 9 (*Ursprung der Bergwerke,* p. 168).

[16] Appendix to Joachimsthaler Bergordnung, 1548, to Art. 104 (*Ebend.,* p. 102).

[17] Kurkölnische Bergordnung, 1669, Part IX, Art. 4 (Brassert, p. 642).

[18] *Op. cit.*, Part II, Art. 3 (Brassert, p. 536). Compare *Bergrechtsspiegel*, Part II, Chap. IV, Sec. 4, p. 195; also Hertwig, *Bergbuch, sub voce* "Watter."

[19] See monograph of Beyers, *in* Brassert, pp. 105, 286, 300.

[20] *Op. cit.* 85.

[21] Halleck, *De Fooz on the Law of Mines*, p. 232.

[22] Rogers, *op. cit.* 457; Alford, *op. cit.* 10.

[23] Lewis, *The Stannaries*, p. 82.

[24] *MacSwinney on Mines* (ed. 3), p. 751.

[25] *Mineral Laws of Derbyshire* (1734 ed.), p. 8.

[26] MacSwinney, *op. cit.* 438; also 439.

[27] *Bainbridge on Mines and Minerals* (ed. 5), p. 144.

[28] Rogers, *op. cit.* 462.

[29] Lewis, *op. cit.* 163.

[30] *Stannary Charters of 1201* A.D. (Lewis, p. 238).

[31] MacSwinney, *op. cit.* 438–439, 408–409.

[32] Alford, *op. cit.* 77.

[33] *Ibid.* 165–166.

[34] *Ibid.* 176.

[35] *Ibid.* 195.

[36] *Ibid.* 210.

[37] *Ibid.* 236.

[38] *Ibid.* 259.

[39] Martin's *Mining Cases*, I: 10, 64, 422, 460.

[40] Rockwell's *Spanish and Mexican Law*, pp. 341, 343.

[41] *Mines and Mining Laws of Latin America* (Bureau of the American Republics, Bulletin No. 40, April, 1892), p. 10.

[42] Chas. Bullman, *Mining Laws of the Republic of Columbia* (1892), p. 78.

[43] *Ibid.* 167.

[44] Mexican Mining Code of 1884. *Mines and Mining Laws of Latin America* (1892), p. 198.

[45] Boquillas Land & Cattle Co. v. Curtis, 213 U. S. 339, 343.

[46] *Mines and Mining Laws of Latin America* (1892), p. 234.

[47] *Ibid.* 260.

[48] *Ibid.* 279.

[49] In a rare pamphlet entitled "Jure Aquarum Metallicarum," published in Germany in 1730, the author quotes this Latin maxim as does the Supreme Court of California (5 Cal. 159, 161) in support of the doctrine of prior appropriation.

[50] John Norton Pomeroy, *The Law of Riparian Rights* (1887).

[51] Irwin v. Phillips, 5 Cal. 140, 147. Yale, *Mining Claims and Water Rights*, pp. 159, 161.

[52] Atchison v. Peterson, 87 U. S. 507, 510–515.

[53] Statutes at Large, 253.

[54] Samuel C. Weil, *Water Rights in the Western States* (ed. 3), contains (Secs. 66–99) one of the finest expositions of this doctrine. See also A. E. Chandler, *Elements of Western Water Law.*

[55] See Edward F. Treadwell, *The Cattle King,* for a most readable account of this epic contest.

THOSE PROTECTIVE TRUSTS WHICH ARE MISCALLED "SPENDTHRIFT TRUSTS" REËXAMINED

BY GEORGE P. COSTIGAN, JR.

IN JULY, 1895, John Chipman Gray, Royal Professor of Law in Harvard University, wrote that Preface to the second edition of his *Restraints on the Alienation of Property,* which has stood ever since as the classic denunciation of so-called spendthrift trusts. He advanced in it three general propositions:

(1) The desirability "of the feeling of imperative duty to use all the money that a man can control for the payment of his debts"[1] which consequently made it the part "of all in authority, and particularly of all judges, to fortify . . . the duty of keeping one's promises and paying one's debts";[2]

(2) "One of the worst results of spendthrift trusts . . . is the encouragement it gives to a plutocracy, and to the accumulation of a great fortune in a single hand, through the power it affords to rich men to assure the undisturbed possession of wealth to their children, however weak or wicked they may be";[3]

(3) The superiority of the "doctrines of laissez faire, of sacredness of contract, and of individual liberty"[4]—"The general repeal of usury laws was the crowning triumph of the system"[5]—over the view that "a main object of law is not to secure liberty of contract, but to restrain it, in the interest, or supposed interest, of the weaker, or supposed weaker, against the stronger, or supposed stronger, portion of the community. Hence, for instance, [we have] laws enacted or contemplated for eight hours' labor, for weekly payments of wages by corporations, for "compulsory arbitration," etc., that is, laws intended to take away from certain classes of the community, for their supposed good, their liberty of action and their power of contract; in other words, attempts to bring society back to an organization founded on status and not upon contract."[6]

These three numbered propositions must be met, but not necessarily seriatim and not necessarily all at once. It is clear that the first proposition is an over-statement. It does not distinguish between just debts and unjust ones, and in respect to just debts it does not allow for conflicting duties, such as those owed to a man's wife and children. The duty of keeping one's promises and paying one's debts is, indeed, a duty to be emphasized, especially by a creditor nation and by creditors, and if a due regard is had to other duties, all must approve of that emphasis. The second proposition, however, seems a gross exaggeration. When one thinks of the boost to plutocracy given to the possessors of property by those devices of practical exemption from full legal and financial responsibility for business-venture failures, known as limited partnerships and corporations, which are, indeed, expressly designed to exempt the limited partners and the shareholders of the corporations from more than a specified partial share of property loss from such failures, the rest of the loss being borne by trusting creditors, he has to smile at the great to-do made over trusts designed by a trustor to give to a favored cestui que trust, for a lifetime or less, out of the trustor's property, to which the cestui's creditors in no way contributed, an income free from interference by such cestui's creditors, whether those creditors were such at the time of the creation of the trust, or first became creditors thereafter.[7] Assurance given to trustors that they may provide spendthrift trusts, whether of limited or of unlimited amounts, for those in whom they are interested, is hardly likely to lead them, or to be an important factor in leading them, to accumulate large fortunes. As a matter of fact, it seems as if only trusts of a nonspendthrift type have played any part in the creation of a plutocracy, and that only a minor one. Even such nonspendthrift trusts as that created by Peter Thelluson, who deliberately sought to pile up accumulations through as long a period of lives as he could figure under the rule against perpetuities, so that a trust fund of about £600,000 personal property and of real property of an annual value of £4500 to £5000 would grow into a fund of anywhere from £19,000,000 to £32,000,000, failed lamentably of attaining that figure because of the litigation to which the trust gave rise, the vicissitudes of investments, and other things.[8] Spendthrift trusts may protect for a lifetime the receipt by the cestui of as much of the income of an accumulated corpus as the state of the investment market and the business judgment of the managing trustees will permit, but they are not intended to amass fortunes and they have no such effect.[9] As for the answer to Professor Gray's third proposition, that must be found, if at all, in the considerations advanced in the rest of this essay.

Perhaps there is no better way of starting a reëxamination of the so-called spendthrift trust doctrine than by considering its historical background. It is true that the doctrine is modern American and that its leading opponent, Professor John Chipman Gray, insisted that "spendthrift trusts have no place in the system of the Common Law,"[10] which would seem to be a negation of any common law historical background for the doctrine. There are, however, certain historical things to remember which bear on our problem, and which Professor Gray, even in his moments of kindliness, overlooked; as when he declared that "The education and support to which any and every person is entitled at Common Law is an education at the public schools and a support as a pauper."[11] That statement has a false implication and, in addition, lets in the effect of legislation as a modifier of the nonstatutory common law and lets in a statutory background of some significance. At the strict nonstatutory common law, and therefore a common law uninfluenced by humanitarian legislation, even a serf was not entitled to support as a pauper or otherwise, but got only what, if anything, it was worth the lord's while or was the lord's pleasure to give him, and, apart from contract, no poor freeman was entitled to support as a pauper or otherwise but got such support, if at all, by an act of private charity or of statutory public provision. As for education at the public schools, that was wholly statutory. Not so long before Professor Gray wrote his harsh pronouncement last quoted above, the question of whether it was proper to tax the unmarried rich or the childless married rich, in order to provide school facilities for the children of small taxpayers or of poor nontaxpayers was vigorously debated in the United States. There was a powerful sentiment in favor of leaving education to individual enterprise and to charity. It will be remembered that this sentiment was so strong in Virginia that in 1817 Thomas Jefferson was unable to get passed by the Virginia legislature a bill for primary schools, each supported and controlled by voters of the ward in which it was located.[12] The English Charity Schools, when at last they were established, furnished as a distinct charity, schooling for those who could not otherwise afford it, and it was strictly in accord with common law notions to have that the fact. Other schools for the poor came by the statutory route. It was not a common law man, but, in that degree at least, a socially minded American, who spoke of one's being "entitled" to an "education at the public schools." The support of paupers and the education of the masses were not common law but social and charitable in origin, and represented a step toward that Social Republic which was itself so abhorrent to Professor Gray.[13] The disagreeable, hard-hearted, and utterly selfish common law man—only less detestable than his fellow-robot, the economic man—has had to yield somewhat to a voluntary charity influence, and to a legislation-supported humanitarianism.

Still other historical background must be noticed, though it was not only not emphasized by Professor Gray, but not even mentioned by him, namely, the unfairness and oppression chargeable to many creditors. It is true that in the history of the common law some debtors have done atrocious things. But every atrocity by debtors is matched by fully as great atrocities by creditors. For every evasion of debt liability by debtors, there will be found an act of oppression or fraud by creditors. Indeed, the shameful treatment of debtors imprisoned for debt during the centuries when such imprisonment flourished in England, and during the time when it flourished at its worst in the United States, of itself supplies the page that is most condemnatory of creditors in the whole long relation of creditors and debtors.[14] The hard-hearted creditor, it is quite safe to assert, has been more ubiquitous and more pernicious than the unscrupulous debtor. It is curious to have the creditor of a cestui so exalted in position and honor, however devious the way in which he became a creditor or got his judgment, that he must be given even all the property which the trustor has donated from his own earnings with restrictions intended to keep it from the clutches of the beneficiary's creditor. In respect of the property supplied in that way, the creditor is seeking to reap where he has not sown, and to take what he was never meant to have. It is a moral theft, even if in a given jurisdiction it is legally sanctioned. In supporting the position of creditors, one should not forget that many are unjust creditors, however legal their claims; that debtors are often only unfortunate creditors made poor by conditions not their fault;[15] that the families of beneficiaries often have claims in conscience to the benefit of the income supplied by the trustors far superior to those of the creditors who seek to profit by the windfall of that income; that hard and fast rules are not always the best rules, and that perhaps it is time for the doctrine of the divine right of creditors to go on its way to join the doctrine of the divine right of kings.

Another bit of historical background which must not be forgotten also escaped Professor Gray. Underlying his diatribe is a curious historical error concerning the power of a creditor at common law to strip his debtor of assets. He might do so, but only if the debtor did not own choses in action or land, and did not take advantage of his opportunities of evasion in other ways. Attention has been directed to the queer results in medieval times of the doctrine of sanctuary and of the rule that an Englishman's house was his castle and not to be broken into to serve civil process. The latter result is detailed in a complaint to King Charles IX, of France, by some French merchants who had been trading in England.

> The English merchant [they wrote] has this privilege, that when he has bought goods and intends to become a bankrupt—he can retire into his house, or even into his shop, provided that the door is closed with a lock or some barrier; and the bailiff cannot touch his goods, nor can any one disturb him nor demand any account from him, nor arrest him or even talk to him, even though the poor ruined creditors may see the bankrupt in his house, with his wife, his factors and servants, publicly selling their goods in front of their eyes, without being able to attach these goods or any of the debtor's real or personal property.[16]

As for choses in action, not until 1838 did a statute permit money, bank notes, bills of exchange, cheques, or bonds to be seized on execution.[17] As for real property,

> From the thirteenth year of Edward I., one-half (Stat. 13 Edw. I. c. 18), and since the year 1838 the whole (Stat. 1 & 2 Vict. c. 110, s. 11), of a man's freeholds has been liable to be taken *in execution of a judgment* for debt or damages against him; the creditor having the right to hold the land so taken till his claim be satisfied out of the profits, and being enabled of late

years to obtain a sale of the property and payment out of the proceeds. See stats. 1 & 2 Vict. c. 110, s. 13; 27 & 28 Vict. c. 112, ss. 4–6.[18]

As for personal property of the debtor, so great was the respect of the law for the right of immunity of the person from other than imprisonment that jewelry and wearing apparel actually worn and personal property held in the hand could not be seized.[19] And most extreme, perhaps, of all was the rule that if the creditor imprisoned his debtor for the debt, the creditor thereby became deprived of all other process for collection.[20] It must have been maddening to certain creditors to see their debtors in the debtors' prisons spending money and displaying property which because imprisonment was an exclusive remedy could not be reached!

Now we are ready to come closer to our specific problem of the spendthrift trust. At once it becomes necessary to say a few words about the common law doctrines of forfeitures on alienation. To our surprise we notice that the common law tolerated, and perhaps welcomed, forfeitures on alienation designed to defeat creditors. From what is sometimes said about spendthrift trusts, one might be led to believe that the common law abhorred any and every defeat of creditors. So far, the leading common law nations have been creditor nations, and naturally they have been strong champions of the duties of debtors to creditors. One might have expected, therefore, that the common law would insist that the duty to pay creditors should prevail over a provision for a forfeiture of an interest in the event that the owner of the interest became indebted and his creditors levied on that interest preparatory to selling it, but such was not the legal development. Even a creditor-nation common-law state, then, may contemplate with equanimity the defeat of creditors of individual debtors by a clause forfeiting certain interests of the individual debtors upon attempted involuntary alienation by creditors wherever third persons attach such forfeiture clauses to the life interests vested by them in the debtors. Forfeitures of estates for years and estates for life are allowed where a condition or conditional limitation for insolvency, bankruptcy of the one having the interest, or for the seizure of the interest on attachment or execution, or for other proceeding to subject the interest to the payment of a debt is attached to the estates.[21] It seems that it is not so much that the common law wants creditors paid whether or no, but that it is opposed to having debtors refuse to pay creditors and still retain the property. No doubt the common law has been forced by statute to contemplate some violation of its preferences, because there are statutory exemptions from execution, statutory denial of access by creditors to trusts created for the indebted cestuis by others, etc., but it does not voluntarily do so. It is something to know that the real cause of distress to the common law is not that creditors go unpaid but rather that they go unpaid when the debtors have property out of which they ought to be paid.

The next thing to notice is the archaic nature of the legal argument for the common law view. "Necessary incidents" or "inseparable incidents" of property interests and "repugnancy" of restraints or of other objectionable conditions are the notions on which the common law hinges its denunciations of such restraints or conditions, yet spendthrift trusts, both those created by equity decisions and those established by statutes, have shown that what the common law calls "necessary" and "inseparable" and "repugnant" are not really such, but are merely a common law judge's, or an English chancery judge's overstatement of preference.[22] As a matter of fact, as Professor Gray of course clearly recognized, whether forfeitures of any particular kind shall be recognized, and whether restraints on alienation, voluntary or involuntary or both, shall be permitted, are purely questions of humanity and of wise public policy. Accordingly, in this discussion, the old-fashioned language of the reports will be dismissed and the question of policy confronted.[23]

Now to come to the spendthrift trust.[24] Why has the spendthrift trust doctrine had such a vogue in the United States? The judicial explanation seems to be that the courts have felt that a donor of property ought to be able to keep the donee's creditors from seizing it sooner or later and thereby sometime or other defeating the gift. It is believed that the courts have not been wholly candid in that explanation. No doubt the reason given has been a factor, and indeed an important factor, in influencing court action,[25] but unquestionably it has not been the sole factor. With respect to the separate use for married women, no doubt an important factor in chancery action was the feeling that the wish of the trustor that the property which he specifically provided for his daughter or other woman relative should be free from any anticipation of income by her and from any possible defeat of the provision for her by her husband or by his creditors was a natural one calling properly for chancery assistance in its fulfillment. That was particularly evident when before marriage the woman established the separate use for herself with her prospective husband's knowledge and possible consent.[26] But in addition, unquestionably, an equally potent reason must have been the pitiable state of hundreds of married women whose husbands, under the legal rules applicable to the married woman's property of various kinds, had each appropriated his wife's personal property in possession (except for a small amount of paraphernalia), reduced her choses in action to possession and realized upon her chattels real, and appropriated the rents and profits of her freehold property, without even supporting her. So, too, in these later times it must often have happened that various beneficiaries of so-called spendthrift trusts were actually incompetent to look after their affairs or were actually spendthrifts, though family pride or inadequate legislation stood in the way of obtaining a judicial decree to that effect and of obtaining the appointment of a guardian or committee, and their defenseless state must have had its influence in the decision that so-called "spendthrift trusts," better called protective trusts, established for them by others, must be enforced.[27] Certainly the need of protection for the beneficiary, at least to the extent of keeping him from becoming a public charge, would seem to be one of the fundamental grounds for the judicial or the statutory establishment of "spendthrift trusts," just as it was one for such establishment of separate uses for married women.

Unfortunately for the good of the spendthrift trust doctrine, and for its more general adoption in what seems to the writer to be its preferable form, in spite of the prejudice aroused against it by Professor Gray, and in spite of the necessary admission that such preferable form is not ideal, the need of the protection for the cestui was not stressed in the spendthrift trust cases, but the supposed freedom of the donor to protect his own acquired property from the creditors of his donee was emphasized, with the result that in many jurisdictions the creators of spendthrift trusts were permitted to provide for the beneficiaries of such trusts, regardless of their real needs or their best good, incomes of any amount—no matter how large—free from the claims of the beneficiaries' creditors. Had the ground of the need of the protection of the beneficiaries been emphasized, it would easily have been made to appear that often only a reasonable amount of income should be freed from the claims of the creditors. In respect to the separate use for married women, naturally any amount of property could be settled to such use, since the protection was only given against her husband and his creditors, and since, the property being all hers in equity and good conscience, if not at law, he and they could not be deemed properly aggrieved by the separate use clause, at least so long as the husband was allowed to have curtesy consummate in her equitable estates of inheritance. But in respect to spendthrift trusts, creditors of the beneficiaries of such trusts may have proper grievances if excessive incomes are provided for their debtors by spendthrift trust provisions while the creditors go unpaid. Had the need of the beneficiary, and not the prideful and lordly disposition of the donor, been the professed judicial ground of the spendthrift trust, the protected income from the amount settled on such trusts would have been kept, with certain exceptions, within only a reasonable income limit fixed by the judges or by the legislature. That was not the openly accepted judicial ground, however, and it was only certain legislatures that forced either the reasonable income limit, or the outside principal or annual income limit in their states. The reasonable income limit exists in New York and a few other states.[28] The outside annual income legislative limit exists in two forms: (1) an annual income fixed sum amount;[29] and (2) the amount of income from a maximum amount of principal.[30]

It is true that, even in its reasonable income form, the spendthrift trust has its opponents. Professor Gray, in his classic Preface, denounced exemptions from execution as well as spendthrift trusts, because of the tendency of such protections to debtors and beneficiaries to make them weaklings,[31] and he especially denounced the New York form of the spendthrift trust because of the snobbish attitude of some of the New York courts in considering it proper to allow more income free from creditors for " 'a gentleman of high social standing, whose associations are chiefly with men of leisure, and who is connected with a number of clubs' " and who must have income "sufficient to maintain his position according to his education, habits and associations," than must suffice a man "who has lived simply and plainly."[32] No doubt there has been a certain amount of indefensible diversity in the New York decisions, some of them being clearly discriminatory and snobbish;[33] but that diversity has come about largely through the wrong theory that the trustor's wishes are the important thing and through an over-emphasis on those wishes and on his supposed knowledge and approval of the scale of living of the beneficiary. The New York courts may be expected to take in the future a saner view in respect of variations of income. If only those courts would make the real needs of the beneficiaries and not the intent of the trustor the vital thing, sound decisions might almost always be looked for.

In a democracy and when human needs are being measured, it is in general undesirable to treat one man by judicial decision better than another without sufficient reason for the discrimination, but at times some variation is unavoidable. Individual human needs vary considerably. For generations distinctions in necessaries have been drawn in respect of infants. A necessary for one infant is a luxury for another. So divorce courts in awarding alimony have properly fixed one amount for one wife and a different amount for another. The wealthy and the less wealthy have differing claims and needs and there is no excuse for courts' not giving that fact a reasonable recognition by making proper but fair diverse provisions for those varying needs. The objection to any award for the support of one person should not be that it varies from the award made to another, but that, if such is the fact, it varies for no sufficient reason or varies more than any reason for variation will justify. No doubt, as Professor Gray pointed out, a few indefensible decisions have been made in the enforcement of spendthrift trusts, but where statutes have not prevented rationality, most of these have probably resulted, not, as he thought, from snobbishness, but from the wrong theory that, because the trustor supplied the trust property, his intent must prevail to the extent of enabling the spendthrift beneficiary in New York to live as nearly as possible as he has been accustomed to do, and in Massachusetts, for example, to have all the trust income, no matter how much it amounts to, free from interference by creditors until after the beneficiary receives it.

While spendthrift trusts may be condemned to the extent that they exceed a reasonable amount of income, how many of such excess incomes are provided by such trusts? The possibilities of such trusts are many; the probabilities are that there really are very few of them. Most spendthrift trusts probably are for amounts which provide only fairly reasonable incomes for beneficiaries who need protection from others.[84] No doubt one whose ideal is the rugged but selfish common law man who, theoretically, always stood on his own feet and unaided defied fate to do its worst, will be impatient with those who have not the same ruggedness and standing ability, and no doubt many of the creditor class will always be irritated, if not shocked, by any protection for debtors through spendthrift trusts and through exemptions from execution. But those who have weathered a world depression in which great numbers of men, without any fault of their own, have been engulfed in financial ruin, and those who have aided in the establishment or maintenance of free-bed hospitals, of orphan asylums, and of all sorts of other charitable social agencies for the refuge or assistance of the misfits, the weak and suffering, the aged, etc., of society, may properly be expected to take a more humane view and to appreciate the fairness of permitting some of the actually and of the possibly weak, and even some of the strong, to be protected by reasonable provision made to keep them from becoming dependent on private or public charity.[85] After all, even the best planned spendthrift trusts have to face the hazards of shrinkage or depletion by business depressions, etc., and it may be doubted if it can be shown that even the largest of such trusts in a jurisdiction which does not limit the size of incomes which are to be free from interference by creditors, have done any but a small amount of harm to the social fabric.[86] It probably will be found, when a proper survey is undertaken, that the beneficiaries of spendthrift trusts, even when not required by tradesmen and others to pay cash, have paid, in general, those bills which ought to be paid. Not all creditors deserve to be paid, though no spendthrift trust antagonist likes to concede that, and probably not many spendthrift trust beneficiaries refuse to pay those who ought to be paid. It has always been true that many inconsiderate rich have treated their tradesmen's bills in a way not to be justified even though such rich were not spendthrift trust beneficiaries. While such rich may be permitted to run up bills, it is hardly likely in these days of credit ratings that spendthrift trust beneficiaries will be allowed to run up bills unless their reputations for paying their bills justify the credit.

When one reflects upon the intemperance of Professor Gray's tirade against exemptions from executions and against spendthrift trusts, one realizes how far we have gone in the direction of social betterment. If only the courts had shown more sense in shaping the spendthrift trust doctrine, first, by restricting the so-called spendthrift cestui's protection against his creditors to only a reasonable amount of support for himself and his dependents (except, perhaps, that the trustor's wife, and his women relatives inexperienced in business, and his children, might be allowed larger incomes[37]), and, secondly, with the possible exception just noted, by figuring that reasonable amount conservatively in view of what ought to suffice for him and his dependents during the time when his creditors have to go unpaid—if only the courts had so proceeded, social betterment would have been served still more. No longer, in most places, may the creditor throw his honest debtor into debtors' prison; and if the debtor has a spendthrift trust created for him by another, and if the trust fund survives in sufficient amount, no longer may the creditor force the spendthrift trust beneficiary debtor and his dependents into the bread line or into the poorhouse. If only the debtor is not allowed to have too much while the creditor goes unpaid, what harm is done? We are accustomed to speak of there being normally only two or three generations from shirt sleeves to shirt sleeves, thereby in substance stating that, in general, the time is short between the creation of fortunes and their dissipation. What is the harm if some part of these fortunes is allowed to assist in keeping some members of the family out of the poorhouse for their lives? Or, to take a more common situation, the life insurance companies have statistics showing the pitifully short time, on the average, that widows receiving unrestricted life insurance money from policies on the lives of their dead husbands manage to retain such money. Why should it not be possible to provide adequate spendthrift trust protection for them against emotional appeals for money and against persuasively presented poor investments, so that they may be kept from becoming dependents on relatives or inmates of poorhouses?

It is true that Professor Gray thought the ultimate effect of exemptions from execution, spendthrift trusts, etc. would be that we should become a nation of weaklings, and Professor Richard B. Powell has recently quoted[38] against spendthrift trusts some casual and impressionistic remarks by Mr. Frederic J. Stimson[39] to show that the spendthrift trust has been the cause of the commercial decline of Boston. Unfortunately, Professor Powell did not quote the passage in full, and so failed to reveal that, apparently, the attack was not against spendthrift trusts, but against all family settlement trusts of the rich. Indeed, Mr. Stimson showed such small comprehension of spendthrift trusts as to assert that they do not exist in New York and to date their beginning in Massachusetts in 1830, which was approximately the New York statutory date, though they did not gain judicial sanction in Massachusetts until 1882, when the case of *Broadway National Bank v. Adams*[40] was decided. Here is a word for word quotation from part of the book:

The next most notable cause of Boston's commercial (I am so far speaking only of that) decline is the "spendthrift trust" decision of Massachusetts courts. (It is not the law in New York or elsewhere.[41]) Somewhere about 1830[42] they decided that a man could tie his children's inheritance up, either by deed or will, so that they could not spend or risk the principal, so that they could make no contract in favor of their creditors which would be binding on their trustees, so that they could not risk their capital in a new enterprise or indeed embark it in any business. Immense wealth had been accumulated in Boston in the first sixty years of the republic: instead of trusting their sons and sending them out at their own risks with all their argosies upon life's seas (as they themselves had done), they distrusted their ability (and this distrust by Boston of the ability of her sons ran through all the post-Civil War times, and in many other ways, as we shall see) and had them all trusteed. No new enterprise could be undertaken by them, for under that court decision they had no capital to risk. Perforce they became coupon-cutters—parasites, not promoters of industry—with the natural results to their own characters. Hence the John M. Forbes type of Bostonian came largely to an end. It was as if the argosies of Venice had been realized and the proceeds placed with Shylock at four per cent. Shylock took no risks, and the Boston Bassanio, bored, spent his four per cent in elegant living—to do him justice, greatly promoting art, charity, public service—but the consequences were disastrous to a Venetian commercial supremacy; and business down-town was left to smaller men, with narrower traditions, taking retail but not wholesale risks. So supine are they that Boston shippers will not complain when, under New York order, they have to ship goods by rail from Boston to New York to be loaded there for Argentina, though the very steamer which takes them to Buenos Aires discharged its cargo in Boston (for Boston still has an import trade) and lay there a week in sight of the Boston man's warehouse. He may not load it there, but must pay tribute to the New York railroad and contribute his own mite to the greatness of New York's harbor by sending his shipment by rail to New York.

And thus, placing all the young intelligentsia under financial guardianship, the natural consequences ensued in other ways. The French *rentier,* however saving, is notoriously an inadventurous person in business. Indeed, the superior energy and initiative—even the imagination—of the British, though "but a nation of shopkeepers," may be ascribed to this. The effect of making Boston's youth, of its best tradition and education, mere four per cent men, was to choke off their own energies and largely divorce business and the Brahmins. True, they were replaced, in the down-town stores and counting-rooms, by some fresh country stock; as, in law or city politics, Harvard has been led by Dartmouth. New Hampshire swarmed into the Hub like the Scots into London. But, however sharp and clever, it may be questioned whether something of the broad vision, almost idealism, in the enterprises of the old Boston merchants, mill-founders, railroad-builders, was not lost in the exchange. Of course, there were notable exceptions; also many sons of the old Boston families moved upon New York, as the New Hampshire and Maine men had moved on Boston. In the eighties and nineties there were far more New Englanders than Knickerbockers at the head of "big business" in New York; and in politics as well. . . .[43]

In the first place, these statements of Mr. Stimson are mere guesses. There is no evidence that spendthrift trusts have weakened strong characters or kept them from developing. Moreover, the argument of Mr. Stimson seems to be directed against all trusts and not merely spendthrift trusts, though he makes that uncertain by using the words "spendthrift trusts," yet making the extraordinary assertion that such trusts are "not the law of New York or elsewhere"! Because a class of caretakers known as trustees manage the fortunes entrusted to them, he seems to say, the beneficiaries become weak or at least have no opportunity and no incentive to do other than receive trust income. That may be any man's guess, but so also may be the view that the strong will make their way even against the handicap, if it be a handicap, of life incomes. In a world where women rarely worked, the fact that women trust-annuitants did not work meant little. In a world where men in general worked, and in view of the apparent circumstance that many strong men's sons have lacked their fathers' strength and initiative, even when no trust funds, let alone spendthrift trust funds, have handicapped the sons, it is not strange that many men, lacking their fathers' abilities, and with sufficient incomes provided for them, passed their time in ease and, where possible, in luxury. The loss to business, if any, may have been the gain of art, literature, and general culture, in spite of the doubts expressed by Mr. Stimson. But, apart from that, if he is right that the best business ability of Massachusetts migrated to New York, the country as a whole was no loser. It is very much to be doubted whether trusts in general, or even spendthrift trusts, whether or not providing only a reasonable income, have been a really deteriorating influence for those who, without such trusts, would not have deteriorated, though a conclusion in respect to that is anybody's guess. At the most the case of Mr. Stimson against trusts in general, and even that against the spendthrift trust, is unproved. Mr. Stimson apparently concedes so much, for he seems to think that Massachusetts has suffered from income trusts but that New York has not. Yet trusts in general have flourished in New York, and spendthrift trusts with only a reasonable amount of income free from the interference of creditors, were known there for generations before Professor Gray's day.

Almost invariably in legal history, incorrect legal premises have led to incorrect results, and the so-called spendthrift trust doctrine is no exception to that statement. On the contrary, that doctrine is an outstanding illustration of the bad consequences of faulty premises. The very name "spendthrift trust" is the outcome of the faulty premise that a trustor, just because he is furnishing the trust property, is entitled to provide that the beneficiary's creditors shall not be paid out of it except to the extent that trust income actually reaches the hands of the beneficiary, and thereafter is voluntarily paid over by the beneficiary or is seized by proper process. A premise like that, once accepted and stretched to its fullest extent, leads to the conclusion that the trust property may be of any amount, and that the income for the beneficiary made free from interference by creditors may be as lavish as the trustor pleases, even if that be so lavish that only spendthrifts could get rid of it. It is the spendthrift trust doctrine in that unadulterated form that has been the subject of the most severe criticism, and that kind, indefeasible as it is except as applied to a very few classes of beneficiaries, has had its bad influence in jurisdictions where the legislature has sought to restrict the exemption to a reasonable income.

And that brings us, at last, to the problem of the man who realizes that he is a spendthrift and who tries to protect himself from ultimately becoming dependent on charity or on the public for support by creating for himself a spendthrift trust. If there is anything in the argument that the beneficiary's need should affect the attitude of the court, then such a beneficiary's need should be met, provided there is no fraud on his existing creditors; that is, provided that he keeps out of the trust assets sufficient to discharge his existing debts. No doubt there is, on the one hand, a danger of defrauding future creditors that must be guarded against; but that is wholly a problem of intent, which may be ascertained, and we are assuming an intent that is legitimate. On the other hand, after the recent experiences of the United States with so-called high-powered salesmanship, there seems clearly to be a grave need that society shall protect those persons who are unable to guard themselves against objectionable importunity and against being thrown to the wolves that infest our society. Nevertheless, since they themselves provide the property to be used for their own reasonable support, free from the claims of their future creditors, and since their protection against such creditors is to be justified only to the extent that sound public policy dictates, it would seem only fair to make each trustor-beneficiary demonstrate his peculiar need for protection—his actual and not merely possible inability to fend off the human vultures seeking to gorge upon his substance. In addition it may be proper to require him, through recorded notices of the trust and through information supplied to commercial agencies and other bodies which furnish credit reports to business people, to spread the news of his self-established spendthrift trust so as to put reasonably cautious future creditors on their guard. Whatever the precautions required to be taken to prevent fraud on future creditors, once they are taken, the "easy mark" should be allowed to assure himself enough spendthrift trust income to keep him at least out of the poorhouse, not so much for his own sake, perhaps, as to save society the expense of his support, and, perhaps, to prevent the ruin of a life which might become of real value to the state.

Undoubtedly, court sanction of the creation by the actual spendthrift or self-recognized incompetent of a spendthrift trust for himself would be something new at the common law and in equity because of its wide departure from the laissez faire of that common law which equity usually "follows." But that is only because the law has not yet faced properly the problem of preventing creditors and others who prey on the weak from stripping the weak of everything they possess and thereby throwing them on the public, or on private charity, for support. No doubt it was a great departure from the common law for the American communities to tax persons able to pay to provide schooling for those children whose parents, unaided, could not provide it. No doubt, as Professor Gray argued, it was quite inconsistent with the common law for a debtor to have a considerable amount of exempt property—in large measure made exempt for the protection of the debtor's wife and children—while his creditor remained unpaid. No doubt bankruptcy statutes are also contrary to the spirit of the common law. But so are the many public institutions where the physically and mentally unfit, the infirm, and the aged are supported and clothed at the public expense. Humanitarian considerations have at least fully as much in their favor as has the ruthlessness of an uninterfered-with struggle for existence in society where the physically weak and the mentally unfit are exterminated. Human life has higher values than the selfishness and the cruelty of the common law could comprehend and always we have to rise above the common law to attain altruistic ends.[44]

It is quite orthodox for law-school teachers to speak disparagingly of the so-called spendthrift trust doctrine, whether that doctrine be unlimited in its scope or be restricted, as in California and New York, to a reasonable income provision for the particular beneficiary. Part of the odium is caused by the unfortunate name, which was designed to prejudice the hearer. The writer of this brief apology does not seek to defend the doctrine in its unlimited form, except in reference to very specially chosen beneficiaries, but he does support it in its California reasonable income form, where common sense is shown in determining the reasonable income in view of the fundamental needs of the cestuis, and in that form he thinks it should be carried farther than it has been so far carried by any court, so that one who is actually a spendthrift and who knows that he will be an easy prey for designing persons who seek to tempt and impose upon wasters, may create such a reasonable income spendthrift trust for himself so long as, and to the extent that, his spendthrift trust is not in fraud of existing creditors or a subterfuge used with fraudulent intent to enable him to speculate to the detriment of future creditors.

The spendthrift trust is chiefly an American innovation, though the English Trustee Act, 1925, supplies an approximation of the California and New York form of it under the name of Protective Trusts,[45] and though, in Scotland, what is virtually the California and New York form of it is well known under the name of Alimentary Trusts.[46] In the married women's separate use cases, the English Chancellor refused to apply the rule that equity follows the law in respect of a use designated for a married woman free from the interference or control of her husband. The reasons for that refusal have met with complete approval, and the Married Women's Separate Property Acts, both in England and in the United States, have taken the additional step of making the legal rules conform to the Chancellor's more enlightened equity notions. The many American courts of chancery jurisdiction which recognized spendthrift trusts have thereby refused to follow in equity the legal rule in respect to restraints on the alienation of life estates,[47] and in some states, even in respect to restraints on alienation of fee simple interests.[48] Moreover, in some states the refusal has met with statutory approval,[49] while, as a result of chancery refusal in that respect, in a few states the law has recognized such restraints on legal life estates,[50] and in at least one state the law has recognized such restraints on legal fee simple estates.[51] Law professors who are excessively given to championing the common law may deplore all that and say with Professor Gray, of the common law system, that its foundation was "justice, the idea of human equality and of human liberty," and that "the general repeal of usury laws was the crowning triumph of the system."[52] But those of us whose ardor for the common law is tempered by an appreciation of its harshness and even cruelty may well advocate help and protection for persons who need to be aided. A society which is coming to recognize that it has a responsibility to its members over and above that met by bread lines and by the poorhouse may well permit those who have property to provide by trusts, whether called "spendthrift" or "protective" or "alimentary" or some better name, for those living persons who at the time need, or some day may need, such provision, a proper income free from the interference of the beneficiary's creditors. It would seem as if only a failure on the part of the courts to place the argument for such trusts on the right ground, or to use common sense in figuring a reasonable income in the particular case, stands in the way of the proper administration of such trusts by the courts and their almost universal approval. Even Professor Gray had to concede:

> My modest task has been to show, that spendthrift trusts have no place in the system of the Common Law. But I am no prophet, and certainly do not mean to deny that they may be in entire harmony with the Social Code of the next century. Dirt is only matter out of place; and what is a blot on the escutcheon of the Common Law may be a jewel in the crown of the Social Republic.[53]

What he failed to acknowledge, and perhaps to see, was that the common law system itself could be improved, was actually being improved, and may be still further improved by the partial replacement of harshness and selfishness by kindly and intelligent treatment and by a reasonable amount of altruism applied to unfortunate debtors. "Spendthrift trusts" do not deserve condemnation: they should receive instead, on their merits, a more sensible and sympathetic application.

NOTES TO COSTIGAN ESSAY

[1] Gray, *Restraints on the Alienation of Property* (ed. 2; 1895), Preface, p. vii.

[2] *Ibid.* iii; also (pp. vi–vii), "Among the causes which have produced the frame of mind in which the doctrine of spendthrift trusts has found a congenial home, there must be placed the attempts to avoid payment of money borrowed by the Nation, or by States or municipalities, either through repudiation, or through technical objections, or through debasement of the coin or currency, which have at times been too successful, and which have exercised so great an influence on political parties. Such things cannot be without a weakening of the moral sense, of the feeling of imperative duty to use all the money that a man can control for the payment of his debts."

[3] *Ibid.* vi. [4] *Ibid.* viii. [5] *Ibid.* viii–ix. [6] *Ibid.* ix.

[7] "The donor owes the donee nothing [in money or property] and gets nothing in return; the transaction concerns him and the donee only. The existing creditor has no right to complain if his debtor should acquire a certain interest, which has cost the creditor nothing but which is walled against his [the creditor's] depredation. The subsequent creditor has no right to complain, for he has extended credit with full knowledge of the debtor's protected title. . . ."—Cothran, J., concurring in Spann v. Carson (1923) 123 So. Car. 371, 116 S. E. 427, 434.

So, from a slightly different viewpoint, Epes, J., for the court in Sheridan v. Krause (Va. 1934) 172 S. E. 508, 515, 91 A. L. R. 1067, 1078–1079, pointed out that "Though it gives lip service to the indisputable principle that a testator is not, unless he has obligated himself to do so, under any obligation whatever to provide for the payment of the debts of his devisee, yet the rule of Hutchinson v. Maxwell [(1902) 100 Va. 169, 40 S. E. 655, 57 L. R. A. 384, 93 Am. St. Rep. 944 against spendthrift trusts, but since changed by statute] made it impossible for a testator to provide in his will for the support and maintenance even of a hopelessly invalided son, whose only source of support has been for years the bounty of the testator, without being forced by law to pay his son's debts as the price of the right to provide for his necessities."

[8] See Thelluson v. Woodford (1805) 11 Ves. 112. It was that trust, under the will of Peter Thelluson, which took effect in 1797, that resulted in the passage of the Thelluson Act of 1800 against accumulations, 39 & 40 Geo. III c. 98, which, with some amendments, is now § 164 of the Law of Property Act, 1925, 15 Geo. 5 c. 20.

An editorial in the London *Times* for July 5, 1858, rehearsed the Thelluson case history. It stated that Peter Thelluson, having £600,000 in money and having land of the annual value of £4500 [some accounts say the land was of the annual value of £5000] died leaving three sons and six grandsons. In his will he provided that, when the last survivor of all the nine children and grandchildren should die, the property left by the testator, and its accumulations in the years, should be divided into three parts, and one-third be given to the "eldest male lineal descendant" of each of his three sons. Thereupon, said the *Times* editorial, "Persons of an arithmetical and statistical turn of mind calculated that this fund, accumulating at compound interest, could not amount to less than nineteen millions at the moment of distribution, and would very probably reach the tremendous figure of thirty-two millions." But, adds the editorial, many chancery suits were brought about the will, and even after the period for distribution arrived in February, 1856, a suit, pending when the editorial was written, was brought to decide who was the eldest male lineal descendant of one of Peter Thelluson's three sons, one being eldest in point of lineage and another eldest in point of years, a question which the House of Lords settled in favor of the eldest in point of lineage in Thelluson v. Rendelsham (1859)

7 H. L. Cas. 429. The years of chancery litigation are mentioned because to that the London *Times* ascribed the fact that at the time for distribution of the estate it was "not much larger than when he [Peter Thelluson] left it." The editorial ended, "It would be fit punishment for that purse-proud, vain, cruel old man, to see that he disinherited his own children only to fatten a generation of lawyers, that he was the dupe of his own subtlety, and that his name, instead of being associated with the foundation of a house of fabulous wealth, is only known in connection with an abortive scheme of vulgar vanity."

The foregoing editorial called forth several letters. One in the London *Times* for July 12, 1858, sought to impute good motives to Peter Thelluson, and one in the London *Times* for July 13, 1858, tried to show that a certain amount of the money which Thelluson left was entrusted to him for investment by French nobles to whom he never accounted. The important thing from our present view is that Peter Thelluson's effort to establish by accumulations an outstanding fortune for his remote descendants was a lamentable failure. Lawsuits accounted for part of that failure, but poor investments, depressions, and wars must have played their part in keeping down the estate.

In (1860) 34 L. T. J. 241, is an item entitled "A Thelluson Will Before Thelluson" which tells about a Dutch estate that by will was to accumulate for one hundred and fifty years and then be divided, and says that the immense principal of the fund, and the accumulations of 40 per cent a year for 50 years, nearly all disappeared before the end of the one hundred and fifty years, owing to the fact there stated that "The bankruptcy of the East India Company in 1775, the revolution and French invasion in 1795, the loss of colonies and trade, the war taxes, and the disastrous annexations to France, have done their work."

If deliberate attempts to swell great fortunes meet such disappointments, the fear that spendthrift trusts, which have a quite different and inconsistent purpose, will swell them, seems quite unfounded.

[9] The demonstration of that fact is perhaps the sole merit of the quotation from Stimson, *My United States* (1931) 76–78, in the text *infra* pp. 97–98.

[10] Gray, *op. cit.*, x. [11] *Ibid.* xi.

[12] Jefferson had better fortune in his efforts to establish the University of Virginia, since that was in the main for the well-to-do. Even there "He found it necessary, however, to meet the objection that it is unjust to take the property of one man to educate the children of another. He says: 'And will the wealthy individual have no retribution? and what will this be? I. The peopling of his neighborhood with honest, useful and enlightened citizens, understanding their own rights, and firm in their perpetuation. 2. When his own descendants become poor, which they generally do within three generations (no law of primogeniture now perpetuating wealth in the same families), their children will be educated by the then rich; and the little advance he now makes to poverty, while rich himself, will be repaid by the then rich, to his descendants when they become poor, and thus give them the chance of rising again.' (Letter to J. C. Cabell, January 14, 1818, in *Early History of the University of Virginia,* 105.) It is of advantage to the state to promote higher education because in colleges and universities are formed 'the statesmen, legislators and judges, on whom public prosperity and individual happiness are so much to depend'; in them 'the interests of agriculture, manufactures and commerce' are promoted, and there the 'mathematical and physical sciences, which advance the arts, and administer to the health, the subsistence, and comforts of human life,' are cherished. In a word, by providing for higher education legislators provide for the 'good and ornament of their country.' (The Report of the Commissioners Appointed to Fix the Site of the University of Virginia, Chap. VIII, §§ 3 and 4.)" Arrowwood, *Thomas Jefferson and Education in a Republic* (1930) 62–63.

[13] Gray, *op. cit.* x.

[14] Perhaps the crowning triumph of the common law was not the repeal of the Usury Acts, but was, instead, the establishment of that highly objectionable imprisonment for debt which came in mainly through English judge-made rules, though, indeed, it was helped along by statutes.—8 Holdsworth, *History of English Law* (1926 ed.) 231–232.

"The result was that in practically every case a creditor could take his debtor's body in execution. But, if he elected to adopt this remedy, as he usually did, no other mode of execution was open to him.

"Constraint of the debtor's person thus became in England a more general method of execution than in many other countries in Europe. Largely because it was introduced in this indirect [nonlegislative] way, a mode of execution which required, and in most countries received, careful limitation and regulation from the Legislature, was almost entirely unregulated. The results can be read in the pages of Dickens; and, long before Dickens wrote, the abuses and the inadequacy of the different modes of execution known to the common law had aroused attention. . . .

"Debtors might be either honest and unfortunate, or dishonest; and in both cases the law was inadequate. To shut up an honest but unfortunate debtor in prison, where he lived on charity or at his own expense, or died of starvation, inflicted much hardship on the debtor without any benefit to the creditor. On the other hand, if the debtor was a dishonest person, who had become insolvent through his own fault, he would very likely be able to secrete some of his ill-gotten gains, and live in comparative comfort in prison, till he forced his creditors to some sort of compromise."—Holdsworth, *op. cit.* 231–233.

As to the debtor dying of starvation, Holdsworth quoted part of what Montague, C. J., said in Dive v. Maningham (Eng., 1551) 1 Plowden 60, 68, which, more fully set forth, was:

"For if one be in execution he ought to live of his own, and neither the plaintiff nor the sheriff is bound to give him meat or drink, no more than if one distrains cattle, and puts them in a pound, for there the owner of the cattle ought to give them meat, and not he that distrained them, no more is the party or the sheriff, who has one in execution, bound to give meat to the prisoner, but he ought to live of his own goods, although he be in for felony, until he be attainted, and this by the course of the common law. For . . . if he has no goods, he shall live of the charity of others, and if others will give him nothing, let him die in the name of God, if he will, and impute the cause of it to his own fault, for his presumption and ill behaviour brought him to that imprisonment." But Holdsworth points out (p. 233, note 1): "14 Elizabeth c. 5, § 38 [37?] and 39 Elizabeth c. 3, § 13 provided for the assessment of a county rate for the relief of these prisoners; but it would appear . . . that its intervention was not very effective."

Certain it is that prisoners for debt at times did starve to death, and they often fared worse in respect to meat and drink than prisoners for crime, unless, at least, they could afford by begging or otherwise to pay for the right kind of both. The horrors to which poor persons imprisoned for debt were subjected have frequently been depicted.

As late as February, 1906, it was said: "As may well be supposed, the consequences of incarceration are, in many cases, disastrous: gone indeed are the horrors of imprisonment for debt, but some of its worst evils are still with us. The wife and children are often forced to seek the shelter of the workhouse; or, to avert this dreaded calamity, the woman, in her husband's absence, chooses rather to become a wanton. Such has been the beginning of many a life of shame. On his release from custody, the man is rarely able to resume his old employment, and it is generally difficult for him to secure a fresh engagement: his home is now broken up and his downfall is complete, while all this ruin has been brought about at the public charge, except in so far as the burden, in the shape of heavy Court fees, has fallen on the shoulders of the injured creditor. . . .

"At the root of the whole mischief lies a vicious credit system, which must needs yield a rich crop of unsatisfied judgments, for it may be taken as certain that so long as credit can be got credit will be had. However stringent the conditions of detention, useless goods will be successfully foisted on the extravagant and unwary, while the reckless and improvident will ever have recourse to the advertising moneylender for loans which it is not within their power to repay."—Atkinson, *Imprisonment for Debt* (1906) 31 Law Mag. & Rev. (ser. 5) 129, 144–145.

In Van Winkle, *Imprisonment for Debt,* 55 Albany L. J. 282, 303, 321, at 325–326, are set forth some of the horrors which such debtors experienced in the American colonies and in the Eastern states of the United States after statehood. New York abolished imprisonment for debt in 1831—the first state to do so. See McAdam, *The Act to Abolish Imprisonment for Debt, etc. Commonly Called "the Stilwell Act" (1880).* At page 10 the author says of the abolition: "There was great rejoicing throughout the state on the part of the poor, unfortunate but honest debtors, and on the part of the humane and charitable, and the lawyers as a class were, may it be said to their honor, almost unanimously in favor of some act to abolish imprisonment for debt."

On the extensive modern use, and the legal phases, of imprisonment for debt, see Thomson, *Imprisonment for Debt in the United States* (1889) 1 Jurid. Rev. 357; and Ford, *Imprisonment for Debt* (1926) 25 Mich. L. Rev. 24.

[15] "But it is sometimes said that most debtors, who do not pay their debts, are in some degree guilty, and merit punishment. This seems to us not quite true. Some debtors, we admit, are mere swindlers and sharpers. Others have become involved by daring speculations. Some are the victims of extravagance. Others fail from want of skill and judgment in conducting their business. We find in the conduct of debtors every moral shade, from gross fraud to the slightest negligence and entire innocence. The high degrees of fraud are comparatively rare. Slighter degrees of misconduct are more common. But judged by the current rules of mercantile honesty, we believe the majority of insolvent debtors upright and honorable."—Anonymous book reviewer *in* (1834) 11 Am. Jurist 289, 291.

[16] Treiman, *Escaping the Creditor in the Middle Ages* (1927) 43 L. Q. Rev. 230–234.

[17] "The common law rule was, that, under the writ of *fi. fa.,* the sheriff could only seize such things as he could sell (Legg. v. Evans, 6 M. & W. 36, 41) . . ."—*Williams on Personal Property* (ed. 18; 1926) 113.

"Debts, being considered as mere rights of action, could not formerly be taken in execution of a judgment obtained against the creditor. But when they are secured by some cheque, bill, note, bond, specialty or other security, the Judgments Act, 1838, provides that under the writ of *fieri facies* the sheriff may seize not only money and bank notes but also the securities above mentioned, and may sue upon them in his own name upon the arrival of the time of payment; but the sheriff is not bound to sue, unless indemnified in the manner prescribed by the Act from the costs of the action. And now, under provisions of the Common Law Procedure Acts, 1854 and 1860, since embodied in the Rules of the Supreme Court, 1883, the Court has jurisdiction to order that all debts owing or accruing to a judgment debtor may be attached [by garnishment] to answer the judgment."—*Ibid.* 268.

[18] *Williams on Real Property* (ed. 21; 1910) 81. For later legislation, see *Williams on Real Property* (ed. 24; 1926) 321–326.

[19] For an American case decided on this common law idea, see Mack v. Parks (1857) 8 Gray (Mass.) 517.

[20] See Holdsworth in note 14 *supra.*

[21] Gray, *op. cit.* §§ 78–80, 101. See also Hartwell v. Mobile Towing and Wrecking Co. (1924) 212 Ala. 313, 102 So. 450; Scott v. Ratliff (1918) 179 Ky. 267, 200 S. W. 462; *In re* Luscombe's Will, (1901) 109 Wis. 186, 85 N. W. 341.

The common law permits conveyances on conditions precedent which do not violate the rule against remoteness of vesting and do not violate any special rule, such as the rule recently repealed by statute in England against gifts to unborn children of unborn children under conditions which would not violate the rule against remoteness of vesting, and trusts of that sort are not treated as spendthrift trusts even though the condition precedent is that the cestui is not to take until he becomes financially solvent and able to pay all his debts apart from the trust fund.—Hull v. Farmers Loan & Trust Co. (1917) 245 U. S. 312, 38 Sup. Ct. 103, 62 L. Ed. 312.

[22] See Miller, J., in Nichols v. Eaton (1875) 91 U. S. 716, 725. That is, of course, strikingly apparent in those jurisdictions where under the influence of the chancery spendthrift trust the law judges recognize restraints on the alienation of a legal life estate (Christy v. Pulliam [1855] 17 Ill. 58; Pulliam v. Christy [1857] 19 Ill. 33); Springer v. Savage (1892) 143 Ill. 301, 32 N. E. 520; Albin v. Parmelee (1904) 70 Neb. 740, 98 N. W. 29, and even such restraints on a legal fee. Hinshaw v. Wright (1928) 124 Kan. 792, 262 Pac. 601, commented upon in (1928) 13 Corn. L. Q. 461, and (1928) 41 Harv. L. Rev. 920. The action of those jurisdictions, however, is probably not in the interests of orderliness of theory. Any recognition of restraints on alienation should be in equity only, where discretion may be exercised and modifications may easily be made. At law, the old rule against restraints on alienation should be maintained. On that old rule see Gray, *op. cit.* §§ 105, 113, 134, 278; Clark v. Clark (1904) 99 Md. 356, 58 Atl. 24; Kerns v. Carr (1918) 82 W. Va. 78, 95 S. E. 606, L. R. A. 1918 E, 568.

[23] "That it shall be alienable by and subject to the debts of its beneficial owner is not an essential element of any estate (legal or equitable, for years, for life, or in fee simple) in the sense that it is a logical impossibility for such an estate to exist without these incidents. Wherever it is held that such provisions are invalid, upon final analysis it will be found the true reason for the holding is not that such provisions are repugnant to or inconsistent with the estate granted or given, but that it is deemed to be against public policy as it is declared by the common and/or statute law to permit them to be attached to the estate in question. The only sense in which they are repugnant to or inconsistent with the estate given is that the law, for reasons of public policy, prohibits the making of such provisions an element or incident of the estate given. If the Legislature should declare that any estate (legal or equitable, for years, for life, or for the duration of a fee simple) might be given to a donee subject to such provisions, the courts would have no trouble in upholding it."—Epes, J., for the court in Sheridan v. Krause (Va. 1934) 172 S. E. 508, 514, 91 A. L. R. 1067, 1077.

Curiously enough, some of the English judges are not sure that there is even a question of policy. In 1904 some of them faced the problem in connection with the Scottish alimentary trust—a form of spendthrift trust like that which exists in California and New York. As the 1931 Supplement to Stroud's *Judicial Dictionary,* 47, states, "By the law of Scotland, a person may create a life interest in favour of another person, and may declare it to be 'Alimentary,' in which case, if it does not exceed a reasonable provision for the donee, then (whether the donee be male or female) there is a restraint on alienation and the diligence of creditors is excluded."

Such a trust, because valid in Scotland, where it was created, was enforced in England in *In re* Fitzgerald [1904] 1 Ch. 573, where a majority of the Court of Appeal gave full effect to a Scottish alimentary trust provision as against the beneficiary's voluntary transfers to creditors, with a clear intimation that it would do so as against attempted involuntary transfers. Against the argument that it was against English public policy to do so, Cozens-Hardy, L.J., said: "It is, however, strongly urged that a strictly alimentary provision for an adult male is not only unknown to and inconsistent with the provisions of English law, as in general it undoubtedly is, but that it is contrary to public policy, and ought therefore to be wholly disregarded in an English Court. I cannot adopt this argument. There is nothing immoral in such a provision. Indeed, there are many instances in which pensions or retiring allowances are by statute made not transferable, or liable to be attached by any legal process. I may refer to the pension allowed to a retiring clergyman under the Incumbents' Resignation Act, 1871, and to the observations of the Court of Appeal on that statute in *Gathercole v. Smith* (1881) 17 Ch. D. 1. Moreover, it has been long settled that at common law, and apart from any statutory enactments prohibiting assignment, certain salaries or pensions are inalienable. For example, the half-pay of an officer.... In my opinion it is impossible to disregard this 'alimentary provision' on the ground of public policy."

And Vaughan Williams, L.J., said: "The English law, in so far as it refuses to give effect to provisions which affect to control the rights of disposition which are attached to an absolute transfer of property, does not seem to me to be a matter regarding 'public order or good morals.' It is, I think, merely a logical development from legal definitions adopted by the English law. But it is true that in its application this law has been made the means of protecting creditors, and yet I do not think that in a country which allows restriction on anticipation in respect of the separate property of a wife, it can possibly be said that to enforce a provision in a Scotch contract inconsistent with this law would be contrary to public order and good morals, even though the result might be to defeat the just rights of a creditor."

To add to Cozens-Hardy, L.J.'s list, the following debt payments are cited in 14 Halsbury *Laws of England* (ed. 1) 94, § 172, as protected from attachment: "(1) wages of seamen, or of servants, labourers or workmen; (2) pay of officers in the public service, including officers of customs; (3) certain pensions payable out of public funds, including police and old age pensions; and (4) maintenance due from a husband to his divorced wife."

[24] "The subject of spendthrift trusts commands the attention of every possessor of property. To the man of wealth it provides a way by which he may make suitable provision for the maintenance and support of another, and yet secure the fruits of his toil from the improvident acts of the object of his bounty. To the reckless and extravagant beneficiary, it offers a means of being saved from himself....

"A spendthrift trust may be defined as a settlement of property in trust for a beneficiary, other than the donor, and so limited that it cannot be alienated by way of anticipation, or be subject to seizure by the creditors of the beneficiary, in advance of its payment to him."—Nathaniel S. Brown, *Spendthrift Trusts* (1902) 54 Central L. J. 382, 383.

There is an occasional suggestion, if not holding, that the beneficiary's interest may be voluntarily assignable by him and yet the restraint on involuntary alienation constitute a valid spendthrift trust (Boston Safe Deposit and Trust Co. v. Luke [1915] 220 Mass. 484, 108 N. E. 64). But except where statutes provide otherwise (*cf.* Binns v. La Forge [1901] 191 Ill. 598, 61 N. E. 382) nearly all the courts assume that the restraint must be against both voluntary and involuntary alienation for a spendthrift trust to exist. See Griswold, *Reaching the Interest of the Beneficiary of a Spendthrift Trust* (1929) 43 Harv. L. Rev. 63, 74–78.

[25] In Lynch v. Lynch (1931) 161 So. Car. 170, 174, 159 S. E. 26, 28, Dennis, J., whose opinion below was adopted as that of the Supreme Court, said that in most of the United States "the validity of spendthrift trusts, either with or without a provision for a cesser, has been sustained, not out of any special anxiety of the law for the protection of the impecunious beneficiary, but rather to protect the donor's right of property, and the right to choose the object of his bounty." So, in *In re* Morgan (1909) 223 Pa. 228, 230, 72 Atl. 498, 499, Stewart, J., declared that "It is always to be remembered that consideration for

the beneficiary does not even in the remotest way enter into the policy of the law; it has regard solely to the rights of the donor. Spendthrift trusts can have no other justification than is to be found in considerations affecting the donor alone." See also Estes v. Estes (Tex. Civ. App.) 255 S. W. 649, 650–655.

[26] For an example of such a happening, see Lloyd's Banking Co. v. Jones (1885) 29 Ch. Div. 221.

[27] See, for example, Cummings v. Corey (1885) 58 Mich. 494, 502–503. See also Tolland County Mutual Fire Ins. Co. v. Underwood (1883) 50 Conn. 493.

[28] Other states are California, Connecticut, Michigan, Minnesota, Montana, North Dakota, Oklahoma, South Dakota, Wisconsin. See 2 Powell, *Cases on Trusts and Estates* (1933) 859 note.

It is true, of course, that logically California need not follow New York except in respect to trusts of real property (see Note [1933] 21 Calif. L. Rev. 142, 144–146, and *In re* Bergman [Dist. Ct., N. Y. 1934] 6 F. Supp. 898), but naturally, like New York, it will treat alike spendthrift trusts of realty and spendthrift trusts of personal property. In Estate of Edwards (1932) 217 Cal. 25, 17 P. (2d) 116, the Supreme Court adopted as its own the opinion of the district court of appeal in *In re* Edwards' Estate (Cal. App. 1932) 11 Pac. (2d) 678, which seems to indicate a desire of the California courts to follow the New York rules as to spendthrift trusts. Professor Turrentine thinks, however, that in California "an equitable life interest in personalty may be made free of creditors' claims, regardless of the size of the trust and of the income therefrom." Turrentine, *Suggestions for Revision of Provisions of the California Civil Code Regarding Future Interests* (1932) 21 Calif. L. Rev. 1, 22. But the only Supreme Court case relied upon by him is Seymour v. McAvoy (1898) 121 Cal. 438, 53 Pac. 946, where the trust was created in 1869, and, therefore, as the court expressly pointed out, was unaffected by the California Civil Code provisions. Whether spendthrift trusts of personal property created since the Civil Code was adopted will be kept, as against the creditors of the spendthrift trust cestuis, within the reasonable limits fixed by the Civil Code for spendthrift trusts of realty is still an open question. In this essay it is assumed that they will be so kept, because that is the New York rule under similar legislation, and because, except perhaps as to widows and special dependents, that ought to be the rule everywhere.

[29] Bank of Union v. Heath (1924) 187 N. C. 54, 121 S. E. 24; N. C. Code Ann. (Michie, 1931) § 1742.

[30] See (1920) 7 Va. L. Rev. 235. The Virginia statute provides that any trust estate "not exceeding $100,000 in actual value" may be held "upon condition that the corpus thereof and income therefrom or either of them, shall be applied by the trustee to the support and maintenance of the beneficiaries without being subject to their liabilities or to alienation by them; but no such trust shall operate to the prejudice of any existing creditor of the creator of such trust." Professor Gray expected the Virginia courts to adopt the spendthrift trust doctrine (Gray, *op. cit.* iv) but in 1902 they repudiated that doctrine in Hutchinson v. Maxwell (1902) 100 Va. 169, only to have the above-mentioned statute of 1919 force it on them. See Dunlop v. Dunlop's Ex'rs (1926) 144 Va. 297, 132 S. E. 351. Now the Supreme Court of Appeals of Virginia applies the statute sympathetically. See Sheridan v. Krause (Va. 1934) 172 S. E. 508, 91 A. L. R. 1067.

[31] "An effect, and at the same time a cause, of the state of mind which favors spendthrift trusts appears in the statutes by which large amounts of property are exempted from execution. In several of the States property, real and personal, to the amount of thousands of dollars, is exempt, and the exemption laws are gloried in as calculated 'to cherish and support in the bosoms of individuals those feelings of sublime independence which are so essential to the maintenance of free institutions.' A community which has accustomed itself to look with complacency on a man holding ten or twelve thou-

sand dollars' worth of his own property, and leaving his debts unpaid, is not likely to be troubled by a man's having a life interest under a trust which his creditors cannot reach."—Gray, *op. cit.* vii, also § 263 and note 1.

In New York a spendthrift trust of the New York type is treated as an exemption from execution and so diminishable by statute without impairing the obligation of contracts.—Brearley School v. Ward (1911) 201 N. Y. 358, 94 N. E. 1001, 40 L. R. A. (n.s.) 1215, Ann. Cas. 1912 B, 251.

[32] Gray, *op. cit.* xi.

[33] By the New York statutes, voluntary alienation by the cestui was prohibited, yet creditors were allowed by involuntary alienation to reach the excess over the amount of income of trusts "necessary for the education and support of the person for whose benefit the trust is created." By another statute, which amended in 1903 a code provision, not exceeding 10 per cent of the income—even of that income necessary for education and support—can be reached by judgment creditors by garnishment.

The New York courts started out to fix income necessary for the education and support of the beneficiary on the reasonable basis of the amount required for the beneficiary, "taking into view his condition in life, his health, and other circumstances and the condition of his family, if any he have," which was stated in those words by way of dictum in Scott v. Nevius (1857) 6 Duer 672, 676. Unfortunately, however, a few New York decisions were indefensible. Professor Gray naturally enlarged on the most extreme (*op. cit.* xi and §§ 294b, 294c). With the exception that Demuth v. Kemp, stated by him, was later disposed of by the Court of Appeals by affirming exclusively on a procedure point the dismissal of the action (Demuth v. Kemp [1916] 216 N. Y. 757, 111 N. E. 1086), an ending to the case which left the discussion of the station in life theory by the Appellate Division (Demuth v. Kemp [1913] 159 App. Div. 422, 144 N. Y. Supp. 690) mere dicta, the New York cases are set out in Part II of Grenville Clark, *Spendthrift Trusts in New York, Needed Reforms in the Law* (1914) 9 Bench & Bar (n.s.) at 59–68. Mr. Clark, because of those decisions, urged that the New York statutes be amended to fix the exemption at $3000, which had been suggested as a suitable maximum by the New York Court of Appeals in a dictum in Brearley School v. Ward (1911) 201 N. Y. 358, 94 N. E. 1001, 40 L. R. A. (n.s.) 1215, Ann. Cas. 1912 B, 251, and which, with the deduction of the 10 per cent which could be reached under the code amendment by garnishment, would make the maximum trust income exemption from involuntary alienation for any beneficiary, $2700 (see Clark, *op. cit.* 114–118), while leaving the whole income restrained from voluntary alienation. Though he may be right that an income of $2700 a year is enough for the sane and adult person who is without dependents, whose case alone seemed to concern Mr. Clark (see *ibid.* 118), any statute or decision should go farther and allow some additional sum, say $600 a year, for each dependent of the cestui and, in the discretion of the proper court, some further sum for each dependent actually requiring a still greater reasonable expenditure to be made on him. For special circumstances to be considered, see Magner v. Crooks (1903) 139 Cal. 640, 73 Pac. 585. If only the courts will use common sense in applying it, the rule of the dictum in Scott v. Nevius, *supra,* is the fairest. But, of course, if they will not use common sense, a sufficiently varied fixed exemption rule should be adopted.

[34] A case like Congress Hotel Co. v. Martin (1924) 312 Ill. 318, 143 N. E. 838, 33 A. L. R. 562, where, in accordance with an Illinois statute, the court was compelled to deny a creditor who had a claim of $6724.16 access to a beneficiary's trust income which that year was $171,737.36, is a startling statutory exception. The Illinois statute makes all trust income, whether labeled spendthrift or not, inaccessible to creditors unless the trust was established by the beneficiary for himself. How much, if any, of the creditor's claim was unjust does not appear, since the statute made the agitation of that

question unnecessary, and whether the creditor was ever paid, in whole or in part, cannot be known. On its face, the conduct of the debtor seems indefensible. It seems a relatively rare happening.

[85] For an interesting discussion, see Mary M. Bartelme, *Spendthrift Trusts* (1894) 50 Albany L. J. 6.

[86] The unnecessary prejudice created by Professor Gray has stood in the way of a fair discussion of even unlimited amounts put in spendthrift trusts for various near relatives by the trustor. Nobody knows how many spendthrift trusts have been created or for whom. It would seem probable that spendthrift trusts in the main have been created for the trustor's widow, for other women relatives or dependents of the trustor, for subnormal persons more or less incompetent, or for inexperienced young people who may mature late so as to seem to need until they are 25 or 30 years old protection against business sharks. Trustors in general do not create trusts with the intention either of increasing the number of weaklings or of showing vindictiveness toward future creditors of the beneficiaries. There would seem to be no serious public policy reason why a trustor, not acting in fraud of his own creditors, should not give from his separate estate as large an amount as he wishes in spendthrift trust for his widow inexperienced in business, the income to be paid her for her life (and certainly there would seem to be even less reason to object to his limiting the spendthrift trust income to a reasonable provision for her), and for his similarly inexperienced women relatives and dependents, nor why he should not do the same for his male children until, at least, they reach an age when they will be reasonably sure to be mature. If it really is the crowning glory of the common law that it succeeded in inducing the repeal in some places of usury laws—something which seems to many of us a reproach and not a glory—it is certainly not a crowning or other glory of that law that widows and other women inexperienced in business who are left unrestricted life insurance money, should be despoiled of it by the rapacious as quickly as the insurance companies tell us is usual. The fundamental assumption made by the opponents of the so-called spendthrift doctrine—and known by such opponents to be quite contrary to fact—that all creditors are praiseworthy, is particularly false where the widows and the fatherless young are concerned. To assert that it is necessarily snobbishness for such persons to be supported by such spendthrift trust provision as their previous station in life calls for, or even in far better state, is ridiculous. The whole subject needs rationalization. If particular judges display snobbishness, the answer is to get new judges of the right kind, instead of throwing widows and orphans to the financial wolves. In connection with other legal doctrines, foolish legal decisions have been made without anybody's thinking that the doctrines themselves should be thrown overboard on that account. Why cannot an equally sensible view be taken of foolish spendthrift trust decisions?

[87] See note 36 *supra.*

[88] 2 Powell, *Cases and Materials on the Law of Trusts and Estates* 847 note.

[89] Stimson, *My United States* (1931) 76.

[40] (1882) 133 Mass. 170.

[41] At the most this only means that New York has a different type of spendthrift trust from Massachusetts.

[42] While there was a dictum in Branan v. Stiles (1824) 2 Pick. (Mass.) 460, suggesting a spendthrift trust of an equitable fee, it was at that time so extreme that nobody took it seriously, and nobody but Mr. Stimson seems ever to have asserted that spendthrift trusts existed in Massachusetts until after the dictum in Nichols v. Eaton (1875) 91 U. S. 716 or until about the time when Broadway National Bank v. Adams (1882) 133 Mass. 170 declared them valid.

[43] Stimson, *op. cit.* 76–78.

[44] If a statute forbids a trustor to create a trust for himself that will be valid against subsequent creditors, as does the New York Personal Property Law § 34, then of course a trustor is forbidden to create a spendthrift trust for himself, whatever his need. His only remedies, if he has any, will lie in guardianship of one kind or another. Even if the trustor may not create a spendthrift trust for himself, the fact that he attempts to do so and, in addition to the spendthrift trust attempted to be set up for himself for life, creates such trusts in remainder for others, will not affect those others unless the conveyance in trust for them is in fraud of his existing creditors (Benedict v. Benedict [1918] 261 Pa. 117, 104 Atl. 581). See Behrends, *Liability under Trusts to Creditors of Trustor* (1929) 3 So. Calif. L. Rev. 75, criticizing what seems perhaps to be a contrary holding in McColgan v. Magee, Inc. (1916) 172 Cal. 182, 155 Pac. 995, Ann. Cas. 1917 D, 1050. That case is considered on another point later in this footnote.

For a careful collection of the authorities, see Griswold, *Spendthrift Trusts Created in Whole or in Part for the Benefit of the Settlor* (1930) 44 Harv. L. Rev. 203. At the end appears the following (p. 222): "If spendthrift trusts are to be tolerated at all, we may well question the soundness of a rule which allows a man to hold the bounty of others free from the claims of his creditors, but denies the same immunity to his interest in property which he has accumulated by his own effort. But, as we have seen, it is well settled by the cases that a man may not validly create a spendthrift trust for his own benefit."

For some cases holding that a trustor may not create a spendthrift trust for himself, see McColgan v. Walter Magee, Inc. (1916) 172 Cal. 182, 155 Pac. 995, Ann. Cas. 1917 D, 1050; Wenzel v. Powder (1904) 100 Md. 36, 59 Atl. 194, 108 Am. St. Rep. 380; Forbes v. Snow (1923) 245 Mass. 85, 140 N. E. 418; Stephens v. Moore (1923) 298 Mo. 215, 249 S. W. 601; Schenck v. Barnes (1898) 156 N. Y. 316, 50 N. E. 967, 41 L. R. A. 395; Ghormley v. Smith (1891) 139 Pa. 584, 21 Atl. 135, 11 L. R. A. 565, 23 Am. St. Rep. 215; Nolan v. Nolan (1907) 218 Pa. 135, 67 Atl. 52, 12 L. R. A. (n.s.) 369; Rienzi v. Goodwin (1915) 249 Pa. 546, 95 Atl. 259; *cf.* De Rousse v. William (1917) 181 Iowa 379, 164 N. W. 896. McColgan v. Walter Magee, Inc., *supra,* went farther and allowed the creditor to reach also the interest of the remainderman under the trust, who happened to be the trustor's wife. That the latter holding was in error unless the trust was in fraud of the trustor's existing creditors and unless the remainderman's interest was needed to pay off those existing creditors, both of which things were uncertain in the report of the case, see Behrends, *loc. cit.* The trust was established in 1905, and the creditor obtained his judgment in 1908.

The nearest to a judicial suggestion, though on the court's part not consciously so, that an actual spendthrift may under certain carefully guarded circumstances establish a spendthrift trust for himself, is probably found in the case of Rehr. v. Fidelity-Philadelphia Trust Co. (1933) 310 Pa. 301, 165 Atl. 380, 91 A. L. R. 99. There the trustor created a trust under which the income was to be paid to herself for life, as a spendthrift trust, with a clause against revocation, the remainder to go as disposed of by her will, or, in default of a testamentary disposition, to be distributed to her next of kin. Later the trustor filed a bill to have the trust declared null and void, but the Supreme Court of Pennsylvania held against termination on two grounds: (1) that the spendthrift trust clause was enough to sustain the trust, and (2) there was no proof of consent by the next of kin to the termination. As is pointed out in substance in (1934) 43 Yale L. J. 342, 343, if the spendthrift trust for the trustor is not valid, there is no use in refusing to terminate the trust on the first ground, as the only restraint on him then will be against voluntary alienation and, if he really is a spendthrift, he will proceed to use his interest as a basis for credit and the creditors thus acquired can reach that intent. In Yale L. J. the article just cited, at pp. 342 and 344, the second ground of the decision is also questioned. If the second ground is unsound, the case provides some slight weight in favor of at least an actual spendthrift's privilege of establishing a spendthrift trust for himself.

[45] Trustee Act, 1925 (15 Geo. 5 c. 19). "33.—(1) Where any income, including an annuity or other periodical income payment, is directed to be held on protective trusts for the benefit of any person (in this section called 'the principal beneficiary') for the period of his life or for any less period, then, during that period (in this section called the 'trust period') the said income shall, without prejudice to any prior interest, be held on the following trusts, namely:—

"(i) Upon trust for the principal beneficiary during the trust period or until he, whether before or after the termination of any prior interest, does or attempts to do or suffers any act or thing, or until any event happens, other than an advance under any statutory or express power, whereby, if the said income were payable during the trust period to the principal beneficiary absolutely during that period, he would be deprived of the right to receive the same or any part thereof, in any of which cases, as well as on the termination of the trust period, whichever first happens, this trust of the said income shall fail or determine;

"(ii) If the trust aforesaid fails or determines during the subsistence of the trust period, then, during the residue of that period, the said income shall be held upon trust for the application thereof for the maintenance or support, or otherwise for the benefit, of all or any one or more exclusively of the other or others of the following persons (that is to say)—

"(*a*) the principal beneficiary and his or her wife or husband, if any, and his or her children or more remote issue, if any; or

"(*b*) if there is no wife or husband or issue of the principal beneficiary in existence, the principal beneficiary and the persons who would, if he were actually dead, be entitled to the trust property or the income thereof or to the annuity fund, if any, or arrears of the annuity as the case may be;

as the trustees in their absolute discretion, without being liable to account for the exercise of such discretion, think fit.

"(2) This section does not apply to trusts coming into operation before the commencement of this Act, and has effect subject to any variation of the implied trusts aforesaid contained in the instrument creating the trust.

"(3) Nothing in this section operates to validate any trust which would, if contained in the instrument creating the trust, be liable to be set aside."

A careful comparison of Trustee Act, 1925, § 33, and Gray, *op. cit.* § 167j, will disclose that the Act seems to vary from the rules set forth by Gray in respect to the rule set forth in § 167j 5 and § 167j 6. The change is in the respect that the trustees, having a discretion to apply the income for the benefit of the cestui or for the other interested parties specified, may apply it for the maintenance or support or otherwise for the benefit of the cestui in the absolute discretion of the trustees and "without" their "being liable to account for the exercise of such discretion."

On the face of the statute there still remain the questions:

(*a*) If the trustees, purporting to act under their discretion to apply the income "or otherwise," actually pay it to the cestui, must they account to creditors under either voluntary or involuntary assignments for any payments made to the cestui?

An American case, in which the special trust provisions of the will and the statute combined presented substantially the provisions in the English statute, says that the trustee may pay the support money to the cestui providing the trustee pays him only what is reasonably necessary for his support and maintenance. See Sheridan v. Krause (Va. 1934) 172 S. E. 508, 518.

(*b*) Do the words "or otherwise for the benefit" remove the seeming restriction in the other words specifying that the income shall be held "upon trust for the application thereof for the maintenance or support," so as, under (ii), to make protective trusts of unlimited amounts of income possible?

Probably "or otherwise for the benefit" has no such strong meaning or effect as is asked about in question (*b*).

Even if both questions (*a*) and (*b*) should be answered in the negative, the Trustee Act section has settled the question considered in Gray's § 167j 6 against Gray's contention there. Since, under the statute, the trustees may apply the income for the cestui's maintenance and support, carefully chosen trustees will do so, and, in consequence, they might as well be allowed to pay that income to the cestui himself. Gray's position in his § 167j 6 would seem to require going to that extent, now that, apparently, the trustees may apply the income for the maintenance and support, at least, of the beneficiary without having to account to the creditors.

[46] See note 23 *ante*. See also Mackay, *Alimentary Provisions* (1913) 25 Jurid. Rev. 290.

[47] The typical spendthrift trust is of course a restraint on an equitable life interest.

[48] Only a few jurisdictions recognize spendthrift trust restraints on equitable fee-simple interests. See Wallace v. Foxwell (1911) 250 Ill. 616, 95 N. E. 985, commented upon in (1913) 7 Ill. L. Rev. 445; Hopkinson v. Swaim (1918) 284 Ill. 11, 119 N. E. 985; Boston Safe Dep. & Trust Co. v. Collier (1916) 222 Mass. 390, 111 N. E. 163, Ann. Cas. 1918 C, 962; Haskell v. Haskell (1920) 234 Mass. 442, 125 N. E. 601.

Yet, "There is no substantial difference between giving a donee an equitable fee-simple estate in real property or an equitable estate of like duration in personal property subject to a spendthrift trust for his support and maintenance during his life and giving the same property to a trustee to be held in trust for him during his life upon the same spendthrift trust, with remainder to him upon termination of the trust. Any difference between the two things is a metaphysical refinement. Where property is given to a trustee to be held for the support and maintenance of a person for a term of years free from his debts and power of alienation, with remainder in the accumulated income and the corpus of the property to the cestui que trust at the end of the trust period, he is given an equitable fee-simple or absolute equitable estate in the property as much as if the spendthrift trust had been for life with remainder to him (*i.e.*, his estate) at his death.

"Where a spendthrift trust is for the life of the cestui que trust, the property is not tied up any longer or any more completely where the remainder passes at his death as a part of his estate than it is where the remainder at his death is devised to another person or reverts to the creator of his estate. So far as the creditors of the cestui que trust are concerned, they are better off where the remainder passes as a part of the estate of the cestui que trust than they would be if it passed to another. In the first case they have the opportunity of ultimately getting their claims paid in whole or in part. In the latter case they have no chance of getting them paid.

"Where it is held not to be against public policy to permit a spendthrift trust of any particular nature to be created for the life of a cestui que trust with remainder in the trust property to another, we are of opinion that there is no substantial reason for holding it against public policy to uphold the same spendthrift trust where the estate given the donee is such that the remainder in the trust property passes at his death as a part of his estate. And we hold that an equitable fee-simple or absolute equitable estate may be given to a person subject to any spendthrift trust for his benefit for his life, or a lesser period, which, under section 5157, would be good if the remainder in the trust property were given to another."—Epes, J., for the court, in Sheridan v. Krause (Va. 1934) 172 S. E. 508, 517.

[49] On spendthrift trust legislation, see Runk, *American Statutory Modifications of the Rule Against Perpetuities, of Trusts for Accumulation and of Spendthrift Trusts* (1932) 80 U. of Pa. L. Rev. 397, 404–410.

[50] See cases cited in note 22 *ante.*

[51] See Hinshaw v. Wright, *supra* note 22.

[52] Gray, *op. cit.* viii-ix.

[53] *Ibid.* x.

JURISDICTION FOLLOWING SEIZURE OR ARREST IN VIOLATION OF INTERNATIONAL LAW

BY EDWIN D. DICKINSON

It is well settled in Anglo-American law that national courts are competent, in general, to adjudicate rights and duties with respect to all things or persons found within the territory which the process of the court controls. Exceptions find an especial justification in considerations of national or international convenience. A situation which seems to have been insufficiently considered, however, is that of the thing or person seized or arrested abroad, in violation of international law, and brought within the state and thus within reach of the process of the state's courts. Should the courts be considered competent, on the basis of physical presence thus procured, to adjudicate in the usual way?

On the one hand, if there are claims to the thing or complaints against the person which require judicial determination, it may be said that the national court should proceed without regard for the antecedent events which gave the court the necessary physical control. It may be urged that only the injured foreign state is in a position to protest against the violation of international law and that, in any event, the alleged violation of international law presents an issue which should be resolved by international negotiation or in an international forum. On the other hand, notwithstanding the desirability of a judicial determination of claims against the thing or of complaints against the person, it may be said that, since the seizure or arrest was made in excess of the state's proper competence, and in violation of the rights of a foreign state, there is in consequence no national competence to invoke local process or to subject the thing or the person to local law. If there is no national competence, obviously there can be no competence in the courts which are only an arm of the national power.[1] To hold otherwise, it may be urged, would go far to defeat the purpose and nullify the efficacy of international law.

The argument for a complete lack of national, and hence of judicial, competence has prevailed in cases in which international right and duty are defined in formal treaty. There is an indirect manifestation of this principle in the rule of extradition which forbids the trial of the extradited person for any offense committed prior to his extradition, other than the offense for which he was surrendered under the treaty. The rule is stated in the leading American case of *United States v. Rauscher* as follows:

> A person who has been brought within the jurisdiction of the court by virtue of proceedings under an extradition treaty, can only be tried for one of the offences described in that treaty, and for the offence with which he is charged in the proceedings for his extradition, until a reasonable time and opportunity have been given him, after his release or trial upon such charge, to return to the country from whose asylum he had been forcibly taken under those proceedings.[2]

There is no occasion to consider here the convenience or policy of this rule as a rule of extradition. Very likely it has been stated too broadly in some of the extradition treaties and it may have been applied too literally in some of the cases.[3] The point to be emphasized is that the rule only permits the subjection of the extradited person to the national law to an extent, at the risk of considerable national inconvenience, which is literally consistent with the terms of the treaty and of the proceedings instituted thereunder. While it is conceded that the individual, as such, has no right of asylum in the foreign state,[4] his objection to the jurisdiction serves as a foil to remind the court of the nation's international obligation. Although his claim to exemption from further prosecution may be without moral foundation, the individual is permitted to make an issue of the right of the state from which he was surrendered to have the extradition treaty respected.[5]

The same rule has been wisely applied, in even more striking circumstances, where the national court was convinced that an international agreement must be implied, in the absence of a formal treaty, in order to escape the conclusion that there had been a violation by national authorities of an obligation of international law. An American case decided by the Texas Court of Criminal Appeals affords a unique example.[6] A United States expeditionary force had been sent into Mexico in "hot pursuit" of bandits. Having apprehended a Mexican, the force discovered upon its return that he was not one of the bandits pursued and he was thereupon surrendered to local Texas authorities, who proceeded to prosecute him for a murder previously committed in Texas. Relying upon the rule of the extradition cases, the defense contended in behalf of the accused that the Texas court was without jurisdiction to prosecute him for the murder until he had been allowed an opportunity to return to Mexico. The prosecution contended that the accused had been abducted or kidnapped without Mexico's consent and consequently that he could be prosecuted for the murder without any breach of treaty obligation. The only information in respect to the source and scope of the expedition's authority which the court had before it was the testimony of the officer in command that he was acting under instructions from the United States Department of War. It was held that an agreement between Mexico and the United States must be presumed, consequently that the rule of the extradition cases was applicable, and that the accused might resist trial for the murder until such time as he should voluntarily subject himself to the jurisdiction of the United States or until the consent of Mexico should be obtained. The entry of the expeditionary force into Mexico for the purpose of apprehending bandits, said the court, would have been "a violation of Mexican territory contrary to the law of nations in the absence of consent of the Mexican Government."[7] Consequently it was to be assumed that the instructions from the Department of War were in accord with a permission granted by the Mexican government. The court concluded that

the same moral obligation that would restrain the United States Government from transgressing the implied limitations upon it under its treaty [of extradition] with Mexico, would necessarily prevail with reference to the agreement resting upon the "comity of nations," and if the legal obligation is the same, the appellant cannot be held for the offense which we are now considering without the opportunity to return to his country in order that it may there determine whether he shall be surrendered for trial under the treaty of extradition.[8]

The principle that national courts, as an arm of the national power, are incompetent to obligate by their process or to subject to the national law a thing or person seized or arrested in violation of an international treaty has perhaps had its clearest and most explicit application in liquor smuggling cases. The leading precedent is the case of "The Mazel Tov," decided by the United States Supreme Court in 1933.[9] "The Mazel Tov" was a vessel of British registry which had been seized by the United States Coast Guard at a point eleven and one-half miles off the Massachusetts coast. In the absence of evidence of communication with the coast, of any act done within territorial waters, or of an intention or attempt to do any act within territorial waters, there was no basis for a proceeding against the vessel under the United States Prohibition Act. In view of the Supreme Court's decision in this case that the Treaty of 1924 between Great Britain and the United States for the prevention of the smuggling of intoxicating liquors had superseded inconsistent provisions of the United States customs laws, so far as those laws authorized the seizure of vessels engaged in liquor smuggling, and had established a comprehensive definition of permissible measures for the suppression of liquor smuggling, there was no foundation for a forfeiture proceeding under the customs laws. In consequence of the fact that the vessel was incapable of a speed exceeding ten miles an hour, there was no case for a seizure under the one-hour sailing rule of the treaty. It was contended, nevertheless, that the facts revealed a violation of United States customs statutes and that the alleged illegality of the seizure was immaterial since the United States, by commencing a forfeiture proceeding, had ratified what would otherwise have been an illegal seizure, since the vessel had actually been brought by the Coast Guard within reach of the process of the national court, and since the claimant by answering to the merits had waived any right to object to the enforcement of penalties imposed by the customs statutes. These contentions the Supreme Court emphatically rejected as inapplicable to the case at bar.

> The objection to the seizure [said the Court] is not that it was wrongful merely because made by one upon whom the Government had not conferred authority to seize at the place where the seizure was made. The objection is that the Government itself lacked power to seize, since by the Treaty it had imposed a territorial limitation upon its own authority.[10]

In other words, had there been nothing more in the case of "The Mazel Tov" than a seizure by one lacking authority, the fact that the possession was acquired by wrongful act would have been immaterial, since the commencement of forfeiture proceedings by the government would have amounted to ratification of the seizure; but a seizure in violation of an international treaty was another and a different matter.[11] Lacking the power to seize, in consequence of the treaty, the United States had no power to subject the vessel to its laws. The objection was not to the jurisdiction of the court alone, but to "the jurisdiction of the United States." The objection was not met by seeking to distinguish between the custody of the Coast Guard and the subsequent custody of the marshal of the court,[12] nor was the defect of jurisdiction cured by an answer to the merits on the part of an individual claimant.[13] The Supreme Court concluded that "to hold that adjudication may follow a wrongful seizure would go far to nullify the purpose and effect of the Treaty." "The ordinary incidents of possession of the vessel and the cargo," said the Court, "yield to the international agreement."[14]

The principle thus emphatically enunciated in the case of "The Mazel Tov" rests, it is submitted, upon a firm foundation of sound logic and wise judicial policy. If the original arrest or seizure is illegal because in violation of treaty, it is logical to conclude that no competence is acquired thereby. Surely the ratification of an illegal act should not purge of illegality. Surely it is a scholastic subtlety which would distinguish the competence of the nation and the competence of the court through which the nation acts. If the original arrest or seizure is in violation of treaty, it would be shortsighted policy which permitted the court to draw a dark curtain before the wrong done by one nation to another, however desirable it may be to impose a well merited penalty or forfeiture upon the individual concerned.[15] Nor should the circumstance be heavily weighed that the injured nation is not a party to the litigation. The issue has been submitted to the court, the property or person which the injured nation is entitled to protect is before the court, and the opportunity to undo the wrong by restoring the property or releasing the person should not be lost. To insist that the decision belongs to a higher forum, when the issue is submitted and the international wrong is conceded or clearly proved, is to abdicate a function which the court, particularly the court of a country in which international law and treaties are regarded as part of the law of the land,[16] ought unhesitatingly to perform. The question is not political but is one clearly within the competence of the national court.[17] If the nation may ratify an illegal arrest or seizure and invoke successfully the aid of its own court, the national judicial process must become a perfunctory proceeding so far as matters of international right and duty are concerned. Anglo-American courts, at least, have not been content to perform so perfunctory a function when issues of international right or duty are presented for their determination.[18]

If the principle thus enunciated is to be approved and its consequences accepted, it becomes necessary to reconsider some of the earlier English and American decisions which are clearly affected by its implications. If the principle is sound as applied to cases involving an arrest or seizure in violation of treaty, it should be applicable likewise in cases involving an arrest or seizure in violation of international law. Yet it has not always been so applied.

At the same term of the United States Supreme Court at which the leading extradition case of *United States v. Rauscher* was decided, the case of *Ker v. Illinois*[19] was decided in reliance upon a distinction which it is difficult to defend upon any but the most refined of technical grounds. An agent of the United States had been sent to Peru to receive the surrender, under the extradition treaty in force with that country, of a fugitive charged with larceny in Illinois. Instead of presenting the extradition papers to the Peruvian government and receiving the surrender of the fugitive in due course, the agent forcibly kidnapped the fugitive in Peruvian territory and returned with him to the United States. Following trial and conviction in Illinois, the case was taken to the Supreme Court of the United States on the plea that the fugitive had been denied a right sanctioned by the treaty with Peru.[20] It was held that, inasmuch as the removal from Peru was accomplished under proceedings in total disregard of the treaty, and inasmuch as the treaty invested the fugitive with no right of asylum in the foreign country, it had not been shown that the fugitive was denied a right conferred upon him by a treaty of the United States. Whether the forcible arrest in Peru, in violation of the rights of that country, should have been available as a defense to the prosecution in the Illinois court, the Supreme Court declined to decide. The decision of that question was said to have been within the province of the state court and not within the competence of the Supreme Court to review on writ of error.

The result in *Ker v. Illinois* is unsatisfactory in both its procedural and its substantive aspects. How much the presentation of the case before the Supreme Court may have contributed to an unsatisfactory result, it is impossible at this date to say with confidence. It would appear that the decision of the Illinois court had raised issues which the Supreme Court should have been competent to review on writ of error;[21] and it seems clear enough that the forcible kidnapping by a United States agent in Peru should have been a complete defense to every assertion of jurisdiction in the United States. The same reasoning which enabled the extradited fugitive in *United States v. Rauscher* to invoke the treaty to his own advantage, "in good faith to the country which had sent him here,"[22] should have enabled the kidnapped fugitive to invoke international law in good faith to Peru. While it is true enough that he had no right of asylum, in relation to Peru, he should have had, in relation to the United States, a right to be released from detention procured by a violation of the universally accepted principles of international jurisprudence.[23]

The outcome in the Ker case was probably influenced by earlier decisions which are still more difficult to defend. There are, for example, a number of decisions of the highest English and American courts which hold that the court's jurisdiction to condemn or forfeit a ship brought within reach of its process is not affected by the fact that the ship was seized within the territorial waters of another state and hence in violation of international law. Thus English and American prize courts have held consistently that captures made in violation of neutral territorial waters will be restored only upon demand of the neutral state. As against an individual enemy or neutral claimant, such captures are regarded as valid.[24] Lord Stowell said that it was "a known principle" of his court that "the privilege of territory will not itself enure to the protection of property, unless the State from which that protection is due, steps forward to assert the right."[25] With respect to this rule, it is to be observed that it is a rule of prize courts, whose decisions are an unsafe reliance in seeking solution of peace-time problems, that it appears to have been formulated under the influence of eighteenth-century notions of neutrality,[26] and preserved, without critical reconsideration, in reliance upon the earlier precedents,[27] and that it is opposed to the more enlightened practice of important Continental countries.[28] It is submitted that the rule is irreconcilable in principle with the doctrine in the case of "The Mazel Tov," discussed above, since a seizure in violation of accepted principles of international law is certainly to be reprehended and discouraged no less than a seizure in violation of treaty, and that the rule ought to be reconsidered and repudiated.

It is not enough, however, to dispose of the prize cases, for there are peace-time cases of forfeiture for breach of municipal law which apply a similar rule. Two such cases were cited and relied upon in argument in the case of "The Mazel Tov." In the case of "The Ship Richmond,"[29] an American vessel was seized by a United States man-of-war in territorial waters of East Florida, then belonging to Spain, and was forfeited to the United States for violation of the Non-Intercourse Act of 1809. In delivering the opinion of the United States Supreme Court, in which sentence of condemnation was affirmed, Chief Justice Marshall said:

> The seizure of an American vessel within the territorial jurisdiction of a foreign power, is certainly an offence against that power, which must be adjusted between the two governments. This Court can take no cognizance of it; and the majority of the Court is of opinion that the law does not connect that trespass, if it be one, with the subsequent seizure by the civil authority, under the process of the District Court, so as to annul the proceedings of that Court against the vessel.[30]

In the case of "The Merino,"[31] American vessels were seized by United States military or naval authorities in the bay of Pensacola, Florida, then belonging to Spain, and were forfeited for violation of laws of the United States prohibiting the trade in slaves. It was held, on the authority of the decision in the case of "The Ship Richmond," that the trespass on Spanish territory was not so connected with the subsequent seizure, under process of the District Court, as to defeat the jurisdiction of that court.

In the case of "The Mazel Tov," the United States Supreme Court sought to distinguish these earlier decisions by pointing out that the earlier cases involved seizures of American vessels and that "the seizures did not violate any treaty, but were merely violations of the law of nations because made within the territory of another sovereign."[32] It is obviously immaterial, however, that the seizures in the earlier cases were of American vessels, just as it is immaterial, in cases like *United States v. Rauscher,*[33] whether the extradited fugitive is a foreign or American national. Moreover, seizures in violation of accepted principles of international law are certainly as thoroughly contaminated with illegality as a seizure in violation of treaty. The reports of the earlier cases indicate that the "more fundamental" objection to the jurisdiction of the United States, as distinguished from an objection to the competence of the court, was pressed by counsel and was rejected on the assumption that the issue thus raised was a political question which the national court was incompetent to decide. Chief Justice Marshall clearly intimated, in the case of "The Ship Richmond," that he considered the issue one which "must be adjusted between the two governments" and one of which the national court could "take no cognizance."[34] In this assumption he was clearly wrong, in the light of later authorities, for the courts have no hesitation in ordering restoration or release, against the executive, where the case has been submitted to the court and a clear violation of accepted international law is admitted or proved.[35] Since the earlier decisions were wrong in principle, and are not distinguishable in fact from such a well considered case as "The Mazel Tov," it should be recognized that they are in effect overruled.

Situations such as those already considered, in which the illegality of the arrest or seizure is admitted or clearly proved, and in which in consequence the troublesome doctrine of political questions is not involved, should be contrasted, in order to complete the picture, with other situations in which the interpretation of a treaty or the application of a rule of international law is in dispute between the two governments concerned. In the latter type of situation, there is a political issue at stake which the national court can hardly be expected to determine. Let us suppose, for example, that it had appeared in the case of "The Mazel Tov" that the interpretation of the treaty between Great Britain and the United States for the prevention of the smuggling of liquor had been a matter of controversy between the two governments, that the government of the United States contended in its international negotiations with Great Britain that the treaty was not intended to affect in any way existing American legislation applicable to liquor smuggling, and that the British government as insistently pressed for a contrary interpretation. It is not to be doubted that the courts of the United States would have adopted the interpretation for which the government of the United States contended.[36] The issue would thus have become political, and judicial determination would have been possible in an international forum only. The United States would thus have made submission to its national courts a perfunctory proceeding in which issues of international law and treaty interpretation were foreclosed before the proceeding began.

Let us suppose, again, that it had appeared in the case of "The Ship Richmond" that the United States had contended in its international negotiations with Spain that East Florida did not belong to Spain or that the seizure was not made within waters which were Spanish territorial waters according to accepted principles of international law. There is no doubt that United States courts would have been required to uphold the seizure, not upon the ground that the contention of the United States was legally correct, although courts in such circumstances are frequently tempted to write a brief in support of their own government's position,[37] but upon the ground that the issue was already concluded by a political decision which the courts were obliged to accept.[38] The government as such has it in its power to submit an issue in respect to the interpretation of a treaty or the application of international law to its own courts, and it is much to the credit of governments in Anglo-American countries that this is done in such a wide variety of cases; but the government also has it in its power to foreclose the issue and when it does so the national court has no competence to pass upon the issue thus concluded.

There is another type of situation in which a similar outcome is all the more striking because inconsistent in a sense with the rule or interpretation for which the government contends in its international negotiations. Let us suppose, for example, that a seizure has been made by French authorities of an American vessel on the high seas. Let us assume that the French government contends that the seizure was authorized by international law or treaties in force, and that the United States government denies the French contention. If the vessel is condemned in due course by a competent French tribunal, is sold to a purchaser at a sale ordered by that tribunal, and is later brought within the reach of the process of a United States court, it is clear that the United States court should regard the French judgment as having effectively divested the original American ownership. The rule was settled accordingly in a series of early decisions of the United States Supreme Court culminating in the famous case of *Williams v. Armroyd*.[39]

In this case, an American vessel and cargo had been seized by a French privateer on the high seas in reliance upon Napoleon's Milan decree interdicting all commerce with English ports or ports under English control. The vessel and cargo were taken into a West Indian port, sold, later condemned by a French prize court, and part of the cargo was sent by the purchaser to the United States. On behalf of the original American owner, it was argued as follows:

This is an appeal by a citizen of the United States to his government for redress for a violation of his neutral rights by a foreign sovereign.... The only question is whether this Court has power to declare void a condemnation founded upon a decree which the legislature and the executive of the United States have declared to be a violation of our neutral rights, and contrary to the law of nations.[40]

Counsel for the purchaser replied:

Whether the proceedings are erroneous, or not, according to our notions of right and wrong... or are founded upon regulations consistent with, or repugnant to, the law of nations, are questions wholly immaterial. The sentence has sealed the proceedings, and those questions can never judicially come before this Court.... Such being the acknowledged effect of a foreign condemnation, the only remedy for the injured party is a resort to the Court of the captors for redress. If that government will not afford it, he must apply to his own, which will make it a national concern to be settled either by negotiation or war, if it be deemed a matter of sufficient importance.[41]

It was held that the original ownership had been divested by capture, sale, and condemnation. The French decree was conclusive on the question of ownership, since the French court had vessel and cargo within reach of its process and since no United States court was competent to review the French proceeding to correct errors arising from the alleged violation of international law. The question of international law at issue between France and the United States was not for United States courts to determine. Although in the outcome the United States court gave effect to a French decree which the United States government had denounced by implication as founded upon a violation of international law, the decision was sound, first, because a court of the United States could not properly pass upon the validity of acts of the French government and, second, because the issue between the French government and the government of the United States had not been submitted and, indeed, could not well be submitted, to a court of the United States. The controversy belonged to a higher forum.

In concluding this study, therefore, it is to be emphasized that the heart of the problem is the competence of the national court to determine judicially a question of the law of nations without encroaching upon the competence of the political departments of national government to control the nation's foreign affairs. The proposition that *disputes between states* with respect to the interpretation of treaties or the application of international law are not within the competence of national courts to determine, should be accepted as a sound principle defining a necessary point of departure. The problem is one of ascertaining and stating the proper limitations circumscribing an accepted principle. That the principle is controlling when the executive has taken a position in an international negotiation or controversy, with respect to the interpretation of a treaty or the application of international law, seems clear enough. The nation must speak in international controversy with one voice and that the voice of the department of government entrusted with the conduct of its international relations. That the principle is not controlling when the executive invokes its own courts to convict, penalize, forfeit, or condemn in a case which turns upon the meaning of a treaty text or of a principle of international law, seems equally clear. When the executive submits to the judicial determination of its own courts, it should abide the outcome of the judicial process. It should not be treated, in the courts of a civilized country in the twentieth century, as litigant and lawgiver in the same contest.

If the executive has already committed the nation to a controlling rule or interpretation, the court should bow to the rule or interpretation thus established, but it should indulge no pretense that it is announcing a rule or interpretation of its own. Its competence is limited in such circumstances to the application of rules of national law or of national interpretation of treaty or international law which it has no power to review. If the executive has not already committed the nation, however, the court should proceed fearlessly and impartially to determine the issue in accordance with the rules of treaties and of international law, which constitute, in Anglo-American jurisprudence at least, an integral part of the law of the land.

If the person or thing which is the subject of controversy has been brought within reach of the court's process by a breach of treaty or of international law, the court should approve no arbitrary or face-saving distinctions. The court is an arm of the nation and its jurisdiction can rise no higher, by virtue of process served within the territory, than the jurisdiction of the nation which it represents. If there was no jurisdiction in the nation to make the original seizure or arrest, there should be no jurisdiction in the court to subject to the nation's law. In terms of American precedents, this means that the underlying principle of *United States v. Rauscher* is correct and that the distinction attempted in *Ker v. Illinois* is arbitrary, unsound, and should be repudiated, that the principle of "The Mazel Tov" is unimpeachable, and that such cases as "The Ship Richmond" and "The Merino" must be relegated to the category of cases discredited and overruled. To hold otherwise would go far to nullify the purpose and effect of the salutary principle, well established in Anglo-American jurisprudence, that "international law is part of our law, and must be ascertained and administered by the courts of justice of appropriate jurisdiction, as often as questions of right depending upon it are duly presented for their determination."[42]

NOTES TO DICKINSON ESSAY

[1] "The jurisdiction of courts is a branch of that which is possessed by the nation as an independent sovereign power."—Marshall, C. J., in The Schooner Exchange v. M'Faddon (1812) 7 Cr. 116, 136.

[2] (1886) 119 U. S. 407, 430, 7 Sup. Ct. 234, 246; Dickinson, *Cases*, 738, 744. See *Re* Alice Woodall (1888) 16 Cox C. C. 478. See also Cosgrove v. Winney (1899) 174 U. S. 64, 19 Sup. Ct. 598; Johnson v. Browne (1907) 205 U. S. 309, 27 Sup. Ct. 539; *cf. In re* Rowe (C. C. A. 8th, 1896) 77 Fed. 161; State v. Rowe (1898) 104 Ia. 323; Cohn v. Jones (Dist. Ct. S. D. Iowa, 1900) 100 Fed. 639; State v. Spiegel (1900) 111 Iowa 701, 83 N. W. 722; Greene v. United States (C. C. A. 5th, 1907) 154 Fed. 401; Collins v. O'Neil (1909) 214 U. S. 113, 29 Sup. Ct. 573; People v. Hanley (1925) 240 N. Y. 455, 148 N. E. 634.

[3] *Cf.* Moore, *Extradition* I, 247.

[4] See Ker v. Illinois (1886) 119 U. S. 436, 7 Sup. Ct. 225; Dickinson, *Cases* 751, discussed *infra* 122.

[5] "As this right of transfer, the right to demand it, the obligation to grant it, the proceedings under which it takes place, all show that it is for a limited and defined purpose that the transfer is made, it is impossible to conceive of the exercise of jurisdiction in such a case for any other purpose than that mentioned in the treaty, and ascertained by the proceedings under which the party is extradited, without an implication of fraud upon the rights of the party extradited, and of bad faith to the country which permittted his extradition. No such view of solemn public treaties between the great nations of the earth can be sustained by a tribunal called upon to give judicial construction to them" (United States v. Rauscher (1886) 119 U. S. 407, 422, 7 Sup. Ct. 234, 242). "In the case of United States v. Rauscher . . . the effect of extradition proceedings under a treaty was very fully considered, and it was there held, that, when a party was duly surrendered, by proper proceedings, under the treaty of 1842 with Great Britain, he came to this country clothed with the protection which the nature of such proceedings and the true construction of the treaty gave him. One of the rights with which he was thus clothed, both in regard to himself and in good faith to the country which had sent him here, was, that he should be tried for no other offence than the one for which he was delivered under the extradition proceedings" (Ker v. Illinois (1886) 119 U. S. 436, 443, 7 Sup. Ct. 225, 229). "It is urged that the construction contended for by the respondent is exceedingly technical and tends to the escape of criminals on refined subtleties of statutory construction, and should not, therefore, be adopted. While the escape of criminals is, of course, to be very greatly deprecated, it is still most important that a treaty of this nature between sovereignties should be construed in accordance with the highest good faith, and that it should not be sought by doubtful construction of some of its provisions to obtain the extradition of a person for one offense and then punish him for another and different offense" (Johnson v. Browne (1906) 205 U. S. 309, 321, 27 Sup. Ct. 539, 543).

[6] Dominguez v. State (1921) 90 Tex. Cr. 92, 234 S. W. 79; Dickinson, *Cases* 755; (1922) 20 Mich. L. Rev. 536; (1922) 31 Yale L. J. 443.

[7] 90 Tex. Cr. 92, 97.

[8] 90 Tex. Cr. 92, 98–99.

[9] Reported as Cook v. United States (1933) 288 U. S. 102, 53 Sup. Ct. 305. See (1933) 27 Am. J. Int. L. 305.

[10] 288 U. S. 102, 121, 53 Sup. Ct. 305, 312.

[11] "At common law, any person may, at his peril, seize for a forfeiture to the govern-

ment; and if the government adopt his seizure, and the property is condemned, he will be completely justified. . . ." (Story, J., in Gelston v. Hoyt (1818) 3 Wh. 246, 310). See also The Caledonian (1819) 4 Wh. 100, 103; Wood v. United States (1842) 16 Pet. 342, 359; Taylor v. United States (1845) 3 How. 197, 205; Dodge v. United States (1926) 272 U. S. 530, 532, 47 Sup. Ct. 191; The Homestead (Dist. Ct. S. D. N. Y., 1925) 7 F. (2d) 413, 415; The Underwriter (C. C. A. 2d, 1926) 13 F. (2d) 433, 434. This proposition may be sound enough, but obviously it does not follow that the government, by proceeding in reliance upon a seizure made in violation of treaty or international law, can acquire for its courts a competence which the seizure could not give. It is lack of competence in the nation, and hence in its courts, that presents the difficulty, not the authority of the individual who made the seizure.

[12] There are cases in which reliance appears to have been placed upon a distinction between the custody of the officer who made the original seizure and the subsequent custody of the court. Some of these cases may be justified on the ground that the original seizure was a permissible exercise of extraterritorial authority in aid of the enforcement of territorial laws. See The Tenyu Maru (1910) 4 Alaska 129; The Grace and Ruby (Dist. Ct. Mass., 1922) 283 Fed. 475; Dickinson, *Jurisdiction at the Maritime Frontier* (1926) 40 Harv. L. Rev. 1, 21. Others, discussed *infra,* are believed to be unsound and to have been virtually overruled by the decision in the case of The Mazel Tov, *supra.* See The Ship Richmond v. United States (1815) 9 Cr. 102; The Merino (1824) 9 Wh. 391.

In civil cases between private litigants, courts decline jurisdiction over a defendant who has been decoyed into the state by fraud or brought by force. "The law will not permit a person to be kidnapped or decoyed within the jurisdiction for the purpose of being compelled to answer to a mere private claim . . ." (Brown, J., in *In re* Johnson (1897) 167 U. S. 120, 126, 17 Sup. Ct. 735, 737). See also Stein v. Valkenhuysen (1858) E. B. & E. 65; Williams v. Reed (1862) 29 N. J. L. 385; Union Sugar Refining Co. v. Mathiesson (1864) 2 Cliff. 304; Metcalf v. Clark (1864) 41 Barb. 45; Dunlap & Co. v. Cody (1871) 31 Iowa 260; Townsend v. Smith (1879) 47 Wis. 623; Abercrombie v. Abercrombie (1902) 64 Kan. 29, 67 Pac. 537; Cavanagh v. Manhattan Transit Co. (Circ. Ct. D. N. J., 1905) 133 Fed. 818; Jaster v. Currie (1905) 198 U. S. 144, 25 Sup. Ct. 614; Beale, *Jurisdiction of Courts over Foreigners* (1913) 26 Harv. L. Rev. 283, 285; (1930) 39 Yale L. J. 889.

The same principle is applied where property is brought within reach of the court's process by fraud or force. See Moynahan v. Wilson (1877) 2 Flippin 130; Copas v. Anglo-American Provision Co. (1889) 73 Mich. 541, 41 N. W. 690; Van Donselaar v. Jones (1923) 195 Iowa 1081, 192 N. W. 22; Abel v. Smith (1928) 151 Va. 568, 144 S. E. 616. In the famous case of The Jewels of the Princess of Orange, in which jewels belonging to a member of the royal family of the Netherlands were stolen, brought to the United States by the thief or his accomplice, and libeled for a violation of United States revenue laws, Attorney General Taney, later Chief Justice of the United States Supreme Court, said: "It is, I think, very clear that the jewels are not liable to condemnation under the laws of the United States. The real owner has done no act that can rightfully subject the property to forfeiture. The party who imported them into this country obtained the possession fraudulently, and without her knowledge, and brought them here against her will. It was not in her power to prevent it; for she did not know who had the possession of them, or where they were to be found, until they were seized. And property thus obtained, and thus introduced against the consent of the owner, stands upon the same footing with that which is cast upon our shores by the violence of the winds and waves, and is entitled to the same protection. It is not liable to forfeiture in either case; and the innocent owner will not be visited with that penalty for an act which it was out of his power to prevent."—(1831) 2 Op. Atty. Gen. 482, 484.

A fortiori a vessel seized in violation of international treaty and brought by force within reach of the court's process should be released. The distinction between the custody of the officer who made the original seizure and the subsequent custody of the court is a mere face-saving device. See United States v. Ferris (Dist. Ct. N. D. Calif., 1927) 19 F. (2d) 925, note 22 *infra*.

[13] It is of course true that an individual defendant may waive an objection which he is personally entitled to make to the jurisdiction of a particular court by appearing and pleading to the merits. See Western Loan and Savings Co. v. Butte & Boston Consolidated Mining Co. (1908) 210 U. S. 368, 28 Sup. Ct. 720; Houston v. Ormes (1920) 252 U. S. 469, 474, 40 Sup. Ct. 369. But such a waiver of personal privilege cannot invest the nation with a competence which it would not otherwise possess. *Cf.* Case of Raymond Fornage, Sirey (1873) Pt. I, 141; Dickinson, *Cases* 648.

[14] Cook v. United States (1932) 288 U. S. 102, 121–122, 53 Sup. Ct. 305, 312.

[15] In so doing, as Judge Hough observed in other and less striking circumstances, the judiciary would be "really contributing to what might become, under conceivable circumstances, a *casus belli*."—The Maipo (Dist. Ct. S. D. N. Y., 1919) 259 Fed. 367, 368.

[16] "It cannot be doubted that all countries governed by the common law have in fact accepted international law as part of the common law; and that the principles of that law which give or withhold jurisdiction are therefore principles of our common law."—Beale, *The Jurisdiction of a Sovereign State* (1923) 36 Harv. L. Rev. 241, 242. See The Paquete Habana (1900) 175 U. S. 677, 700, 20 Sup. Ct. 290.

[17] The contrary has been argued in reliance upon cases in which the political departments of government had foreclosed the issue by expressly asserting an authority to make the seizure or arrest. *Cf.* Buron v. Denman (1848) 2 Ex. 157; The Marianna Flora (1826) 11 Wh. 1; Jones v. United States (1890) 137 U. S. 202; *In re* Cooper (1892) 143 U. S. 472. This argument has undoubtedly influenced some of the decisions. See The Ship Richmond v. United States (1815) 9 Cr. 102; The Tenyu Maru (1910) 4 Alaska 129; The Grace and Ruby (1922) 283 Fed. 475. See also State v. Brewster (1835) 7 Vt. 118, 121; Ker v. People (1884) 110 Ill. 627, 640; United States v. Unverzagt (Dist. Ct. W. D. Wash., 1924) 299 Fed. 1015. But the cases relied upon are not in point and the argument is clearly mistaken where the issue has not been thus foreclosed by political decision, where it is admitted or proved that the seizure or arrest was made in violation of treaty or international law, and where the executive has submitted to the court for the purpose of securing condemnation or conviction. *Cf.* Le Louis (1817) 2 Dods. 210; The Paquete Habana (1900) 175 U. S. 677, 20 Sup. Ct. 290; United States v. Ferris (Dist. Ct. N. D. Calif., 1927) 19 F. (2d) 925, Ann. Dig., 1927–1928, Case No. 127; Williams, *Federal Practice* (ed. 2) 14; (1923) 36 Harv. L. Rev. 609, 613.

[18] See Dickinson, *L'Interprétation et l'application du droit international dans les pays anglo-américains,* Académie de Droit International, Recueil des Cours (1932) II, 305.

[19] (1886) 119 U. S. 436; Dickinson, *Cases* 751.

[20] "A final judgment or decree in any suit in the highest court of a State, in which a decision in the suit could be had, where is drawn in question the validity of a treaty, or statute of, or an authority exercised under, the United States, and the decision is against their validity; or where is drawn in question the validity of a statute of, or an authority exercised under any State, on the ground of their being repugnant to the Constitution, treaties, or laws of the United States, and the decision is in favor of their validity; or where any title, right, privilege, or immunity is claimed under the Constitution, or any treaty or statute of, or commission held or authority exercised under, the United States, and the decision is against the title, right, privilege, or immunity specially set up or claimed, by either party, under such Constitution, treaty, statute, commission, or authority, may be re-examined and reversed or affirmed in the Supreme Court upon a writ of error. . . ."—U. S. Rev. Stat. § 709. See 28 U. S. C. A. § 344.

[21] See U. S. Rev. Stat. § 709, quoted note 20 *supra.*

[22] 119 U. S. 436, 443, 7 Sup. Ct. 225, 229, *supra* note 5.

[23] There are decisions to the effect that when a person is held on a criminal charge the court need not inquire into the circumstances of his apprehension. It has been said that "in criminal cases the interests of the public override that which is, after all, a mere privilege from arrest" (Brown, J., in *In re* Johnson (1897) 167 U. S. 120, 126, 17 Sup. Ct. 735, 737). See Travers, *Des Arrestations au cas de venue involontaire sur le territoire* (1917) 13 Rev. de Droit Int. Privé et de Droit Pénal Int. 627. But decisions relying upon this proposition have not been founded upon an adequate consideration of the effect to be attributed to an arrest abroad in violation of treaty or international law. See *Ex parte* Scott (1829) 9 B. & C. 446; State v. Brewster (1835) 7 Vt. 118; Ker v. People (1884) 110 Ill. 627; United States v. Unverzagt (Dist. Ct. W. D. Wash., 1924) 299 Fed. 1015, Ann. Dig., 1923–1924, Case No. 161; *Ex parte* Ponzi (1926) 106 Tex. Cr. 58, 290 S. W. 170. Cases of arrest abroad pursuant to an informal agreement are not in point since there is no violation of treaty or international law in such circumstances. See People v. Rowe (1858) 4 Parker Cr. 253; People v. Pratt (1889) 78 Cal. 345, 20 Pac. 731; Travers, *op. cit.* See also *Ex parte* Brown (Dist. Ct. N. D. N. Y., 1886) 28 Fed. 653; *In re* Ezeta (Dist. Ct. N. D. Calif., 1894) 62 Fed. 964; *Ex parte* Wilson (1911) 63 Tex. Cr. 281, 140 S. W. 98. The American interstate cases are not controlling. State v. Smith (1829) 1 Bailey (S. C.) 283; Dow's Case (1851) 18 Pa. St. 37; State v. Ross (1866) 21 Iowa 467; *In re* Miles (1880) 52 Vt. 609; Mahon v. Justice (1888) 127 U. S. 700, 8 Sup. Ct. 1207; Kingen v. Kelley (1891) 3 Wyo. 566, 28 Pac. 36; (1923) 36 Harv. L. Rev. 609. And even among the American interstate cases there are a few decisions *contra.* See State v. Simmons (1888) 39 Kan. 262, 18 Pac. 177; State v. Jackson (Dist. Ct. E. D. Tenn., 1888) 36 Fed. 258; see also Commonwealth v. Shaw (1885) 6 Crim. L. Mag. (Pa.) 245. The question is not political. See note 17 *supra. Cf.* State v. Brewster (1835) 7 Vt. 118, 121; Ker v. People (1884) 110 Ill. 627, 640; United States v. Unverzagt (Dist. Ct. W. D. Wash., 1924) 299 Fed. 1015, Ann. Dig., 1923–1924, Case No. 161; Travers, *op. cit.* 642, 646. In principle, in the international cases, there should be no jurisdiction to prosecute one who has been arrested abroad in violation of treaty or international law.

The complete lack of jurisdiction has been asserted in noteworthy language in United States v. Ferris (Dist. Ct. N. D. Calif., 1927) 19 F. (2d) 925, Ann. Dig., 1927–1928. Case No. 127, Hudson, *Cases* 676, a prosecution of members of the crew of a foreign ship for conspiracy to violate the Prohibition and Tariff acts following seizure of the ship some 270 miles off the west coast of the United States. In sustaining pleas to the jurisdiction, Judge Bourquin said: "Hence, as the instant seizure was far outside the limit, it is sheer aggression and trespass (like those which contributed to the War of 1812), contrary to the treaty, not to be sanctioned by any court, and cannot be the basis of any proceeding adverse to the defendants. The prosecution contends, however, that courts will try those before it, regardless of the methods employed to bring them there. There are many cases generally so holding, but none of authority wherein a treaty or other federal law was violated, as in the case at bar. That presents a very different aspect and case. 'A decent respect for the opinions of mankind,' national honor, harmonious relations between nations, and avoidance of war, require that the contracts and law represented by treaties shall be scrupulously observed, held inviolate, and in good faith precisely performed—require that treaties shall not be reduced to mere 'scraps of paper'." After referring to United States v. Rauscher, 119 U. S. 407, 7 Sup. Ct. 234, and Ker v. Illinois, 119 U. S. 436, 7 Sup. Ct. 225, Judge Bourquin concluded: "It seems clear that, if one legally before the court cannot be tried because therein a treaty is violated, for greater reason one illegally before the court, in violation of a treaty, likewise cannot be subjected to trial. Equally in both cases is there absence of jurisdiction."

[24] The Twee Gebroeders (1800) 3 C. Rob. 162, 162 note; The Anna (1805) 5 C. Rob. 373; The Purissima Conception (1805) 6 C. Rob. 45; The Eliza Ann (1813) 1 Dods. 244; The Bangor [1916] P. 181; The Düsseldorf [1920] A. C. 1034, 1037; The Valeria [1921] 1 A. C. 477; The Pellworm [1922] 1 A. C. 292; The Anne (1818) 3 Wh. 435; The Santissima Trinidad (1822) 7 Wh. 283, 349; The Lilla (1862) 2 Sprague 177; The Sir William Peel (1866) 5 Wall. 517; The Adela (1867) 6 Wall. 266; The Florida (1879) 101 U. S. 37, 42.

[25] The Purissima Conception, 6 C. Rob. 45, 47.

[26] Possibly also under the influence of eighteenth-century uncertainty in respect to the nature and extent of territorial waters.

[27] *Cf.* The Santissima Trinidad (1822) 7 Wh. 283, 349 (claim to restitution by an individual claimant where a capture had been made on the high seas by a belligerent vessel equipped in United States ports in violation of neutrality); The Appam (1917) 243 U. S. 124, 37 Sup. Ct. 337, Dickinson, *Cases* 781 (claim to restitution by individual claimant where a belligerent prize captured on the high seas had been laid up in a United States port in violation of neutrality).

[28] The prize tribunals of France, Germany, and Italy apparently consider a capture made in violation of neutral territorial waters as "absolutely illegal irrespective of whether the neutral power in whose waters the capture was made intervenes or not."—Garner, *Prize Law* 227–230. See also Colombos, *Law of Prize* 117–120.

[29] (1815) 9 Cr. 102.

[30] 9 Cr. 102, 104.

[31] (1824) 9 Wh. 391.

[32] 288 U. S. 102, 122, 53 Sup. Ct. 305, 312.

[33] 119 U. S. 407, 7 Sup. Ct. 234, discussed *supra* at p. 118.

[34] 9 Cr. 102, 104. In the case of The Merino, it was argued for the United States, in reliance upon the case of The Ship Richmond, that "the trespass on the Spanish territory cannot be so connected with the subsequent seizure, under the process of the Court below, as to invalidate the seizure (The Richmond, 9 Cranch 102). If there was any offence against the sovereignty of Spain in the original seizure, that is a matter to be adjusted between the two governments."—9 Wh. 391, 399.

[35] See The Charming Betsy (1804) 2 Cr. 64; Le Louis (1817) 2 Dods. 210; The San Juan Nepomuceno (1824) 1 Hagg. Adm. 265; The Antelope (1825) 10 Wh. 66; The Paquete Habana (1900) 175 U. S. 677, 20 Sup. Ct. 290; The Pellworm [1922] 1 A. C. 292.

[36] See Pearcy v. Stranahan (1907) 205 U. S. 257, 27 Sup. Ct. 545; Sullivan v. Kidd (1921) 254 U. S. 433, 41 Sup. Ct. 158, Ann. Dig., 1919–1922, Case No. 252; Crandall, *Treaties* (ed. 2) 364.

[37] *Cf.* The Leonora [1918] P. 182, [1919] A. C. 974; Yntema, *Retaliation and Neutral Rights* (1919) 17 Mich. L. Rev. 564.

[38] Foster & Elam v. Neilson (1829) 2 Pet. 253, 307; Williams v. Suffolk Insurance Co. (1839) 13 Pet. 415, 420; Jones v. United States (1890) 137 U. S. 202, 221, 11 Sup. Ct. 80; Moore, *Act of State in English Law* 35.

[39] Rose v. Himely (1808) 4 Cr. 241; Hudson v. Guestier (1808) 4 Cr. 293, (1810) 6 Cr. 281; Williams v. Armroyd (1813) 7 Cr. 423. See also Schooner Exchange v. M'Faddon (1812) 7 Cr. 116.

[40] 7 Cr. 423, 431.

[41] 7 Cr. 423, 427, 429.

[42] The Paquete Habana (1900) 175 U. S. 677, 700, 20 Sup. Ct. 290.

THE STORY OF THE CRIMINAL JURY

In the Civil Law and in the Common Law

BY THE HON. ROBERT L. HENRY

REPUBLICAN ROME had an institution which resembled our criminal jury. Originally crimes were tried by the *comitia,* the assembly of the people, on the accusation of a magistrate. Later, in order to avoid the necessity of assembling all the people for the trial of every crime, it became the custom to appoint *quaestiones,* or commissions, at first special, and then permanent. Each commission was presided over by a magistrate, a *quaestor*. The other members constituted the *consilium,* the jury, or body of judge assessors. In the early Republic the latter was chosen exclusively from among the senators; but by the Lex Sempronia, of 123 B.C., and subsequent statutes the list of those eligible to jury service was enlarged, though it continued to be restricted to notables. The votes of a majority of the jury decided the verdict of the court, which (whether in accordance with the opinion of the magistrate or otherwise) was final.[1] There is nothing in the constitution of such a court or in the procedure to suggest a division into separate organs, one to decide questions of law and the other questions of fact. It is evident that the popular judges in the general assemblies and on the commissions decided both.

The contrast with the civil tribunal of the time is radical. It is doubtful whether the popular courts at any time had to do with purely civil controversies other than those relating to wills, adoptions, and other family affairs. At any rate, from a very early date we see such matters taken care of outside the assemblies. Questions of law were referred to a judicial magistrate, the *praetor,* those of fact to an arbiter or *judex,* who was a layman. In civil matters submission to the court was by mutual consent. Both parties went voluntarily before the magistrate; or the debtor, who had put himself under the power of his creditor by the noxal contract, was brought there by the latter. Until late in the Republic, the state did not help by even so much as an official summons. The judex, if one was necessary to determine the facts, was selected by the parties, or assigned to them by the magistrate.

In Anglo-Saxon England the development was similar. In the course of time the criminal court, which had consisted of all the people, contracted; during the past seven or eight hundred years it has consisted of a presiding magistrate and of twelve popular judges, and both in composition and in function is similar to the *quaestio* of Republican Rome.

There are slight differences. The members of the quaestio were drawn from the aristocratic classes. The modern criminal jury is most democratic. It should be noted, however, that in medieval England there were qualifications: for the ordinary person who was subject to the jurisdiction of the hundred court, the tribunal consisted of twelve knights or freemen, representing the hundred; and the popular judges had to be of rank at least equal to that of the accused, since the latter was entitled to the judgment of his peers. The decision of the Roman tribunal was by majority vote, while that of the common law criminal jury must be unanimous. But neither that difference nor the one concerning the qualification of jurors goes to the essence of the matter.

Fundamentally the similarity is striking. In each we see a presiding magistrate who regulates the proceedings, advises the jurors as to the law, and helps them to come to a decision as to the facts. In each the popular judges have the final say. In each their decision of "guilty" or "not guilty" involves a determination of law as well as of fact.

In Anglo-Saxon England, as in ancient Rome, the popular courts concerned themselves with offenses only. By an application of modern juristic theory it might be said that proceedings which depended on private initiative were not criminal, that the test is whether the right of action lies in the state or in the individual. But modern theory does not in any way fit early institutions. The test for them should be whether or not the acts repressed, for which a sanction is provided, are of the same nature as those which we consider crimes today. Such were certainly the offenses treated of in their tables of compositions.

Contracts were not inexistent, as has been assumed, but they were taken care of without the intervention of the court. As in ancient Rome, they were self-executing. The debtor by the *wed* and *borh* ceremony (performed when the contract was entered into) placed himself in the surety's power. The latter, if the debtor failed to perform, discharged the debt and then took execution himself upon the debtor.[2]

By the twelfth century, civil debts could be sued upon before the popular courts; and by these is meant not only the communal courts, that is, the courts of the hundreds and of the counties, which were the assemblies of the people as in Anglo-Saxon times, but also the other local courts of the time, the seignorial and the borough courts, for they also were constituted in the same manner as the communal. The people, who were the suitors of the court, were the doomsmen or judges.

Contracts had from time immemorial been contracted by precisely the same formalities as those employed for the formation of the procedural contract used in penal matters. The ancient procedure for the recovery of money compositions was essentially one of debt. The offer of suit by the plaintiff, and the defense by compurgation by the defendant, the wager of law, were suitable for civil debts.

There was no reason why a civil suit should not take place before the people assembled as a court, at the same sessions which handled criminal matters, and such came to be the practice. But in civil matters the people had comparatively little to do, and that little was routine. And in the most important civil cases, those which took place before the communal courts when assembled before the justices, and those in the central courts of the king, the people had nothing whatever to do with the judgments.

There is no evidence that, in the ordinary sessions of the local courts, civil suits were handled in a different manner from penal. Certainly the suitors were present when both civil and penal matters were decided; and they gave judgments in the one as in the other. In civil matters as well as in penal, there had to be a decision concerning who should make the proof. There was not, however, a choice with respect to what the proof should be. Plaintiffs in contract cases, if their suits were challenged, had to prove by witnesses, and defendants in all civil cases by wager of law. For centuries, inquests were little used and then only by the consent of the parties.

It has been said on this subject that "to the last, trial by jury has no place in the ordinary procedure of our old communal courts." The term "ordinary" excludes the sessions of the popular courts which took place before the justices, for certainly juries of several sorts took part in them in penal matters. It likewise excludes courts merchant, which before the close of the Middle Ages were using the inquest to a considerable extent. With respect to such ordinary sessions it should be pointed out that the suitors, the hundred court itself, took the place of one kind of jury present at the sessions before the justices—that is, the twelve representatives of the hundred—which eventually became our criminal jury.

It is interesting to note, however, that a radical distinction was made between civil and criminal proceedings when the local courts came before the justices at the county seats, as also when the case came up before a central court of the king. In both events, in civil affairs, in the thirteenth century, except in the petty and grand assizes, concerning land, "there are no recognitors, no representatives of 'the country' at hand."[3] This means that only for that limited class of cases was the inquest used on the civil side. Of course on the criminal side there was the jury of the twelve hundredors, and two sorts of inquests, the information-giving and the inquest of proof. With respect to the important courts, then—the central courts, and the sessions of the local courts before the justices—it may be said that the people did not insist on the right to have a judgment of their peers, except in penal matters. Magna Carta provided, "No freeman shall be arrested or detained in prison or deprived of his freehold, or outlawed, or banished, or in any way molested, unless by the lawful judgment of his peers and by the law of the land," and, in another section, "Fines must only be imposed by the oath of honest men of the neighborhood."[4] Clearly, only criminal matters are referred to, unless the clause "deprived of his freehold" should be construed to guarantee the inquest as used in the new forms of action, grand and petty assize, which it was probably not meant to do.

In civil matters the people were quite content not to pronounce the judgments. So, if we remember that for several centuries of their history in England the popular courts did not concern themselves with non-penal matters, and that from the thirteenth century on such courts when assembled for the decision of the most weighty matters—that is, before the justices—did not do so either, and that no attempt was made to insist on popular judges for civil matters before the central courts, we see a phenomenon not greatly different from that of ancient Rome in which the popular courts functioned for criminal matters only. We see two, three, or four juries of the people taking part in a single criminal case. This is in striking contrast to civil trials, in which there was either no jury at all (unless one is pleased to call the *secta* of the plaintiff and the oath-helpers of the defendant, juries), or at most one, an inquest summoned to determine a question of fact. Among the several juries taking part in a penal case we can always identify one and often two as representing the hundred court. Also there are always two judgments rendered by such a jury, or juries; one when presentment is made or the charge avowed, the other when guilt or innocence is determined. Each is a judgment involving the determination of both fact and law. In civil affairs we can never find a jury representing the hundred.

The civil inquest in the twelfth century and later did not render a judgment,[5] though such inquests did sometimes answer questions of law as well as of fact. Eventually, by the sixteenth century, we do get a civil jury which looks very much like the twelve hundredors used in criminal cases; but such a jury had quite a different origin, and even today is not exactly the same institution as the criminal jury, for the latter decides mixed questions of fact and of law, while it became settled comparatively early that the civil jury's province was to decide on the facts only.

The story of the jury would be truly confusing if we should fail to discriminate between civil and criminal juries on the one hand and between the various sorts of juries employed in a criminal case on the other. The term "jury" by itself means nothing except that the members are sworn. It was applied to inquests whose sole function was to give information, to juries of neighbors who made the proof, to civil juries who judged facts, and to criminal juries who judged both facts and law. It is not names which signify, but the function served; yet names should be accounted for. The jury representative of the hundred, which has come down to us as the criminal jury, was no doubt called a "jury" because that name was applied to all the various popular groups taking part in legal proceedings; and because in fact it was sworn, though for another purpose, and not in its sovereign capacity as a popular court.

All the groups summoned to the county seat when the royal justices presided, whether they were primarily inquests or something quite different, were put through the same catechism, after having been sworn to tell the truth. That was to permit the Crown to get information about the commission of crime from every available source. It should be noted, however, that when afterwards at the trial, perhaps many weeks later, the same jury of the twelve hundredors, or another one, pronounces "guilty" or "not guilty," it is not sworn, but the jury of twenty from the four vills, who are the neighbors on whose verdict or truth-telling the accused puts himself, is sworn.[6]

It has been suggested that because, in the twelfth and thirteenth centuries, the same jury of twelve commonly served for the presentment and for the trial, this jury having been sworn once, it was not necessary to put it under oath again;[7] but this hardly explains the difference in the treatment of the two groups at the trial, for at times it did happen that a different jury of twelve functioned at the trial, and at other times it happened that the same jury of twenty *villani* made presentment and later acted as the proof-making inquest of neighbors.[8] Why, in the latter event, swear them twice; why, in the former, fail to swear the second jury of twelve? Evidently at the trial the latter acted in its sovereign capacity, and therefore did not have to be sworn.

In order to trace with certainty the separate story of the criminal jury, we must study the criminal court as a whole and at each stage in its history note the functions performed by the several organs which constitute it, without being led astray by the names which may chance to be applied to them. For it is the function which determines the nature. Wherever we see a definite function served by an organ at one period, we can be reasonably certain that the organ which serves the same function at a later was developed from the corresponding organ at the earlier. It will be sufficient for this purpose to analyze the criminal court at three different epochs: (1) the early Anglo-Saxon, (2) that of the twelfth and thirteenth centuries, and (3) that of today.

If we begin with our criminal court of today, we observe that it consists of three or four organs, each serving separate purposes. First, there is the judge who presides, regulates the procedure, and advises the jury as to the law. Secondly, there is the grand jury which sits as a separate body, the functions of which are to inform, and to decide who shall be tried. Thirdly, there are the witnesses who make the proof. We may not consider these as an organ of the court, but should include them for purposes of comparison with the court at other periods. Fourthly, there is the petty jury to judge the facts and apply the law.

Now, going back to Anglo-Saxon times when the court consisted of the assembly of the whole people, we may observe a differentiation beginning for the performance of the several operations of which criminal judicial proceedings consist. The accusation was brought either by the injured party or by the representative of the family whose member had been killed or injured. The accuser was backed up by his suit. Together they may be considered the accusing group, or jury. It should be noted, however, that such a group does not correspond exactly to its successors in the accusing function, that is, to the inquest, or to the modern grand jury. The criminal informing-inquest was not had on private initiative, and the grand jury in addition to the informative or accusing function also has to judge whether the accused shall go to trial or not. The influences which brought about such changes will be discussed later. It is sufficient here to point out the identity of function served.

Secondly, there is the judging group which in early times consisted of all the people. They decided, in the first stage of the proceedings, whether or not the accusation was in due form, whether the act charged constituted an offense, and what the customary penalty was. The accused, if he did not deny, was required to give security to pay the customary composition. If he denied, the court ordered a trial and prescribed the mode. In this part of the proceedings the popular court performed functions which are now served by the grand jury. In the second stage of the proceedings the function of the court was quite simple. As the modes of trial were by compurgation or ordeal, it did not have to go through processes of analyzing and weighing evidence, and of coming to decisions often very difficult, as is the lot of its modern representatives the members of the criminal petty jury. It had merely to determine whether the required number of oath-helpers had sworn according to custom, or how an ordeal had resulted, and then on such a basis to order an acquittal, or the execution of the sentence previously defined.

Thirdly, we note the proof-making group, the jury of oath-helpers, which was later succeeded by the jury of neighbors, and still later by modern witnesses.

In early times compurgation was the normal and most usual method of proof for freemen. It is true that the oath-helpers differed in certain important respects from their successors. They did not always know the facts personally. Also they were not impartial, as they were selected by the accused from among his relatives or friends. Yet they were generally persons who did know the facts. And it did happen frequently that persons of ill repute, or persons believed to be guilty, could not muster the required number of compurgators. So to a large extent the three institutions of compurgation, proof inquest, and witnesses correspond in personnel; and they certainly perform the same function, that of making the proof.

Going forward several hundred years to the time of King John, we observe that, though the popular courts are still going strong and are still attended by a very considerable proportion of the populace, influences have been at work to bring about their contraction, for the serving of their principal function, that of judging, to a group of twelve, the rest of the populace being present, first, for the purpose of informing the Crown, and secondly, in order to be available to be formed into proof inquests of the neighbors.

There were several causes which brought about the contraction. The first and principal one was the burden which court service put on the suitors. As court business increased, the attendance of all the people at all sessions was more than could be borne. In the first place, many men obtained exemption from the burden. In the second, as far as the local meetings of the hundred court were concerned, a distinction was drawn between full sessions, at which the view of frankpledge was taken and at which all persons owing suit had to be present, in order that it might be ascertained that everyone who ought to be, was in pledge, and ordinary sessions, at which a much smaller representation was acceptable. At the latter the presence of the chief pledges would seem to have sufficed. As for the sessions of the hundred at the county seat, when the royal justices on circuit presided, the burden of suit was obviously far heavier than when the court met in its own locality. Such sessions might continue for many weeks, necessitating a like absence of the suitors from home. It early became settled that at such sessions the hundred should be represented by twelve of its members.[9] More would hardly have been reasonable to demand for such service. It may even sometimes have been difficult to find that many available; for it should be remembered, first, that the hundredors had to be knights or freemen, and that in the twelfth and thirteenth centuries the depressed classes formed the greater part of the population; and secondly, that a large proportion of the remaining freemen had obtained exemptions. That the number twelve should be chosen was most natural, since that number had for centuries tended to become the normal one for various judicial organs. The number of chief pledges in a hundred approximated twelve; hence the number of suitors at the minor sessions of the court held locally tended to be about the same. Twelve was also the normal number of compurgators required of the accused in a criminal trial. So, by a simple process of contraction, induced by practical necessity and guided by a traditional feeling concerning the minimum number of popular judges required, we might have arrived at precisely the sort of criminal court which we have today, consisting for trial purposes of a presiding magistrate and of twelve representatives of the people of the district.

The story does not appear quite so simple as that, however, though such is, in fact, its main thread. For one thing, it does not account for the grand jury. For a full understanding, we must trace the development not only of the jury of twelve, by itself, but also that of the other organs taking part in the administration of criminal justice. Though in a strict sense the group of twelve hundredors, with its presiding magistrate, constitute the court—for it alone can judge—yet in a broader sense the court may also be considered as consisting of a larger body, including in its make-up all the juries taking part. We must in fact consider the latter as well as the jury of twelve, for purposes of comparison with both earlier and later periods.

When the royal justices held the sessions, there were summoned to the county seat, from each hundred, not only the twelve representatives of the hundred, but also the reeve and four men from each of its vills. There came perhaps seventy or eighty or more men from each hundred, a very considerable proportion of its male inhabitants. The latter groups, which were composed for the most part of *villani,* that is, of the unfree, were present for two purposes: first, they were called to furnish to the Crown information concerning what crimes had been committed in the hundred, and concerning what persons were suspected; and secondly, they were there to be available for the formation of inquests of neighbors, to make proof in trials.

Their first or accusing function was now in an official capacity. In the time of King Alfred all charges had been brought on private initiative. Offenses had been looked upon primarily as against individuals or family groups. It was they who got the *wer,* the money composition. The *bot,* which went to the lord, and the *wite,* due the king, were comparatively insignificant. But in the course of several centuries the proportionate shares of lord and king grew; until by the time of King John, in cases of felony they got everything—lands, personalty, and the body of the convict. When such had become the situation, private initiative could no longer be relied on. The king as the chief interested party had to bring the accusations; and in order to furnish himself with the necessary information he resorted to the inquest. The second function served by the representatives of the vills, that is, of serving on inquests of neighbors, came about through radical changes which took place in the mode of proof.

The normal proof for freemen, in the early Anglo-Saxon period, was compurgation. But side by side with it, and likewise of very ancient origin, was the ordeal. The latter seems to have been the method of trial for the unfree, those who did not belong to a family or group of standing, and who could not in the nature of things muster the necessary oath-helpers. But as we approach the time just before the abolition of the ordeal in 1215 A.D., we see it as much the commonest method of proof in matters of serious crime. The reasons for that were several. In the first place the depressed classes had increased enormously, so that they had come to be about two-thirds of the population. In the second, the criminals came for the most part—that is, in a considerably larger proportion than two out of three—from the depressed classes. In the third place, the ordeal had come to be used extensively for freemen. Probably at all times some of the latter were put to the ordeal: when, for example, they were generally believed to be guilty and could not get the required oath-helpers to stand with them.

By the twelfth century, however, the king, who was the party chiefly interested, had contrived to make compurgation for crime so difficult, by complicated formulas, and by the rule that a slip or a faltering on the part of an oath-helper meant conviction, that freemen were freely choosing the ordeal, in which they had about an even chance of escape, in preference to their traditional right of trial by compurgation. Then, besides the two ancient methods, a third was being tried out, the inquest of neighbors. It was one which could be used by mutual agreement. It was a sort of two-sided compurgation. Instead of one party to whom the proof was awarded picking out the oath-helpers, both parties put themselves on the oaths of those who knew the most about the facts. The sheriff or bailiff chose them impartially. He summoned the neighbors of the accused. In practice at the eyres such men were already present in court. It was only necessary to form into a jury the reeve and four men from each of the four nearest vills. When such a jury came to give its verdict, it might make the proof for either party. If it said "not guilty" it was in effect making compurgatory proof for the accused. If it said "guilty" it was doing so for the Crown. Probably that is the reason why the decision of our juries must be unanimous. It was necessary in compurgation for the accused to muster the required number of oath-helpers, generally twelve, and for all these to support him by their oaths. If one failed him, the proof was not made. It would seem only fair that the Crown likewise should have to make the proof of "guilty" by the oaths of the full member.

Suddenly, in 1215, the Lateran Council forbade the clergy to take part in the ordeal ceremony. The decree was promptly obeyed in England and the ordeal disappeared. The trial by compurgation as used in criminal matters had to a large extent been assimilated to the ordeal and was already seldom used because of its difficulty. The field was left with only one available method of trial, that by inquest of the neighbors. There was the difficulty that it could only be used by agreement of the parties; but a method was soon devised to compel the consent of the accused—the *peine forte et dure.*[10]

Pollock and Maitland give us an excellent description of just how the three types of juries performed the functions required of them—of presenting, judging, and proving. The first stage of the procedure is the charge and the decision that the accused shall go to trial. When the sheriff is on his turn of the hundreds,

The representatives of the vills make presentments to a jury of twelve freeholders which represents the hundred, and then such of these presentments as the twelve jurors are willing to "avow" or make their own, are presented to the sheriff.[11]

When the justices begin their session they have before them the sheriff, the coroners, and the bailiffs of the hundreds and liberties. They have before them what is in theory "the whole country," that is to say, all the suitors of the county court who have neither sent excuse nor failed in their duty. They have before them a jury of twelve men representing each hundred; the boroughs, and some privileged manors, also send juries. The process whereby these juries were selected was this: the bailiff of the hundred chose three or four knights who chose the twelve. There were also present the reeve and four men from every township.[12]

When the county is assembled at the county seat before the justices, a proceeding similar to that which took place before the sheriff on his "turn" is gone through with, except that it begins by the questioning of the representatives of the hundred.

Before the abolition of the ordeal in 1215 the justices, having received the statements of the hundred-jurors, turn to the representatives of the four neighboring vills, who at this point are sworn to make the answer. If these villani agree with the hundredors in declaring that the person in question is suspected of a felony, then he goes to the water.[13]

After 1215, the person against whom a presentment is made is brought to court and is asked how he will acquit himself of the charge.

By this time there is but one mode of trial or proof open to him, namely, a verdict of the country. His choice lies for good and ill upon the oath of his neighbors. . . . The hundred jury without being again sworn—it has taken a general oath to answer questions truly—is asked to say in so many words whether this man is guilty or no. If it finds him guilty, then "four townships" are sworn and answer the same question. If they agree with the hundredors, sentence is passed.[14]

It looks as if, in the normal trial, in the time of King John, the hundredors and sometimes even the same four vills which make presentment also pronounce on the question of guilt or innocence in the second stage of the proceedings, that is, at the trial. We should expect that. Most crimes were committed by members of the hundred within the hundred district. The hundredors, who constitute the court, naturally judge in both stages of the case, as they have from time immemorial in the Anglo-Saxon popular assemblies. It is natural also, ordinarily, for more or less the same villeins to act as the accusing inquest and as the jury of neighbors, though it might readily happen that the crime was committed in one neighborhood, within the hundred, and that the accused lived in another. Should the latter occur, it would then be the four vills where the act took place who would accuse, and the four vills nearest to where the accused lived who would constitute the jury of neighbors, to whose verdict he would appeal. It might happen that the crime was committed in one hundred and that the accused lived in another. Such a case would go to the county court. The hundred and the county courts were both of general jurisdiction. The former naturally handled the greater part of the legal business, and the latter only had to be appealed to when justice could not be had impartially in the former. In a case, then, involving persons of two or more hundreds, the accusing hundredors and their supporting vills would come to the county court from one hundred, and the trial hundredors and the neighbors upon whose verdict the accused put himself, from another.

The notion grew that a man's indictors will not be impartial in trying him. By a statute of 1352 the general rule was established that a man's indictors are not to be put upon the inquest which tries him.[15] There is after that, then, a definite separation of the popular court into two divisions, one operating in what we have come to call grand jury proceedings, and the other at the trial.

In course of time the two groups which make the presentments, that is, the twelve hundredors and the representatives of the vills, are consolidated into one large group, which eventually becomes our grand jury of twenty-three. That number was probably selected because the presenting jury decided by majority vote, and the traditional feeling was very strong that no one should be sent to trial without the judgment of twelve of his peers. Blackstone tells us that no one in England can be convicted of crime without the concurrence of twenty-four of his peers, twelve on the presenting jury and twelve on the trial jury. The grand jury undoubtedly is derived from that of the twelve presenting hundredors, reënforced by a number of other men drawn from the vills. It had the double function of having to give information of its own personal knowledge—and therefore it had to be large, and of judging whether the evidence was sufficient to justify the accused being put to trial—and therefore it had to contain the twelve representatives of the hundred.

In avowing, or consenting, or presenting, it gave a judgment. The famous words of Magna Carta, that "No freeman shall be arrested or detained in prison, or deprived of his freehold, or outlawed, or banished, or in any way molested, unless by the lawful judgment of his peers and by the law of the land,"[16] were not ill chosen. They mean exactly what they say. The phrase *judicium parium* refers to the judgment of the popular court. It is quite obvious what were the evils against which the prohibition was aimed. King John and his minions were arresting freemen and putting them into prison without first getting the consent of the people. If the king could not lay hands on them because they had fled, he was declaring them outlawed or banished, or, if they had freeholds, was seizing their property. The prohibition did not refer to trials at all, but to the preliminary proceedings, corresponding to those which with us take place before grand juries. At that time such matters were markedly important. They were the primary safeguards of the people's liberties.

The provision of Magna Carta referred to has been considered the most important one in the charter of our liberties. It has been traditionally thought that the judgment referred to meant the judgment of a jury; and because the jury, which in recent times has seemed most important as the bulwark of liberties, has undoubtedly been the jury of trial, it has been assumed to refer to such a jury, that is, to the petty jury. Scholars have pointed out that it could not be our common law jury which was referred to, since it was several centuries later that jury procedure in its present form evolved. Also the phrase evidently did not refer to the method of proof, novel at that time, of the verdict of one's neighbors. It seems clear that it was the judgment of the twelve hundredors who had to "avow" an accusation before the accused could be arrested or put to trial, which the framers of Magna Carta had in mind.

But it happened also that the same twelve hundredors (at the time of King John) commonly pronounced the judgment of "guilty" or "not guilty"; so tradition is substantially correct in identifying "judgment of his peers" with the jury. It was the judgment of the tribunal, which has come down to us in the dual form of the grand and the petty jury. Their judgment was required at each of the two stages of the proceedings.

That the twelve hundredors were doomsmen or judges there can be hardly any doubt. It has been well said,

> If what we were seeking for were a court in which, at the bidding of its president, the inhabitants of a district, or some selected group, perhaps twelve, of such inhabitants, deemed the dooms, we should have no difficulty in discovering the origin of the trial by jury. Everywhere we find such courts, for during the earlier Middle Ages it is the exception, rather than the rule, that the judgment should be made by the lord or president of the court or by a group of professional justices.[17]

But the same learned authors go on to say

> But what the jurors or recognitors of our twelfth century deliver is no judgment; they come to "recognize," to declare, the truth; their duty is, not *judicia facere;* but *recognoscere veritatem*.[18]

Obviously in the last sentence they are talking about the inquest. There cannot be the slightest doubt that the inquest had its origin in the inquest, and not in the doomsmen. It is equally clear that inquests were called "juries," and that those used in civil cases were actually transformed in the course of several centuries into such juries as are used in civil cases today. Therefore such juries did not originate in the doomsmen.

The jury of twelve hundredors, however, was not an inquest. It was never so called. And it did not originate in the inquest, but in the doomsmen. The learned authors go on:

When both the jury and the body of doomsmen are already established institutions, the transformation of doomsmen into jurors may be possible, and this transformation may actually have taken place in our manorial courts.[19]

That is exactly what happened, not only in the manorial courts, but also in the communal. When the hundred-courts came to the county seat to be presided over by royal justices, they became juries of twelve for criminal proceedings. The significance of that seems to have been overlooked by the learned authors. Apparently they fail to realize that there were several sorts of juries, and that these may not all have had the same origin. "But," they say, "that the jury should have originally grown out of a body of doomsmen seems almost impossible." That is quite accurate, if one thinks only of the inquest jury. That the twelve hundredors came also to be called a jury was accidental, as I have just explained.[20]

As for the term "verdict," applied to the judgment of the criminal jury, it may readily be accounted for. All the juries summoned to the county seat for criminal proceedings were sworn *veritatem dicere*. So was the inquest or jury in civil suits. It was quite natural to use the word "verdict," loosely, to apply to the pronouncements of all juries on all occasions. Indeed, even in the "avowing" and the finding of "guilty" or "not guilty," it was not a serious misdescription, as what the hundredors said concerned facts more than law. When, for example, a murder had been committed, there would seldom arise the question, what murder was. The matter of interest was nearly always the question, Was the accused the one who had committed it?

The fact that the jury of the hundredors was questioned by the justices along with all the other juries concerning what crimes had been committed, in order to make use of every available source of information, and as a preliminary to such questioning was sworn to tell the truth, did not take away from it its sovereign capacity to pronounce judgments either in the first stage of the proceedings, in which it "avowed" presentments, or in the second, in which it pronounced a verdict of "guilty" or "not guilty."

In order to trace the history of the criminal jury from this point on, it is necessary to take into consideration the story of its civil counterpart, although the latter had an entirely distinct origin, and in the thirteenth century was performing a quite different function. The reason is, that the two juries ultimately became very similar, a development caused by the influence that one exercised upon the other.

It is clear that the civil jury was derived from the inquest, that is, from the inquest in its secondary form as a method of proof, which in turn was a combination of the inquest in its original form as a simple means of gathering information, and as compurgatory proof. No other explanation is possible. We see the proof inquest used in civil cases in the thirteenth, fourteenth, and fifteenth centuries, and in its place in the sixteenth, the civil jury, very much as it is today. It is true that the latter differs radically from the former. The members of the inquest were those who knew the most about the facts. Such persons are excluded from the modern jury. The transformation needs some explanation; yet there can hardly be any doubt that it did take place. Likewise we have seen in the thirteenth century, on the criminal side, among the three or four juries taking part in a single case, two which were called inquests and which certainly were inquests: one serving the primary function of such a body, simply furnishing information; the other, the inquest of neighbors, being used to make the proof. Thus, among the numerous juries going about at that time, the only type used on the civil side, and two varieties used on the criminal, were called inquests and were derived wholly or in part from the inquest in its original form.

It is more or less accepted theory that the common law jury, without distinguishing whether the civil or the criminal jury is meant, had its origin in the Frankish inquest. That would be substantially correct if the modern jury were looked upon as a single institution. There can be no doubt that the Norman kings were familiar with the inquest before they came to England, and that they and their successors used it for all sorts of purposes fiscal and judicial. They employed it in its primary form to get information concerning what crimes had been committed and what persons were suspected, and in its secondary form as a method of proof (the compurgatory-proof idea having been incorporated into it), in both criminal and civil cases. Therefore the Frankish inquest was the basis for all the various juries employed in judicial proceedings, in medieval times, except one, namely, the jury of twelve hundredors in criminal affairs. We should recognize, in strict accuracy, that the modern jury is not a single institution; that the criminal and the civil jury are distinct; that the latter did originate in the inquest, but that the former did not, though it may in its development have been considerably influenced by it.

The two juries, civil and criminal, have each had a separate history and at the same time a common one. The details of the story of the former concerning its initial use in the novel writs having to do with possession and ownership of land, and its spread to the quasi-criminal action of trespass, and eventually through the action of assumpsit into the contract field need not concern us here; but we must trace the influence that each had upon the other through the centuries when they existed side by side.

Superficially, from the beginning, the two were alike. The grand assize was composed of twelve lawful knights of the district in which the disputed tenements lay: the petty assize, of twelve free and lawful men of the neighborhood.[21] The jury of hundredors in criminal proceedings also consisted of twelve, and they had to be knights or freemen. There is no danger of confusing the latter with the jury of twenty neighbors, five from each of four vills, and consisting of villeins, which made up the jury of neighbors in criminal cases. But although alike in appearance, the juries of the assizes and the juries of the hundredors were quite different. In the one the twelve men represented the hundred, and in the other they did not; and the functions of the two were different. As a matter of fact the assize jury corresponded to the jury of villani. They both were inquests of neighbors. Both were composed of the men who knew the most about the facts. We must keep in mind that in civil affairs there was a single jury, if any, and for the trial only; in criminal, a double one at each of the two stages. Of the latter the hundred jury was the court itself; the others were information-giving and proof-making inquests.

It is easy to see how the two juries of twelve would tend to become more and more alike. It would happen that a civil jury would not of its own personal knowledge know the facts. Suppose the persons who knew the most about them were villani, and therefore not eligible to sit on an assize jury. In such a circumstance it was their duty to inform themselves from those who did know, before they came to court, or afterwards before they gave their verdict. Thus they would in effect become judges, at least of fact. Indeed they not infrequently judged law also, since in saying whether A was entitled to a piece of land rather than B, difficult questions of law might be involved.

The hundred jury in criminal matters did not usually know the facts, either. When it acted in the first stage of proceedings, it got its information from the representatives of the vills at home, that is, before coming to court. In the second stage of the proceedings, before giving its verdict of "guilty" or "not guilty," it consulted the groups from the vills who knew the most about the facts. It is certain that the villani had to tell their tales individually in order for the hundredors to be able to make up their minds concerning what charges to avow or what verdicts to render. It is true that the groups from the vills were formed into inquests, consisting of five representatives from each of four vills, and as such they appear to speak to the sheriff on his turn, and when coming before the justices either to confirm a presentment or to make the proof; but such an appearance, and such speaking as a unit, is nothing more than a formal reporting.

The substance was the same whether the matter was civil or criminal; in either, the jury was informed by the witnesses out of court. A formal difference remained until the end of the thirteenth century; that is, the criminal witnesses continued to be formed into a body which spoke as a unit on certain occasions, while the civil witnesses did not. But with the beginning of the fourteenth century the four vills are no longer mentioned as a part of the *patria* which says that men are "guilty" or "not guilty."[22] The assimilation of criminal witnesses and of civil is then complete, which leaves the two juries functioning in much the same way.

The details of their stories in the fourteenth and fifteenth centuries are still obscure,[23] but since we know what they developed into by the sixteenth century we can picture to ourselves fairly well what must have occurred. In the first place, witnesses came to be questioned in the courtroom. It would seem that bringing them in was essential to the proper administration of justice. How else could abuses such as subornation or intimidation be checked? Why not let the judging jury get its information openly before the eyes and under the control of the magistrate, rather than at the tavern? It was hardly a radical step. The inquests had for centuries come into the presence of the magistrate to report, and he had been at liberty to question them. Also, the right to challenge had grown apace, and had come to be applied to the criminal jury as well as to the civil. Even at an early date challenges had been allowed against persons selected or about to be selected for an inquest. "The jurors must be free and lawful, impartial and disinterested, neither the enemies nor the too close friends of either litigant."[24] But it may well be doubted whether that applied to the twelve representatives of the hundred. There might be a choice with respect to which of two hundred-juries should try a case, but there were no extra hundredors present from a particular hundred. The twelve representatives had to sit during the whole session, of perhaps many weeks, for all cases in which the hundred was concerned. But with the discontinuance of the old eyres, and with the great social changes which took place (serfdom disappeared), conditions had become quite different. It became possible to provide a panel of free and lawful men of sufficient size to permit challenges and the selection of a special criminal trial jury for each case.

In the development which had taken place the civil jury had traveled a much longer road than the criminal. It had been transformed from an inquest which declared the facts of their own personal knowledge into a judging body. It had become the court, so far as judging the facts is concerned. As for its relation to the law, although in its early days it frequently pronounced itself on mixed questions of fact and law, it became settled that such was not in its province; that it should confine itself to facts. And that was quite proper, because in origin it was merely a proof-making body. But even making such a jury judge of fact was a most unfortunate historical accident. The accident was not in the substitution of the inquest for the older methods of proof; there was some logic in that; the proof inquest served as a natural transition between primitive proof and modern proof by witnesses. The error lay in assimilating the civil jury to the criminal, in making it almost though not quite equal in power to the latter. There was no basis for that, either in history or in reason. The primitive popular court, as we have seen, did not concern itself with civil matters. Between the twelfth and sixteenth centuries there continued to be a popular court for criminal matters, in the twelve representatives of the hundred; there was not a corresponding popular civil court.

The inquest, to be sure, was used in both criminal and civil affairs. From 1215, it became the only method of proof in the former. In striking contrast, it was used comparatively little on the civil side; the greater number of the civil cases both in the local and in the central courts continued to be settled by the old methods of proof. It is true that comparatively early the trial by battle was superseded, in land cases, by the assize or the inquest. Also, where there was a specialty, written proof was allowed. By far the greater number of cases, parol contracts and the rest, were settled by the compurgatory system—as far as contracts were concerned, by witnesses-proof for the plaintiff, and always by wager of law for the defendant.[25]

It was a long process, extending over three hundred years, before the inquest came to be used generally in civil matters. Within that period the inquest entirely disappeared in criminal cases, having been broken up into witnesses testifying singly and in the courtroom; the witnesses to which the civil inquest had had to resort had likewise been brought before the magistrate, and the inquest itself was converted into a fact-judging body. By that time the civil jury was looked upon as the same institution as the criminal; and as such it has enjoyed the protection of the English and American constitutions, which guarantee a judgment of one's peers, or jury trial.

In that way an institution which nobody really wants and which is very poorly adapted to serve the function required of it, has been fixed in our social structure and will be difficult to get rid of. In practice we have to a large extent abandoned it. Most fortunately a large number of the cases with complicated states of fact go to the equity side of the court where there is no jury; and in the greater number of law cases the jury is waived by mutual consent.

Probably the only useful function the civil jury can now, on occasion, serve is to provide more than one mind for the judicial process. It is possible for a single judge to see things askew, for various reasons.

If there is more than one judge, a judicial deliberation is ensured and individual idiosyncracies are guarded against. If we had benches of three judges for important cases, as they do under the civil law system, there would be no reason whatever for the the civil jury. It is obvious that trained and experienced judges are better able to struggle with complicated facts than is a jury.

But it is entirely different with the criminal jury. The facts and the law involved are usually comparatively simple. To be sure, the question in a murder mystery may crack the brains of anyone; but there is usually just one question involved and that question a matter of intense popular interest, and a jury can usually do about as well as the judge, if it is allowed the benefit of the latter's aid. But even if it is an instrument comparatively inefficient, there are overwhelming reasons for its retention for criminal affairs. The people demand it, and the judge should be relieved of the full responsibility.

If the civil jury should be abolished tomorrow, the people would not care. They would scarcely know that it had disappeared. Most of them never sue nor are sued. They think of the law as concerned chiefly with crime. The criminal jury for eight hundred years has been looked upon as the bulwark against official oppression, and though at the present time there is less danger from that sort of thing than in former ages, the people are certainly not ready to trust their lives and liberties to a single judge. The experience of the civil law in Europe shows that the people are not willing to trust even a professional bench composed of three judges. And the responsibility in criminal cases is too great, certainly, for a single judge. In doubtful cases the decision would prey on his mind, and his life might even be endangered by a convict or the convict's relatives or friends.

The criminal jury, in contrast to the civil, has hardly changed at all in eight hundred years. In its beginning, as the popular court contracted to twelve of its representatives, it was the ultimate judge of fact and law; and it is so today. The judge has acquired considerable power, such as that of being able to set aside a verdict, but no one can be declared "guilty" or "not guilty" without the decision of a jury, and such a decision necessarily involves both fact and law.

To be sure, in some states statutes now require juries to take the law from the judge; but there is no practical way to compel them to do so. If they do not approve the law as given to them they are likely to bring in verdicts of "not guilty" when the facts clearly show the contrary. Such statutes are unfortunate. They are induced by the theory that the judge's province is the law and the jury's is the facts. Such a theory has a historical basis only as applied to civil courts, and whenever an attempt has been made to put it into effect with respect to criminal courts, it has caused trouble. It is one of the causes of the breakdown of the administration of criminal justice in America. Its application to criminal justice in modern civil-law countries caused so much difficulty that it has there been abandoned.

The same theory has caused in most of our states the further blunder of prohibiting the judge from helping the jury with the facts. A jury is really a poor instrument for sifting, weighing, analyzing, and synthesizing conflicting and complicated evidence. The judge by his training and experience is far better qualified for the test. The jury should be allowed to get all the help it can from the judge. If the latter is allowed to comment on the evidence and summarize the case, the jury in criminal matters can act with a reasonable degree of certainty; without such help, it must frequently go astray. These two developments with respect to the functioning of the criminal jury show how dangerous it is to effect changes without a knowledge of the history of our institutions, and without the benefit of the experience of other systems of law with similar institutions.

Historically, the judge was not the arbiter of the law. The king or the lord, or their representatives, presided over the popular courts. But the law was customary. It lay in popular memory. In Iceland and among many of the Teutonic peoples on the Continent there was an officer called the "law speaker" whose special function it was to know the law and to declare it. The law was something which everyone knew in a general way; but as it grew more detailed and complex it became desirable, in the absence of books, for someone to make it his business to know the law in all its details, to serve as a book the better to preserve tradition. In Anglo-Saxon England we do not find such an officer, but there must always have been someone present more learned in the law than the rest. When king or lord presided, it would naturally be his chancellor or legal adviser. Where sheriff or bailiff held court, that officer himself would probably be familiar with the law and the procedure. When professional judges come upon the scene, it is they whose function it is to advise the popular representatives as to the law. And such has in effect continued to be the situation in our criminal courts to this day. The common-law criminal juries are still the ultimate judges of law and fact, except where certain comparatively recent state constitutions or statutes have hamstrung them by forbidding them to decide matters of law.

In the civil law there is a big gap in the story of its criminal jury. Not long after Rome became an empire its popular courts disappeared. When in the Middle Ages there was a revival of the study of the civil law and a reception of it throughout western Europe, it was the courts and procedure of the late Empire, and not those of Republican Rome, that were looked to as a model. But on the procedural side it was a question, whether the popular courts of the various Teutonic peoples which overran the Empire could withstand the tendency to absolutism of the feudal system. The fact is, the people were unable to defend their ancient liberties by ensuring the survival of such courts. There was no Runnymede and no Magna Carta on the Continent. The feudal lords were able to get all the administration of criminal as well as of civil justice into the hands of their servants, the professional judges.

When, however, absolutism was overthrown by the French Revolution, the civil law returned to the jury for the trial of crimes. It was not adopted for civil or commercial matters, or for minor offenses. Nor did the French go so far as to put it into the first stage of criminal proceedings, in imitation of our grand jury system. They were content with having it for criminal trials only. The reason for introducing such an institution in France was that the people distrusted the judges, and desired a check on the latter's power in matters involving life and liberty. For this same reason most of the other civil law countries followed the example of France.

Although the jury was taken over by the modern civil law frankly in imitation of the common law system, its adoption may be looked upon as a return to an ancient tradition, to the system of Republican

Rome. For Napoleon derived much of his inspiration from the Rome of Caesar and Augustus; his Code of Criminal Procedure, which is still in use in France, shows the influence of the Roman tradition. Incidentally, in going back to that tradition, several much-needed reforms were effected in the jury system.

In the first place, the common law rule requiring unanimity in the verdict was done away with. It is a requirement which with us causes innumerable acquittals and miscarriages through the stubbornness or subornation of minorities, when the accused are clearly guilty. A decision by a majority vote as in ancient Rome was substituted. The size of the majority is kept secret. No juror is allowed to tell how he or anyone else voted. In a jury of twelve it amounts to a seven to five majority at the least. It is a reform which has accomplished its purpose without apparently having endangered the innocent.

In the second place, an expeditious system of selecting the jurors is provided for. From thirty to forty members of the jury list are required to be present in court before the trial opens. The names of those who are to appear are notified to the parties not earlier and not later than the day before. The names of the jurors present are put into an urn. The president of the court in the presence of the accused and of the prosecuting attorney draws out the names one at a time. The accused first and then the prosecutor can challenge any that they see fit. No questions are asked of the jurors and no reasons are given for the challenges. Each side is allowed an equal number of challenges. The process goes on until twelve unchallenged jurors are drawn, except that no more challenges are allowed when the number of names left in the urn, plus those already accepted, equals twelve. The whole proceeding can take but a few minutes. The possibility of one or more of the jurors dropping out in the course of the trial because of illness or some other imperative cause is guarded against by the selection of supernumeraries, whenever the trial is expected to be long drawn out. The latter sit through the case; but they take no part in the deliberation if they are still extra numbers.

In the third place, France attempted to get a selective jury similar to that of ancient Rome, and of a much higher average in character, ability, and education than that of the common law. The French Code of Criminal Procedure[25] provides that the jury list shall be made up from the following: (1) members of the electoral college; (2) officers of the army and navy on the retired list; (3) doctors and *licenciés* (i.e., holders of research or professional degrees, mere holders of the *baccalauréat* degree not being considered learned enough) of one or several of the faculties of law, science, or letters; (4) doctors of medicine; (5) members and correspondents of the Institute of France; and (6) notaries of more than three years' service. The last-named are required to have an education and a training at least as high as that for admission to the bar, and are important officials. But with the enlargement of the electoral college (which had been at first a small group) by the widening of the suffrage, the plan to restrict membership in juries to high-brows and leading citizens broke down. The result is that today the personnel of the French jury is not of much higher average intelligence than that of the American: it consists of all sorts of persons.

But France also did something which was not a reform: it provided in its code that the jury were to be judges of fact only; they were not even to be instructed as to the law, as is the common law practice. Having once seized upon the theory, which in reality does not apply to the criminal jury at all, that the judge's province is the law and the jury's the facts, the French pushed it to its logical conclusion. In 1881 they went still farther and imitated the example of the American states which prohibit the jury from getting any help and advice from the professional judge: by a law of June 19 of that year, the president of the court was forbidden to sum up. But now France has at length come to realize the impracticability of separating questions of fact and law, and the inadvisability of trying to withdraw from the criminal jury the right to judge law as well as fact.

By 1932 the scandal of the criminal jury had become so great that something had to be done about it. They were letting off persons whom everyone knew to be guilty. The chief trouble was either that the juries did not approve the law, or that the minimum penalties prescribed by statute were too great, or that the judges were in the habit of fixing penalties with a severity which shocked the public conscience. Rather than have guilty persons suffer the prescribed or usual penalties, juries acquitted.

The law of March 5, 1932, provides that judges and jury must deliberate together and concur: (1) when the question is, whether the facts constitute an offense penally punishable; (2) when the question is, whether the act committed is excusable; (3) to fix the penalty. Such provisions clearly permit the jurors to take part in judging the law, and in effect do away with the code sections which confine them to facts and which provide for no instructions by the judges as to the law. Incidentally, they permit the latter to participate in the deliberation as to the facts, and therefore virtually abrogate the law of June 19, 1881. Theoretically, when there is only a question of fact the jury retains the right to deliberate and to decide alone. But juries want to be helped by the judges in the weighing and analysis of the evidence, and they want to consider the problem as a whole, including the fixing of the penalty. The door is open for a joint deliberation on all matters of law and fact. What will take place is that the three judges and the twelve jurors will retire to the deliberation chamber; the president of the court will summarize the case and expound the law applicable; all will take part in the discussion; and all questions of law and fact will be decided by a majority vote. Though the two organs of the court have not been amalgamated in form, they do virtually constitute a single college, just like the quaestor and the concilium of ancient Rome.

Italy, aroused by similar jury scandals, and for the express purpose of doing away with the impractical attempt to separate questions of law and fact, has by legislative decree of March 23, 1931, gone the whole way toward unifying questions of law and fact, and for the trial of crimes has substituted five judge assessors to sit with two professional judges. The court sits as a bench of seven.[26] They deliberate together on all questions of law and fact, and have equal votes. The judge assessors are appointed by royal decree from a list made up by the ministry of justice from the following: (1) members of the Great Council of the Fascisti: (2) senators and deputies; (3) members or secretaries of the academies of sciences, letters, and arts; (4) governors of communes of more than 10,000 inhabitants and certain other high civil officials in active service, or retired; (5) officers of the army and navy on the retired list; (6) persons who have published scientific or literary works of merit; and (7) persons who have university degrees. The list is strikingly reminiscent of ancient Rome, where the jury list was made up at first of senators only, and later of senators plus certain other notables. The judge assessors serve without pay and give only a limited amount of time to the work. As only the most distinguished and most learned people are eligible for the office, it is considered a high honor to be on the list. The appointments are coveted and there is no desire to shirk the service. The judge assessors wear the "toga," or magisterial robe, and enjoy sitting on the bench and their association with the professional judges.

The fact that the popular courts in the form of the criminal jury have persisted now for some eight hundred years in Anglo-Saxon countries; the fact that they functioned in the form of the quaestio in Republican Rome for perhaps six hundred years; the fact that as soon as the peoples of Europe became free and assumed control of their governments that reëstablished the popular court in the form of the jury for criminal trials, and that this institution has already survived for nearly one hundred and fifty years, would seem to indicate a deep-seated and universal desire on the part of the people to participate in the administration of the criminal law. We must retain such popular participation in some form.

But it may be that our common law criminal jury system needs reform. In its present condition it is wasteful of time, expensive, inefficient, and to a large extent ineffective. We may well consider the reforms which the modern civil law has found it necessary to adopt, such as the decision by a majority vote, and the method of forming a jury without loss of time. Italy has shown us a way by which it is possible to insure that our popular judges shall be of quality, a way to get the best citizens to perform the service.

The experience of both France and Italy shows the futility, the impracticability, and the undesirability of attempting to separate questions of law and of fact, and of having them decided by different organs of the court. It should induce us at least to return to common law tradition, by doing away with those statutory provisions which hamstring our criminal juries by providing that they must take the law from the judge, and with those others which deprive them of the help of the judge in coming to a decision as to the facts, by enacting that he must not comment on the evidence or sum up the case. If we would really have an efficient jury system we should follow the example of France and Italy and provide for a joint deliberation of judge and jury on all questions of law and of fact, not forgetting to include also the matter of fixing the penalty, for it was the absence of the right of the jury to participate in that matter which was the chief cause of the breakdown of the system in the civil law countries. Such provision would permit each element in the court to perform the function it is best capable of, and place the responsibility and power where they should be. The judge, being the most expert in the law, would have the task of informing the jury in that subject. Likewise, his training and experience would come into play in helping them sift and weigh the evidence. The presence of the members of the jury who would make all the ultimate decisions of both fact and law involved in the question of "guilty" or "not guilty" and in the fixing of the penalty, would ensure a thorough deliberation, would relieve the judge of the full responsibility (which is as it should be in matters involving life and liberty), and would continue to afford full protection for the people against official oppression.

NOTES TO HENRY ESSAY

[1] See Hunter, *Roman Law* (ed. 4), p. 56.

[2] See Henry, *Forms of Anglo-Saxon Contracts*, Mich. L. Rev. XV, May and June, 1917. See also Pollock and Maitland, *History of English Law* (ed. 2; Cambridge, 1899, hereafter referred to as P. & M.), II:645.

[3] P. & M., II:617.

[4] Chaps. XXXIX and XX to XXII.

[5] P. & M., I:139–140.

[6] P. & M., II:647.

[7] *Ibid.*

[8] *Ibid.*, II:648.

[9] *Ibid.*, 645.

[10] *Ibid.*, 651.

[11] *Ibid.*, 643.

[12] *Ibid.*, 645.

[13] *Ibid.*, 647.

[14] *Ibid.*, 647.

[15] Stat. 25 Edw. III stat. 5, C. 3; P. & M., II:649.

[16] Chap. XXXIX.

[17] P. & M., I:139.

[18] *Loc. cit.*

[19] P. & M., I:139, n.

[20] See above, p. 149.

[21] P. & M., II:621.

[22] *Ibid.*, 649.

[23] *Loc. cit.*

[24] *Ibid.*, p. 621.

[25] See Henry, *Contracts in the Local Courts of Medieval England* (London, 1926).

[25] Secs. 381–382.

[26] The idea of judge assessors for criminal trials is not new in modern court procedure. The Mixed Courts in Egypt have had, for more than fifty-eight years, a *Chambre correctionnel* (i.e., a Misdemeanor Court) consisting of three professional judges and four judge assessors.

ARMY COURTS-MARTIAL

BY HUBERT D. HOOVER

THE EXTRAORDINARY criminal jurisdiction exercised through courts-martial and applicable to persons in the active military service of the United States finds authorization in the federal Constitution. The fourteenth clause of Section 8, Article I, of that basic ordinance empowers the Congress to "make rules for the government and regulation of the land and naval forces" the raising and support of which are in the same section expressly provided for. And by the Fifth Amendment, which guards against encroachment by the national government upon the traditional rights of the people, it is stipulated that no person shall be held to answer for a capital or otherwise infamous crime unless on the presentment or indictment of a grand jury "except in cases arising in the land or naval forces, or in the militia, when in actual service in time of war or public danger."[1]

So far as they concern the army as distinguished from the naval forces, the powers thus delegated have been exercised throughout our constitutional history by the Congress in the recognition or enactment of codes designated as Rules or Articles of War. The code at present in effect was enacted on June 4, 1920.

The Articles of War set up, as the basic machinery for this specially ordained juristic structure for the government and regulation of the land forces, a system of courts-martial wholly penal in jurisdiction and with processes essentially summary in operation. The system is designed to ensure, by orderly and effective means, prompt and exact obedience to law and to lawful commands of constituted authority by those persons and elements which make up the military organization that by its strong arm provides for the common defense and ultimately guarantees constitutional and democratic forms of government within the nation. It finds its moral justification in the necessity of national self-preservation, for which purpose it is but one of the weapons placed in the hands of those persons who are charged with the duty of supporting by force, if need be, the integrity of established borders and institutions.

Were the system of courts-martial molded in the common law forms of the civil courts of the land there would be, quite obviously, no need for it. It departs from those forms, nevertheless, only to the extent which, in Anglo-Saxon experience, its summary nature has appeared to require. For example, the military courts perform their functions, by Constitutional sanction, without the jury forms so indelibly written into the punitive common law, yet they retain something at least of the guiding principle of the jury system—the principle that human life and liberty should not be taken away because of infractions of the law until disputed guilt shall have been determined by a body of unbiased men chosen from the culprit's countrymen and governed by the laws which have allegedly been violated. The common law jury is composed of persons traditionally known as peers of the accused. The court-martial is composed of fellow-members of the army, subject to the same code of laws and equals thereunder. The military responsibilities and legal powers of the officer sitting on the court-martial differ from the responsibilities and powers of the private soldier accused before the court, but the officer sitting on the court and the soldier on trial enjoy equally the fundamental rights of citizenship and are equally amenable to the processes and penalties of the military law which is being enforced.

Although the military system differs from the common law system of civil law in some more or less superficial characteristics of the fact-finding body utilized in its criminal processes, it is designed to protect with equal fidelity the personal liberties and rights guaranteed by the Bill of Rights written into the federal Constitution by the amendments and otherwise. Such basic procedural and substantive rights as the requirement of a thorough and impartial investigation before trial, and protection from double jeopardy and from compulsory self-crimination, as well as the privileges of counsel and of speedy trial are specifically guarded by the Articles of War (Art. 17, 24, 40, 70).

Historical.—The history of the Articles of War is written in the long struggle between the people of England and the Crown. The Crown, exercising its asserted royal prerogative, insisted on the processes and tribunals of the military in the trials of all persons, civilian and military, in war and in peace.[1] The people with signal success found ways and means to preserve hard-won rights and individual liberties through civil courts. In the Petition of Right protest was registered against the exercise of military law through military courts in time of peace, even in the trials of soldiers and mariners, that is, members of the land and naval forces, and the Crown's approval of this petition would seem to have been a recognition that military law could exist only by consent of Parliament. Abhorrence of a military code was closely associated in the minds of the people with hatred of a standing or professional army, which was viewed as a special instrument of tyranny. In the Bill of Rights of 1688 the maintenance of a standing army in time of peace, without the consent of Parliament, was declared illegal.

But circumstances alter cases. A year later the King and Parliament were in accord with respect both to the need of a regular army and to the necessity of effective discipline therein. The Ipswich Mutiny of 1689 (certain troops, mainly Scotch, who adhered to the cause of the Stuarts, refused to obey the order of William the Third to proceed to Holland and marched in the opposite direction) had revealed the inadequacy of the control of His Majesty's troops. Under the restrictions imposed on the Crown, a mutineer or a deserter was treated as an ordinary felon, and was tried, if at all, at the assizes by a petty jury on a bill found by a grand jury, just as was any person not a member of the army. His punishment, on conviction, was both slow and uncertain, and, worst of all, it was administered by agencies not responsible for the successful performance by the army of the missions assigned to it. Furthermore, at this same time the military powers on the Continent were threatening the established order for the preservation of which the King and Parliament were united by their common interest. It was therefore decided that the survival of the existing order not only demanded trained soldiers but also required that these soldiers must be held to strict discipline. In order to enforce such discipline it was needful to restrict liberties by a sharper penal code and a more stringent method of procedure than were available through the existing civil tribunals. It was recognized, moreover, that in order to be really effective, a system of military punishment must be administered by the authority responsible for the military operations. The best results were to be expected from unified control.[2]

As a result of the conditions confronting all concerned, the Parliament enacted the first Mutiny Act, effective April 12, 1689.[3] This Act was for a period extending only to November 10, 1689, but at the end of six months it was renewed for a year and was renewed thereafter by succeeding Parliaments until 1879. Among other things, it prescribed "Death or such other Punishment as by a Court-Martiall shall be Inflicted" for the offenses of desertion and participation in a mutiny, provided for the convening of courts-martial by Their Majesties, by the General of Their Army, and by other officers commissioned to that end, and defined the composition of the courts to be convened.

The penal processes of courts-martial thus received in England for the first time the sanction of a representative legislative body. Articles of War which, prior to the Mutiny Act, had been promulgated by royal prerogative and which were admittedly effective in an army serving abroad, were not superseded by the Act but were, so far as they were not inconsistent therewith, impliedly recognized as being in force. In 1718 the promulgation of articles by the Crown, to be operative within the kingdom as well as beyond seas, was expressly authorized by the renewal of the Mutiny Act; and in 1803 Parliament expressly approved the application of the articles at home as they had theretofore applied abroad.[4]

Articles of War, or at least written military codes, had existed for some time before they received statutory recognition. There is evidence, indeed, that, prior to the first written codes, as far back as the times of the Greeks and Romans, purely military offenses, such as desertion, mutiny, and wrongful sale of arms, were recognized in the armies and were punished by penalties peculiar to military custom, that is, by decimation (death of every tenth man), maiming, expulsion from camp, labor on fortifications or other hard labor, and the like. Among the early Germans the punishments, including death, were administered through instrumentalities of the chief officers commanding troops.[5]

Written codes involving military jurisdiction, blending with the civil, appeared as early as the fifth century in the Salic Laws. Other written military codes appeared during the Middle Ages.[6] In 1190, Richard the First, of England, addressed an ordinance to his crusading subjects about to proceed by sea to the Holy Land, prescribing summary punishments to be meted out for certain offenses which might be committed. "Whoever," he ordained, "shall slay a man on shipboard, he shall be bound to the dead man and thrown into the sea.... If any man shall utter disgraceful language or abuse, or shall curse his companion, he shall pay an ounce of silver for every time he has so abused him," and so on.[7]

In 1385, Richard the Second ordained "Statutes, Ordonnances and Customs, to be observed in the Army" which contained some twenty-six "Items" or articles defining military offenses and prescribing punishments therefor.

> Firstly [the Articles commanded] all manner of persons ... shall be obedient to our Lord the King, to his constable and mareschall, under penalty of everything they can forfeit in body and goods.

Among other rules conceived to maintain order in the armed forces was a requirement,

> that every one be obedient to his captain and perform watch and ward, forrage, and all other things belonging to his duty, under penalty of losing his horse and armour, and his body being in arrest to the mareschall till he shall have made his peace with his lord and master, according to the award of the court.

Rioting was forbidden on pain of losing horse and armor, and arrest at the King's will,

> and if it be a boy or page he shall lose his left ear.

Failure well and faithfully to stand watch, always a high duty of every soldier, was punishable by decapitation. Numerous other offenses were forbidden on pain of death by beheading or hanging or by drawing and hanging. Lesser offenses were less sternly punished.[8] Henry the Fifth and Henry the Eighth prescribed military codes,[9] and Articles of War covering a wide range of offenses, promulgated by Charles the Second, were in effect at the time of the adoption of the first Mutiny Act.[10]

The articles of Charles the Second, as well as subsequent decrees and enactments of articles, closely followed a Code of Articles issued by Gustavus Adolphus, of Sweden, in 1621. These "Articles and Military Laws to be observed in the wars," embracing one hundred and sixty-seven subdivisions, covered the field of military wrongs with an elaboration not before attempted, and prescribed the composition of military courts as well as many details of their procedure.[11]

The first American Articles of War were adopted by the Provisional Congress of Massachusetts Bay on April 5, 1775. In the spirit of the times they recited that,

> Whereas the great law of self-preservation may suddenly require our raising and keeping an Army of observation and defence, in order to prevent or repel any further attempt to force the late cruel and oppressive Acts of the British Parliament, which are evidently designed to subject us and the whole Continent to the most ignominious slavery. And whereas, in case of raising and keeping such an army, it will be necessary that the Officers and Soldiers in the same be fully acquainted with their duty, and that the Articles, Rules and Regulations thereof be made as plain as possible; ... It is, therefore, Resolved, That the following Articles, Rules and Regulations for the Army, ... be, and are hereby earnestly recommended to be strictly adhered to, by all Officers, Soldiers, and others concerned, as they regard their own honour and publick good.[12]

The punitive enactments and the composition of the military courts provided for were patterned after the existing articles in effect in the British Army, which had been ordained by George the Third in 1765. Articles of War adopted by the second Continental Congress on June 30, 1775, likewise followed the form of the British articles. Additional articles were enacted by the Continental Congress on November 7, 1775; and on September 20, 1776, revised Rules and Articles of War, which survived the Revolution, were enacted.[13]

The Congress, acting under its Constitutional prerogative, first spoke on the subject of military jurisdiction on May 31, 1786, revising the existing Rules and Articles in certain respects, and in 1806 it completely overhauled the previous enactments. Following the Civil War, the articles were restated and reënacted (June 22, 1874). Amendments were adopted from time to time and on August 29, 1916, the Articles were again restated and reënacted. On June 4, 1920, they were amended through the vehicle of the revamped National Defense Act,[14] following a searching inquiry by the Congress into the administration of military justice in the army of some four million men recruited during the World War.[15] The Code of 1920 remains unchanged.

Present articles and Manual.—The present code contains one hundred and twenty-one articles, fifty-three of which define the jurisdiction of the various types of courts-martial with respect to persons and subject-matter, the composition and methods of convening the courts, their procedure, the statutes of limitation, the methods of punishment, the systems of review, and the execution, suspension, and remission of sentences. Forty-two of the articles are punitive, defining offenses and prescribing punishments. The remaining articles cover miscellaneous subjects including the composition and powers of courts of inquiry (fact-reporting bodies without the power to punish), disciplinary powers lodged in commanding officers without the intervention of courts-martial, relations of the military to the civil authorities, and kindred subjects.

Article 38 authorizes the President to prescribe the procedure, including modes of proof, in cases before military tribunals so far as the rules so prescribed are not inconsistent with the Articles of War. Pursuant to this power and in the exercise of his Constitutional authority as Commander-in-Chief of the Army, the President has from time to time published Manuals for Courts-Martial. The Manual now in effect was promulgated in 1928. It fills in many details of procedure, prescribes rules of evidence, fixes maximum limitations upon punishments that may be adjudged in cases in which statutory limitations are not laid down, states policies in the administration of military justice, and carries numerous forms designed to aid in the practical application of the Articles of War by the officers of the army who are called upon to apply them while in the immediate command of troops. All officers of the line, that is, of the combatant branches, receive theoretical and practical instruction in the Articles and sufficient grounding in the elements of military law to ensure working familiarity with the Manual. In the War Department at the seat of the national government, and at the principal administrative centers of the army elsewhere, are stationed officers of the Judge Advocate General's Department, trained in the legal profession, who are charged with supervision of the administration of the law and regulations by the officers in the field.

Transitory nature of courts.—Courts-martial, of which there are three kinds—general, special, and summary, are, under the Articles of War, called into being as necessity arises, by a military order of the President as commander-in-chief or by officers of the army in command of troops and vested with the convening power. By a similar military order the courts may be dissolved when their functions have been fulfilled. They have no inherent permanency of duration, as have the civil courts. They are not courts of record and their jurisdiction is special and limited. They meet wherever the military authority convening them may direct, whether at home or abroad, and their jurisdiction is in no wise territorial. The officer or soldier charged with violation of the Articles of War while on the high seas or in foreign lands is subject to trial before any court-martial wherever sitting, by proper order of the officer under whose command the offender may happen to come. The courts being of limited jurisdiction, each record of trial (a separate and complete record of each trial is required) must show upon its face all jurisdictional facts, that is, the lawful composition of the court, the details of procedure as prescribed by law, and the amenability to trial by the court of the person accused.

Courts-martial not part of federal judiciary.—Although courts-martial proceed by Constitutional and statutory sanction and are distinctly judicial in form and action, they are not a part of the federal judiciary, that is, they are not among the "inferior courts" which the Congress, under Section 1, Article III, of the Constitution "may from time to time ordain and establish." The power to provide for trial and punishment of military offenses is entirely independent of the power of the Congress exercised under Article III of the Constitution.[16] As a result, the federal statutes governing procedure and jurisdiction of courts of the judicial branch of the government of the United States are not, *proprio vigore,* applicable to courts-martial.[17]

This system of military tribunals, it is clear, is neither more nor less than an arm of the executive branch of the government, a judicial instrumentality provided by the Constitution and by statute to the President as commander-in-chief for the purpose of aiding him in his effective command of the army and in the maintenance of discipline therein. The function of the courts does not differ from that of their predecessors, the British courts-martial, of which Clode has said, "It must never be lost sight of that the only legitimate object of military tribunals is to aid the crown to maintain discipline and government of the Army."[18] As the object of maintaining an army is to win battles when the use of armed force in the common defense can no longer be avoided, so the object of establishing a judicial system within the army is to ensure that cohesion of effort and quick obedience to law and orders which give temper to the sword when drawn.

That a military court is but an instrumentality of the executive branch of the government is forcefully illustrated by the fact that it comes into being only by virtue of an order issued by a designated military commander as provided by Articles of War 8, 9, and 10, and by the fact that the sentence which it adjudges may not be carried into execution until after the sentence has been approved by the sign manual of the officer who appointed the court, or by the officer who may be exercising for the time being the duties of the officer whose command carried the power to convene the court, and, in some circumstances, until confirmation by the President or some lesser military authority. The authority of the reviewing officer to approve a sentence fixed by the court and the authority to confirm are limited only in that the court must have acted within its lawful sphere and according to the forms prescribed by law. Power to disapprove and thereby vacate the sentence, to mitigate it, or to remit portions of it at the time of action on the proceedings by the reviewing and confirming authorities, is wholly discretionary.

Proceedings not reviewable by civil courts.—The proceedings of military tribunals which have acted within the reach of their jurisdiction in respect to subject-matter and persons and according to the requirements of law, are not subject to revision by the civil judiciary, through writ of prohibition, certiorari, writ of error, or appeal. Mr. Justice Wayne,[19] speaking for the Supreme Court of the United States in a proceeding involving the legality of a sentence adjudged by a naval court-martial, expressed the completeness of military jurisdiction and the finality of the proceedings of military tribunals thus:

With the sentences of courts-martial which have been convened regularly, and have proceeded legally, and by which punishments are directed, not forbidden by law, or which are according to the laws and customs of the sea, civil courts have nothing to do, nor are they in any way alterable by them. If it were otherwise, the civil courts would virtually administer the rules and articles of war, irrespective of those to whom that duty and obligation has been confided by the laws of the United States, from whose decisions no appeal or jurisdiction of any kind has been given to the civil magistrate or civil courts.

Although there is no appeal to the civil courts from a sentence adjudged by a military tribunal which has had jurisdiction of the person and offense and which has acted within the scope of its legal powers, the person imprisoned under the sentence may avail himself of the remedy of habeas corpus in the federal civil courts for the purpose of testing the legality of his detention, that is, for the purpose of determining whether the military court had jurisdiction and whether it acted within the law. Such a proceeding cannot, of course, be made to perform the functions of a writ of error, for the civil tribunal will not go into the merits of, or try, the military cause. It will go no farther than to release the prisoner if it finds the sentence absolutely void.[20] For obvious reasons the civil tribunal will not, through the vehicle of habeas corpus, inquire into the validity of a sentence of a military court, which does not involve confinement, but imposes punishment such as a fine, forfeiture of pay, or dishonorable separation from the military service.[21] As indicated, mere errors of procedure or the improper reception of evidence are not open to consideration upon the application for a writ of habeas corpus, for such errors do not go to the jurisdiction of the court or to its lawful authority to sentence.[22]

It may be added that state courts are without power to inquire into the legality of the restraint of a person sentenced by a military tribunal, for in such a case the prisoner is held by authority of the United States, and a state cannot authorize its courts to exercise judicial power, by habeas corpus, within the jurisdiction of another and independent government. Upon learning, judicially, that the prisoner is held by authority of the United States, the state court will not attempt an adjudication, but will leave remedial action to the federal courts.[23]

Army courts-martial as courts of law.—But the fact that military tribunals are free, within the scope of their jurisdiction and statutory powers, from control by the civil judiciary, and are designed and maintained as aids to the executive branch of the government, does not mean that they are not courts of law. Facts are determined judicially according to established rules of evidence which follow, substantially, the common law as incorporated, with variations, into the criminal procedure of the civil federal judiciary. As observed above, a person accused before a court-martial of the commission of an offense is guaranteed the fundamental rights of a preliminary hearing to determine probable cause for trial, of being informed precisely of the charges against him, of a speedy trial by a court free from favor, prejudice, and bias, of representation by counsel if desired, of confrontation of witnesses under oath, of calling witnesses in his own behalf, of protection against unwillingly being made a witness against himself, of protection against unreasonable searches and seizures, of the presumption of innocence, and of protection against double jeopardy.

The court-martial, though not functioning as a jury of a civil tribunal, is analogous thereto, the members being sworn to "well and truly try and determine, according to the evidence, the matter" before them, and to "administer justice, without partiality, favor or affection" (Art. 19). Determination of the facts is reached through findings of guilty or not guilty. Depending on the severity of the sentence, a finding of guilty requires a two-thirds or unanimous vote. Failure of the necessary proportion of the court to agree upon a finding of guilty automatically results in a finding of not guilty. Disagreements are not possible.

While the military court is the trier of facts, it also exercises some of the ordinary functions of the trial judge of the civil court, passing upon challenges to its own members, arraigning the accused, entertaining special pleas to the jurisdiction and pleas in bar of trial or in abatement, granting continuances, and adjudging sentences. Upon interlocutory questions arising during the proceedings of general courts-martial, one of the members, designated by the appointing authority, because of his special qualifications, as "law member," is empowered to make rulings binding upon the court. But in the absence of a law member the court itself makes the rulings, going into closed sessions, that is, excluding from its presence all persons except the members, and voting upon the action to be taken. Among other things, the court may punish as for contempt any person who uses menacing words, signs, or gestures in its presence, or who disturbs its proceedings by riot or disorder (Art. 32).

It is, however, a peculiarity of the military tribunal, as observed, that its findings and sentences are not self-executing but can be carried into execution only upon the formal approval of the sentences by the military authority through whose order the court was convened, and, in some cases, only upon confirmation by higher authority following approval by the appointing authority. The appointing and confirming authorities thus become reviewing authorities, and though they may not reverse the action of the court in acquitting an accused of any charge or part thereof, they are specially charged with the duty of considering the propriety of the decisions upon questions of law reached by the court, weighing the evidence in order to determine whether the findings ought to be approved or disapproved, and judging with respect to the propriety of the sentences imposed. In a very real sense, therefore, the reviewing and confirming authorities are entrusted with judicial duties which make them, in effect, a part of the court on whose proceedings they pass judgment.

Appellate review of proceedings.—It will be seen from what has been said in respect to reviewing and confirming authorities that the sentence of a court-martial may not be carried into execution without a review of the proceedings upon which the sentence is based, and that this review amounts to an automatic examination on appeal. This appeal pertains to the facts as well as to the law of the case.

Provision is also made for self-acting appellate review of every case after the sentence has been acted upon by the reviewing authority, this review being made by an officer or officers with special legal training and being designed to ensure compliance with the law by the reviewing and confirming authorities as well as by the courts. Division and higher commanders are provided with staff sections composed of members of the Judge Advocate General's Department, the legally trained component of the military establishment, whose duty it is to examine the records of all trials held within their commands and to advise in respect to corrective or other action on the records. As will be more fully outlined below, certain classes of cases are also formally reviewed in the office of The Judge Advocate General, the legal adviser of the Secretary of War and of the bureaus of the War Department at Washington.

Prior to the World War, sentences of courts-martial involving authorized punishments, including such punishments as dishonorable discharge of enlisted men in times of peace and war, dismissal of officers below the grade of brigadier general in time of war, and the death penalty in time of war—all punishments of the greatest severity but not then requiring confirmation by the President—were carried into execution upon approval, or approval and confirmation, by commanders in the field and without prior authorization by the War Department or the Commander-in-Chief. Abuse or fear of abuse of such plenary power, the composition during the World War of courts-martial of officers recently taken from civil life and therefore lacking in experience and military judgment, and the recognized fact that these punishments when once carried out could not be undone (dishonorable discharge and dismissal, branding the former soldier or former officer as unfit to wear his country's uniform, involve changes of status from soldier or officer to civilian and, once executed, are beyond the power of disapproval, pardon, or remission by executive authority), led to the promulgation by the War Department, in January, 1918, of General Order No. 7, which forbade the execution of sentences of dishonorable discharge, dismissal, or death until after examination in the War Department by The Judge Advocate General of the records of trial on which they were based. A branch of the office of The Judge Advocate General was set up at general headquarters of the American Expeditionary Forces in France for the purpose of acting upon records of trials in the zone of operations. As a result, after the promulgation of this order, sentences involving dishonorable discharge, dismissal, and death were not carried into execution until after appellate review by the chief legal officer of the War Department or by his immediate assistants.

The board of review.—The principle of automatic appellate review by an independent legal authority, that is, by an authority not acting under the control or direction of the commander of troops in the field, was carried into the revised Code of 1920, through the enactment of a new Article of War, Article 50½, and by incidental amendments of other articles, Article of War 50½ requires The Judge Advocate General to constitute, in his office, a Board of Review of not less than three officers of the Judge Advocate General's Department, which board, in collaboration with The Judge Advocate General, is, in effect, a supreme court of appeals in respect to the administration of military justice.

Any record of trial in which there has been adjudged a sentence requiring approval or confirmation by the President, that is, a sentence respecting a general officer, a sentence adjudged by a court-martial convened by the President, a sentence extending to the dismissal of an officer or the suspension of a cadet of the Military Academy, or a sentence to death in time of peace, is required to be examined by the Board of Review, which submits its opinion in writing, and by The Judge Advocate General, who also submits his opinion, prior to submission of the case to the President for his action.

In addition, Article 50½ provides that no authority shall order the execution of any sentence of a general court-martial involving the penalty of death, dismissal not suspended, dishonorable discharge not suspended, or confinement in a penitentiary, unless and until, with the approval of The Judge Advocate General, the Board of Review shall have held the record of trial upon which the sentence is based legally sufficient to support the sentence; except that sentences of dishonorable discharge or confinement in a penitentiary, if based solely upon findings of guilty, may be carried into execution by the reviewing or confirming authorities without such prior holding. If the Board of Review, with the concurrence of The Judge Advocate General, holds a record of trial legally insufficient to support the findings or sentence or any part thereof, the convening authority must take action in conformity with such holding. If, in such a case, The Judge Advocate General and the Board of Review do not agree, their respective opinions are transmitted to the President for his decision and final action on the record of trial.

In disapproving or vacating a sentence the execution of which has not theretofore been ordered, the President or any reviewing or confirming authority may authorize or direct a rehearing before a court composed of officers not members of the court which first heard the case. Upon such rehearing the accused person may not be tried for any offense of which he was found not guilty at the first hearing, and the sentence adjudged at the rehearing may not exceed that previously adjudged. Rehearings are not infrequently directed in cases in which the findings or sentences are held legally insufficient because of the commission at the trials of errors of law injuriously affecting the substantial rights of the accused. Appeals being automatic in operation, rehearings are directed without regard to application therefor by the accused persons. They are designed as much to protect the government in the final conviction and punishment of offenders as to protect those persons accused whose rights have been injuriously affected by errors at their trials.

All records of trial by general court-martial other than those which must be examined by the Board of Review before the sentences involved may be carried into execution, are, under the requirements of Article of War 50½, examined in the office of The Judge Advocate General. This class of cases includes many in which sentences to dishonorable discharge have been suspended by the reviewing authorities. Examination and a written opinion by the Board of Review are required in every case of which the record of trial, on examination by the assistants of The Judge Advocate General, is found legally insufficient to support the findings or sentence, in whole or in part, unless corrective action may be taken administratively through remission of the sentence or a portion thereof. In cases in which the Board of Review is of the opinion that corrective action which cannot be accomplished administratively is necessary, the record of trial, together with the views of The Judge Advocate General, is submitted to the President for vacation of the findings or sentence or other appropriate disposition, as he may determine.

Reversible error.—Reviewing authorities, The Judge Advocate General and the Board of Review, in passing in appellate capacities upon the findings and sentences of courts-martial, proceed in the light of, and under the restrictions of, Article of War 37, which provides that the proceedings of a court-martial and its findings and sentence shall not be held invalid or disapproved "in any case on the ground of improper admission or rejection of evidence or for any error as to any matter of pleading or procedure" unless, in the opinion of the examing authority, "after an examination of the entire proceedings, it shall appear that the error complained of has injuriously affected the substantial rights of an accused." Thus, there is no presumption that error is reversible or fatal to the validity of the proceedings. On the contrary, before reversal is authorized, it must appear affirmatively that the error did in fact injuriously affect the substantial rights of the accused. This legal rule is in conformity with federal criminal practice, and appears to be in accord with the modern trend in other civil jurisdictions.

General courts-martial.—The Articles of War provide three distinct kinds of courts-martial—general, special, and summary. The general court-martial, composed of not fewer than five officer members, may be appointed by the President, the commanding officer of a territorial division or department, the superintendent of the Military Academy, the commanding officer of an army, an army corps, a division, or a separate brigade (the normal brigade consists of two regiments), and, when empowered by the President, by the commanding officer of any district or of any force or body of troops. If the commanding officer is the accuser or prosecutor of the person to be tried, the court is appointed by competent superior authority. No officer is eligible to sit as a member of a court when he is the accuser or is a witness for the prosecution (Art. 8). All members are subject to challenge for cause, and all members except the law member are subject to peremptory challenge (each side is entitled to one peremptory challenge, Art. 18). The law member must be chosen from among the officers of the Judge Advocate General's Department or from officers of other branches of the service selected as specially qualified to perform the duties required (Art. 8).

For each general court-martial the appointing authority is required to detail an officer as trial judge advocate, and another as defense counsel, and assistants to both are appointed when necessary. The trial judge advocate prosecutes in the name of the United States and, under the direction of the court, prepares the verbatim record of the proceedings. The defense counsel represents the accused at the trial unless the latter has other counsel, military or civil, of his own selection. Civil counsel are not provided at public expense.

General courts-martial have the power to try any person subject to military law for any crime or offense made punishable by the Articles of War. They may impose any punishment authorized by the Articles, within maximum limitations prescribed by the President from time to time (Par. 104c, *Manual for Courts-Martial*). Included in the punishments they may impose are death, dismissal (dishonorable separation from the military service, of an officer), loss or suspension of rank (of an officer), dishonorable discharge (of a noncommissioned officer or soldier), detention of pay, forfeiture of pay and allowances, fine, reprimand, admonition, confinement at hard labor, hard labor without confinement, reduction in grade of a noncommissioned officer, and restriction to specified limits (a modified form of restraint by confinement). Murder and rape, for which the death penalty is prescribed, are punishable by courts-martial, within the geographical limits of the states of the Union and of the District of Columbia, only when the country is at war (Art. 92). Under the maximum limitations prescribed by the President, the death penalty may not be adjudged by courts-martial in times of peace for offenses other than murder and rape.

Special courts-martial.—The military tribunal next in importance is the special court-martial. Consisting of any number of officers not fewer than three, this court may be appointed by the commanding officer of any district, garrison, fort, camp, or other place where troops are on duty, by the commanding officer of a brigade, regiment, detached battalion (there are three battalions in the normal infantry regiment), or other detached command. As in the general court-martial, the accuser may not appoint the court, and no officer who may be the accuser or a witness for the prosecution is eligible to sit as a member. Special courts-martial do not have law members, but a trial judge advocate and a defense counsel are appointed for each court.

A special court-martial has power to try any person subject to military law for any crime or offense punishable under the Articles of War except those offenses for which the death penalty is authorized. It does not have power to adjudge confinement at hard labor in excess of six months, or to adjudge forfeitures in excess of two-thirds pay per month for six months (Art. 13), or the equivalents of these penalties.

Summary courts-martial.—Summary courts-martial may be appointed by the commanding officer of any garrison, fort, camp, or other place where troops are on duty, or by the commanding officer of a regiment, detached battalion or company, or like command, or of a detachment of troops, or by higher authority. When but one officer is present with a command he becomes the summary court-martial for that command (Art. 10). Summary courts-martial have, in general, the power to try only noncommissioned officers and private soldiers, and noncommissioned officers are exempted from trial thereby unless by the authority of an officer competent to bring them to trial before a general court-martial. These courts do not have power to adjudge confinement at hard labor in excess of one month, restriction to limits for more than three months, or forfeiture or detention of more than two-thirds of one month's pay (Art. 14).The summary court, as its name implies, is designed to provide a vehicle for prompt punishment of minor offenses and is not resorted to in cases of serious infraction of discipline or for the punishment of offenses involving moral turpitude. It is, however, a highly effective instrument for bringing home to the recruit, and to the older soldier as well, the necessity of orderly conduct and obedience to established regulations. It is axiomatic with the military man that the unfaltering obedience and unified effort so essential on the battlefield is best inculcated by training the soldier to conform to the rules of the barracks, the camp, and the drill field.

Jurisdiction of courts-martial wholly criminal.—The jurisdictional powers of military courts are limited strictly to punitive measures. With the determination of civil rights—title to property, enforcement of contracts, redress for tortious acts, they have nothing to do. As happens with respect to any purely criminal court, the forfeitures and fines they adjudge accrue to the government and never to the injured individuals. To be sure, they recognize as violations of Articles of War 95 and 96, dishonorable neglect to pay just debts and other dishonorable or discreditable acts on the part of officers and enlisted men which may be civil wrongs, but this recognition springs from the disgrace or discredit brought upon the military service through the wrongful conduct, and the military courts make no effort to adjudicate the civil rights involved or to provide remedies for the aggrieved parties. Or, to state the matter in another way, the surrender by military personnel to the extraordinary jurisdiction of courts-martial, a surrender which results when their status is changed from that of civilian to soldier, is only sanctioned by the Constitution as a means of perfecting the military arm of the nation for the accomplishment of its missions. It extends its boundaries in the field of the soldier's rights as a citizen no farther than is needful to the end in view.

Military jurisdiction.—Article of War 2 fixes with particularity the classes of persons who are amenable to military jurisdiction. They include all (*a*) officers; (*b*) members of the Army Nurse Corps; (*c*) warrant officers; (*d*) noncommissioned officers and private soldiers of the Regular Army of the United States; (*e*) volunteers; (*f*) persons lawfully called, drafted, or ordered into or to duty, or for training in the military service of the United States (this class includes the National Guard, the Officers' and Enlisted Reserve Corps, and men selected by compulsory process in emergencies); (*g*) cadets of the Military Academy; (*h*) members of the Marine Corps when detached for service with the army by order of the President; (*i*) retainers to the camp and persons accompanying or serving with the armies (such as clerks, welfare workers, mechanics, etc.) when without the territorial jurisdiction of the United States and, in time of war, such retainers and persons accompanying or serving with the armies in the field at any place; (*j*) persons under sentence adjudged by court-martial (though they may have been dishonorably discharged and may thus have become civilians); and (*k*) inmates of the Regular Army Soldier's Home at Washington, D. C.

Authority for the legislative designation of these classes of persons as subject to military law is found in the constitutional grant to the Congress of the power to make rules for the land forces (Cl. 14, Sec. 8, Art. I). All are members of the army in active service, or, because of their relation to the army incident to their employment or status, are in fact so closely associated therewith as to necessitate, for purposes of discipline and for the success of military operations, their treatment as constituent parts of the armed forces. The modern tendency in military affairs is, through compulsion or otherwise, to place in the uniform of the soldier all persons who may be useful in the administration, supply, maintenance, and movement of the army. In former times armies in the field were followed by swarms of civilians—clerks, cooks, teamsters, laborers, contractors, sutlers, but during the World War the military units of the American Army in the field were self-contained, at least in respect to all their essential functions.

But the Congress has also seen fit by the Articles of War to provide for the punishment by military tribunals of certain persons though they be civilians wholly unconnected with the army. Thus, it is provided that whoever relieves the enemy with arms, supplies, etc., or harbors, protects, communicates with or gives intelligence to the enemy (Art. 81), or who is found lurking or acting as a spy (Art. 82), shall be punished by a military tribunal. By Article of War 94, it is provided, also, that former members of the army are amenable to trial by courts-martial, after their discharge and separation from the military service, for frauds committed against the United States and certain of its instrumentalities while the offenders were in the active military service.

In respect to the offenses of spying and aiding the enemy by giving him supplies and information, it is noteworthy that both are punishable in time of war only, since they can only be committed when an enemy exists. Both directly affect the safety and success of operations of the armies in the field. Both are essentially violations of the laws of war. Aside from usage or the unwritten law of war that has invariably permitted punishment of civilians by military tribunals for these offenses, it may be that legal justification for the inclusion of civilian offenders as persons amenable to such trial and punishment may be implied from the Constitutional grant of power to the Congress to make rules for the "government and regulation of the land . . . forces," and from the exception of "cases arising in the land . . . forces," from the operation of the guaranty of grand jury action by the Fifth Amendment. The question has not been directly and authoritatively passed upon. Colonel Winthrop, whose *Treatise on Military Law and Precedents* ranks foremost among the commentaries on American military law, questions the constitutionality of the article declaring amenability to military jurisdiction of civilians giving aid to the enemy but not coming within the definition, according to military usage, of spies. He concedes, however, that the legislative expressions covering the subject have remained on the statute books during our Constitutional history, and that their constitutionality must be presumed pending a contrary ruling by the courts.[24]

Discharged officers and soldiers who as members of the military establishment have committed frauds against the government or its instrumentalities, were also probably declared by the Congress to be amenable to trial by courts-martial upon the theory that theirs are cases "arising in the land . . . forces," and that punishment for these offenses is essential to the proper government and regulation of the army, for which the Congress is authorized to legislate. The fact that the articles involved have remained on the statute books for many years without any authoritative ruling adverse to their constitutionality favors the view that they will be upheld if and when they are challenged in the Supreme Court of the United States.

FOOTNOTES TO HOOVER ESSAY

[1] Bl. Comm. 414.

[2] Carbaugh, *Military Law and Wartime Legislation* (published under supervision of the War Department, 1919) "Historical Note" 1; Winthrop, *Treatise on Military Law and Precedents* 8; Davis, *Treatise on Military Law* 3.

[3] Statutes of the Realm, 55; 1 Wm. & M. c. 5.

[4] Winthrop, *op. cit.* 9.

[5] *Ibid.* 5.

[6] *Ibid.* 5, 6.

[7] 2 Grose, *History of the English Army* 63; Winthrop, *op. cit.* 1411.

[8] Grose, *op. cit.* 64–69; Winthrop, *op. cit.* 1412.

[9] Winthrop, *op. cit.* 1415.

[10] *Ibid.* 1434.

[11] *Ibid.* 1416.

[12] *Ibid.* 1470.

[13] *Ibid.* 1489.

[14] 41 Stat. 787.

[15] See *Manual for Courts-Martial* (1921), Introduction, p. vii.

[16] Dynes v. Hoover, 20 How. 79.

[17] Winthrop, *op. cit.* 54.

[18] Clode, *Military Forces of the Crown* II, 361.

[19] Dynes v. Hoover, 20 How. 65, 82; see also *Ex parte* Vallandigham, 1 Wall. 243; *In re* Grimley, 137 U. S. 147; Johnson v. Sayre, 158 U. S. 109; United States v. Maney, 61 Fed. 140.

[20] *Ex parte* Mason, 105 U. S. 697; Wales v. Whitney, 114 U. S. 575.

[21] Wales v. Whitney, *supra.*

[22] *In re* Grimley, *supra* note 19.

[23] Tarble's Case, 13 Wall. 397; Robb v. Connolly, 111 U. S. 624; Ableman v. Booth, 21 How. 506.

[24] Winthrop, *op. cit.* 105–107.

INTERNATIONAL ENGAGEMENTS AND THEIR INTERPRETATION BY THE PERMANENT COURT OF INTERNATIONAL JUSTICE*

BY MANLEY O. HUDSON

IN ALMOST EVERY CASE which has come before the Permanent Court of International Justice, either for judgment or for advisory opinion, the Court has been confronted with the necessity of dealing with an international engagement,[1] and the issues drawn have called for the Court's determining whether an engagement existed or what interpretation was to be placed upon the text of an engagement admitted to exist. The law of treaties and of the interpretation of treaties is by far the largest subject in the Court's jurisprudence. Indeed, the value of this jurisprudence for general purposes is limited by the fact that the Court is usually dealing with a specific text, and the texts are seldom the same in two different cases. Yet the Court has appreciated the necessity of maintaining a consistent attitude in dealing with the texts which have come before it, and the result has been both a clarification of the legal situations to which the texts have related and a significant contribution to the approach to be made in international law to the interpretation and application of conventional arrangements.

The form of engagements. For the present purpose, the term "international engagement" is borrowed from Article 18 of the Covenant of the League of Nations as a general term applicable to the assumption of an international obligation. It is broader than the term "treaty," also employed in Article 18 of the Covenant, or the term "treaties and conventions" employed in Article 36 of the Statute of the Court; it is also broader than the term "agreement" if that term is taken to involve action by more than one State. The Court has shown a decided preference for this term in its frequent references to the obligations resulting from "engagements." In the case relating to the *Austro-German Customs Régime,* the Court said of a provision in the Geneva Protocol

* The substance of this essay will appear as a chapter in a forthcoming treatise on the Permanent Court of International Justice.

of 1922 that "though it took the form of a declaration,[2] Austria did thereby assume certain undertakings in the economic sphere"; adding that "from the standpoint of the obligatory character of international engagements, it is well known that such engagements may be taken in the form of treaties, conventions, declarations, agreements, protocols, or exchanges of notes."[3]

The undertaking of engagements.—No case has arisen which compelled the Court to lay down rules governing capacity to enter into international engagements, though it has declared that "the right [power] of entering into international engagements is an attribute of State sovereignty."[4] Nor have any rules been laid down by the Court in respect to the conditions of validity of engagements,[5] or to the formalities necessary for entering into an engagement; it has not even adverted to the effect of noncompliance with the formality of registration required by Article 18 of the Covenant.[6] In the *Eastern Greenland Case,* an oral reply "given by the Minister for Foreign Affairs on behalf of his Government in response to a request by the diplomatic representative of a foreign Power, in regard to a question falling within his province," was held to constitute an "undertaking" which was "binding upon the country to which the Minister belongs."[7] In the advisory opinion on the *Jurisdiction of the European Commission of the Danube,* the Court refused to consider an interpretative protocol signed by delegates to the European Commission attending the Danube Conference in an advisory capacity, as "an international agreement between the parties to the Definitive Statute" of the Danube.[8] In its reply to the request for an advisory opinion concerning *Eastern Carelia,* the Court gave no answer to the question whether a declaration inserted in a *procès-verbal* at the time of the signature of the Treaty of Dorpat constituted an engagement; the question was said to be, "in the very nature of things, a question of fact."[9] In the judgment in the *Free Zones Case,* the Court treated a manifesto of the Royal Sardinian Court of Accounts, issued on royal orders following a favorable reception by the King of Sardinia of a request of the Canton of Valais based on Article 3 of the Treaty of Turin, as a "concord of wills" which conferred on the delimitation of the zone of St. Gingolph "the character of a treaty stipulation."[10] In the opinion on *German Minority Schools in Upper Silesia,* an arrangement adopted by the Council of the League of Nations and accepted by Germany and Poland was said to be "valid and binding for both countries."[11]

It has been recognized in several cases that an engagement may be undertaken by a State as a consequence of its agent's declaration before the Court. In the *Mavrommatis Case,* the British agent made a declaration which was incorporated in the Court's judgment, with the statement that its binding character was beyond question.[12] In the case relating to *German Interests in Upper Silesia,* the Polish agent made various declarations in respect to the binding character of which the Court was in no doubt.[13] In the *Free Zones Case,* the Swiss agent made, in the oral proceedings, a declaration which was incorporated in the judgment of the Court, and in the operative part of the judgment the Court placed it on record.[14]

It may also be noted that the same text may serve several purposes: it may constitute an international engagement and a provision of national law, and its legal consequences may depend upon the aspect in which it is to be considered. Thus the Statute of Memel was regarded by the Court as "a conventional arrangement binding upon Lithuania," because it was an annex to the Convention of May 8, 1924, and referred to in Article 16 of that Convention, though the Statute had also "been enacted as a Lithuanian law."[15]

Effectiveness of engagements.—The Court has not been called upon to fix the precise time when an international engagement becomes effective. In the *Oder Commission Case,* reference was made to the "ordinary rules of international law amongst which is the rule that conventions, save in certain exceptional cases, are binding only by virtue of their ratification."[16] In the judgment on *German Interests in Upper Silesia,* it seems to have been admitted that a "principle of good faith" requires a signatory to ratify, but it was found to be unnecessary to "consider the question whether, and if so how far, the signatories of a treaty are under an obligation to abstain from any action likely to interfere with its execution when ratification has taken place."[17] In determining its jurisdiction in the *Mavrommatis Case* the Court recognized the Lausanne Protocol which came into force after the proceeding was instituted as having effects which "extend to legal situations dating from a time previous to its own existence";[18] on another occasion, however, it refused to "examine the question whether" this protocol might, before its ratification, "have produced certain legal effects as regards the contracting parties."[19] In that case, also, it was recognized that a later may prevail over an earlier instrument.[20]

Performance of obligations undertaken.—The Court has acted upon the principle of *pacta sunt servanda,* though without frequent reference to it, and has repeatedly declared that international engagements are binding on the parties thereto. Throughout its jurisprudence, the assumption runs that States will in good faith observe and will carry out the obligations which they have undertaken. Hence, little hospitality has been shown to reasons advanced by parties for the nonfulfillment of their obligations. In the opinion on *Exchange of Greek and Turkish Populations,* the principle was declared to be "self-evident" that "a State which has contracted valid international obligations is bound to make in its legislation such modifications as may be necessary to ensure the fulfillment of the obligations undertaken."[21] It follows that a State cannot rely upon its own constitution or legislation as an excuse for nonperformance of its obligations. In the case concerning the *Polish Nationals in Danzig,* it was said that "a State cannot adduce as against another State its own Constitution with a view to evading obligations incumbent upon it under international law or treaties in force."[22] In the opinion on the *Jurisdiction of Danzig Courts,* it was made clear that Poland could not rely upon her own failure to enact legislation for the purpose of avoiding the obligations undertaken with Danzig.[23] In the opinion on the *Greco-Bulgarian Communities,* it was declared to be "a generally accepted principle of international law that in the relations between Powers who are contracting parties to a treaty, the provisions of municipal law cannot prevail over those of the treaty."[24]

At various times, excuses for nonperformance have been advanced, usually in the form of limitations on the extent of the obligation undertaken. In the *Wimbledon Case,* two dissenting judges would have excused nonperformance of Germany's obligations with respect to the Kiel Canal: "If, as a result of a war, a neutral or belligerent State is faced with the necessity of taking extra-ordinary measures temporarily affecting the application of such conventions in order to protect its neutrality or for the purposes of national defense, it is entitled to do so even if no express reservations are made in the Convention."[25] This view was not shared by the Court, however. In the *Serbian Loans Case,* the impossibility of performance contended for was found not to exist, and in the *Brazilian Loans Case* no basis was found for a defense of impossibility of performance based on *force majeure;*[26] but the judgments intimate that these might in a proper case be excuses for nonperformance. In the *Eastern Greenland Case,* Judge Anzilotti was willing to consider the effect of a mistake if it was "of an excusable character," but he concluded that no mistake had been made.[27]

Rebus sic stantibus.—The Court has not been confronted with a necessity of deciding on the so-called *clausula rebus sic stantibus.* In the opinion on *Nationality Decrees in Tunis and Morocco,* the French agent contended that certain treaties had "lapsed by virtue of the principle known as the *clausula rebus sic stantibus*"; the Court was of the opinion that any pronouncement on this point would involve "recourse to the principles of international law concerning the duration of the validity of treaties," but it was unnecessary for it to make such a pronouncement in that case.[28] In the *Free Zones Case,* the principle of the *clausula* was invoked in the earlier stages;[29] in the final judgment, it was considered at some length.[30] The French agent's contention was that the zones were created in 1815 "in view of and because of the existence of a particular state of facts," namely, that the Canton of Geneva was a free trade area which by the zones became an economic unit with other territory; that this state of facts disappeared when "the institution of Swiss Federal Customs in 1849 destroyed this economic unit"; and that in consequence the Court should declare the stipulations creating the zones to have lapsed. The Court stated that "to establish this position it is necessary, first of all, to prove that it was in consideration of the absence of customs duties at Geneva that the Powers decided, in 1815, in favour of the creation of the zones." As this was not proved to the Court's satisfaction, "the French argument fails on the facts," and it therefore became

> unnecessary for the Court to consider any of the questions of principle which arise in connection with the theory of the lapse of treaties by reason of change of circumstances, such as the extent to which the theory can be

regarded as constituting a rule of international law, the occasions on which and the method by which effect can be given to the theory if recognized, and the question whether it would apply to treaties establishing rights such as that which Switzerland derived from the treaties of 1815 and 1816.

This statement leaves wholly unanswered the question whether the *clausula rebus sic stantibus* has become a principle of international law.[31]

Effect of engagements on States not parties.—On several occasions the Court has had to deal with the effect of international instruments upon the position of States which are not parties to them. In general, a treaty may create rights for States not parties if this is clearly intended,[32] but it cannot impose obligations on such States.[33] In the case relating to *German Interests in Upper Silesia,* Poland relied upon the Armistice of November 11, 1918, and the Protocol of Spa of December 1, 1918; though Poland was not expressly a party to either instrument at the time of its signature, it was asserted that by virtue of being one of the Allied and Associated Powers Poland was entitled to be considered a party from the time of its recognition, accorded in the peace negotiations.[34] The Court found "no subsequent tacit adherence or accession on the part of Poland." As the instruments made no provision for adhesion, it was said to be

just as impossible to presume the existence of such a right—at all events in the case of an instrument of the nature of the Armistice Convention—as to presume that the provisions of these instruments can *ipso facto* be extended to apply to third States. A treaty only creates law as between the States which are parties to it; in case of doubt, no rights can be deduced from it in favour of third states.[35]

This language was so guarded as to leave open the general question of rights of third States. In the *Free Zones Case,* the Court held that "Article 435 of the Treaty of Versailles is not binding upon Switzerland, who is not a party to that Treaty, except to the extent to which that country accepted it."[36] Switzerland had acceded to the Declaration of the Powers of March 20, 1815, and in consequence it was found to be unnecessary to "consider the legal nature of the Gex zone from the point of view of whether it constitutes a stipulation in favour of a third party." It was added *obiter* that:

It cannot be lightly presumed that stipulations favourable to a third State have been adopted with the object of creating an actual right in its favor. There is, however, nothing to prevent the will of sovereign States from having this object and this effect. The question of the existence of a right acquired under an instrument drawn between other States is therefore one to be decided in each particular case: it must be ascertained whether the States which have stipulated in favour of a third State meant to create for that State an actual right which the latter has accepted as such.[37]

Judges Altamira and Hurst, dissenting in this case, made

every reservation in regard to a theory seeking to lay down, as a principle, that rights accorded third parties by international conventions to which the favored State is not a party, cannot be amended or abolished, even by the States which accorded them, without the consent of the third State.[38]

International engagements and private individuals.—In general, it may be said that an international engagement entered into by two States creates rights and obligations for those States only, and it does not of its own force confer rights or impose obligations on individuals, though this may be the consequence of its incorporation into the municipal law of a State which is a party. This was recognized by the Court in its advisory opinion on the *Jurisdiction of Danzig Courts:* "it may be readily admitted that, according to a well established principle of international law, the *Beamtenabkommen,* being an international agreement, cannot as such create direct rights and obligations for private individuals."[39] However, the parties may accomplish that result, and in that case an intention was found to adopt "definite rules creating individual rights and obligations and enforceable by the national courts"; the Court therefore held that the *Beamtenabkommen* governed the relations between the Polish Railways Administration and the Danzig officials, and constituted a part of the latter's "contract of service."

Interpretation and application.—The Court may be called upon to interpret a provision in a treaty apart from any question of its application.[40] "There seems to be no reason why States should not be able to ask the Court to give an abstract interpretation of a treaty; rather would it appear that this is one of the most important functions which it can fulfill. It has, in fact, already had occasion to do so in Judgment

No. 3."[41] However, the Court is usually called upon to interpret the text of an instrument in connection with some problem of its application, and the cases are rare in which an abstract question of interpretation will be presented. Many instruments confer on the Court jurisdiction over disputes or differences in respect to the "interpretation and application" of their provisions; the word *or* is sometimes employed instead of *and,* but *and* may be construed to be both alternative and cumulative.[42] Just as interpretation will usually be connected with application, any difference in respect to the application of a provision will almost invariably involve some question of its interpretation. In the *Mavrommatis Case,* the term "application" used in a contract was thought to be broader than the term "execution," the latter involving "a form of application."[43] In the judgment on *German Interests in Upper Silesia,* differences of opinion in respect to interpretation and application were said to "include differences of opinion as to the extent of the sphere of application,"[44] and they were held to include also differences relating to reparations for nonapplication.[45]

If it is true that interpretation is usually connected with application, this may very well influence the conception to be entertained of the nature of the function of interpretation. The consequences of a particular interpretation must be given greater importance in the discharge of that function, if interpretation and application are not dissociated. This was recognized by the Court in its opinion on the *Interpretation of the Treaty of Lausanne,* when it said that "any article designed to fix a frontier should, if possible, be so interpreted that the result of the application of its provisions in their entirety should be the establishment of a precise, complete and definitive frontier."[46]

The function of interpretation.—The process of interpreting the text of an international instrument[47] is not to be viewed as a search for some preëxisting meaning. It may be true, as was said in the opinion on *Access to German Minority Schools in Upper Silesia,* that "in accordance with a rule of law," an interpretation once arrived at is to be given "retrospective effect," "in the sense that the terms . . . must be held to have always borne the meaning placed upon them by this interpretation";[48] yet this does not mean that the interpretation merely gives form to a meaning which previously existed. Interpretation involves *giving* a meaning to the text. Few terms of art may be said to exist in international law, and as the terms employed in international instruments seldom have an exact meaning,[49] they can be interpreted only as content is given to them. This is not a matter of a mechanical operation; it is not a process which performs itself automatically. Results have to be kept in mind,[50] judgment must be exercised, many factors must be appreciated. Given a text, the Court may have to "look to its practical effect rather than to the predominant motive that may be conjectured to have inspired it."[51] There may be no danger in saying that it is the function of the Court to "ascertain the precise meaning" of a text,[52] if the nature of this process is kept in mind. Yet it serves little purpose to say that the Court must look for a "true meaning," or that "the question in every case must resolve itself into what the terms of the treaty actually mean."[53] Such expressions sometimes serve merely to hide the operations through which the Court must pass before it can arrive at a determination of the meaning to be given to a text. It is more proper to say that "the duty of the Court is to interpret the text as it stands, taking into consideration all the materials at the Court's disposal."[54]

Of course the Court does not enjoy a complete freedom in the process of interpretation thus conceived.[55] It is always under a duty to respect the text before it; unlike a legislative body, it cannot substitute a new text. Nor can any complete list be made of the "materials at the Court's disposal" for explaining the given text.[56] Canons or technical rules of interpretation can serve but a limited usefulness, and none of them can be of rigid and universal application. Within wide limits the Court must have a free hand; and it must be bound by no hard and fast rules of its own making.[57]

This has been appreciated by the Court. Fortunately, it has formulated but few rules, and most of those formulated have been stated in such guarded form as to leave it open to the Court to refuse to apply them; it would be difficult to say that all of them have been applied by the Court.

Authentic interpretation.—The Court must of course follow any interpretation of an instrument agreed upon by the parties to it, after the instrument has taken final form, but it has been scrupulously attentive to the facts in finding any such agreement. In the *Jaworzina Case,* it refused to admit the power of the Conference of Ambassadors to give a binding interpretation of its own previous decision after the task entrusted to the Conference had been fulfilled, saying: "it is an established principle that the right of giving an authoritative interpretation of a legal rule belongs solely to the person or body who has power to modify or suppress it."[58] Apart from this principle, it was said also that "the opinion of the authors of a document cannot be endowed with a decisive value when that opinion has been formulated after the drafting of that document and conflicts with the opinion which they expressed at the time."[59] In the case concerning the *Polish Postal Service in Danzig,* it was said that "a so-called authentic interpretation of a judicial decision is in effect a new decision," and the Court denied that the proper meaning of a decision could be altered by an expression of a personal opinion by its author.[60] In the case relating to the *Jurisdiction of the European Danube Commission,* an "interpretative protocol" annexed to the minutes of the Danube Conference was treated as a part of the preparatory work which could not prevail against the text of the Statute drawn up by the Conference.[61]

Intention of the parties.—The judgments and opinions of the Court contain numerous references to the "intention of the parties" as a guide for interpretation. It is of first importance that the definitely entertained and expressed intentions of the parties should be effectuated,[62] and in some cases the results reached by the Court may be so explained. Yet it is necessary to be on guard against the use of this criterion merely as a palliating description of a result which has been arrived at by some other method than the ascertainment of intention. The simple case is relatively rare in which the parties may be said to have foreseen and endeavored to effect a solution of the precise problem presented. The parties seldom proclaim their intention in unmistakable terms; and even if an intention is proclaimed, it must be found to have been expressed in the text.[63] More often, the problem raised before the Court was not foreseen when the instrument in question was being drafted, neither the particular problem nor a general class which would cover the particular problem; nor, if it was foreseen, was its solution definitely agreed upon. The compromises which are inevitable in framing international instruments frequently result in the acceptance of a "formula" which is possible only because it does not foreclose the contentions of any party. No great experience in international conferences is required to know that terms are sometimes employed in treaties of which no common understanding is reached in advance.[64] In some situations, a lack of clarity may even be a *desideratum;* the chief desire may be to continue uncertainty.[65] Where a text is not consciously "so framed as to perpetuate the divergence of views which had arisen," however, a "formula" may be chosen which will leave the solution even of the definitely foreseen problem to await future developments.[66]

It is precisely these kinds of situations which are calculated to produce the differences of which the Court will be seised: either (1) a situation was not foreseen, or (2) it was foreseen and no definite provision was made for it. In a case involving an unforeseen situation, it can only be conjectured what the parties might have thought or said if their attention had been directed to a given possibility; the Court may very properly be asked to deal with this situation, though it cannot do so by a simple reference to the intention of the parties, and any reliance on assumed intention would be artificial.[67] This was recognized in the advisory opinion on the *Convention concerning Employment of Women at Night* when the Court said:

> the mere fact that, at the time when the convention . . . was concluded, certain facts or situations, which the terms of the convention in their ordinary meaning are wide enough to cover, were not thought of, does not justify interpreting those of its provisions which are general in scope otherwise than in accordance with their terms.[68]

Also, where the "facts or situations" were foreseen and no definite provision was made for them, the Court may be called upon to apply a "formula," and to give it a content based upon considerations other than intention. Important as it may be, therefore, that effect be given to the intentions of the parties, it must be recognized that the problem of interpretation is not so simple that it can be resolved by a mere statement of that principle. In fact no purpose is served by an assumption that the Court's function is so limited.

It is also possible that a treaty may contain provisions which were envisaged to apply to situations which could not be foreseen, and in such a situation the task of interpretation may be still less confined to a mere effectuation of intention.

"Natural" meaning.—Throughout the Court's jurisprudence, a tendency is manifest to seek first the so-called "natural" meaning of the terms to be construed, and, once it is found, to weigh other considerations with a disposition to say that the "natural" meaning is not to be disturbed.[69] This may be a wise tendency, and no objection is to be made to a term which has a soothing effect and which tends to avoid arousals because of its indefinite content. Yet there may be some danger in allowing the "natural" meaning to overcome the results of other investigations. Numerous substitutions have been made for the term from time to time: a meaning may be described as "literal,"[70] "grammatical,"[71] "ordinary,"[72] "normal,"[73] "logical,"[74] "reasonable."[75] It is often said that the meaning is "clear"[76] or "sufficiently clear,"[77] in spite of the fact that the States concerned do not place the same construction on the text, or that some members of the Court do not agree with this conclusion.[78] It would be difficult to say that the various adjectives are always used by the Court synonymously, or that any one of them is used as a term of art. "Natural" seems to have reference to ordinary usage.[79] On one occasion standard dictionaries were consulted to determine usage, though "common use" was made to yield to context.[80] The legal terminology of the States concerned is not necessarily controlling.[81] Ordinary usage must clearly yield to the usage of the time, place, and occasion, however, and the Court has therefore admitted that "natural" meaning may be displaced. It has been laid down as "a cardinal principle of interpretation that words must be interpreted in the sense which they would normally have in their context, unless such interpretation would lead to something unreasonable or absurd."[82] In the advisory opinion on the *Convention concerning Employment of Women at Night,* a willingness was expressed "to find some valid ground for interpreting the provision otherwise than in accordance with the natural sense of the words"; but the grounds on which it had been suggested that the natural meaning could be displaced, did not "appear to the Court to be well-founded."[83]

Context.—Even in arriving at the natural meaning of terms, the Court insists upon looking at them in their context, and it early announced that "the context is the final test."[84] The context is not simply the particular sentence, or the particular paragraph in which the term to be construed occurs.[85] It may be (*a*) a particular part of the instrument, or (*b*) the instrument as a whole, or (*c*) the texts of the instrument in different languages, or (*d*) the texts of several interrelated and interdependent instruments.

A particular part of an instrument.—The various parts of a single instrument may be quite independent, either because of the history of their drafting or because each deals completely with a distinct subject-matter. Thus, in the judgment in the *Free Zones Case,* though it was said to be "impossible to interpret the second paragraph without regard to the first paragraph" of Article 435 of the Treaty of Versailles, that Article was taken by itself, independently of other articles in the same treaty, to form "a complete whole," both because of its position in the treaty and because of its origin.[86] In determining the competence of the International Labor Organization, the Court has considered Part XIII of the Treaty of Versailles as a whole;[87] and it has referred to "the entire framework of Part XIII."[88] In the *Wimbledon Case,* also, the provisions relating to the Kiel Canal, Section VI of Part XII of the Treaty of Versailles, were held to be "self-contained"; and it was said that "they would lose their *raison d'être*" if they had to be interpreted in connection with other sections of that part of the treaty.[89] However, one part of an instrument may be dependent on another part in connection with which it must be construed; thus in the judgment concerning *German Interests in Upper Silesia,* the Court held that a "system of rules relating to large scale industry," forming part of the Geneva Convention, should be construed as a whole.[90]

An instrument as a whole.—In some cases, the Court has insisted that "the treaty must be read as a whole, and that its meaning is not to be determined merely upon particular phrases which, if detached from the context, may be interpreted in more than one sense."[91] Thus in the advisory opinion concerning the *Interpretation of the Treaty of Lausanne,* the Court not only read Paragraph 2 of Article 3 in the light of Paragraph 3 but also inquired whether any other articles of the Treaty were "calculated to throw any light upon the scope of Article 3."[92] This is especially so when the treaty sets up a *régime.* The Court in such cases tends to construe the provision before it by reference to its place in a whole system. This may be seen in the Court's construction of provisions relating to Danzig and to Memel. In the advisory opinion concerning the *Polish Postal Service in Danzig* it was said that "the construction which the Court has placed on the various treaty stipulations is not only reasonable but is also supported by reference to the various articles taken by themselves and in their relation one to another."[93] In the case concerning the interpretation of the *Memel Statute,* there being no clear provision governing the question in dispute, the Court stated that "the Convention of Paris of 1924 and the Statute annexed to it must be considered as a whole in order to understand the *régime* which the Four Powers and Lithuania intended to establish for the Memel Territory."[94] In the same case the Court rejected an argument of the applicants on the ground that "such an interpretation would destroy the general scheme of the Convention of Paris of 1924 and the Statute annexed to it."[95] Nevertheless, the Court has refused in some cases to allow its construction of a part of a treaty to be influenced by other parts.[96]

Texts in different languages.—International instruments may be embodied in texts in different languages,[97] without provision with respect to which is to prevail if a difference arises;[98] in such a situation, it may be better to speak of several versions of a single text.[99] The versions in all languages must be considered together, and a meaning is to be given to the composite.[100] Ordinarily, neither version should be subordinated to the other, though a history of both should be taken into account. This was recognized in the second advisory opinion relating to the *Competence of the International Labour Organization.*[101] The rule was formulated in the *Mavrommatis Case* that "where two versions possessing equal authority exist one of which appears to have a wider bearing than the other," the Court "is bound to adopt the more limited interpretation which can be made to harmonize with both versions and which, as far as it goes, is doubtless in accordance with the common intention of the parties."[102] In that case it was held that "the wider meaning of the English text appears to be the only one which does not nullify the expression *contrôle public* in the French version." "Especial force" was said to be given to the rule "because the question concerns an instrument laying down the obligations of Great Britain in her capacity as Mandatory for Palestine and also because the original draft of this instrument was probably made in English." The latter ground smacks of a reference to *travaux préparatoires* for taking account of the fact that the text in one language was constructed by the process of translating from another language, and the Court has frequently stated that this should be done only in cases of doubt.

Related and interdependent instruments.—Two or more instruments may be so related, or so interdependent, that the text of one must be construed with reference to the other. This was found by the Court to be true of the Polish-Danzig Convention of November 9, 1920; "in case of doubt as to the meaning of its provisions, recourse may be had to the Treaty of Versailles, not for the purpose of discarding the terms of the Convention, but with a view to elucidating their meaning."[103] In its judgment relating to *Minority Schools in Upper Silesia,* it was "presumed" that provisions in the Polish Minorities Treaty, which had been incorporated into the later Geneva Convention, were not thereby given a different meaning: "there is a presumption that the provisions of the Convention are in conformity with the principles underlying the Minorities Treaty."[104] In the case concerning *German Interests in Upper Silesia,* the application of the Geneva Convention was found to be "hardly possible without giving an interpretation of Article 256 of the Treaty of Versailles and the other international stipulations cited by Poland," and it was held that the "interpretation of other international agreements is indisputably within the competence of the Court if such interpretation must be regarded as incidental to a decision on a point in regard to which it has jurisdiction."[105] In the advisory opinion on the *Jurisdiction of the European Commission of the Danube,* the Court spoke of "the whole system of international acts applicable before the War to the Maritime Danube."[106] In the advisory opinion on *Danzig and the International Labour Organization,* Judge Huber thought that the Covenant of the League of Nations and Part XIII of the Treaty of Versailles were "organically connected."[107]

Nature and purpose of an instrument.—A consideration of the setting of an instrument necessarily leads to appreciation of the office it was designed to serve, and the Court has frequently referred to the "nature,"[108] "spirit,"[109] "scheme,"[110] "purpose,"[111] "function,"[112] "intention,"[113] "tenor,"[114] "rôle,"[115] "object,"[116] "aim,"[117] or "system"[118] of, or "principles underlying"[119] an instrument.[120] That interpretation is to be favored which will make the instrument effective to serve its purpose. No rules of interpretation, therefore, can be of universal validity, applicable in the same way to all international instruments.[121] Such appreciation has been shown by the Court, particularly in connection with its interpretation of treaties for the protection of minorities. In the advisory opinion on *German Settlers in Poland,* the Court rejected a contention that the competence conferred on the Council of the League of Nations by the Polish Minorities Treaty did not apply to Poland's exercise of rights conferred by the Treaty of Versailles, stating:

The main object of the Minorities Treaty is to assure respect for the rights of minorities and to prevent discrimination against them by any act whatsoever of the Polish State. . . . If the Council ceased to be competent whenever the subject before it involved the interpretation of such an international engagement, the Minorities Treaty would to a great extent be deprived of value. . . . In order that the pledged protection may be certain and effective, it is essential that the Council, when acting under the Minorities Treaty, should be competent, incidentally, to consider and interpret the laws or treaties on which the rights claimed to be infringed are dependent.[122]

Later it was said that "an interpretation which would deprive the Minorities Treaty of a great part of its value is inadmissible."[123] The same attitude was shown in the construction of the words "interpretation and application" in Article 23 of the German-Polish Convention of May 18, 1922, when the Court took account

not only of the historical development of arbitration treaties as well as of the terminology of such treaties, and of the grammatical and logical meaning of the words used, but also and more especially of the function which, in the intention of the contracting Parties, is to be attributed to this provision.[124]

When called upon to interpret an international labor convention, the Court considered "the fact that the improvement of the lot of the manual worker was the aim of Part XIII" of the Treaty of Versailles.[125] In the case relating to *German Settlers in Poland,* however, the Court refused to give weight to an alleged purpose of de-Germanization where this would involve an extension inconsistent with the provisions of a treaty.[126] In an opinion on the *Competence of the International Labour Organization,* it was said that "the Court, in determining the nature and scope of a measure, must look to its practical effect rather than to the predominant motive that may be conjectured to have inspired it."[127]

The jurisprudence of the Court does not establish any rigid timetable for the various steps in the process of interpretation. Yet it is to be noted that, in the opinion on the *Convention concerning Employment of Women at Night,* the Court did not take account of the policy to be served by an instrument until after it had arrived at a conclusion in respect to the "natural" meaning of terms in the Convention, and then only for the purpose of determining whether the "natural" meaning could be displaced. This was made the target of a brilliant dissent by Judge Anzilotti, who protested that it is not "possible to say that an article of a convention is clear until the subject and aim of the convention have been ascertained." "The first question which arises," he said, "is what is the subject [Fr., *objet*] and aim of the convention."[128]

Use of travaux préparatoires.—It is doubtless a sound principle that when negotiations have resulted in an instrument which is formalized by signature and possibly by ratification, that instrument should ordinarily be taken to embody the whole of the agreement reached in the course of the negotiations. Additions to the instrument are not to be made as a consequence of a study of preliminary drafts which were not incorporated into the text which was signed; nor are subtractions to be made by that means. A preliminary question may arise in respect to what is the text which was agreed upon.[129] Yet after it is disposed of, the construction of the text cannot be arrived at without a consideration of its setting, and the development of the negotiations forms a part of the history which constitutes that setting. Where a dispute revolves about issues connected with the preparation of a text, as did the dispute concerning the *Interpretation of the Treaty of Lausanne,* it would be merely stultifying to say that *travaux préparatoires* cannot be examined.

While the Court has always been careful to trace the history of the negotiations which have led to the signing of an instrument, it has shown itself somewhat reluctant to make use of preliminary drafts, *travaux préparatoires*.[130] The actual rules formulated on this subject have been stated in such a way as to leave the Court wide latitude; and it is doubtful whether the Court's practice has been in any way circumscribed by such formulations. Even when the use of *travaux préparatoires* has been said to be excluded, they have usually been used to confirm conclusions reached. The rule has frequently been stated that "there is no occasion to have regard to preparatory work if the text of a convention is sufficiently clear in itself."[131] This leaves the door open for saying that *travaux préparatoires* must be resorted to because the text is not "sufficiently clear";[132] on this point, individual judges have sometimes dissented from the majority's view. On a few occasions the Court has shown a willingness to refer to *travaux préparatoires* without referring to this rule.[133] In the case relating to *Polish Nationals in Danzig,* where a text was found to be not "absolutely clear," the Court thought it "useful, in order to ascertain its precise meaning, to recall here somewhat in detail the various drafts which existed prior to the adoption of the text now in force";[134] yet one judge in this case found the text to be "so clear that a reference to the *travaux préparatoires* of the convention seems hardly justifiable."[135] Even in cases where the text has been found to be "sufficiently clear," however, usually the Court does not altogether refuse to examine *travaux préparatoires,* and it sometimes uses them to buttress the conclusions which have been reached independently. Thus, in its second advisory opinion, after the Court had reached its conclusion "on the construction of the text itself," it was observed that "there is certainly nothing in the preparatory work to disturb this conclusion."[136] In the *Lotus Case,* after a construction was given to the expression "principles of international law" as used in the Lausanne Convention, it was said that "the records of the preparation of the Convention . . . would not furnish anything calculated to overrule the construction indicated by the actual terms" of the article, and *travaux préparatoires* were gone into to justify this statement.[137] In the opinion on the *Interpretation of the Treaty of Lausanne,* a text was found to be "sufficiently clear," yet the Court proceeded to consider it "in the light of the negotiations."[138] With reference to the bonds in question in the *Serbian Loans Case,* the Court said that "as the words themselves are not ambiguous, there is no occasion to refer to the preliminary documents. But if these are examined, it will appear that they tend to confirm the agreement for gold payments."[139] In its interpretation of the *Convention concerning Employment of Women at Night,* the Court was "so struck with the confident opinions expressed" that it was "led to examine the preparatory work of the Convention," disclaiming any intention "to derogate in any way from the rule" laid down relating to *travaux préparatoires;* its conclusion was only confirmed in consequence.[140]

The conclusion to be drawn from the jurisprudence is that, while the Court professes a willingness to look into *travaux préparatoires* only for the purpose of resolving a doubt concerning the text, it has on many occasions done so to confirm constructions concerning which it had no doubt. In spite of the frequency of these occasions, it must be said that the Court has not exercised a complete freedom in the use of *travaux préparatoires;* a resort to them only after a conclusion has been reached is not the same as a resort to them before the conclusion is formulated.[141]

Once the decision is taken that *travaux préparatoires* may be resorted to, the Court has not been very definite in saying how far they may be relied upon. It has said, however, that "preparatory work should not be used for the purpose of changing the plain meaning of a text."[142] Judge Anzilotti has formulated a more definite rule, that preparatory work is to be "adduced not to extend or limit the scope of a text clear in itself, but to verify the existence of an intention not necessarily emerging from the text but likewise not excluded by that text."[143] Under the approach made by the Court, it seems improbable that it will have a case in which it admits the "plain meaning" to be clear and in which it will feel compelled by the *travaux préparatoires* to assign a different meaning to the text.

One quite definite ground for refusing to consider *travaux préparatoires* was stated in the advisory opinion relating to the *Jurisdiction of the European Commission of the Danube.* The history of certain articles of the Treaty of Versailles having been invoked, the Court said:

> The record of the work preparatory to the adoption of these articles being confidential and not being placed before the Court by, or with the consent

of, the competent authority, the Court is not called upon to consider to what extent it might have been possible for it to take this preparatory work into account.[144]

Perhaps it is a somewhat different question whether *travaux préparatoires* may be admitted as evidence. Usually they are admitted without question, and in consequence they constitute a part of the judges' background of knowledge, whatever rule may be formulated concerning their use. In connection with the second advisory opinion, the objection was made that such materials should not be considered by the Court, not that they should not be admitted as evidence.[145] In the case relating to the *Oder Commission*, however, the Court was asked to rule that no attention should be paid to passages in the Polish case and counter-case which referred to records of the preparatory work of the Treaty of Versailles, namely, the minutes of the Commission on Ports, Waterways and Railways; and by its order of August 20, 1929, the Court ruled that these minutes should "be excluded as evidence from the proceedings in the present case."[146] The chief ground of this order was that "three of the parties concerned in the present case did not take part in the work of the conference which prepared the Treaty of Versailles."[147]

Legal background.—Any international instrument must be interpreted in the light of the prevailing international law, by which the parties must be taken to have charted their course.[148] Judges Anzilotti and Huber insisted on this point in the *Wimbledon Case,* stating that "treaty limitations cannot be interpreted as limiting" a State's right of self-protection, "even though these stipulations do not conflict with such an interpretation."[149] In the judgment relating to *German Interests in Upper Silesia,* the Court took the "generally accepted international law" to constitute, at least in part, "the basis of the Geneva Convention."[150] In the case relating to the *Jurisdiction of the Oder Commission,* the Court found it proper to explore "the principles underlying the matter to which the text refers," and Article 331 of the Treaty of Versailles was "interpreted in the light of these principles," namely, "the principles governing international fluvial law in general";[151] and in interpreting Article 338 of the same treaty, it was said to be "hardly justifiable to deduce from a somewhat ill-chosen expression an intention to derogate from a rule of international law so important as that relating to the ratification of conventions."[152] In the opinion on the *Interpretation of the Treaty of Lausanne,* the Court took the provisions of the Covenant concerning unanimity to be subject to the "well-known rule that no one can be judge in his own suit."[153] In some degree, also, the Court might take account of the municipal laws of the parties as a part of the legal background of an instrument, though in the opinion on the *Exchange of Greek and Turkish Populations* it showed itself reluctant to do so.[154] It has also referred to the "precedents supplied by international practice."[155]

Political and social background.—Quite clearly, the Court would not be justified in dealing with an international instrument as if it had been concluded *in vacuo.* It must take account of the general setting in which the parties acted if it would understand their purposes, and its construction of an instrument may very properly be influenced by factors of a political or social significance. International legislation which the Court must apply is frequently designed to deal with such factors. As the Court has phrased it, "the making of laws, whether national or international, is a political act and as such may involve the application of political principles."[156] If international law is to be builded on sound foundations, it is no more possible to ignore the political and social phases of the prevailing international order than it is possible to ignore similar phases of the prevailing national order in the building of municipal law.[157]

This has been appreciated by the Court in a long course of action. In the judgment on *German Interests in Upper Silesia,* the Geneva Convention was interpreted "in the light of war-time legislation," and a city was included in the term "national."[158] In the *Jaworzina Case* extended reference was made to the general political situation in which decisions had been taken for defining the Polish-Czechoslovak frontier, by the Supreme Council and the Conference of Ambassadors.[159] In determining the nature of the vote to be taken by the Council of the League of Nations under Article 3 of the Treaty of Lausanne, the Court had in mind the "political position" of certain States which might require them to "bear the larger share of the responsibilities and consequences."[160] The Definitive Statute of the Danube was viewed by the Court with reference to "the historical facts upon which it rests."[161] The construction placed on the treaties which related to the proposal of an *Austro-German Customs Régime* was preceded by a reference to "the existing political settlement which has laid down in Europe the consequences of the break-up of the Austro-Hungarian monarchy"; the existence of Austria was thought to be "an essential feature" of that settlement, and the Court's conclusions were based on this background of "circumstances."[162] This was surely a sounder attitude than that taken by a minority of the Court which was not "concerned with political considerations" and which saw the question presented as "purely legal."[163] In the advisory opinion on *Polish War Vessels in Danzig,* the Court "took notice," as of a "matter of history," of the assurances given to Poland of a free and secure access to the sea,[164] but it found no reasons for assuming that these assurances had not been completely fulfilled in the later agreements. In the advisory opinion on the treatment of *Polish Nationals in Danzig,* an interpretation of the treaty provisions was made "in the light of the circumstances which led to the creation of Danzig as a Free City."[165] In the opinion concerning the *Greco-Bulgarian Communities,* the Court insisted on the "traditional conception" of a "community" in Eastern countries, and held that the Greco-Bulgarian Convention should be taken to embody that conception.[166]

Analogous provisions.—An aid to the interpretation of a text may sometimes be found in analogous provisions either in the same instrument, or, more rarely, in an instrument to which other States are parties. Even if a part of a treaty or convention is taken to be a self-contained whole, analogies may be drawn from other parts; thus, in the *Wimbledon Case,* though the provisions of the Treaty of Versailles relating to the Kiel Canal were said to be self-contained, the wording of Article 380 was "compared with that of the other provisions to be found in Part XII."[167] In the opinion concerning *German Settlers in Poland,* the Court drew upon analogies in Article 75 of the Treaty of Versailles relating to Alsace-Lorraine, and in other articles, in its application of Article 256 of the same Treaty.[168] In the *Chorzow Case,* the Court refused to draw any conclusion from the terminology in general arbitration agreements, for interpreting a compromissary clause in the

Geneva Convention, though it found some analogy in the classification of disputes in Article 13 of the Covenant and Article 36 of the Court's Statute.[169] In interpreting the *Convention concerning the Employment of Women at Night,* the Court was willing "to attach some importance" to provisions in the eight-hour-day convention, also drawn up by the Labor Conference in 1919, because of its "similarity both in structure and in expression."[170] The Court, however, has declared it to be a general principle of interpretation that "an obligation imposed on one contracting party cannot be based on the fact that it is mentioned in the annex to a section of a treaty dealing with a different subject-matter."[171]

Action by the parties.—In the process of *giving* a meaning to a text, the Court cannot ignore action which may have been taken by the parties to an instrument, either contemporaneously with its drafting or subsequently,[172] though, as the Court said in the *Brazilian Loans Case,* "where reference is had to the conduct of the Parties as an aid to interpretation, it is necessary to consider whether that conduct itself permits of but one inference."[173] Contemporaneous action by the parties, related to the instrument itself, may be taken to indicate the purpose which the instrument was designed to serve.[174] In an advisory opinion on the *Competence of the International Labour Organization,* the Court relied upon the inclusion of an item in the agenda of the first International Labor Conference, "as a contemporaneous practical interpretation made by the High Contracting Parties of the scope of the competence which they had conferred upon the International Labour Organization."[175] Subsequent action taken by the parties may also furnish some indication of the purpose with which an instrument was concluded, though great caution must be exercised in finding such an indication. In its opinion on the *Interpretation of the Treaty of Lausanne,* the Court declared that "the facts subsequent to the conclusion of the Treaty of Lausanne can only concern the Court in so far as they are calculated to throw light on the intention of the parties at the time of the conclusion of the treaty."[176] It seems doubtful whether this limitation has always been observed, however.

In an advisory opinion on the *Competence of the International Labour Organization,* a willingness was expressed "if there were any ambiguity"[177] to "consider the action which has been taken under the Treaty" for the "purpose of arriving at the true meaning"; and though no ambiguity was found to exist, the Court did refer to action taken under the Treaty.[178] In a later opinion on the same general subject, the Court referred to the actual exercise of competence by the International Labor Organization in the convention on the use of white lead in painting.[179] In these two cases, the function of interpretation bore a close resemblance to the function exercised by certain national courts in passing upon the constitutionality of legislation, and in the second case the Court pointed out that

> it is not an unusual thing, in countries in which legislative power is limited by a fundamental charter, for the courts, in deciding whether certain legislation is constitutional, or *intra vires,* to resort to practice, national or international, for the determination of the extent of a particular governmental power.[180]

Such action by national courts is based upon a reluctance to disturb a course of action under legislation and upon a desire to taken into account the results of a particular interpretation given in practice to a constitutional provision. It would seem that the consideration of subsequent action by the Court in these two cases was based upon a similar reluctance and a similar desire; in other words, the Court has not observed the limitation placed upon itself in the opinion relating to the *Interpretation of the Treaty of Lausanne.* With the lapse of time, intentions entertained by the draftsmen of an instrument may lose some of their importance, and a course of action by those who must live with and under the provisions of the instrument may assume a correspondingly greater significance. In the advisory opinion relating to the *Jurisdiction of Danzig Courts,* the fact that the *Beamtenabkommen* had been actually put into force by the parties was taken to indicate their intention that it should govern directly the relations between the Polish Railways Administration and the Danzig officials.[181]

What has been said applies to action which is common to all the parties to an instrument. Action taken by a single party may involve an admission which will militate against some position it may assume,[182] but it is not otherwise to be taken into account in interpretation.

Liberal or restrictive interpretation.—The Court has not attempted to formulate any general principle that instruments must be liberally or strictly construed. A national court may be justified in adopting a policy of the liberal construction of treaties to which the State is a party, for it will seldom be called upon to construe a treaty with other States before it;[183] an international court before which States only may be parties would not be justified in adopting any such principle. If any "rules as to a strict or liberal construction" are to be followed, they "can be applied only in cases where ordinary methods of interpretation have failed."[184] No rules for extensive interpretation have been formulated;[185] and where specific rules for a restrictive interpretation are announced,[186] a caveat is usually entered to avoid their automatic application. First, the Court has adopted a rule of restrictive interpretation of texts conferring jurisdiction upon itself. "Every special agreement, like every clause conferring jurisdiction on the Court, must be interpreted strictly"; yet it was added that this rule is not to be so applied that the special agreement would fail to enunciate the question in dispute and prejudge the answer,[187] or to have "appropriate effects."[188] Again, it has been said that limitations on the exercise of sovereign rights must be strictly construed; but this is only "in case of doubt,"[189] and in applying this rule in the *Wimbledon Case* the Court felt itself "obliged to stop at the point where the so-called restrictive interpretation would be contrary to the plain terms of the article and would destroy what has clearly been granted."[190] In the *Oder Commission Case,* it was contended that, where a text is doubtful, that construction should be given to it "which imposes the least restriction on the freedom of States"; the Court thought that, while the argument was "sound in itself," the rule was to be "employed only with the greatest caution." "Only when in spite of all pertinent considerations, the intention of the parties remains doubtful," is that interpretation to be given "which is most favorable to the freedom of States."[191] In the advisory opinion concerning the *Interpretation of the Treaty of Lausanne,* it was said to be a sound principle that "if the wording of a treaty provision is not clear, in choosing between several admissible interpretations, the one which involves the minimum of obligations for the parties should be adopted"; but the text was said to be clear.[192]

A clear illustration of restrictive interpretation is to be found in the interpretation of texts which form an exceptional part of a system or régime into which they must be fitted. Thus, in the case concerning *Nationality Decrees in Tunis and Morocco,* it was said that, since Paragraph 8 of Article 15 of the Covenant is "an exception to the principles affirmed in the preceding paragraph," it "does not therefore lend itself to an extensive interpretation."[193] In the case concerning the *Mavrommatis Concessions,* "a strict interpretation" was given to Article 6 of the Lausanne Protocol as "the only one which is in harmony with the system of the Protocol."[194] In the judgment on *German Interests in Upper Silesia,* it was said that "the liability to expropriation of rural property constitutes, under the Geneva Convention, an exception; in case of doubt as to the scope of this provision, its terms must therefore be strictly construed."[195]

Special rules of interpretation.—On a few occasions the Court has formulated special rules of interpretation which were borrowed from municipal law. Thus, in the *Mavrommatis Case,* it held that, as between Article II of the Palestine Mandate and the Lausanne Protocol XII, "in cases of doubt, the Protocol being a special and more recent agreement should prevail."[196] In the *Serbian Loans Case,* the Court being called upon to interpret provisions in a bond declared that "the special words, according to elementary principles of interpretation, control the general expressions."[197] In the *Brazilian Loans Case,* it was said to be "a familiar rule for the construction of instruments that, where they are found to be ambiguous, they should be taken *contra proferentem*"; and it was held that an ambiguity in a prospectus of the loans might be resolved against the Brazilian Government which was responsible for it, that meaning being given which the terms "would naturally carry to those taking the bonds under the prospectus."[198] The Court has also applied the maxim *expressio unius exclusio alterius.*[199]

NOTES TO HUDSON ESSAY

[1] In the *Serbian* and *Brazilian Loan Cases,* before the Court under special agreements, no other treaty engagements were involved.—Publications of the Court, Series A, No. 20/21. In the *Lotus Case,* however, the question submitted referred to Article 15 of the Convention of Lausanne of July 24, 1923.—Series A, No. 10.

[2] The multipartite instrument mentioned, denominated "Protocol No. 1," contained bilateral "declarations." For the text, see 12 League of Nations Treaty Series 385; 2 Hudson, *International Legislation* 882.

[3] Series A/B, No. 41, p. 47. The list given by the Court cannot have been intended to be exhaustive; the terms "arrangement," "act," "statute," and "modus vivendi" are common, and other names of instruments are sometimes employed. The choice of a name for an instrument is frequently determined by political considerations, and the name selected often has no juridical significance.

[4] Series A, No. 1, p. 25; Series B, No. 10, p. 21.

[5] Dissenting judges have addressed themselves to conditions of validity, however. See Judge Schucking in Series A, No. 1, p. 47; Judge Negulesco in Series B, No. 14, p. 126; Judge Anzilotti in Series A/B, No. 53, p. 92.

[6] It may be doubted whether the Court should give any effect to an unregistered treaty or engagement concluded by two members of the League of Nations since January 10, 1920. The practice ought to be adopted of citing the League of Nations Treaty Series when reference is made to registered treaties or engagements. Perhaps an exception must be made in the application of Article 18 of the Covenant, of special agreements for the reference of disputes to the Court; certainly most of the special agreements to date have not been registered with the Secretariat of the League of Nations.

[7] Series A/B, No. 53, pp. 71, 73. Judge Anzilotti said in this case that "there does not seem to be any rule of international law requiring that agreements of this kind must necessarily be in writing, in order to be valid."—*Ibid.* 91.

Possibly an agreement may be expressed in a map, also. In the *Jaworzina Case,* confirmatory evidence was found in maps, though it was said that independently maps could not be regarded as conclusive proof (Series B, No. 8, p. 33). In the *Monastery of St. Naoum Case,* the map in question was unsigned and its authenticity was not established. —Series B, No. 9, p. 21.

[8] Series B, No. 14, pp. 32–34. Judge Moore referred to the interpretative protocol as a "legally unclassified paper."—*Ibid.* 81.

[9] Series B, No. 5, p. 26. *Sed quaere.*

[10] Series A/B, No. 46, p. 145. See also Series A, No. 24, p. 17.

[11] Series A/B, No. 40, p. 16.

[12] Series A, No. 5, p. 37.

[13] Series A, No. 7, p. 13.

[14] Series A/B, No. 46, pp. 170, 172. In this case, Judge *ad hoc* Dreyfus, dissenting, called attention to the limitations of the Swiss constitution which might prevent the Swiss declaration from being binding (*ibid.* 209). In the order in the case relating to the *Southeastern Territory of Greenland,* it was stated that where intentions have "been officially proclaimed before the Court, the latter must not and cannot presume that the two Governments concerned might act otherwise than in conformity with the intentions thus expressed."—Series A/B, No. 48, p. 287.

[15] Series A/B, No. 49, p. 300.

[16] Series A, No. 23, p. 20.

[17] Series A, No. 7, p. 40. See also *passim*, Series B, No. 6.

[18] Series A, No. 2, p. 34. In this case, Judge Moore, dissenting, said that "the doctrine that governments are bound to ratify whatever their plenipotentiaries, acting within the limits of their instructions, may sign, and that treaties may therefore be regarded as legally operative and enforceable before they have been ratified, is obsolete, and lingers only as an echo from the past."—*Ibid.* 57.

[19] Series A, No. 5, p. 39.

[20] Series A, No. 2, p. 30; *cf.* Series A, No. 15, p. 59.

[21] Series B, No. 10, p. 20.

[22] Series A/B, No. 44, p. 24.

[23] Series B, No. 15, pp. 26–27.

[24] Series B, No. 17, p. 32.

[25] Series A, No. 1, p. 36.

[26] Series A, No. 20/21, pp. 40, 120.

[27] Series A/B, No. 53, p. 92.

[28] Series B, No. 4, p. 29.

[29] Series A, No. 22, pp. 29, 36, 41.

[30] Series A/B, No. 46, pp. 156–158.

[31] In the first phase of the *Free Zones Case,* Deputy-Judge Negulesco expressed the view that Article 19 of the Covenant of the League of Nations "confirms the validity of the clause *rebus sic stantibus* and at the same time rejects any claim to apply it unilaterally."—Series A, No. 22, p. 30.

[32] In the *Wimbledon Case,* Judge *ad hoc* Schucking, dissenting, expressed the view that "a legally binding contractual obligation cannot be undertaken to perform acts which would violate the rights of third parties."—Series A, No. 1, p. 47.

[33] Agreements forming part of a general continental settlement, such as those concluded at the end of the World War, may be viewed as exceptional. The Commission of Jurists which dealt with certain questions involved in the Aaland Islands dispute in 1920, emphasized the "European character" of the Convention of March 30, 1856, and the intention thereby to create "European law" (League of Nations Council Document 69 [20/4/238], 1920, pp. 25–26). However, in a dissenting opinion on the *Jurisdiction of the European Commission of the Danube,* Judge Negulesco expressed the view that "decisions of the Great Powers, met together as the Concert of Europe, . . . have never been held to be legally binding upon States not represented in the Concert."—Series B, No. 14, p. 95. See also Series A, No. 24, p. 27.

[34] Series C, No. 11-II, pp. 616 ff.

[35] Series A, No. 7, pp. 28–29. *Cf.* Lord Finlay's dissent, asserting that on analogy to "contracts on behalf of companies not yet incorporated," the "Allied States made the Armistice on behalf of Poland, which was about to become a State."—*Ibid.* 84.

[36] Series A/B, No. 46, p. 141.

[37] *Ibid.* 147–148. *Cf.* Series A, No. 22, pp. 20, 26; and the dissenting opinions of Judge Negulesco and of M. Dreyfus (*ibid.* 36–37, 43–44).

[38] Series A/B, No. 46, p. 185.

[39] Series B, No. 15, p. 17.

[40] Interpretation is the process of giving a meaning to a text; application is the process of determining its consequences in a given situation. *Cf.* the explanation by M. Ehrlich in Series A, No. 9, p. 39.

As the Court stated in the judgment relating to *German Interests in Upper Silesia*, "the interpretation of other international agreements is indisputably within the competence of the Court if such interpretation must be regarded as incidental to a decision on a point in regard to which it has jurisdiction."—Series A, No. 6, p. 18.

[41] *German Interests in Upper Silesia*, Series A, No. 7, pp. 18–19. Judgment No. 3 related to the Treaty of Neuilly.

[42] Series A, No. 6, p. 14; No. 7, p. 18. But *cf.* the views of Judge Rostworowski in Series A, No. 6, p. 35.

[43] Series A, No. 5, p. 48.

[44] *Ibid.* No. 6, p. 16. *Cf.* pp. 29–30.

[45] *Ibid.* No. 9, pp. 20–24.

[46] Series B, No. 12, p. 20.

[47] Of course the interpretation of a treaty does not "fall solely within the domestic jurisdiction of a single State."—Series B, No. 4, p. 30. In the interpretation of international instruments, an international tribunal should be on its guard against the improper use of analogies based on the interpretation of private instruments by national courts.

[48] Series A/B, No. 40, p. 19.

[49] The chemical formulas in the 1931 Opium Convention are exceptional. See League of Nations Official Journal (1931) 1795.

[50] See *e.g.* Series A, No. 5, p. 49, and No. 22, p. 13; Series B, No. 12, p. 20. This process is sometimes hidden under an imputation to the parties of an intention to arrive at "the best possible solution of the difficulty." See *e.g.* Series B, No. 14, p. 27. Judge Anzilotti has found it to be "a fundamental rule in the interpretation of legal texts" that "when there are two interpretations, one of them attributing a reasonable meaning to each part of the text and the other not fulfilling these conditions, the first must be preferred."—Series A/B, No. 41, p. 62.

[51] Series B, No. 13, p. 19.

[52] Series A/B, No. 44, p. 33.

[53] Series B, No. 2, pp. 23, 39.

[54] Series A/B, No. 44, p. 40.

[55] Dealing with national courts' function of interpretation, Austin characterized the process here described by the terrifying epithets of *bastard* and *spurious* interpretation. —Austin, *Lectures on Jurisprudence* (ed. 3) II, 597, 1029.

[56] The following statement in the *Chorzów Factory Case* indicates that this has been appreciated by the Court: "For the interpretation of Article 23 [of the Geneva Convention between Germany and Poland], account must be taken not only of the historical development of arbitration treaties, as well as of the terminology of such treaties, and of the grammatical and logical meaning of the words used, but also and more especially of the function which, in the intention of the contracting parties, is to be attributed to this provision."—Series A, No. 9, p. 24.

[57] The Court has also refused to be "bound by the views of the interested Governments" in giving an advisory opinion.—Series A/B, No. 44, p. 35.

[58] Series B, No. 8, p. 37.

[59] *Ibid.* 38.

[60] Series B, No. 11, p. 31.

[61] Series B, No. 14, p. 32.

[62] It has been suggested that the criterion of intention is "hardly applicable" to "treaties imposed by force."—Lauterpacht, *Function of Law in the International Community* (1933) 272.

[63] Series A/B, No. 43, p. 144.

[64] In 1919, the writer served as a member of the commissions which drafted the articles in the Treaty of Versailles and in the Polish Minorities Treaty relating to the Kiel Canal and as a member of the drafting committee of the 1919 International Labor Conference. While he shares fully the view expressed by Lord Halsbury in Hilder v. Dexter (1902) A. C. 474, 477, that "the worst person to construe" a text "is the person who is responsible for its drafting," a refreshing of recollection from the official records only confirms his impression that the conferences which drafted these texts did not have their attention drawn to the precise problems presented to the Court in the cases which have called for their interpretation and application.

[65] This may have been true of the provision relating to the Danube, of which the Court said that its authors "were not all well acquainted with the situation which existed before the War between Galatz and Braila," but that they had agreed to maintain "that situation whatever it may have been."—Series B, No. 14, pp. 31–32.

[66] In the *Free Zones Case,* Judges Altamira and Hurst insisted that account should be taken "of human psychology and more particularly of Governmental psychology."—Series A/B, No. 46, p. 182.

[67] It has been suggested that it is the duty of the judge "to find what, having regard to the available data, was the intention of the parties or what the intention of the parties must be presumed to have been" (Lauterpacht, *op. cit.* 130). This makes a farce of the criterion of intention.

[68] Series A/B, No. 50, p. 377.

[69] See especially Series A/B, No. 50, pp. 373, 378.

[70] Series A, No. 9, p. 24.

[71] *Loc. cit.;* Series A, No. 23, p. 26.

[72] Series B, No. 11, p. 37.

[73] *Ibid.* 39; Series A/B, No. 41, p. 61 (dissenting opinion).

[74] Series A, No. 9, p. 24.

[75] Series B, No. 7, p. 20; No. 11, p. 39.

[76] *Ibid.* No. 7, p. 20; Series A/B, No. 50, p. 373.

[77] Series B, No. 12, p. 22.

[78] In the advisory opinion on the *Convention concerning Employment of Women at Night,* a majority of the Court found the terms of Article 3 "in themselves clear and free from ambiguity"; while Judge Anzilotti found them, "to say the least . . . ambiguous."—Series A/B, No. 50, pp. 373, 388.

[79] In one case, the Court referred to the "etymology" of the word and the "current practice of the language."—Series B, No. 10, p. 18.

[80] Series B, No. 2/3, pp. 33, 35.

[81] "If an expression, not in itself of a legal nature, is used in a convention which derives legal consequences from it, it does not in the least follow that" a criterion for interpreting the expression "must be sought in the legislation of the respective contracting States."—Series B, No. 10, p. 21.

[82] Series B, No. 11, p. 39. See also Series A/B, No. 41, p. 60. In a dissenting opinion in the *Eastern Greenland Case,* Judge Anzilotti said that "a literal interpretation fails where it would lead to absurd or inconsistent results."—Series A/B, No. 53, p. 82.

[83] Series A/B, No. 50, pp. 373, 378.

[84] Series B, No. 2, p. 35. See also No. 11, p. 39.

[85] A scientific approach to the problem might also insist on the "context of situation."

[86] Series A/B, No. 46, p. 140. In this case, it was also a matter of some importance to say whether a reference to Article 435 in the special agreement was to be construed as a reference to that article and its annexes.—See *ibid.* 182.

[87] Series B, No. 2, pp. 23, 25.

[88] *Ibid.* No. 13, p. 18.

[89] Series A, No. 1, p. 24.

[90] *Ibid.* No. 7, pp. 33, 48. See also No. 15, p. 31.

[91] Series B, No. 2, p. 23. See also Series A/B, No. 49, p. 317. "A law cannot set up a rule in one article and, changing its mind, a contrary rule in the next article. Any such interpretation must be ill-founded."—Judge Nyholm in Series B, No. 14, p. 76.

[92] Series B, No. 12, p. 21. But see *ibid.* 22.

[93] *Ibid.* No. 11, pp. 39–40.

[94] Series A/B, No. 49, p. 317. See also *ibid.* 321.

[95] *Cf.* Series B, No. 6, p. 37.

[96] Series A, No. 17, p. 42.

[97] Where a text is in one language, it must of course be given a meaning in that language.—Series B, No. 10, p. 18.

[98] This is true of the Covenant of the League of Nations and the Statute of the Court.

[99] The Court frequently refers to the English and French "versions" of its judgments and opinions.

[100] The statement in 1 Oppenheim, *International Law* (ed. 2) 586; (ed. 3) 704; (ed. 4) 765, that in this case "each party is only bound by the text in its own language," seems clearly erroneous; nor can his statement be accepted that "a party cannot claim the benefit of the text in the language of the other party." Oppenheim's statement may have been due to the views expressed by English courts in such cases as Rex v. Brixton Prison [1912] 3 K. B. 190, 197. *Cf.* Ehrlich, *L'Interprétation des Traités* (1928) 24 *Recueil des Cours, Académie de Droit International,* 95–104.

[101] Series B, No. 2. If one version is clear and the other is not, the former might be allowed to prevail.—*Reparation Commission v. German Government* (1923–1924) Ann. Dig. 334.

[102] Series A, No. 2, p. 19.

[103] Series A/B, No. 44, p. 32.

[104] Series A, No. 15, p. 33. It seems difficult to justify the Court's willingness in this case to consider a German argument based upon the attitude taken by Poland in negotiating an agreement with Danzig, even though the Court did not attach "much importance" to the argument.—*Ibid.* 40.

[105] Series A, No. 6, p. 18.

[106] Series B, No. 14, p. 55.

[107] *Ibid.* No. 18, p. 30.

[108] Series A/B, No. 50, p. 388.

[109] Series B, No. 16, pp. 19, 24.

[110] Series A/B, No. 49, p. 317.

[111] Series A, No. 15, p. 33; Series B, No. 17, p. 19.

[112] Series A, No. 9, p. 24.

[113] Series B, No. 6, p. 25.

[114] *Ibid.* No. 14, p. 52.

[115] *Ibid.* No. 12, p. 23.

[116] Series A/B, No. 44, p. 27; Series B, No. 6, p. 25; No. 8, p. 40; No. 13, pp. 19, 28; No. 17, p. 21.

[117] *Ibid.* No. 13, p. 18; No. 17, p. 21; Series A/B, No. 50, p. 383—(Judge Anzilotti dissenting).

[118] Series A, No. 5, p. 49; Series B, No. 14, p. 37.

[119] Series A/B, No. 43, pp. 142, 157; Series A, No. 1, p. 23; No. 23, p. 26.

[120] Mr. Hyde states the task of the interpreter to be "to get at the truth concerning the design of the parties as exemplified by their treaty." See his studies in (1930) 24 Am. J. Int. Law 1; (1933) 27 *ibid.* 502.

[121] Thus, the Covenant of the League of Nations may have to be interpreted less strictly than many other international instruments. In a memorandum signed by President Wilson, M. Clemenceau, and Mr. Lloyd George on May 6, 1919, it was said that "the articles of the Covenant are not subject to a narrow or technical construction."—Miller, *Drafting of the Covenant,* I, 489. See also Ray, *Commentaire du Pacte de la Société des Nations* (1930) 12 ff.

[122] Series B, No. 6, p. 25.

[123] *Ibid.* No. 7, p. 17.

[124] Series A, No. 9, p. 24. See also *ibid.* 25.

[125] Series A/B, No. 50, p. 374. See also Series B, No. 3, p. 57.

[126] Series B, No. 6, p. 37.

[127] *Ibid.* No. 13, p. 19.

[128] Series A/B, No. 50, p. 383.

[129] See Series B, No. 14, p. 34.

[130] This term may also be applied to materials other than preliminary drafts. Using it in this broader sense, the Court may be said to have referred to *travaux préparatoires* in the *Jaworzina Case,* when it expressed a willingness to study instructions given to representatives composing the Conference of Ambassadors in interpreting a decision of that Conference.—Series B, No. 8, p. 26.

[131] Series A, No. 10, p. 16; Series B, No. 14, p. 28; Series A, No. 20/21, p. 30; Series A/B, No. 47, p. 249; No. 50, p. 378.

The Supreme Court of the United States has followed a similar rule with reference to national legislation.—Standard Fashion Co. v. Magrane-Houston Co. (1922) 258 U. S. 346, 356; Ozawa v. U. S. (1922) 260 U. S. 178, 194; Van Camp & Sons v. American Can Co. (1929) 278 U. S. 245, 253; U. S. v. Missouri Pacific R. R. Co. (1929) 278 U. S. 269, 278.

[132] The mere fact that the Council has asked for an interpretation of a provision ought not to cast doubt upon its clarity. *Cf.* Series B, No. 12, p. 25.

[133] See the *Mavrommatis Case,* Series A, No. 2, p. 24; No. 5, p. 47; Series B, No. 9, pp. 17–18; No. 10, p. 16. In their individual opinions, the judges frequently refer to *travaux préparatoires; e.g.* Series A, No. 22, p. 32.

[134] Series A/B, No. 44, p. 33.

[135] *Ibid.* 56.

[136] Series B, No. 2, p. 41.

[137] Series A, No. 10, p. 17.

138 Series B, No. 12, p. 22. See also No. 14, pp. 28–31.

139 Series A, No. 20/21, p. 30.

140 Series A/B, No. 50, pp. 378–380.

141 The element of time may be less important than is here indicated. Where *travaux préparatoires* are referred to in documents or argument before the Court, they will doubtless have been studied even before any conclusions are reached; this fact robs the actual formulations by the Court of some of their importance.

142 Series B, No. 14, p. 31.

143 Series A/B, No. 50, p. 388.

144 Series B, No. 14, p. 32. For the correspondence of the Registrar with the President of the Conference of Ambassadors at Paris, see Series C, No. 13–IV, pp. 2172, 2188.

145 Series B, No. 2, p. 41; Series C, No. 1, pp. 187–189.

146 Series A, No. 23, pp. 41–43.

147 This refers to Denmark, Germany, and Sweden. As to Germany, the statement is somewhat surprising, though it is true that Germany was not represented in the Commission on Ports, Waterways and Railways of the Preliminary Peace Conference at Paris; Denmark and Sweden were not parties to the Treaty of Versailles.

148 The following statement by the French-Mexican Claims Commission seems to be apposite: "Every international convention must be deemed tacitly to refer to general principles of international law for all questions which it does not itself resolve in express terms or in a different way."—*Georges Pinson Case* (1928) (1927–1928) Ann. Dig., Case No. 292.

149 Series A, No. 1, p. 37.

150 Series A, No. 7, p. 42. *Cf. ibid.* 21.

151 Series A, No. 23, pp. 26, 29.

152 *Ibid.* 20.

153 Series B, No. 12, p. 32.

154 *Ibid.* No. 10, pp. 19, 21.

155 *Ibid.* No. 7, p. 17.

156 *Ibid.* No. 13, p. 22.

157 This is admirably shown in the foundations of the public law of the United States as they were laid by Chief Justice John Marshall, and in the decisions of the United States Supreme Court with reference to the Fourteenth Amendment to the Constitution of the United States.

158 Series A, No. 7, p. 74.

159 Series B, No. 8, pp. 20–22.

160 *Ibid.* No. 12, p. 29.

161 *Ibid.* No. 14, p. 28.

162 Series A/B, No. 41, p. 42. Judge Anzilotti also insisted in this case that "account must be taken of the movement... the aim of which is to effect the political union" of Austria and Germany.—*Ibid.* 70.

163 Some of the criticism of the Court's opinion in this case was due to a failure to appreciate the nature of the judicial process which had to be followed in order to reply to the questions put.

164 Series A/B, No. 43, p. 144.

165 *Ibid.* No. 44, p. 27.

[166] Series B, No. 17, p. 21.

[167] Series A, No. 1, p. 23.

[168] Series B, No. 6, p. 38. *Cf.* Series A, No. 7, p. 30.

[169] Series A, No. 9, pp. 22–23.

[170] Series A/B, No. 50, pp. 380–381.

[171] Series A, No. 3, p. 9.

[172] *Cf.* M. Ehrlich's statement, Series A, No. 9, p. 43.

[173] Series A, No. 20/21, p. 119.

[174] In the *Jaworzina Case,* one of the contemporary documents relied upon was not related to the decision to be interpreted.—Series B, No. 8, pp. 33, 38. See also No. 14, p. 58.

[175] Series B, No. 13, p. 19. However, this result might have been rested on reading Part XIII of the Treaty of Versailles as a whole. See also Series B, No. 8, p. 33.

[176] Series B, No. 12, p. 24.

[177] *Cf.* Series A, No. 20/21, pp. 38, 119.

[178] Series B, No. 2, p. 39.

[179] *Ibid.* No. 13, p. 19.

[180] *Ibid.* p. 20. This is particularly true of the Supreme Court of the United States.

[181] *Ibid.* No. 15, pp. 18, 20–21.

[182] See Series A, No. 3, p. 8.

[183] The Supreme Court of the United States has frequently stated that "treaties are to be liberally construed."—See Jordan v. Tashiro (1928) 278 U. S. 123; Nielsen v. Johnson (1929) 279 U. S. 47.

[184] Series B, No. 11, p. 39.

[185] However, the Court said in the *Jaworzina Case* that as the object of a clause in a decision was "one of equity, it must not be interpreted in too rigid a manner."—Series B, No. 8, p. 40.

[186] In their individual opinions, judges have sometimes referred to rules of restrictive interpretation as "presumptions"; *e.g.* Series A, No. 9, p. 40.

[187] Series A/B, No. 46, pp. 138–139, 167.

[188] Series A, No. 22, p. 13. See also No. 24, p. 14.

[189] *Ibid.* No. 1, p. 24; No. 24, p. 12; Series A/B, No. 46, p. 167.

[190] Series A, No. 1, pp. 24–25. In this case, Judge Schucking declared that "all treaties concerning servitudes must be interpreted strictly" (*ibid.* 43). Judges Anzilotti and Huber were reluctant to interpret a treaty so as to limit a State's self-protection, and this consideration was said to apply "with particular force in the case of perpetual provisions without reciprocity which affect the interests of third States."—*Ibid.* 37.

[191] Series A, No. 23, p. 26.

[192] Series B, No. 12, p. 25.

[193] *Ibid.* No. 4, p. 25. See also Series A, No. 2, p. 85; No. 7, pp. 22, 42.

[194] Series A, No. 5, p. 49.

[195] *Ibid.* No. 7, p. 76.

[196] Series A, No. 2, p. 31. *Cf.* No. 7, p. 29.

[197] *Ibid.* No. 20/21, p. 30. *Cf.* No. 7, p. 33.

[198] *Ibid.* No. 20/21, p. 114.

[199] Series A/B, No. 42, p. 121.

LA PROTECTION DES FAIBLES PAR LE DROIT

PAR LOUIS JOSSERAND

LA PROTECTION DES FAIBLES est assurément une des préoccupations les plus constantes du législateur contemporain; elle représente pour lui un but de prédilection, un des articles de foi qui sont inscrits à l'ordre du jour de la politique juridique mondiale: à ce titre, elle ressortit au droit commun législatif comme aussi au droit naturel, tel que nous le concevons aujourd'hui.

Ce n'est pas à toute époque et sans contestation qu'elle obtint cette place d'honneur; une doctrine d'airain lui fut parfois contraire, celle qui prétendait identifier la force avec le droit ou subordonner celui-ci à celle-là. Le droit, affirmait-on, est «la politique de la force»;[1] il est «une force vive»;[2] «la mesure de la puissance de chacun»;[3] et, de même que «celui qui a la force a le droit»[4] ainsi celui qui est faible n'a pas de droit ou n'est investi que d'un droit inférieur, en rapport avec son infirmité.

Cette conception brutale, matérialiste et pessimiste, que notre fabuliste français a condensée dans la formule fameuse, «La raison du plus fort est toujours la meilleure», s'expliquait et recevait son application dans les communautés primitives, à l'âge des cavernes, quand «la force tenait lieu de droit et d'équité,» ou encore à l'époque médiévale, alors que tout titulaire d'un droit devait être capable de le défendre les armes à la main; mais de nos jours, et depuis longtemps déjà, elle exprime une contre-vérité, et le moment n'est pas éloigné où elle fera sourire, après avoir fait trembler; elle sera reléguée, telle une panoplie très ancienne et assez ridicule, dans le musée historique des idées périmées, et nos descendants auront peine à réaliser qu'on ait pris pour le droit lui-même, qui est avant tout, suivant la juste définition de Leibniz, «une puissance morale», ce qui n'est que sa caricature et ce que l'un de nos anciens juristes, Jean Bodin, appelait «le droit des voleurs.»

Car, comme on l'a fort bien écrit, «c'est une singulière illusion qui nous fait voir parfois, dans les commandements de la loi, la consécration de la force: une injonction du droit n'est nullement un impératif imposé par le fort au faible; c'est un impératif imposé à tous par le sentiment de la masse ou la conscience populaire.»[5] Et, à considérer le soin jaloux, l'empressement mis par les législateurs à voler au secours de la faiblesse, on serait tenté de dire, en renversant l'aphorisme émis par Jhering, que le droit est la politique de la faiblesse; il est tout au moins la politique de la protection des faibles par les pouvoirs publics; Thomas Mann n'a-t-il pas constaté, avec un parfait dédain d'ailleurs, que «la loi est l'amie du faible; elle veut tout aplanir; si elle pouvait, elle aplanirait le monde . . .»? Suivant la remarque d'un philosophe du droit, «l'idée du droit est si peu celle de la force, qu'elle n'éclate nulle part avec plus d'énergie qu'en présence de la faiblesse. Si le droit est une puissance, il est dans notre esprit la puissance des faibles comme des forts.»[6] Il est même davantage encore, la puissance des faibles par la puissance des forts; il est l'armure forgée par ceux-ci pour protéger ceux-là, armure de plus en plus efficace, de plus en plus protectrice; en vérité, les faibles sont partis à la conquête du droit.

Et, pour eux ce droit s'est modifié, non seulement dans ses aspects secondaires, mais dans son essence et dans son tréfonds même; il s'est rénové pour s'humaniser. Le concept du droit subjectif a bénéficié de cette rénovation profonde dont il atteste la réalité pratique; jadis, les droits tels que la propriété, la puissance paternelle, ou la puissance maritale, étaient considérés ainsi que des pouvoirs conférant à leurs titulaires des prérogatives absolues, sans contre-partie effective; on y voyait des rapports unilatéraux qui mettaient tous les avantages du même côté, tous les devoirs de l'autre. Puis cette conception simpliste et fruste a vieilli; si elle a reçu un regain de vitalité sous l'action de la Révolution française et par le truchement de la *Déclaration des Droits de l'homme et du citoyen,* marquée au coin d'un individualisme outrancier, elle est tombée, depuis bien des années déjà, dans un discrédit qui s'accuse toujours davantage. Désormais, les droits sont considérés comme des rapports synallagmatiques, imposant à leurs titulaires, en compensation des prérogatives qu'ils leur assurent, des obligations plus ou moins nombreuses et étendues; comme des valeurs relatives et sociales qui doivent être utilisées conformément à l'esprit de l'institution: *l'idée d'équilibre des droits a supplanté le dogme de la souveraineté;* tous les droits ou presque se sont harmonisés en se rangeant sous le signe de l'altruisme; on s'efforce d'assurer à chaque humain son dû, non pas en considération de sa force brutale, de sa puissance, mais bien plutôt de sa valeur sociale, et aussi de sa faiblesse, de son infirmité; on se préoccupe de protéger les faibles plutôt que d'exalter les forts, et, de même qu'on entoure un objet fragile de soins plus attentifs, ainsi la conscience collective veille jalousement sur les plus faibles habitants de la ruche.[7]

Car c'est bien désormais la conscience collective qui est la source première et unique du droit; la règle juridique est élaborée, non par un homme, ou par une oligarchie, ou par un parti, mais par la communauté tout entière dont le Verbe législatif n'est que le mode de révélation officiel, non point exclusif d'ailleurs, car il existe d'autres «organes d'expression du droit»;[8] une loi qui ne répondrait pas aux nécessités, aux aspirations du milieu social pour lequel elle est intervenue, serait condamnée à la stérilité, au non-usage; le législateur moderne ne peut plus remonter les grands courants d'opinion, puisqu'il est lui-même porté par ces courants, puisqu'il est l'interprète de cette opinion: le droit moderne est un phénomène de génération, sinon toujours spontanée, du moins toujours universelle; il sort des entrailles de la nation, et c'est bien pourquoi il pratique plus que jamais, et dans tous les domaines, une politique de protection des faibles, objets de la sollicitude commune.[9]

C'est cette politique que nous voudrions examiner de plus près en essayant d'analyser l'évolution dont elle fut le centre au cours des siècles et qui se poursuit de nos jours encore; la courbe qu'elle décrit est délimitée par les idées suivantes qui en constituent les trois lignes essentielles:

1° Les faibles que protège le droit contemporain ne sont pas toujours ceux que l'on protégeait autrefois;

2° Les mesures de protection auxquelles on a recours ne sont pas toujours celles qui étaient utilisées jadis;

3° Les faibles sont protégés à tel point qu'on se préoccupe à l'inverse de garantir le public contre les mesures de préservation instituées à cette occasion: le garant veut être lui-même garanti.

Une triple évolution se poursuit dans ces trois directions dont nous allons tenter de préciser le sens et la portée.

Nous tirerons, en manière de conclusion, la moralité juridique de cette étude.

I

Les faibles d'aujourd'hui ne sont pas toujours les faibles d'autrefois.

Une évolution à double action s'est accomplie qui a abouti à une transposition de la notion de faiblesse, envisagée sous l'angle juridique: la multitude des faibles, des opprimés, ne comprend plus les mêmes unités, ni les mêmes catégories qu'autrefois; l'oppression exercée par la vie en communauté a changé de nature et d'incidence: d'une part, il est des personnes telles les femmes, jadis considérées comme des faibles, comme des êtres inférieurs, qui sont parvenues de nos jours, presque partout, à la plénitude du statut juridique; tandis qu'à l'inverse il est des individus ou des catégories sociales qui, exposés à de nouveaux ou plus pressants dangers, issus de la vie moderne, ont appelé sur eux l'attention et la protection des pouvoirs publics, tels les ouvriers, les clients des grandes compagnies, les piétons. Certaines causes de faiblesse, de dépendance ont disparu, dans le même temps que d'autres causes apparaissaient et se développaient: la concentration des entreprises, la mécanisation de l'activité humaine.

Examinons le double courant qui s'est ainsi établi et grâce auquel certains faibles sont rentrés dans la normale tandis que d'autres catégories sociales en sont sorties et ont appelé sur elles la protection des pouvoirs publics.

I. *Il est des faibles qui sont rentrés plus ou moins complètement dans la normale, qui ne sont plus protégés ou défavorisés, ou qui le sont moins qu'autrefois.* On songe aussitôt dans cet ordre d'idées et dans cette direction, aux incapacités artificielles (ou du moins nous semblant telles aujourd'hui), qui atteignaient jadis certaines personnes: l'esclavage a disparu de la communauté civilisée; la mort civile qui imitait si cruellement la mort véritable, n'est plus qu'un fâcheux souvenir;[10] quant aux étrangers, ils jouissent, en général, des mêmes droits privés que les nationaux.

Mais ce ne sont pas là les seuls exemples d'accession à la plénitude du statut juridique: les femmes, les mineurs, les prodigues, les personnes morales tendent à une capacité accrue, et, par conséquent, à une protection diminuée.

1. Les *femmes.* En ce qui les concerne, le mouvement libérateur est bien près d'être consommé: incapable dans les sociétés peu évoluées, la femme est devenue, de nos jours, presque complètement et universellement capable, au moins dans le domaine du droit privé.[11]

A vrai dire, la *capitis deminutio* qui la frappait jadis s'expliquait, moins par la «*levitas animi*» et la «*fragilitas sexus*» invoquées par les juristes romains, que par d'autres causes variées, successives, et multiples: par la constitution autocratique de l'Etat et de la famille; par le culte de la force physique; par l'influence de la tradition romaine et des Pères de l'Eglise, et aussi, à une époque moins reculée, par l'insuffisance d'instruction, de culture. Tant de facteurs puissants et convergents avaient condamné la femme à demeurer, sa vie durant, sous une puissance perpétuelle, *patria potestas,* tutelle, *manus* ou *mondium,* puissance qui existait, non point dans son intérêt, mais dans celui de l'Etat, de la famille, de l'ordre public, et des bonnes mœurs. Lorsque ces facteurs de servitude disparurent ou s'atténuèrent, il était naturel que l'infériorité juridique de la femme fût elle-même abolie ou palliée. La famille est devenue, un peu partout, une république domestique; la force physique a cessé de régner dans les relations d'ordre privé; le droit romain a vu s'affaiblir son empire; la femme a accédé à l'instruction et, du même coup, aux carrières libérales, à de nombreuses fonctions publiques, voire, dans certains pays, aux fonctions électives. Dès lors, son incapacité devenait injustifiable et anachronique; on ne comprenait plus que la moitié du genre humain se trouvât protégée et infériorisée par rapport à l'autre moitié; seule la faiblesse appelle la protection, comme seule l'indignité appelle des sanctions juridiques: ayant cessé d'être faible et méritant tous les égards, la femme a cessé d'être incapable, et, du même coup, d'être protégée.

La réforme s'est accomplie ou est en voie de s'accomplir, d'abord pour la femme célibataire, plus tard pour la femme mariée; à l'heure actuelle, on peut dire que, dans tous les pays civilisés, la femme, célibataire et majeure, possède dans les relations du droit privé, la même capacité que l'homme. Quant à la femme mariée, son incapacité a disparu, non seulement dans les pays *anglo-saxons*[12] comme aussi chez les peuples régis par de grandes codifications récentes: *Allemagne;*[13] *Suisse;*[14] *Turquie;*[15] *Chine;*[16] mais aussi dans certains pays latins, en

Italie,[17] en *Espagne,*[18] en *Roumanie,*[19] elle ne subsiste plus guère qu'en *France,* en *Belgique,* et dans certaines républiques *sud-américaines.*[20] Encore a-t-elle subi, dans ces derniers pays, des correctifs notables, à raison tant de l'institution des biens réservés[21] que de la législation relative au commerce,[22] aux Caisses d'épargne,[23] aux pensions civiles ou militaires,[24] au droit syndical;[25] aux sociétés de secours mutuels,[26] etc....

Somme toute, la femme a cessé ou cessera prochainement de figurer dans la catégorie des faibles, des opprimés, des assujettis: le droit privé mondial, en l'émancipant, lui a retiré du même coup la protection dont il l'entourait jadis.

2. Les *mineurs.* Ces incapables n'ont pas bénéficié et ne pouvaient pas bénéficier d'une évolution aussi complète et aussi effective que celle qui a profité à la femme; ils continuent et ils continueront à figurer dans la catégorie des faibles et des protégés: c'est que l'incapacité qui les frappe n'est nullement factice et arbitraire; elle est naturelle et justifiée; elle existe par définition même: qui dit minorité dit faiblesse, donc nécessité d'une protection juridique.

Toutefois, des efforts ont été faits et s'accentuent pour inclure les incapacités tenant à l'âge dans des limites aussi resserrées que possible et pour modeler l'infériorité juridique sur l'infériorité naturelle dont elle doit épouser exactement les contours sans jamais les dépasser.

a) D'une part, on admet l'existence, entre le temps de complète incapacité et celui de la pleine capacité, d'une période intermédiaire au cours de laquelle le mineur bénéficie d'un statut de demi-capacité et de moindre protection.[27] Certains codes ont même établi, entre le premier stade et le deuxième, des frontières précises et rigides, se conformant en cela à la tradition romaine: dès qu'il atteint l'âge de sept ans, l'enfant sort de la période de l'*infantia* et voit s'atténuer sensiblement l'incapacité dans laquelle il se trouvait jusqu'alors; des dispositions de ce genre se retrouvent tant dans le code civil *allemand*[28] que dans le code civil de la République de *Chine.*[29]

b) De plus, cette capacité restreinte du mineur parvenu à l'âge du discernement tend à l'elargissement: non seulement ce mineur est investi de la pleine capacité délictuelle et quasi-délictuelle,[30] mais une législation touffue, qui se retrouve en tous pays, lui ouvre l'épargne,[31] le droit syndical,[32] etc....

c) Le mineur, parvenu à un certain âge—quinze, seize, dix-huit ans, suivant les cas et suivant la législation—accède à la capacité soit en devenant commerçant,[33] soit par le jeu de l'émancipation,[34] ou même à raison d'une déclaration de majorité qui lui octroiera la capacité du majeur lui-même.[35]

d) Enfin, dès qu'il atteint l'âge de la majorité, l'ex-mineur voit s'abaisser toutes les barrières élevées par la loi à raison du jeune âge; les restrictions, jadis formulées dans certains pays pour des actes particulièrement graves, disparaissent aussitôt. C'est ainsi qu'en *France,* une loi du 2 février 1933 vient d'assimiler l'âge de la majorité matrimoniale à la majorité tout court: du moment que le jeune homme ou la jeune fille atteint l'âge de vingt-et-un ans, il est capable de contracter mariage, sans avoir à solliciter de ses parents ni autorisation ni conseil.

L'incapacité tenant à la jeunesse se trouve ainsi atténuée par toute une série de palliatifs, comme est affaiblie par une répercussion nécessaire, la protection aménagée par le législateur en faveur des mineurs parvenus à l'âge de discernement.

3. Les *prodigues.* C'est une question de savoir s'il convient de frapper les prodigues d'une incapacité plus ou moins complète et de protéger contre leur propension à la dissipation tant leur famille qu'eux-mêmes: sont-ils à considérer comme des faibles, dangereux pour leur propre avenir comme pour celui de leur entourage, et, spécialement, de leurs héritiers présomptifs?

Sur ce problème aussi, une évolution s'est dessinée, dans le sens du libéralisme, tout au moins pour ce qui est de la *France.* Anciennement, avant la Révolution, le prodigue était interdit et placé en tutelle, comme le mineur ou l'aliéné; il était incapable de s'obliger comme de faire son testament.[36] Mais notre code civil français s'est montré moins sévère, en autorisant seulement la nomination d'un conseil judiciaire qui doit assister le prodigue dans les actes les plus graves et en excluant donc tout régime de représentation; d'une part, le prodigue peut accomplir seul, en principe, les actes de la vie civile; d'autre part, pour les actes particulièrement dangereux (aliénation, emprunt, procès, etc....) une simple autorisation suffit à l'habiliter, à le relever de son incapacité. L'évolution s'est donc poursuivie dans le sens de l'atténuation de l'incapacité et de l'allégement des mesures de protection.

On s'est demandé s'il ne convenait pas d'aller plus loin dans la voie du libéralisme: il s'est trouvé des économistes pour soutenir que le prodigue en faisant circuler ses biens, fait œuvre économiquement utile,[37] comme il s'est trouvé un tribunal pour déclarer que c'est bien plutôt l'avare qui, ennemi des intérêts généraux de la société, devrait être l'objet de mesures de rigueur: la même thèse avait été présentée déjà: au cours des travaux préparatoires, par le président de la commission de rédaction du code Napoléon, Tronchet.[38]

Cependant, la plupart des législations admettent que la prodigalité est une cause d'incapacité et qu'elle justifie même l'organisation d'une tutelle.[39] Du moins, le droit de provoquer cette mesure est-il, en général, réservé aux proches parents ainsi qu'au conjoint du prodigue, tandis que le code Napoléon l'accorde, solution excessive, à toute la parenté.[40]

4. Les *personnes morales.* Comme certaines personnes humaines, les personnes morales ont vu développer leur capacité en même temps que se relâchait l'appareil protecteur, d'ailleurs établi dans l'intérêt de l'Etat plutôt que dans le leur; pour elles, la progression est particulièrement saisissante, puisqu'elles sont parties de l'inexistence totale pour aboutir à une personnalité et à une capacité plus ou moins étendues. L'essor dont elles ont bénéficié est un des phénomènes les plus remarquables et les plus constants du droit mondial contemporain: tandis que le code Napoléon ne disait rien à leur sujet, le code civil *italien* de 1865 les mentionne déjà, cependant que le code civil *espagnol* de 1889 leur consacre un chapitre, au lieu que le code civil *allemand* leur fait les honneurs d'un titre entier,[41] comme aussi le code civil *suisse*[42] et le code civil de la République de *Chine*:[43] la progression est donc continue, au point que l'on peut augurer de l'âge d'une codification d'après la place qu'elle réserve aux personnes juridiques.

En *France,* l'essor de la personnalité morale fut une loi constante au cours du dernier demi-siècle: non seulement les *sociétés* acquièrent la personnalité, grâce à la jurisprudence, d'abord en matière commerciale, puis dans le domaine civil,[44] mais les *associations,* c'est-à-dire les groupements à but non lucratif, reçoivent, en 1901, un statut assez libéral, puisqu'une simple déclaration suffit, indépendamment de toute autorisation des pouvoirs publics, pour leur conférer une large capacité, en matière contractuelle comme dans le domaine judiciaire;[45] puisqu'aussi les *syndicats professionnels,* reconnus et réglementés par la loi du 31 mars 1884, ont vu leur personnalité singulièrement développée par la loi du 12 mars 1920, de même que les *sociétés de secours mutuels* acquièrent la jouissance de certains droits moyennant un simple dépôt de leurs statuts effectué à la mairie.[46]

Tous ces groupements ont cessé d'être les mineurs qu'ils étaient autrefois; ils sont sortis de la période embryonnaire au cours de laquelle ils végétaient; ils ne sont plus des faibles, mais bien des forts, et qui ont parfois tenté d'abuser de leur force; d'opprimés qu'ils étaient, certains d'entre eux font maintenant figure d'oppresseurs: ils ont conquis au soleil la place à laquelle ils pouvaient légitimement prétendre; ils ont changé de catégorie juridique et sociale.

II. *Il est de nouveaux faibles qui sont sortis récemment de la normale au point d'appeler sur eux la protection du droit.* De nouvelles catégories de faibles sont apparues qui ont provoqué de nouvelles mesures de protection juridique.

Ces faibles d'un nouveau genre, ces faibles «up to date», présentent une caractéristique qui leur est commune: leur faiblesse n'est point inhérente à leur être même; elle n'est point permanente et continue; elle se présente comme intermittente et discontinue; elle est professionnelle ou contractuelle ou fonctionnelle; elle est fonction d'une situation déterminée; elle ne se manifeste que dans les moments où le patient se trouve pris dans l'engrenage d'un ordre économique ou social déterminé et pour lui oppressif; il l'éprouve et il la subit, en quelque sorte *ès qualités,* en tant que travailleur, ou en tant qu'industriel ou commerçant, ou en qualité de client d'une grande compagnie, ou encore en tant que piéton et dans ses rapports avec les autres usagers de la voie publique.

1. Le *travailleur*—et nous entendons par là principalement l'ouvrier, mais aussi à l'occasion l'employé—se trouve, vis-à-vis du patron, plus exactement vis-à-vis de l'établissement dont il constitue un rouage, dans une situation de dépendance juridique et économique qui s'est aggravée tant avec la concentration des capitaux et des entreprises qu'avec la mécanisation de la vie industrielle et commerciale: d'une part, la liberté contractuelle ne saurait exister pratiquement et spon-

tanément entre un ouvrier isolé et une puissante compagnie: celle-ci ne s'attardera pas à discuter avec celui-là les conditions du contrat de travail, mais elle prétendra lui appliquer un règlement élaboré à l'avance et par ses soins; elle lui imposera sa loi. D'autre part, la mécanisation de l'industrie expose l'ouvrier à des risques nouveaux et redoutables contre lesquels il importe de le prémunir, ou dont il convient, s'ils viennent à se réaliser, de l'indemniser: sous l'angle économique comme sous l'angle juridique, la rupture d'équilibre est très accusée qui se produit au détriment de l'ouvrier et qui appelle des mesures de redressement.[47]

2. L'*industriel* et le *commerçant* eux-mêmes passent parfois de la catégorie des forts dans celle des faibles, car eux aussi peuvent être victimes du double phénomène de la concentration des capitaux et de la mécanisation de la vie: la constitution de cartels, de syndicats, de trusts, aura pour conséquence d'établir des monopoles de fait et de tuer les petites entreprises;[48] la concurrence, par ses propres excès, va se dévorer elle-même; il faudra venir au secours des plus faibles qui risquent d'être absorbés, annihilés par les plus forts.

3. Les *clients des grandes compagnies* subissent de plus en plus la loi de celles-ci, car ils ne sauraient prétendre traiter à égalité avec une puissante administration de chemins de fer ou avec une compagnie d'assurances; les conditions des opérations qu'ils passent avec ces sociétés ne sont point débattues; les tractations sont réduites au strict minimum, puisque la compagnie est armée d'un règlement, par elle élaboré et auquel le client se contentera d'adhérer, si mieux il ne préfère s'abstenir; on ne discute pas les conditions d'un transport, au guichet d'une station de chemin de fer, mais on se contente d'entrer dans le modèle d'un contrat préparé à l'avance; on conclut un *contrat d'adhésion* dans lequel on subit la loi du plus fort, sans plus: il faudra, de toute justice, que le droit vienne au secours de tant de faiblesse.

4. Le *piéton*, lui aussi, a changé de catégorie économique et juridique: jadis en sécurité sur la voie publique, il a maintenant à compter avec des usagers mieux armés que lui et dont les véhicules, mus par des moteurs mécaniques, sont pour lui un danger de tous les instants. L'homme de la rue se trouve dans une situation subordonnée et dangereuse par rapport à l'automobiliste qui occupe, vis-à-vis de lui, une

position dominante, sans aucune réciprocité. L'équilibre ainsi rompu doit être rétabli, sur le terrain juridique, par des mesures appropriées, destinées à garantir le faible contre le plus fort, contre l'automobile, contre le tramway, contre l'avion.

Envisagé sous ces différents angles et dans ces différentes situations, l'homme subit la tyrannie de forces supérieures avec lesquelles il est aux prises, avec lesquelles il engage, avec lesquelles il doit engager une lutte inégale qui rappelle celle du pot de terre contre le pot de fer; victime de l'ordre social, économique, scientifique, il est dominé par des forces collectives ou mécaniques redoutables; l'équilibre rompu, en fait, à son détriment, doit être, autant que possible, rétabli, et c'est le droit qui opérera ce redressement; comme toujours, la loi s'affirme ici l'amie du faible à qui elle assure la sécurité que lui refusait le seul jeu des forces économiques et sociales: le juridique aura pour mission de corriger et d'amender l'économique; et plus le déséquilibre aura été grand, plus le risque couru aura été grave, et plus énergique et efficace devra s'affirmer le redressement par le droit.[49]

Entre cette nouvelle catégorie de faibles et l'ancienne, une série de différences sont à noter:

1° Comme nous l'avons déjà signalé, tandis que la faiblesse des femmes, des mineurs, des prodigues, voire de certaines personnes morales, tient à leur être dont elle s'affirme partie intégrante, celle des ouvriers, des petits commerçants ou industriels, des clients des grandes compagnies, des piétons, n'est qu'intermittente et occasionnelle, fonctionnelle.

2° De plus, tandis que la première est imposée systématiquement par la loi, la deuxième dérive seulement du jeu des forces économiques et mécaniques: elle est un résultat, non un but en soi.

3° Les remèdes auxquels on a recours pour venir en aide à ces deux catégories de faibles ne sont pas de même nature.

Mais nous touchons ici au deuxième aspect de l'évolution que nous avions annoncé.

II

Les mesures de protection utilisées aujourd'hui, ne sont pas toujours celles auxquelles on avait recours jadis.

Dans la conception traditionnelle et qui est restée en vigueur, la faiblesse était prémunie contre les abus de force par un système d'incapacités : le mineur, la femme mariée, le prodigue, certaines personnes morales sont déclarées incapables de s'obliger, ou d'aliéner, ou de se léser par leurs engagements, ou de plaider, etc. . . . : c'est donc le protégé lui-même qui devient le centre du régime protecteur institué à son occasion; on paralyse son activité, on l'immobilise, on le fixe sur place afin de lui éviter des déconvenues; ou bien l'acte juridique sera complètement interdit, ou bien il devra être accompli par le représentant de l'incapable, ou encore, parfois, par l'incapable lui-même, mais autorisé, assisté d'un curateur, d'un conseil, d'un mari, du tribunal.

Mais la conception moderne du protectorat des faibles est profondément différente de l'ancienne : généralement, sinon toujours, ce n'est pas la personne du protégé qui devient le siège des mesures protectrices qui ont une incidence tout autre; c'est la partie adverse que l'on atteint et dont on paralyse, dont on conditionne l'activité; c'est le plus fort que l'on maîtrise afin qu'il n'exploite pas injustement le plus faible; le handicap est pour lui, non pour sa victime désignée.

Les procédés employés dans cette voie et en vue de ce but sont fort nombreux et très variés : les uns sont *préventifs,* tandis que d'autres sont *sanctionnateurs.*

I. *Mesures préventives.*

Elles affectent elles-mêmes des aspects divers :

1. Il arrive que le législateur proscrive certaines clauses, de nature à mettre le faible à la discrétion du fort. Les dispositions prises dans cet ordre d'idées sont fort nombreuses et varient avec les législations. Pour ce qui est du droit *français,* nous signalerons que, dans le contrat de *transport,* les clauses tendant à exonérer le transporteur de la responsabilité qui lui incombe à raison de la perte ou des avaries des marchandises qui lui avaient été confiées, sont frappées de nullité;[50] que, dans le *gage,* pareil traitement est infligé à la clause qui autoriserait le créancier, à défaut de paiement, à s'approprier la chose engagée ou à en disposer sans observer les formalités prescrites par la loi;[51] que, dans le contrat d'*assurance,* une multitude de clauses tendant à sacrifier les intérêts de l'assuré sont également frappées par la loi.[52]

2. Le législateur prend des mesures afin d'éviter que, dans les contrats intervenus entre de puissantes compagnies et leurs clients, des clauses soient insérées subrepticement et par surprise, qui n'auraient pas été effectivement connues du destinataire. Notamment, il est à craindre que, dans les polices d'assurance ou dans les titres de transport, des conditions draconiennes ne soient sournoisement glissées dans le corps d l'*instrumentum,* lequel est rédigé par l'assureur ou par le transporteur, de sa seule autorité et sans qu'il en eût conféré avec ses clients. Aussi exige-t-on que, dans la police d'assurances, les diverses clauses soient insérées en *caractères apparents,*[53] et même, pour celles qui édictent des nullités ou des déchéances, en *caractères très apparents.*[54] Plus généralement, la jurisprudence française se réserve la faculté de rechercher si la clause introduite dans un contrat d'adhésion a bien effectivement été connue de celui à qui elle est opposée,[55] en cas de négative, il n'en est point fait application à celui qu'elle visait.

3. En ce qui concerne les ouvriers et aussi parfois les employés, la législation ouvrière édicte toute une série de mesures destinées à assurer la sécurité, la santé, la dignité du travailleur; toute une police de l'industrie est ainsi aménagée, cependant qu'une tutelle est exercée par les pouvoirs publics en vue d'assurer l'observation exacte de la réglementation légale du travail industriel ou commercial.[56]

II. *Droit sanctionnateur.*

Si les mesures préventives sont demeurées infructueuses, si le faible a été exploité, s'il a été blessé, si l'équilibre a été effectivement rompu entre les intérêts en présence, alors interviennent des mesures de réparation: lorsqu'on n'a pu prévenir le mal, on doit s'efforcer de le guérir ou de l'apaiser; tel est le rôle des sanctions juridiques qui interviennent alors et dont nous ne retiendrons que celles qui intéressent le droit privé.

1. Lorsque, dans la formation d'un contrat, l'une des parties a été dominée par l'autre qui a exploité sa faiblesse ou sa détresse, il est juste et il est désirable que l'acte tombe, vicié qu'il est dans son origine: la lésion, du moins si elle a été volontairement, consciemment causée à la victime, doit être pour celle-ci, une cause de nullité ou de rescision du contrat.

C'est là une idée juste et féconde, qui tend à s'acclimater dans les législations contemporaines; elle a peu pénétré jusqu'ici dans le droit *français,* qui n'attribue à la lésion un caractère dirimant que dans un petit nombre de contrats ou encore si elle a été subie par un mineur; mais elle est devenue familière à d'autres pays et son succès s'affirme pour ainsi dire chaque année.[57] La disposition-type à cet égard est celle du code civil *allemand* qui frappe de nullité «l'acte juridique par lequel quelqu'un, en exploitant le besoin, la légèreté ou l'inexpérience d'autrui, obtient, pour lui ou pour un tiers, qu'en échange d'une prestation on promette ou que l'on fournisse des avantages patrimoniaux qui excèdent de telle sorte la valeur de la prestation, qu'en tenant compte des circonstances, ces avantages soient, par rapport à la prestation, dans une disproportion choquante.»[58] La formule, encore qu'assez lourde et indigeste, a fait fortune; on la retrouve, sous une forme approchée, dans le code fédéral *suisse* des obligations,[59] dans le code civil des *Soviets,*[60] dans le code civil de la République de *Chine,*[61] dans le code *libanais* des obligations,[62] comme aussi dans le projet *franco-italien* d'un code des obligations.[63] Dans ces différents pays et d'après ces différents textes, la rupture volontaire de l'équilibre des intérêts vicie le contrat dans son origine et dans son essence; elle fait de lui un contrat mort-né.

2. La théorie de l'*abus des droits,* ancienne par ses origines, jeune par son essor et par sa systématisation, figure au premier rang parmi les idées-forces qui viennent au secours du faible et qui tendent à mettre le droit au service de la justice. Elle est issue de ce postulat que les droits subjectifs ne sont point absolus, mais relatifs; qu'ils doivent être exercés, non dans un but quelconque, mais en fonction de leur esprit, de leur finalité; qu'ils ne sauraient davantage se rebeller contre leur fonction sociale qu'un cours d'eau ne pourrait refluer vers sa source; qu'ils ont pour mission d'assurer le règne de la justice, non celui de l'illégalité; que ce sont des armes à utiliser, non à tort et à travers, mais à bon escient, dans le plan social, *civiliter;* leur titulaire, s'il les fait dévier de leur direction, commet une faute, volontaire ou non, et engage donc sa responsabilité: *summum jus, summa injuria.*[64]

Il en va ainsi non seulement si ce titulaire a agi malicieusement, méchamment, mais aussi du moment qu'il a détourné, fût-ce inconsciemment, son droit de sa destination, du moment qu'il en a faussé l'esprit: le *détournement des droits privés* est illicite au même titre et pour les mêmes raisons que le *détournement de pouvoir*: le droit privé s'apparente ainsi, pour ce qui est de l'essence et de l'utilisation des droits, au droit administratif.

Cette thèse féconde trouve son application avec l'immense majorité des droits: propriété, action ou défense en justice, voies d'exécution, puissance paternelle, puissance maritale, libertés individuelles et libertés comparatives, droits issus des contrats, etc.... C'est seulement si le titulaire peut invoquer un *motif légitime* qu'il exercera son droit impunément; sinon, il devra réparer les dommages causés par son initiative incorrecte.

Il est manifeste qu'un tel *standard,* essentiellement social et moralisateur, est de nature à fournir au faible un rempart efficace contre l'aggression du plus fort; avec lui, c'est la fin qui justifie les moyens; ce ne sont plus les moyens qui justifient la fin. Aussi comprendra-t-on qu'il pénètre dans toutes les législations modernes pour assouplir, pour canaliser et pour moraliser le droit subjectif: son essor est un des phénomènes cardinaux du droit moderne contemporain.[65]

3. Plus généralement, la théorie de la *responsabilité,* elle-même en pleine transformation et en plein développement, s'efforce de venir au secours de la faiblesse; de plus en plus, elle s'aménage en vue d'assurer une réparation à ceux qui, professionnellement ou non, journellement ou d'aventure, sont aux prises avec des puissances redoutables auxquelles ils doivent s'abandonner purement et simplement, sans être à même de les diriger efficacement: en présence du déchaînement de forces mécaniques qu'il n'a déclenchées que pour en devenir le sujet et l'esclave, l'homme en est réduit à un rôle passif qui fait parfois de lui une victime; du moins faut-il qu'il obtienne une réparation, qu'il trouve, dans le domaine juridique, la sécurité que lui refuse le monde physique: de là l'élargissement du concept de la responsabilité qu'on s'efforce de mettre au diapason de la vie moderne, de son intensité et de ses risques.

Le problème a été abordé de plusieurs côtés; des procédés nombreux ont été imaginés afin de refouler l'antique notion romaine de la faute aquilienne, de la faute prouvée, laquelle n'est plus à la mesure du monde contemporain. Tous ces procédés se ramènent, dans les grandes lignes, à deux vastes techniques, à deux disciplines de grand style: d'une part, on s'est efforcé d'*objectiver* la responsabilité, d'autre part, on a tenté de la ramener au concept contractuel, de la «*contractuelliser.*»

a) L'*objectivation* de la responsabilité affecte elle-même différents aspects et plusieurs degrés.

Parfois—et c'est la solution la plus radicale—on l'a assise sur le concept du *risque,* en la dissociant ainsi complètement de la notion subjective et romaine de la faute; l'auteur du dommage est responsable, non pas en tant que coupable, mais en tant que «faiseur d'actes», à raison de son initiative et parce que c'est lui qui a créé, dans son intérêt ou dans sa fonction, le risque aujourd'hui réalisé: bien que moralement irréprochable, il doit indemniser la victime de son geste, de son initiative, de son action. Avec cette thèse, l'objectivation de la responsabilité est complète et le nœud gordien se trouve tranché qui, pendant des siècles, avait uni indissolublement les deux concepts de la faute et de l'obligation délictuelle; le demandeur obtient satisfaction sans avoir à prouver l'imprudence ou la négligence du défendeur; le fardeau de la preuve qui pesait jadis si lourdement sur ses épaules, se trouve allégé: victime de sa faiblesse, il a du moins pour lui, devant les prétoires, la force effective du droit: il sera indemnisé.

Cette conception—la seule qui convienne à une société agissante comme la nôtre,[66] puisqu'elle fait très justement de la responsabilité la rançon de l'autorité et de l'initiative humaines,—a été consacrée par les législations et les jurisprudences de maints pays, soit en ce qui concerne les accidents éprouvés par les ouvriers au cours de leur travail et mis d'autorité à la charge du chef d'entreprise,[67] soit pour les accidents de chemins de fer,[68] soit encore pour les accidents d'automobile: dans ce dernier ordre d'idées, il y a lieu de réserver une mention spéciale, à raison de son importance et de son caractère récent, à la loi fédérale *suisse* du 15 mars 1932 sur la circulation des véhicules automobiles et des cycles, qui, confirmée par un *referendum,* édicte la responsabilité de plein droit du détenteur, à raison des dommages causés par l'emploi du véhicule,[69] n'admettant comme causes d'exonération que la force majeure ou la faute grave du lésé ou d'un tiers.[70]

La jurisprudence, moins hardie et moins puissante que le législateur, ne pousse pas aussi loin l'objectivation de la responsabilité: respectueuse de la tradition, elle maintient, du moins en *France,* la notion de la faute, mais en la rendant aussi peu gênante que possible, grâce à des présomptions: lorsqu'un dommage a été causé par une chose inanimée—automobile, locomotive, ascenseur, batterie mécanique, etc. . . .—elle considère que le propriétaire, plus exactement le gardien de cette chose, doit être présumé en faute, et elle maintient cette présomption envers et contre tout, réserve faite seulement de la force majeure, du fait des tiers et de la faute de la victime. Les derniers arrêts de la Cour de cassation française vont plus loin encore en évoquant, non plus une présomption de faute, mais seulement une ***présomption de responsabilité.***[71] Ainsi ce concept de la faute, venu des profondeurs du droit romain, s'estompe de plus en plus dans le passé; après l'avoir effectivement consacré, nos tribunaux se sont contentés de lui faire quelques politesses; aujourd'hui, ils tendent à l'oublier complètement, du moins lorsque le dommage a été causé par l'intermédiaire d'une chose ou d'un animal: l'objectivation de la responsabilité se réalise ainsi par étapes successives, sans que le but à atteindre soit jamais perdu de vue.[72]

b) Juge et législateur ont eu parfois recours à un tout autre procédé pour améliorer la situation de la victime d'un dommage: ils se sont efforcés de faire passer le délictuel dans le contractuel, de «contractueliser» la responsabilité en la rattachant, bon gré mal gré, à un contrat précédemment intervenu entre la victime et celui à qui on veut imposer le fardeau de la responsabilité.

Dans ce but, on fait produire au contrat, d'autorité, des obligations jusque-là insoupçonnées: par exemple, on considérera que, dans le transport de personnes, le transporteur promet au voyageur la sécurité absolue au cours du voyage; si donc ce voyageur est tué ou blessé c'est que le contrat a été inexécuté et la responsabilité du transporteur se trouvera engagée, contractuellement et cela de plein droit, au moins jusqu'à la preuve contraire qui ne pourra résulter que de la force majeure ou de la faute de la victime. Le demandeur se trouve ainsi, dans le procès en indemnité, dans une situation très favorable: ayant prouvé l'accident de transport, il va demeurer sur la défensive et voir venir son adversaire.

La jurisprudence *française* a ainsi inclus de vive force une obligation de sécurité absolue soit dans le transport de personnes,[73] soit dans les jeux forains,[74] soit dans le contrat conclu entre le directeur d'un manège et ses clients[75] ou encore dans le contrat d'hôtellerie.[76]

Il est à noter que, pour le transport de personnes, cette thèse dite de la *responsabilité contractuelle* a été législativement consacrée en *Belgique*[77] et dans le *Grand-Duché de Luxembourg.*[78]

III

Des mesures sont prises pour protéger le public contre le régime de protection institué en faveur des faibles.

Le protectorat dont bénéficient les faibles n'est point sans danger pour le public qui peut en subir fâcheusement et injustement la répercussion : il est à craindre que la faiblesse ne devienne une force à raison de l'inaptitude qu'elle implique, pour celui qui est atteint, à jouer un rôle sur la scène juridique; il en est ainsi du moins pour la faiblesse telle que la concevait la tradition avec son cortège d'incapacités et de nullités, armes à double tranchant, susceptibles de blesser des innocents et de causer des dégâts injustifiés. Aussi des mesures sont-elles prises pour sauvegarder les droits du public et pour secourir la bonne foi.

1. Ce sont d'abord, autant que possible, *des mesures de publicité*: des dispositions sont prises, par les législations des divers pays, pour divulguer l'état civil des personnes en faisant connaître leur âge, leur mariage, leur régime matrimonial, leur divorce, leur interdiction, etc.... Grâce à ce régime de publicité, qui gagnerait à être développé, nous pouvons traiter en connaissance de cause, renseignés que nous sommes sur la capacité de notre contre-partie; nous savons si nous avons en face de nous un faible, un incapable, spécialement protégé par le droit.

2. Dans une conception qui tend à prévaloir, on admet que la victime d'un *délit* ou d'un *quasi-délit* commis par un incapable—enfant ou aliéné—a droit à une réparation pécuniaire : encore qu'irresponsable l'auteur du fait dommageable pourra être condamné à réparer, au moins partiellement, le préjudice causé. En pareille occurrence, et en vertu d'une curieuse objectivation de la responsabilité, c'est moins la

personne que le patrimoine lui-même qui se trouve obligé, dans une mesure que le juge arbitrera en toute équité.[79]

3. De plus, et pour ce qui est des incapables doués de discernement; il est généralement admis qu'ils n'ont plus droit à la protection du législateur lorsque, dans les tractations qui ont précédé la conclusion d'un contrat, ils se sont rendus coupables de manœuvres dolosives, frauduleuses, en vue de faire croire à leur complète capacité ou à l'assentiment de leur représentant légal: la sanction, qui consiste dans le refus de l'action en nullité, est alors adéquate à la faute commise: le mensonge devient la vérité et l'acte conclu sous son empire est inattaquable.[80]

4. Enfin, malgré l'annulation du contrat qu'il avait passé irrégulièrement l'incapable demeure tenu dans la mesure de l'enrichissement par lui réalisé et conservé.[81]

IV

Conclusion

Ainsi, en tout pays,[82] des mesures sont prises pour venir au secours des nouveaux faibles, de ceux qui subissent l'oppression des forces économiques et sociales du monde contemporain; ainsi se renouvelle, dans ses fondements comme dans sa réalisation, le sujet dont nous venons de donner une sommaire esquisse.

L'étude de cette évolution universelle nous amène, entre autres, aux conclusions suivantes:

1° Les raisons qui déterminent, de nos jours, la faiblesse de certains individus et qui les infériorisent par rapport aux autres, sont d'ordre économique ou mécanique: elles n'ont donc, à la différence de celles qui motivèrent, dans le passé, certaines infirmités juridiques, rien d'artificiel, rien d'arbitraire; elles correspondent à une réalité brutale, non à des préjugés ou à une mystique sociale.[83]

2° C'est pourquoi le remède consiste, non plus dans des incapacités, mais tout au contraire dans des avantages, dans des privilèges: les mesures de protection ont leur siège, non dans la personne du protégé, mais bien plutôt dans la personne de son adversaire, de son oppresseur, de son contradicteur possible; on réfrène la force plutôt qu'on ne souligne, qu'on ne consacre officiellement et directement la faiblesse.

3° *Le nouveau système est dominé par l'idée de risque*: ceux qui doivent être protégés et sur lesquels les pouvoirs publics établissent un protectorat effectif, ce sont ceux qui courent des risques anormaux, exceptionnels, injustes: les ouvriers au travail, les voyageurs en cours de transport, les piétons qui traversent la chaussée, ce sont ceux qui se trouvent en état d'*insécurité matérielle* et à qui on confère, pour cette raison, un surcroît de *sécurité juridique*: ceci compense cela, autant qu'il est possible.

Comme toujours, le problème de responsabilité est un problème d'équilibre des droits: lorsque l'un des plateaux de la balance s'élève alors que l'autre s'abaisse, le droit intervient pour remettre les choses dans l'ordre, pour ramener le fléau à la position horizontale. La tâche est de plus en plus difficile, à mesure que la vie se complique et qu'elle devient plus intense; le besoin se fait alors sentir d'asseoir la responsabilité sur des bases plus larges que celles dont avait pu se contenter le peuple romain; il faut, de toute nécessité, faire appel à des notions nouvelles, plus amples et plus fécondes que celle de la faute aquilienne, et, au premier rang, à la notion de risque; dans une société où se multiplient les risques de toute nature, les systèmes de responsabilité et de protection des faibles ne peuvent être rationnellement basés que sur la notion même du risque; en pareille occurrence, le législateur doit faire de l'homéopathie juridique et combattre le mal par le mal lui-même qui devient son propre spécifique; tout autre traitement serait inopérant, parce qu'il passerait à côté du problème et qu'il ne serait pas exactement approprié à la situation: aux grands maux les grands remèdes.

NOTES TO JOSSERAND ESSAY

[1] Jhering, *Zweck im Recht* (traduction française de De Meulenaere, *L'Evolution du droit*), p. 169.

[2] Jhering, dans *La Lutte pour le droit.*

[3] Schopenhauer.

[4] Gœthe, dans le second *Faust.*

[5] G. Cornil, *Le Droit privé*, p. 20.

[6] Fouillée, *L'Idée moderne du droit*, p. 59.

[7] On a pu dire que la grande idée qui préside à l'évolution du système juridique moderne, est celle de l'*humanisation des pouvoirs* conférés aux individus ou aux collectivités —Emilio Novoa, *El derecho de los débiles* (Madrid, 1930), p. 135.

[8] G. Cornil, *op. cit.*, p. 46 et suiv.

[9] V. Emilio Novoa, *op. cit.*

[10] En France, la mort civile a été abolie par une loi du 31 mai 1854.

[11] V. Paul Gide, *Etude sur la condition privée de la femme.*

[12] En Angleterre, ce sont les *Acts* de 1870 et de 1882 qui ont accordé à la femme mariée la même capacité qu'à la femme célibataire.

[13] C. civ. *allemand*, art. 1 et suiv.

[14] C. civ. *suisse*, art. 13 et suiv.; art. 163.

[15] Le c. civ. *turc* est reproduit du c. civ. suisse.

[16] C. civ. de la République de *Chine*, art. 12 et suiv.

[17] L. *italienne* du 17 juillet 1919.

[18] Constitution de la nouvelle République *espagnole*, art. 25, 36, 40, 43.

[19] L. *roumaine* du 20 avril 1932, modifiant l'art. 194 du c. civ. *roumain* de 1865. V. Alexandre C. Angelesco, *L'Abolition de l'incapacité de la femme mariée roumaine;* Popesco-Ramniceano, «L'Abolition de la femme mariée en Roumanie», *Bulletin de la Société de Législation comparée*, 1933, p. 186.

[20] Pour le *Brésil*, v. Rodrigo Octavio, «La Codification du droit civil au Brésil», *Rev. trim. dr. civ.*, 1930, p. 1029.

[21] V. pour la *France*, la loi du 13 juillet 1907, modifiée par celles du 19 mars 1919 et du 8 juin 1923; pour la *Belgique*, la loi du 20 juillet 1932. (Un commentaire de cette dernière loi a été donné par Mme Gevers dans la *Belgique judiciaire*, 1933, fasc. 1.)

[22] C. comm. *français*, art. 5.

[23] V. pour la *France*, les lois du 8 avril 1881 et du 20 juillet 1895, art. 16.

[24] L. 28 déc. 1922, art. 26.

[25] L. 31 mars 1884, art. 4, mod. par l. 12 mars 1920.

[26] L. 1er avril 1898, art. 3, par. 2.

[27] V. sur ce point pour le droit *français*, L. Josserand, *Cours de droit civil positif français*, 2e éd., t. I, n° 312 et suiv.

[28] C. civ. *allemand*, art. 104 et 106.

[29] C. civ. de la République de *Chine*, art. 13, para. 2: «le mineur qui a accompli sa septième année a une capacité d'exercice des droits restreinte.»

[30] «*Malitia supplet œtatem*», c. civ. *Français*, art. 1310.

[31] Loi *française* du 20 juillet 1895, art. 16.

[32] Loi *française* du 31 mars 1884, mod. par celle du 12 mars 1920, art. 4.

[33] C. comm. *français*, art. 2 et 6.

[34] C. civ. *français*, art. 481 et suiv.

[35] C. civ. *allemand*, art. 3; c. civ. de la République de *Chine*, art 13, para. 3. Pour la *Suisse*, v. Rossel et Mentha, *Manuel de droit civil suisse*, t. I, p. 78.

[36] Pothier, qui s'explique sur ce point, dénonce le caractère arbitraire et factice des mesures prises contre le prodigue (Pothier, *op. cit.*, t. II, pp. 29, 58).

[37] *Sic*, Cauwès, *Cours d'économie politique*, 3ᵉ éd., t. I, nº 415 et 424; comp. Colson, *Traité d'économie politique*, 2ᵉ éd., t. I, p. 119.

[38] Fenet, *Travaux préparatoires*, t. X, p. 684 et suiv.

[39] *Sic*, c. civ. *allemand*, art. 6; c. civ. *suisse*, art. 369 et suiv.; avant-projet de code du droit *musulman algérien*, art. 239.

[40] C. civ. *français*, art. 490 et 514.

[41] C. civ. *allemand*, art. 21 à 89.

[42] C. civ. *suisse*, art. 52 à 89.

[43] C. civ. de la République de *Chine*, art. 25 à 65.

[44] Req. 23 fév. 1891 (D.P. 1891, 1, 337; S. 1892, 1, 73).

[45] L. 1ᵉʳ juillet 1901, art. 6.

[46] L. 1ᵉʳ avril 1898, art. 4.

[47] V. Pic, *Traité élémentaire de législation industrielle*, 6ᵉ éd., *passim*.

[48] J. Tchernoff, *Ententes économiques et financières*, Paris, 1933.

[49] V. les arrêts du Conseil d'Etat français, du 24 déc. 1924 (D.P. 1925, 3, 9, note de M. J. Appleton) et du 29 déc. 1926 (S. 1927, 3, 105, note de M. Hauriou).

[50] C. com. *français*, art. 103, § 3, ajouté par une loi du 17 mars 1905.

[51] C. civ. *français*, art. 2078, § 2.

[52] L. *française* du 13 juillet 1930 sur *le contrat d'assurance terrestre*, art. 2.

[53] L. *française* du 13 juillet 1930, art. 8, § 1.

[54] Même loi, art. 9.

[55] *Sic*, Paris, 15 mars 1922, *Rev. trim. dr. civ.* 1922, p. 896; comp. civ. 31 juillet 1930, S. 1931, 1, 281 avec la note de M. Gény.

[56] V. Pic, *op. cit.*, p. 357 et suiv.

[57] V. L. Josserand, *Les Mobiles dans les actes juridiques du droit privé*, nº 96 et suiv.

[58] C. civ. *allemand*, art. 138.

[59] C. fédéral *suisse* des obligations, art. 21.

[60] C. civ. des *Soviets*, art. 33 et 150.

[61] C. civ. de la République de *Chine*, art. 74.

[62] C. *libanais* des obligations, art. 214. Ce code, promulgué le 9 mars 1932, entrera en vigueur en oct. 1934.

[63] Projet *franco-italien* de code des obligations, élaboré par le Comité d'Union législative, art. 22.

[64] Sur cette théorie de l'*abus des droits*, v. L. Josserand, *De l'esprit des droits et de leur relativité*, Paris, 1927; *Cours de droit civil positif français*, 2ᵉ éd., t. II, nº 428 et suiv.; *Sur la relativité des droits*, dans la *Revue internationale de la théorie du droit*, de Brno, 1928, p. 143.

[65] V. c. civ. *allemand*, art. 226 et 862; 1353, 1357, 1358; c. civ. *autrichien*, art. 1295; c. civ. *suisse*, art. 2; c. civ. des *Soviets*, art 1er; c. civ. de la République de *Chine*, art. 148; projet de c. civ. *polonais*, art. 18; projet *franco-italien* du code des obligations, art. 74; code *libanais* des obligations, art. 124.

[66] Comme on l'a justement constaté, «the best way to secure proper care and caution in present-day society is to throw the risk of damage upon the person who chooses to act» (Rufus C. Harris, «Liability without Fault», *Tulane Law Review*, 1932, p. 368).

[67] V. pour la *France*, la loi du 9 avril 1898 et les lois subséquentes intervenues dans le même ordre d'idées. En *Amérique*, les mêmes principes ont prévalu dans les Workmen's Compensation Acts, adoptés dans la plupart des Etats-Unis (Burdick, *Law of Torts*, 4e éd., p. 17).

[68] L'Organisation objective de la responsabilité des entreprises de transport a été assurée par différentes lois, *prussienne, allemande, autrichienne, hongroise, suisse*. V. notamment la loi *allemande* du 7 juin 1871 qui consacre le système de la responsabilité légale, du fait de l'exploitation (Haftpflicht).

[69] Loi *suisse* du 15 mars 1932, art. 37, § 1.

[70] Même loi, art. 37, § 2.

[71] Ch. réun. 13 fév. 1930 (D.P. 1930, 1, 57, avec les conclusions de M. le Procureur Général Paul Matter, le rapport du conseiller M. Le Marc Hadour, et la note de M. G. Ripert).

[72] Sur le mouvement d'objectivation de la responsabilité dans les *Etats-Unis d'Amérique*, v. outre l'étude précitée de Rufus C. Harris, les ouvrages de Wigmore, *Responsibility for Tortious Acts*, de Burdick, *Law of Torts*, de Thayer, *Liability without Fault*, 1916.

[73] Civ. 21 nov. 1911 (S. 1912, 1, 73, note de Ch. Lyon-Caen).

[74] Nancy, 26 juin 1925; Paris, 22 fév. 1926 (D.P. 1927, 2, 27, note de M. Lalou); *Lyon*, 7 déc. 1928 (D.P. 1929, 2, 17, note de L. Josserand).

[75] Lyon, 1er avril et 21 oct. 1922 (D.P. 1924, 2, 51).

[76] Lyon, 24 juin 1920 (D.H. 1922, 2, 40).

[77] Loi *belge* du 25 août 1891, art. 4.

[78] Loi *luxembourgeoise* du 8 fév. 1908.

[79] (1) V. c. civ. *allemand*, art. 829; C. féd. *suisse* des obligations, art. 54; C. *libanais* des obligations, art. 122, para. 3; projet de code *franco-italien* des obligations, art. 76.

[80] (2) V. c.civ. de la République de *Chine*, art. 83; projet de code *franco-italien*, art. 75.

[81] (3) *Sic*, c. civ. *français* 1312.

[82] L'*Angleterre* ne suit ce mouvement qu'avec lenteur: c'est que, dans ce pays, la tradition revêt une autorité particulière et oppose une force d'inertie difficilement surmontable; le respect du passé hypothèque lourdement l'avenir; notamment le droit jurisprudentiel n'est pas doué, en Angleterre, de la vertu évolutive qui, en France, lui permet de s'adapter à de nouvelles conditions économiques ou sociales. V. sur ce point une étude de F. P. Walton, «Delictual Responsibility in the Modern Civil Law», dans la *Law Quarterly Review*, janv. 1933, p. 70, et notamment pp. 92 et 93.

[83] Suivant la juste remarque de Rufus C. Harris (*op. cit.*), «Back of all doctrine, economic interests are the final and determining influences which eventually shape and vitalize all legal dogma of each generation.»

SOME RECENT SUBROGATION PROBLEMS IN THE LAW OF SURETYSHIP AND INSURANCE*

BY STEPHEN I. LANGMAID

VAST EXTENSION within recent years of the use of both suretyship and insurance as protective devices has naturally reflected novel problems, the solutions of which are frequently perplexing. It is not, however, with the construction of such contracts or the rights of the obligee that this essay is concerned, but rather with the intricate relations arising out of the multiplication of sureties and insurers in a single set of circumstances. In view of the present economic condition, with its numerous insolvencies and bankruptcies, questions involving the rights of sureties both for and with other sureties, as well as sureties for different principals, will in increasingly frequent measure press upon the courts for answer.

The fundamental problems between a principal and his surety and between cosureties have been worked out with considerable unanimity of opinion. The surety is entitled to complete indemnity, complete subrogation, or complete exoneration as against his principal; but as against his cosurety he is entitled only to contributive indemnity, contributive subrogation, and contributive exoneration. Subrogation, while frequently possessing advantages in excess of those obtainable by a simple suit for indemnity or contribution, is nevertheless but a device or aid for securing indemnity or contribution, while the bill for exoneration is only a sort of anticipatory indemnity or contribution in the nature of *quia timet* relief. Simply stated, the purpose is to put the ultimate loss, as between the parties concerned, where it fairly belongs. If a surety is made to pay, it is only just that he should recover in full from the principal debtor directly by indemnity or through the creditor by subrogation. Where there are two cosureties, each fully liable, and one is made to pay more than his share, the doctrine of contribution permits equalization of loss between them. The equities

* This essay has appeared in 47 Harv. L. Rev. 976.

between these obligors are conceded to be equal, and that one should bear the whole burden while the other escapes scot-free merely because the creditor chose the former is repugnant to our theory of justice. It is this principle that lies at the foundation of the relations to be considered; only an examination of the equities in each case will produce the true solution.

SURETY AND QUASI-SURETY

PROCEEDING from the simpler to the more complex questions, there will be first considered disputes arising between a true surety on the one hand, namely, one whose obligation is based upon contract the express object of which is to bear the risk of nonperformance by a principal, and on the other hand one who is actually liable to the creditor of the first but whose liability rests either upon rules of law independent of contract or upon a contract whose purpose is not suretyship. The latter, to give him a concise name, may be called an involuntary surety, a surety by operation of law, a constructive surety, or a quasi-surety. An example will clarify. A bailee under bond for the proper return of the property sells it to a third person who pays value and acts in good faith but who, nevertheless, is technically a tortfeasor to the bailor. The latter may collect from the bailee, the surety on the bond, or the purchaser, but payment in full by any one will satisfy the bailor's claim. If either the surety or the purchaser pays, he can come back upon the bailee. On the contrary the bailee, the "primary" debtor, has recourse against neither of the others. Thus in substance the bailee is principal with two sureties. What are the relations between the bond surety and the quasi-surety? Four solutions are possible. (1) The law might leave the loss between the two as the creditor's choice of collection has dictated. Such a result, however, is inconsistent with the equitable principles which, as indicated, lie behind the theory that the choice of remedy by the creditor must not be permitted to determine the rights of recourse between surety and principal and between cosureties. Imposition of the burden should not depend upon chance or capricious choice, the relative ease of collection by the creditor from one rather than the other, or, certainly, upon collusive arrangements by the creditor and one of them to throw the loss on the other.[1] (2) The ultimate loss should rest on the quasi-surety. (3) The ultimate loss should rest on the bond surety. (4) The two should be considered cosureties and contributive subrogation decreed.[2]

It is at once obvious that the usual statements in the books that the surety will, upon payment, be subrogated to all the rights and remedies of the creditor, will not be helpful, since they lead either to mutually exclusive results or to a ceaseless circle. The answer to the bailment case will be found in a consideration of the relative equities. Are they equal or is that of one superior to that of the other? The bond surety knowingly and intentionally undertook a risk, while the purpose of the quasi-surety's act was directed essentially to obtaining the property with as little risk as possible. Yet his act contributed with that of the bailee to fix and mature the bond surety's obligation, and, conceding knowledge of the law, he also consciously assumed the danger of lack of title in the bailee. To hold the bond surety primarily liable is in effect to give the quasi-surety the benefit of security for which he neither arranged nor paid. The opposite result, however, gives the bond surety the benefit of the quasi-surety's obligation, compelling the latter to pay twice for the goods and to bear the burden of the bailee's default when the bond surety has guaranteed performance to the bailor. Is it material that the bond surety has been compensated for bearing the risk?[3] If the bailee had not given bond, the quasi-surety would have recourse against no one save the bailee, while if the bailee had willfully or negligently destroyed the property, the bond surety would have no recourse against anyone save the bailee. Under these considerations, is it possible to conclude with assurance that the equity of either is superior? Are the equities not rather equal with the result that either is entitled to contributive subrogation against the other? Yet in cases of this sort the courts seem to have disregarded the possibility of contributive subrogation, sometimes saying that in order to have subrogation, the plaintiff's equity must be greater than the defendant's and that equality of equities is fatal to subrogation.[4] If such a statement were correct, the ordinary surety could never have contributive subrogation against his cosurety, a conclusion refuted by numerous authorities.[5] Furthermore, if the equities of surety and quasi-surety are in truth to be regarded as equal, the conception means that the ultimate loss will lie where the creditor's choice has first put it.

A growing number of decisions deny both partial and complete subrogation to the contractual surety as against the quasi-surety who has acted in good faith, and without negligence, where to allow subrogation would cause affirmative loss, and not mere deprivation of gain.[6] Stress is occasionally laid upon the hardship of imposing liability at all upon the quasi-surety. The decision in the bailment situation, previously considered, falls within this group.[7] Cases putting the primary responsibility upon the contractual surety are fairly typified by *American Bonding Co. v. State Savings Bank*,[8] in which a court officer issued false jurors' certificates that were bought in good faith by a bank and paid by the county. The surety on the clerk's bond, who had satisfied judgment to the county for the money so paid, was denied recovery against the bank.[9]

To be included in this last group are certain other cases, presenting a different sort of factual situation. An employee without actual or apparent authority signs checks in his employer's name or raises genuine checks, which are cashed by the employer's bank. The preliminary question arises, whether the employee's fidelity surety is liable at all. Clearly, the employee's act has not affected legally the depositor's account with the bank, for that account is purely a debtor-creditor relationship; contrary to popular phraseology the depositor did not own any *res* in the hands of the bank and in paying the checks the bank did not part with anything belonging to the depositor.[10] The depositor had merely a chose in action against the bank; he still has it intact. Consequently, while the employee has caused the bank loss, he has not caused the employer loss. The situation differs from that of a fire loss for which a tortfeasor is liable. The insured owner has actually suffered the loss of his building, whatever remedy he may have against the tortfeasor. While, to be sure, as a practical matter the expenses of litigation may be necessary to compel the bank to pay, it is doubtful whether the ordinary fidelity bond against "loss" through the acts of the employee protects the employer against such contingent expenses as may be made necessary by his acts and, even if so, the liability of the surety should be restricted to their amount.[11] But following a decision holding the surety liable,[12] the same surety unsuccessfully sought subrogation to the employer's claim against the bank.[13] In *Grubnaw v.*

Centennial National Bank[14] an apparently contrary but possibly distinguishable result was reached. There the surety seems to have paid without litigation, taking an assignment from the employer. In spite of the fact that a good deal of the discussion is inconsistent, the court seemed to consider the surety liable. However, considerable stress is laid upon the assignment. If, as a matter of law, the surety was not liable, no reason is apparent why the surety could not buy the claim against the bank as a means of settling a disputed controversy of its own liability to the employer. Yet if in truth both surety and bank are liable, and the primary responsibility is conceived to rest upon the surety, the assignment would be futile.[15] As well might it be urged that the ordinary principal, by taking upon payment an assignment from the creditor of the latter's claim against his surety, could obtain recourse against his own surety.[16]

Where the quasi-surety, although acting in good faith, has not taken due care, the majority of decisions impose the primary liability upon him. Thus, in *Cooper, Myers & Co. v. Smith*,[17] a state official abstracted a warrant drawn by the auditor, and, after forging the name of the payee, sold it to a bank which collected from the state treasury. After stating that the bank, having procured the money by means of the forged indorsement, was bound to restore the amount to the state, whether or not the bank was innocent of actual wrong or negligence, the court held that the bank which had refunded could not recover from the official's surety because the particular circumstances involving the purchase were such as reasonably to challenge inquiry and the exercise of care.[18] But the distinction was clearly made that in the absence of such "negligence," subrogation would be granted. In another case, however, in which an employee deposited checks payable to his employer to his own credit in the defendant bank, which collected and allowed withdrawals by the employee against the credit, a Kentucky court[19] denied subrogation to the employee's surety. Stress was laid upon the harshness of the rule making the bank liable to the employer; it was thought that the equity of the surety, paid to bear the risk, was inferior to that of the bank which had received no benefit from the transaction. The liability of the purchaser to the "creditor" in such a case as *Cooper, Myers & Co. v. Smith* was an absolute one not dependent on negligence. Carelessness, however, in not taking steps for his own protection is apparently sufficient to turn the scales in determining the relative equities of the surety and the quasi-surety.

Difficult to reconcile with this trend is the treatment of the quasi-surety whose liability is founded upon negligence toward the creditor, as where a fiduciary, otherwise innocent, is made liable to the beneficiary for failure to supervise properly the conduct of his embezzling cofiduciary. Here the few cases in point regard the liability of the latter's surety as "primary" in relation to the negligent fiduciary.[20] Yet if there is any distinction, the negligence of the fiduciary toward the beneficiary might be thought to entitle him to less consideration than when the quasi-surety's liability is absolute and his fault has consisted in not properly safeguarding his own interests. To be sure, the negligent fiduciary has been guilty merely of an omission, when the law required of him an active duty, whereas in the cases presented in the preceding paragraph positive action on the part of the quasi-surety contributed to the surety's liability. Whether this distinction will justify the more lenient treatment of the former may be seriously questioned, and the result should be compared with the subrogation of the fire insurer to the insured's cause of action against one through whose negligence to the insured the loss has occurred.

When the act of the quasi-surety cannot be said to have caused the ripening into liability of the contingent obligation of the surety, this added factor should be considered in balancing the equities.[21] Certain stockbrokerage cases offer an illustration. A stock broker has in his possession, for safe-keeping only, securities belonging to *A*; he also has securities of *B*, which he is authorized to pledge for his own debts. Both lots are effectively pledged by the broker to *C*, who thus obtains a valid security claim to all. Realization of the debt by sale of some of the securities leaves others free. If the creditor uses *A's* securities to satisfy the claim, *A* is subrogated to the right of the creditor as against *B's* securities.[22] The case is merely one of marshaling, a prominent aspect of subrogation.[23] Whatever one may think of the solution reached by the courts in the cases earlier discussed, the soundness of this result is clear. While the possible imprudence of the involuntary or quasi-surety in entrusting the indicia of ownership to the broker may be regarded as the cause of the subjection of his interest to the debt of the broker, the act can hardly be considered as prejudicing the voluntary surety or causing the lien to ripen upon his securities.

On a somewhat similar principle, in a case in which the treasurer of a taxing district used its funds to make good his defalcation as administrator of an estate, the district was subrogated to the rights of the beneficiaries of the estate against the surety on the administrator's bond.[24] While the district was never a surety, its money was used without its consent to satisfy obligations for which the surety had bound himself. However, apparently on the view that such a conclusion is unsound, the North Carolina court denied subrogation in an analogous case. A sheriff gave a bond to the state for county taxes, another for state taxes. He used county tax money to settle state taxes with the state treasurer, who was ignorant of the true facts. The surety on the county tax bond, who had paid the deficit in county tax money resulting from the misappropriation, was denied recourse against the surety on the state tax bond.[25] Analysis discloses that, by virtue of the fact that the state could properly retain the county tax money in settlement of state taxes, the principal by his wrongful conduct has thrown upon the county tax surety the obligation of the state tax surety, whereas the former was in no way the cause of the liability of the latter.

An interesting problem, presented by a Minnesota decision,[26] brings out the importance of still another factor that may affect the result. *P* bought materials from a corporation in which he held stock, the corporation obtaining a statutory lien on the stock for the price of the materials. *P* had previously assigned the stock to *A* to secure a loan, but absence of notice to the corporation afforded priority to the lien of the corporation. Since *A's* interest became subordinated to the corporation's lien, it might be said that *A*, in respect to the stock, became an involuntary surety. *S*, who was *P's* surety, paid for the materials, but was held not entitled by subrogation to priority over *A's* interest. In the absence of reliance by *S* on the apparently unencumbered ownership of *P*, the result is sound, since *A's* interest arose prior to the inception of *S's* obligation and the perfecting of his lien. That this is the explanation appears from another appeal in the same cause.[27] A different lender had made a loan to *P* before the materials were bought upon an agreement that when new stock was issued to *P* it should be held by the lender as collateral. The stock was not issued until after the debt for materials had been incurred. Under these circumstances the surety was accorded the prior claim.[28]

Certain other decisions may depend upon the interpretation of statutes. Thus, in *Knoll v. Marshall County,* a statute, besides requiring saloon keepers to give bond for payment of liquor taxes, made the claim for taxes a lien on the interest of lessors of the saloon keepers. The bond surety was denied subrogation to the county's lien.[29] Construction of a statute was in part the explanation of a decision holding that, as between a depository surety of a bank and the state depositors' guaranty fund, the obligation of the former was secondary.[30] Also a county, absolutely liable under statute for state taxes collected by its treasurer, has been subrogated to the state's remedy against the sureties on the bond of the official.[31]

The reports also furnish a few examples in which both parties may be called quasi-sureties. Thus where a public treasurer, absolutely liable for public funds, lawfully deposits them in a bank, he is completely subrogated to the government's claim against the stockholders on their obligations as such.[32] Bearing in mind the theory upon which stockholders' double liability is founded, the result seems sound.

INSURER AND QUASI-INSURER

INSURANCE CONTRACTS, other than life and accident, are contracts of indemnity, and thus closely allied to suretyship, but in order to avoid confusion are here treated separately.[33] The general purposes of both are alike, namely, to protect against loss. Because of the same element of indemnity and the policy of preventing double recovery for the insured, the courts are confronted with the same problem in respect to the person upon whom the ultimate loss should rest, but one seldom, if ever, finds a suretyship case cited in an insurance case or *vice versa.* Explanation may be found in the lamentable practice of considering each branch of the law as a more or less water-tight compartment. Although in many cases the equities appear equal, the principle of contribution is consistently ignored in both.

The insurer's subrogation against a tortfeasor is a commonplace, and not infrequently is available against even a "tortfeasor" who has acted in good faith, without negligence, and when his causal connection with the loss is of the most shadowy sort. Thus an employer who has used the greatest care in his selection of an employee and has most diligently instructed him, may nevertheless find himself saddled with liability for the tort of that employee. The situation is closely analogous to suretyship. The insured, whose property has been destroyed through the tort of the employee, may sue the fire insurer, the employer, and the employee. If the employer pays the loss, he will have redress against the employee; likewise the insurer would be subrogated to the insured's claim against the employee. The latter may be called the principal, while the employer is his quasi-surety and the insurer his contractual surety. Certainly it is not self-evident that the insurer should be subrogated as against the employer. While the liability of the employer to the injured person who has *in invitum* suffered damage may rest upon the sound policy of putting the loss upon one who engages in the business or undertaking, it is not so clear that as between insurer and employer the loss should fall entirely upon the latter. The insurer for a premium willingly undertakes the risk; the employer, if cognizant of the law, likewise consciously assumes the risk for which he must, if at all, hope for reimbursement out of the profits of the business or recourse against the employee, an asset of decidedly questionable value. In what respect, then, does the problem differ from that of the surety of the bailee and the *bona fide* purchaser from the bailee, in which the surety was denied relief from the purchaser?[34] Yet a failure to recognize this similarity is apparent from the numerous decisions which uniformly permit complete subrogation against the employer. The inconsistency of one group's denying any subrogation, while the other grants it completely, points clearly to the fundamental equality of the equities, and is itself the strongest argument for contribution.

Analysis of analogous cases further substantiates this inconsistency. In two early English decisions[35] an insurer was completely subrogated to the insured's cause of action against a hundred which by statute was liable for damages occurring therein and caused by rioters, without regard to whether the public officials could have prevented it. The causal relation of the hundred to the loss was most attenuated, if it can be said to have existed at all. Yet contributive subrogation was not even suggested. A theft insurer has been completely subrogated to the insured's claim against a bailee who was technically a converter because of an innocent and nonnegligent misdelivery to a thief.[36] In a case, however, in which property was stolen from a bailee as a result of his negligent custody, the complete subrogation granted to the theft insurer accords with the distinction taken in the majority of suretyship cases upon the effect of the quasi-surety's "negligence."[37] But again difficult to reconcile is the full subrogation permitted a liability insurer to the insured's claim on an expressed or implied warranty without reference to personal negligence.[38]

In a recent Missouri decision it appears that a company had forgery insurance protecting against loss through forgery of the names of payees upon its checks. Before a certain check was received by the payee, his signature was forged and the check cashed with the defendant bank, which in turn collected from the drawee bank. Although the report does not indicate that the deception of the defendant was in any way caused by its carelessness, the insurer upon payment was subrogated to the insured's claim against the defendant.[39] The Supreme Court of the United States was confronted with an interesting problem in 1932.[40] A policy protected a bank against losses through payment of checks bearing forged indorsements. Such checks were cashed and debited to the depositor. Since the depositor upon receipt of monthly statements and vouchers did not give prompt notice of the forgeries, the debit, originally invalid, became good. Upon a later demand by the depositor, however, the bank recredited him. In an action by the bank against the insurer, the conceded original liability of the insurer was held to have been discharged much as the liability of a fire insurer may be destroyed by the insured's release of a tortfeasor, since the recrediting amounted to a release of a then valid debit against the depositor's account. The peculiarity of the case is that the insured did not at the time of the original payment of the checks have any claim against the depositor. The clear implication is that after the validation of the debit as between bank and depositor the loss falls upon the latter and not upon the insurer. If the validation of the debit is based on the theory that the bank, by reason of the failure of prompt notice, is prejudiced in its recourse against the forger and subsequent indorsers, if any, as well as against the person to whom payment was made, the decision must rest on the theory that the insurer is likewise prejudiced in its claim to subrogation to such recourse. But it will be observed that if the validation of the debit occurs even when the depositor had no reason to suspect the forgeries, the case is similar to those in which the quasi-surety's obligation is absolute without regard to negligence.

Another group of cases presents a situation in which the tortfeasor who is without fault has no recourse against another tortfeasor, and in which, consequently, it would be possible to treat the tortfeasor and the insurer as coinsurers with contributive relief *inter se* as the consequence. However, this solution seems to be either ignored or rejected. Thus, a fire insurer has been completely subrogated to the shipper's claim against a common carrier who was liable in spite of the fact that the fire was purely accidental;[41] and in cases in which absolute liability is imposed by statute upon railroads for fires caused by the operation of trains, fire insurers are given by the courts the complete benefit of the liability.[42] No reason is apparent why it is not possible to consider an insurer as a coinsurer with a third person, who has, as part of a larger contract, expressly assumed the very risk covered by the insurance. Yet if a lessee is bound to repair all injuries to the premises, the lessor's insurer in England is given the complete benefit of the covenant even without misconduct on the part of the lessee.[43] Several recent decisions, however, take the opposite view, denying any subrogation to the insurer.[44]

In a separate category are those cases in which the contractual obligation does not expressly purport to cover the loss, but still is absolute and not excused thereby.[45] It is generally conceded that if a mortgagee insures solely in his own behalf and at his own expense, the insurer will be completely subrogated to the mortgage debt even in the absence of any subrogation clause.[46] Yet in the closely analogous situation of vendor and vendee, the authorities are divided on the question whether the vendor's insurer is subrogated to the obligation of the vendee to pay the price in spite of the fire, or whether the vendee shall have the benefit of the insurance, with apparently no support for a division of the loss.[47] The mortgage and contract of sale cases are to be distinguished only with difficulty from the standpoint of insurance law. The undoubted tendency of the American courts to give the vendee the benefit of the insurance is probably to be attributed chiefly to the feeling that the rule placing the risk of loss upon the vendee is harsh and perhaps, as a novel matter, questionable, whereas the same qualms do not appear to be felt in the mortgage case. Yet the retention of legal title until full payment of the price serves the same purpose as a mortgage, particularly when the vendee has gone into possession. There is of course the practical distinction that the mortgage is usually a long-term transaction, and the ordinary mortgagor adverts to the desirability of insurance, whereas many contracts of sale contemplate a speedy closing and, during the short interval before execution of the deed, the untutored purchaser does not realize that the risk of loss is upon him, and that consequently he needs insurance.

A few miscellaneous problems are entitled to brief mention. Is a building contractor, who, as between himself and the owner, is bound to rebuild in spite of the destruction of the partially completed structure, entitled to the benefit of the owner's insurance on the building?[48] A fire insurer paying for the destruction of a party wall has been held subrogated to the insured's claim against the adjoining landowner who subsequently used the rebuilt wall.[49] In a recent decision it appeared that a loan broker, by forging the name of the plaintiff's attorney to a certificate of title, secured title insurance from the plaintiff for a lender. The supposed borrower-mortgagor was a nonexistent person whose name the broker forged to the note and mortgage. By forging also the name of the supposed borrower to the lender's check the broker collected from the drawee bank. Denial of subrogation to the title insurer against the bank was placed on the ground that the plaintiff was negligent in not discovering the forgery of its own agent's signature before granting the insurance, while the defendant bank was not negligent in failing to discover the forged indorsement.[50] Another title insurance case offering less difficulty is *St. Paul Title Insurance and Trust Co. v. Johnson*,[51] in which the insurer of a mortgagee was subrogated against the mortgagor who gave bond to pay off any prior mechanic's liens. It would seem clear that the mortgagor who has had the benefit of the work should be ultimately liable; to compel him to pay does not subject him to a positive loss.

Many of the questions previously considered might be obviated by a subrogation clause in both suretyship and insurance contracts, broad enough to cover all possible claims of the creditor or the insured against third persons. No legal obstacle normally stands in the way of a surety by express stipulation becoming surety *for,* rather than *with* or as principal debtor *to,* another surety, whether that other surety's obligation precedes or follows in point of time; nor is there such an obstacle in the way of the insurer similarly protecting itself.

SURETY OF A SURETY

IT SEEMS to be generally settled that the surety of a surety upon payment to the creditor will be completely subrogated to the latter's rights against the ultimate principal. This is well illustrated by an English decision,[52] in which the bail of a surety arrested on civil process was subrogated to a mortgage given the creditor by the surety's principal. A possible qualification, however, must be noted, namely, that as against the ultimate principal the surety's surety will be placed only in the position in which the surety himself would have been placed had he made the payment. Thus, a second surety upon payment was subjected to a set-off of the principal against the original surety that had arisen prior to the subrogee's obligation.[53]

Following from the rule just mentioned and from the rule that a surety may have only contributive subrogation against his cosurety, a surety of a surety is only entitled to contributive subrogation against a cosurety of the latter. In other words, his right does not rise higher than the right which his immediate principal would have had upon payment. Thus, in *Crow v. Murphy*[54] judgment had been obtained against two cosureties. The surety on a stay bond was permitted only contributive subrogation to the claim of the creditor, whom he paid, against the other original surety. Presumably, if it had been the latter who paid, he would have had contributive subrogation against the surety of his cosurety. As between two cosureties, each is principal for part and surety for the remainder; consequently, in respect to the surety of one of two cosureties, the other cosurety is principal only for a part, although the ultimate principal is principal for the whole.

The same rule should govern in respect to coprincipals with a surety for one of them, since, as between those who are really coprincipals, each is principal for a part and surety for the rest, as is true of copurchasers.[55] This view receives support in a Pennsylvania decision. A tort judgment was obtained against *A* and *B* for injuries sustained by the concurrent negligence of their respective employees. Both *A* and *B* appealed, and the surety on *A's* bond paid the affirmed judgment. After deciding that contribution was permissible between *A* and *B* in spite of the fact that they were technically tortfeasors, the court held that the surety was only entitled to contributive subrogation to the judgment against *B*.[56]

A related problem concerns the relation between sureties of different principals, where payment by one of the sureties satisfies the claims of the common creditor. It has been argued that there cannot be contribution between sureties of different principals, since there is no identity of risk when the two bonds are separate and distinct and the principals different.[57] But what rational explanation can be given for such a view, which ignores the basic reason for the whole doctrine of contribution between those who are subject to a common burden, and whose denial in the sort of case under consideration, as in the more usual one of cosureties of the same principal, makes the ultimate loss depend upon the choice, capricious or collusive, of the creditor? Denial of contributive relief to the paying surety may well operate, if the creditor so elect, to cast the entire loss upon the surety who took the smaller risk. Is not contribution a better solution, in spite of the difference in risk?[58] The plausible sound of the argument that the risks must be identical and the principal the same person ignores the justice of the situation and takes no account of analogous problems in the law.[59]

Should not their relation be governed by the relation between their respective principals? Support for this view may be found. Thus in a Minnesota case *A* had obtained a state permit to cut timber, giving bond for payment of timber cut. Before any cutting *A* assigned the permit to *B*, who, in conformance with the statute, also gave bond to the state. As between the sureties on the two bonds it was decided that the surety of *B* must bear the whole loss, since if *A* had to pay, he could have had recourse against *B*, while *B's* surety could not have had recourse against *A*.[60] The principle is further illustrated by *Southern Surety Co.*

v. Tessum,[61] a case in which two coguardians gave separate bonds, and the surety of the misappropriating guardian paid. The court denied the paying surety a recovery from either the other guardian, who was liable to the ward by reason of negligent inattention, or from his surety, since as between the two guardians the primary responsibility was upon the defaulter.[62] If the decision is correct in denying recovery against the negligent guardian,[63] *a fortiori* it is correct in respect to his surety. Assuming, however, that the court was in error on the former point, since the negligent inattention was a cause of the loss and therefore matured the obligation of the defaulter's surety, it by no means follows that the court was in error in refusing relief against the negligent guardian's surety. The latter was entirely innocent, in no way a cause of the loss, and therefore his equities appear greater than those of the surety of the embezzler.[64]

Difficulty, however, arises in a different situation. A county treasurer deposits public funds in a bank in excess of the amount of the depositary bond of the bank. A statute forbids the excess deposit. Upon the failure of the bank the depositary surety pays the county the full amount of its bond while the treasurer's official surety pays the excess. How is the dividend of the failed bank, applicable to the county's claim, to be distributed between the two sureties? It is a truism in the law of subrogation, applicable alike to sureties and insurers, that partial subrogation is not available to the prejudice of the creditor or insured. Until payment in full of the principal obligation or obligations, secured wholly or in part by the surety's or insurer's promise, the creditor and insured have the superior claim to the obligations of the principal as well as to securities consisting of property of the principal pledged for those obligations.[65] An English distinction grafted upon that doctrine permits a surety for only part of a debt upon full payment of that amount, to be subrogated *pro tanto* to the creditor's claim against the bankrupt estate although the result is to diminish the creditor's dividend.[66] Those decisions allocating to the bank's surety that proportion of the dividend which the amount of the depositary bond bears to the total claim of the county, only the balance going to the treasurer's surety, have in part at least been based on this distinction.

If the English doctrine is repudiated,[67] some other ground for permitting the prorating must be found. Is there a basis in the illegality of the excess deposit? As against the county, the obligee of the bond, it has been held that the official's violation of the statute, designed for the protection of the county, cannot be taken advantage of by the bank's surety so as to secure a prorating.[68] Moreover, in spite of his violation of the statute, the officer, subordinately to the county's claim for complete relief, might be subrogated to the county's claim against the bank.[69] This would depend on the importance attached to the doctrine of *in pari delicto,*[70] for the treasurer could well argue that the general creditors of the bank would not be improperly prejudiced by a wrong which was to the county and not to them, and which presumably increased the assets of the estate. But assuming that the treasurer has subrogation against the bank itself, does it follow, when the bank's surety is involved, that the treasurer should be given preferred subrogation? Cannot the surety say to the treasurer, with considerable plausibility, that it had every reason to expect that the statutory limit would not be exceeded, and that it would be prejudicially affected by the treasurer's preferred subrogation? Thus, if $10,000 is the amount of the bond and the deposits are $12,000, while the rate of dividend is 20 per cent, the treasurer who pays $2,000 will be made whole and there will be only $400 for the bank's surety, whereas, if the limit had not been exceeded, the bank's surety would have received much more.[71] On this line of reasoning there would be prorating of the county's dividend as between the treasurer and the depositary surety.[72]

However the previous question be answered in respect to the treasurer himself, it does not necessarily follow that his surety will not occupy a position superior to the depositary surety. The argument may be made that the illegal act of the treasurer was not the "proximate cause" of the loss as between himself and the bank, since the bank could have carried out its full obligation to the county in spite of the illegal deposit, and that as between the two innocent sureties of the principals the one whose principal's default was the "proximate cause" should be postponed.[73] Or a slightly different argument might be employed. If, on the one hand, the treasurer, in spite of his violation of law, may have full recourse against the bank, then, following the usual rule, the sureties should stand in the same relation *inter se* as the principals themselves stand. On the other hand, if the treasurer is denied such recourse solely on grounds of public policy, his surety is not properly affected by these considerations and he should be treated as if the treasurer did have such complete recourse. So far as the actual decisions go there is a sharp split, some allowing the depositary surety that proportion of the dividend which the amount of its bond bears to the total claim of the county, the remainder going to the official's surety,[74] while others give the treasurer's surety the preferred claim to the entire dividend.[75]

LIABILITY INSURERS

WHILE THE MATTER of subrogation of the liability insurer raises certain points that might have been considered previously, the entire subject has been postponed for separate treatment, owing to certain peculiarities not present in the situations already reviewed.

What is the nature of a liability policy? Before the advent of fairly recent legislation the usual policy was a contract indemnifying the insured, not against liability but against loss, and in consequence it followed that the insurer was not liable until the insured paid off his liability to the third person; the so-called "no action" clause compelled this result.[76] In other words, the tortfeasee was neither the insured nor the beneficiary of the policy. Since this result permitted the escape of the insurer when the insured tortfeasor was insolvent, there were enacted statutes of various types[77] all designed to prevent that escape and to afford the tortfeasee the benefit of contracts for which the insurer had been paid. The statute may, on the one hand, require the policy to be written so as to make the injured person a beneficiary as well as the insured in somewhat the same fashion as a fire policy issued to a mortgagor and made payable to the mortgagee. On the other hand, the policy may be required to be virtually an indemnity against liability, although the maturity of the obligation may be conditioned on judgment against the insured, with provisions therein making the benefit of the contract, really an asset of the insured for which he has paid, available to the tortfeasee by a process in the nature of execution even though it may be sought by a separate action against the insurer. The point, however, must be emphasized that the insurer is not an insurer of the tortfeasee, nor, since the paying insurer obviously has no recourse against the insured, a surety of the tortfeasor. It follows that the insurer cannot seek subrogation to the tortfeasee's remedy against others; like other insurers it seeks normally subrogation to the insured's, the tortfeasor's, remedy against others.

This introduction leads to the question, When may a paying tortfeasor have recourse against a third person? As obviously the problem is too large to be treated here in detail, suffice it to state that in certain circumstances he may obtain complete and in others contributive reimbursement from another. But often when two tortfeasors appear to stand on a parity, contribution will be denied upon reasons of policy which must be regarded as questionable, except possibly when the two are conscious and willful wrongdoers.[78] Their weakness is shown by the fact that the same arguments of public policy have not been sufficiently strong to invalidate liability policies, even those insuring against the consequences of one's personal negligence.[79] The inconsistency of these two positions is probably an historical accident.

With respect to subrogation the law is clear that if and when the tortfeasor is entitled either to contribution or complete indemnity from his fellow, his liability insurer will be subrogated, partly or completely, against the cotortfeasor.[80] Thus if an employer is rendered liable solely by the negligence of his employee, his liability carrier will be subrogated to the employer's right of complete indemnity.[81] The employer is virtually the surety of the employee and, as the indemnitor of a surety, the insurer is subrogated to the surety's right against his principal.[82] Conversely, if, as between *A* and *B, B* would be entitled to complete indemnity from *A,* then *A's* insurer would have no relief against *B.*

Can, however, the liability insurer of one tortfeasor force contributive or total reimbursement from the insurer of the other?[83] Let us assume, as has been held, that the insurer of one employer, *A,* is subrogated to the latter's claim for contribution against another employer, *B,* in a case in which the injury occurred through the negligence of the respective employees of the two.[84] If *B* then pays the contributive share to *A's* insurer, he may secure indemnity from his own insurer with the result that the loss is shared by the two insurers. Suppose, however, that *B* is insolvent. In the absence of the statutes previously referred to, and under the old type of policy, no way seems open to either *A* or *A's* insurer to compel *B's* insurer to contribute, since even the tortfeasee had no remedy against the latter.[85] Will the result be different under a policy containing the provisions required by the statute? A fairly typical enactment requires insertion of a provision to the effect that insolvency or bankruptcy of the insured shall not release him from payment of damages for injury or loss suffered during the life of the policy, and that if judgment is secured against the insured, then action may be brought against the company "by the injured person or his heirs or personal representatives."[86] It may be thought that such an act, designed primarily to protect the tortfeasee, may not have been phrased in terms broad enough to aid the other tortfeasor, and consequently his insurer by subrogation.[87] If *A* may recover contribution from *B,* he is really a surety in part for the latter, and therefore upon payment to the judgment creditor should be partly subrogated to the latter's statutory remedy against *B's* insurer. If one of two principal debtors, each of whom is bound to the other to pay one-half the debt, gives a mortgage to the creditor and later transfers the property to one who assumed the grantor's obligation, it would seem that the other principal, upon full payment, should be contributively subrogated not only to the mortgage, but also to the personal obligation of the grantee to the creditor. The grantee, as between himself and the grantor, has become the principal obligor; likewise *B's* insurer is primary obligor in respect to *B.* On this theory *A's* insurer would be subrogated to *A's* right of subrogation against *B's* insurer, with the result that contribution is worked out between the two insurers. But even a rejection of this idea, based upon the premise that the tortfeasee is the beneficiary of the policy, does not exhaust the possibilities. If the policy permitted by the statute indemnifies against liability,[88] then, in spite of the fact that *A* is not the "person injured" within the meaning of the statute, so that he cannot bring an independent action on the policy, it does not follow that he cannot by garnishment against his fellow reach the insurance contract which is the latter's asset,[89] and one that should now be available to *A* only, since performance of the contract would enure only to his benefit and not to general creditors of the insured.[90] On this theory *A's* insurer, by subrogation to *A's* remedy, could also force contribution from *B's* insurer. If such contributive relief is not possible, the result is that the tortfeasee, by collecting in full from *A* or *A's* insurer, may throw the entire loss upon *A,* to remain there if perchance *A* has no insurer, or upon *A's* insurer while *B's* insurer goes scot-free. The more or less capricious choice of the tortfeasee may determine the ultimate situation, and the way is again open to collusion.[91]

Suppose that *A* is liable to the tortfeasee solely on the doctrine of *respondeat superior* while *B* is personally negligent. If *A* pays, he can recover complete indemnity from his employee. If contribution is permissible between that employee and *B,* then, since the employee and *B* are coprincipals, *A,* and consequently *A's* insurer by subrogation to *A's* claim, should be able to obtain at least contributive subrogation against *B,* following the usual rule that a surety—and *A* is virtually a surety for his employee—stands in the position of his principal against the coprincipal as respects subrogation to the claim of the creditor. But should not *A* be entitled to complete subrogation against *B*? *A* is personally innocent while *B* is personally negligent. If, as has been seen, the contractual surety of a fiduciary is completely subrogated against the one who colludes with the fiduciary and also against a quasi-surety where the latter is merely negligent,[92] one may urge that the involuntary surety *A* should be completely subrogated to the tortfeasee's claim against *B.* The latter's personal wrong in conjunction with the wrong of *A's* employee has created *A's* liability.[93] Conversely *B* and *B's* insurer would have no claim against *A.*

We may now consider a situation and a jurisdiction in which contribution is denied between the tortfeasors on assumed grounds of policy, although otherwise *A* and *B* are on a parity, and both are personally negligent. *A's* insurer pays the tortfeasee. Relief against *B,* partial or entire, has been denied the insurer for the simple reason that *A* had no claim to which his insurer may be subrogated.[94] While the result seems *prima facie* logical, it violates the good sense of the old maxim *ratione cessante, cessat lex.* The stated reasons for denying contribution between the tortfeasors themselves have no application to the insurer, who is innocent of any wrong and whose every interest is opposed to the commission of wrong.[95] Nor is there validity to the argument, sometimes employed, that the rule against contribution should not be evaded by an assignment of the tortfeasee to a straw man who pays with funds furnished by the tortfeasor,[96] since the insurer pays out its own money without chance for reimbursement from its own insured. Exonerating the cotortfeasor is at the expense of the insurer, not of the tortfeasor. The insured tortfeasor escapes the actual burden through the validity of the insurance contract and not by an evasion of the rule against contribution. The insurer's claim for relief is not stained by his own turpitude or wrong. If the rule between the tortfeasors is based upon its supposed deterrent effect, surely that purpose can be better consummated by imposing an obligation upon the tortfeasor to the insurer of the cotortfeasor. Since denial of contribution is based not on the merit of the defendant but on the demerit of the plaintiff, there appears reason for allowing contributive relief to the insurer against the other tortfeasor, whose conduct has contributed to the liability of the insurer. Judicial support for such a conclusion is to be found in a New York decision which, while not squarely in point,[97] suggests that where the two tortfeasors can be considered on a parity the law should treat the case for the protection of the insurer as if the insured did have a claim for contribution.[98] An earlier New York case lends further support to this view.[99] An appeal surety of one tortfeasor was allowed contributive relief against the other tortfeasor, although the wrong was an intentional and malicious one. The opinion is significant, for, while admitting that contribution would be denied between the tortfeasors, it declared that the surety did not come within the same reprobation of the court.

NOTES TO LANGMAID ESSAY

[1] The danger of collusion was strongly emphasized in Pace v. Pace's Adm'r (1898) 95 Va. 792, 30 S. E. 361.

[2] Throughout this essay no attempt will be made to examine the entirely distinct problem of the ratio of contribution. The difficulty of determining the ratio might sometimes conceivably induce an indolent court to accept the easier, if less just, solution of complete subrogation in behalf of one party rather than the other. Difficult as the determination might be, the attempt would achieve more just results. The courts have not been deterred by a similar difficulty in partly concurrent insurance or suretyship. See note 58 *infra.* Nor will attention be paid to the various ways in which the main problem of "primary" and "secondary" liability may arise.

[3] An occasional case has stressed this element, *e.g.,* Baker v. American Surety Co. (1916) 181 Iowa 634, 159 N. W. 1044.

[4] American Surety Co. v. Citizens Nat. Bank, 294 Fed. 609, 616 (C. C. A. 8th, 1923): "The right of subrogation is an equitable right, and where equities are equal the right does not exist and there can be no relief." One may wonder whether such a statement is not attributable to general remarks employed in entirely different situations. If a surety should pay off the debt which is also secured by a mortgage of the principal's land, which mortgage is discharged of record by the creditor without the surety's concurrence, the surety would lose his equitable claim to the mortgage as against a subsequent purchaser in good faith who relied on the recorded release (Richards v. Griffith [1891] 92 Cal. 493, 28 Pac. 484; Orvis v. Newell [1845] 17 Conn. 97; Gaskill v. Wales [1883] 36 N. J. Eq. 527; Wolford v. Bias [1916] 79 W. Va. 349, 90 S. E. 875). In such an event the purchaser has been misled by appearances, and it is not too much to ask the surety to prevent such misleading appearances. Furthermore, the purchaser can use his "legal title" both offensively and defensively against the surety. But this is so different from the problem under discussion that further elaboration is of little avail. Here there are two persons liable at one and the same time to a third, and it is not a case where, after the liability of one is fixed, subsequent conduct or inaction has led to a change of position on the part of another.

[5] See Sheldon, *Subrogation* (ed. 2; 1893) § 140. Note particularly Furnold v. Bank of Mo. (1869) 44 Mo. 336. A judgment against several cosureties became a lien on their lands. One sold his land for full consideration to the plaintiff, who later, to protect himself, paid the judgment. He was allowed contributive subrogation to the judgment liens on the property of the other sureties; note that in effect the plaintiff, in respect to his interest in the land, became the surety of his grantor.

[6] National Surety Co. v. Arosin, 198 Fed. 605 (C. C. A. 8th, 1912); American Surety Co. v. Lewis State Bank, 58 F. (2d) 559 (C. C. A. 5th, 1932); Washington Mechanics' Sav. Bank v. District Title Ins. Co., 65 F. (2d) 827 (App. D. C. 1933) (denying the bond surety recourse against the quasi-surety but stating that, had the latter paid, it would have no recourse against the former since the equities of neither were superior to those of the other); Cooper, Myers & Co. v. Smith (1918) 139 Minn. 382, 166 N. W. 504 (quasi-surety suing contractual surety). See also American Surety Co. v. Citizens Nat. Bank, 294 Fed. 609 (C. C. A. 8th, 1923) (but also dependent on the view that the alleged quasi-surety was not liable to the creditor). *Contra:* National Surety Co. v. Bankers Trust Co. (1930) 210 Iowa 323, 228 N. W. 635 (employee forged name of employer to drafts belonging to latter and cashed them with defendant, which was not the drawee; the fidelity

surety paid and took an assignment of the claim against the bank; held, three judges dissenting, for the surety against the bank which was liable for conversion; nothing said to indicate that the bank was negligent); National Surety Co. v. National City Bank of Brooklyn (1918) 184 App. Div. 771, 172 N. Y. Supp. 413 (by fraudulent means an employee procured superior to sign checks made payable to fictitious persons on defendant bank and secured payment; fidelity surety given recourse, although nothing to indicate negligence on part of bank; query whether surety liable at all. See pp. 248–249 (*infra*); Seward v. National Surety Co. (1929) 120 Ohio St. 47, 165 N. E. 537 (questionable because the quasi-surety was not even the cause of the loss).

[7] Northern Trust Co. v. Consolidated Elev. Co. (1919) 142 Minn. 132, 171 N. W. 265.

[8] (1913) 47 Mont. 332, 133 Pac. 367.

[9] While it was conceded in the case for the purpose of argument that the bank was bound to refund to the county, this conclusion may be doubted. See Langmaid, *Quasi-Contract—Change of Position by Receipt of Money in Satisfaction of a Preëxisting Obligation* (1933) 21 Calif. L. Rev. 311, 331.

[10] See Grubnaw v. Centennial Nat. Bank (1924) 279 Pa. 501, 504, 124 Atl. 142, 143: "In honoring the forged check it [the bank] used its own money, not the depositor's."

[11] *Contra:* Champion Ice Mfg. & Cold Storage Co. v. American Bonding Co. (1903) 115 Ky. 863, 75 S. W. 197; Alabama Fid. & Cas. Co. v. Alabama Penny Sav. Bank (1917) 200 Ala. 337, 76 So. 103 (on rehearing; based entirely on the Champion case); Grand Lodge, Knights of Pythias v. Fidelity & Dep. Co. (1922) 223 Ill. App. 516 *semble*. But see Padgett v. Young County, 204 S. W. 1046, 1052 (Tex. Civ. App. 1918); *cf.* Bristol Trust Co. v. National Surety Co. (1922) 97 Conn. 198, 116 Atl. 251.

[12] Champion Ice Mfg. & Cold Storage Co. v. American Bonding Co. (1903) 115 Ky. 863, 75 S. W. 197.

[13] American Bonding Co. v. First Nat. Bank (1905) 27 Ky. L. Rep. 393, 85 S. W. 190. In Baker v. American Surety Co. (1916) 181 Iowa 634, 159 N. W. 1044, the case before the court did not require determination of the surety's liability; it was held, however, that, assuming liability, it could not have recourse against the bank.

[14] (1924) 279 Pa. 501, 124 Atl. 142.

[15] United States v. National Surety Co., 298 Fed. 536 (D. R. I. 1924); Louisville Trust Co. v. Royal Indemnity Co., 20 S. W. (2d) 71 (Ky. App. 1929). In American Bonding Co. v. State Sav. Bank (1913) 47 Mont. 332, 133 Pac. 367, the assignment taken by the paying surety proved useless.

[16] Sheldon, *Subrogation* § 46.

[17] (1918) 139 Minn. 382, 166 N. W. 504.

[18] *Accord:* National Surety Co. v. State Sav. Bank, 156 Fed. 21 (C. C. A. 8th, 1907); Richfield Nat. Bank v. American Surety Co., 39 F. (2d) 387 (C. C. A. 8th, 1930) (bad faith); Fidelity & Deposit Co. v. Farmers' Bank, 44 F. (2d) 11 (C. C. A. 8th, 1930) (same); American National Bank v. Fidelity & Deposit Co. (1907) 129 Ga. 126, 58 S. E. 867 (depositary of receivership funds honored receiver's checks without requisite signature of judge; while nothing to indicate knowledge of receiver's fraudulent intent, bank treated as a knowing participant in breach of trust); Fidelity & Dep. Co. v. Queens County Trust Co. (1919) 226 N. Y. 225, 123 N. E. 370 (depositary of bankruptcy funds honored checks of trustee in bankruptcy without requisite countersignature of officer of court; bank should reasonably have been put upon inquiry); Bunting v. Ricks, 2 Dev. & Batt. Eq. 130 (N. C. 1838); United States Fid. & Guar. Co. v. United States Nat. Bank (1916) 80 Ore. 361, 157 Pac. 155; Rivers v. Liberty Nat. Bank (1926) 135 S. C. 107, 133 S. E. 210 ("gross negligence" on part of bank); Dobbins v. Carroll (1916) 137 Tenn.

133, 192 S. W. 166 (surety of master in chancery subrogated to claim of beneficiary against one who purchased nonnegotiable notes from master and later collected from maker); *cf.* Mendel v. Boyd (1902) 3 Neb. Unoff. 473, 91 N. W. 860.

In the recent case of Martin v. Federal Surety Co., 58 F. (2d) 79 (C. C. A. 8th, 1932), the authorities are elaborately discussed and the decision put expressly on the above-mentioned distinction. *Cf.* National Surety Co. v. Webster Lumber Co. (1932) 187 Minn. 50, 244 N. W. 290.

[19] Louisville Trust Co v. Royal Indemnity Co., 20 S. W. (2d) 71 (Ky. App. 1929), (1930) 43 Harv. L. Rev. 500.

[20] *In re* Whitney's Estate (1932) 124 Cal. App. 109, 11 Pac. (2d) 1107 (contributive subrogation denied the bond surety); Southern Surety Co. v. Tessum (1929) 178 Minn. 495, 228 N. W. 326, (1930) 14 Minn. L. Rev. 423, (1930) 39 Yale L. J. 749; Adams v. Gleaves, 10 Lea 367 (Tenn. 1882). *Contra:* Hewlett v. Beede (1905) 2 Cal. App. 561, 83 Pac. 1086 (negligent executor denied relief against the sureties of the embezzling executor, although it was admitted he could recover from his coexecutor; not cited in the later California case of *In re* Whitney's Estate, *supra*).

If a third person collude with the surety's fiduciary, the surety will be subrogated to the creditor's claim against that party (American Bonding Co. v. National Mechanics Bank [1903] 97 Md. 598, 55 Atl. 395; Blake v. Traders' Nat. Bank [1887] 145 Mass. 13, 12 N. E. 414). So also where the third person has knowingly accepted trust funds in satisfaction of the debt of the principal. Hall v. Windsor Sav. Bank (1923) 97 Vt. 125, 121 Atl. 582.

[21] An agent liable under contract with his employer for all moneys collected, including those collected by subagents, has been subrogated to the employer's remedy against the surety on the bond of the subagent. Hough v. Aetna Life Ins. Co. (1870) 57 Ill. 318.

[22] *In re* Wilson, 252 Fed. 631 (S. D. N. Y. 1917); *In re* Toole, 274 Fed. 337 (C. C. A. 2d, 1921). For a detailed consideration of the respective rights of different classes of brokers' customers, see Oppenheimer, *Rights and Obligations of Customers in Stockbrokerage Bankruptcies* (1924) 37 Harv. L. Rev. 860; Tillinghast, *Problems of Distribution in Bankruptcies of Stockbrokers* (1930) 44 *ibid.* 65; Holohan, *Contribution among Securities Pledged by a Defaulting Stock Broker* (1930) 4 So. Calif. L. Rev. 1.

[23] Compare the rule of sale in inverse order of alienation where a mortgage covers several lots subesquently sold by the mortgagor. The first purchaser paying the full value of the lot and taking an unqualified warranty deed becomes in effect, if involuntarily, in respect to his land the surety of the mortgagor. The second purchaser takes his lot subject to the equity of the first. See Sheldon, *Subrogation* § 75.

[24] First Taxing Dist. v. Gregory (1922) 97 Conn. 639, 118 Atl. 96. *Accord:* Pittsburgh-Westmoreland Coal Co. v. Kerr (1917) 220 N. Y. 137, 115 N. E. 465.

[25] Liles v. Rogers (1893) 113 N. C. 197, 18 S. E. 104; *cf.* Fidelity & Deposit Co. v. Gill (1914) 116 Va. 86, 81 S. E. 39.

[26] Benson v. Saffert-Gugisberg Cement Const. Co. (1924) 159 Minn. 54, 198 N. W. 297.

[27] Benson v. Saffert-Gugisberg Cement Const. Co. (1924) 161 Minn. 269, 201 N. W. 424.

[28] *Accord:* Young v. Vough (1873) 23 N. J. Eq. 325; Klopp & Stump v. Lebanon Bank (1863) 46 Pa. 88; see (1925) 9 Minn. L. Rev. 292.

[29] (1901) 114 Iowa 647, 87 N. W. 657. Compare Wanack v. Michels (1905) 215 Ill. 87, 74 N. E. 84. A statute made the owner of premises knowingly leased for a dram shop liable with the saloon keeper to those injured by the sale of liquor. The liquor dealer was

also required to give bond for payment of such damages. The surety paid a judgment against both seller and lessor but was denied contribution from the lessor. One may agree with the result and not with the reasoning, which was that, if the lessor had paid, he could not have recovered from the saloon keeper since he was an intentional wrongdoer, hence not a surety for him or cosurety with him. If the court is right in this respect, it might be thought to follow that the bond surety would be entitled to complete indemnity from the lessor. But one may question the application of the rule of no indemnity between tortfeasors in this case. While technically the lessor became a tortfeasor, yet leasing for the purpose was not illegal nor was the sale of liquor illegal, and as between the two tortfeasors the saloon keeper was the one in a position to control the immoderate use of intoxicants, the prevention of which with its consequences was the object of the statute. It would seem, therefore, that the lessor should be entitled to full indemnity from the lessee and from the surety as well.

[80] Rogers v. National Surety Co. (1927) 116 Neb. 170, 216 N. W. 182 (so far as the decision depends on the view that there can be no contribution between a surety and a "guarantor," the criticism of Merrill, *Contribution between Sureties and Guarantors* [1932] 2 Idaho L. J. 1, appears eminently sound); *cf.* Cleary v. Fidelity & Deposit Co. (1928) 117 Neb. 478, 221 N. W. 107. But *cf.* State v. Citizens' State Bank (1929) 118 Neb. 337, 224 N. W. 868.

[81] Elder v. Commonwealth (1867) 55 Pa. 485.

[82] Bank of Midland v. Harris (1914) 114 Ark. 344, 170 S. W. 67; Johnson v. Wallace (1916) 123 Ark. 74, 184 S. W. 835.

[83] Accepting the definition that a contract of suretyship is one to answer for the debt, default, or miscarriage of another (1 Brandt, *Suretyship and Guaranty* [ed. 3; 1905] § 1), one may ask why theft insurance is not suretyship, since the contract indemnifies against the breach of legal duty not to commit theft. Likewise, while fire insurance usually protects against fire loss resulting from pure casualty or the act of a tortfeasor, yet in respect to the latter type of fire the contract is like theft insurance. Even if usually principal and surety are parties to one and the same contract, this is not necessarily so, and at least most suretyship incidents apply when they are not, and even when the principal is unaware that his obligation is secured by a surety's undertaking. One making a guaranty without the knowledge of the principal may be denied the benefit of the ordinary rule that the cause of action for reimbursement, for the purpose of the statute of limitations, runs from the time of payment, yet may secure reimbursement through subrogation, with the qualification that so far as the statute is concerned he will stand in the shoes of the creditor (Leslie v. Compton [1918] 103 Kan. 92, 172 Pac. 1015). Usually in suretyship there is a named principal, while theft insurance protects against all thieves; yet would fidelity suretyship (frequently termed fidelity insurance) be any the less such because it protects against the acts of a group of unnamed employees? If it be urged that the distinction is that in suretyship the liability of the principal is contractual, whereas in insurance the liability of the "principal," namely, the one against whom subrogation is available, is delictual, even this breaks down, since the liability of the faithless employee is frequently delictual, based upon the relationship rather than upon contract. Furthermore, as will be seen, there are not lacking examples in which the insurer is subrogated to purely contractual claims of the insured against third persons. See p. 255 *infra.*

[84] Northern Trust Co. v. Consolidated Elevator Co. (1919) 142 Minn. 132, 171 N. W. 265.

[85] Mason v. Sainsbury (1782) 3 Doug. 61; Clark v. Inhabitants of the Hundred of Blything (1823) 2 B. & C. 254.

[86] Potomac Ins. Co. v. Nickson (1924) 64 Utah 395, 231 Pac. 445. In Farmers' Fire

Ins. Co. v. Johnston (1897) 113 Mich. 426, 71 N. W. 1074, a fire company was denied subrogation to the insured's cause of action against his vendor for fraudulent representations of value, on the assigned ground that the representations did not cause the fire. A simpler basis would seem to be that since the insurer paid only the value of the goods at the time of destruction—unless the policy was a valued one and the value was based on the fraudulent representations of the vendor—the insurer did not pay a loss for which the defendant was liable, for in an action against the seller the measure of recovery would be, at most, the difference between the actual value and the represented value.

[37] Stevens v. Stewart-Warner Co. (1916) 223 Mass. 44, 111 N. E. 771.

[38] London Guar. & Accident Co. v. Otis Elevator Co. (1927) 86 Ind. App. 150, 155 N. E. 182; John Wanamaker v. Otis Elevator Co. (1920) 228 N. Y. 192, 126 N. E. 718. While the two policies contained express subrogation clauses, no attention was paid them by the courts, and under the tort subrogation cases they would appear unnecessary.

[39] Royal Indemnity Co. v. Poplar Bluff Trust Co. (1929) 223 Mo. App. 908, 20 S. W. (2d) 971. Although the matter is not discussed, the liability of the insurer on the policy may have been on the ground that the insured's failure to notify its bank promptly after receiving the vouchers validated the bank's debit against the insured, and thus the insured sustained a loss. As the drawee bank would have been entitled to recover its payment from the defendant bank, the theory of the insured's claim against the defendant must be that upon its reimbursement of the drawee bank—for that is what the validation of the debit amounts to—the insured was subrogated to the drawee's claim against the defendant. The insurer then claims by way of double subrogation.

[40] Aetna Casualty & Surety Co. v. Phoenix Nat. Bank (1932) 285 U. S. 209.

[41] Hall & Long v. Nashville & Chattanooga R. R., 13 Wall 367, 372–73 (U. S. 1871): "It has been argued, however, that these decisions rest upon the doctrine that a wrong-doer is to be punished; that the defendants against whom such actions have been maintained were wrong-doers; but that, in the present case, the fire by which the insured goods were destroyed was accidental, without fault of the defendants, and therefore that they stood, in relation to the owner, at most in the position of double insurers [note the suggestion of contribution]. The argument will not bear examination. . . . The law raises against him [the carrier] a conclusive presumption of misconduct, or breach of duty, in relation to every loss not caused by excepted perils. Even if innocent, in fact, he has consented by his contract to be dealt with as if he were not so. He does not stand, therefore, on the same footing with that of an insurer, who may have entered into his contract of indemnity, relying upon the carrier's vigilance and responsibility." The answers to the arguments are obvious. The presumption is a pure fiction. Whether the insurer could have justifiably relied upon subrogation, at least in the absence of an express subrogation clause broad enough to include the claim, must depend on the law, and therefore the argument begs the question. The carrier is hardly a cause of the loss except in the most technical way, when, for example, fire spreading from adjoining premises destroys the goods without any fault on its part.

[42] Crissey & Fowler Lumber Co. v. Denver & R. G. R. R. (1902) 17 Colo. App. 275, 68 Pac. 670; Hart v. Western R. R., 13 Metc. 99 (Mass. 1847). But see Home Ins. Co. v. Atchison, T. & S. F. R. R. (1893) 19 Colo. 46, 48, 34 Pac. 281, 284. Judging from these cases, one may expect complete subrogation in other types of absolute liability such as that presented by Rylands v. Fletcher, L. R. (1868) 3 H. L. 330. It is not perhaps without significance that statutes have been enacted which in effect give the benefit of the insurance to the railroad company. Leavitt v. Canadian Pac. Ry. (1897) 90 Me. 153, 37 Atl. 886; Farren v. Maine Cent. R. R. (1914) 112 Me. 81, 90 Atl. 497; Lyons v. Boston & Lowell R. R. (1902) 181 Mass. 551, 64 N. E. 404; Boston Ice Co. v. Boston & Me. R. R. (1913) 77 N. H. 6, 86 Atl. 356.

[43] Darrell v. Tibbitts (1880) 5 Q. B. D. 560. After the insurer paid the lessor, the lessee recovered from a tortfeasor and with the proceeds made the repairs. The action was by the insurer to recover from the insured the insurance money. Although the greater number of references to the case ignore the recovery from the tortfeasor, and Brett, J., reached his result independently of it, it must be noted that the actual decision left the ultimate loss not on the lessee but on the tortfeasor. To deny recovery in the action meant double indemnity for the lessor. It is significant that Cotton, L. J., expressly repudiated any distinction between subrogation to tort claims and to contract claims. *Accord:* but with the element of recovery by the contractor against a tortfeasor lacking: North British Mercantile Ins. Co. v. London, Liverpool & Globe Co. (1876) 5 Ch. D. 569 (bailee under contract absolutely liable for fire loss); Larner v. Commercial Union Assur. Co. (1926) 127 Misc. 1, 215 N. Y. Supp. 151.

[44] Burford & Co. v. Glasgow Water Co. (1928) 223 Ky. 54, 2 S. W. (2d) 1027 (denying a fire insurer subrogation to the insured's claim as a "beneficiary" of a contract between the city and a water company), (1928) 37 Yale L. J. 1160; Plate Glass Underwriters' Mut. Ins. Co. v. Ridgewood Realty Co. (1925) 219 Mo. App. 186, 269 S. W. 659. *Contra:* Powell & Powell v. Wake Water Co. (1916) 171 N. C. 290, 88 S. E. 426.

United States v. American Tobacco Co. (1897) 166 U. S. 468, is distinguishable. An insurer paid the Company for the loss of unused internal revenue stamps, the full value of which was recoverable from the government. The allowance of subrogation against the United States was not to cause it an affirmative loss but merely to compel it to reimburse taxes paid in advance for privileges not used.

[45] See Note (1928) 28 Col. L. Rev. 202.

[46] Leyden v. Lawrence (1911) 79 N. J. Eq. 113, 81 Atl. 121; Milwaukee Mechanics' Ins. Co. v. Ramsey (1915) 76 Ore. 570, 149 Pac. 542; see 3 Joyce, *Insurance* (ed. 2; 1917) §§ 3563, 3564. The same is true with other types of lienors (Interstate Ice & Power Corp. v. United States Ins. Co. [1926] 243 N. Y. 95, 152 N. E. 476). The Massachusetts cases seem to stand alone in cutting the Gordian knot by ignoring the indemnity nature of the contract and permitting the mortgagee to collect and keep both the insurance money and the debt (King. v. State Mut. Fire Ins. Co., 7 Cush. 1 [Mass. 1851]; Suffolk Fire Ins. Co. v. Boyden, 9 Allen 123 [Mass. 1864]; International Trust Co. v. Boardman [1889] 149 Mass. 158, 21 N. E. 239 (insurance by attaching creditor). This result of course offers a powerful temptation to a dishonest mortgagee. The question is not of much practical importance at present owing to the use of the standard mortgage clause whereby both mortgagor and mortgagee are protected, and subrogation of the insurer provided for only when the mortgagor has violated a condition of the policy.

[47] See Vance, *Insurance* (ed. 2; 1930) § 172. Allowing the insurer subrogation: Rayner v. Preston (1881) 18 Ch. D. 1; Castillain v. Preston (1883) 11 Q. B. D. 380; *cf.* White v. Gilman (1903) 138 Cal. 375, 71 Pac. 436; Brownell v. Board of Education (1925) 239 N. Y. 369, 146 N. E. 630, Note (1925) 25 Col. L. Rev. 477. Awarding the vendee the benefit of the insurance: Brady v. Welsh (1925) 200 Iowa 44, 204 N. W. 235; Godfrey v. Alcorn (1926) 215 Ky. 465, 284 S. W. 1094; Standard Oil Co. v. Dye (1929) 223 Mo. App. 926, 20 S. W. (2d) 946; *cf.* Dolan v. Spencer (1933) 92 Colo. 389, 21 Pac. (2d) 411 (awarding the optionee the benefit of insurance carried by the optionor), (1934) 47 Harv. L. Rev. 532.

[48] Foley v. Manufacturers' & Builders' Fire Ins. Co. (1897) 152 N. Y. 131, 46 N. E. 318, suggests that an affirmative answer might be given. *Cf.* Michael v. Prussian Nat. Ins. Co.(1902) 171 N. Y. 25, 63 N. E. 810. It has been decided that if both parties carried insurance, the contractor's insurer, who paid the contractor who then rebuilt, was not entitled to any subrogation against the owner's insurer. Schultz v. Home Ins. Co. (1917) 205 Ill. App. 297.

[49] Monteleone v. Harding (1898) 50 La. Ann. 1147, 23 So. 990.

[50] New York Title & Mortgage Co. v. First Nat. Bank of Kansas City, 51 F. (2d) 485 (C. C. A. 8th, 1931), (1932) 30 Mich. L. Rev. 800.

[51] (1896) 64 Minn. 492, 67 N. W. 543 (while the policy contained an express subrogation clause, no attention is paid it in the opinion). Would a title insurer be subrogated to the insured's claim on the covenants of a predecessor in title?

[52] Goddard v. Whyte (1860) 2 Giff. 449. *Accord:* Leake v. Ferguson, 2 Gratt. 419 (Va. 1846); Frederick Snare Corp. v. Globe Indemnity Co. (1922) 201 App. Div. 505, 194 N. Y. Supp. 353. Commercial Casualty Ins. Co. v. Capital City Surety Co. (1928) 224 App. Div. 500, 231 N. Y. Supp. 169.

[53] Ursini v. Piazza (1925) 101 Conn. 736, 127 Atl. 350 (query, if this would be so had the offset claim arisen after the surety's surety paid). In Putnam v. Tash, 12 Gray 121 (Mass. 1858), a guarantor to a bank of all notes to be discounted for a third party was denied subrogation to the bank's claim against the maker of a note of which the third party was payee, when, by reason of failure of consideration between maker and payee, the latter had really become principal.

[54] 12 B. Mon. 444 (Ky. 1851); *cf.* Furnold v. Bank of Mo. (1869) 44 Mo. 336.

[55] See Sheldon, *Subrogation* § 169.

[56] Goldman v. Mitchell-Fletcher Co. (1928) 292 Pa. 354, 141 Atl. 231. Probably the same view is responsible for Hill v. Wright, Williams & Co. (1861) 23 Ark 530. In Taul v. Epperson (1873) 38 Tex. 492, judgment was obtained against *A* and *B*, and became a lien on *A's* land. *A* did not sue out a writ of error, and when *S*, the surety on *B's* supersedeas bond, paid the affirmed judgment, he was decreed complete subrogation to the judgment lien upon *A's* land. But no information is given concerning the relations between *A* and *B*. A similar unsatisfactory case is Robinson v. Sherman, 2 Gratt. 178 (Va. 1845).

[57] National Surety Co. v. Massachusetts Bonding & Ins. Co., 19 F. (2d) 448 (C. C. A. 2d, 1927), *cert.* denied (1927) 275 U. S. 548. But see Note (1927) 76 U. of Pa. L. Rev. 75. In Southern Surety Co. v. Nichols (1927) 239 Mich. 158, 214 N. W. 137, the court contented itself, if not others, by stating that the rule is "elementary."

[58] Nelson v. Century Indemnity Co., 65 F. (2d) 765 (C. C. A. 9th, 1933); Agren v. Staker (1928) 46 Idaho 36, 267 Pac. 460; Goldman v. Mitchell-Fletcher Co. (1928) 292 Pa. 354, 141 Atl. 231.

In so-called partially concurrent insurance of the same insured, the various insurers contribute, however difficult may be the problem of determining the proportions; yet clearly the risks are not entirely identical. See Richards, *Insurance* (ed. 3; 1910) § 318; Notes (1911) 24 Harv. L. Rev. 487, (1927) 40 *ibid.* 878; *cf.* Burnett v. Millsaps (1881) 59 Miss. 333 (sureties); Cherry v. Wilson (1878) 78 N. C. 164 (same). But see Exchange Mut. Indemnity Ins. Co. v. Zurich General Accident, Fire & Life Ins. Co. (1924) 122 Misc. 386, 202 N. Y. Supp. 720.

[59] Even when there are different obligations of the same principal, sureties on those obligations may be brought into relation with each other. Thus, suppose two obligations of the principal with collateral securing both. *A* is surety on one and *B* on the other. While the creditor may apply all the collateral in satisfaction of the obligation for which *A* has bound himself in spite of the demand of *B* that it be prorated between the two debts, it does not follow that after payment by *B*, he may not properly demand as against *A*, who has been relieved of liability by the application of the security, that *A* reimburse him for an amount equivalent to that which would have inured to *B's* benefit had the creditor himself prorated the security. Wilcox v. Fairhaven Bank, 7 Allen 270 (Mass.

1863); Cory v. Leonard (1874) 56 N. Y. 494. In the proper circumstances there may possibly be contribution between insurers of different persons. Ramsdell v. Insurance Co. of No. Am. (1928) 197 Wis. 136, 221 N. W. 654.

60 Aetna Casualty & Surety Co. v. Equitable Surety Co. (1920) 145 Minn. 326, 329, 177 N. W. 137, 138: "The surety holds the same relation as the principal in respect to the obligations of a bond, hence the equitable considerations which should determine the primary liability as between the principals ought to be applied as between their respective sureties." *Accord:* Nelson v. Century Indemnity Co., 65 F. (2d) 765 (C. C. A. 9th, 1933); Commercial Casualty Ins. Co. v. Capital City Surety Co. (1928) 224 App. Div. 500, 231 N. Y. Supp. 169; Bender v. George (1879) 92 Pa. 36; Goldman v. Mitchell-Fletcher Co. (1928) 292 Pa. 354, 141 Atl. 231; Padgett v. Young County, 204 S. W. 1046 (Tex. Civ. App. 1918). It is merely an application of the same rule that makes the relation between separate sureties of cosureties dependent on the relation between the co-sureties. Furnold v. Bank of Mo. (1869) 44 Mo. 336. The same is true as between insurers of different persons (Schultz v. Home Ins. Co. [1917] 205 Ill. App. 297; North British & Mercantile Ins. Co. v. London, Liverpool & Globe Co. [1877] 5 Ch. D. 569). St. Paul Title Ins. & Trust Co. v. Johnson (1896) 64 Minn. 492, 67 N. E. 543, subrogated the title insurer of a mortgagee against the mortgagor and his sureties on a bond to the mortgagee to pay off prior mechanics' liens.

61 (1929) 178 Minn. 495, 228 N. W. 326.

62 In Union Nat. Bank v. Legendre (1883) 35 La. Ann. 787, the court reasoned that since an employee, who connived to aid his fellow employee in embezzlement, could not recover from the latter's fidelity surety, his surety could stand in no better position. Since here, however, the principals are willful wrongdoers, with contribution in respect to them denied only on grounds of policy, there is little to choose between their sureties, and contributive relief between them would appear proper. See p. 264 *infra.*

63 See p. 250 *supra.*

64 *Accord:* Adams v. Gleaves, 10 Lea 367 (Tenn. 1882). But it may be that the rule given above must yield to a minor qualification. In Commonwealth v. Stratton, 7 J. J. Marsh. 90 (Ky. 1831), a creditor obtained judgment against *P* and *S,* his surety. After issuance of execution against *P,* the sheriff, in violation of law, levied upon a later execution in favor of another creditor of *P* and as a result *S* had to pay. The recovery of *S* against the sheriff's surety was based on the ground that under the statute the sheriff's bond protected anyone injured by the sheriff's official acts, and consequently the actual decision does not depend upon subrogation to the claim of the creditor. An interesting point, however, is suggested by the opinion. The court said that *P* could not have recovered on the sheriff's bond since he was not injured by the sheriff's appropriation of his property to a different debt. Assuming that *S* was not directly within the protection of the sheriff's bond, would he still not be entitled to subrogation to the creditor's remedy on the bond, since the sheriff's wrongful act destroyed the prior claim of the creditor to have *P's* property applied on the judgment?

65 Wilcox v. Fairhaven Bank, 7 Allen 270 (Mass. 1863).

66 This refinement is said to be inapplicable to a surety for a whole debt with liability limited to a certain amount. See Ellis v. Emmanuel (1876) 1 L. R. Ex. D. 157. Whether a case falls within one class or the other is frequently difficult to determine. See 2 Williston, *Contracts* § 1253. The English doctrine is discussed and the American cases reviewed in Note (1931) 29 Mich. L. Rev. 753; Note (1931) 41 Yale L. J. 141; (1920) 34 Harv. L. Rev. 94; (1924) 37 *ibid.* 392; (1921) 21 Col. L. Rev. 293; (1922) 70 U. of Pa. L. Rev. 245; (1933) 1 Chi. L. Rev. 155.

67 United States v. National Surety Co. (1920) 254 U. S. 73; Jenkins v. National

Surety Co. (1928) 277 U. S. 258; Board of Health v. Teutonia Bank & Trust Co. (1915) 137 La. 422, 68 So. 748; Knaffl v. Knoxville Banking & Trust Co. (1915) 133 Tenn. 655, 182 S. W. 232. But see Cole v. Myers (1916) 100 Neb. 480, 160 N. W. 894, in which it was made, in part at least, the basis of the decision, as well as in those cases relying upon it. See note 74 *infra*.

[68] Commissioner v. Chelsea Sav. Bank (1910) 161 Mich. 691, 125 N. W. 424, 127 N. W. 351. Nor can the bank's surety take advantage of a statute forbidding deposits of public funds in excess of a percentage of the bank's paid-in capital. People of Sioux County v. National Surety Co. (1928) 276 U. S. 238; Scotts Bluff Co. v. First Nat. Bank (1927) 115 Neb. 273, 212 N. W. 617.

[69] Ordinarily, perhaps, the question would not arise. If the officer himself is liable to the county for the excess amount only, the county's dividend would not usually satisfy the county's claim. The point, however, might become of consequence if the treasurer is absolutely liable for the public funds and in addition is forbidden to deposit more than a certain percentage of the bank's paid-in capital.

[70] In *In re* Stinger's Estate (1921) 61 Mont. 173, 201 Pac. 693, a guardian made an unwarranted loan of funds, but after full payment to the ward and despite the "clean hands" argument, was subrogated to the ward's claim against the maker of the note. In State *ex rel.* Davis v. People's State Bank of Anselmo (1924) 111 Neb. 136, 198 N. W. 1018, a county treasurer, who made an improper deposit in excess of 50 per cent of the paid-up stock of the bank, but who apparently had not reimbursed the county, was, as representative of the county, allowed recovery against the state depositors' guaranty fund. See Aetna Casualty & Surety Co. v. Village of Maywood (1931) 262 Ill. App. 206, 221, *cert.* denied, Ill. Sup. Ct., Oct., 1931 term: "As between the bank which failed to repay money deposited with it and a village treasurer who made the mistake of trusting the bank when *technically* she ought not to have done so, there can be no question in a court of conscience as to which would have the superior equities, . . ." (Italics inserted.) *Cf.* Forest County v. Poppy (1927) 193 Wis. 274, 213 N. W. 676. But *cf.* Rowley v. Towsley (1884) 53 Mich. 329, 19 N. W. 20. In Wilkinson v. Babbitt, Fed. Cas. No. 17,668 (W. D. Mo. 1877), an internal revenue deputy collector, in violation of law, deposited funds in a bank that failed. The collector was forced to pay but was denied subrogation to the government's preferred claim against the bank. This decision is particularly obnoxious, since the collector was apparently not privy to the deputy's act and was really only a surety for the deputy.

[71] Probably not $2000, because, if the excess deposit had not been made, the assets would likely be less and consequently the dividend rate smaller.

[72] Compare United States Fid. & Guar. Co. v. Title Guar. & Surety Co., 200 Fed. 443 (D. Md. 1912). But *cf.* State *ex rel.* Davis v. People's State Bank of Anselmo (1924) 111 Neb. 136, 198 N. W. 1018; Cleary v. Fidelity & Dep. Co. (1928) 117 Neb. 478, 221 N. W. 107.

[73] United States Fid. & Guar. Co. v. Title Guar. & Surety Co., 200 Fed. 443 (D. Md. 1912). Compare the cases holding that where two tortfeasors are liable to a third person, the one with the "last clear chance" to avoid the injury may have complete indemnity from the other. See Leflar, *Contribution and Indemnity between Tortfeasors* (1932) 81 U. of Pa. L. Rev. 130, 151.

[74] United States Fid. & Guar. Co. v. McClintock, 26 F. (2d) 944 (D. Wyo. 1927) (subsequently overruled on other points by Jenkins v. National Surety Co. [1928] 277 U. S. 258); Ortonville v. Hahn (1930) 181 Minn. 271, 232 N. W. 320 (statute relieved officer for funds lawfully deposited); Cole v. Myers (1916) 100 Neb. 480, 160 N. W. 894 (officer apparently liable for excess deposit only); Minshull v. American Surety Co.

(1927) 141 Wash. 440, 252 Pac. 147 (under state law treasurer liable even for funds lawfully deposited).

[75] National Surety Co. v. Salt Lake County, 5 F. (2d) 34 (C. C. A. 8th, 1925) (stress laid upon fact that the treasurer was obligee of the bank's bond and suggested the answer might be different if bond had run to the county); Aetna Casualty & Surety Co. v. Village of Maywood (1931) 262 Ill. App. 206, *cert.* denied, Ill. Sup. Ct., Oct., 1931 term (the most fully considered case), (1931) 26 Ill. L. Rev. 448, 684.

[76] See Vance, *Insurance* § 178.

[77] *Ibid.*

[78] The whole subject is ably treated by Leflar, *op. cit., supra* note 73.

[79] Messersmith v. American Fid. Co. (1921) 232 N. Y. 161, 133 N. E. 432.

[80] Underwriters at Lloyds of Minneapolis v. Smith (1926) 166 Minn. 388, 208 N. W. 13; Frankfort Gen. Ins. Co. v. Milwaukee Elec. Ry. & Light Co. (1919) 169 Wis. 533, 173 N. W. 307 (two tortfeasors liable through negligence of their respective employees).

[81] Steinfield v. Massachusetts Bonding & Ins. Co. (1920) 79 N. H. 422, 111 Atl. 303; see Leflar, *op. cit., supra* note 73, at 148.

[82] Hackensack Brick Co. v. Borough of Bogota (1916) 86 N. J. Eq. 143, 97 Atl. 725.

[83] While not strictly in point, see the interesting case of New York Cons. R. R. v. Massachusetts Bonding & Ins. Co. (1920) 193 App. Div. 438, 184 N. Y. Supp. 243, *aff'd* without opinion (1922) 233 N. Y. 547, 135 N. E. 912, where the same company was insurer of both.

[84] Frankfort Gen. Ins. Co. v. Milwaukee Elec. Ry. & Light Co. (1919) 169 Wis. 533, 173 N. W. 307.

[85] But *cf.* Beacon Lamp Co. v. Travellers Ins. Co. (1900) 61 N. J. Eq. 59, 47 Atl. 579, modified on appeal, Travellers Ins. Co. v. Moses (1901) 63 N. J. Eq. 260, 49 Atl. 720.

[86] Cal. Stat. 1919, c. 367.

[87] Metropolitan Casualty Ins. Co. v. Union Indemnity Co. (1930) 229 App. Div. 827, 242 N. Y. Supp. 807, 243 N. Y. Supp. 904, *aff'd* without opinion (1931) 255 N. Y. 591, 175 N. E. 326, (1931) 16 Corn. L. Q. 400.

[88] See Vance, *Insurance* § 178.

[89] Anoka Lumber Co. v. Fidelity & Cas. Co. (1895) 63 Minn. 286, 65 N. W. 353; Maryland Casualty Co. v. Peppard (1915) 53 Okla. 515, 157 Pac. 106; Hoven v. Employers' Liability Assur. Corp. (1896) 93 Wis. 201, 67 N. W. 46. Or by a bill in equity. Capelle v. United States Fid. & Guar. Co. (1922) 80 N. H. 481, 120 Atl. 556.

[90] Anoka Lumber Co. v. Fidelity & Cas. Co. (1895) 63 Minn. 286, 65 N. W. 353; see 1 Williston, *Contracts* §§ 362–64; *cf.* Merchants' Mut. Auto Ins. Co. v. Smart (1925) 267 U. S. 126. But *cf.* Voss v. Stranahan (1929) 248 Mich. 390, 227 N. W. 542, (1930) 28 Mich. L. Rev. 1060.

[91] It is one of the serious objections to the cases denying contribution between tortfeasors that such collusion is rendered possible. See Leflar, *op. cit., supra* note 73, at 137.

[92] See pp. 249, 250 *supra.*

[93] In Sutton v. Champagne (1917) 141 La. 469, 75 So. 209, a parent, liable by statute for the torts of his child, was given complete indemnity against the person whose negligence coöperated with the child's.

[94] Adams v. White Bus Line (1921) 184 Cal. 710, 195 Pac. 389, but *cf.* Salter v. Lombardi (1931) 116 Cal. App. 602, 3 Pac. (2d) 38; United States Cas. Co. v. Cincinnati, N. O. & T. P. Ry. (1927) 218 Ky. 455, 291 S. W. 709; Fidelity & Cas. Co. v. Christensen

(1931) 183 Minn. 182, 236 N. W. 618 (1932) 27 Ill. L. Rev. 78, 30 Mich. L. Rev. 804; Leflar, *op. cit., supra* note 73, at 144; Fiorentino v. Adkins (1931) 9 N. J. Misc. 446, 154 Atl. 429; Royal Indemnity Co. v. Becker (1930) 122 Ohio St. 582, 173 N. E. 194, (1931) 79 U. of Pa. L. Rev. 507 (nor by becoming supersedeas surety of the tortfeasor did the liability insurer better his position, although as surety to the tortfeasee it was insisting on subrogation to the claim of the tortfeasee and disclaimed subrogation through the tortfeasor. But *cf.* Smith v. Fall River Joint Union High School Dist., 26 Pac. (2d) 37 (Cal. App. 1933); Cain v. Quannah Light & Ice Co. (1928) 131 Okla. 25, 267 Pac. 641.

[95] *Cf.* Schubert v. Schubert Wagon Co. (1928) 249 N. Y. 253, 164 N. E. 42.

[96] See Leflar, *op. cit., supra* note 73, at 141.

[97] White Plains v. Ellis (1920) 113 Misc. 5, 184 N. Y. Supp. 444, *aff'd* without opinion (1922) 200 App. Div. 869, 192 N. Y. Supp. 920.

[98] Inasmuch as insurance is doubtless invalid which would protect one against liability founded on willful and conscious wrongdoing directed to the consummation of injury, the problem will not arise in the case of such a tort.

[99] Kolb v. National Surety Co. (1903) 176 N. Y. 233, 68 N. E. 247. While Smith v. Fall River High School Dist., 26 Pac. (2d) 37 (Cal. App. 1933) did not perhaps call for an opinion on the measure of recourse, certain statements may be thought to indicate that the appeal surety of one tortfeasor would be allowed complete recourse against the other. See also Agren v. Staker (1928) 46 Idaho 36, 267 Pac. 460.

THE CONSTITUTION AS AN INSTITUTION*

BY K. N. LLEWELLYN

MEN LIMP ALONG for years or decades with an outworn, performance-baffling framework of their thought, until some child, inadequately taught to "see," cries out that the king in question has no clothes. New understanding comes typically as a scattered qualification of the existing ways of thinking. Scattered and occasional, not sustained or consistent; and qualification, not reorganization.

The king in question here is the Constitution of the United States. His supposed clothes consist of our now prevailing theory of constitutional law. It is too much to argue that that theory does not exist; the trouble is that it does. But it is high time that the untutored bystander set up his outcry. The theory does not serve to clothe. It leaves naked most of what needs covering; and what it covers, it fetters, where it should leave free.

This is no discovery. Bentley saw and said in 1908 all that should have been necessary to force Constitutional law theory into total recon-

* This essay represents an effort to round out, on the side of Constitutional law theory, some implications of the point of view presented before the League for Industrial Democracy at Camp Tamiment in June, 1933, to appear in *A New Constitution for America*, ed. Paul Blanshard; my first phrasing of the idea appears in (1933) 3 Nat. Encyc. 239.

I owe many suggestions to the work of Max Radin and James Landis. But most of all I am indebted to Bentley's magnificent study. And for needed help in clarifying both theory and presentation I owe thanks to Ambrose Doskow, Milton Handler, Herbert Wechsler, and Emma Corstvet. For further development *re* the idea of official behavior as the central material for legal theory, see *A Realistic Jurisprudence* (1930) 30 Col. L. Rev. 431; *re* the conception of interested groups, see *Legal Institutions and Economics* (1925) 15 Am. Ec. Rev. 665, *Law Enforcement and Law Observance* (1928) 1928 Proc. Conf. Soc. Work 127, and *What Price Contract* (1931) 40 Yale L. J. 704; *re* the common law judicial process and the government of cases by rules, see *Legal Tradition and Social Science Method* in *Essays on Research in the Social Sciences* (1931) 89, esp. 105 ff.; *Law and the Modern Mind, a Symposium* (1931) 31 Col. L. Rev. 82; *Some Realism about Realism* (1931) 44 Harv. L. Rev. 1222, 1236 ff.; and *Präjudizienrecht und Rechtsprechung in Amerika* (1933) § 52 ff.; also *Bramble Bush* (1930) c. 4, 5; *re* attitudes or sets of people and institutions, and the interaction of diversified groups of institutions, see *Behind the Law of Divorce* (1931) 32 Col. L. Rev. 1281, esp. 33 *ibid.* 249 ff., the third portion of which will include particular study of the influence of laymen's practices on lawmen's attitudes and ethics.

struction.[1] McBain, in 1927, saw and said it again, and more accessibly, and was indorsed and supplemented by Landis.[2] It has been implicit always, and explicit often, in the magnificent work of Beard.[3] Indeed, any student of Bryce[4] ought to have moved forthwith into action; on such insight-in-practice rests the full import of his best work and thought.

But none of these men *carried through* his insight. Bentley, more interested in government than in constitution, more interested in general sociological theory than in either, limited his remarks on the nature of a constitution to a dozen pages. Bryce, in spite of his description of the English Constitution in terms which apply to *any* constitution, allowed himself to be misled in America by the presence of a Document and of a theory.[5] This, even though in dealing with our government he could wrestle toughmindedly with such of its unofficial aspects as Tammany. Beard was not greatly interested in personal reform of legal absurdities; his work has run to stress on extra-legal actualities. McBain, finally, although his very theme was The Living Constitution, and although he demonstrates beyond cavil (especially in his early chapters) the existence of a living Constitution which completes, alters, aye, and overrides the Document, moves then into discussion of what our Constitution *ought* to be. Some other scholar, before or since, may have milked the insight for all that it has to give. I do not know. But this stands clear: if he has, his work has found no hearing among constitutional lawyers. It is up to Constitutional laymen to take a hand.[6]

The argument of this paper runs somewhat as follows: The existing theory of our Constitutional law once had some point and value; as applied to a code some century and a half old, it has ceased to serve. It covers perhaps half of what the Court actually does, but covers that half in such manner as to throw the other half into Stygian black. A theory which suffers from any such misrepresentation of the facts confuses and distorts issues.[7] It cannot help but lead, repeatedly, to purblind action. And action which is intellectually purblind, even when it is informed by considerable intuition, registers an unfortunate number of misses on occasions when bull's-eyes are needed. A recanvass of the nature of any working constitution, and especially of ours, as being in essence not a document, but a living institution built (historically, genetically) in first instance *around* a particular Document, would make clear both the fact of and the reasons for the major vagaries of the Court's action. It would lay the foundation for an intelligent reconstruction of our Constitutional law theory. The practice of the Court to date offers indication that such reconstruction would be healthy. Indeed, the times make it rather clear that *some* reconstruction is on the way; they call for getting clear the issues involved, before the reconstructon occurs.

THE ORTHODOX THEORY AND ITS MERITS

THE FRAMEWORK of orthodox Constitutional theory consists of a number of propositions which to a new Adam or the well-known sudden visitor from Mars would seem appalling. Indeed, save for the blinders of familiarity, they would appall the thinking man of here and now.

(1) There is the notion that the primary source of information about what our Constitution comes to, is the language of a certain Document of 1789, together with a severely select coterie of additional paragraphs called Amendments. Is this not extraordinary? The Document was framed to start a governmental experiment for an agricultural, sectional, seaboard folk of some three millions. Yet it is supposed to control and describe our Constitution after a century and a half of operation; it is conceived to give basic information about the government of a nation, a hundred and thirty millions strong, the population and advanced industrial civilization of which have spread across a continent.

(2) There is the notion that rulings of the Supreme Court on Constitutional points *interpret* or *apply*, seldom do more than *merely* interpret or apply, this Document as Amended. This notion is a corollary of the first.

(3) From the two flows a third: that the next best source of information about what the Constitution is, lies in the aforementioned rulings of the Supreme Court.[8]

(4) Related to these notions are two others: one, that the only amendments to the Constitution are the Amendments.

(5) The other—a sort of premise to the theory at large—that "writ-

ten" and unwritten constitutions are different in their fundamental nature.

As to such propositions or notions, or any which are cousin to them, it will be argued here that they are hopelessly misdescriptive of the facts about our Constitutional life; and that, further (and in this case by consequence) they are seriously ill-adapted to achieve the major purposes to which Constitutional law theory is designed. As descriptions, each contains a kernel of truth; but a kernel so *relatively* small that the contrary would be closer to accuracy than the proposition.

The attack just launched contains two distinct counts: inadequacy of description, and inadequacy of functioning. Obviously, the second does not *per se* follow from the first.[9] Very bad descriptions may on occasion be extremely serviceable tools of thought. And certain items to the credit of the conceptual structure above suggested need to be set down, on the side of how it works. The matter of description is reserved.

(*a*) To begin with, the theory indicated affords lawyers and judges a most convenient vocabulary. It affords them, as well, a filing cabinet for the classification of Constitutional questions which, though distinctly inconvenient, is at least workable. As texts and digests demonstrate.

(*b*) For judges, it offers a refuge from responsibility. The words of the Document seem repeatedly to guide decision. They seem repeatedly even to control decision. Where they do either, they open escape from facing or, indeed, from seeing issues. Where they can be made to seem to do either, they open escape from answering in public for the manner of deciding issues. It is a bit amusing, in this connection, to reflect that the power of the judges to pass on Constitutional issues at all, like the practice of submitting many such issues to them for final decision, derives in no slightest manner from the words of the Document on which the judges purport to rest the decisions which they make, but instead from precisely such considerations as this same manner of decision tends to keep from consciousness.[10]

(*c*) The theory affords further a comforting sense of definite and tangible continuity—which could be had by other means. But it also offers a thing not easily to be had by other means—an even more comforting sense of solid permanence, of an *unchanging* foundation from which to face a changing, unreckonable world. "The Constitution does not change; it is merely interpreted."

(*d*) The theory, moreover, coincides with practice at least in this, that it recognizes the final official arbiter set up by practice (*not*, I repeat, by the Document) to determine constitutional controversy that refuses otherwise to get settled. From this derives an advantage both practical and esthetic. There is a single designated authority to determine, in the ordinary pinch, what is permitted by the Constitution and what is not. This does not remove all doubt; often the oracle has not spoken; often its pronouncements are more authoritative than lucid. But constantly reduce the area of doubt the oracle does. The esthetic advantage, meanwhile, lies in one's relative ability under the orthodox theory to know just what the Constitution "means." It "means"—under that theory—what the Supreme Court says it means, and neither more nor less. Here again, there remain doubts, but much is gained for the theorist. And much for practice as well: for by thrusting the bridge of "meaning" between the words and new events, it becomes possible to remodel to some extent the going Constitution without departing openly either from the words of the consecrated Document or from a theory almost as sacred as Itself. If no such remodeling had been achieved, it hardly needs argument that either Document or theory would have been junked these many years.

(*e*) Lastly, the orthodox approach provides for the guildsmen of the law and for the layman a reasonably single line of ideology about the Constitution and its part in the national life. This makes easy and likely the symbolization of the existing government by the Document of 1789. It provides for the existing form of government that sanctity which only century-long tradition can afford. The old and the new are *identified* in the minds of men, and all that is new is clothed with the ancient glory—which might be threatened, if the general public came to perceive the facts about the working Constitution; at the least, such perception would afford a platform for inconvenient agitation.[11]

Doubtless the orthodox theory can list other assets; surely, however, none that compare with these in value. The major assets being thus in the reckoning, let us turn to consideration of the liabilities.

We shall not expect to find these liabilities out in the open. They do not wait for us by appointment, with pink carnations in the left lapel. For any theory without *some* heritage of truth and workability dies young indeed; this one is finishing out its third half-century. Moreover, devices called by a faulty theory to its aid, when results are needed which the theory lacks power to produce alone, are not merely correctives. They serve also to save face.[12] Their purpose is to save the theory from its own implications, but without letting either faultiness of the theory or fact of rescue come to attention. Their operation is therefore not outright and aboveboard. They slink to cover when their work is done. Which is why they are not made consciously a part of *regular* equipment, *regularly* employed, called on *whenever* needed. Which in turn is why they are but partial correctives.

THE PRIVATE LAW BACKGROUND

Before bringing the implications of a face-saving corrective technique to bear upon Constitutional law it is as well to take stock of the situation on the private side.[13] It paves the way. The orthodox theory that *rules decide cases* has been splintered sufficiently in recent years to make no longer shocking the proposition that they do not. We know already something of the dodges and devices by which that theory was enabled to maintain itself in the teeth of fact. Finally, and by no means to be disregarded, our constitutional lawyers are case-trained men. The dodges used in private law have their analogues in the Constitutional field.

To begin with, the theory that rules decide cases seems for a century to have fooled not only library-ridden recluses, but judges. More, to have fooled even those skillful and hard-bitten first-hand observers of

[13] The argument will proceed: The discrepancy between theory and fact found in private law is exaggerated in the Constitutional field, because under a code of rigid words no easy and gradual rewording of outmoded rules in such manner as to hide the changes made in their content, is possible. The consequence is that with growing age all force in the actual words of a code withers and dies. What is left, and living, is not a code, but an institution. Many of the institution's roots trace back through time into the code. *Many do not.* But the living institution is neither the dead code nor its "interpretation." It is not even by any parthenogenesis descended from its great-grandmother code alone. It is new, it is different, it is growing; and in its blood run so many other streams that resemblance to the code is seldom strong and always confined to single traits.

judicial work, the practitioners. This fact amazes; for the theory flew in the face of common sense and professional experience. If rules decided cases, one judge would be as good as another, provided only the rules had been adduced before him. Yet who knew better than the lawmen that judges, one by one, had earned their reputations as great, or run-of-the-mine, or rather awful? If rules decided cases, law stood still (and, as we remember, the theory was at its blindest drawn out to that conclusion); whereas growth and change of law were as striking in nineteenth- and twentieth-century America as they have ever been. If rules decided cases, able lawyers would be unable to disagree, nor could there be dissenting votes save by incompetents, nor could an honest and informed judge face reversal. Yet I take the theory still to dominate our legal ideology, if one should take a census of the guild.

Why so? How so? Extended rehearsal here of the learning in the field would be offensive; a summary must do. The effective reasons fall into three groups, one dealing with the points where the theory really reflects reality, one with those where it reflects in distortion a certain segment of the relevant reality, the third with points at which its patent departure from reality is psychologically obscured.

A. Situations where rules are certain, and the theory that rules decide cases rather accurately reflects reality:

(1) Uncontested cases, very often.

(2) Cases where the facts-in-court are standardized in terms of rules; so, for example, when divorce testimony is fitted into the very verbal model set up by some appellate ruling on, say, desertion, or adultery.[14] Or, often enough, the affidavits which precede a labor injunction. But to fit here, such cases must normally be also uncontested.

(3) There are the cases where the facts-in-life are standardized, whether with an original eye to possible litigation (lease forms) or chiefly by way of extra-legal institutionalization and conventionalization (checks, notes). In cases of this last kind the classification of the facts may be so clear that rules can "decide" cases even out of court. Life does build on regular judicial action; and perception of regularity is often communicated by words describing it; and if one sees fit, he *may* think of such rules-for-judging as conform to the ways-of-judging as being the immediately operative factor.[15]

To avoid improper inference from the foregoing, it must be remembered that never, when the facts are in dispute, can rules decide the case. At best, they set the framework for decision, and the bounds within which it is to move. No less important: if there is any slightest doubt about the classification of the facts—though they be undisputed —the rule cannot decide the case; it is decided by the classifying.[16] Finally, even where rules are clear, semi-perceived or unperceived practice of action, thought, or emotion, is commonly a far more effective factor than any verbal formula.

B. Situations in which, even at times when the rules are uncertain, there is a certain distorted approach to reality in the theory that rules decide cases:

(1) The situation-types out of which both rules and legal concepts are developed set the framework of approach to any legal problem-situation. The concepts developed out of such situation-types set the framework of thinking about, or even of *perceiving*, the problem. The number and kind of categories available for sizing up the case is pretty well limited by tradition. Some of this tradition is expressed, more or less accurately, in rules. And it makes a difference whether the issue is posed in terms of "corporation or association?" or of "*société anonyme* or *commandite?*"[17]

(2) Over and above this, and even in cases for which no rule exists as yet, these categories show, each one, a certain shadowy totality, so organized that it tends to develop or expand along one line, and not along another. These tendencies are real; they are observable in judicial behavior. They are expressed in rules only when an overgeneralization of past decisions happens to include the true prediction. But (a point falling rather under C) once a judge has decided that "this is a sale and not an agency," he comes under their influence—and often enough *thinks* his then discovery of "the true rule" of Sales to do the deciding.[18] Moreover, the verbal formulations we call rules contribute *somewhat* to the shape and tendency of any category; as Williston remarks, the accepted constellation of past decisions goes far to determine our way of reading them, and to constrain their possibilities.[19]

(3) Rules limit the range of decision in the case, in that they require the decision to be justified. They also limit the choice of justification,

and so affect the precedent-value of decision. That is, legal *practice* does all these things, and enough of the practice is effectively expressed (or misexpressed) in rules to make rules partly operate as such.

C. Factors which, even when the theory that rules decide cases fails wholly to meet the situation, still keep that discrepancy from conscious recognition:

(1) Under a theory that rules decide cases, the actual fluidity of precedent is *experienced* only during the search for a theory, after the impact of a case. This experience is largely wiped out by the immediately following justification of the theory in deductive, rigid terms.

(2) Man (even though he learned square roots in high school) finds more than one *right* answer hard to conceive of. And if decision is to be "by rules," the rules must be dealt with as presaging, nay, as forcing, that single one "right" answer. Hence reinterpretation of a precedent becomes in thought merely the search for *the* "true rule" which it "must" contain.[20]

(3) Whence the insertion between creation and consciousness of creation of those most majestic and baffling of masks—"interpretation" and "application" of that which, before the process, had not been present to be interpreted or applied.

(4) Our orthodox common law presses upon the judge two demands together. He is to abide by precedent and statute. *But he is also to do justice.* The two demands drive into inconsistency.[21] But satisfying either tends to satisfy the conscience. What satisfies the conscience lulls the mind.

Such factors afford some indication of how the myth of legal certainty, once put into the world, has been able to maintain itself. And the matters listed under B and C suggest some of the sleights in use to *corriger la fortune* when the theory deals out an unfortunate hand. Against this background of common theory—and of common law techniques anent the manipulation of the fifth ace—constitutional cases are decided; but with a difference. For when changes in common law cumulate to the point where even the willful blind may be expected to perceive the change, some judge rewords "the" rule into a wholly different rule tailored more neatly to the current course of decision—one more device to save the face of an insolvent theory. The words of a rigid code do not permit reformulation of the sort. Despite this, our theory of Constitutional law maintains itself. The concentration of unseeingness which has made this possible must be regarded as a notable intellectual achievement. The French, dealing with a code a decade younger, were unable to keep themselves deceived beyond a century. The will was indeed there. With the adoption of the code they promptly junked the insight of Portalis.[22] But the flesh was weak. By the turn of the new century Gény's obvious sanity had downed even the "systematic" lawyer's will to shut his eyes. In Germany, war and inflation did the work within two decades and a half. Gény had gone before; the first gun in Germany was fired by a certain "non-Aryan" Kantorowicz in 1907. It remade "Aryan" German legal theory. Meantime, the "earthy common sense"[23] of common lawyers has built footing under footless theory for a century and a half. A feat, I say!

ON THE NATURE OF A CODE

A CODE, whether constitutional or other, and whatever its nature or backing, begins of necessity as an experiment.[24] Both as a whole, and in each of its parts. As to the parts, one need only refer to the successive Amendments of the Document of 1789, and most particularly to numbers eighteen and twenty-one. As to the whole, one thinks of Weimar and Hitler; or of those successive slavery-question Compromises any one of which *might* have entered permanently, as each did enter very temporarily, into our own working Constitution.

A code begins as an experiment. A successful code is an experiment that works. It incorporates the wisdom of the past. It selects from the present those trends which have a future, and so is in part a prophecy that will be fulfilled. Yet the portent of death is laid on it by two forces, one of fact and one of theory. Man cannot see too far into the future. It will never be long before the code is antiquated or inadequate: this the portent of fact. And that of theory: a code purports to be exclusive and all inclusive, for present and future. Which means that in due course it will be made to "contain" what it does not contain. Practices and cases will ivy upon its walls, and kill the stone.[25]

When we turn to our own Document in the light of this, we find (with surprise) that certain of its phrasings still state parts of the working Constitution with some accuracy. We have in fact a legislature in two houses. It bears the name Congress. The first of these facts has significance. We have a President. That also has significance. The Senate contains two Senators from each state; each sits for six years. That has significance as well. There is more. The Government borrows money upon the credit of the United States. There are heads of departments. The pocket veto is expressly foreseen and provided. Over and above the very considerable number of matters of vital moment (Congressional privilege of debate; control of interstate commerce) there are a number of minor rule-of-the-road provisions still more or less in force: entitulations, qualifications for office,[26] and the like. There are, moreover, provisions of rare incidence, such as impeachment, which have perhaps a prophylactic value even when they fall short of actual use. Such a one as succession of the Vice-President enjoys the curious distinction of being regularly applied when the contingency arises, without ever being seriously reckoned with beforehand—unless by the wives of vice-presidential candidates. All these things, and the rarity of Amendments, make a lasting tribute to the skill of the experimenting Framers. The thought that the nation could work on indefinitely with little more than the original language as its sacred Code has proved correct. The device of enumerating blanket powers leaves the Document, in appearance, still "controlling," despite range or mass of concrete action taken "under" them.

Yet the appearance cheats. Wherever there are today established practices "under" or "in accordance with" the Document, *it is only the practice which can legitimatize the words as being still part of our going Constitution.* It is *not* the words which legitimatize the practice. This is the first principle of a sane theory of our Constitutional law. Its necessity is patent wherever practice has flatly abrogated a part of this "supreme law of the land." Discretion in the electoral college is the classic example; can any doubt that if that college should today disregard their mandate, such action would be contrary to our Constitution? Yet "vote by ballot"—the original language, repeated in the Twelfth Amendment—is a strange way of saying "act as rubber stamps."

INTENT, THE NATURE OF THE CASE, AND PRACTICE

To MAKE CLEAR why the principle which obviously holds *re* abrogation requires extension no less to "interpretation" and most especially to far-flung "application," one needs to look a little into the sequence of action "under" a code. One *caveat:* the argument will not at this point undertake to distinguish in terms between the *basic* aspects of governmental practice and the "mere detail," though illustrations will be chosen only from what seems to me to be the former field. Later, some effort will be made to find criteria to help mark one off from the other.

And it will be remembered that this inquiry into the practice of the Court is not for the purpose of showing what all lawyers know: that the Court has indefinitely extended, has nobly pieced out, has skillfully remade the meaning of the Documentary words. The purpose is rather to make plain the *manner* of the retailoring, and the *source* of the new patterns in the nature and needs of government, in order that the real nature of the Constitution as an Institution may stand forth, and the essential conformity of a theory built in those terms to the court's tradition-hallowed practices may cease to be obscured.

At the beginning of a code experiment, intent of the language has a clear and proper bearing on men's actions. Some changes are toward, some older things are to be carried forward. The words have as their function to guide action. The words are thus—at the beginning—best read in terms of the legislative history. Cases already have been put in the debate. But even here, intent cannot rule purely. Some cases have *not* been put in the debate. Resort must then be had to language and circumstance, to "obvious" rather than to real intent. Forthwith sets in the overwhelming tendency of clear-cut words, in law as in life, to usurp exclusive attention whenever they are met.—All this is buttressed by the traditions of our law. Hence the rise of orthodox Constitutional theory was, if not inevitable, almost so. A good code being, as indicated, a successful experiment, and one reaching some distance out into so much of the future as wise men might foreguess, the treatment in terms of real plus "necessary" intent does little harm—for some good time. Indeed it furthers mightily the standing of the code while the latter is working its way into traditional acceptance. Such treatment has, that is to say, political value. While the code is young, "intent" contributes to stability.

But the older the code, the less the need for such treatment, and the greater the need for departing from it. Some cases, as has been mentioned, were *not* put in the debate. The "glass" in which the future shows is metal none too highly polished. The outward sign of the newer inward grace is Marshall's word: "We must remember that it is a *Constitution* which we are expounding." Thus is signaled a treatment of the Document in which the vital element becomes the need and circumstances of the case. This also, however, and most unfortunately, darkly. The language is still: "which we are *expounding*." The voice of Jacob speaks over pseudo-hands of Esau: *pseudo*-interpretation. The present need is thus served *as if* by ancient meaning; more recent wisdom clothes itself in ancient words; the road over fiction has begun. More, and worse: it is not conscious fiction. Clothed as it is in the language of original intent and language of the Document, the newer method of dealing does not overthrow or displace the old. Rather does it creep in silently, alongside, but leave the old still nominal master of the house. By its own phrasing it invites confusion. By its own verbal expression it invites its own inventors, in any subsequent case, to overlook it, or to throw it out.

In curiously similar fashion the working Constitution creeps in beside the Document, always in deference, always in nominal subjection. Not being clothed in words, it can be unobtrusive—so much so that even in the occasional instances (electoral college; the President's power over war-making, or dependence on him to initiate legislation, appropriation, or other) in which practice flouts the Document, no man sees the flouting, thanks to the observance of the form—thanks also to the now ingrown *institution* of simply *taking* the Document, without thought or inquiry, as being *the* dominant factor.

But the President's position as head of his party, as dispenser of patronage, as limited by the "courtesy of the Senate" as long as administration Senators are good—are these not basic to the framework of our government? Or the expected second term? Or the unconstitutionality of a third? There is only one reason for considering such matters extra-

Constitutional: the no-longer-reasoned ideology which simply *takes* the Document as both dominant and all containing. Do I mean that the Supreme Court would, on demand, declare the third election of a president to be void? Of course not.[27] I mean that institutions which sit so firmly that the Supreme Court never gets a chance to pass on variations from them attain the zenith of fundamental law's perfection.

Neither, as has been indicated, would I deny the shaping influence of the Document—which is to say, of men's ways and attitudes with reference to the Document—upon the going Constitution.[28] The argument is, that there is only one way of knowing whether, and how far, any portion of the Document is still alive; that is to watch what men are doing and how men feel, in the connection. If their doing and feeling squares more or less roughly with the language, so much the luckier for the language; if not, so much the worse. Whether the one or the other, it is the action and the attitude which give the light. The argument is, further, that most of the going framework of our Leviathan is hardly adumbrated in the Document. As a criterion of what our working Constitution is, the language fails in both directions. It affords neither a positive nor a negative test.

Here and there the two do square. Some—enough—instances above. But, to repeat, the working Constitution is in good part utterly extra-Documentary (the privilege of Senatorial filibuster; the powers of the Conference Committee; the President's power of removal; the Supreme Court's power of review; the party system; the campaign fund). This, plus the less frequent fact of abrogation, ought to be enough in itself to kill the cock robin of orthodox theory (who cares who did it, if it be done?) and to dethrone the Words. But the Words put forward a cover first to be disposed of. Vital organs of the working Constitution, while not described or prescribed by the Document, are urged to be merely its "applications"—or merely the "application" of its words "as interpreted." Let us tug a little at the texture of this cover, to test its strength. The argument is simple enough, if I may shift the figure: once tails have come to dwarf and wag dogs, "dog" ceases to be a convenient or significant concept for classifying the things that really matter. It becomes inconvenient, first, in lumping disparate things together—white-slaving, railroad consolidation, Federal Trade Commission, prize-fight films, radio control, drug traffic, conceivably migratory birds, certainly N. R. A. (and so child labor, *and barbers*)—all in one basket marked "regulate commerce among the several States." This is tradition, but it is not sense. The unifying feature is not "regulate commerce"—the verbal excuse—but "things which seem to call for centralized regulation"—the fact. What matter whether any of them had been successfully hung upon the taxing power, or the treaty power, or the money power? Yet the greater inconvenience lies in obfuscation of those vibrant tails which have become the things that count in life. When the offshoot-of-an-offshoot-of-an-offshoot turns giant and permanent, its great-grand-parentage no longer gives clue to what it is. "To provide for the common defense" as an objective, and "to raise and support Armies" and "to make Rules for the Government and Regulation of the land and naval Forces," as powers, are limited by certain Documentary provisions on quartering of troops and martial law, and by others on taxation, appropriations, due process, and equal protection of the laws. They are extended by the provision concerning all laws necessary and proper. But it is not these provisions which have meaning in our lives. Nor are these provisions in any intelligible sense being "applied." There is nothing to apply. We are told, not to have an army, but that we *may* have one. As a grant of power, the provisions provide a verbal peg on which a billion-dollar budget *can* still be hung. The peg has meantime ceased to be of interest. It has been used. Its service is done. What is of interest, are the ingrained ways of the people who consume the billion, supported by the ways of those who provide it: provision for service-disabled veterans as a national institution, awards to other veterans as a national racket, the use of air forces (forces not mentioned, if I remember rightly, in the Document) for show purposes as a national amusement and for propaganda purposes as a national indulgence, the interesting bottle-necked promotion system, non-conscription in time of peace, the Officers' Reserve, the undiscoverability of colored or Jewish West Point graduates. These things are living Constitution, acted on, suffered by all, and in appropriate quarters passionately approved. They might, under the Document, be wholly different. But they are not. Their connection with the Document is so remote and inconclusive as to require a detective novelist to trace. I repeat that it is they, and not the Words, which carry living meaning. Stronger examples under other general powers are legion. It takes, for instance, a person gifted with a keen and abstract intellect to figure the Documentary basis for the Department of Labor or that of Agriculture.

Let me digest the argument thus far:

(1) The orthodox theory breaks down when practice abrogates and negates the Document. (For example, the President has *de facto* and with Vox Populi's approval the power to make war; could, indeed, if he wanted to, "declare" it.)

(2) The orthodox theory leaves wholly uncovered a mass of fundamental governmental structures and norms which do not happen to be mentioned in the Document, even by innuendo (say, the party system).

(3) The orthodox theory of "interpretation" or "application" of the Document, or of "exercise of powers," lacks all perspective and obscures all meaning. An inch from the eye is a clause of the Text; the whole living world behind is "covered" by it. Only because the Supreme Court has been so good at three-card monte,[29] has made so much *seem* to be where it was not, have the Document and its Theory been able to survive so long.

(4) In result, it is institutions which test whether there is still force in the Words, and how much force, and what that force is. It is institutions which validate the Words, not the Words which validate the institutions.

Hence it behooves us to look into the institutions. From such an inquiry the foundations of a saner theory may, with luck, emerge.

We shall inquire first into the nature of institutions in general; then into the general attributes of that peculiar institution of government, the working Constitution; then into the problem of how the Constitution can be distinguished from other phases of government. This over, we can turn from fact to theory, from description to the pressing matter of what to do about it.

ON THE NATURE OF AN INSTITUTION

AN INSTITUTION is, in first instance, a set of ways of living and doing. It is not, *in first instance,* a matter of words or rules.[30] The existence of an institution lies first of all and last of all in the fact that people do behave in certain patterns *a, b,* and *c,* and do not behave in other conceivable patterns *d* to *w*. And the probability that an institution will continue coincides with whatever probability there is that people will continue so to behave. Every living constitution is an institution; it *lives* only so far as that is true. The difference between a "written" and an "unwritten" constitution lies only in the fact that the shape of action in the former is *somewhat* influenced by the presence of a particular document, and of particular attitudes toward it, and particular ways of dealing with its language.[31]

A national constitution is a somewhat peculiar institution in that it involves in one phase or another the ways of a huge number of people —well-nigh the whole population. If, like ours, it is a firmly established constitution, it involves ways of behavior deeply set and settled in the make-up of these people; it involves not patterns of doing (or of inhibition) merely, but also accompanying patterns of thinking and of emotion—attitudes, for example, potent and largely predictable, toward the verbal symbol "Constitution" and toward any person supposed to be attacking "It."

As an institution of major size, then, our working Constitution embraces the interlocking ways and attitudes of different groups and classes in the community—*different* ways and attitudes of *different* groups and classes, but all cogging together into a fairly well organized whole.

Perhaps it is as well to stop for an illustration. Any family is an institution. Any family is made up of persons. But not every aggregation of persons is a family. The persons in a family have one or another trait in common: either they live together, or they are related by blood, or both. We shall take for further development a case in which these two common factors concur. Yet what appears at once is the *divergence* of the ways of action of the persons concerned, in spite of the common factors. Mr. Hubb goes out to work and provides for payment of the bills. When he rises, his breakfast has been attended to; and the bathroom has been left free for his shaving. He, and no other, reads the newspaper while he eats. Before he leaves for his train, he fixes the furnace; and he receives certain instructions concerning things to be brought back on his return. There is no need to go on. It is obvious that Mr. Hubb's patterns of behavior are not those of Mrs. Hubb, nor those of the maid, nor those of little Lorna. But it is equally obvious that the patterns of all four intercog like the wheels of a clock, and make a *whole* go round which we choose to call "a family," and which is more than and different from the constituent parts. It is obvious, moreover, that Mr. Hubb's behavior lies in good part in patterns, expected and reckoned with by the others; and normatized. If he should fail to come home to dinner, or should forget the ordered purchases, or should gamble away his pay check at a poker game, Mrs. Hubb would not only be upset in her coöperation, but would *feel* aggrieved. Meanwhile, each other member of the family contributes her own quite diverse patterns to the interlocking whole that goes on *as* a whole.

Now what holds of the gearing together of the ways of single persons into a small group holds of the gearing together of the ways of whole groups into a still larger whole. A factory combines management personnel, foremen, operating labor, repair staff, shipping clerks. A national corporation combines different factories (now taken as units) with the commercial divisions of the head office, the selling staff, the directors, the varied security-holders. A national government —but, again, why go on? The essential fact is that the larger the number of persons concerned, and the more intense their participation, (*a*) the more intricate the detail of the patterned clockwork, (*b*) the greater the range of room for slipping gears, (*c*) the larger and more internally complex the units which must be taken as units, if discussion is to remain intelligible.

THE CONSTITUTION: SPECIALISTS, INTERESTED GROUPS, PUBLIC

To sum up: No institution consists of *like* ways among all the persons concerned. It is the unlikeness plus the complementary cross-play of the organized ways which is the most convenient criterion for marking off an "institution" from a mere "way" or simple culture-trait.

As to our working Constitution, even in so rough a sketch as this, it will pay to distinguish three categories of persons whose ways are concerned. The first are the *specialists in governing*. The second are what we may term the ***interested groups:*** aggregations of people more or less organized around some interest, who direct pressure upon the specialists or upon the general public in furtherance of their own particular desires. The third are those who, in respect to any given issue, are left over—call them the *general public*. They are important, as will appear; but important rather as is the audience in a theater, as distinguished from actors and stage hands, or from author and producer. Plays succeed or flop. So do constitutions. So does constitutional change. The audience, however, ***initiates*** neither play nor change.

By specialists in government I mean those persons whose business is governing in general, or, perhaps more accurately, persons *so far as* they enter into the *general* business of governing. This includes most official officeholders, be they legislators, executives, administrators, or judges. But when, say, a legislator conceives his job to include getting the silver or aluminum or power people what they want merely because they want it, he will for my present purpose be dividing his time between specialization in government and activity as a member of an interested group. The classification by persons, or by offices, in other words, serves merely as an approximation to a classification of activity and attitude.

Somewhat obviously to be included among these specialists would be such party officials as devote a good share of their time to the problems of *de facto* government: Mr. Croker, Mr. Penrose, Mr. Curry. Beyond this, as suggested, the group shades off in terms of more or less time, more or less intensity, more or less success or influence, of persons partly specializing on such other matters as, say, road construction, saloon-keeping, labor union management, corporation law practice, gangsterism, or investment banking. The general position here to be maintained is that these specialists occupy, with reference to what the working Constitution is and how it changes, the key position, with various of the interested groups serving now to induce, now to inhibit, one or another change. One small group of specialists, the judges, hold a peculiar veto power, called on fairly often, exercised only occasionally. The general public hold a further veto power, but one exercised rarely indeed. Referendum and recall of judicial decisions were devices aimed at furthering the exercise. Elections are an indirect and rather ineffective device for the purpose. Riot and revolution—when successful—are its final expression. In all but odd cases this power of the general public operates not as a veto of action taken, but as a deterrent from taking action—for fear of what *might* happen.[32]

THE RÔLE OF THE SPECIALISTS

IT HAS BEEN URGED THUS FAR that a working constitution is an institution, that it is an institution highly complex in nature, that it can be viewed with some adequacy as the interaction of the quite different ways and attitudes of three diverse categories of people, and that of these *the specialists in government stand at the focus.* I propose now to concentrate for a time upon the ways of these last. For not only is it they who are the prime movers in preserving so much of the Constitution as is preserved; it is also they who in all save most peculiar situa-

[32] *Excursus: On the nature of these concepts.*—It will be obvious that the categories thus laid down flow one into another, and even overlap. A man may be today an independent officeholder, tomorrow a lawyer with important political influence, the day after a bought-and-paid-for official working for an interested group. He may be president of the Civic Club and be simultaneously fighting a rate case for some utility. Neither he nor any other may, in the rate case, be able to tell whether his conception of good government, his conception of his clients' interest, his personal prestige and satisfaction in victory, his love of the game as such, or his prospective fee, is his fundamental drive. In so far the three "descriptive" categories fail of accurate descripton. And as of these, so of the other categories here suggested. "Way," for example, is the roughest inaccurate generalization of individual acts of individual people, all of a given line of acts being treated for convenience *as if* they were interchangeably alike. Of course, under the microscope, they are not so alike. Yet often, *for the purpose in hand,* the differences can safely be sunk in the similarities. The turning back of the clock at one session of a legislature can be treated as "the same" as at another. The fact that three new opposition members may protest, or even that some session may go by without clock-turning becoming necessary, does not obscure the presence of a governmental "way" general and predictable enough to warrant conceiving and applying the category. But in the main, the presence of a way is not a question of yes-or-no, but of more-or-less: *so far as* there exists significant regularity and significant uniformity of action in a given circumstance among certain people, *to that extent* there exists "a way" among those people. Attendance at roll calls of important legislative sessions (or, alternatively, pairing) may be regarded as a way rather well established. Similarly, *so far as* certain individuals are active regularly and in coöperation, they can be said to be "a group." For example—despite absences for fence-building or junketing—a legislative house. Again, *so far as* ways interlock in complement, they build into "an institution." The orderly progress of parliamentary debate is, for example, distinctly more an institution in this country than in some others. It is not, to be sure, when examined in detail, a way, but a complex. Only the speaker presides. Only one member holds the floor at a time; the others sit. "The rules of order" hold for all, but the predictable action of individuals which they call for is *different* action by *different* individuals,

tions—on eleven occasions in our history, to be exact—arrange all amending of that Constitution.

Surely there are few superstitions with less substance than the belief that the sole, or even the chief process of amending our Constitution consists of the machinery of Amendment. Party system and campaign fund, protective tariff and secret ballot, patronage and Senatorial filibuster, judicial review and national banking: these sit as firmly, and most of them weigh as heavily, in our governmental structure as did ever indirect election of Senators or the power of the federal courts to entertain a suit against one State brought by a citizen of another. They were put into our working Constitution by the specialists. Two of them (filibuster and review) could each be taken out by the vote of a single body of specialists. Their disappearance is less likely in fact than was, let us say, the coming of the income tax, and hardly more so

all organized into a going whole. The difference between "way" and "institution" is thus commonly merely one of emphasis and level of discourse. Where thought of as a unit in a larger whole, a complex may be treated as "a way," though the same complex, when treated as a subject for nicer analysis, would be thought of as an integration of interlocking parts.

The *outer* boundaries of a group or of an institution are almost never sharply marked. Each shades off into its neighbors. Some ways or men are closely, others not so closely, tied into the perceptible core. Are lobbyists, or pages, or inactive Senators, as much "The Senate" as floor leaders? The United States Steel Corporation—meaning thereby the persons *with* their significant ways and attitudes—might in one connection be considered to be the managing personnel, in another that personnel plus major stockholders, in still another that personnel plus all stockholders, and so on through bondholders, interested bankers, white-collar staff, laborers, customers—or even customers of customers. A "basic" outfit is of necessity an outfit with outward boundary undefined.

The farther out one goes, to be sure, the slighter the nexus, the greater the outward range and angle-spread of radiation, the more disturbing the dynamic context of other groups and institutions built around other types of center. Yet the *core* is always clear—as clear as the boundary, in any given discussion, must be arbitrary. There is, certainly in a complex society, no escape from this fact: that the marking off of "*an* interest," "*a* group," "*an* institution" is an artificial abstraction from a complexly concrete mass of phenomena; nor any escape from the correlative fact: that the boundaries drawn will always be indefensible, save as they become useful and significant *for the purpose in hand*. Hence all that is intended by the use of such terms, unqualified, is, throughout this paper, twofold: first (and descriptively) that in significantly high measure the attributes of the concept are present in fact in the life around us; second (and theoretically) that any increasing quantum of their presence, or of their range or intensity where present, would strengthen the truth-value of the proposition announced concerning them.

[Throughout the foregoing my lasting indebtedness to Max Weber will be obvious. And Sumner must be added, and Ehrlich, and W. I. Thomas, and Underhill Moore, and that relentless teacher that *facts* must be regarded, A. L. Corbin. The last will not agree with my views; but he will recognize his contribution to them.]

than a territorial reorganization of States into Regions, or the alteration of the two-Senator allotment. This feature of highly probable permanence is, as will appear, one essential criterion of what is Constitution, and what is not. Here it suffices to note that the amendment of the living Constitution to include these phases has been the work either mainly or exclusively of the specialists in government, and that the process of Amendment has not been found requisite in that work.

Whether it be to continue or to repeat, let me attempt further to make a seemingly unorthodox position unambiguous: *the working Constitution is amended whenever the basic ways of government are changed.* The reform of Cannon's committee rules was a striking example; they had been fundamental. The entrance of the federal government into control of the air was a second. The N. R. A. may be hoped to be a third. Indeed, *amendment occurs typically by action of the relevant specialists alone,* and without alteration of the language of the Document. Of their own motion they can, and of their own motion or under pressure from interested groups they do, change the manner of government in vital aspects, widen it startlingly, ring out old pieces of the Constitution as bells ring out an Old Year. It is they who have remade the pattern of government as we have passed from a dominantly agricultural into a dominantly industrial and on into a dominantly financial economy. It is they who have tinkered, twisted, invented, on the governmental side, either to further shifts in economic institutions or to catch up with such shifts; to attempt some adjustment of the emergent new to the persistent old. By legislation—by executive or administrative practice—by building the wherewithal to elect or control executives or legislators. The Document has been blotted out like the original text upon a double palimpsest.

"By action of the relevant specialists alone." Often a single person (a President) or a single group; more often several groups in active or passive concert. Occasionally, as mentioned, one peculiar group intrudes a veto: the judges. Their power so to do, if called upon, is the most vital reason for invoking the cumbersome machinery of Amendment. It is not the only reason. Neither, thanks to the awkwardness of the machinery, is their veto often an occasion for its invocation. In the main, when the judges interpose their Nay, men shrug and suffer. Yet this much is patent: unless the judges have vetoed, or unless it is confidently believed that if called upon they will veto, Amendment is in the main unnecessary, and is rarely resorted to. When their veto occurs or is anticipated, the *working* Constitution (which includes judicial review) prescribes Amendment as the sole available process of amending.[33] This, not because the Document so says, nor because the proposed amendment varies from the Document, or from its judicial "interpretation." *It is because one body of the relevant specialists happens to be unwilling to let the proposed amendment pass.* Why else are we concerned about the personnel of the Court?

Yet of certain Amendments, such as those on woman's suffrage or direct election of Senators, or, say, one admitting some hitler-like[32a] foreign-born to the Presidency, the use of the formal machinery would be reasonably predictable (unless perhaps in a time of overwhelming emergency) even though the Court's veto might *not* be expected. For the working Constitution consists not merely in powers of the specialists, nor merely in their existing ways of action; it includes no less their *attitudes* toward the Document and its language. It embraces deep-seated inhibitions among many of the most influential guildsmen (not judges alone) against departing openly from its express language, or even, at times, from what is thought to be the "intent" of less express wording. In this the specialists resemble the members of the undifferentiated general public—save that some of the specialists have some knowledge of what the express language of the Document happens to be. The specialists are, then, self-limited in their powers of amending; or, more accurately, they are limited in their discovery of their own *de facto* powers, or in the use of those discovered, by traditions concerning the Document which have shaped their imaginations and their consciences in the very process of becoming specialists.

THE RÔLE OF THE GENERAL PUBLIC

LESS POTENT, I suspect, and if not that, then less frequently operative, are inhibitions based on the attitudes of the general public (from which distinguish at this point interested groups). Two factors characterize the general public's rôle. There is an unreasoned, unreasoning, tradition-founded loyalty to a symbol of national unity and permanence.

Along with this there is a pervasive ignorance and indifference concerning almost all detail. The loyalty, so far as I can observe, is chiefly to a phrase, without more: "The Constitution." It runs in infinitely decreased measure to the Document of 1789—which is currently enough supposed to begin: "When in the course of human events" or: "We hold these truths to be self-evident." Rather is the second line of loyalty to a slightly idealized picture of the Nation-As-It-Stands—including elections (pruned in dream of fraud, or blackjack, or of the triumph of the wicked enemy), including the present incumbents of highest office (somehow made National by panoply), including Prosperity (around the corner), including the People (always with silent elimination from that concept of particular objectionable elements, the negative selection varying to taste), including finally American Prestige as painted by pulp-paper fiction, grade-school history books, and Fourth of July orations. All of which is somehow identified with the War of Independence and with a Document, and conceived loosely as having existed, with minor aberrations, from the glorious beginning.

This popular loyalty, though real, is blind. It is almost empty of *specific* content. Therefore (*a*) it leaves the specialists free to shape and reshape the working Constitution in *almost* any way they please, and *almost* to any extent on which they get together—whether they get together by concerted action or by drift. But (*b*) the combination of intense loyalty to a symbol with total emptiness of concrete content means an ever-present latent possibility that the symbol may become attached in the popular mind to *any* concrete content at all. And persons opposed to any projected change may work the hook-up. And simple and clear language in the Document may mightily facilitate such an arrangement, even though it should fail to stir the inhibitions of the specialists at large, or of the judiciary in particular.

Here, then, lie both the scope and the limits of the leeway which the general public affords the specialists. And be it noted that the scope is more real than the limitations. For the most potent limitation lies inside the skulls of the specialists. Whereas the public not only know nothing of the real operation of the Constitution—they also care nothing about it. What difference whether income taxation rests on "interpretation" or Amendment? What matter—to most—whether the Eighteenth

Amendment be on the books, and, if on the books, whether it or a Volstead Act do the forbidding; whether New York has thirty-nine representatives, or fifty-two, or eighty-seven; whether Congress or the States regulate longshoremen's accident compensation; whether impeachment of judges calls for majority, two-thirds, three-fourths, or unanimous vote; whether "to receive ambassadors" does or does not imply the power of refusing recognition to a foreign government? What farmer cares whether a mortgage moratorium or scaling-down clashes with the impairment of contracts clause? One can indeed in normal times conceive an uproar if the electoral college should proceed to perform its original Documentary function, or if the President should seek to dissolve Congress by action of the military arm. Bounds there are. But they are ample—as against the *general* public. The interested groups remain.

THE RÔLE OF THE INTERESTED GROUPS

WHEREFORE ONE OTHER TYPE OF LIMIT should be mentioned. When action by the specialists on a point of Constitutional change pinches the personal toes of Albert Jones too sharply, Albert is likely to react as he does to less fundamental change of similar effect. If part of a group, he fights effectively to block or undo the change. If only one of an unorganized class, he groans and gets nowhere, unless the pressure is painful and sustained enough to lock his fellows and himself together into an interested group.[84]

For the effective block upon Constitutional change which ranges too far or in a direction undesired—alongside the self-limitation of the specialists and the looming specter of the Court—is the pressure of these interested groups. They are plentiful; and many or most of them are single-minded, and motivated in a fashion which reminds one of the Economic Man. To the extent that they are groups at all, they are organized; to the extent that they have found intelligent leadership, they are effectively organized, and their organization is effectively applied where it will do *them* the most good. They "see" bosses; they persuade administrators; they lobby bills into the legislature and out of committee, or out of the legislature and permanently into committee; they draw the teeth of legislation in passage, or in the process of its "application"; or, if the bill serves them, they get teeth into it, and give "due" unofficial aid in its enforcement; they discover barriers in the language of the Venerable Document, or in the cases "under" it, and press those barriers upon the courts. Nor is this all. They also "educate" the public; they offer generous aid in framing and forcing the issues of political campaigns. And I take the presence of such groups, and their activities in squeezing upon the specialists either directly or by way of first stirring the theretofore disinterested public, to be *essential* components of the working Constitution of these United States. It is hard, without them, to see how our government would govern. The mind of a mere professor staggers in void when he attempts to conceive Manufacturers' Association, Beet Sugar Interests, Public Utilities, Federation of Labor, Magazine Publishers, Oil, or United Realtors abstracted from the national scene. Certain it is that, without such groups, governing would become for persons of this day and age unrecognizable. Yet I do not find them mentioned in the Document, save under an obsolescent clause about "the right of the people peaceably to assemble and petition the Government for redress of grievances." And even this clause touches only that relatively ineffective fraction of the Interested Groups which has to "assemble" in order to bring its grievances, or wants, to bear.

CONSTITUTION VERSUS MERE WORKING GOVERNMENT

IT HAS NOW BEEN ARGUED that a working Constitution is an institution, and so consists of the ways and attitudes of varied people; which last may be summed up more or less adequately as the going scheme of government under which those who do it, do it; and those who get something out of it proceed about getting something out of it; and those who take it, take it—sometimes hard.

But it will properly be urged that a constitution is not the governmental machine at large, but rather its *fundamental* framework, whereas most of what has been said here would apply both to the whole of that machine and to the least consequential of its parts. Hence there remains the problem, within the totality of going government, of marking off how much and which parts are to be regarded as basic to the whole,[35] and, therefore, as the working Constitution.

The discussion above,[36] with reference to the nature of an institution and the inevitable character of its gradual shading off into surrounding complexes of ways (be they complementary, competing, or merely cross-currents fulfilling other needs) will have made clear my belief that, whatever one takes as being this working Constitution, he will find the edges of his chosen material not sharp, but penumbra-like. The penumbra will of necessity be in constant flux.[37] New patterns of action develop, win acceptance (sometimes suddenly), grow increasingly standardized among an increasing number of the relevant persons, become more and more definitely and consciously "the thing to do," proceed to gain value as honored in tradition—that is, become things to be accepted in and of themselves without question of their utility—until they take on finally, to more and more of the participants, the flavor of the "Basic." Pragmatic values may of course, for some, remain in the foreground. There is no lack of men who know precisely what they can do or get away with under the existing set-up or some phase of it. But as long as pragmatic evaluation remains *exclusively* in the foreground, the way or institution is on trial. Take, as an instance, the history of the tariff, or of the air forces, or of the parcel post.

Even as new ways win their way, so old ways obsolesce, lose sanctity by non-observance. They are no longer present, even in imagination, to observe. Both growth and decline are *normally* gradual; they are gradual as to both regularity of occurrence and range of persons affected. So that there will of necessity be constant differences of opinion (capable of capitalization by interested parties for their immediate ends) in respect of the fact: what is or is not the practice? And in respect of the norm:[38] what exceptions, if any, are to be made, and when, and how? And in respect of the intellectualization: how to reconcile competing analogies in application to a present problem? All of which is no new matter to lawyers who have watched the institution of courts-at-work; or the particular institution of the Supreme Court of the United States. Finally, it will be no new thing to lawyers who have watched the twisting and expanding power of all the ill-defined concepts of our law, to be reminded again that the ways of government, as

[36] Note 32 *supra.*

they interlock and play one upon another, generate *attitudes* not only of general and specific approval (in the main) of whatever happens to have become existing practice, but also attitudes less capable of definition—*sets,* or built-up predispositions in the participants, to deal with situations those participants have previously never met or thought of, *along the lines* of the ways they know—so that in certain measure both direction and nature of new developments can be predicted; and could, if it were possible to foresee the stimuli which will be presented, be predicted with a very fair measure of accuracy. This has been mentioned, anent the theory that rules decide cases. But it needs restressing at this point. Much of any sane theory of Constitutional law must turn on it.

Thus the penumbra-border of the Constitution ranges through practices which are marked with varying definiteness and consistency in individuals; and vary in range as to the individuals who share such practices; ranges through varying attitudes as to possibility of departure from such practices under stress; and through varying degrees of clarity and certainty as to what the response to some new situation—in action or in normatization, or in both—will prove to be. And within the field of the penumbra (which, I insist again, will remain present wherever one seeks to draw the line) opinions will divide as interests clash. It is thus in the penumbra or on its edges that *judicial* problems lie. Moreover, because the penumbra is in its nature indefinite, while words are relatively sharp in outline, the most conscientious attempt at pure description will in this region embody gross idealization. For the describer, in choosing which of the halfway features to stress and which to scant, must be guided by his judgment of tendencies and trends. His description must, whether he will or no, embody a prophecy.

Nor is this all. The penumbra is the region in which institutions are only *partly* fixed. The question is whether a given change, or (less often) a given move toward crystallization, is *to be approved.* To appeal to definite institutions for a sure criterion is footless: there are no institutions which, on the point in hand, are definite. The appeal must therefore be not only to an idealized description, but to a normative *ideal* of what the given institution *should* be and do. The argument of this paper is that the total "set," that is, the resultant development-tendency of existing and formative practice, plus the need and nature of the case, provide a basis for constructing such an ideal which is workable, healthy, and within decent limits capable of consistency;[39] whereas the language of the Document and its "intent" offer a basis utterly self-inconsistent, unworkable, and heavy with the fragrance of a charnel house.

CONSTITUTIONAL PRACTICE

THE FIRST THING TO FIND OUT is what is definitely Constitutional, because it is definitely Constitution. Any practice, to be so designated, must fulfill requirements: (1) of existence (which includes highly probable continuance) and felt importance; and (2) of Constitutional function. One might set the scheme up roughly as follows:

I. To be unambiguously a part of the working Constitution a practice or institution must

(1) Be regular in occurrence among the relevant actors, whenever the occasion arises; and the overwhelming bulk of passive participants, or relevant non-participants, must allow of its occurrence. Say: election of a President every four years, or succession of the Vice-President, or the necessity of a two-thirds majority to impeach.

Be it noted that there is no intention to exclude the Constitution character of two or more *alternative* devices to a single end, when both or all are *de facto* capable of being called on, when the number of alternatives is limited, and when the shape of each is certain. Today, for example, Amendment by way of convention vote is again Constitution. But I doubt whether the initiation of Amendment by application of state legislatures any longer is.

(2) It must consist of or include ways of official officeholders whose action or passivity has real importance, direct or indirect, to more than the participants. Thus the practice of pairing, as distinguished, let us say, from the practice of writing personal correspondence during a Congressional debate. Or the patronage or pork-barrel or lobbying system as contrasted with the style of letter-carriers' uniform. This predicates that the way or institution shall be one *of government,* and *significant* to government.

(3) The actors, and any non-actors in a position to block or modify action, must *feel* that the way or institution is not subject to abrogation or material alteration. They need not feel that it is right or wise (pork barrel again) if they are clear that it is permanent. But in the normal situation the two feelings coincide. This is intended to exclude such matters as lines of intrenched favoritism or graft, where opinions divide, or where written law and practice are at odds, and each from time to time observed. It is intended to exclude practices which, even though long established, have not acquired in the relevant minds the intangible atmosphere of unquestioned rightness or of course of nature. Seniority in committee rank would, I suspect, belong; so would the use of an income tax, and of its graduation; the particular percentages of the income tax would not at present—but some day may.

(4) The feeling just described may leave room for alteration or abrogation of the practice or institution under really severe stress (say compulsory scaling down of debts at last worst,[40] or the definitive revaluation of the dollar); but if we are to have unambiguous Constitution there must be in the offing no felt likelihood that any stress will arise sufficient to overcome the inhibition against (or, less ideally, the mere felt impossibility of) departure. Which is why so much of the Constitution of 1928 has ceased today to be unambiguous—or even ambiguous—Constitution.

Negatively: it is not essential that the practice or institution shall be in any way related to the Document; nor that it be old, if it in any other manner acquire the look and sense of future permanence; nor that the *machinery* of change be complex or cumbersome, if the *likelihood* of change approaches zero.

II. *In addition,* each way or institution which is to rank as clear-cut Constitution must have some one of certain attributes of function. Either:

(1) It must form part of the framework of procedure within which the acting officials go about the doing of their official business (consultation with the Cabinet; hardly the Inaugural Ball); or of the framework in terms of which they coöperate with other officials (the Conference Committee; the President's message; his consultation with floor leaders); or of the division of official business between themselves

and other officials (severance of the Departments); or of the scheme of things under which they procure leads as to policy, or test out their own views on policy (the lobby; the practice of administrative press release; public offerings of government obligations).

(2) Or it must form part of the framework of procedure under which the officials are recruited (party system; the Senatorial quota; the patronage function of the Postmaster General).

(3) Or it must be a portion of the framework of going government in terms of which important relevant portions of the community at large have organized their activities as on a permanent base (tariff; limitation of commission powers over public utilities; until a few years back, the then second-class postage rates and the then confinement of "national" banks to a single office).

To the extent that any one of these attributes is lacking, I should regard the phenomena in question as entering into the penumbra of the working Constitution—so, for example, of a matter on which there are few precedents, or no precedents, but the handling of which is measurably predictable, should it occur; or of a matter on the relative importance of which skilled observers might differ; or of a practice under which a seemingly growing minority is becoming restive; or of prevailing doubt on whether an emergency already impending may not require a drastic departure. In such cases, the ways or institutions are typically on their way into the working Constitution, or on their way out of it; and in situations of infrequent occurrence they may remain for decades or centuries in this sort of limbo.

So far as this core of living Constitution is definite, even the orthodox theory admits it as "Constitutional." *Established* executive, administrative, or legislative practice the Court merely accepts. It would consider intervention only in the event of attempted change in them. It might then inquire into such questions as: whether the established practice had created private vested rights; or which of the relevant specialist-groups had power to do the changing; or whether the procedure of the change was an admissible procedure; or, even, whether the older practice had not become an inherent part of our institutions (thus as to notice and a hearing before revocation of license; or uniformity of plan in the exercise of discretion in successive cases).

THE PROBLEM OF LEEWAY AND GIVE

WHICH BRINGS US BACK to the trite truth that the troubling judicial problems lie in the penumbra. Indeed, the mere fact that change is attempted brings the relevant institution or practice into the penumbra. Its universal sway is thereby challenged.

And there appears a road fork at which orthodox theory and sane theory of Constitutional law must part company. The orthodox theory purports to turn, for the ideal picture which will settle doubts, to the Documentary text. And sane theory would, as indicated, join in the view that guidance must in such event be sought from ideal pictures. But a sane theory would utterly disregard a Documentary text *if any relevant practices existed* to offer a firmer, more living basis for the ideal picture. The judge's first duty would be study not of the Text nor (though these are distinctly less obnoxious because influenced by life) of the decisions. His first duty would be study of the structure and functioning of going government. Really not two matters, but three: structure, *and* functioning, *and* function. Moreover, sane theory would approach the study of these matters with an outlook fundamentally at odds with the rigid attitude inculcated by orthodoxy. For the major problem that sane theory must work out is the problem of *leeway* in the governmental structure. No institutional structure can be viable save insofar as it contains within itself the wherewithal for give, for readjustment, for self-sanation. Some parts of the structure need less of this, some parts need more. But everywhere the extent of readjustment-leeway grows greater in fact (it must) as the strain for readjustment is increased. This is not merely to rehash in different words the "emergency" concession which orthodoxy has been forced to make to fact; nor to repeat that dodging of responsibility and concession of leeway which is found in leaving some things untouched, as being "political" questions, and others as being "the exercise of sound discretion." Rather is it to insist that what semi-orthodoxy knows as "emergency," "political question," or "discretion" are in fact but isolated examples of *the regular course of daily business,* met always and everywhere; and that the central problem for the judiciary is to build a theory in those terms. How much give does the structure afford, at any point, and to whom, and how far and in what direction does the give increase with growing strain? *This calls for a theory built, from the bottom up, in terms of scope for change.* Only *in* the penumbra do judicial problems lie. A theory to solve those problems must be a theory *of* the penumbra.

The manner of framing the question is psychologically of huge importance. "Is this within the powers granted by the Document?" throws the base-line of inquiry back a century and a half, constricts the vision to the static word, turns discussion into the channels of logomachy. It invites, and too often produces, artificial limitation of attention to the non-essential, the accidental: to wit, what language happens to stand in the Document, or in some hoary—or beardless—text of its "interpretation." What is the sense in arguing, for example, whether this is a tax upon a thing or one upon a privilege? The real questions are (*a*) whether it is an indecently discriminatory[41] tax; and (*b*) whether the institution of such a tax too seriously disturbs the existing apportionment of powers between states and nation; the *existing* apportionment, not the apportionment described in any Document. Or again, what sense in arguing whether this is "property," or whether it is being "taken," or whether the confiscatory statute is "due process"? Any expectation may have value, any valuable expectation may be likened to property, or made into property by judicial fiat, any change in law upsets some expectations, any such upset is a deprivation, any argument on "taking" is a quibble, and the confiscatory statute is "due process," if it stands. The only real question is, again, whether the deprivation is indecently discriminatory: who is being penalized, and how much, for the benefit of someone else? Can the gain achieved be regarded as at all commensurate to the cost? Were the expectations the kind we want to see perpetuated? Does the need press?

Contrast the effect of framing the question thus: "Is this within the leeway of change which our going governmental scheme affords? And even if not, does the nature of the case require the leeway to be widened to include it?" The base line then becomes so much of the past only *as is still alive,* and the immediate future comes to bear as well. The tone and tendency of the very question is dynamic. The "nature of the case" invites attention to explicit policy. While that continuity with the past which, if not a duty, is wisdom quite as well as a necessity, is carefully preserved—only that the past concerned is that embodied not in an ancient Text, but in a living Government.

THE PERSONNEL PROBLEM UNDER A SANE THEORY

Four things appear, I trust, from the foregoing.

First, that there is no disposition, under this approach by way of practice and institution, to disregard the normative and ideal element in Constitutional law. As stated, in the penumbra the only guidance lies in idealizations. The quarrel is with turning to the Document as their source, in any case in which living practice with a function, or formative practice with a function, exist to serve as better base-lines.

Second, that there is no quarrel to be had with judges *merely* because they disregard or twist Documentary language, or "interpret" it to the despair of original intent, in the service of what those judges conceive to be the inherent nature of our institutions. To my mind, such action is their duty. To my mind, the judge who builds his decision to conform with his conception of what our institutions must be if we are to continue, roots in the deepest wisdom. I may differ with him in his choice of an ideal. I may feel, say in the *Coppage* and *Abrams* and *Adkins Cases,* that he was quite misguided. But I cannot simultaneously defend the dissents in those cases and deny the implicit premise common to majority and to dissent: to wit, that certain fundamental features of our institutions need expression in the rulings of the Supreme Court of the United States, whatever be the language of the Document.

The third point is therefore, obviously, that a sane theory of Constitutional law would no more be a substitute for adequate personnel than is the prevalent modified and halfway reworking of the ancient orthodoxy. The only guaranty of judicial wisdom will remain the judge.

Yet I submit that a sane theory would, should it ever be achieved and accepted, be a gain.

(*a*) There are certain cases in which I suspect the majority to have used an approach related in its fundamentals to the approach which I advocate as sound—but with a sorry difference. To *institutions* they looked. But not to *governmental* institutions.

Observe the difference. When new regulation hits a field of laymen's action, you have an interplay of government and non-government. No man with sense will deny that non-government (the market, or social life) is *infiltrated* with aspects of prior government. Neither, on the other hand, will any man deny that, say in the market, self-maintenance and traditional ways of bargaining outweigh such governmental factors, if an assessment had to be made. When governmental folk attempt to intervene and re-regulate various *predominantly* non-governmental practices, we have a contact and interaction of men predominantly specializing in running things in the alleged interest of most-of-us and men predominantly specializing in running things in the interest of themselves, and the alleged interest of certain associates of theirs. The area of contact and conflict is clear, and single. But the *way of approaching* that area has meaning for results. If the practices and institutions (and the ideology thereof) in the foreground of attention are *non*-governmental, you get the sadder decisions in the cases under the Fourteenth Amendment. Not only do existing institutions set the norm in such cases. There is worse. Judges see these institutions not as they *are,* but through the spectacles (*a*) of what they may have been, (*b*) of the honorably received ideology about them—which is of necessity vastly older than themselves. Troublesome excrescences tend to be overlooked, in that sweet ideology—say, of laissez-faire. The picture fits into a background shaped in unthinking childhood, uncritically accepted, all deviating and modern factors slighted. Contrast with this an approach by way of the institutions of *government.* These no judge has met until his manhood. They come to him not by way of a confusing and obfuscating ideology imbibed before he either thought or observed, but through the observation and critique of a grown man. The factors in the foreground of attention are the new factors. Let him approach the area of contact and conflict from that angle, and he asks not: "Can we permit this tradition-hallowed way of doing to be altered?" but: "Has governmental regulation not been extended further than this, within our history?" It is not enough to look naïvely to *institutions* for a norm. Such looking—at the *non-*

governmental phase of institutions—has been the curse of the worst Supreme Court decisions. The eye must be directed—as in the dissents in the Free Speech cases—*at the practices of specialists in government, and at the ideal of what their job is*. Perhaps these two (as in the Free Speech cases) may be inconsistent. Despite that, with this criterion of measurement, the base-line of judgment shifts a hundred yards or more to the left.

(*b*) The admission of issues of policy to free discussion in court as being the very crux of the point of law will of course never make intelligence or insight grow from solid ivory, nor will it undo mental and emotional arteriosclerosis. But if any man conceives the vocabulary in which legal discourse is cast to be without serious immediate and long-run effect on legal behavior, he is ignorant of the ways of language and of men. *Control,* that vocabulary does not; *prejudice,* it must.

(*c*) To study the processes of government is to open the eyes to governmental needs. To ponder on their function is to open the eyes to their effects. To study the Words of a Document, on the contrary, is to invite inattention to either effects or needs. And whereas knowledge of needs and effects may not be wisdom, wisdom without such knowledge remains a limping horse.—

The fourth point which I hope has become obvious is that I am not urging, nor need any sane revision of Constitutional law theory urge, that order in change be disregarded, nor that the continuity of institutions be cut. On the side of words and formulae alone, the ease with which the existing patter can be made to compass such radical departures as non-consensual, compulsory regulation of enterprise and action never heretofore regulated is evidenced by the past year's judicial extensions of the concept "affected with a public interest." We need, then, few new formulae in order to make decision conform to the demands of life. We need only a new attitude to guide the use of ancient formulae, and an earth-rooted theory to give continuity to the results.

Save as to one phase of the theory of precedent in Constitutional decision, which, for all the necessity of its revision, must be considered minor.

PRECEDENT IN CONSTITUTIONAL AND PRIVATE LAW

The genesis in Constitutional cases of a procedure appropriate only to private law is understandable. The training of the judges has regularly been a training on the private side, and almost regularly on the side of pure common law. The assumption of power to review legislation was itself bottomed on private law reasoning. It came into exercise as a mere incident in settling a private dispute of man with man, or group with group.

But the *persistence* of such private law procedure in Constitutional cases for a century after the significance of the latter has been realized, is hard to understand. To be sure, a case for a certain ideological conservatism in private law doctrine of precedent can be made—speciously—persuasive. (1) The *range* of the decision, in its aspect of establishing a precedent, is rarely wide. (2) Therefore the chance is *relatively* great that the accidental parties who happen to be litigating will typify the relevant conflicting interests; that the court will therefore, by looking merely at the record, gain some fair insight into the underlying policies. (3) Private law courts exist for the very purpose of settling officially controversies which do not otherwise get settled; and to that end nose count of judges is a reasonable means. (4) The fluidity of phrasing in the rules laid down, moreover, leaves much room for unnoticed extension, restriction, or change of direction, in any further case. (5) Private law precedents, where hopelessly bad, leave open the resort to a higher instance: the legislature. The legal *system,* that is, leaves explicit room for the correction of judicial blunders. Again, we can afford the nose count—because, where we have to, we can undo its results.

But these attributes, all of them, are regularly lacking in Constitutional cases. There the range of a precedent is wide; the chance of adequate information coming before the Court is slight; the controversy comes with the whole weight of legislative judgment cast in advance on one side; the Text construed is unchanging, inelastic even in "interpretation"; *and there is no appeal from the Court's decision, save to the Court itself.*

In such a situation mere nose-count decision of unconstitutionality is a monstrosity. It means applying to a decision which limits legislative powers the voting technique evolved to accomplish mere decisions between individuals, or to make precedents which the legislature is expected to correct if they are wrong. It is to let those judicial votes which are backed by legislature and executive weigh no more heavily *on matters of policy in change* than those judicial votes that run counter to both executive and legislative views. If ever the borrowing of institutions to be turned to uses for which they were not designed was blind and silly, it has been here. The minimum of readjustment needed is to require unconstitutionality of statutes to call for six[42] votes in a Court of nine.

Nor is this all. There is no appeal, I say, from the Court's precedent, save to the Court itself. This in a world of constant growth and change; this in a nation of expanding business and financial centralization, piled-up complexity, rising pressure of population. This in controversies in which the rulings purport to limit, as things stand, *for all future time* the *powers* of the government. Certainly, in this situation, one would expect to see a Court alive to its responsibilities ready to reopen any precedent on unconstitutionality as much as ten years old, ready to inquire whether the once decreed denial of power *still* could be maintained. Almost one would be tempted to urge that there should be recognized two types of precedent; rulings on Constitutionality, which would not thereafter be subject to challenge; rulings on unconstitutionality, which would at regular intervals be laid bare to reëxamination. Almost—for, let it peal out again from the bell towers: there is no appeal from the Court's precedent to any save the Court itself, or (has it been twice in our history?) to Amendment, or to a revolution. The Court has indeed reversed itself quite often enough to demonstrate some definite absence of infallibility among its members. But in its *working* ideology, from day to day, the tacit assumption of past infallibility controls. Judges are mortals, mortals are prideful, and common law, private law, tradition—however unsuited to the case—dominates judicial imagination. *Ruat coelum!*

Meantime, the machinery for easing the grip of precedent would be so simple. There is the well-known but little used announcement that, whereas in this case we abide by our precedent, yet in all cases arising hereafter we shall rule as follows, etc.—a procedure explicitly recognized as Constitutional by the Great Court itself, in what may yet become the epoch-making case of *Great Northern Ry Co. v. Sunburst Oil & Refining Co.*[43] There is the now unorthodox but once freely practiced procedure (still echoing in the wariness with which we eye *in private law* the case of first impression) of refusing in a novel case, not obvious in all its bearings, to lay down any precedent as such. Surely there is enough of precedent in the make-up of man to render legal fetishism on the subject quite dispensable.

THE TRULY FUNDAMENTAL WITHIN THE CONSTITUTION

ALMOST, I SAID, ONE WOULD BE TEMPTED to the twofold division of rulings just set forth. And in respect to rulings of *un*constitutionality I should yield gladly to the tempter. But there have been occasional rulings on Constitutionality—rare, but bothersome—which must be reëxamined and some day disavowed. Again one enters into the region of the ideal pictures, this time on a more airy level where little enough basis is found in governmental practice to make the pictures even a partial reflection of reality—where, therefore, opinions divide and become unprovable—where the explicit or implicit social and governmental philosophy of judges must control.

There are certain persistent areas of judicial problems which no acceptance of such a theory as is here sketched can remove, and which no indulgence of presumptions in favor of the national government's action can greatly lessen. Legislators—including the Congress—can and do go off half-cocked. They are tempted constantly to confiscate rather than to compensate. They are tempted, in emergency or panic, to make haste overhastily. Likewise executives. But oversudden change by way of government costs hugely. Discriminatory change often distributes the burden with indecent inequality.—Meanwhile, changes in method of changing are even now under way; consider the application of the assessment principle in the A. A. A. Will its extension some day make outright police-power confiscation unconstitutional?[44]

We have, moreover, a federal system, and some division of powers among governmental organs. Some guiding lines of distribution, as between federal and local (or other sub-) authorities, there must always be. The actual lines of distribution are inane. The federal government should be doing much that the states now do (taxation of interstate enterprise; what cure is there for double taxation, save in centralizing the tax?). Most of the more local governmental machinery needs utter reconstruction, and it is far from certain that state boundaries, or even territorial (for example, regional) lines afford the sound lines of such reconstruction. And so *ad infinitum*. More: changes are already under way: consider the guild-building non-territorial philosophy implicit in the N.R.A.

Finally, persons in power, if freed of all restraint, grow in their good time most uncomfortably arbitrary. The individual, or the subgroup, needs not only policing by, but protection from the government. Added to which, the lesser, but better, philosophy of American governmental institutions has it that only in wide freedom of minority expression can the solution of future problems, dark to us yet, be had. Hence—with the mind on such cases as those of Abrams, Rosika Schwimmer, and Our Adolf—the "almost" in the paragraphs above.

Here, then, over and above (1) the great region where governmental practice without reference to the Document gives the answer, and (2) the region where governmental quasi-practice, seen in the light of its function and functioning, and qualified by the going range of leeway and by the emergent need, affords without reference to the Document the foundations of the needed norm—here (3) is the region where the job of the Court is, now and again, to *control* the course of governmental practice by reference to an ideal found not in that practice, but in the nature of what our government should be.[45] In the light of this, I grow impatient with this mourning that the day of the Court is over; that it has no course left except to rubber stamp, no choice except to abdicate or perish. The Court is faced with a reconstruction of Constitutional law theory as big with portent as the work of Marshall.[46] But again, so far as I can see, without reference to the Document. True, one can rally, if one chooses, round the Bill of Rights. But to what end? The privilege against self-incrimination is today a misfit. The privilege to keep and bear arms, applied to modern weapons, needs infringement, and by national control. The paragraphs which still have meaning have it not because they stand in the Text, but because we need some similar meaning in our lives.

There is, in a word, one reason and one only, for turning in this day to the Text. A "written constitution" is a system of unwritten practices in which the Document in question, by virtue of men's attitudes, has *a little influence. Where it makes no important difference which way the decision goes,* the Text—in the absence of countervailing practice—is an excellent traffic-light. Aside from such cases, any Text of fifty years of age is an Old Man of the Sea. For the rest, the Constitution is an institution. And 1933 has come—and gone.

One matter in conclusion. The view advanced here *sounds* unorthodox. It sounds unorthodox only because it puts into words the *tacit* doing of the Court, and draws from that doing conclusions not to be avoided by a candid child. Whatever the Court has *said,* it has repeatedly made concessions to governmental practice and governmental need.[47] Whatever the Court has *said,* it has repeatedly turned to established governmental practice in search of norms. Whatever the Court has *said,* it has shaped the living Constitution to the needs of the day as it felt them. The whole expansion of the due process clause has been an enforcement of the majority's ideal of government-as-it-should-be, running free of the language of the Document. Whatever the Court has *said,* it has departed from its own precedents whenever it saw fit to do so. It has refined and whittled precedents into unrecognizability, or shifted the line of their development from East to West. Whatever the Court has *said,* it has in deciding repeatedly weighed policy to a degree exceedingly unusual in private-law decision. But all of this has, in the main, been *sub silentio.* All of it has, in the main, occurred on first and third Mondays, with the second and fourth devoted slavishly to Sinbad's rider. All of this undermining of the ancient orthodox approach has taken place in prudery, with averted eyes. It minds one of some Victorian virgin tubbing in a nightgown. Yet the year, in fact, insists on being 1934. Theory that can face fact, including that fact, is what we need.

NOTES TO LLEWELLYN ESSAY

[1] *The Process of Government* (1908) *e.g.*, 295, 325 ff. Why so profound and incisive a book has found so little echo, I cannot make out. Morris Cohen led me to it. I feel like entitling this essay *A Rediscovery of Bentley.*

[2] McBain, *The Living Constitution* (1927) perhaps especially c. 1; to which add Landis' review (1928) 41 Harv. L. Rev. 545.

[3] Perhaps especially in *American Government and Politics* (ed. 1; 1910; ed. 6; 1931) and *The American Leviathan* (1930).

[4] *The American Commonwealth* (ed. 1; 1888; last ed., 1928).

[5] In order to forestall misconception: I am not arguing that the United States *ought to* have the sort of constitution loosely designated as "unwritten." I am arguing that they *have* such a constitution, and that nobody can stop their having such a constitution, and that whether anyone likes that fact or not, the fact has been there for decades, and must be dealt with by any theory that purports to do a theory's work.

[6] Again, to forestall misconception: I am not by trade a constitutional lawyer. Therefore, this essay may be shot through with errors in delicate detail. It does purport, for all that, to talk sense in rugged outline. Indeed, its author suspects that it is hard for any person unblest with child-like innocence of most of the technique to talk sense in a field so ridden by archaic nonsense.

[7] I have no quarrel with Pound's insight that certain formal postulates of legal thinking are mere postulates, not purporting to depict the fact.—*A Comparison of Ideals of Law* (1933) 47 Harv. L. Rev. 1, 9. I should joyously go further, and urge that no postulate of thinking (legal or other) could ever square wholly with the facts. To theory, facts will remain eternally unregenerate. But there remains the question of degree. There are approximations which serve well, whereas there are also absurdities so violent as to be clumsy, crazy tools. A postulate of thinking has to be close *enough* to the material thought about to get (granted due intuitional correctives) adequate results, to get them consistently, and to get them as economically as the material allows of. And the argument here is that, in respect to our Constitution, the ancient postulates—even as quasi-corrected—have ceased to perform in any such fashion. *Sit eis terra levis.*

[8] In a slightly modernized form, the phrasing would be "an even better source of information." The argument will be that this emendation logically involves flat rejection of the first two premises. For it recognizes the fact of creation by the Court. Once such creation is recognized *and the implications of the recognition fairly faced,* there is no stopping short of some such conclusions as this essay offers. For that reason I leave the bold, but consistent, older orthodoxy in the text. The newer insights among constitutional lawyers as clear-eyed even as T. R. Powell and Frankfurter are still tradition-ridden halfway houses.

[9] See note 7 *supra.*

[10] The accomplishment of judicial review is a major instance of the leeway allowed to specialists in government—even by other specialists in government. The reasoning was clear: there is a clearly stated "supreme law of the land"; *someone* must measure lesser law against it, and the lesser law must yield, or the Document cease to have effective legal force *pro tanto.* Thus far, there can be no quarrel. The next proposition of the Court: *We* are the appointed Someone! and in event of dispute the *ultimate* Someone!—that proposition carries them into territory which *under the Document* is unstaked. They occupy that territory. No one challenges their title seriously. Occupation—and assiduous cultivation—

produce title under any number of theories. The important thing here is that important and sustained action, however founded in theory, met with no consistent vigorous challenge in fact—and therefore became a portion of the working Constitution.

[11] Although the question remains always: Inconvenient to whom? On the values and presuppositions of truth-telling in such circumstances, see *The Conditions for, and the Aims and Methods of Legal Research* (1930) Am. L. S. Rev. 670, 671 n.

[12] It is at this point that I differ partly from Jerome Frank in his conception of the "myth" of legal certainty. Face-saving implies *acceptance* of things untrue which *could* be seen to be untrue. But it does not *necessarily* imply their conscious acceptance in spite of *conscious* perception of their falsity. *Cf.* Frank, *Law and the Modern Mind* (1930) *e.g.*, at 9, 37. And Frank's otherwise illuminating presentation seems to me to wobble now and again between those two ideas.

[14] *Cf.* Marshall and May, *The Divorce Court, I. Maryland* (1932) c. 5.

[15] *Cf.* John Dickinson, *Legal Rules: Their Function in the Process of Decision* (1931) 79 U. of Pa. L. Rev. 833, 846 ff., with the corrective by Frank, *What Courts Do in Fact* (1932) 26 Ill. L. Rev. 645, 649 ff., and 761 ff.

[16] Walter Wheeler Cook has devoted a deal of fruitful attention to this problem of the minor premise. *Cf. The Utility of Jurisprudence in the Solution of Legal Problems,* in (1928) 5 Lect. on Leg. Top. Assn. Bar of City of N. Y., 337 ff.

[17] I know few values of comparative law study comparable to that of discovering how far such traditional categorization guides decision. Features that the Anglo-American lawyer views as fundamental fade out of sight; features which to him are meaningless assume importance. And yet, abroad and here, *facts* press (over three decades) with the same bulldog refusal to be downed. Where necessary, they reshape the legal categories. Compare, *e.g.*, German and Anglo-American results in the field of Agency (conversation with Höneger), or French and American results in the field of industrial and auto liability. On the latter, see Deák, *Automobile Accidents: A Comparative Study of the Law of Liability in Europe* (1931) 79 U. of Pa. L. Rev. 271.

[18] For an illustration see Note (1928) 28 Col. L. Rev. 66.

[19] Williston, *Some Modern Tendencies in the Law* (1929) 62.

[20] Goodhart, *Determining the Ratio Decidendi of a Case* (1930) 40 Yale L. J. 161 will remain the classic illustration of the best work that can be done upon this premise. An intelligent reader asks a single question: Why such a futile premise?

[21] *Legal Tradition and Social Science Method, supra* note *, at 106.

[22] Cornil, *Autorité de la loi et autonomie de la jurisprudence* (1928) I Acta Acad. Universalis Juris. Comp. 128, quotes Portalis skillfully and extensively. "Codes of peoples make themselves over the years, but properly speaking no man makes them."

[23] Outside of Constitutional law theory, the phrase is warranted. *Cf. Bramble Bush* (1930) 128 ff.; 65. I should like to make very clear that my objections in this essay do not go to the major lines of the Court's action. They go to a theory which turns *much* important action into lines at odds with the general tenor of a glorious record.

[24] In this I am in full accord with H. Jahrreiss, *Berechenbarkeit und Recht* (1927) 22 ff.; *cf.* 1928 Proc. Conf. Soc. Work, *loc. cit. supra* note *.

[25] Whether one prefers ivy or stone is in law as in architecture a question of taste; and in the one case as in the other, taste varies by epoch. But taste (with due allowance for W. I. Thomas' magnificent and yet unpublished theory as to the *occasional* effects of fad) determines commonly less what happens than how the happening is judged.

[26] *Cf.* McBain, *op. cit. supra* note 2, at 29.

[27] The Supreme Court is not the final arbiter of Constitutionality. It is merely the *official organ* for final pronouncement. Hence, it moves within limits. In the case put, the limits would, by popular action, have expanded to fit.

[28] There is no question that the Text has influenced the course of growth. Let me take a single illustration. The money and borrowing powers have excused first a National Bank, then a national banking system, then a Federal Reserve System, all, as it happened, making little initial allowance for the needs of either industrial or agricultural banking. One step toward filling out the system was found in the securities affiliates. Their connection with the Document escapes my untrained eye; the giddy trapeze-work of Constitutional theory is not for mere commercial lawyers. Yet I have heard nothing of serious challenge to the constitutionality of the affiliates—prior to the crash. (For post-crash challenge, *cf.* Note [1933] 33 Col. L. Rev. 324.) More, had they been managed as befitted their possibilities, to produce a national banking system integrated with intelligence and operated with some sense of public responsibility, I think the position inescapable that after ten years of operation they never would have been successfully challenged on the Constitutional point. Not the innovation, nor the transparent hypocrisy of the devices used to innovate, but varying sense in respect to which way lay pressing need, has been the determinative factor in their history. Yet even these remote securities affiliates *showed the marks* of the Document's influence. They were, nominally, separate corporations, with segregated assets; they could, as national banks could not, cross city and state lines, and scatter offices throughout the country; their operations were not subject to national banking examination—in a word, by forcing a branch of banking outside of the "banking" system built primarily upon the *money* power, the Document contributed its effective part to irresponsibility and to the semi-collapse of its materially more legitimate offspring.

The Document thus plays its part. It serves not only as above suggested, in forcing growth *out of* certain institutional channels; it also at times forces growth *into* certain channels; and sometimes it checks growth for a time (income tax; child labor; minimum wage) or even chokes it off entirely. Of this last, illustrations in the tax field are too familiar to warrant listing. The most dramatic example is still the effect on flow of capital into non-private enterprise of the exemption of state and municipal obligations from federal taxation, plus the unanticipated later arrival of the income tax. To be sure, that exemption was laid down not by the Document, but by Marshall; but in this matter of shaping, the text and what the Court has thus far made it stand for, flow at any given moment indistinguishably together. And it is, as I have insisted to boredom, not the Document itself, but men's actions and attitudes with reference to it, which have effect. Their actions more than their attitudes: Marshall certainly had no conscious intent thus to undermine the scheme of private enterprise; yet what agitator has ever done so effective a job of boring from within?

The apparent concessions thus made to theoretical difference of written and unwritten constitutions should, however, not be read as meaning so very much. Both illustrations rest vastly more on practice than on the Text. And the deflection of later development by the historically acquired set-up of existing practice—and thought—is found no less with an "unwritten" constitution. Consider the history of the King's Council; or, more concretely, the effect of the existing system of peer-creation on the reform of 1911.

[29] Three-card monte, like the shell-game, depends on the undoubted fact that the practiced hand is quicker than the unpracticed eye. A major technique is the diversion of attention. While occasional courts must be recognized as consummate artists in the legal branch of these games, one feels that most judges could profit by intelligent attendance at the county fair. This judgment is perhaps unjust. For after all, it is only the unpracticed eye that needs to be deceived.—I have elsewhere expressed my belief that until the pre-

vailing theory of case law is reformed, judicial card-sharping is the part of wisdom, decency, and duty.—*Legal Tradition and Social Science Method, op. cit. supra* note *, at 106 ff.

[30] Some institutions—for instance, our present Constitution—have found words and rules serving them as midwife or even as ancestor; but in the main it is action which comes first, to be followed by delayed perception of that action, then by rationalization of the action delayed still longer, and finally by conscious normatization of what has been perceived or rationalized. Before these latter processes have been worked out, the lines of the action commonly have shifted. Veblen's eyes were keen: "A man's ethics are modelled on the conditions of his grandfather's time."

[31] *Cf.* note 28, *supra.*

[32a] By the editor's courtesy, and in defiance of the form-book, I am permitted to retain the lower case h.

[33] As an alternative, there is the remodeling of the Court—say, by way of increase of numbers; or even by way of introducing a retiring age sweetened, let us say, by duly attractive pension. But these are still in the realm of expediency and experiment.

[34] Such as, for example, appears to be again emerging among farmers. Or must one subdivide into cotton-, corn-, tobacco-farmers, and the like?

[35] Basic to the government scheme as a governmental scheme. There is no need to insist at length that while order in some form is basic to any society, yet economic and some social factors are likely to condition the governmental institutions on levels far deeper than those on which governmental institutions in turn condition them. Such exceptions as the remaking of the Soviet economic and social world under the aegis of government demonstrate the *possibilities* inherent in sustained and intelligent leverage by way of organized power; the First William affords a lesser illustration, and the Second Roosevelt may be offering another. Still, the normal course of events has been for government to drift a deal more than it controlled.

[37] This ought to need no discussion; but as long as an orthodox theory of Words and Intent befogs the constitutional landscape, the most obvious features of that landscape need explicit pointing out.

[38] Throughout this essay "norm" is used to designate a standard of Oughtness for behavior; "normative," not "normal," is the relevant adjective. Is-ness of behavior is designated by "way" or "practice." "Functioning" refers to the observable results of ways or institutions: What do they *do?* "Function" is used, on the other hand, to denote some purpose or end served, some value gained, by the way or institution; it is intended to incorporate two subjective elements: any end described as a "function" is conceived for the moment as having, (*a*) in the eyes of the person judging, (*b*) value for the whole of the society. The persons viewed as doing the judging are, save where the reference is patently to myself, the judges.

[39] Only within decent limits, in a society formed of pluralistic tendencies and needs, behind which no one of us has yet been man enough—or God enough—to descry a unity *with communicable meaning.* Formulas of unity we have enough of; but the formulas stand dumb before the concrete problem.

[40] "Last worst" does not indicate my own views on the subject; quite the contrary; save that I am interested in machinery for future control of debt creation quite as much as in machinery for shrinking the bulk of debt already incurred.

[41] I make no attempt here to define "indecent" in this connection. That is a job for Constitutional lawyers. I insist only that the definition must be worked out, first in terms of the going leeway for change which our governmental scheme affords; second, in

terms of the felt need in question; third, in terms of the range of policy choice properly open *to officials whose business is policy-shaping.* This last will shift somewhat with shift in practice. Confiscatory police power is now, as we know, one legitimate available means, subject to spasmodic veto of the Court. A segregation ordinance is bad; a zoning ordinance is good. But one can conceive a shift in practice toward the approach by way of compensation or assessment. Granted such a shift, one would expect to find the Court developing some decent theory for controlling the use of confiscation; for example, that restrictions placed upon all members of a group in the apparent long-range interest of all could stand, in spite of the immediate penalization of some; that intangible values not capable of reasonable estimation would remain open to confiscatory regulation; that even demonstrable values could be wiped out by new regulation where enough remained to permit the partial wiping out to be felt as a legitimate taxation of the line of enterprise. Or one could conceive of an attempt to estimate the chanciness of any line of investment or enterprise in terms of the unforeseen march of events, with a view to affording government greater freedom to intervene where there had been less reason to build firm, vested, expectations; or, to move from the opposite pole, more freedom to intervene where the extra-governmental outlook showed a firmer wherewithal to stand the intervention without ruin.

[42] If the change in the theory of unconstitutional precedent suggested *infra* were not to prevail, this figure should then read seven, or eight.

[43] (1932) 287 U. S. 358.

[44] *Cf.* note 41 *supra.*

[45] If a lawyer will consider the difference in process and attitude of a judge when he conceives himself (*a*) to be reading a statute, and (*b*) to be passing on the inherent powers of a court—say in regard to notice and a hearing, or to punishment for contempt—he will see at once the effect of "the nature of the case" as a base-line for decision. He will also perceive that judges can go as magnificently wrong from that base-line as from the other. There *is* no guaranty of judicial wisdom but the judge. But the worst wrong-going has been pretty regularly in cases in which the judge's premises were hidden even from himself. A realistic theory would come close to forcing them into expression. It would do more. Explicit realism among the judges would unchain realism among the other specialists. If the personnel problem *should* persist in bothering, it would be remembered that there is no Documentary specification of the number of judges on the Court.

"... to make our economic and social structure capable of dealing with modern life is the joint task of the legislative, the *judicial* and the executive branches of the national government."—President Roosevelt's message to Congress, N. Y. *Times,* Jan. 4, 1934, at 1.

[46] Even leaving aside the long-run job of theory reconstruction, consider that of immediate statesmanship. If the first batch of cases arising under the new legislation happens to present instances of administrative arbitrariness, the temptation is strong to restrict the leeway which government and the country need. But if not, the temptation is strong to open a leeway which in more stable times may lead to grave abuse. To keep the double issue clear, irrespective of the accidents of the case; to grant the leeway, and yet retain a purchase for control of its abuse—if this is not worthy of a Marshall's statesmanship, what judicial problem ever was?

[47] Stone's opinions in tax cases are a cumulative and lovely classic example. Stone deals with the precedents, in such cases, to three-quarters from the angle here suggested: "*What will they let us do?*" The implicit nub is always governmental need. The precedents—or more accurately, the resulting versions of them—are not a *ratio,* but an excuse, or, shall we say, a "justification"?

OUR NON-CITIZEN NATIONALS, WHO ARE THEY?

BY DUDLEY O. MCGOVNEY

UNLESS THE READER HAS TIME for some interesting and intricate curiosities of American law he should pass this essay by. To determine exactly and completely the difference in American law between the status of non-citizen national and that of citizen national would be an interesting and profitable exercise in analytical jurisprudence. It would involve a cataloguing of all the legal relations that are peculiar to each status. I had hoped to introduce the present essay with an exhaustive study of these distinctions but time has not permitted and I have limited my theme to the question, What persons have this status of non-citizen national with respect to the United States?

By the Treaty of Paris, which became effective April 11, 1899, Spain "relinquished" sovereignty over Cuba and "ceded" Puerto Rico, other Spanish islands in the West Indies, the Philippine Islands, and Guam to the United States. What effect did the cession have upon the nationality of the inhabitants of those islands?

The parties to the treaty expressed no intention of altering the status of resident aliens of British, German, Chinese, or other alien nationality. Those who were aliens both to Spain and to the United States continued to be aliens to the United States.

As to the inhabitants who were Spanish subjects the treaty contained these provisions:

ARTICLE IX

Spanish subjects, natives of the Peninsula, residing in the territory over which Spain by the present treaty relinquishes or cedes her sovereignty, may remain . . . or may remove. . . . In case they remain in the territory they may preserve their allegiance to the Crown of Spain by making, before a court of record, within a year[1] from the date of the exchange of ratifications of this treaty, a declaration of their decision to preserve such allegiance; in default of which declaration they shall be held to have renounced it and to have adopted the nationality of the territory in which they may reside.

The civil rights and political status of the native inhabitants of the territories hereby ceded to the United States shall be determined by the Congress.

It will be noted that these two paragraphs of the treaty dealt with two classes of persons: (1) "Spanish subjects, *natives of the Peninsula,*" that is, of the Spanish mother-country, the Iberian Peninsula and adjacent islands,[2] and (2) "native inhabitants" of the *ceded* islands. The use of the word "ceded" in the second paragraph excluded the Cubans from its provision. The first paragraph, however, applied to Cuba as well as to all the ceded islands; hence the generality of the expression, that the Spaniards born in the Spanish mother-country who remained either in Cuba or in any of the ceded islands, without declaring their election to retain Spanish nationality, should acquire "the nationality *of the territory in which they may reside.*" In respect to all the ceded islands this was definitely American nationality; as for Cuba, her national character was yet to be determined. It is sufficient here thus to direct attention to the peculiar factors that made the status of the Cubans a separate problem, one not included in this essay.

As to the Philippines and Puerto[3] Rico, let us take the easier point first, that is, the "Spanish subjects natives of the Peninsula," in the first paragraph, before passing to "the native inhabitants of the territories" dealt with in the second paragraph.

It will be noted that Spanish subjects natives of the Peninsula residing, at the date of the treaty, in Cuba or the ceded territory had an option of remaining or removing, and that those who remained had an option of retaining or losing Spanish nationality. The treaty did not expressly provide the latter option for those who removed. The Supreme Courts of the Philippines and of the United States have held[4] that this option of removal was intended to be an option to remove without incurring any change in nationality, so that by removal Spanish nationality was retained and American rejected, without the necessity of any declaration.

What is the meaning of "natives" in the expression "natives of the Peninsula"? Frequently the word is used in the sense of indigenous people or in a racial sense. Thus, "natives of the Peninsula" might have been taken to mean persons of Spanish blood or Spanish ancestry.

In the main, this sense has been rejected in favor of "born in" the Peninsula.

Thus the United States District Court for Puerto Rico held that a person born in Puerto Rico and of adult age at the date of ratification of the treaty, although both his parents were of Spanish blood and his father a native of the Peninsula, did not under the treaty have a privilege of retaining Spanish nationality if he remained in Puerto Rico.[5] He became involuntarily an American national.

The same court held in several cases, however, that a Spaniard born in peninsular Spain who gave the name of his wife and minor children in the document[6] filed for the purpose of expressing his election to retain Spanish nationality for himself thereby elected for them also, and that this election was operative to preserve the Spanish nationality of the wife, regardless of the place of her birth, and likewise to preserve the Spanish nationality of the minor children during their minority, regardless of the place of their birth.[7] In several of these cases the children whose Spanish nationality was held thus to be preserved were born in Puerto Rico;[8] they were not "natives of the Peninsula" as the courts conceded. As to the minors, this judicially evolved rule, that the father's or guardian's[9] election served for them also, was coupled with a limitation that they retained Spanish nationality only provisionally, during minority, and that upon coming of age, or within a reasonable time thereafter, they must elect for themselves to retain Spanish nationality, a failure then to elect resulting in the acquisition of American nationality as of the time of attaining majority, or perhaps at the expiration of the reasonable time period.[10]

This judicial interpretation seems to have been judicious. A parent born in the Peninsula may have had residing with him in the ceded territory a child or children born in the Peninsula, also a child or children born in the ceded territory, and all still minors at the date of cession. The treaty was silent in respect to minors. It did not purport to confer upon them capacity to elect for themselves. It did not authorize them to elect upon coming of age. The only election expressly mentioned was one to take place within a year[11] of the cession. The inference was reasonable that the election for minors born in the Peninsula was to be made by their parents or guardians. From this it was but a short step to extend the parent's or guardian's election to the minor children born in the ceded territory. It should be noted, however, that these judicial decisions were contrary to the opinion of two Secretaries of State, Hay in 1899, and Lansing in 1918, both of whom, the latter more explicitly, took the position that a parent's or guardian's election sufficed only with respect to minors who had been born in the Peninsula.[11a]

The reason assigned by the courts, namely, that the treaty should be construed as not intending to create diversity of nationalities within families, seems a good one. This extension in respect to some minors, as stated above, was made only in behalf of the minor children of natives of the Peninsula whose fathers or guardians elected, expressly or impliedly, in their behalf within the period fixed by the treaty. It did not enable a minor, whose parent or guardian had not elected for him, to elect Spanish nationality upon coming of age if that event occurred after the period fixed in the treaty. Such a minor, if he remained in the ceded territory, became *nolens volens* an American national, just as did adult natives of the Peninsula who remained in the ceded islands and made no election within the treaty period.

The opinions in these cases make it clear that the courts took the words "natives of the Peninsula" to mean persons born in the Peninsula but believed that it would be giving the treaty a harsh literalness to hold that a wife or the minor children though not natives of the Peninsula should acquire a new nationality although the husband or father elected to retain the old. In one opinion the court by solemn dictum gave assurance that no further exceptions would be made beyond wives, widows, and minor children of natives of the Peninsula.[12]

It has been said that about five or six thousand Puerto Rican Spaniards born in the Peninsula elected to retain Spanish and reject American nationality.[13] I have seen no corresponding statement with respect to the Philippines.

As to other classes of Spanish subjects inhabiting the islands at the time of cession they became American nationals without choice. This was the result of the lack of any treaty provision to the contrary.[14] These included approximately seven million persons in the Philippines and approximately eight hundred thousand in Puerto Rico.

There were without doubt some persons then inhabiting the ceded islands who were not Spanish nationals. The greater part of the population of the Philippines were the descendants of the "aborigines" who occupied the islands when Magellan "discovered" them, but there had been some Chinese and Japanese immigration for centuries, and more recently there had been immigrants of other Asiatic stocks and of European stocks. Some of these immigrants and perhaps some of their descendants were aliens to Spain. These did not become American nationals. They were no doubt relatively few compared to the total number of inhabitants, but to them as individuals the rules determining their status were important. These rules are to be found in the Spanish law. The courts under the American régime have found ascertainment of these rules quite difficult and in fact have not seriously sought to ascertain them.[15] Most of the judicial decisions dealing with this question have been concerned with the status of persons of Chinese descent residing in the Philippines at the cession. There are baffling obscurities in the Spanish nationality laws that none but a very competent Spanish legal scholar could resolve. I venture, however, in an appendix to this essay to discuss some of the difficulties and to indicate the remainder. I relegate this matter to an appendix not because it is not interesting, not because it is not important, but because the non-specialized reader might find it tedious. The curious will be interested in that peculiar Spanish institution, *vecindad,* and other matters.

It is a matter for wonderment what dictated to the American treaty commissioners the choice of words used in the second paragraph of Article IX of the treaty: "The civil rights and political status of the native inhabitants ... shall be determined by the Congress." It is perfectly obvious that Congress, being the sole legislature over any territory of the United States not included in the States, may determine the civil rights and political status of the inhabitants, subject to the limitaions of the Constitution. Could such a treaty stipulation relieve Congress of any of those limitations? Not the Americans who negotiated the treaty but the subsequent ingenious statesmanship of the Supreme Court invented the mysterious doctrine of "unincorporated territory,"[16] whereby until Congress "incorporates" newly annexed territory the governmental power of Congress over it is subject to some only of the limitations of the Constitution, that is, subject to those and those only which the Supreme Court deems "applicable." I mention this doctrine merely to dismiss the supposition that the status of "unincorporated territory" which the Supreme Court has conferred upon Puerto Rico and the Philippines was the product of this paragraph of the treaty. It is true that in *Downes v. Bidwell,* Justice White, delivering the opinion which gave the doctrine of unincorporated territory the rationalization that has since been accepted by the Court, rested in part upon this paragraph, but he conceded that it was unessential. While he seemed to admit that immediate incorporation might be produced by a treaty provision expressly so providing "if the treaty be not repudiated by Congress," he said that a treaty of cession silent in respect to incorporation produced the effect of annexation without incorporation just as did a treaty that expressly stipulated against incorporation.[17] Two years later the Court held that the annexation of Hawaii by joint resolution of Congress did not "incorporate" that territory, although no reservation was made in the resolution of power in Congress to determine the civil and political status of the inhabitants.[18] Moreover, the doctrine of "unincorporated territory" as it has developed has no relation to the "political status" of the inhabitants of the territory, if by that is meant citizenship *vel non*. Thus the Supreme Court continued to hold Puerto Rico to be unincorporated territory after Congress had conferred United States citizenship upon all "citizens of Puerto Rico."[19] Moreover, the only limitations on Congress that the Supreme Court has so far held inapplicable to Puerto Rico and the Philippines are the requirements of uniformity in import duties and of juries in criminal cases. Under the decision in *Downes v. Bidwell,*[20] so long as Puerto Rico remains "unincorporated," Congress can levy special import duties upon goods coming to the continental United States from Puerto Rico although the shipper and consignee are both citizens. Trial without jury may still continue in Puerto Rico, so the Court holds,[21] notwithstanding that Puerto Ricans are now citizens.

There is no doubt whatever that President McKinley, Secretary of State Hay, and members of the Supreme Court had in their minds a fear of a dire handicap upon the United States in dealing with the Philippines if upon annexation all classes of Spanish subjects therein became citizens of the United States. That this turned out to be, in the main, a bugaboo, does not show that it was not a motive in the negotiations. Justice White even expressed the fear that if the inhabitants of these islands acquired citizenship the United States could never relinquish its sovereignty over them.[22] If that were true, we cannot now grant independence to the Philippines, because a considerable number of citizens of the United States have become permanent residents of those islands, have their homes there, and are as much "citizens of the Philippines" as are the non-citizen nationals that reside there. In the fervent controversy that raged between political parties and between members of the Court over the annexation of millions of remote islanders it is not strange that ill-founded apprehensions were entertained.

While the negotiation was proceeding, Secretary of State Hay had cabled to the American peace commissioners:

> The President wishes to know the opinion of the Commission as to inserting in treaty provisions on the subject of citizenship of inhabitants of Philippines which will prevent extension of that right to Mongolians and others not actually subjects of Spain; also whether you consider it advisable to provide, if possible, for recognition of existence of uncivilized native tribes in same manner as in Alaska treaty, perhaps leaving to Congress to deal with status of inhabitants by legislative act.[23]

The apprehension of the President that the status of inhabitants not subjects of Spain would be affected by annexation was clearly a misapprehension. Obviously they would remain aliens subject to the full power that Congress has over aliens residing anywhere in the United States. The misapprehension may have been imbibed from the inaccurate statement commonly made that upon cession the "inhabitants" acquire the nationality of the new government, in the absence of stipulations to the contrary,[24] instead of the correct statement that this principle operates only in respect to the nationals of the ceding country.

The reference by the President to the Alaska treaty gave the clue upon which the Commission acted. In several other treaties of cession of territory to the United States it had been stipulated that the subjects of the ceding power remaining in the territory should become "citizens."[25] The treaty with Russia in 1867 contained a novel variation. It declared that the Russian subjects who remained in Alaska *"with the exception of uncivilized native tribes,* shall be admitted to the enjoyment of all the rights, advantages and immunities of citizens of the United States." In the light of our present-day knowledge and terminology, these "uncivilized tribes" came to us as non-citizen nationals. Being Russian subjects, their nationality changed, but they did not acquire citizenship. Nevertheless, the Supreme Court held[26] in 1905 that Alaska had been "incorporated" because of the express words of incorporation in the treaty and an intent of Congress inferred from its extending in 1868 the internal revenue and customs laws to that territory. I suppose that the treaty power is capable of giving the status of non-citizen national to newly annexed people even though their territory is "incorporated" by the treaty or by Congress. The treaty is the law applicable to them. The declaration of the Fourteenth Amendment that all persons born in the United States and subject to its jurisdiction are citizens may doubtless be construed as not applying to persons born in territory that was foreign at the time of their birth, even though it has been assumed to confer citizenship upon some persons[27] born in the United States before its adoption.

It seems therefore that the intent of the second paragraph of Article IX of the Treaty of Paris was likewise to limit the effect of the cession to a change of nationality without conferring citizenship upon our new nationals. The fear that statesmen and judges felt that some evil consequence would follow if all the people ceded to us by Spain should thereby acquire citizenship of the United States, had only one sensible ground. That was that somewhere in the Constitution there must inevitably be found a Constitutional right of a citizen to migrate freely throughout the empire, to reside in any part, in any territory or any state of his choice. It may be that this idea was behind the refusal of citizenship to American-born Indians until after the policy of the United States to shunt them about where it pleased was abandoned. Fear of the effects of a right of free migration was the controlling motive behind Chief Justice Taney's dictum that a free Negro born in one of the states was not a citizen of the United States. He conceded that a citizen of the United States residing in a state is a citizen of that state[28] and by Article IV, Section 2, Clause 1 of the Constitution a state citizen has a Constitutional right of ingress and egress to and from any state. True, he was speaking of the lack of power of any state to forbid ingress of citizens of other states. He was not considering whether *Congress* might forbid migration of citizens of the United States. It might be said, consistently with the point he made, that so long as a citizen of the United States has not gained residence in any state, that is, while he has residence in a territory only of the United States, Congress might forbid his migration to any other state or territory. If so, it might with respect to Filipinos and Puerto Ricans, assuming that they became citizens of the United States at the cession. We have subsequently lost our fear with respect to Puerto Ricans, if the fear ever extended to that quarter. We have found them a mixture of whites and Africans quite homogeneous with the similar elements that constitute the greater part of the population of the continental United States. But whether one has little or much belief in the importance of race purity, one must recognize the social and governmental risks involved in the presence of large numbers of a race toward which a considerable part of the community has a racial antagonism. It required no great prophet to forecast that the coming into any of our states of large numbers of Malay Filipinos would develop a racial hostility. Now, it is possible for a court to concede that a citizen has a Constitutional right of free migration which neither a state nor Congress can abridge and at the same time hold that a non-citizen national does not. The Commerce Clause, by negative implication perhaps, denies to the states power to forbid entry of non-citizen nationals, but no decision or principle so far articulated would compel the Supreme Court to hold that Congress could not do so. If this was the thought of the statesmen and judges, its potency cannot be denied.

The State Department, the Attorney General, Congress, and the Supreme Court have assumed that the paragraph validly accomplished its purpose of conferring nationality without citizenship upon the ceded people. The Supreme Court has not squarely so decided, but in *Toyota v. United States*[29] it assumed in a deliberate dictum that Filipinos may become citizens by naturalization by bringing themselves within the narrow provisions of an act of Congress applicable to them, an absurd assumption if they are already citizens.

We have, on the one hand, no statutes which enable an alien to acquire the status of non-citizen national. On the other hand our naturalization statutes enable some aliens and some non-citizen nationals to become citizens. That is, naturalization under the present statutes of the United States is a process of attaining citizenship, not a process of attaining nationality merely.

The Treaty of Paris was incomplete with respect to two points which may reasonably be regarded as within the scope of matters dealt with:

(1) Nothing is said in the treaty with respect to Spanish subjects residing in the ceded territory who had been born neither in that territory nor in the mother-country. Spanish law declared that children of a Spanish father are Spanish nationals even though born abroad. This class of Spanish nationals, doubtless few in number, were not given an option, if they remained in the ceded territory, to elect to preserve their Spanish nationality.

(2) Although the treaty reserved to Congress the determination of the civil rights and political status of the native inhabitants of the ceded territory, it did not expressly make a like reservation with respect to those natives of the Peninsula who remained and acquired the new nationality by failure to retain the old.

Were these two classes of Spanish subjects incorporated into American citizenship by force of the cession and only the "native inhabitants" given the status of non-citizen nationals? If the doctrine is that it requires an express reservation in a treaty of cession to prevent the subjects of the ceding power from becoming at once citizens of the United States, it would seem logical to give the reservation no more scope than it expressly has. Chief Justice Marshall once questioned[80] whether cession of territory to the United States did not operate of itself to confer citizenship upon the resident subjects of the ceding power without express provision for citizenship, but Marshall lived before the concept of nationality without citizenship evolved. The doubts to which I have just directed attention seem never to have troubled any American statesman. The fact is that very little thought has been applied to the peculiar status of the persons with whom this essay is concerned. Attorney General Griggs[81] assumed that when it is said that these persons are nationals of the United States that concludes the whole subject. In that respect they do not differ from President Roosevelt or Chief Justice Hughes, who also are nationals of the United States. The point of difference is that these distinguished nationals are also citizens, while at least the greater number of the persons who underwent a change of nationality upon the Spanish cession became non-citizen nationals. I suggest the possibility that a few of them became citizen nationals. At least I put the question, If particular language of the treaty was essential in order to prevent acquisition by the ceded people of citizenship in addition to nationality, what is the status of that class of the ceded people to which the reservation of the treaty did not apply?

What has Congress done in exercise of the power reserved, if that is a correct way of putting it, to determine the political status of these ceded people? It assumed from the outset that they were indeed non-citizen nationals. Thus the passport law which previously authorized the issuance of passports to citizens only, was modified in 1902 for the benefit of these new nationals, so as to read: "No passport shall be . . . issued to . . . any other persons than those owing allegiance, whether citizens or not, to the United States."[32]

In 1906, with reference to these new nationals, an addition was made to the naturalization law. Previously the naturalization law gave the opportunity for individual naturalization upon application and proof of prescribed qualifications to aliens only.[33]

The addition extended the "applicable provisions" of that law to "all persons not citizens who owe permanent allegiance to the United States, and who may become residents of any State or organized Territory of the United States, with the following modifications: The applicant shall not be required to renounce allegiance to any foreign sovereignty. . . ."[34]

The "applicable provisions" phrase turned out either an intentional or an unconscious joker, since it has been construed to make the racial discrimination with respect to aliens applicable to this extension, with the result that non-citizen nationals may become citizens under this Act of 1906 only if they are "white persons" or persons of "African descent."[35] Whether Congress intended this race discrimination is doubtful, but the significant point is that Congress recognized the status of these new nationals to be that of non-citizen nationals and gave to some of them, at least, an opportunity to become citizen nationals. The greater number of our non-citizen nationals, being Malays, were by this construction excluded from the privilege—even those who have become permanent residents within the states. One trifling opportunity to acquire citizenship has been given them. By Act of May 9, 1918, any "native-born Filipino," whatever his race, is eligible to naturalization upon honorable discharge after service for three years in the United States Navy, Marine Corps, or Naval Auxiliary.[36]

The legislation just discussed did not change the status of our islander non-citizen nationals. It merely gave an opportunity to some persons to elect to change into citizen nationals provided they satisfied the requirements.

Significant were the Acts of 1900[37] for Puerto Rico and of 1902[38] for the Philippines. The earlier declared, "all inhabitants continuing to reside" in Puerto Rico "who were Spanish subjects on April 11, 1899, and then resided in Porto Rico, and their children born subsequent thereto, shall be deemed and held to be citizens of Porto Rico, and as such entitled to the protection of the United States." The later statute, using identical terms, declared the same classes of persons in the Philippines to be "citizens of the Philippine Islands." Both statutes excepted those natives of the Peninsula who had elected to reject American nationality under the terms of the treaty.

Obviously these statutes did not change the international status of these persons. From the date of cession they had been nationals of the United States. The statement that they were entitled to the protection of the United States had some value as a direction to diplomatic and consular officers of the United States. Otherwise it was merely declaratory that the United States recognized them to be eligible to protection by the United States in relation to other countries, that is, recognized them as being nationals of the United States. As to declaring them "citizens of Porto Rico," and "citizens of the Philippine Islands," those were statutory designations that meant nothing of themselves and would only have such meaning as would result from subsequent legislation ascribing specific privileges, immunities, duties, and liabilities to "citizens of Porto Rico," or "citizens of the Philippine Islands." They were merely handy names of reference to the persons included.

These statutes defined who were members of these classes, namely, (*a*) those who met three conditions: (1) being Spanish subjects on April 11, 1899, and (2) residing in the islands on that date, and (3) continuing to reside therein, or (*b*) being a child, subsequently born, of persons falling within group (*a*).

"Residence" under points (2) and (3) means permanent residence or domicile, so that a native of Puerto Rico, who presumably had retained domicile there but who had lived in Chile from 1884 to 1901, was within the statute, notwithstanding his absence both on April 11, 1899, and on the date when the statute went into effect, April 12, 1900.[39] The provision for children born subsequently has much significance, as we shall see.

No later legislation by Congress has modified the status of "citizens of the Philippine Islands."

By the Jones Act (for Puerto Rico) of March 2, 1917,[40] all "citizens of Porto Rico" as defined in the Act of 1900, mentioned above, were declared "citizens of the United States."[41] So terminated the status of non-citizen national for these persons and the new status of citizen national supervened. There was a curious exception: the statute provided that any of these persons might "retain his present political status" by sworn declaration within six months in a district court of "intention not to become a citizen of the United States." It is said that 288 persons "unfortunately for themselves followed the independence movement"[42] and rejected American citizenship. Obviously they did not understand the legal relations involved. Refusal of citizenship nowise diminished their subjection to the United States. It seems that Congress also erred in giving them the opportunity to elect to remain non-citizen nationals. By Act of March 4, 1927,[43] these persons were given another opportunity to become citizens of the United States by making a sworn declaration of "allegiance to the United States."[44] This was odd in view of the fact that they already owed allegiance to the United States just as fully in the status of non-citizen national as in that of citizen national. The change in status was significant but the mode provided for signalizing the change was inappropriate. The intricacies involved in distinguishing nationality from citizenship probably never will be widely understood.

As stated above, Congress has not conferred citizenship upon those persons who became non-citizen nationals of the United States by virtue of the annexation of the Philippines. This doubtless is consistent with its intention to grant independence to those Islands, in contrast with its intention to retain Puerto Rico permanently as a part of the United States. In the Jones Act (for the Philippines) of August 29, 1916,[45] this policy toward the Philippines was declared and a more autonomous government with enlarged powers was established there. Consistently with this purpose, this inchoate independent nation was given power to determine what additions should be made to its "citizenship." Perhaps, after all, Congress acted wisely in creating the statutory category, "citizens of the Philippine Islands." This probably contributed to the sense of national unity among these people. It may have been assumed by them to have more meaning than a legal analysis would disclose. This statute, after repeating the provisions of the Act of 1902 (mentioned above) which declared who were "citizens of the Philippine Islands," added:

> The Philippine Legislature ... is hereby authorized to provide by law for the acquisition of Philippine citizenship by [*a*] those natives of the Philippine Islands ... [who did not acquire Philippine citizenship by the Act of 1902], [*b*] the natives of the insular possessions of the United States, and [*c*] such other persons residing in the Philippine Islands who are citizens of the United States, or who could become citizens of the United States under the laws of the United States if residing therein.[46]

Acting under this authority the Philippine legislature enacted a "naturalization law" in 1920.[47] The only persons who may become "Philippine citizens" under this act are the three categories given above, (*a*), (*b*), and (*c*). Class (*c*) is thus phrased in the Philippine law: "(*c*) citizens of the United States or foreigners who under the laws of the United States may become citizens of said country if residing therein."

The remainder of the statute follows the plan of the naturalization statute of the United States with variations in substance. Thus, Section 2 states grounds of personal disqualification of individual members of the classes (*a*), (*b*), and (*c*) given above; for example, being opposed to organized government, practicing or believing in the practice of polygamy, conviction of crimes involving moral turpitude, insanity, or having an incurable contagious disease.

Section 3 states personal qualifications required to be shown: age, twenty-one years; five years' residence; good conduct; holding real estate in the Philippines worth not less than one thousand pesos, or having some known trade or profession; and speaking and writing English, Spanish, or some native tongue—except that those falling in class (*a*) need none of these qualifications except that of age.

The oath to be taken by a person about to receive a certificate of naturalization includes this: "I recognize and accept the supreme authority of the United States of America in the Philippine Islands and will maintain true faith and allegiance thereto"; also the oath-taker pledges to obey the laws of the Philippine Islands, and the legal orders and decrees of the authorities duly constituted therein, and faithfully to defend its government. Quite properly, swearing allegiance to the Philippine Islands is not required.

The very next statute enacted by the Philippine legislature contained this:

> Whenever the Philippine flag is hoisted in public jointly with the American flag, both shall be hoisted and lowered at the same time. The American flag shall be placed above the Filipino flag when both are in a vertical line . . .[48]

In addition to the naturalization statute mentioned above, the following provisions have been made by the Philippine legislature for the acquisition of Philippine citizenship:[49]

> Sec. 13(*a*) Any woman who is now or may hereafter be married to a citizen of the Philippine Islands, and who might herself be lawfully naturalized, shall be deemed a citizen of the Philippine Islands.
>
> Sec. 13(*b*) Children of persons who have been duly naturalized under this law,[50] being under the age of twenty-one years at the time of the naturalization of their parents, shall, if dwelling in the Philippine Islands, be considered citizens thereof.
>
> Sec. 13(*c*) Children of persons naturalized under this law who have been born in the Philippine Islands after the naturalization of their parents shall be considered citizens thereof.

The authority delegated by Congress and the "naturalization law" enacted in pursuance of it suggest many questions and comments. Only a few will be indulged in here. One remark may be made, not pertinent to the subject of this essay, namely, that with respect to class (*c*) Congress imposed upon the Philippines the race distinctions in the naturalization law of the United States.[51] The extreme case is that a Malay, a subject of Siam and not a native of the Philippines, is ineligible to be made a citizen of the Philippines though residing there, because not eligible to become a citizen of the United States if residing here. Was Congress of two minds in this legislation? It wanted to give to the people of the Islands through their legislature some authority to determine who might become members of their political society, but feared to give them an unlimited voice. Was it under the impression that any person made a "citizen of the Philippine Islands" by this delegated authority necessarily became a national of the United States? Did Congress fear that some implication might be drawn from the Constitution to deny power in Congress to forbid migration of non-citizen nationals from the Philippines to the continental United States? Or conceding constitutionality, may not Congress have desired to avoid increasing the necessity for such a law? In spite of strong urging Congress long refrained from forbidding the migration of Malay citizens of the Philippines to the States. If the Philippine legislature had been authorized to "naturalize" into Philippine citizenship foreign-born alien Chinese and Japanese, the demand for an exclusion of "Philippine citizens" from the continental United States would have been increased.

Is it true that aliens who become "citizens of the Philippine Islands" under this law thereby become nationals of the United States? If so, they become non-citizen nationals. No authority is given to the legislature of the Philippines to naturalize aliens into citizens of the United States. With respect to the international problem, there is no doubt that Congress may delegate to a subordinate organ of government power to enact an American nationality law. If the United States should extend protection abroad to an alien converted into a citizen of the Philippine Islands under this law, the country upon whom the demand was made would have no basis for rebutting an assertion by the United States that the person was a national of the United States. It is doubtful, however, whether this is the intent of the law. Congress may only have intended to regard the status of citizenship of the Philippine Islands as a status having wholly to do with the internal affairs of the Philippine Islands—an authority to admit these aliens, while remaining alien to the United States, to equal privileges with the body of citizens of the Philippines. It may be a situation analogous to one formerly existing when twenty-two states of the Union and organized territories gave voting rights at all elections to aliens who had merely declared intention to become citizens. They thus held a sort of local citizenship without being either citizen or non-citizen nationals of the United States.

If this be the true construction of the Act of Congress, the Philippine legislature misconceived it by requiring an alien who becomes a citizen of the Philippines under this law to take an oath of allegiance to the United States. That assumes acquisition of American nationality.

Class (*a*) of this statute presents matter of interest—"natives of the Philippines" who were not made citizens of the Philippines by the Act of 1902 or its provisions as repeated in the Act of 1916. Those Acts, as we have seen, conferred that status upon all Spanish subjects who became American nationals by the cession, and their children born subsequently. There may have been and doubtless were some Spanish subjects born in the Philippines who at the time of cession had established domicile abroad and who subsequently returned to the Islands as aliens. If so, class (*a*) may have been designed for them, but their number seems too insignificant to have gained legislative recognition. There are two larger categories which a natural reading of the word "natives" includes, namely, (1) persons born in the Philippines before the cession whose parents failed to claim[52] Spanish nationality for them, alien *ante-nati,* that is, alien to Spain and alien to the United States notwithstanding the cession, and (2) persons born there of alien parents since the cession, the *post-nati* of alien parentage. I shall later present an argument for the position that the *post-nati* of alien parentage acquire United States citizenship at birth. If so, they may be regarded as falling within class (*c*) of the statute, which determines what citizens of the United States may become citizens of the Philippine Islands. But it seems that they and all other citizens of the United States *born in the Philippines,* if birth there confers citizenship, are included in class (*a*) as natives in order to give them the benefit of the provision that no qualification but age of majority is required for "naturalization" of persons in class (*a*),[53] whereas other citizens of the United States falling in class (*c*) have to show various qualifications to become "citizens of the Philippine Islands." This reconciles the provisions and avoids construing them as overlapping.

The question whether the Fourteenth Amendment is operative in the Philippines or in Puerto Rico is a fundamental one which I am reserving to the conclusion of this essay. It is one of the most perplexing difficulties of the subject in hand. Suffice it to say here, still postponing that issue, that if Congress assumed that the Constitution does not impose the rule of *jus soli* on the Philippines, that is, to make all persons born there since the cession citizens of the United States, it has nevertheless authorized the Philippine legislature to adopt it as a principle in Philippine naturalization. The attentive reader has already noticed that Congress has imposed no race discrimination with respect to "naturalization" of class (*a*), and that the Philippine legislature has provided but a single qualification—the age of majority.[54] Really, with reference to an alien, regardless of race, born in the Philippines before or since the cession, this law in effect confers upon him the privilege of electing at majority the status of citizen of the Philippines, subject to his renouncing his former allegiance, if any, and taking the prescribed oaths of obedience and allegiance. It is citizenship of the Philippines by election at majority, because of birth in the territory, as distinguished from outright *jus soli,* as applied in the Fourteenth Amendment to give citizenship of the United States at birth because of birth in the United States.

So far as class (*b*), "natives of the insular possessions of the United States," includes those natives of Puerto Rico who are now citizens of the United States, class (*b*) clearly overlaps class (*c*) in part. So far as it includes natives of Puerto Rico born before the cession who were not Spanish subjects and whose status has not since changed, class (*b*) overlaps the provision in class (*c*) for aliens. So far as class (*b*) includes persons born in Puerto Rico since the cession, of alien parents, the difficult question again arises, whether the Fourteenth Amendment has been operative in Puerto Rico. There is one further possibility, namely, that there may be a few natives of Puerto Rico who were Spanish subjects at the date of the cession who still are non-citizen nationals of the United States, remnants of the small group that rejected citizenship of the United States in 1917.[55] This privilege given to persons of class (*b*) is also unqualified by any distinctions in respect to race, but individuals of this class must be free from all the disqualifications of Section 2 and must possess all the qualifications of Section 3. This class (*b*) provision seems to be little more than an empty gesture of sympathy for the natives of other islands possessing the rather derogatory status of "insular possession."

Finally, attention should be directed to some degree of anomaly in "naturalizing" a citizen of the United States into a citizen of the Philippines (class *c*). If he is an anarchist, assassinationist, or polygamist (has any of the disqualifications of Section 2) he is ineligible; and why not? Equally, he is ineligible if he lacks any of the qualifications of Section 3, unless the place of his birth puts him in class (*a*). The grant of this privilege to citizens of the United States is consistent with the interpretation that citizenship of the Philippines is a status purely local and internal. Nevertheless, a citizen of the United States who petitions for this privilege is required, like others, to swear allegiance to the United States, as well as obedience to the local government and laws.

Much of this discussion of the "naturalization" law of the Philippines is, strictly speaking, irrelevant to the theme of the essay—except that part of it which presents the pros and cons of the question whether the Philippine legislature is authorized to admit some aliens to the status of non-citizen nationals of the United States. Perhaps the right answer to this question is that Congress did not intend to confer nationality of the United States upon those aliens who may become "citizens of the Philippine Islands" under this "naturalization" law of the Philippine legislature. This statutory category has important local uses; it designates a class of persons who have certain local privileges. Congress has found it convenient to continue the category, "citizens of Porto Rico," even though it has conferred United States citizenship on all who had that status in 1917.[56] In 1927 Congress enacted that "all citizens of the United States who have resided or who shall hereafter [after March 4, 1927] reside in the island for one year shall be citizens of Porto Rico."[57] Obviously it is the intention of Congress to give citizens of the United States, wherever born or whatever their title to that status, the maximum of local privileges in Puerto Rico, unless they are only transiently there.

Citizenship of the Philippine Islands is likewise, it seems, a purely local status.[58] The greater number of the persons who possess this status also have the status of non-citizen nationals of the United States; some may be citizens of the United States; some may be aliens, since some persons of the two classes last named are eligible to Philippine citizenship under the Philippine "naturalization" law. There is no provision of American law whereby a citizen of the United States becomes a non-citizen national by becoming a citizen of the Philippines; nor, if my conclusion is correct, is there any provision of law whereby an alien who becomes a citizen of the Philippine Islands under its "naturalization" law ceases to be an alien. It is true that an alien in acquiring Philippine citizenship is required by law to forswear his former allegiance and to swear allegiance to the United States; and in order to reach the conclusion which I have reached, I am required to assume that these requirements as applicable to aliens are beyond the authority delegated by Congress. The inconsistencies of the legislation force some construction.

We come now to grapple with some major difficulties of our subject.

Not only the Philippine Islands but also Puerto Rico remains "unincorporated territory." Has the Fourteenth Amendment, declaring that "all persons born . . . in the United States and subject to the jurisdiction thereof, are citizens of the United States," been operative in those islands since the cession? This question concerns chiefly children born in the islands, since the cession, of alien parents. It therefore concerns a small portion only of the persons born in the islands since the cession. The greater number of the persons born there since the cession are children of those Spanish subjects who became non-citizen nationals by the cession. We have already seen that Congress enacted that Spanish subjects residing in the islands at the cession, except those who elected to retain Spanish nationality, "and their children born subsequent thereto," should be "citizens of Porto Rico" and "citizens of the Philippine Islands," respectively. While I have argued that this "citizenship" is a local status internal to the islands, it is not inconsistent therewith to find implicit in these declarations an intent that the status of these children *in all respects* was to follow the status of their parents, and that since the parents were non-citizen nationals of the United States the children also should have that status. The question arises, Why are not these subsequently born children citizen nationals at birth by virtue of the Fourteenth Amendment? Consistently with precedents in our law, children born in the United States of parents who are non-citizen nationals are likewise non-citizen nationals, notwithstanding the Fourteenth Amendment. Congress acted within the precedents in prescribing the status of these subsequently born children. While our law has always followed the principle of *jus soli* in respect to acquisition of citizenship, it has followed the principle of *jus sanguinis* in respect to non-citizen nationality. All the precedents we have are to that effect, and none is to the contrary. It has always been said that the declaration of *jus soli* in the Fourteenth Amendment was declaratory of the prior law, and adopted to overcome the dictum of *Dred Scott v. Sandford*.[59] That dictum was that while American-born Negroes owed permanent allegiance to the United States they were not citizens of the United States. Chief Justice Taney and the two associates who concurred with him reasoned that it had never been the intention of the American people to include American-born Negroes in our citizenship. This opinion was not new.[60] It was accepted as law by state courts, by Congress, and the people, and the express affirmation of the Fourteenth Amendment was deemed necessary to wipe out the exception. So long as the view prevailed that American-born Negroes were non-citizen nationals, to use the modern terminology, their children generation after generation had followed the status of their parents. If the dictum was true in 1856, it had been true from 1789. The common law rule of citizenship *jure soli* by exception did not apply to Negroes, and the principle of *jus sanguinis* applied so as to give to the children of non-citizen nationals the same status, though they were born in the United States.

Even after the adoption of the Fourteenth Amendment it was likewise held that American-born tribal Indians were not citizens, regardless of where in the United States they were born.[61] While there were dicta of judges calling them aliens, these were inadvertences, because there could be no denying that the Indians owed permanent allegiance to the United States and were, in modern terminology, non-citizen nationals. To them likewise the principle of *jus sanguinis* applied—that the child, no matter where born, of a tribal Indian parent followed the status of the parent.

If it is admitted, as I think it should be, that the treaty power of the United States can annex people without conferring citizenship on them, Congress may say, as I think in effect it has said, that the descendants of these non-citizen nationals shall to the end of time follow the status of their forebears. The Fourteenth Amendment may be operative in the Philippines and Puerto Rico in respect to persons other than the subsequently born children of the new nationals of 1899, just as it is in the United States, but the children born of our Filipino nationals, whether born in the Philippines or in any other part of the United States, are not within its operation, just as American-born tribal Indians were outside its scope and American-born Negroes were outside the scope of the common law rule declared in the Amendment.

While the logic of precedent excepts the children of non-citizen nationals from the operation of the Fourteenth Amendment and makes it possible to recognize it as operative in the Philippines and Puerto Rico, there is an element that may lead to the opposite conclusion when the question reaches the court of last resort. If the Amendment does operate in the islands, then every child born there since the cession of alien parents is not merely a national but also a citizen of the United States. It is not new, though it may seem odd, that the child of an alien born on American soil acquires at birth a station superior to the child there born of non-citizen national parentage. For many generations that difference prevailed between children born in the United States of Negro or Indian non-citizen parentage and the children of aliens born here. The rule of the Fourteenth Amendment is repugnant to some persons because it makes no racial discrimination, and no doubt these persons will protest against any conclusion that has the effect of giving United States citizenship to the children born in the Philippines since April 11, 1899, of alien parents of Chinese or Japanese blood. The number of the latter is insignificant, and of the former almost so. It must be remembered that the children subsequently born in the Philippines of parents of Chinese blood who were subjects of Spain at the cession are non-citizen nationals following the status of their parents. I assume that no great harm will come from recognizing as citizens children born since the cession, in the Philippines and Puerto Rico, of alien parents of European stock. Whether the inexpediency of recognizing as citizens of the United States a few Chinese born since the cession in the Philippines will weigh heavily on the judicial mind, must be left to the future.

If my conclusion is correct, Congress in authorizing the Philippine legislature to grant citizenship of the Philippines to all persons born in the islands was, in respect to the children born of alien parents since the cession, dealing with citizens of the United States. With respect to *ante-nati* of parents alien to Spain who failed to acquire Spanish nationality by any rule of Spanish law, the Fourteenth Amendment would not operate retrospectively; the place of birth was not American at the time of birth.

Turning again to Puerto Rico, the question whether the Fourteenth Amendment has been operative there since the cession, or now is operative there, is on the same footing. Puerto Rico has been and still is "unincorporated territory." In the Jones Act[62] for Puerto Rico there is a provision which I have not yet discussed. That Act, it will be remembered, extended citizenship of the United States to all who had become non-citizen nationals by the cession of Puerto Rico. There was the additional provision that

> any person who is born in Porto Rico of an alien parent and is permanently residing in that island may, if of full age, within six months of the taking effect of this Act, or if a minor, upon reaching his majority or within one year thereafter, make a sworn declaration of allegiance to the United States

and thereby acquire citizenship of the United States. What adults were referred to and what minors? The use of the present tense in "is born" and "is residing" might not, taken alone, be conclusive that the Act referred to those persons only who were born of alien parents before

March 2, 1917; but the adults were required to make a declaration of allegiance within six months from that date. Clearly, then, the only adults in contemplation were those born before 1917. Persons who were adults at that time necessarily were *ante-nati,* that is, born before the cession, April 11, 1899. The Fourteenth Amendment, if operative in Puerto Rico after the cession, would not apply retrospectively to them. As to the minors referred to, who were they? It seems that the only minors included are those born before March 2, 1917. Now, doubtless some who were then minors had been born before April 11, 1899. Being born of parents alien to Spain they were aliens to Spain at the cession unless their parents "claimed"[63] Spanish nationality for them. Such persons were aliens to the United States after the cession. But the language of the Act respecting minors is broad enough to include all persons born of alien parents in Puerto Rico between April 11, 1899, and March 2, 1917. My opinion is that to this extent Congress was indulging in unnecessary legislation. Congress apparently felt that, since birth in the United States generally confers citizenship, birth in Puerto Rico should have the same result, irrespective of race or nationality of the parents; or, at least, that the privilege of becoming citizens should be extended to persons so born. The result is substantially the same as it would be if the Fourteenth Amendment were operative in Puerto Rico both retrospectively and prospectively. On the assumption, which seems correct, that the Amendment did not operate retrospectively, this legislation by Congress was necessary to give to *ante-nati* aliens the privilege of citizenship; but, if my opinion is correct, it was superfluous in respect to the *post-nati* of alien parentage. In 1927 Congress gave to all the persons born in Puerto Rico of alien parents covered by the Act just discussed who had failed to take advantage of the privilege to become citizens a new period for election, one year from March 4, 1927.[64] This statute did not enlarge the class dealt with; it also applied to those persons only who were born in Puerto Rico before March 2, 1917, and then resided there.

What of persons born in Puerto Rico of alien parents since March 2, 1917? By the last legislation affecting the Puerto Rican situation, the Act of June 27, 1934, "all persons born in Puerto Rico on or after April 11, 1899," and hereafter, "and not citizens, subjects, or nationals of any foreign power" are declared to be citizens of the United States. The text is given below.[65] It seems to mean that persons born in Puerto Rico between the date of the cession and June 27, 1934, are deemed now to be citizens provided at birth or subsequently they have not acquired a foreign nationality; and persons there born after June 27, 1934, are or will be citizens at birth unless by the laws of some other country they are nationals of that country at birth. Thus, a child born hereafter in Puerto Rico of alien parents who are French nationals will not be born an American citizen because by the law of France he will be a French national at birth. In short, the statute confers American citizenship upon those children born in Puerto Rico whose parents are aliens only if otherwise they would be stateless. This assumes that the Fourteenth Amendment is not operative in Puerto Rico, for under it birth "in the United States" confers American citizenship regardless of the laws of all other countries. Why does Congress desire to avoid double nationality of persons born in Puerto Rico although on like facts if the birth occurs "in the United States" double nationality results? Why is not our national policy of unrestricted *jus soli* applicable there?

It is interesting to note that if the Fourteenth Amendment is not operative in Puerto Rico or the Philippines, the status of a child born in those islands, since the cession, one of whose parents is a citizen of the United States, rests upon a forced construction of the act of 1855 and that of May 24, 1934.[66] There is no other provision of American law that confers citizenship upon the child of a citizen, solely because of such parentage.[67] The Act of 1855, both in its original and in its revised form[68] and the Act of 1934 apply only to children "born out of the limits and jurisdiction of the United States."

It would be a forced construction to say that the Philippines and Puerto Rico are outside the limits and jurisdiction of the United States. The Court might, however, arrive at a decision upon a less artificial basis by a resort to judge-made law, with a conventional concealment of its legislative action, by imputing to Congress an intent that these Acts should *completely* supplement the *jus soli* principle. It could be said that since children born of a citizen parent in what is unequivocally the "United States" and children born "out of the limits and jurisdiction of the United States" are citizens, *a fortiori* children born of a citizen parent in ambiguously appurtenant territory are intended to be citizens, or are citizens regardless of a fictitious Congressional intent. By such a *tour de force* the Court, the case arising, may take care of the numerous children born in our "unincorporated territories" of American citizen parents and thus reduce the practical necessity for holding the citizenship provision of the Fourteenth Amendment operative in those territories. Or the Supreme Court may hold that provision operative in "unincorporated territory" without conflict with any decision, or with any dictum in any approved opinion, or with any doctrine heretofore announced by the Court.

It is true that Judge Hamilton of the so-called Federal Court for Puerto Rico has held that the citizenship provision of the Fourteenth Amendment is not operative in Puerto Rico. He reasoned that the "Insular Cases decided that the Constitution did not follow the flag" and that no part of the Constitution is operative in annexed territory until Congress "extends" it there, except certain "inherent natural rights of man" of which acquiring citizenship by birth on the soil was not one.[69] It is obvious that Judge Hamilton was following the "extension" theory announced in the opinion of Justice Brown, in *Downes v. Bidwell,* a theory with which no other member of the Court concurred.

Finley Peter Dunne, the humorist, said, "Mr. Justice Brown delivered the opinion of the Court, eight justices dissenting." The actual fact is stated in the official report, that Mr. Justice Brown "announced the conclusion and judgment of the Court."[70]

Chief Justice Taft, twenty years later, giving the opinion of a unanimous Court, said,"The *Insular Cases* revealed much diversity of opinion in this Court as to the constitutional status of the territory acquired by the Treaty of Paris ending the Spanish War, but the *Dorr Case*[71] shows that the opinion of Mr. Justice White of the majority in *Downes v. Bidwell,* has become the settled law of the court."[72] The opinion of Justice White laid down several propositions, the starting point of which was that the Constitution is the source of the power of Congress wherever it governs and "it follows that that instrument is everywhere and at all times potential in so far as its provisions are applicable."[73] His sixth formulation is nearest to a summary:

As Congress in governing the territories is subject to the Constitution, it results that all the limitations of the Constitution which are applicable to Congress in exercising this authority necessarily limit its power on this subject. It follows also that every provision of the Constitution which is applicable to the territories is also controlling therein.[74]

I shall not make the vain attempt to explain the reasoning upon which that mysterious status of "unincorporated territory" was imputed to Puerto Rico (and to the Philippines); it is sufficient to say that this status was asserted to be a factor in determining what limitations of the Constitution are applicable to Congress in governing those regions and what provisions of the Constitution are applicable to them. It is clear, however, that the proposition that the Constitution is eclectically applicable to territories and to Congress in governing them was meant to include "unincorporated territory." This appears clearly in the statement:

From these conceded propositions it follows that Congress in legislating for Porto Rico was only empowered to act within the Constitution and subject to its applicable limitations, and that every provision of the Constitution which applied to a country situated as was that island, was potential in Porto Rico.[75]

The point actually decided in *Downes v. Bidwell* is stated in Justice White's conclusion:

The result of what has been said is that whilst in an international sense Porto Rico was not a foreign country, since it was subject to the sovereignty of and was owned by the United States, it was foreign to the United States in a domestic sense, because the island had not been incorporated into the United States, but was merely appurtenant thereto as a possession. As a necessary consequence, the impost in question assessed on merchandise coming from Porto Rico into the United States after the cession was within the power of Congress, and that body was not, moreover, as to such imposts, controlled by the clause requiring that imposts should be uniform throughout the United States; in other words, the provision of the Constitution just referred to was not applicable to Congress in legislating for Porto Rico.[76]

The opinion will be searched in vain for any formula or standard by which may be determined what other limitations upon Congress are applicable in its government of Puerto Rico or the Philippines. In *Dorr v. United States,*[77] in holding that the requirement of juries in criminal trials did not apply to the Philippines the Court said that unincorporated territory "is to be governed under the power existing in Congress to make laws for such territories and subject to such constitutional restrictions upon the powers of that body as are applicable to the situation."[78] The right to trial by jury was considered not a "fundamental right which goes wherever the jurisdiction of the United States extends"[79] and in view of the fact that jury trial was unknown to the people of the Philippines the Court concluded that "it was not intended" to "hamper" Congress in governing them by imposing the requirement of jury trial,[80] "to whatever other limitations it may be subject, the extent of which must be decided as questions arise."[81]

Balzac v. Porto Rico[82] contributes nothing to the evolution of a test for determining what provisions of the Constitution are applicable to unincorporated territory, merely reaffirming that the jury requirement is not, the contested point being resolved by holding that Puerto Rico was still unincorporated.

The only rationalization of these decisions that seems sensible is that the necessities of statesmanship and expediency require that Congress be freed from some of the limitations of the Constitution in legislating for some parts of American territory, especially where the lack of familiarity of the inhabitants with American institutions makes some of them unworkable there. This is true of the jury system, particularly in the Philippines. It seems in retrospect not so obvious, however, that like considerations made it necessary to hold that Congress could levy tariff duties on goods entering the continental United States from Puerto Rico and the Philippines. It may be that the Court felt an impulse to announce a general principle in its first case, in order to remove the anxiety felt in many quarters over the annexation of remote and dissimilar peoples, and in excess of zeal overstepped the requirements of the principle.

Formerly I contended[83] in the light of the actual decisions and the predominating language of the opinions that the Court was merely holding that some *limitations* on Congress contained in the Constitution did not apply to Congress in legislating for unincorporated territory; that these cases nowise question the applicability to every part of the United States of a rule of law enacted in the Constitution which in no accepted sense is a limitation on Congress. Such is the declaration that "all persons born . . . in the United States . . . are citizens. . . ." The attentive reader has noticed, however, that while Justice White spoke almost continually about what limitations of the Constitution are applicable *to Congress* in governing unincorporated territory, he also spoke of what "provisions" of the Constitution are "applicable to the territories."

Of the term "United States" in the Fourteenth Amendment it will be asked, in the language of Chief Justice Marshall, "Does this term designate the whole, or any particular portion of the American empire?"[84] Justice Brown's individual opinion in *Downes v. Bidwell* was that "United States" in general in the Constitution refers only to the Union of States, excluding even the "organized territories," and that the Constitution applied only to that Union of States.[85] He pointed to the difference in the language of the Thirteenth and Fourteenth Amendments, the former abolishing slavery "within the United States, or any place subject to their jurisdiction," the latter speaking of birth "in the United States" without any addition. This was by way of arguing that no part[86] of the Constitution was operative of its own force outside the area included in the States unless made so by its own explicit language. Since Justice Brown did not admit the distinction between incorporated and unincorporated territories, it is obvious that his line of reasoning went too far. It tended to prove that the citizenship provision of the Fourteenth Amendment did not apply even in the continental "organized territories" of the United States until extended there by Congress, although the contrary has always been assumed.

In summary, it appears that it is an entirely open question whether the citizenship provision of the Fourteenth Amendment is operative in Puerto Rico, the Philippines, and other "unincorporated territory," and that the Supreme Court is free to decide it according to its appreciation of the requirements of statesmanship and expediency. If the Court accepts the theory of the precedents discussed in this essay, that the children of non-citizen nationals wherever born follow the status of their parents, it may well decide that the Amendment is operative in unincorporated territory, for the rule referred to denudes the problem of its only embarrassing element. Only those children who were born in such territory after its acquisition, of alien and citizen fatherhood, would be citizens at birth under the Amendment. That is, there is one highly desirable result favoring that conclusion and one that may seem adverse. As to those unincorporated territories which the United States intends to retain permanently, such as Puerto Rico, a rule that children born there of alien fatherhood are citizens would seem a perfectly normal application of an American principle. The legislation for Puerto Rico shows that Congress considers that a desirable result.

As to any unincorporated territory that the United States intends to cast off, Congress may provide that upon independence persons born there since the annexation, of alien parents, though citizens of the United States, shall lose their American citizenship and nationality and become solely nationals of the new nation.

What effect upon the status of our Philippine non-citizen nationals is worked by the Philippine Independence Act of March 24, 1934? Brief summarization of the scheme of the Act will aid. It authorizes a constitutional convention in the Philippines at a date to be fixed by the Philippine legislature, not later than October 1, 1934, to draft a constitution for the new Commonwealth of the Philippine Islands. The Act specifies some provisions which Congress requires shall be contained in the constitution. After the President of the United States certifies that the proposed constitution conforms to these requirements it is to be submitted for ratification to the Philippine voters. On July 4 next after ten years' operation of the government set up under this commonwealth constitution, the President of the United States is to proclaim the withdrawal and surrender of all "jurisdiction, control or sovereignty . . . over the territory and people of the Philippine Islands," and those Islands will become an independent, foreign country.

The constitution of the Commonwealth contemplated by the Act is an interim constitution for the ten-year transition period and the one to be in force when the new nation assumes its separate and equal station among the powers of the earth. Amendments made to it during that period must have the approval of the President of the United

States. Among the "mandatory provisions" that this transition constitution must contain is this: "All citizens of the Philippine Islands shall owe allegiance to the United States."[87] This means that until independence is proclaimed by the President, which cannot be done until the lapse of at least ten years, the status of non-citizen nationality continues to be possessed by those "citizens of the Philippine Islands" who now possess it.

With this provision may be compared another transition provision of the Act, a provision that became operative upon acceptance of the Act by the concurrent resolution of the Philippine legislature passed on May 1, 1934.[88] It is to be operative from that date until independence is finally proclaimed. This provision is that "for the purposes of" the laws of the United States (except Section 13(*c*) of the Immigration Act of 1924) relating to immigration and to exclusion and expulsion of aliens, "citizens of the Philippine Islands who are not citizens of the United States shall be considered as if they were aliens."[89] The people affected are not declared to be aliens; they still owe allegiance to the United States; the Act merely means that migration of these nationals into other parts of the United States, except the Territory of Hawaii,[90] is forbidden on nearly the same terms as is the immigration of aliens. The Act assigns to the Philippine Islands an immigration quota of fifty a year. There are no racial limitations on this quota, a result brought about by the exception above mentioned making Section 13(*c*) of the Immigration Act of 1924 inapplicable. This quota of fifty is merely sentimental, psychological, or what you will. Annually, fifty "Filipinos," irrespective of race, may enter the continental United States for permanent residence during the transition period. In addition, others may come as temporary residents and visitors under the non-quota provisions of the immigration laws. There is a definite warning in the Act that after independence the race discrimination of Section 13(*c*) of the Act of 1924[91] will apply to the Philippine Islands. I call the fifty per year quota sentimental because I cannot see that the coming of fifty Philippine citizens a year for *permanent* residence in the United States has any relation whatever to the program of preparing the Philippine Islanders for independence. It is the non-quota immigrants who come and return that may contribute to that program.

The essential thing in this legislation, for the topic of this essay, is that Congress believes now that it has Constitutional power to forbid migration of non-citizen nationals from one part of the United States to another. If Congress can forbid all but fifty, it can forbid all. The individual right of a person excluded because the quota is exhausted is the same as it would be if there were no quota. If there were any doubt about Congress' having such a power at any time the present exercise of it may be distinguished as applied to non-citizen nationals who are on the verge of becoming aliens.

There is no provision in the Act to determine the effect of independence upon the nationality of citizens of the United States who may be inhabitants of the Islands when the United States relinquishes its sovereignty. Will the usually stated rule apply, that in the absence of reservations by treaty or otherwise the nationals of the former sovereign, residing in the territory, lose their former nationality and become exclusively nationals of the new sovereign? Congress has surely been remiss in not prescribing that American citizens inhabiting the Islands shall have an election to reject the new Philippine nationality when independence occurs. As we have seen,[92] when Spain relinquished her sovereignty over Cuba, the treaty by which the United States required her to do so gave to Spanish subjects born in Spain, who then resided in Cuba, a privilege of rejecting the new nationality of independent Cuba. So Congress should have prescribed an election in favor of those citizens of the United States, residing in the Philippines, who owe their citizenship to birth in other parts of the United States, and of their citizen children born in the Philippines. This would have excluded from the privilege of election those citizens of the United States who became citizens by reason of birth in the Philippines of alien parents since the cession, assuming my theory of the status of these persons to be correct. Though citizens *jure soli,* they have no attachment to the continental United States and should follow the status of the territory in which they were born; while children born in the Philippines of parents who were citizens of the United States have at least a tie of parentage to the continental United States. Perhaps Congress may yet fill up this hiatus in its legislation. If it does so, the argument for the doctrine that the Fourteenth Amendment has not been applicable in the Philippines will be shorn of the last shred of expediency. The notion that Congress cannot in relinquishing territory cast off some citizens of the United States is a mere abstraction as applied to the children of aliens who became citizens by birth in territory which the United States has temporarily held, a territory which the United States has proclaimed from the beginning was not to be retained permanently against the will of the greater number of its inhabitants.

Upon the independence of the Philippines the status of non-citizen national of the United States will terminate with respect to more than 13,000,000 persons, who will become aliens. The "citizens of Puerto Rico" have passed out of that status in the other direction, by becoming citizens as well as nationals. The Negroes and the Indians also passed out by the latter route.

After the independence of the Philippines will there remain no non-citizen nationals of the United States? There are the possible remnants of the 288 intransigeant Puerto Ricans who rejected citizenship in 1917. Then there are the Alaskan "uncivilized tribes" under the treaty of 1867. The members of these tribes became nationals without citizenship,[93] notwithstanding that Alaska was "incorporated." Presumably they consisted of both Indians and Eskimos. All Indian non-citizen nationals among them who had not previously acquired citizenship were made citizens by the Act of 1924,[94] which declared "all Indians born within the territorial limits of the United States" to be citizens. Some legislation of the United States indicates that in statutory terminology Congress regards Indians and Eskimos as distinct categories.[95] If Congress intends uniform meaning of its terms, the Act just quoted does not include the Alaskan Eskimos. On this assumption the Eskimos who became non-citizen nationals in 1867 and their descendants have that status now, if the principles propounded in this essay are correct.[96] Unless it is considered undesirable to give them the privilege of voting, now limited in Alaska to citizens,[97] there is no reason why Congress should not confer citizenship upon the Alaskan Eskimos.

Whether the citizens of the Republic of Hawaii were non-citizen nationals for several months after the transfer of sovereignty to the United States, August 12, 1898, is uncertain. The doubt is unimportant. By an Act of April 30, 1900,[98] United States citizenship was imposed upon all who had been citizens of the Republic of Hawaii on the day of the transfer. This Act also declared the Constitution and all laws of the United States not locally inapplicable to have the same force and effect in the Territory of Hawaii as elsewhere in the United States.[99] This legislation undoubtedly "incorporated" the Hawaiian Islands,[100] if they were, temporarily, only appurtenant but unincorporated territory.[101] It follows that all persons, including numerous children of Filipino parentage,[102] born in Hawaii since annexation, or at least since April 30, 1900, became citizens of the United States at birth by virtue of the Fourteenth Amendment, unless the thesis of this essay is correct—that no matter where in the United States a child of a non-citizen national is born, the child follows the status of the parent. This brings us to point out that the Philippine Independence Act does not deal specifically with those of our Filipino nationals who have become permanent residents of the continental United States—about 45,000 by the census of 1930. The Act does not require their removal. Will they as "citizens of the Philippine Islands" become aliens, when those Islands become independent—along with persons then residing in the Islands? By some confusion of thought we may say that those who are residents here at that time are not distinguishable from those resident there. But it must be recalled that the status of "citizen of the Philippines" as it exists now is not an international status but a purely internal American status. If we say that those who are residents of the Islands must abide by the majority vote for independence and lose their American nationality without their personal consent, it takes more arbitrary determination to cast off these American nationals who reside in the continental United States and who do not participate in the vote. It takes some obscuration to assume that there is a Filipino nation before it is brought into existence. What precedent is there for holding that, upon a change of sovereignty over a territory, those formerly connected with that territory but permanently removed from it undergo a change of nationality? If *A,* an independent nation, annexes the whole of the territory of *B,* another independent country, it may well be that all nationals of state *B* wherever they reside at the time become nationals of state *A.* Their former state disappears and for them it is the new nationality or none. Our case is quite different. Why should American nationals residing in retained territory lose that nationality because another part of our territory is exscinded, even though the latter is territory in which they or their ancestors resided at the time it was annexed to the United States?

I think that there is no precedent upon which Congress could legislate, nor any principle in the absence of legislation upon which a court could hold, that, upon independence of the Philippines, American nationals of Filipino extraction who then have permanent residence in the United States cease to be nationals. If they do not, they also remain as non-citizen nationals, they and their descendants, even though born in the continental United States, until Congress sees fit to make them citizens. To these should be added several thousands of Filipinos residing in Hawaii, and their descendants.

There remain for brief consideration those persons whose nationality was affected by our acquisition of Guam, of the Virgin Islands, of American Samoa, and of the Panama Canal Zone, and the descendants of those persons.

Guam is one of the islands ceded by Spain by the Treaty of Paris. To it as well as to the Philippines and Puerto Rico the provision of Article IX applied—that the political status of the native inhabitants should be determined by Congress. Congress has enacted nothing as yet affecting the status of these native inhabitants of Guam. The treaty denied them citizenship and they and their descendants remain as they came to us, non-citizen nationals. It may be noted that there is no indication of intention to relinquish American sovereignty over Guam.[108]

The contrary is true of the Virgin Islanders. The treaty by which Denmark ceded the Virgin Islands to the United States, effective January 17, 1917, declared that Danish citizens who then resided there and remained there, in default of formally electing to preserve Danish citizenship, "shall be held to have renounced it, and to have accepted citizenship in the United States."

In spite of this definite conferring of citizenship, a respect in which the treaty differed from the Treaty of Paris ceding the Philippines, Puerto Rico, and Guam, the Danish treaty added a clause resembling yet differing from the second paragraph of Article IX of the Spanish treaty: "The civil rights and the political status of the inhabitants of the islands shall be determined by the Congress, *subject to the stipulations contained in the present convention.*" No clause like the one that I have italicized appears in the Spanish treaty. It may refer both to the stipulation that these former Danish nationals shall have the status of citizens of the United States and to other stipulations concerning property rights and "private, municipal and religious rights and liberties."

Notwithstanding these differences a Circuit Court of Appeals has said that the Virgin Islands became a part of the United States as "unincorporated territory" and that Congress had not yet done anything to incorporate them.[104] The complete understanding of the Supreme Court's decisions with respect to unincorporated territory shown in Circuit Judge Woolley's opinion is persuasive of the soundness of the specific application to the Virgin Islands.

This conclusion that the Virgin Islands have the status of "unincorporated territory," notwithstanding that most of their inhabitants were made citizens by the treaty of annexation, confirms the theory expressed above that the doctrine of unincorporation is independent of the citizenship of the inhabitants.

I have not undertaken to study the Danish law in order to determine who of the residents of the Virgin Islands were Danish nationals at the cession. It is immaterial to the question who are our non-citizen nationals, because those who were Danish nationals either became aliens to the United States by rejecting American nationality or they became citizens of the United States. It is obvious that the United States did not acquire any non-citizen nationals by the annexation of the Virgin Islands.

Congress in an excess of legislative zeal has purported to confer American citizenship by statute upon the Danish citizens who became American citizens by the treaty.[105] Congress has gone further. It has conferred citizenship upon certain classes of persons born in the Virgin Islands before the cession, provided that on February 25, 1927, the date of the statute, they had no foreign nationality, or, in the language of the Act, "are not citizens or subjects of any foreign country." These classes consist of persons who, born in the Islands, resided there at the cession and resided either in the Islands or "in the United States or Porto Rico" on February 25, 1927; or resided "in the United States" at the cession and resided in the islands on February 25, 1927. This is not all. Five years later than the above-mentioned Act, Congress conferred citizenship upon all persons born in the Islands before June 28, 1932, and residing at that date in any part of the American empire in its most extensive sense, provided they then were not nationals of any foreign state.[106] The Senate Committee on Immigration, in its report accompanying the bill, assumed that there were a few stateless aliens ("in the status of 'persons without a country' ")[107] among these persons born in the Virgin Islands and residing in American territory and thought it desirable to confer American citizenship upon them. Obviously, as the Committee reported, very few persons were affected by the Act.[108]

More meaningful legislation is Section 3 of the Act of 1927:

All persons born in the Virgin Islands of the United States on or after January 17, 1917 (whether before or after February 25, 1927), and subject to the jurisdiction of the United States, are hereby declared to be citizens of the United States.[109]

This is a paraphrase of the Fourteenth Amendment. It is a flat application of the *jus soli* to birth in the Virgin Islands since the cession. This provision and the treaty which conferred citizenship upon all Danish nationals residing in the Islands at the cession (except those who rejected it) covered the whole ground, especially if "residence" is construed to mean "domicile."

Of course, the question arises whether the citizenship provision of the Fourteenth Amendment was operative in the Virgin Islands from the date of the cession, so that Section 3 of this Act, just quoted, was unnecessary. In view of the judgment of Congress that the rule embodied therein may operate there without harm to the people of the continental United States, it seems that a court would not readily have found any reason based upon expediency or statesmanship for holding the citizenship provision of the Amendment inapplicable there. Of course, so long as the *jus soli* rule applies there by statute, it will remain an academic question whether it exists there apart from statute.

What of the natives of American Samoa? There is some doubt in respect to when, and how, those islands became definitely a part of the United States. John Bassett Moore, an eminent authority, states that they passed "under the exclusive jurisdiction of the United States" by virtue of the treaty concluded on December 2, 1899, between the United States, Germany, and Great Britain, although by that treaty the latter two powers merely renounced in favor of the United States all their rights (?) over those islands.[110] In 1902 Attorney General Knox seems to have had some doubt[111] but came to the conclusion that the Island of Tutuila had ceased to be foreign territory. One thing is certain, that from soon after that treaty the United States has governed the islands through resident naval officers acting under the direction of the Secretary of the Navy. Congress in a joint resolution, February 20, 1929, after reciting that "certain chiefs" of the eastern Samoan Islands (now called American Samoa) had agreed on April 10, 1900, and July 16, 1904, to cede "all rights of sovereignty" over the islands,[112] resolved "that said cessions are accepted, ratified and confirmed, as of April 10, 1900, and July 16, 1904, respectively." The resolution placed the islands under the government of the President of the United States, until Congress shall provide otherwise.

There is nothing in the treaty of 1899 nor in the joint resolution of Congress touching the political status of the inhabitants of these American islands. It is a safe guess that American Samoa is "unincorporated territory," and another that the subjects of these islands who acquired American nationality when they passed under the jurisdiction of the United States are non-citizen nationals. Both of these guesses correspond with those made by the American Samoan Commission, appointed in 1929 to study conditions there and report recommendations for Congressional legislation.

They recommended that the islands "be not erected into an organized Territory at the present time but be given a provincial status as a body politic under the name of 'American Samoa' with its own bill of rights and not the United States Constitution as its guaranty of personal liberties. . . ."[113] Evidently they thought some parts of the Constitution inapplicable there and did not believe immediate "incorporation" wise. Nevertheless, and quite consistently, they proposed that the islanders be made citizens. This is proposed in Section 3 of their bill for an Organic Act for American Samoa in these words: "That all persons of full or part Polynesian blood who were inhabitants of American

Samoa on February 20, 1929, and their children born subsequent thereto, are hereby declared to be citizens of the United States of America."[114] In the report accompanying the bill, it is said, "the Samoans are capable of accepting and should receive full American citizenship."[115] The bill passed the Senate in the Seventy-first Congress, but died in the House.

If the citizenship provision of the Fourteenth Amendment is operative in unincorporated territory, the provision given above for subsequently born children is unnecessary in respect to those born in the islands, and unnecessary for those born outside the limits of the United States, for, on the assumption that the fathers are made citizens, the Act of 1855 makes such children citizens. If the Fourteenth Amendment has been applicable since American Samoa became a part of the United States, the only legislation necessary for the purpose in hand is to confer citizenship on those Samoans who were living at the date of annexation. If Congress is in doubt about the operation of the Fourteenth Amendment in American Samoa, it should, in addition to declaring those persons living at the date of annexation to be citizens, also declare, as it did with respect to the Virgin Islands, that all persons born there since the cession and hereafter shall be citizens. What possible good can be accomplished by limiting citizenship of the United States to the Polynesians there born? Why not extend it to children born there to fathers who are aliens and even to the children born there of all fathers who are citizens of the United States?

There is no objection to limiting "citizenship of American Samoa" to persons of full or part Polynesian blood, as this is a purely local status, the object of the restriction being to exclude the white man and others, even those who may be citizens of the United States, from participation in the government. The bill mentioned above and another which has passed the Senate in the Seventy-third Congress and which is now pending in the House both so limit Samoan citizenship.

The new bill proposes to declare: "Section 4 (*a*). All persons of full or any part Samoan blood born in American Samoa after the effective date of this Act . . . to be citizens of the United States."

This assumes that the citizenship provision of the Fourteenth Amendment is not operative in American Samoa, and purports to adopt for that territory a similar statutory rule limited to persons of a particular blood. The new bill also declares "all persons of full or any part Samoan blood who are inhabitants of American Samoa on the effective date of this Act, and their children born subsequent thereto ... to be citizens of the United States" with the privileges of electing to retain any foreign nationality now possessed, if any. Why substitute "Samoan blood" for "Polynesian blood," shifting to the vague from the relatively definite? Why choose the date on which the statute, if enacted, takes effect instead of the date of formal annexation as the time factor in determining what persons are affected by the legislation?

Finally, there is the Panama Canal Zone. The treaty between the Republic of Panama and the United States by which the latter obtained its present rights in the Canal Zone, notwithstanding its ambiguous avoidance of specific language of cession, is assumed by the Supreme Court of the United States to have ceded that area to the United States.[116] The treaty was silent in respect to the effect of the cession upon the nationality of the citizens of the Republic of Panama residing in the ceded area. No provision for election being provided, it seems that all such persons lost their former nationality and became nationals of the United States,[117] doubtless non-citizen nationals. This status they and their descendants retain because no legislation by Congress has prescribed otherwise. The Canal Zone doubtless has the status of "unincorporated territory" and whether birth there to alien parents since the cession confers citizenship is subject to the doubt whether the citizenship provision of the Fourteenth Amendment is operative in such territory.

CONCLUSION

For the curious reader who has persisted through this long discussion of an intricate, uncoördinated, and uncertain part of American law I shall summarize what in my opinion is the answer to the question, Who are our non-citizen nationals?

(1) More than 13,000,000 of those persons who bear the statutory designation, "citizen of the Philippine Islands"; but not all of them, because some persons in that category seem to be aliens, and some are undoubtedly citizens of the United States. Independence will leave us a number of Filipino non-citizen nationals, in the absence of further

legislation—those then permanently residing in the remainder of the United States, now numbering more than 100,000, including those who reside in Hawaii and the continental United States.

(2) A possible handful of Puerto Ricans.[118]

(3) Doubtfully, the Eskimos in Alaska in 1867 and their descendants wherever born.

(4) Those inhabitants of Guam who acquired American nationality in 1899 and their descendants wherever born.

(5) The Samoan Islanders who acquired our nationality upon annexation and their descendants wherever born.

(6) Those former citizens of the Republic of Panama who became American nationals upon the cession of the Canal Zone, and their descendants wherever born.

(7) If the Supreme Court holds that the citizenship provision of the Fourteenth Amendment is not operative in Guam, Puerto Rico, or American Samoa, or the Canal Zone, the children born there under American sovereignty to alien parents will be aliens unless Congress legislates to make them either citizen nationals or non-citizen nationals. Congress has twice given an election to become citizens to all aliens born prior to March 2, 1917, in Puerto Rico. Congress has also provided that all persons born in Puerto Rico since the cession and in the future are citizens of the United States at birth, unless at birth they acquire the nationality of some foreign country by its laws.[119] This fails to confer citizenship upon many persons born in Puerto Rico of alien parentage. However, Congress by statute has applied the rule of the Fourteenth Amendment to the Virgin Islands so that all persons born there at any time subsequent to the cession have or will become citizens at birth. Of course the Fourteenth Amendment is operative in Hawaii and Alaska so as to make every person born there a citizen, except, as elsewhere in the United States, children whose fathers are non-citizen nationals.

When one considers the slight distinction between the status of citizen and that of non-citizen national *so long as the person in question resides outside of the States,* a subject for another essay, there is little reason for perpetuating the status of non-citizen national.

APPENDIX

Spanish Nationality Law in Force Prior to the Cession

The Spanish Constitutions of 1812, 1837, 1845, 1856, and 1876, the last-named being in force at the time of the cession, each declared the following groups to be Spaniards, that is, Spanish nationals:

1. All persons born in Spanish dominions.

2. The children of a Spanish father or Spanish mother, even though born outside of Spain [Spanish territory?].

3. Foreigners who have obtained letters of naturalization.

4. Those who without such letters have acquired *vecindad* in any Spanish town.

If these were the only pronouncements of Spanish law the status of the majority of the residents of the ceded islands would be easy of determination, except only for the obscurities of *vecindad* in Rule 4. But there were both a royal decree and legislation that seemed to modify Rules 1 and 2 if such methods of law making were operative though in conflict with the constitution in force.

There was the Royal Decree[1] of November 17, 1852, concerning "Aliens and their Classification in Spain," but it seems that this was not extended to the Philippines and Puerto Rico.[2] The Law of July 4, 1870,[3] on the same subject, however, was by its terms extended to the "Spanish provinces beyond the seas." It became effective in the Philippines September 18, 1870.[4] Both these instruments purported to modify Rule 1, by declaring children born in Spanish territory of alien parents or of an alien father and a Spanish mother to be aliens unless they "claim" Spanish nationality.[5] The mode of making claim was not specified. Secondly, Rule 2 was modified by an enactment stating that a child born outside of Spanish territory of a Spanish mother is not a national if the father is alien.

The Civil Code of 1889,[6] in derogation of the Constitution of 1876, then in force, again qualified Rule 1, to the same effect as the Decree of 1852 and the Law of July 4, 1870, adding only a clarification of the mode of claiming Spanish nationality for the child born in Spanish territory of alien parents: first, the parents must record an election of Spanish nationality for the child during its minority, and secondly, upon coming of age the child must record an election for himself. By Royal Decree of July 31, 1889, the Civil Code of 1889 was extended to Cuba, Puerto Rico, and the Philippines to become effective in each twenty days after publication in the local official gazettes.[7]

It is difficult for an American lawyer to regard as valid legislation in derogation of the reigning constitution, but it is said that Spanish writers support the provisions of the Civil Code of 1889 as against the constitution.[8] If so, the Law of July 4, 1870, would seem superior to the constitution of 1856. I should add that the Civil Code of 1889 re-announced Rule 2 in its original constitutional form, repealing, it seems, the variation made in that rule by the Law of July 4, 1870.

The constitutions mentioned two modes of naturalization, modes by which aliens might acquire Spanish nationality, (1) letters of naturalization and (2) by acquisition of *vecindad*. By the Constitution of 1812 letters of naturalization were obtainable from the Cortez. Subsequent constitutions were silent as to what organ of government might issue them. It seems that under them until 1860 there was no established mode of obtaining letters; by a law of that year they might be issued by royal decree. The Law of the Civil Register of June 17, 1870, added that letters granted by royal decree were not operative until recorded in the civil register of the town in which the applicant was domiciled and were recordable only upon the applicant's renouncing his former allegiance and swearing to support the constitution.[9] The institution of civil register was not extended to Puerto Rico until the Royal Decree of August 16, 1884,[10] and if ever extended to the Philippines it was not until after 1889.[11] It is a safe assumption that few if any aliens residing in the ceded territory at the time of the cession had become Spanish nationals by receiving letters of naturalization.

Acquisition of *vecindad* may have been a more prolific mode of naturalization of aliens. Not until after the cession, by the Royal Decree of November 6, 1916, was the institution of *vecindad* as a mode of acquiring Spanish nationality cleared of the confusion and ambiguities that had existed because of the vague and various provisions of the earlier laws.[12] With this later clarification we are not concerned.

Vecindad under the earlier laws was an institution wholly without a parallel in American law. A law of March 8, 1716,[13] enumerated numerous modes of acquiring this status. Each was stated as sufficient in itself. They included conversion to the Catholic faith, establishment of domicile by one who lived on his own resources, marriage with a native-born person, settling and acquiring real estate, settling to practice a profession or a mechanical employment or to run a retail store, and living ten years as a householder. The law seems to indicate that *vecindad* resulted as a matter of law from the existence of any one of these fact situations, without any necessity for governmental consent or approval. An order of August 14, 1841,[14] addressed to the Governor Captain General of the Philippines introduced a requirement of official consent. By it aliens desirous of settling in the Philippines were required to apply to the Governor or to the Spanish home government for consent, to be granted if deemed advisable and advantageous to the country. Aliens already settled and those settling thereafter with consent might obtain *vecindad* in the towns of their residence "in accordance with law," presumably the Law of March 8, 1716, but only upon application to the Governor, "who may grant it or deny it as may best answer the national interests." Moreover, this order stated: "These grants of *vecindad* which must be preceded by a hearing from the municipal governments concerned, shall be provisional until confirmed by the supreme government." This last expression probably did not refer to the Spanish home government. Even if the Governor's consent alone was sufficient, the process of becoming a Spanish national by acquiring *vecindad* had become more like modern processes of naturalization. The Law of July 4, 1870, which extended to the provinces beyond the seas, declared that aliens who obtain *vecindad* in any town of the Spanish provinces beyond the seas in accordance with the law should be regarded as Spaniards. Article 25 of the Civil Code of 1889 further modified this mode of acquiring Spanish nationality. By its provisions the acquisition of *vecindad* no longer operated without further act to confer Spanish nationality. It required that a person who had acquired *vecindad,* in order to become a Spanish national must renounce his former allegiance, take oath to the constitution, and have himself inscribed in the civil register as a Spanish national. We have seen, however, that the institution of the civil register came in Puerto Rico only fifteen years before the cession, and not before 1889, if ever, in the Philippines.

There seems to be only one reported case in which Spanish nationality at the time of cession has been recognized as resulting from the acquisition of *vecindad*. A native of China immigrated to the Philippines in 1839 or 1840. He adopted the Catholic religion, married a woman who was a Spanish national, acquired a domicile first in Vigan, later in Manila, engaged in business, and acquired real estate. The court said that "by virtue of all these acts" he became a "nationalized citizen in accordance with the laws in force in these Islands."[15] That there is only one reported judicial decision does not establish rarity of instances to which the rule was applicable.

One further rule of Spanish law should be mentioned, namely, a Spanish woman married to an alien is an alien. This rule was extended to the provinces by the Law of July 4, 1870. The Civil Code of 1889 added that upon termination of the marital status the woman might regain Spanish nationality by declaration before the Civil Registrar of her domicile.

So much for the rules for determining what inhabitants of the ceded islands had Spanish nationality, and the alienage of the relatively few who were not Spanish nationals. Be it recalled that all who were not aliens to Spain became American nationals except those Peninsulars who elected to reject the new status.

NOTES TO McGOVNEY ESSAY

[1] Extended to eighteen months with respect to the Philippines by a supplementary convention between Spain and the United States, signed March 29, 1900.—Foreign Relations, 1900, p. 889. For need of this extension see *ibid.*, 1899, pp. 714 ff.; abstract in 3 Moore's Dig. 321.

[2] The United States State Department expressed opinions that "natives of the Peninsula" included natives of the Balearic and Canary Islands.—3 Moore's Dig. 321.

[3] The change of name from Porto Rico to "Puerto Rico" was officially made by Act of Congress, May 17, 1932, 47 Stat. 158.

[4] *In re* Bosque (1902) 1 Phil. Rep. 88; Bosque v. United States (1908) 209 U. S. 91.

[5] Calderin v. Fabian y Fabian (1908) 4 P. R. Fed. Rep. 153. And see Laborde v. Laborde (1907) 2 P. R. Fed. Rep. 493, especially pp. 502, 510.

[6] The United States military government in Puerto Rico had issued a general order, No. 132, dated August 31, 1899, by way of directing the manner in which the treaty privilege of election might be exercised. In part, it read:

"II. For the purpose of permanent record and the protection of the parties concerned a document will be prepared in duplicate in each case by the municipal judge setting forth the following facts: (*a*) the name and surname of the interested party, his or her age, nationality (specifying the province), civil status and profession, trade and occupation; (*b*) names of wife and children, should there be any, and the names of the applicant's parents. . . .

"III. Unmarried women (natives of the Peninsula), of legal age, will make declaration in the same manner as men."—Quoted in *Ex parte* Garcia (1918) 10 P. R. Fed. Rep. 516, 536.

The failure to provide explicitly for election by married women seems to imply an administrative interpretation that a wife's nationality would be preserved by the husband's election. As to minors, the implication is not so strong. The express limitation of the provision for unmarried women to those of legal age implied that minors could not elect for themselves. Yet the document was merely to state the names of children (not limited to minors) and contained no statement that the parent elected on behalf of the children. It may be that the Spaniards who executed these documents assumed this to be the purpose of giving their children's names.

[7] Rios de Rubio v. Burset (1906) 2 P. R. Fed. Rep. 189 (wife born in the Republic of Mexico); Echcandia v. San Sebastian (1916) 9 P. R. Fed. Rep. 153 (wife born in Puerto Rico); Martinez de Hernandez v. Casañas (1907) 2 P. R. Fed. Rep. 519 (minor children born in Puerto Rico); *Ex parte* Garcia (1918) 10 P. R. Fed. Rep. 516 (same); and see Rodriguez y Pujals v. Argueso y Flores (1907) 2 P. R. Fed. Rep. 517 (place of minor's birth not stated).

[8] The last three cases just cited.

[9] In one case it was held that an election made by a native of the Peninsula to preserve the Spanish nationality of his minor niece, whose guardian he appears to have been, was effective. The girl, it also appears, was the daughter of a native of the Peninsula.—Martinez de Hernandez v. Casañas (1907) 2 P. R. Fed. Rep. 519.

[10] *Ex parte* Garcia (1918) 10 P. R. Fed. Rep. 516.

[11] See note 1 *supra*.

[11a] M. S. Department of State, Mr. Hay, Sec. of State, to the Sec. of War, December 21, 1899; Mr. Lansing, Sec. of State, to the Spanish Ambassador, April 15, 1918.

[12] Martinez de Hernandez v. Casañas, note 9 *supra,* at pp. 532–533.

[13] Compare Rodey, J., *In re* Bonnet y Jaspard (1906) 2 P. R. Fed. Rep. 70, 75, with the statement in 10 P. R. Fed. Rep. at p. 519.

[14] "Manifestly the nationality of the *inhabitants* of territory acquired by conquest or cession becomes that of the government under whose dominion they pass, subject to the right of election on their part to retain their former nationality by removal or otherwise, *as may be provided.*"—Boyd v. Thayer (1892) 143 U. S. 135, 162, italics added. If the word "inhabitants" in the first line of this quotation be changed to nationals of the ceding power residing in the territory, the statement expresses the accepted opinion.

[15] See the concurring opinion of Malcolm, J., in United States v. Lim Bin (1917) 36 Phil. Rep. 924, 927.

[16] For a very comprehensive discussion see Coudert, Evolution of the Doctrine of Territorial Incorporation (1926) 26 Col. Law Rev. 823.

[17] Downes v. Bidwell (1901) 182 U. S. 244, 339.

[18] Hawaii v. Mankichi (1903) 190 U. S. 197.

[19] Balzac v. Porto Rico (1922) 258 U. S. 298.

[20] *Supra* note 17.

[21] Balzac v. Porto Rico, *supra* note 19.

[22] Downes v. Bidwell (1901) 182 U. S. 244, 315.

[23] Foreign Relations, 1898, p. 961.

[24] See for example, the quotation and remark *ante* note 14.

[25] See the treaties of cession of Louisiana and of Florida, quoted in 3 Moore's Dig. 313, 314, and the Treaty of Guadalupe Hidalgo, *ibid.* 318.

[26] Rassmussen v. United States (1905) 197 U. S. 516.

[27] It has always been assumed that the Fourteenth Amendment wiped out the dictum of the Dred Scott case, and gave citizenship to all American-born Negroes, *ante-nati* as well as *post-nati.* This assumption is not affected by the decision that the Amendment did not confer citizenship upon American born Indians either *post-nati* or *ante-nati,* since the court held that the words "subject to the jurisdiction" in the Amendment were inserted for the purpose of excluding Indians.—Elk v. Wilkins (1884) 112 U. S. 94.

[28] This rule existed before the adoption of the Fourteenth Amendment. See Gassies v. Ballon (1832) 6 Pet. 761.

[29] (1925) 268 U. S. 402, 409.

[30] Speaking of the Florida treaty, Marshall said: "This treaty . . . admits the inhabitants of Florida to the enjoyment of the privileges, rights and immunities of the citizens of the United States. It is unnecessary to inquire, whether this is not their condition, independent of stipulation."—American Insurance Co. v. Canter (1828) 1 Pet. 511, 542.

[31] (1901) 23 Ops. Att'y Gen. 401, 402.

[32] Act of June 14, 1902, 32 Stat. 386.

[33] When we speak of ineligibility of persons to naturalization because lacking in racial or some other prescribed qualification, we have reference to this statutory opportunity for individual naturalization under the statutes as they now stand. Congress may, of course, make any alien or non-citizen national eligible to acquire citizenship, regardless of his race or other condition, or it may collectively naturalize, confer citizenship upon,

a class of persons regardless of race or personal qualifications. Thus, American Indians were always racially ineligible under the statutes providing for individual naturalization, but by the Act of June 2, 1924, 43 Stat. 253, all non-citizen Indians born in the United States were collectively converted into citizens—without privilege of rejecting this change of status.

[34] Act of June 29, 1906, § 30, 34 Stat. 606, 8 U. S. C. § 360.

[35] Toyota v. United States (1925) 268 U. S. 402, 410.

[36] 40 Stat. 542, 8 U. S. C. § 388. See Toyota v. United States (1925) 268 U. S. 402, 409.

[37] Act of April 12, 1900, 31 Stat. 77, 79.

[38] Act of July 1, 1902, 32 Stat. 691, 692.

[39] Mr. Hill to Mr. Lenderink, April 29, 1901.—For. Rel. 1901, p. 32. Accord: an opinion of Knox, Attorney General (1902) 24 Ops. Att'y Gen. 40; an opinion of Hay, Secretary of State, Mr. Hay to Mr. Hardy, Feb. 26, 1904.—For. Rel. 1904, p. 805. So conversely, it was held that a Spanish subject born in the Peninsula and physically residing in Puerto Rico before and during the period for recording election to retain Spanish nationality retained it without such election because, being a minor at that time, he had his legal residence or domicile at the domicile of his parents in Spain.—Rivera v. Pons (1908) 4 P. R. Fed. Rep. 177.

[40] 39 Stat. 951, 953.

[41] This Act also conferred citizenship of the United States upon all natives of Puerto Rico who were temporarily absent April 11, 1899, who had returned, were permanent residents, and were not "citizens of any foreign country." The chief value of this was to cure the ambiguity as to the residence requirement of the Act of 1900, *supra*, p. 334.

[42] Hamilton, J., in *Ex parte* Ramirez (1918) 10 P. R. Fed. Rep. 549, 550; see also *Ex parte* Morales (1918) 10 P. R. Fed. Rep. 395, 397.

[43] 44 Stat. Pt. 2, 1418.

[44] A further opportunity was open to them, namely, naturalization under the Act of June 29, 1906, § 30, 8 U. S. C., § 360, discussed *ante*, p. 333. For the applicability of this provision to the Puerto Ricans who rejected citizenship in 1917, see *Ex parte* Morales (1918) 10 P. R. Fed. Rep. 395. See also another provision for naturalization available to those who had enlisted in the armies of the United States.—*Ex parte* Ramirez (1918) 10 P. R. Fed. Rep. 549.

[45] 39 Stat. 545.

[46] 39 Stat. 546. The letters (*a*), (*b*), and (*c*) have been added for convenience in reference.

[47] Act No. 2927, March 26,1920.—15 Public Laws, P. I., 267.

[48] Act No. 2928, March 26, 1920.—*Ibid.*, 271.

[49] Act No. 3448, November 30, 1928.—24 Public Laws, P. I., 26.

[50] "This law" means the naturalization statute No. 2927 to which Act No. 3448 is an addition.

[51] The Supreme Court of the Philippines has held that a person of Chinese blood born *in China* (cf. note 53), though he maintained a permanent residence in the Philippines from 1881 to the date of his application in 1925, was ineligible to naturalization because of his race.—Lucio v. Government of the Philippine Islands (1928) 51 Phil. Rep. 596.

[52] See the rule of Spanish law on this point, discussed in the Appendix to this essay, at p. 364.

[53] See Go Julian v. Government of the Philippine Islands (1923) 45 Phil. Rep. 289 where a person of Chinese blood born in the Philippines after the cession, his parents being aliens, was held eligible to naturalization as a member of class (*a*) to which the racial discrimination does not apply, reading class (*a*) as not cut down by the provision for class (*c*), that is, considering the latter to refer to those aliens who are not natives of the Philippines.

[54] The disqualifications stated in Section 2 of the statute, stated above at p. 336 apply to this class, but of the qualifications prescribed in Section 3, that of age only applies.

[55] See *ante,* p. 335.

[56] Subject to the election stated *ante,* p. 335.

[57] Act of March 4, 1927, 44 Stat. Pt. 2, 1418.

[58] It is, of course, a local status. The question is whether it carries with it also a national status—whether all "citizens of the Philippine Islands" are necessarily also nationals of the United States.

[59] (1857) 19 How. 393.

[60] Attorney General Legare, in 1843, had placed free Negroes born in the United States in an intermediate status between full citizenship and alienage. He designated them "denizens."—(1843) 4 Ops. Att'y Gen. 147. See also opinion of William Wirt (1821) 1 Ops. Att'y Gen. 506 and the opinion of Marcy, Secretary of State, given in 1855.—3 Moore's Dig. 880.

[61] Elk v. Wilkins (1884) 112 U. S. 94.

[62] *Ante,* note 40.

[63] See the rules of Spanish law discussed in the Appendix to this essay, *infra,* p. 364.

[64] Act of March 4, 1927, c. 503, § 2, 44 Stat. Pt. 2, 1418.

[65] "All persons born in Puerto Rico on or after April 11, 1899 (whether before or after the effective date of this Act) and not citizens, subjects, or nationals of any foreign power, are hereby declared to be citizens of the United States. *Provided,* that this section shall not be construed as depriving any person, native of Puerto Rico, of his or her American citizenship heretofore otherwise lawfully acquired by such person; or to extend such citizenship to persons who shall have renounced or lost it under the treaties and/or laws of the United States or who are now residing permanently abroad and are citizens or subjects of a foreign country. . . ."—Act of June 27, 1934, c. 845, 48 Stat. ——.

[66] The Act of 1855, 10 Stat. 604, confers citizenship at birth upon a child born, theretofore or thereafter, "out of the limits and jurisdiction of the United States," having a citizen father who has resided in the United States prior to the child's birth. The Act of May 24, 1934, c. 344, § 1, 48 Stat. 797, 8 U. S. C. § 6, applies the same rule where either the child's father or mother is a citizen who has previously resided in the United States, provided that where one parent is an alien, the other a citizen, the child is not a citizen at birth, but may become such by residing in the United States the five years immediately preceding its eighteenth birthday and taking an oath of allegiance within six months after attaining the age of twenty-one years. This Act applies to births after the taking effect of the Act, and, it seems, for the future, cuts down the Act of 1855, which conferred citizenship at birth on the child in case the mother was an alien as well as in case she was a citizen, provided the father was a citizen.

[67] Except a provision of the naturalization law that gives citizenship to the minor children of a naturalized alien provided the children are dwelling in the United States.—R. S. § 2172, 8 U. S. C. § 7. I say "solely" above because a child born of a citizen father "in the United States" is a citizen because of the place of birth.

[68] 8 U. S. C. § 6.

[69] Maysonet v. Zamorano (1919) 11 P. R. Fed. 412.

[70] 182 U. S. at p. 247. "Opinion of the Court" is the erroneous caption to each page of Justice Brown's opinion.

[71] Dorr v. United States (1904) 195 U. S. 138.

[72] Balzac v. Porto Rico (1922) 258 U. S. 298, 305.

[73] 182 U. S. 244, 289. [74] *Ibid.* 291. [75] *Ibid.* 293. [76] *Ibid.* 341–342.

[77] (1904) 195 U. S. 138. [78] *Ibid.* 143. [79] *Ibid.* 148. [80] *Ibid.* 148. [81] *Ibid.* 149.

[82] (1922) 258 U. S. 298.

[83] American Citizenship (1911) 11 Col. L. Rev., 231, 326, at pp. 338 ff.

[84] Loughborough v. Blake (1820) 5 Wheat. 317, 319.

[85] After referring to the Articles of Confederation, the Ordinance for the Northwest Territory, and the Constitution, he said, "It is sufficient to observe in relation to these three fundamental instruments that it can nowhere be inferred that the territories were considered a part of the United States."—182 U. S. 250, 251.

[86] Even Justice Brown admitted exceptions to his generality. "There is a clear distinction between such prohibitions as go to the very root of the power of Congress to act at all, irrespective of time or place, and such as are operative only 'throughout the United States' or among the several States. . . . We do not wish, however, to be understood as expressing an opinion how far the bill of rights contained in the first eight Amendments is of general and how far of local application."—182 U. S. p. 277.

[87] Section 2(*a*), ¶ (1).

[88] The resolution is published in Department of State Press Releases, Weekly Issue No. 240, p. 248.

[89] Section 8(*a*), ¶ (1).

[90] "Citizens of the Philippine Islands who are not citizens of the United States shall not be admitted to the continental United States from the Territory of Hawaii (whether entering such Territory before or after the effective date of this section)," unless they are "nonimmigrants" or "nonquota immigrants," etc. [section 8(*a*), ¶ (2)], but Filipino immigration into that Territory "shall be determined by the Department of the Interior on the basis of the needs of industries in the Territory of Hawaii."—Section 8(*a*), ¶ 1.

It is said that in 1931 there were about 64,000 Filipinos in Hawaii, where they are considered an essential labor supply in the sugar and pineapple plantations.—Bruno Lasker, *Filipino Immigration* (1931) pp. 159, 160, 324.

[91] Section 14.

[92] *Supra,* p. 324.

[93] Mr. Justice White makes this assumption in Downes v. Bidwell (1901) 182 U. S. 244, 335.

[94] Act of June 2, 1924, 43 Stat. 253. Some Alaskan Indians acquired citizenship under the Act of Congress of February 8, 1887, which provided: "Every Indian born within the territorial limits of the United States who has voluntarily taken up, within said limits, his residence separate and apart from any tribe of Indians therein, and has adopted the habits of civilized life, is hereby declared to be a citizen of the United States." 24 Stat. 390.

[95] See 48 U. S. C. §§ 49, 169, 357.

[96] But see *In re* Minook (1904) 2 Alaska 200. It has been said that acting under authority conferred by Congress in the Organic Act of 1912 for Alaska, the Alaska Territorial legislature in 1915 "passed a law permitting the Alaska natives to become citi-

zens under the following conditions . . ." This is a double error. First, the Organic Act does not confer the alleged authority. Secondly, the territorial statute (2 Sess. Laws, Alaska, 52) does not purport to confer citizenship. Its purpose was to enable those Indians who acquired citizenship under the Act of Congress of February 8, 1887, 24 Stat. 390, quoted in note 94 *supra,* to prove that fact and obtain a certificate that the proof had been made.

The erroneous statement is in George Washington Spicer, *The Constitutional Status and Government of Alaska* (1927) 45 Johns Hopkins Studies in Historical and Political Science, No. 4, p. 43, and is repeated in Luella Gettys, *The Law of Citizenship in the United States* (1934) p. 148.

97 48 U. S. C. §§ 73, 135.

98 8 U. S. C. § 4.

99 31 Stat. (1900) 141, 48 U. S. C. § 495.

100 Neuss, Hesslein & Co. v. Edwards (1929) 30 F (2d) 620, 622, dictum; see Farrington, Governor of Hawaii v. Tokushige (1927) 273 U. S. 284, where the due process of law clause of Amendment V was regarded as operative in the Territory of Hawaii, a result probably not dependent upon "incorporation." Notwithstanding this dearth of judicial decision the statement in the text is a confident prediction of ultimate decision.

101 See Hawaii v. Mankichi (1903) 190 U. S. 197.

102 See note 90 *supra.*

103 Though Guam was acquired from Spain by the Treaty of Paris, April 11, 1899, and is sometimes thought of as related to the Philippines, it was acquired under Article II, whereas independence is now being offered to those islands only which were ceded by Article III and the supplemental treaty concluded November 7, 1900.

104 Soto et al. v. United States (1921) 273 Fed. 628, 633.

105 Act of February 25, 1927, c. 192 § 1(*a*), 44 Stat., Pt. 2, 1234.

106 Act of June 28, 1932, c. 283 § 5, 47 Stat. 336.

107 Sen. Rep. No. 641, 72 Cong. 1 Sess. (1931–1933) 3.

108 The bill was inspired by Paul M. Pearson, Governor of the Virgin Islands.—*Op. cit.* pp. 4–5.

109 The Committee report accompanying this bill said of this section merely this: "Section 3 provides for persons hereafter born in the Virgin Islands of the United States. The rule of citizenship already provided in the Fourteenth Amendment to the Constitution of the United States." Sen. Rep. No. 650, 69 Cong. 1 Sess., (1926) 2.

110 1 Moore's Dig. 553.

111 He said: "By the treaty referred to, the exclusive sovereignty of the United States over it [Tutuila] appears to be asserted by us and recognized by Great Britain and Germany, which nations formerly shared with us a protectorate." (1902) 23 Ops. Att'y Gen. 630.

112 "In 1900 an American warship arrived at Pago Pago and anchored in its harbor. At this time the chiefs of the island of Tutuila voluntarily ceded their diminutive domain to the United States. In 1904 the chiefs of the three tiny islands, the Manua group which lay 65 miles farther east, followed suit."—Moore and Farrington, American Samoan Commission's Visit to Samoa, (Washington, 1931) 1.

"The sovereignty of the United States over American Samoa is hereby extended over Swains Island, which is made a part of American Samoa. . . ."—Joint Resolution of March 4, 1925, c. 563, 43 Stat. 1357.

113 Sen. Doc. No. 249, 71 Cong. 3 Sess. (1931) 7. 114 *Ibid.* 17. 115 *Ibid.* 6.

[116] Wilson v. Shaw (1907) 204 U. S. 24, 32.

[117] (1907) 26 Ops. Att'y Gen. 376.

[118] *Supra,* p. 335.

[119] Act of June 27, 1934, discussed *ante,* pp. 346–347.

NOTES TO APPENDIX

[1] Flournoy and Hudson (1929), Nationality Laws, 530.

[2] 16 Phil. Rep. at p. 182.

[3] Flournoy and Hudson, 531.

[4] 16 Phil. Rep. at p. 184.

[5] For an example of such a claim, see Gely de Amadeo v. Riefkohl (1910) 5 P. R. Fed. 420.

[6] Its articles on Spanish nationality are translated in Flournoy and Hudson, 537.

[7] This decree is printed in 1 Manresa, Codigo Civil Español, ed. 2 (1903) p. 22.

[8] Zeballos, I, 317.

[9] 1 Manresa, *op. cit.* 146.

[10] 2 *ibid.* 798.

[11] 16 Phil. Rep. at p. 185.

[12] The reform is fully explained by J. Trias de Bes, La naturalización española por título de vecindad según las últimas y recientas disposiciones.—Rev. gen. de legis. y jur. (1917) 289.

[13] Translated in Flournoy and Hudson, 528.

[14] *Ibid.* 529.

[15] Sy Joc Lieng et al. v. Sy Quia et al. (1910) 16 Phil. Rep. 137, 180.

GROWING LAWLESSNESS OF TREES*

BY SAYRE MACNEIL

TREES, WHETHER DISMEMBERED into roots, timber, boughs, leaves, fruit, nuts, or standing alone or in groves, have since Eden been intimately involved with every human instinct and emotion. Roots, fruits, and nuts satisfy our hunger and quench our thirst. Without firewood our cooking and warmth is scant. Trees shelter us from sun, wind, and rain. The house of timber still has advantages in earthquakes. Log dugouts or wooden rafts first teach us how to dare fresh or salt waters. Deadwood, Lone Oak, Lone Pine, Palo Alto, Palo Verde, and a host of other place names embody the benign memory of trees as guides and landmarks long after the very site of the tree is forgotten. Our self-regarding instinct warms when we are referred to as "tall as a tree," "straight as a tree," or when "hearts of oak" are attributed to us. Love, whether of man and dryad, Apollo and Daphne aforetime, of a monarch for Fair Rosamond in a bower, of adventurers in the Forest of Arden, marks our racial course past the Shade of the Old Apple Tree. Men of many times and places delight to carve not only their names and initials but also hearts and other mystic symbols in the bark of sympathetic, helpful trees. Our instincts of awe often center around trees. The Oracle of Dodona generally selected an oak. The Golden Bough of Lake Nemi is aptly chosen by Frazer as the symbol for a vital cross-section of the life of early and modern man. Why do youngsters delight in the Maypole? Why did grown-ups pursue legal remedies in respect of rights of common regarding them? What did a Liberty pole mean a century and a half ago? Why a *pole?* Why are flagpoles of wood? Is it not more economical for mass production to make them of metal, as we have shifted the material of the oil derrick and the electrical transmission line? Why are you saying to yourself, "Flag poles are different"? I have said nothing of the centuries of varied and tender emotion revolving around the Christmas tree, nor need I remind you that the symbol of Christianity is more

*A topic ignored in recent crime surveys.

than two crosspieces of wood. No wonder that trees are respected and beloved.

Trees are also to be hated and feared.[1] Around a tree and a serpent centers the Fall of Man. Pious anger destroying the groves of idolaters marks the progress of Israel. The laws of Canute will carry the same spirit into English law. Our own poet bids us "beware the pine tree's withered branch," and white paint and red reflectors warn the night motoring party that even on the king's highway all the king's horses and all the king's men must turn out for the ancient oak or sprawling sycamore. Hemlock killed Socrates. Belladonna is a graceful flattering name for a shrub; the druggist must suffer if he omits the skull and crossbones from the bottle of extract or if he mislabels it "dandelion."[2] Vividly does Mr. Kipling's *The Knife and the Naked Chalk* illustrate how the children of the downs loathe trees while their neighbors of the weald pine away if taken from them. Today the breeds are generally mixed. Each of us is apt to be a confusion of tree lover and tree hater. Few are tree neutrals.

Has this clash of feelings shown any mark on our law? If the answer is "No," then will some rationalist, who knows neither love nor fear for trees, explain how so many trees, in cases involving economically a few shillings or a few dollars, have found their way into the highest courts of so many kings, and received such patient and prolonged hearings before the judges?

SOME TREES IN PRIMITIVE LAW

TREE LAW IS IMMEASURABLY OLD. The early records bristle with references which hark back to far earlier centuries. Even an unlearned essayist (who at the time of writing was not even aware of the fascinating collection of ancient and English law in John Evelyn's *Sylva*) can pick them at random from the translations though lacking the wisdom to explain or correlate them. In the Laws of Manu (wherein are intermingled religion, government, revenue, law, business, morals, manners, diet, and health),[3] I have caught at least seventeen specific references to trees.

The householder is bidden to pass by "well-known trees," as well as earth mounds, idols, and other objects or men, "turning his right hand towards them."[4] Not only should he keep distant at night from the roots of trees[5] (though the hermit in the forest should use the roots as his only dwelling),[6] but also he should not make use of "red exudations from trees and [juices] flowing from incisions."[7] Herbs and trees as well as birds and animals, if destroyed for sacrifices, are destined for a nobler rebirth.[8] One of the hells is that of the forest with sword-leaved trees.[9] The king's palace should be supplied with trees as well as water,[10] and in respect of his taxes the king takes the sixth part of trees as well as of meat and honey.[11] Along with royal prerogative runs kingly duty. He must settle boundary disputes, marking the true lines by specified trees or clustering shrubs such as bamboo.[12] He must protect forests, natural and artificial groves and the like by the triple guard of sentries, patrols, and spies.[13] Penalties in compensatory[14] and exemplary[15] fines follow injuries to trees, objects of wood, or roots. Loss of caste results to the misguided man who cuts down green trees for firewood, as well as to him who studies bad books, practices the arts of dancing and singing, has intercourse with women who drink spiritous liquor, or is an atheist.[16]

Frederick Goodwin's fragments and attempted reconstruction of Rome's Twelve Tables indicate:[17]

1. Boundaries are governed by Solon's law. My fence, wall, house, trench, well, have definite "set-back" requirements, much more in the manner of the restrictions of a modern subdivision's set of building restrictions, or of a zoning ordinance, than in the spirit of the conception of seisin or the maxim *cuius est solum* etc. "An olive or vine must not be planted within nine feet of a neighbour's land, nor other trees within five feet."[18]

2. "Trees which cast their shadow on adjoining land may be lopped up to fifteen feet from the ground."[19]

3. "Fruit which falls on adjoining land may be collected by the owner of the fruit every third day."[20]

4. Penalties for wrongfully felling another's tree are fixed at a lump sum.[21]

From India via Rome to early England, in newsreel fashion, let us examine flashes of the law from King Alfred to Henry the First.[22]

King Alfred's Laws fixed payment and "wite," according to size, for "every great tree" and other trees, burned or hewn without the owner's leave.[23]

13. If at their common work [felling trees (?)] one man slay another unwilfully, let the tree be given to the kindred, and let them have it off the land within xxx. days; or let him take possession of it who owns the wood.[24]

Trees may incite our awe instincts or our fear instincts in two opposing directions. Compare the little girl who "when she was good she was very, very good, and when she was bad she was horrid." King Alfred is protector of the good tree, with the one hand, and avenger toward the wicked tree, with the other. King Canute opens up a new aspect of the wicked tree. "And we earnestly forbid every heathenism: heathenism is . . . that they worship heathen gods, and the sun or the moon, fire or rivers, water-wells or stones, or forest trees of any kind; . . ."[25]

In the laws of King Henry the First, the parents of the man killed by timber in work with others have the same right to the timber as that conferred by King Alfred.[26] Far more remarkable: If a man falls upon another from a tree or any apparatus, so that the man fallen upon is killed or injured, the man falling shall be held innocent by the ancient laws if he can prove that he could not help it; or if anyone obstinately and against public opinion presumes to demand revenge or the blood money, let him ascend if he wishes and similarly crush the defendant.[27]

Out of many isolated items in the field of law I invite you to glance at a few topics in which either the lawlessness or restlessness of growing trees, or the awe or hate which men bear to them have caused the tree law to deviate substantially from the familiar juristic patterns.

1. *Is a Growing Tree a Movable or an Immovable? Real or Personal?* A very neat legal maxim ought to put all well-behaved trees in their proper places. *Quicquid plantatur solo, solo cedit.*[28] Growing crops, because of the needs of husbandry, their fleeting, transitory nature, marketable for cash today, frostbitten tonight, have to be treated as outside the maxim.[29] But how can abiding trees (trees "which may by possibility endure forever" and therefore serve as the measuring stick for a determinable fee simple[30]) escape the legal logic? The land itself (save for the occasional lawlessness of earthquakes, "wild waters," and human violators of the duty of lateral support) is immovable. The tree

planted in the land yields to the land. Therefore the tree is immovable. Oak, ash, and elm generally obey this law. Perhaps they are pleased at being allotted the higher dignity in the ranks of property. Timber trees, useful for building houses, such as oak, ash, and elm,[31] are accorded dignity in our law books, as they were accorded dignity ere we had law books or houses.

In India, even a fruit tree such as the mango may share the dignity of true English timber trees. In a district where its wood "was often used not only for building houses, but also for boats, fences, furniture, carriages, &c.," my landowner grandfather made a deed of gift of a mango tree to your father, who failed to register the deed as deeds of immovables other than "standing timber" must be registered. A generation later I took the mangoes. Your suit for possession of the mango tree succeeds in spite of the lack of registration, though the court suggests that other mango trees elsewhere might be different![32]

Suppose I am lord of the manor. You are my guest and neighbor. You want firewood. You want a deer for your barbecue spit. With lordly gesture and stilted speech, I say, "I grant you that tree to carry it away the next day after to your own use, and that deer to hunt and take." There is no seal. There is no writing signed by the lord. Nevertheless, somehow, you have "a power coupled with an interest," and tree and deer may become as effectively yours (together with the requisite privileges of ingress and egress to take them) as though we had sent the coach to town to bring us the services of conveyancer and clerk.[33] Yet on many occasions a "grant" of standing timber is subject to the Statute of Frauds,[34] recording laws, and other earthy incidents. Perhaps the explanatory clue is that you and I did not treat the tree as tree, but as firewood. We pictured your cutting it quickly and turning it into chattel. Were there many trees and the grantee had years to remove them and so would "derive a benefit from the further growth of the trees and their nourishment from the land," then Dean Pound's Aristotelian nourishment theory[35] would apply, and the trees be kept in the realm of the land law.

The restlessness of a growing tree may similarly play havoc with the symmetry of our doctrines of prescription. For far more than a score of years the branches of your oaks and elms grew over my freehold. Had it been your invading eaves or cornice, a prescriptive right to maintain them would have arisen. Not so, however, of your boughs. Just as the airplane's varying flights acquire no prescriptive right of way,[36] so the growing, wind-blown, snow-weighted, or sun-seeking branches can build you no easement.[37] Is not that oak or elm tree an odd type of immovable?

2. *Can I Do What I Will with My Tree?*—The answer is "No." Avoiding cruelty to animals, I may slay my steed as I please, whether it be gallant Dobbin or motor-vehicular Lizzie. Guarding against violation of another's right of lateral support, I may whimsically turn my hill into a pit. I may kill my weeds or vegetables (whether or not I can tell which is which) at will. Barring duties to an insurer, or other very specific third persons, I may destroy my house according to my pleasure. Cutting my trees may prove a more serious matter.

The venerable native black walnuts, poplars, silver-leaf maples, and catalpas in the line of the highway easement were planted by John More and belonged to John More. The public did not own them or any proprietary interest in them because it had never taken or paid for them. If they fell, if More or anyone else cut them, the wood was More's. Yet the owner was properly punished under rather general statutory enactments for cutting them.[38] Suppose further, that the landowner's trees lie far within his boundaries. The American sovereign here also may speak with almost the unfettered authority of Charlemagne, or William the Conqueror, not only to penalize the stranger who cuts California's so-called holly, or "any Christmas tree,"[39] but also to command the lord of the land itself: "Spare that tree."[40]

Note well the wholly different technique with which the courts approach the problem where the sovereign commands his landowning subject to destroy "weeds."

1. There is no such common law duty. Not even the Texan railroad need curb its destructive Johnson grass.[41] Nor need the English landed gentry (in spite of the powerful arguments of a Bray) take any pains whatever to keep down their thistles.[42] Neither is a statute to be loosely construed to cast such a duty on the owner of the New South Wales "station" in respect of loftier "prickly pears."[43]

2. When even the modern sovereign sets out to formulate commands for the destruction of weeds, it is wise to begin with a preambulatory tirade of abuse. This closely parallels the technique by which courts sometimes shear the invading trees of their usual legal privileges by first calling them "noxious." The weeds should first be cut off from the fellowship of the "kindly fruits of the earth." Thus "weeds" may be defined to include "all rank vegetable growth which exhale unpleasant and noxious odors, and also high rank vegetable growth that may conceal filthy deposits."[44] That incidentally might, according to one or another set of senses or sensibilities, include almost any growing thing.[45] Poison ivy has recently been planted near Pittsburgh to protect scenic rocks from sign painters. Warnings, however, akin to the "cross dog" signs were given.

Marijuana weed with its puzzling narcotic qualities has been uprooted and burned by California deputy sheriffs. Lucky is the owner of a vacant lot who has not paid a "weed tax" or special assessment for the clearing of his lot. Such exercises of police power are part of the life we take for granted. Rice seems at first blush far removed from the list of weeds. But if the life of rice is wagered against the life of pines, then the sovereign may place rice on the black list of noxious weeds.[46]

3. *Noxious Trees.*—As we shall see in a succeeding section, our courts are exceedingly tolerant toward a tree which grows restless on its home freehold and breaks and enters the close of a neighbor. The falling tree, which injures a man, may involve someone's having to pay or to suffer by primitive or by modern law.[47] Even the invading tree may involve its guardian in liability. To evoke this result, however, it seems necessary to outlaw the tree. The proper magic is to term the tree "noxious," thus throwing it into the botanical Fiddler's Green along with proscribed weeds. The leading case is *Crowhurst v. Burial Board.*[48] Defendant seventeen years before planted two yew trees in a country churchyard. If nuisance may be "a right thing in a wrong place, like a pig in the parlor instead of the barn yard,"[49] then we have the authority of Gray's *Elegy* that this yew was *prima facie* no nuisance. One knows, or ought to know, however, that cattle frequently eat yew leaves and are sometimes poisoned thereby. The branches of the yews invaded plaintiff's air space. Plaintiff was tenant for a term

of three years. His horse nibbled the yew leaves and died. The nibbling was done on both sides of the line. Plaintiff sued and won. No horse of mine ever had any yew leaves to eat and mayhap my impressions formed only on reading English poetry predispose me in favor of yew trees, that they belong in English country churchyards just as much as horses belong in neighboring fields. Some inherited defect of sight or smell keeps me from grasping the nicety of the analogies to the yew tree which the court found most helpful. These were a reservoir, a hog house, lime pits and kilns for tanning and dyeing, and a high dung-heap. Accordingly it is hard for me to see (1) any wrong in planting the yew in the churchyard;[50] (2) any wrong in preventing the yew's branches from growing according to yew's law rather than man's rules; (3) why, in short, the burden of keeping the horse from the yew should not lie with the horseman rather than the Burial Board; (4) whether some problem of "prior in time is prior in right" is not involved, in which event the yew was senior to the horse; (5) what science, art, or learning will safely enlighten the planter of trees, or the cultivator of "natural" trees with respect to what trees may sometime thereafter be judicially anathematized as "noxious."

Note, however, that a slender thread of the ban of the "noxious" cuts across American as well as English decisions. It savors distinctly of the children of the downs rather than the sons of the forest.[51] Note, further, that the application of the anathema is extremely vague. Noxious to man we readily understand, and therefore noxious to cattle. But what about noxiousness to other vegetation, to premises generally, or to a well?

In *Ackerman v. Ellis*[52] you sued me, alleging that I, intending to injure you and make your farm adjoining my land unfit for habitation and tillage, carelessly planted poisonous or noxious trees, viz., thirty-five spruces in a row, and other trees (unspecified) so close to the line that roots, branches, limbs, and leaves hang over and make the premises barren, incommodious, and unfit for use. I demurred. The court says

> the fact that spruce trees are neither poisonous nor noxious is not so universally known that the court will take judicial notice of it. On the contrary, so far as there is any common knowledge on the subject, we are in-

clined to think it is that coniferous trees (including spruce) have a poisonous or noxious effect upon all vegetable growth within the spread of their branches.

Regardless of the goodness or badness of the trees, continues the court, any overhang of any tree is *pro tanto* a nuisance. You are, in the language of the court

entitled to [your] action for damages against the person who is responsible for their presence there . . . and this is so without regard to the extent of the damage resulting therefrom, the insignificance of the injury going to the extent of the recovery and not to the right of action.[53]

The American case on the "noxious" tree which troubles me most involves mulberry trees and a well in Mississippi.[54] The scene is set in the city of Aberdeen. In Japan, as in the Valley of the Po, the mulberry is valued as the foster mother or wet nurse of the silk worm. The court finds: "The white mulberry is a valuable ornamental shade tree, quite common in Aberdeen." When you bought your home and I bought my adjoining home, yours contained a domestic water well three feet from the boundary, mine had two white mulberry trees planted "long anterior" to either purchase and locate from seventeen to twenty feet back of the line. Eventually my mulberry roots "penetrated [your] well, polluted the water and rendered it unfit for domestic purposes." You requested me to cut down the trees or to permit you to do so. I refused. You sued and recovered $25 in the justice court. This the circuit court reversed on the ground that you had no cause of action. You appealed.

You argued that the invading roots were a nuisance which by ruining your well had caused serious and permanent harm.

I countered thus: Valuable shade trees are not a nuisance. These were there when I bought the land. When the roots invaded it was up to you to cut them to the line.

The court decided against me. It says:

It seems to be settled law that overhanging branches are a nuisance and it must follow that invading roots are. The person intruded on by branches may cut them off; it must be true that one may cut off invading roots; it must be true that he who is injured by encroaching roots from his neighbor's tree can recover the damages sustained by them. The right of action seems clear.

Referring to the injury to the well, the court remarks:

That proves the noxious character of the trees.

The fact that I did not plant the trees does not excuse me. I cannot maintain a nuisance after notice even though I did not start it. But I need not destroy the trees if I can otherwise keep the roots from your well.

4. *Boundary or "Line" Trees.*—Where the trunk of a tree grows partly on my lot and partly on your lot, so that its nourishment is derived from both freeholds, wisdom akin to the judgment of Solomon needs invocation. We are dealing with ancient, weighty, and unique matters. For weak analogies one must range from the drawn sword which ought to lie untouched between the bride and the proxy for the bridegroom, to the Sacred Cod which at the moment of writing should have hung in the Chamber of the House of Representatives on Beacon Hill, to the four legal types of party wall[55] with their attendant mysteries, and to the monument which it is tort, crime, and sin to remove.

Here our case law begins not with boundary trees strictly speaking, but with trees whose trunks are so near to the boundary that substantial nourishment is taken from a neighbor's soil. Dean Pound has identified the essential clash of conflicting English cases with the clash of ancient and pervading conceptions. Since Aristotle said that plants are composed of the elements of earth and water drawn from soil by roots, and since the form of the tree is the material of earth and water realizing the idea of a tree, so surely the Roman law and several centuries of English law must call such a tree common property. To part of this the Teutonic notion of the exclusiveness of seisin says "Nay"; if *A* planted the tree on his own land, and is seised of the trunk, which is the main thing for the jury to base its verdict upon, then, in spite of the invasion of roots and branches, all the tree is *A's*.[56]

The Aristotelian nourishment theory is best illustrated in *Waterman v. Soper.*[57]

It was ruled by *Holt* chief justice at *Lent* assizes at *Winchester*, upon a trial at *nisi prius* 1697–8. 1. That if *A*. plants a tree upon the extremest limits of his land, and the tree growing extended its root into the land of *B*. next adjoining, *A*. and *B*. are tenants in common of this tree. But if all the root grows into the land of *A*. though the boughs overshadow the land of

B. yet the branches follow the root, and the property of the whole is in *A.* 2. Two tenants in common of a tree, and one cuts the whole tree; though the other cannot have an action for the tree, yet he may have an action for the special damage by this cutting; as where one tenant in common destroys the whole flight of pigeons.

No such notion of common tenancy of the tree either as a boundary tree or as a robber of nourishment occurs to Crew, C. J., in his dictum about the fruit of the tree growing "in an hedge" in *Mitten v. Faudrye.*[58] *Masters v. Pollie*[59] bluntly followed the seisin theory. Plaintiff brought trespass *quare clausum fregit,* adding asportation of his boards by way of aggravation. Defendant justified that a huge tree grew between the two closes, though apparently the main trunk or body of the tree [60] was on plaintiff's soil; that part of the roots grew into and derived nourishment from his soil; that plaintiff felled the tree, carried it into his close, and sawed it into boards; that defendant entered and took part of the boards as his. The plea was held bad. The court conceded that if plaintiff had planted the tree in defendant's soil the result would have been otherwise, Montague, C. J., pointing out that in the instant case the plaintiff was not able to limit the roots of the tree, how far they should grow and go. Though the roots grow in your close, the whole tree is mine.[61]

Long afterward the court in *Holder v. Coates*[62] had to choose between Aristotle and seisin. Seisin won. The common-law jury just could not handle Aristotle. They had quite enough trouble with seisin. The trunk was all on my land. Some roots surely invaded your land. I cut the tree. You brought trespass. Evidence was conflicting in respect to the whereabouts of the tap root. There was no doubt that nourishment was derived from both freeholds, but the jury were charged not to find for either party according to the proportion of nourishment. They were charged to determine on whose land the tree was first planted and find for the owner of that land. When they could not tell in whose ground the tree first grew, I took the verdict on stipulation. Littledale, J., was clear that the seisin rule was preferable.

New Hampshire questioned the nourishment theory except in occurrences of true line trees where either neighbor may have trespass *quare clausum fregit* if the other cuts the tree.[63]

New York gave exhaustive study to $25 worth of line trees felled between two adjoining farms.[64] The line trees involved were natural woodland growth. I cut them to build a fence to the line. You brought trespass and claimed statutory treble damages. I claimed the quite extreme right to cut and remove all the line trees. The jury was charged to award you "the value of such proportion of the trees" as were on your soil. On my exception to the charge, Hogeboom, J., in rendering the decision of the Supreme Court, flatly denied that such line trees are held by tenancy in common. They were the result neither of combined effort nor of purchase "nor of any of the ordinary modes of acquiring title, by which a tenancy in common was created." *Cuius est solum* applies "whether it be the grass and herbage, the plants and bushes, or the more lordly trees." I owned the part of the tree on my soil. You owned the part on yours. Nevertheless, neither you nor I can in such a circumstance do what we will with our own because (1) a monument must be preserved and (2) the destruction of my portion may destroy or injure your portion. Therefore both trespass[65] and injunction "in a proper and sufficiently important case" are available. The Supreme Court affirmed the judgment.

On appeal the Court of Appeal affirmed the judgment. Where the trunk is on my land, the court (by Allen, J.) preferred the seisin theory. He thought it consistent with this theory to call the ownership of the soil several "while the tree, standing and growing partly on the soil of each, not capable, as an entire thing of several ownership by the two, would be the property of the two in common, and as tenants in common." Destruction of the common property by one tenant in common grounds an action of trespass by the other.[66]

The New Hampshire and New York line trees involve natural growth. Iowa has applied the tenancy in common rule to a planted line of cottonwoods and protected them by injunction.[67]

The tenancy in common theory of line trees, in spite of its theoretical difficulties, seems to work in rural life. When we come to the vacant city lot, or the residence lot, the boundary tree refuses to adjust itself to one owner's ambition "fully to improve" his freehold by the usual store building covering the lot. In Connecticut a line maple tree came twice before the highest tribunal.[68] Its trunk stood half and half on each lot. It was forty years old. Defendant sought to hew it to the line in order to build a residence with a twenty-foot wall. The lower court enjoined "such interference with the tree . . . as will destroy or injure same." On appeal the injunction was modified to apply only to the trunk, permitting the lopping of boughs and roots "up to the line, even though that were practically to the trunk of the tree." The decision was reconciled with the earlier leading case of *Lyman v. Hale*[69] on the ground that the nourishment theory, while rejected with respect to trees where the trunk stands on one freehold, was quite consistent with the "common" theory of line trees. Sharp analysis leads the court to conclude that for many reasons it is not technically correct to call the relationship of the owners "tenancy in common"[70] though the term is "probably well enough and sufficiently accurate for practical purposes"—"the tenancy in common of a tree is of peculiar nature, if there be such a tenancy at all." In addition, however, to each man's owning the part of the trunk that is on his land, each has *also* the right "to demand that the owner of the other portion shall so use his part as not unreasonably to injure or destroy the whole." Such view comes closest to that of the party wall owned each part in severalty with mutual cross-easements.[71]

5. *Invading roots and boughs.*—If the roots of my tree invade your subsurface or the boughs invade your air space, the following problems arise: (1) Who owns the fruit and wood in or over your soil? (2) To what extent, if any, am I liable to you? Ultimately we may decide that the two questions depend from the same principles.

(1) Aside from occasional vestiges of the Aristotelian nourishment notions discussed in connection with boundary trees, the authorities are fairly clear that the fruits of the invasion are mine. This seems at war with either (*a*) the application of the doctrine *cuius est solum* to your freehold, or (*b*) the general common law theory of the exclusiveness of your seisin. It is probably in direct conflict with bucolic tradition and belief in many a locality in the English-speaking world.[72]

The language of Viner's Abridgement that "if trees grow in the hedge, and the fruit falls into another's ground, the owner may go in and take it"[73] has puzzled critics because of the possibility of some peculiar magic of the "line" tree's being involved and because "it might be argued that the applies only to the case of A's fruit being carried on to B's land without any fault of A, as, for instance, by the action of the wind."[74] However, in *Mitten v. Faudrye,*[75] Doderidge, C. J., uses substantially the identical words in a context which seems to me clearly to involve the fruit falling from invading boughs.

Lyman v. Hale,[76] the leading American case, is squarely in point, ably argued, well considered, and has received the joint accolade of Kent and Holmes.[77] The pear tree's trunk was well back of the line on my land. Large roots invaded your soil. Branches overhung your land. From the latter you plucked and kept as your own six bushels of pears. I brought trespass *quare clausum fregit.* The trial judge charged the jury in your favor. The verdict was for you. The Superior Court affirmed it. My motion in error was made in the highest court. Was all this really a contest over six bushels of pears before the learned arguments had even begun? I fancy not. They argued *pro* and *con* the doctrine *cuius est solum*. They argued the doctrines of line trees. They argued prescriptive rights and whether trespass was the proper remedy. Bissell, J., wrote the opinion. The decision was for me on all points. The opinion is too fine an admixture of careful study of old cases and sharp Connecticut insight into the ways of trees and adjoining Yankee landowners for me to attempt a paraphrase.[78]

I see no satisfactory basis of distinction, once we abandon the Aristotelian-nourishment theory, with respect to title between invading fruit and invading wood of roots or branches. I should place title to root, branch, fruit, and nut in the owner of the trunk. However, I would hesitate to certify what the law is as to the wood. Belcher, C. C., in the second case of *Grandona v. Lovdal,*[79] expressly gives such wood to the owner whose land is overhung. The owner of the trees maintained them "for the purpose of supplying himself with fuel and hop-poles," and it was argued that he should not thereby use "plaintiff's land for his own profit and advantage." To which the court replied: "The fuel and hop-poles growing over plaintiff's land were his, and could have been claimed by him against the defendant." Possibly the court was thinking of the fact that some of the trees involved were line trees. Possibly the chief commissioner had in mind some analogy of puzzling precedents involving the falling of the clippings from my hedge or tree upon your land.[80] I should think the topic difficult enough without giving title of fruit to one and of wood to the other.

(2) As to my liability and your rights and remedies for my tree's trespasses, courts and text writers[81] almost unanimously *say* that the invasion is a nuisance. Aside from the rare and puzzling "noxious tree" decisions, I have found only one case where the courts help you either in law or in equity.[82] The other cases say that you have a remedy. That remedy is self-help. You may hew or lop the invading roots and branches to the line.[83] You may do this freely. You do not even have to give me notice[84] as you must do (except in emergencies) in the usual case of self-abatement of private nuisance.[85]

The following American cases illustrate the failure of judicial remedy.

Countryman v. Lighthill.[86] In Stark, Herkimer County, New York, my maple tree overhangs your garden some five to fifteen feet. You make some showing that your shaded berry bushes bear more lightly than those in the sun. I refuse to trim on your request. You sue for damages and on rather sketchy findings of fact win six cents damages which the county court affirms. The Supreme Court, however, denies you even such scant relief. It says: "But it would be intolerable to give an action in the case of an *innoxious*[87] tree whenever its growing branches extend so far as to pass beyond the boundary line and overhang a neighbor's soil." It bids you use self-help and clip them. "The overhanging branches of a tree, not poisonous or noxious in its nature, are not a nuisance, *per se,* in such a sense as to sustain an action for damages. Some real, sensible damage must be shown to result therefrom."[88]

Jumping from New York to California, we find one row of cottonwoods appearing twice before our Supreme Court. My long 534-foot line of cottonwood trees was some score and odd years ago by my grantor planted from eight to twelve feet behind the common boundary of our ranches. They grew fast and luxuriantly. You allege a rather horrible condition of impoverished land, ruined crops, and broken fences. The trial court finds, however, no destruction of crops, and an ability to plow and cultivate substantially as close as to any fence, no land impoverished, fences crowded over "a few inches" and despite my doing some trimming every few years an overhang ranging from six to twenty feet. It concludes there is no damage and no relief.[89] The Supreme Court affirms this. You are advised that your property is not injuriously affected nor your personal enjoyment lessened.[90] Again you are bidden to use self-help.[91]

In the rather rather confused case of *Tanner v. Wallbrunn*,[92] my maple's boughs overhung your brick store and when swept by the wind took bricks from your flue tops and made holes in your roof whereby rain water injured your leather goods. Invading roots caused minor harm to your foundations. If, because the legal remedy is trespass on the case, substantial harm must be shown in order to recover, the roof situation ought to be enough. Furthermore, as lopping will have to be repeated as the boughs grow again, if the invasion is a tort, it is of a type peculiarly susceptible to an equitable bill of peace. You sought a mandatory injunction. The court admitted the nuisance. It emphasized your remedy of self-help. It indicated (the boughs had been cut before hearing) that in no event could you have injunctive relief. It suggested that you might have an action at law for the branches but probably would not have for the roots.[93]

High-water mark of this tree-loving tendency may find evidence in a recent Massachusetts case.[94] You proved that the roots of my poplar tree so clogged your sewers and drain pipes that they had to be dug up and cleaned "several times"; that the roots grew under your cement cellar and caused cracks therein, though the cracks were not as yet serious. Surely here is substantial money loss and the assurance of more trouble to come. Neither injunction nor damages were awarded. The plaintiff is bidden to help himself by cutting the roots to the line. Obviously he had better keep the tools handy, since the poplar roots will grow again. The Supreme Judicial Court of Massachusetts says that the invading roots involve the same principle as the shade of the earlier maple which made the house "damp and unhealthy."[95] There may be such harm to you, but there is no legal wrong. The court says flatly, "The principle involved is that an owner of land is at liberty to use his land, and all of it, to grow trees."

And now for a final anomaly. In most of the fields of our law the rise of the king's courts and the rise of parliaments have tended to choke, hamper, or restrict the remedies of self-help. Criminal law is largely substituted for private justice. In many places, the "duty to retreat" limits warriors' privileges of self-defense. My primitive self-help, if I am disseised of my freehold or if my chattel is taken, has been greatly whittled away. The action of replevin is given to put bonds on the landlord's right of distress. When through centuries the flood beats generally and continuously against self-help, why should tree law be such a marked exception? Normans, Borderers, and their successors exercised self-help in a manner which too frequently became the occasion of a ballad of bloodshed and burning. May it be that Normans and Borderers, Daniel Boones and Forty-Niners, and the descendants of each of them, found something about trees that caused them to be generally moderate and judicious in lopping to the line? Has experience shown that, even when tree lover and tree hater hold adjoining freeholds, they can best settle informally the problems of tree trimming? May this be a secret which every judge knows but none tells?

Before attempting any summary or conclusion of the legal results of this desultory ramble among trees and law, a fond father pauses to decide a simple question: Which path would I choose for my own Hugh or Jim? Shall I give the paternal advice of Scott's laird in *The Heart of Midlothian?*—"Jock, when ye hae naething else to do, ye may be aye sticking in a tree; it will be growing, Jock, when ye're sleeping." Pay is low and competition strong in the untried legions of the new reforestation army.

Is it better to bid them pursue the mighty footprints of tree-felling Paul Bunyan and his Ox Babe—last of the American demigods? So long as the oak leaves in Dodona rustle ambiguously toward such easy questions, it seems safer to let the lawless trees continue to make and break their own legal fetters.

NOTES TO MACNEIL ESSAY

[1] So thought the false accusers of the chaste Susanna when the mastic tree and the holm tree gave occasion to the youthful Daniel for the first successful essay at the art of cross-examination of which I am aware. So thought the wicked when a king dispensed saintly justice under an oak tree in Vincennes.

[2] Thomas v. Winchester (1852) 6 N. Y. 397.

[3] References are to Laws of Manu (Bühler trans.) 25 Müller (ed.) *Sacred Books of the East.*

[4] Laws of Manu IV, 39, p. 135.

[5] *Ibid.* IV, 73, p. 140.

[6] *Ibid.* VI, 26, p. 203.

[7] *Ibid.* V, 6, p. 170. Compare maple syrup and the eternal war between parent and child over chewing-gum. Extracts "from pure flowers, roots and fruit" are permitted.—V, 10, p. 171.

[8] *Ibid.* V, 40, p. 175.

[9] *Ibid.* XII, 75, p. 500.

[10] *Ibid.* VII, 76, p. 228.

[11] *Ibid.* VII, 131, p. 237.

[12] *Ibid.* VIII, 246, 247, p. 298. Compare the puzzling treatment of "line trees" and "boundary trees" in English and American cases, sec. 4 *infra.*

[13] *Ibid.* IX, 265, 266, p. 389.

[14] *Ibid.* VIII, 285, p. 304.

[15] *Ibid.* VIII, 289, p. 305. The Hindu deity's ability to override the distinctions between real and personal property helped him to avoid England's difficulties in extending the protection of criminal law to trees. See 4 Bl. Comm. 233, 245–246.

[16] *Ibid.* XI, 65, p. 443; XI, 167, p. 465. See also penances for injuries to trees and plants at XI, 143, 145, p. 459.

[17] References are to Frederick Goodwin, *The XII Tables* (London, 1886).

[18] *Ibid.* p. 22, T. VII, fr. 2, citing D. 10.1.13.

[19] *Ibid.* p. 23, T. VII, fr. 9, citing D. 43. 37.1.9. Compare this brevity, clarity, and certainty with the English-American case law on "Noxious Trees," sec. 3 *infra,* and "Invading Roots and Boughs," sec. 5 *infra.*

[20] *Ibid.* p. 23, T. VII, fr. 10. What California lawyer dare give an unqualified opinion (citing authority) on what our law on this may be? *Cf.* "Invading Roots and Boughs," sec. 5 *infra.*

[21] *Ibid.* p. 24, T. VIII, fr. 11, citing Pliny, H.N.xviii.1. The learned author suggests that, before the Lex Aquilia (B.C. 287), no *damnum injuria* protected the thing attached to or severed from realty; hence the need for a special remedy. So Manu's way was simpler than Rome's as well as England's. Other references to Roman tree law occur in 3 Kent, Commentaries (Holmes, ed.; 1873) 438 note (*a*); and in Pound, *Juristic Science and Law* (1918) 31 Harv. L. Rev. 1047, 1049–1050.

[22] References are to 1 Thorpe, *Ancient Laws and Institutions of England* (by Royal command under direction of the Commissioners of Public Records, 1840).

[23] *Ibid.* p. 71. Laws of King Alfred, sec. 12. See index heading, "Hewing or burning another's trees," for several other penalties in early English law.

[24] *Ibid.* p. 71. This reminds us of a *deodand* and I have endeavored unsuccessfully to refresh my recollection of examples of trees treated as *deodands.* My most learned preceptor suggests that I may have confused a law of Draco's regarding the right of kindred to the falling bough which kills the traveler. Knowing none of Draco's laws, I could not confuse them with anything. Blackstone confines the *deodand* to chattels personal. I suppose that a tree would have been too much "of the earth" for the analogy to be arguable before him, although he cites Aeschines to the effect that the well which drowned a man must be filled up. (I saw where just that had been done in a small Tuscan town, except that it was a woman who was drowned.) 1 Bl. Comm. (Sharswood, ed.; 1895), 300, and see Christian's note. See also for analogies Pound, *Outlines of Lectures on Jurisprudence,* p. 22. I found no light on tree law in the Twelve Tables of Gortyna or the Code of Hammurabi.

[25] *Ibid.* p. 379. Laws of King Cnut: Secular ordinance, sec. 5. Strong in conviction, prompt in action is the prophet who cuts down the sacred grove. Ordinarily in our law you must give me notice before you use self-help to abate a nuisance caused by me. But with respect to your right to lop my invading boughs without notice, see "Invading Roots and Boughs," sec. 5, *infra.*

[26] *Ibid.* p. 600. Laws of King Henry I, Chap. xc. SI QUIS VOLENS ALIQUOS INTER SE DIMICANTES DIVIDAT. Sec. 6.

[27] *Ibid.* p. 600, sec. 7.

[28] On the maxim, which arises as a gloss to Bracton's text, see 7 Holdsworth, *History of English Law* (1926) 485–486; Elwes v. Brigg Gas Co. (1886) L. R. 33 Ch. D. 562 (the maxim inapplicable to a buried "pre-historic boat"); State v. Martin (1906) 141 N. C. 832, 53 S. E. 874.

[29] Penhallow v. Dwight (1810) 7 Mass. 34 (standing ripened corn is personal property as between heir and executor, or for purposes of levy of execution). Compare the felled hemlock trees lying in place which pass on conveyance of the land. Brackett v. Goddard (1866) 54 Me. 309.

[30] See examples of determinable fees in Challis' *Real Property* (ed. 3, 1911) 256. "As long as such a tree shall grow . . . during the time that such a tree shall grow . . . as long as such a tree stands."

[31] These "are timber, throughout all England; and other trees are timber in particular parts of the country, by special custom." Craig, *Legal and Equitable Rights and Liabilities as to Trees and Woods* (London 1866) 11. Several pages of examples follow.

[32] Krishnarao v. Babaji (1899) I. L. R. 24 Bombay 31, by Parsons, J.: ". . . a mango tree which is primarily a fruit tree might not always come within the term [immovable], but in this respect the custom of a locality has to be considered." For discussion of this and other tree cases, see Haribans Sahai, *Immoveable Property: Standing Timber.—II.* (July 16, 1906) 3 Allahabad L. J. 213, 217.

[33] Thomas v. Sorrell (1674), Vaughan's Rep., 330, 351. This was just prior to the Statute of Frauds. But similarly when the Dame family orally decided to treat a house as a chattel, the court treated it like a chattel. Dame v. Dame (1859) 38 N. H. 429. I have trouble, however, in reconciling such decisions with the implications of the laconic doctrine of Coke in Liford's Case (11 Co. Rep. 46b, 50a) where "it was said, that timber trees cannot be felled with a goose quill." *A fortiori,* none save Paul Bunyan can sever them with spoken words.

[34] See Flett, *Property in Growing Trees* (1895) 40 Cent. L. J. 230.

[35] See "Boundary or Line Trees," sec. 4 *infra.*

[36] Smith v. New England Aircraft Co., Inc. (1930) 270 Mass. 511, 170 N. E. 385.

[37] Lemmon v. Webb [1895] A. C. 1, affirming decision of Court of Appeals [1894] 3 Ch. 1.

[38] County of Santa Barbara v. More (1917) 175 Cal. 6, 164 Pac. 895, where the conflicting authorities are collected.

[39] Cal. Stats. (1927) 530 amending Penal Code sec. 384a.

[40] Opinion of Justices, 103 Me. 506 (1907); for an interesting exercise of municipal power to prevent cutting of pine trees, see Town Council of Summerville v. Pressley (1889) 33 S. C. 56, 11 S. E. 545.

[41] Gulf, Colorado & Santa Fe Ry. Co. v. Oakes (1900) 94 Tex. 155, 58 S. W. 999. A Texas statute "directed solely against railroad companies" which prescribed a penalty in favor of adjoining landowners for permitting Russian thistles or Johnson grass to mature on the railroad right of way was upheld against attacks under the due process and equal protection clauses by a divided court in Missouri, Kansas & Texas Ry. Co. v. May (1904) 194 U. S. 267, 24 Sup. Ct. 638.

[42] Giles v. Walker (1890) 24 Q. B. D. 656, 657; per Coleridge, L. J. "There can be no duty between adjoining occupiers to cut the thistles, which are the natural growth of the soil."

[43] Sparke v. Osborne (1908) 7 Commonw. L. Rep. 51, High Court of Australia. This case uses the statute involving the *Opuntia vulgaris* (not the same variety of *Opuntia* as any of the southern California prickly pears) for one of the most searching studies of the relations of neighbors in respect of trees and weeds to be found in the books.

[44] City of St. Louis v. Galt (1903) 179 Mo. 8, 77 S. W. 876, 63 L. R. A. 778. The court admits that what is a weed in one place may be a flower in another. "It is a matter of common knowledge that decaying vegetable matter produces disease." Malaria is cited as an example.

[45] The court firmly resisted the city's contention that sunflowers could be weeds. One wisely hesitates to abuse sunflowers in open court. Particularly should this be so when one's next-door neighbor is often called the "Sunflower State" and has selected said flower as an emblem of power (Kans. Laws [1903], ch. 479, sec. 1, p. 725). When aforetime a stranger asked another, "Sirrah! Do you prefer red roses or white roses?," wise men often replied, "Whichever is your favorite, gentle Sir!" Note that when the modern sovereign raises a "weed" to share the throne under the title and honor of "State Flower," even the overriding prerogative of the "emergency clause" may be invoked. See Legislation Note—Emergency Legislation (1931) 44 Harv. L. Rev. 851, 854, citing Session Laws So. Dak. (1903) ch. 219, p. 293 (the Pasque Flower—*Anemone patens*—with the motto "I lead") and Colo. Laws (1899) ch. 139, p. 349 (the white and lavender columbine). I have not been able to find any contemporaneous legislation for the protection of these flowers which would lend point to the assertion of emergency.

[46] See Town Council of Summerville v. Pressley (1889) 33 S. C. 56. The opinion is very valuable and affords hints to our sovereigns of cheaper possibilities of restricting farm production than many of those currently advocated. The police power over rice culture on grounds of health developed early. See Green v. Mayor of Savannah (1849) 6 Ga. 1.

[47] Even here the falling tree carries far vaster immunity than the falling wall, cornice, or other man-made thing. Noble v. Harrison (1926) 2 K. B. 332; Chambers v. Whelen, 44 F. (2d) 340 (C. C. A. 4th, 1930). *Contra:* Brandywine Hundred Realty Co. v. Cotillo,

55 F. (2d) 231 (C. C. A. 3d, 1931). However, the interesting juristic place of trees in or near the public highway should be a story in itself.

[48] L. R. 4 Exch. Div. 5 (1878). In the highly questionable case of Pickering v. Rudd (1815) 1 Starkie 56, the fact that my Virginian creeper [it was a tree to Lord Ellenborough] growing on the wall of your home and barber shop, though "very ornamental to the prospect" from my house, was "noxious" and "mischievous to some extent" to your premises, was admitted by the pleadings.

[49] Per Sutherland, J., in Village of Euclid v. Ambler Realty Co. (1926) 272 U. S. 365, 388.

[50] Emphasis is sometimes laid upon whether the tree is "planted" by defendant or his predecessor in title or is "natural growth."

[51] A polite way of hinting that it may be "sheep herders' doctrine."

[52] (1911) 81 N. J. L. 1, 79 A. 883.

[53] The case seems to me opposed to the weight of American authority. See sec. 5, "Invading Roots and Boughs," *infra*. Compare South Carolina's tenderness for conifers at the expense of both liberty and rice in Town Council of Summerville v. Pressley, *supra* note 46. Perhaps the power of trees meets its match when so ancient, revered, and frequently hallowed an institution as the well is the other real party in interest.

[54] Buckingham v. Elliott (1884) 62 Miss. 296.

[55] Fry, J., in Watson v. Gray, L. R. 14 Ch. D. 192 (1880), lists the following: (1) tenancy in common; (2) ownerships in severalty; (3) sole ownership of wall by *A* subject to *B's* easement; (4) ownerships in severalty with mutual cross-easements.

[56] Pound, *Juristic Science and Law* (1918) 31 Harv. L. Rev. 1047, 1049–1053, also *Interpretations of Legal History*, p. 89. Query: Is there not also involved a Roman notion (discussed in Skinner v. Wilder [1865] 38 Vt. 115) that neighborly amenity requires me to keep back from the line a respectful distance in my planting contrasted with our notion that only the sovereign can force us, with difficulty, to "set back" either buildings or trees? In Bliss v. Ball (1868) 99 Mass. 597, where defendant justified girdling non-invading maple trees on the highway easement because their shade "made his house damp and unhealthy," the court in sustaining the huge (in tree cases) verdict of $400 went almost out of its way to say: "As against adjoining proprietors, the owner of a lot may . . . cover it with a thick forest. . . . It is no violation of their rights."

[57] (1697–8) 1 Ld. Raym. 737; same case 3 Wilson 120.

[58] Popham 161; same case *sub nom.* Millen v. Fawdry, Latch 119.

[59] Rolle 141 ([1620] K. B. 17 Jac. 1). Three years later, however, the same court in *Anon.*, 2 Rolle 255, held that a true line tree deriving nourishment from both parcels was held in tenancy in common.

[60] "corps del maine part del' arbor."

[61] Bracton is cited. Dean Pound, *op. cit., supra* note 56, at 1049, calls this an error, since Bracton followed the Institutes verbatim. The explanation probably lies in the note to printed editions of Bracton mentioned by Holdsworth: "*Quicquid plantatur, seritur, vel inaedificatur, Omne solo cedit, radices si tamen egit.*"—*7 History of English Law* 485.

[62] Moody & Malkin 112 (C. P. *nisi prius* 1827). The reporter's note (p. 114) influenced later American cases. See, *e.g.*, Dubois v. Beaver (1862) 25 N. Y. 123.

[63] Griffin v. Bixby (1841) 12 N. H. 454. I infer that the trees were felled and removed. The line trees involved were natural woodland growth marked as monuments. They were analogized to the tenancies in common of mete stones, *pro metis et bundis*, Co. Litt. 200, *b* and of old party walls by common user.

[64] Relyea v. Beaver (N. Y. Sup. Ct. 1861) 34 Barb. 547, which became on appeal Dubois v. Beaver (1862) 25 N. Y. 123.

[65] On strict common law theories of procedure it seems to me that trespass would lie *if* the relationship is tenancy in common, but that if we follow the analogy of cross-easements in a party wall the action would be trespass on the case. Probably, however, the precedents for trespass were too well established to make the point arguable.

[66] He distinguishes line trees from party walls, but apparently is considering only one of the four types of party wall, viz.: each owns his portion in severalty subject to cross-easement in favor of the other.

[67] Musch v. Burkhart (1891) 83 Iowa 301, 48 N. W. 1025. The facts are a bit blind in respect to whether the trees were so planted by one owner on his own account or pursuant to some mutual arrangement. The fact that plaintiff had valued the trees at $200 did not make the legal remedy adequate.

[68] Robinson v. Clapp (1894) 65 Conn. 365, 32 A. 939; (1896) 67 Conn. 538, 35 A. 504. The second hearing upheld the discretion of the trial judge in refusing to enjoin defendant from cutting the part of the trunk upon his own soil even though the tree would be killed. A balancing of the interests indicated that plaintiff should rely on his damages at law.

[69] *Infra.* p. 388.

[70] The usual unity of possession of cotenants is wanting because the possession of each must be confined to the part that is on his side. Also (1) accounting is not possible between the cotenants where, as here, no fruit but only ornament and shade are involved. (2) No partition either in kind or by judicial sale is practicable. Further puzzles are that (1) the aliquot undivided shares of the cotenants are continually changing, and accurate determination thereof at any instant would often cost more than the tree was worth, and (2) a cotenancy in real property arising neither through descent, limitation, purchase, prescription, gift, grant, nor covenant is hard to tie into our scheme of conveyancing. See also arguments of practicability in Skinner v. Wilder (1865) 38 Vt. 115.

[71] I see no reason to suppose that a line tree is more or less of a line tree because it is (1) natural growth, (2) planted by either or both owners, (3) originally planted on one freehold but with the trunk gradually spreading so that it rises from both. I assume also that, at least under the Connecticut theory, each keeps as owner the wood or fruit cut or taken on his side of the line.

[72] The trial judge in Lyman v. Hale (1836) 11 Conn. 177, charged the jury that "the universal practice in Connecticut has been for each to take the fruit overhanging his own land."

[73] A Tit. Trees (E).

[74] See comment on Lemmon v. Webb, in (1895) 31 Canada L. J. (n.s.) 41.

[75] Popham 161 (K. B. 22 James I 16); same case, Millen v. Fawdry, Latch 119.

[76] 11 Conn. 177 (Sup. Ct. of Errors 1836).

[77] Kent, *op. cit., supra* note 21, at 438, note (*a*), calls it "the best considered, and is not only the latest, but the most simple and definite rule on the subject."

[78] "The other judges ultimately concurred in this opinion; Williams, Ch. J., having at first dissented, on the ground of a decision of the Superior Court in *Hartford* county . . . and the general understanding and practice in *Connecticut* among adjoining proprietors."

Accord with principal case: Skinner v. Wilder (1865) 38 Vt. 115, a fine combination of scholarship and country horse-sense—trespass *quare clausum fregit* with a count for trover lies where the invaded landowner takes the overhanging apples; Hoffman v. Armstrong (1866) 46 Barb. (N. Y.) 337. Verdict for $1000 sustained in action of battery. The adjoining landowner *A* had sought forcibly to prevent the picking of overhanging cherries by a representative of *B*, the owner of the trees, "standing on the premises or fence" of *B*. Affirmed (1872) 48 N. Y. 201.

[79] (1889) 78 Cal. 611, 618, 21 Pac. 366.

[80] See dicta in Lambert v. Bessey, Sir T. Raymond 421 (K. B. 32–33 Car. II). (I cut my hedge of thorns; they fell on your land *ipso invito*. It was a trespass when they fell and when I entered to retake them); also same case Bessey v. Olliot, *loc. cit.* 467 (K. B. 34 Car. II). Parker, J., in Newkirk v. Sabler (1850) 9 Barb. (N. Y.) 652, 655, puts three pretty cases. If my tree blows down and falls on your land I may enter and retake it. The same is true of my fruit. "But if the owner of a tree cut the loppings so that they fall on another's land, he can not be excused for entering to take them away, on the ground of necessity, because he might have prevented it."

[81] *E.g.*, Pollock, *Torts* (ed. 5; 1897) 562—such invasion a nuisance whether the tree be noxious or not.

[82] Smith v. Giddy (1904) L. R. 2 K. B. 448, is dead against me. Elm and ash trees overhanging and interfering with the growth of fruit trees may invoke damages and injunction. Brock v. Connecticut and Passumpsic Rivers R. R. Co. (1862) 35 Vt. 373, is hardly in point. The court approved an injunction for the farmer against the railroad's willow hedge. But apparently the railroad had only an easement and this may well have been an excessive user thereof. The court expressly reserves decision respecting the problem should it arise between adjoining farmers.

[83] My cases begin with Croke, J.'s, dictum in Morrice v. Baker, 3 Bulstrode 196 (K. B. 10 Jac. 1).

[84] Lemmon v. Webb (1895) A. C. 1; (1894) 3 Ch. 1. A truly fascinating case, whether upon the spirited argument before Kekewich, J., on appeal to the Court of Appeal, or in the House of Lords. The costs and expenses must have been several hundred times the money interests involved. As a psychological matter it is interesting to see that every judge involved *wished* to decide in favor of the loser. Note the handling of the problems of costs.

[85] Perhaps this is because of the fact that in the usual tree case the "nuisance" may be abated without entering another's close. I infer that there is an "incomplete" privilege to enter if necessary to lop boughs. Otherwise with respect to high boughs the remedy becomes dust and ashes in the mouth. In such cases the careful lawyer will urge prior notice and request for removal. Notice is better in *every* case.

[86] (1881) 24 Hun. (N. Y.) 405.

[87] Note that the maple leaf is the Canadian emblem.

[88] See also Harndon v. Stultz (1904) 124 Iowa 440, 100 N. W. 329. Injunction against willows denied despite their making substantial amount of farm land unproductive. They would have been line trees but for defendant's disclaimer. Self-help is sanctioned for a specified period conditioned on there being no unnecessary damage to defendant's land.

[89] Grandona v. Lovdal (1886, Dept. 1) 70 Cal. 161, 16 Pac. 623; Grandona v. Lovdal (1889, Bk.) 78 Cal. 611, 21 Pac. 366.

[90] Note that if my brick wall through fire came to slope a few inches over your lot, you could compel me to remove it (Meyer v. Metzler [1875] 51 Cal. 142). Here, however, the overhang hinders your raising your own building.

[91] You are given one unusual crumb of comfort. When you hew to the line, the prospective fuel and hop-poles are yours. So far as this applies to trees which are true line trees, this rule is well founded; otherwise it seems anomalous.

[92] (1898) 77 Mo. App. 262.

[93] I can only explain the variation as grounded upon the requirement of substantial harm as part of the cause of action.

[94] Michalson v. Nutting (1931) 275 Mass. 232, 175 N. E. 490.

[95] Bliss v. Ball, *supra* note 56.

THE CONSTITUTION AND RECOVERY LEGISLATION: THE RÔLES OF DOCUMENT, DOCTRINE, AND JUDGES

BY DOUGLAS B. MAGGS

WHEN FRANKLIN D. ROOSEVELT became President in March, 1933, there was an insistent demand for action to end or at least to alleviate the depression. It was a demand for action opposed to American customs and traditions, for action which would work fundamental alterations in basic American institutions. Faith in "natural economic forces" had waned. Governmental action interfering in economic affairs was sought. Action by the federal government, for local and state governments were obviously impotent. Prompt action. Roosevelt called for, and Congress enacted, the statutes known as the recovery legislation.[1] These statutes did effect a fundamental redistribution of legislative, governmental, and economic power. Congress delegated vast legislative power to the President, to his appointees, and (in effect) to associations of business men. The federal government invaded fields hitherto controlled exclusively by the states. Many of the powers of the managers of business enterprises were transferred to associations of those managers and to public officials. Whether the recovery legislation has been or will be efficacious in ending or even in alleviating the depression are questions with which this paper is not concerned. It is concerned with assertions which have been made as to its constitutionality.

That the Supreme Court of the United States will uphold all the recovery legislation and most of the official action thereunder is the conclusion reached by those commentators whose writings reveal what I consider to be the view generally accepted by informed persons as to the relative importance, in the decision of constitutional cases, of the written Constitution, the doctrines of constitutional law, and the statesmanship of the judges. The relative importance of those three factors is, it seems to me, misconceived by other commentators who conclude that much of the recovery legislation is clearly unconstitutional or that the Supreme Court can uphold important parts of it only by distinguishing or overruling and repudiating past decisions and doctrines in such a way as to subject its members to accusations of intellectual dishonesty and to ridicule and contempt. That which this group misconceives is not explicitly dealt with by the other group. There seems, then, to be a need for an explicit discussion of the relative importance of judge, doctrine, and document in constitutional law cases. This paper is an attempt to meet that need and to indicate what will be the relative importance of those factors in the decision of the constitutional questions raised by the recovery legislation.

THE CONSTITUTION—DOCTRINE—THE JUDGES

I

UNDOUBTEDLY most of the recovery legislation is "unconstitutional," if that word be given the meaning it has in England. There is, in England, no written constitution; there are no legal limitations upon the power of Parliament; no statute enacted by Parliament is ever treated as void by the courts on the ground that it is inconsistent with the British Constitution. Yet there is a British "Constitution" and it is not unusual for a member of Parliament to urge in opposition to a proposed statute that it is "unconstitutional." He means that, in his opinion, the proposed statute is opposed to British customs and traditions, that its enactment would effect a fundamental alteration in basic British institutions, that it would change something which he and, he thinks, most other Englishmen, had regarded as permanent. Such a *proposed* statute is "unconstitutional," in the English sense. But if and when it is enacted, the statute is no longer unconstitutional. Its enactment has altered the British "Constitution."

According to American usage, to say that a statute is unconstitutional is to predict that the judges will treat it as void. There is an American "Constitution" in the English sense—the aggregate of American institutions, customs, traditions; it is the primary interest of the student of political economy and of the lawyer *qua* student of political economy. But our judges do not treat as void statutes which are inconsistent with that "Constitution." The Constitution upon the basis of which they do treat statutes as void consists of a written document and the doctrines of constitutional law. Large segments of American institutions, customs, and traditions are not rendered immune from legislative change by that document and those doctrines. Nevertheless, it is, I believe, in large part due to an unconscious confusing of the two senses of the word "unconstitutional," that many conservatives, distrustful of anything new, are now attaching that epithet to much of the recovery legislation.[2]

II

The constitutional validity of *some* statutes can be predicted with assurance from the words of the written Constitution—the document—alone. It contains some clauses so worded that practically no construction or interpretation is needed. Any intelligent reader with some knowledge of history prior to 1789, when the Constitution was adopted, can predict accurately what applications the Supreme Court will make of those clauses.[3]

Most of the clauses in the document, however, are not so worded. Congress, for example, is empowered "to regulate Commerce with foreign Nations, and among the several States."[4] What laws are "regulations"? What activities are "Commerce"? What commerce is "Commerce with foreign Nations, and among the several States"? Here the inquirer may not rest content with the document. He must turn to the Supreme Court reports. They will reveal what doctrines the Court has derived by construction and interpretation from the commerce clause.

The Constitution, then, comprises the document and also the doctrines which the Supreme Court justices derive from it by construction or interpretation. These two parts of the Constitution are partially independent, since construction and interpretation are not processes which yield the same results to all persons. The doctrines derive, not from the document alone, but also from the judges' social, economic, and political philosophies. Within limits set by the extensibility and contractibility of the words used in the light of the known relevant historical data, the construer or interpreter of a clause in the Constitution (or a statute, or will, or other document) is free to pronounce and should pronounce a construction or interpretation which will lead to results he believes to be desirable. Within the specified limits, the judge creates constitutional law not found in the document. And he does this with intellectual honesty and without usurping the authority conceded to the written Constitution. The limits vary for each clause; they are usually, because most of the clauses are phrased in general terms, extremely wide. Within those limits, the judge is called upon to be a statesman creating wise constitutional law, making wise decisions.[5]

The judge may exceed these limits. He may err in determining them. More important, he may intentionally usurp the authority generally conceded to the document. Regard for the public welfare under the conditions of today—conditions vastly different from those of 1789—may prompt him to do so. He may believe that, had the framers of the document foreseen the conditions of today, they would have laid down rules other than those they did lay down. Realizing the extreme difficulty of securing an amendment to the document by the method it prescribes, he may well find in these considerations irresistible temptations to surreptitious judicial amendment.[6]

Nor is this all. I have distinguished two parts of the Constitution—the document and the doctrines which the Supreme Court justices derive from it by construction or interpretation. In the creation of the second part, the words of the written Constitution—the document—have played and do play an important rôle. *There is a third part of the Constitution the content of which derives not at all from the document.* The judges have held since the latter part of the nineteenth century that certain clauses of the document authorize them to pronounce doctrines not deducible by construction or interpretation from the document.[7] The due process clauses of the Fifth and Fourteenth Amendments, they hold, authorize them to declare invalid as unconstitutional any statute not specifically authorized by other clauses of the document, which they deem arbitrary, capricious, or unreasonable. Under them, the judges pronounce doctrines as to the reasonableness of statutes relating to procedure, to jurisdiction to tax, to the regulation of public utility rates, to any and every subject—doctrines constituting in no sense of the word construction or interpretation of language found in the written document.[8] In pronouncing these doctrines, which constitute the third and last part of the Constitution, the judges act wholly as statesmen.[9]

To summarize to this point, the Constitution upon the basis of which the Supreme Court will treat a statute as void consists of the written document and of the doctrines of constitutional law which the judges will apply. These doctrines are of two kinds: doctrines which the judges of the past have derived or the judges of today will derive by construction or interpretation from the document; and doctrines, the content of which derives not at all from the document, announced under the authority held by the judges to be conferred upon them by the due process clauses. In creating these doctrines, the judges are called upon to be statesmen; with respect to doctrines of the first kind, their statesmanship is limited by the words of each clause and the known relevant historical data, but with respect to doctrines of the second kind their statesmanship is wholly unlimited. Moreover, doctrines purporting to be derived by construction or interpretation from the document may be, on the contrary, the result of usurpation by the judges, perhaps impelled by motives of statesmanship, of the authority conceded by all to the document. As against the words of the document, the part played by the statesmanship of the judges bulks large.

III

There are other considerations which make the rôle of the judges as statesmen even more important.

In the first place, the existence of doctrines announced and decisions rendered by their predecessors, even when the judges of today adhere to them, does not narrow as much as is sometimes assumed, their freedom to reach results they believe to be desirable. There is considerable room for statesmanship in the development and application of accepted doctrines and decisions;[10] the doctrines and decisions do not destroy, but merely limit, the freedom of the judge to decide as he thinks he ought.[11] Moreover, examination of the Supreme Court reports reveals that as to many matters the Court has laid down conflicting doctrines and rendered conflicting decisions without admitting the existence of the conflict. As to many subjects both doctrine and decisions are confused. This confusion, this multiplicity and heterogeneity of precedent, permits the judges of today to select that one of existing doctrines, those past decisions, which will indicate in the case before them the decision which they think wise.

Secondly, many of today's doctrines of constitutional law embody tests of such a nature that the doctrine does little, if anything, more than direct the judges to decide the case before them as they think best. As will appear later, this is true of most of the doctrines pronounced under the due process clauses, which do little more than ring the changes on the word "unreasonable"; it is true of the doctrine which has to do with the delegation of power by Congress to the President and others; it is frequently true of doctrines allocating power between the federal government and the states. Where doctrines embody such tests not only do they restrict judicial statesmanship hardly at all, decisions applying them are authoritative only for the narrow points decided and later cases can be easily distinguished from them.

Finally, the rôle of the judges as statesmen is tremendously increased by the fact that the Supreme Court's tradition permits and modern practice makes not unusual the repudiation of doctrine and the overruling of past decisions.[12] Changes in the judges' approach which have occurred in the past twenty years or so make this of especial significance today. The opinions of Mr. Justice Holmes and Mr. Justice Brandeis and the writings of commentators such as Thomas Reed Powell have brought it about that the judges of today are more fully conscious than were their predecessors that what doctrines shall be created, what decisions rendered, has depended and does depend more upon the wisdom of the judges than upon the wording of the document. This realization, coupled with the contagious effect of Mr. Justice Holmes's skepticism as to the power of any human being to achieve ultimate wisdom,[13] has made some of the judges less willing than were their predecessors to veto changes in our institutions deemed by Congress to be necessary. Coupled with Mr. Justice Brandeis's insistence that the judges' decisions will be wise ones only if they inform themselves fully as to the facts, to the needs the questioned legislation was enacted to meet,[14] the judges' realization that their task is that of statesmen has made some of them more willing than were their predecessors to reëxamine their initial uninformed disapproval of questioned legislation. Realizing that they are statesmen attempting to reach wise decisions, some of the judges are today influenced less by traditionally accepted ideas about the respective spheres of government and business, of state and federal governments, of Congress and the President, and more by the growth and general acceptance of new ideas concerning the proper allocation of those spheres. For all these reasons, the judges' deference to the decisions and doctrines of their predecessors has been lessened. For if those decisions and doctrines were not deductions from the written Constitution, but merely the wisdom of the judges of yesterday, they should not be binding upon the legislatures or judges of today—surely not if they were pronounced by judges who had not fully informed themselves as to the facts, or if since their pronouncement the factual situation has changed, or if they were the result of views of policy which have become outmoded. And to the extent that the deference of the judges to precedent has been lessened, the freedom of the judges of today to act as statesmen is increased.

IV

All that I have written sums up to this: The freedom of the judges of today to decide cases as they think best (resulting from the part their own wisdom plays in construing and interpreting clauses in the written Constitution, in pronouncing doctrines under the due process clauses, in the development and application of doctrines and past decisions, in determining whether or not to repudiate old doctrine and overrule past decisions) is so great that their statesmanship plays a far greater part in the determination of what statutes are constitutional than do either the words of the document or the pronouncements of their predecessors.

The judges, like other statesmen, have been influenced by prevailing sentiment with respect to "the historical rights of Englishmen," "Anglo-Saxon" traditions of individual liberty, and American traditions, customs, and institutions.[15] But, again like other statesmen, they have felt the needs of a society which has become more and more unlike the America of pre-Revolutionary or pre-Civil War days.[16] Their statesmanship has reflected that sentiment and those needs, as it has reflected the rest of their social, economic, and political philosophies. Consequently, although the Supreme Court justices could veto practically any statute, the area within which they are likely to veto statutes that are likely to be enacted by legislators who are products of the same general environment as the judges, is fairly narrow. Moreover, the area is further restricted by a consideration not yet mentioned—the fact that past decisions upholding Congressional legislation are less likely to be overruled than are past decisions invalidating it.

As a single economic and social unit has been fashioned out of a congeries of quasi-independent states, the federal government has extended its control further and further over matters once within the exclusive control of the states. With few and minor exceptions the Supreme Court has been able to hold these extensions of federal control valid. It has permitted extension after extension, each going farther than the preceding ones. And *once the Court has upheld an extension of federal control it has never retraced its steps and overruled that holding*. Similarly, as a simple agricultural society has become a complex, interdependent, industrial one, government (federal and state) has gradually limited the liberty and the property rights of individuals and corporations. There have been notable exceptions, but more than 99 per cent of this regulation has been upheld. Decisions invalidating particular regulations have been overruled from time to time, but *once the Court has upheld an extension of governmental regulation of personal and property rights it has never overruled that holding*. In short, decisions limiting governmental power, decisions denying federal power, are likely to be overruled; decisions upholding governmental power, in general, or federal power, are not. Moreover, no delegation of power by Congress has ever been invalidated; successive delegations, each greater than the preceding, have been upheld.[17]

What statutes the Supreme Court justices are likely to veto depends primarily, then, on what statutes have been upheld in the past. Secondary in importance, because likely to be overruled, are the past decisions invalidating statutes and the doctrines announced in those decisions. In some few cases, the words of the document play an important part. Prevalent attitudes, in which the judges share, toward existing institutions bulk large. Within the limits which these considerations tend to fix, what statutes are constitutional depends upon what nine men happen to be justices of the Supreme Court of the

United States, upon their social, economic, and political philosophies they hold, and upon the extent to which they believe judges should go in vetoing legislation.[18] Their choices are not based solely upon their judgments concerning the wisdom of the particular statute before them: their decision will be a precedent tending to establish the validity or invalidity of other statutes already enacted or possible of future enactment; the judges are influenced, therefore, by their judgments concerning the wisdom of other statutes.

The judges' growing realization of the nature of their rôle and of the necessity of their being informed if their decisions are to be wise, their growing skepticism as to the finality of their own wisdom and even more of the wisdom of their predecessors, their tendency more and more to adopt a policy of laissez faire for legislatures and especially for Congress—these are the most significant developments in constitutional law today.

* * * * *

Three types of attack are made upon the constitutionality of the recovery legislation. It is contended that it unconstitutionally interferes with personal and property rights and with the freedom of business enterprisers to operate their businesses as they want to operate them, that it unconstitutionally delegates Congressional power to the President and to others, and that it involves invasions by the federal government of fields reserved by the Constitution to state control. Learned articles have appeared in several legal periodicals discussing in detail constitutional questions raised by these contentions. It is not the purpose of this paper to deal with them in detail. But I shall discuss each of the three types of questions separately, attempting to show, in the light of the foregoing exposition of the judicial process in constitutional cases, what will be, as to each, the rôle of the document, of doctrine, of the judges.

Attacks of the first type—contentions that the Constitution guarantees a minimum of individualism, that its mandate with respect to governmental control of business is laissez faire, and that the recovery legislation violates that guaranty and that mandate—are based wholly upon the doctrines (and decisions applying them) announced by the judges in the exercise of the authority which they have claimed, during the past half-century, is conferred upon them by the due process clauses. These attacks invoke neither the words of the document nor doctrines deducible by construction or interpretation (in any true sense of those words) from it; they invoke solely the doctrines which I have called the third part of the Constitution. To substantiate the position I have taken that these doctrines are wholly the result of the judges' statesmanship and not at all the result of construction or interpretation of the document in any true sense, I shall, before discussing the due process attacks upon the recovery legislation, attempt a review of so much of constitutional history as is necessary for a full understanding of the power claimed by the judges under the due process clauses.

THE HISTORY OF THE JUDGES' POWER UNDER THE DUE PROCESS CLAUSES

I

THE INITIAL ASSUMPTION by the judges of power to declare statutes unconstitutional is not adequately accounted for, as Mr. Chief Justice Marshall asserted it to be,[19] by the mere fact that there was a written Constitution. In France a written Constitution did not lead to judicial review of the constitutional validity of statutes. When the Constitution was adoped it was not generally accepted that law is a command of a political superior to a political inferior; the notion that law is that which commands the right, that law is discoverable, not made by human beings, was widely accepted. This identification of "ought" with "is" has a long history. Natural law, natural rights, deriving from Greek and Roman thought, persisting throughout and beyond the Middle Ages, have often meant more than "ought-to-be-law" or "ought-to-be-rights"; at many times throughout antiquity and the Middle Ages it was asserted that any human enactment violating natural law was not binding.[20] The colonists had cited Coke's claim of power for the courts to nullify Acts of Parliament contrary to "right reason" in support of their refusal to recognize English statutes hurtful to their pocket books. It is in the light of these ideas and of the then prevalent social compact theory, of Cicero, Grotius, Puffendorf, and Locke, that the Declaration of Independence with its inalienable rights is to be interpreted.[21] Impressed as they were with Montesquieu's notion that the judiciary was a branch of government coördinate with the legislature, it is easy to understand why the judges seized upon the written Constitution as empowering them to nullify statutes which they thought infringed the rights to secure which government was instituted.[22]

In the period immediately following the adoption of the federal Constitution, the really doubtful question was whether, in addition to invalidating statutes which they thought violative of constitutional provisions, the judges would nullify statutes which were inconsistent with their conceptions of natural law and natural rights. In 1798, in delivering the opinion of the Supreme Court in *Calder v. Bull,*[23] Mr. Justice Chase, by dictum, unequivocally claimed for the judges power to do this; Mr. Justice Iredell delivered a separate opinion protesting against the assumption of such power.[24] Iredell's rebuke did not silence the adherents of natural law. In 1810, in *Fletcher v. Peck,*[25] the Supreme Court held invalid a Georgia statute revoking a land grant, which had been procured by fraud, after the land had been bought by an innocent purchaser. Mr. Chief Justice Marshall stretched the impairment clause to cover the case.[26] But he did not place the decision upon the written Constitution alone; he expressed doubt whether the Georgia constitution's grant of "legislative power" to the state legislature authorized the revoking statute—whether power to enact such a statute could be said to be "legislative power"—and he definitely held, as an alternative ground of decision, that the revoking statute was void under "general principles which are common to our free institutions."[27] Mr. Justice Johnson, unwilling to stretch the impairment clause as his brethren had done, placed his concurrence in the decision solely on this ground—in his own words, "on a general principle, on the reason and nature of things; a principle which will impose laws even on the Deity."[28] *Fletcher v. Peck,* nevertheless, really marks the end of the judges' open avowal of power to nullify statutes not violative of the written constitutions because inconsistent with their conceptions of natural law. For it showed the availability, so far as state statutes were concerned, of the impairment clause as a peg for the views of Marshall and his federalist associates as to the sanctity of property rights.[29] That clause was extended still further; it became the basis for the doctrine that state legislatures may not impair vested rights.[30] This doctrine did not forbid all impairments of vested rights; in effect, it forbade only unreasonable impairments of them[31]—in other words, it forbade impairments worked by statutes inconsistent with the judges' conceptions of natural law.

The necessity of finding for invaded rights an origin which could be called "contractual," even in the broad sense that Marshall gave to that term, restricted the availability of the impairment clause as a peg for the invalidation of statutes upon the basis of natural law. As Jacksonian Democrats were appointed, Marshall gradually lost control of the Court, and the veto power exercised by the judges under the impairment clause at first ceased to expand and finally began to contract. In 1827, the Chief Justice and his never-failing adherent, Mr. Justice Story, were able to muster but one other of the Court's seven members to vote in favor of Webster's contention that the impairment clause should be extended so as to serve as a peg for the doctrine of the liberty of contract—for natural law objections to state bankruptcy laws applicable to debts contracted after their enactment.[32] In 1833, Marshall conceded that nothing in the federal Constitution prevented a state from taking private property for public use without compensation.[33] After Marshall's death, in 1837, the Supreme Court, under Taney's leadership, cut down the availability of the impairment clause by the adoption of the rule that public grants must be construed strictly against the grantee.[34] Until several decades after the Civil War, state legislation was not subject to invalidation by the Supreme Court upon the ground that it was inconsistent with natural law or invaded natural rights, *i.e.*, that it was unreasonable.[35]

II

Today, the due process clauses of the Fifth and Fourteenth Amendments[36] are held to render invalid all statutes, whether relating to procedure or substantive law, which the judges deem to be violative of natural law or natural rights. The words "life," "liberty," and "property" in those clauses have been given such extended meanings that every statute adversely affecting an individual is held to deprive him of one or another of them. Whether or not a statute is valid depends, therefore, wholly upon whether it is "law" within the meaning of that word as it is used in the due process clauses. And it is "law" only if the judges deem it to be not arbitrary, capricious, or unreasonable—*i.e., not inconsistent with their conceptions of natural law, not violative of what they deem to be fundamental, or natural, rights.* The subsidiary doctrines which have been laid down under the due process clauses are nothing more nor less than the judges' versions of natural law, of natural rights. The Taney court's limitation of Marshall's impairment clause doctrines was of no avail. The Supreme Court's final position gives it more power than even Marshall claimed for it; in all but theory, Mr. Justice Chase's claim of power for the judges to invalidate statutes not violative of the provisions of the written Constitution but inconsistent with the judges' conceptions of natural law and natural rights[37] has won out. How did this occur?

Most of the original state constitutions contained clauses forbidding deprivations of life, liberty, or property otherwise than by the law of the land. These clauses, copied after chapter 39 of Magna Carta, sometimes substituted "without due process of law" for "otherwise than by the law of the land." With one or two exceptions,[38] these clauses were at first held by the state courts to be, not restrictions upon the legislature, but merely directions that executive and judicial action must be in accordance with law, *i.e.,* either the common law or the law enacted by the legislature. Later they came to be regarded as limitations upon legislative power to alter and prescribe modes of procedure.[39] Finally, there was a revival in some state courts of the practice, already abandoned by the Supreme Court of the United States, of overthrowing statutes on natural law grounds. The state constitutions' grants of "legislative power" to state legislatures were said to embrace only the power to tax, the power of eminent domain, and the "police power." As a New York judge put it in 1843, the power delegated to the legislature by the clause granting it legislative power does not "reach the life, liberty, or property of a citizen . . . when the sacrifice is not demanded by a just regard for the public welfare"[40]—*i.e.,* by what the judges deem to be a just regard for the public welfare. The next step, an assertion that the law of the land and the due process clauses were a mandate to the judges to protect persons and property against unreasonable laws, was a short one.[41] This construction of the state constitution's due process and law of the land clauses was far from universal and was not unchallenged,[42] but it was stated as settled law, elaborated, and whole-heartedly approved by Judge Cooley in his *Constitutional Limitations*. This work, published in 1868, the year of the adoption of the Fourteenth Amendment, was for forty years at least the standard lawyer's and law student's text on constitutional law and was constantly cited and relied upon by the courts.

The due process clause of the Fifth Amendment, applicable to the federal government, had received no such construction when it was copied by the Joint Committee on Reconstruction and inserted in what became, in 1868, the Fourteenth Amendment. It was thought by Mr. Justice Story in 1833 to relate to modes of procedure only.[43] It had been invoked in but two cases, one in 1855 and another in 1857, and these cases had done nothing to clarify its meaning.[44] What, if any, limitation on the power of state legislatures, its framers, the Congress which proposed it, and the state legislatures which ratified it, intended the due process clause of the Fourteenth Amendment to have, has never been and probably never can be ascertained.[45]

It was twenty years after the adoption of the Fourteenth Amendment before the view that its due process clause authorized the judges to invalidate all statutes they thought to be arbitrary and unreasonable finally prevailed. In the end that view was asserted not only with respect to the due process clause in the Fourteenth Amendment but also with respect to that in the Fifth Amendment. Widespread acceptance of the views of state court judges in the forties and fifties given currency by Judge Cooley's universally read treatise, the rapid industrialization of the country and the never-ending advocacy of able counsel employed by corporations and individuals of great wealth and economic power to combat statutes regulating industry,[46] the convictions and dominating personality of Mr. Justice Field,[47] the judges' fright at the Granger and Populist movements and other rumblings of discontent—these are some of the influences which contributed to the result.

The development was marked by aberrations. It began with the first *Legal Tender Case*,[48] decided in 1870, which held invalid, by a vote of four to three, the federal Legal Tender Act. Among other grounds of invalidity, the majority cited, as a makeweight, the due process clause of the Fifth Amendment. The invocation of this clause because of the alleged injustice of the law was denounced by Mr. Justice Miller as substituting "our ideas of policy for judicial construction, an undefined code of ethics for the Constitution, and a court of justice for the national legislature."[49] Two years later, the decision was overruled; Mr. Justice Field, now in dissent, not only disagreed with Miller's interpretation of the due process clause but went further and, quoting the language of Mr. Justice Chase in *Calder v. Bull* in 1798, reiterated the latter's claim for the judges of power to invalidate unjust laws even though they violated no provision of the written Constitution.[50] In 1874, in *Loan Association v. Topeka*,[51] with only one justice protesting, the Supreme Court did invalidate on natural law grounds, without reference to the Fourteenth Amendment or any other provision of the written Constitution, a Kansas statute authorizing a city to donate money to a manufacturing concern to encourage it to establish its works in the city. The opinion (written not by Field but by Miller!) invokes limitations upon the powers of legislatures "which grow out of the essential nature of all free governments," "implied reservations of individual rights, without which the social compact could not exist"; from them it deduces a rule that taxation must be for purposes deemed by the judges to be "public."[52] But in most cases before 1885, Field's views were expressed in dissenting opinions. The Fourteenth Amendment was first invoked in 1873 in the *Slaughter House Cases*.[53] The majority, over the dissent of Field and three other justices, who relied more upon the privileges and immunities clause of the Fourteenth Amendment[54] than upon its due process clause, held that the grant of a monopoly to certain butchers in New Orleans did not infringe the constitutional rights of other butchers; they insisted that the Fourteenth Amendment was not intended to make the United States Supreme Court "a perpetual censor upon all legislation of the States, on the civil rights of their own citizens, with authority to nullify such as it did not approve as consistent with those rights, as they existed at the time of the adoption of this amendment."[55] Again, in *Munn v. Illinois*[56] and several companion cases,[57] decided in 1877, it was held, over Field's vehement dissents, that the Fourteenth Amendment did not prevent a state from fixing the rates to be charged not only by railroads but also by grain elevator operators and that when the state had fixed such rates the court had no power to review their reasonableness and to invalidate them if the judges thought them too low to yield a fair return on the property of the owner. But Field's dissents persisted. Majority opinions, although upholding questioned statutes, began to meet him on his own ground—began to attempt to demonstrate the reasonableness of the statutes. In 1898, in *Smyth v. Ames,*[58] the railroad attorneys finally persuaded the court to overrule the decision in *Munn v. Illinois* that the reasonableness of legislatively fixed rates was not subject to judicial review. Field's view of the power of the Supreme Court under the due process clauses had finally become unquestioned law.[59]

III

In the past decade, constitutional theory as to the power claimed by the judges under the due process clause has been simplified. Until then, there was much talk of the "police power." State statutes interfering with life, liberty, or property were said to be valid under the due process clause of the Fourteenth Amendment only if they were exercises of the power to tax, the power of eminent domain, or the "police power."[60] Countless attempts were made to define, or rather describe, the "police power." For a time there was controversy whether it extended only to the protection of the peace, good order, morals, and health of the community, or also to the promotion of the general welfare. There were disputes whether or not the federal government possessed "police power." By a curious confusion of ideas, it was suggested that Congress' power to tax was not subject to the limitation of reasonableness held to be created by the Fifth Amendment due process clause.[61] Now the term "police power" is obsolescent. The considerations formerly held to determine whether or not a statute was "within the police power" are now held to go to "reasonableness" and the due process clauses are held to require that every exercise of any governmental power, whether the general governmental powers retained by the states or the special powers delegated to the federal government, be reasonable. The extra term is being dropped.[62] Distinct bodies of doctrine have been developed concerned with what statutes dealing with particular subjects—*e.g.*, procedure, taxation, regulation of business—are reasonable and therefore "law" within the due process clauses.

To say, as I have said, that in creating these doctrines, in determining their content, the judges have been wholly free to act as statesmen does not disclose the influences that have induced the judges to pronounce the particular doctrines which they have pronounced. Negatively, it does assert that those doctrines have not been derived from the words of the document. It implies the part played by the accidental presence upon the Court of men with definite views as to what institutions the country should have,—as to what existing institutions must be left unaltered if the country is to persist. On the other hand the prevailing American emotional attachments to the "historical rights of Englishmen," to "Anglo-Saxon" traditions of individual liberty and individual rights, to American customs and institutions, would have been reflected in doctrine and decision whatever men had been upon the Court.[63]

Here, as elsewhere in constitutional law today, it is of the utmost significance that some of the judges, at least, are becoming increasingly unwilling to veto Congressional legislation on the basis of their own or their predecessors' wisdom. This fact is peculiarly important here because so much of existing due process doctrine embodies tests which do little more than direct the judge to decide cases as he thinks they ought to be decided.

THE RECOVERY LEGISLATION AND DUE PROCESS OF LAW

UNPRECEDENTEDLY drastic limitations upon the liberty of business enterprisers to operate their businesses as they want to operate them are imposed by the National Industrial Recovery Act and the Agricultural Adjustment Act and the subordinate legislation (the codes, etc.) authorized by them. The Securities Act and the banking and railroad legislation also constitute far-reaching extensions of governmental control over business. The calling in of gold coin, the reduction of the gold content of the dollar, and the annulment of the gold clauses in private and public contracts are striking interferences with the liberty and property of individuals. The expenditure of public funds for relief of banks, of industry, of farmers, of home owners, of the unemployed entails the exaction of money from taxpayers for unwonted uses.

One thing is certain. No clause of the written Constitution and no doctrine deducible by construction or interpretation therefrom prevents government from thus regulating business or from thus interfering with the liberty or property of individuals or corporations. The document and doctrines thus deducible therefrom furnish no basis for claims that the mandate of the Constitution with respect to governmental control of business is laissez faire. So far as they are concerned, the Constitution permits the adoption of any form of relationship between government and business. The document does guarantee certain fairly clearly defined individual rights,[64] but it is clear that the recovery legislation does not infringe the rights thus guaranteed.[65] Its constitutionality (apart from questions of the delegation of legislative power and of federal government interference in fields reserved to the states, which are considered in later sections) depends wholly upon the "third part" of the Constitution—the due process doctrines which derive not at all from the document. I shall attempt to state the principal questions which are likely to be raised and to indicate the extent to which their decision will depend upon the statesmanship of the Supreme Court justices.

I

That a statute expending funds derived from taxation is invalid unless the purpose of the expenditure is deemed by the judges to be a "public purpose" was first announced as a limitation upon government growing out of "the essential nature of all free governments";[66] later the doctrine was subsumed under the due process clause. Phrased as it is, this is one of the doctrines which involve a test that does little more than direct the judges to decide as statesmen would. Past decisions have upheld most questioned expenditures.[67]

So far as most of the statutes comprising the recovery legislation which authorize the expenditure of public funds are concerned, there is no way in which the constitutional question whether the expenditure is for a public purpose can be brought before the Court. The statutes under which the federal government has lent or given money to banks, industry, farmers, home owners, and the unemployed do not compel action or penalize nonaction by anyone other than the taxpayers from whom the money distributed is exacted. Except for the proceeds of the processing taxes, the funds expended are funds raised by general taxes. And the Supreme Court has held that a taxpayer has too remote and slight an interest in funds raised by general taxation to be entitled to question the validity of statutes authorizing their expenditure.[68] Nor can a state, as *parens patriae* of its citizen taxpayers, question such statutes.[69]

The money turned over to farmers under the Agricultural Adjustment Act is raised by a special tax—the processing tax. Persons from whom it is exacted, therefore, do have a sufficient interest to question whether it is being expended for what the judges deem to be a "public purpose." The answer to that question, it is obvious, will depend wholly upon the statesmanship of the judges.[70]

II

The calling in of gold coin and payment therefor of a smaller number of paper dollars than could be procured for the gold were there a free market, the reduction in the gold content of the dollar, the annulment of the gold clause in private and public contracts raise questions so unlike any question upon which the Supreme Court has ruled in the past, that no relevant due process doctrines or decisions exist. Consequently, the test of validity is the fundamental due process test—are the statutes, in view of needs to meet which they were enacted, arbitrary, capricious, and unreasonable or does their tendency to advance the public welfare outweigh the burdens they impose upon individuals? In the invalidation of statutes by reason of this test the judges must determine how far it is wise for them to go in preferring their own views of policy if these differ from those of Congress; in the application of such a test, statesmanship alone is called for.[71]

III

Some of the extensions of government control over industry are, it is clear in view of existing doctrine and past decisions, unlikely to be held invalid under the due process clause of the Fifth Amendment. The Securities Act, the Act providing for the insurance of bank deposits, and the Emergency Banking Act (which provides for limitations on banking and foreign exchange transactions) are similar to and are little if any more drastic interferences in the field of private enterprise than statutes which the Court has upheld in the past.[72]

There remain for consideration the attacks which will be made upon the National Industrial Recovery Act and the Agricultural Adjustment Act and the subordinate legislation thereunder. These Acts and the codes and licenses which to date have been promulgated under them contain provisions, binding upon some or all industries, which can be grouped under four heads: labor provisions, price-fixing provisions, production-limitation provisions, miscellaneous trade practice provisions.

Hours of work are limited, minimum wages are fixed, child labor is forbidden, employers are prohibited from interfering with their workmen's freedom of organization, a variety of regulations of working conditions are imposed. Past decisions, based upon the fundamental due process tests of reasonableness, of balancing the social gain against the restrictions upon liberty and property rights, make it practically certain that all the regulations of working conditions, the prohibition of child labor, and the limitation of hours of work will be upheld.[73] Past decisions invalidating the outlawry of "yellow dog" contracts[74] have recently been overruled in effect by a decision[75] which renders practically certain the upholding of the prohibition against interference by employers with the freedom of organization of employees. The fixing of minimum wages is the only labor regulation the upholding of which is at all doubtful. A 1923 decision by a narrowly divided Court held invalid the fixing of minimum wages for women.[76] Criticism of the holding has been almost entirely adverse.[77] The N.I.R.A. codes will not raise the question whether the 1923 decision should be overruled. Not only have conditions changed, but the social gains sought to be achieved are very different from those sought by the statute invalidated in 1923. Then the tendency, if any, of a local minimum wage to protect and promote the health and morals of women was held by five of the justices not to outweigh the interference with freedom involved. Whether a nation-wide minimum wage for men as well as women, intended not only to benefit the workers but also to benefit industry as a whole by creating, through increased purchasing power of the workers, a better market for the products of industry, is reasonable is a very different question—a question the answering of which involves statesmanship alone.

Prices for petroleum and for milk are now fixed directly; indirectly, the prices for certain agricultural products are sought to be raised by the processing tax; sales below cost or below a fair market value or below published price lists are forbidden in certain industries.[78] When this regulation was undertaken, doctrine invalidated governmental price fixing except in businesses "affected with a public interest" or "clothed with a public use." No satisfactory definition of these phrases had been formulated; in reality they were labels used after the judges, as statesmen, had decided to permit price fixing in a particular business.[79] Now this doctrine has been repudiated. Over the dissent of Justices McReynolds, Van Devanter, Sutherland, and Butler, the fixing of prices for milk by the State of New York was upheld on March 5, 1934, by Chief Justice Hughes and Justices Brandeis, Stone, Roberts, and Cardozo.[80] Writing the majority opinion, Mr. Justice Roberts said: "The phrase 'affected with a public interest' can, in the nature of things, mean no more than that an industry, for adequate reason, is subject to control for the public good."[81] The subdoctrine repudiated, the fundamental due process test of reasonableness is all that is left. Constitutionality depends upon the judges.

In the petroleum and lumber industries maximum production figures are set for each industry as a whole and quotas are allocated to individual producers; in the cotton and wool textile industries the number of hours of plant activity is limited; before the capacity of existing plants in the cotton textile, lace, ice, and some other industries may be increased, the equivalent of a certificate of public convenience and advantage must be procured. The only past decision relevant to the validity of these regulations is *New State Ice Co. v. Liebmann*.[82] There it was held by six of the justices (the Chief Justice and Mr. Justice Roberts voting with the four who constituted the minority in the *New York Milk Case*) that the requirement of a certificate of public convenience and advantage as a prerequisite to entrance into a business was permissible only in the case of businesses "affected with a public interest" and that the ice business in Oklahoma was not so affected. The *Milk Case* undermines this decision. Much of Mr. Justice Roberts' language in the latter case is reminiscent of Mr. Justice Brandeis' already classic dissent in the *Ice Case*.[83] It seems certain that the Court as at present constituted will regard all regulations as to limitation of production and entry into business as subject only to the fundamental due process test of reasonableness. Again constitutionality depends upon the statesmanship of the judges, and upon the extent to which they will prefer their own views of policy if these differ from those of Congress and the agencies to which Congress has delegated power to make such regulations.

The trade practices outlawed by the codes are practices some of which are regarded as injurious to consumers, some as injurious to competitors. No past decisions lay down doctrines particularizing the general due process test.

* * * * *

Due process decisions in the past, and the doctrines announced in them, gave some basis for claims that the Constitution's mandate with respect to governmental control of business was laissez faire. But so many regulatory statutes have been upheld, so many invalidating decisions overruled and doctrines repudiated, that there is today no basis for such claims. Moreover, doctrine at all times has been so phrased that any regulatory statute would be upheld if the judges thought the public interest involved was great enough to outweigh the interference with liberty and property involved. The rôle of the judges far overshadows the rôle of doctrine; the words of the document have never, in this field, played any part.[84]

THE RECOVERY LEGISLATION AND THE DELEGATION OF LEGISLATIVE POWER

MANY OF THE STATUTES which comprise the recovery legislation delegate legislative power to the President or to others. The N.I.R.A. codes are the most conspicuous example of the subordinate legislation which Congress has authorized.

The document does not expressly forbid the delegation of legislative power by Congress. Article I, Section 1, provides that "All legislative Powers herein granted shall be vested in a Congress of the United States." The judges have derived from these words, by construction and interpretation, a doctrine that legislative power is non-delegable. *But,* Congress has delegated important legislative powers to the President and to others many times. A number of these delegations have been questioned; none has ever been invalidated.[85] The delegations upheld have been labeled delegations of "quasi-legislative power" only.

The truth is that the complexity of the problems with which legislatures must deal today, the need for the particularization of general policies and for the formulation and frequent readjustment of subordinate policies and specific rules by informed experts, have made subordinate legislation an essential part of the machinery of government.[86] As Elihu Root has said, "the old doctrine prohibiting the delegation of legislative power has virtually retired from the field and given up the fight."[87]

Doubtless a Congressional enactment empowering the President to promulgate what laws he pleased upon any subject would be held invalid by the judges. Somewhere short of such a statute the judges will draw the line. The recovery legislation does leave to the President and the other delegates wider discretion than did any of the statutes upheld in the past. Whether, notwithstanding the exigency which led to their passage, they will be held to go too far, will depend upon the judges' statesmanship, not upon the document, existing doctrines, or past decisions.

THE RECOVERY LEGISLATION AND THE INVASION BY THE FEDERAL GOVERNMENT OF FIELDS RESERVED TO THE STATES

THE FEDERAL GOVERNMENT possesses only those powers delegated to it by the Constitution. An Act of Congress, or subordinate legislation or official action thereunder, will be held invalid unless it can be referred to powers conferred on Congress by the document. But by interpretation and construction of the document, the Supreme Court has discovered many powers not evident to one reading it. As the United States has become economically and socially more and more a single unit, the federal government has gradually extended its control and the Court has felt able to justify practically all these extensions.

I

Most of the statutes which comprise the recovery legislation are clearly within powers of Congress long recognized by the Court. To the currency and fiscal powers, held to result from the power to coin money, from the taxing power and from other powers, can be referred all the legislation and official action relating to currency and inflation, the invalidation of the gold clauses, the regulation of banks and of dealings in foreign exchange, the calling in of gold. For the greater part of this regulation, the commerce clause is also a possible peg. To a spending power expressly or impliedly conferred by the clause granting Congress the power to tax, can be referred the Farm Credit Act, the Home Owners' Loan Act, the Public Works Act, the Tennessee Valley Authority Act, the Civilian Conservation Corps Act, the Emergency Relief Act, the National Employment Service Act. The contention once made that the federal spending power may be exerted only in fields directly related to other powers possessed by the federal government has long been abandoned;[88] moreover, since these statutes authorize the expenditure of funds raised by general taxation only, no one will have sufficient interest to attack them.[89] To the commerce clause can be referred the Emergency Railroad Transportation Act and parts, at least, of the Tennessee Valley Authority Act; to that clause and to the power over the mails can be referred the Securities Act.

II

The National Industrial Recovery Act and the Agricultural Adjustment Act (with the possible exception of the processing tax levied under the authority of the latter) are, I believe, referable only to the commerce clause.[90] Applications of the subordinate legislation promulgated under these statutes may be attacked as federal interference in fields reserved by the Constitution to state control, but the statutory provisions authorizing the codes and licenses are not themselves subject to such attack. The N.I.R.A. provides that violation of a code shall be a criminal offense only if it occurs "in any transaction in or affecting interstate commerce." The A.A.A. authorizes licenses (imposing as conditions provisions comparable to those in the N.I.R.A. codes) for the handling of agricultural products "in the current of interstate or foreign commerce" only. Congress has expressed its intention that codes and licenses shall have the widest application it has power to give them. If a code or license cannot constitutionally be applied to a particular transaction, the statutes do not authorize its application thereto. Codes and licenses have been applied and are now being applied to transactions formerly controlled by state law. Are these applications violative of the Constitution and therefore of the statutes?

The document, doctrine, and past decisions leave it uncertain to what transactions the power of Congress extends. The document makes no attempt to define what activities are interstate (or foreign) commerce activities. Doctrine and past decisions make it clear that transportation of persons, things, or ideas across state lines falls within but does not exhaust the category. What other activities fall within it is far from clear. Moreover, doctrine makes it certain that Congress may regulate, under the commerce clause, some activities which do not themselves constitute interstate commerce, because of the effect those activities have upon interstate commerce activities; but doctrine does not make clear what non-interstate commerce activities Congress may thus regulate nor what effect they must have upon interstate commerce activities to render Congressional regulation of them permissible.

Decisions either upholding or invalidating state regulation of a particular activity are sometimes thought to indicate the field of Congressional competence under the Commerce clause. But since Congress may sometimes regulate intrastate commerce activities, it is clear that they do not. Moreover, decisions upholding or denying state competence as to a particular activity do not necessarily indicate even whether that activity is interstate or intrastate commerce. Interstate activities are affeced by intrastate activities and by regulations of the latter; the converse is also true. Doctrine asserts that state statutes are invalid if they "unduly" burden, obstruct, or interfere with interstate commerce activities. A state statute may be held invalid either because the activity it directly affects is interstate commerce (and its effect thereupon constitutes an "undue" interference therewith) or because, although the activity is intrastate commerce, this particular regulation of it indirectly affects and unduly interferes with other, interstate commerce, activity. Similarly, a state statute may be held valid either because the activity it directly affects is intrastate commerce (and it involves no indirect "undue" interference with other, interstate commerce, activity); or because, although the activity is interstate commerce, this particular regulation of it does not constitute an "undue" interference therewith. Even when the Court has placed a decision explicitly upon one rather than the other of these alternatives and definitely characterized a particular activity as interstate (or as intrastate) commerce, it may later treat the case as resting upon the other alternative.[91]

Decisions that state statutes regulating particular activities do or do not involve "undue" interferences with interstate commerce are not, therefore, relevant authority upon the question whether Congressional power under the commerce clause extends to those activities. The validity of a Congressional statute founded on the commerce clause depends upon whether the activities it regulates either constitute interstate commerce or so affect interstate commerce that the particular Congressional regulations imposed are valid.[92] The document does not furnish a test. The only relevant doctrines and decisions are those which relate specifically to the validity of Congressional statutes.

Doctrine permits Congress to regulate intrastate commerce activities to the extent necessary to preserve, protect, and foster interstate commerce. Upon the basis of this doctrine, past decisions have permitted further and further extensions of Congressional power.[93] The concept of a "stream of interstate commerce," including many intrastate commerce activities, has been employed.[94] It has been asserted that where intrastate activities are so intermingled with interstate commerce activities that the latter can be regulated effectively only if the former are subjected to the same regulation, Congress may regulate both.[95] It is probably true that all intrastate activities have some remote effect upon interstate commerce and that conceivable Congressional legislation could so regulate them as to foster interstate commerce. Somewhere short of that, the Supreme Court will probably draw a line limiting Congressional power under the commerce clause. Neither the document, existing doctrines, nor past decisions furnish any basis for prediction where that line will be drawn. They do indicate that codes and licenses can be validly applied far outside the field of interstate commerce itself. But whether, for example, a minimum wage provision in an N.I.R.A. code can be validly applied to a Chicago barbershop depends wholly upon the judges' statesmanship.

III

The N.I.R.A., the A.A.A., and perhaps the Securities Act raise questions of another type. It is sometimes contended that these statutes, or parts of them, though they constitute exertions by Congress of powers granted to it by the Constitution, were enacted for the purpose of achieving results in fields control over which is reserved by the Constitution to the states and that they are therefore invalid. The *Child Labor Cases*[96] are cited in support of these contentions. The first case, decided in 1918, invalidated a Congressional prohibition of the shipment in interstate commerce of the products of child labor. The second, in 1922, invalidated a Congressional tax upon mines and factories in which child labor was employed. Both statutes were regarded by a majority of the Court as unconstitutional invasions by Congress of powers reserved to the states by the Tenth Amendment. It is now urged that the exclusion of oil produced in violation of the N.I.R.A. code from interstate commerce, the exclusion of prospectuses forbidden by the Securities Act from interstate commerce and from the mails, and the levying of the processing tax under the A.A.A. are unconstitutional for the same reason.

There are two alternatives open to the court. The first derives from the fact that the written Constitution's grant of authority to Congress is phrased in terms of powers, not fields of control. The Preamble states that the promotion of the general welfare is one of the objects to secure which the Constitution was ordained. It is possible for the Court to take the position that Congress is authorized to exert any power delegated to it for the purpose of promoting the general welfare in any field. The second alternative derives from the Tenth Amendment, which provides that powers not delegated to the federal government are reserved to the states. The court has held that certain of the powers of Congress are exclusive, that the states may not regulate matters falling within the scope of these exclusive powers. It is possible for the Court to take the position that similarly certain of the powers reserved to the states by the Tenth Amendment are exclusive, that Congress may not exert its powers so as to regulate (or at least not for the purpose of regulating) matters falling within these exclusive state powers.

Until the *Child Labor Cases* were decided, doctrine and decisions indicated that the Court had taken the first of these alternative positions.[97] These earlier decisions were not overruled, nor were they satisfactorily distinguished, in the *Child Labor Cases*. Doctrine is now confused.[98] It is probable, though not certain, that the Court will eventually draw a line somewhere, preserving for the states exclusive control of some matters. But with doctrine confused and past decisions contradictory, where that line will be drawn depends wholly upon where the judges believe it should be drawn.

* * * * *

There is a written constitution in France. The French judges do not claim power to treat as invalid statutes they think inconsistent with it. But it does not follow that French legislators do not feel restrained, because of the existence of the written Constitution, from enacting laws forbidden by it.

In Australia there is also a written Constitution. The judges there do treat as invalid any statutes which they may think inconsistent with its provisions. Doctrines construing and interpreting those provisions do derive in part from the statesmanship of the judges. But the Australian judges do not claim power to pronounce doctrines of constitutional law which derive not at all from their written Constitution.

This power to invalidate statutes upon the basis of wholly extra-documental constitutional law was not exercised by the Supreme Court of the United States during the first century of its existence. During most of our history, the Court confined itself to functions similar to those exercised by the Australian courts—the American constitutional system then resembled closely the Australian. Between such systems and our present system, there is a gap as large as that which separates such systems from the French system.

The rôle of the judges under our present system—with the due process clauses held to authorize them to treat as invalid all statutes which they deem to be unwise or unjust—renders relatively insignificant the rôle of the written Constitution. It is possible that a majority of the nine justices of the Supreme Court may vote against the constitutionality of minor parts of the recovery program. If they do, it will not be because of the words of the document, or because of doctrine or past decisions. It will be because they believe those parts of the recovery program to be so unwise that they think the Court should invalidate them.[99]

NOTES TO MAGGS ESSAY

[1] Chief among the statutes known as the recovery legislation, all enacted in 1933, are:

National Industrial Recovery Act, 48 Stat. 195
Public Works Act (N.I.R.A., Title II), 48 Stat. 200
Agricultural Adjustment Act, 48 Stat. 31
Emergency Relief Act, 48 Stat. 55
Unemployment Relief Act, 48 Stat. 22
Employment Service Act, 48 Stat. 113
Home Owners' Loan Act, 48 Stat. 128
Farm Credit Act, 48 Stat. 257
Emergency Banking Acts, 48 Stat. 1, 2, 5, 20, 72
Banking Act, 48 Stat. 162
Securities Act, 48 Stat. 74
Act Amendatory to Reconstruction Finance Corporation Act (47 Stat. 5) 48 Stat. 141
Emergency Railroad Transportation Act, 48 Stat. 211
Tennessee Valley Authority Act, 48 Stat. 58
Credit and Currency Expansion Act, 48 Stat. 51
Gold Clause Annulment Resolution, 48 Stat. 112

[2] There is nothing novel in their conduct. A generation ago, conservatives reacted similarly to workmen's compensation acts and other unprecedented legislation. Speaking for a majority of the Supreme Court, Mr. Justice McKenna protested against this attitude in German Alliance Insurance Co. v. Kansas, 233 U. S. 389, 409, 58 L. Ed. 1011, 34 Sup. Ct. 612 (1914): "Against that conservatism of the mind, which puts to question every new act of regulating legislation and regards the legislation invalid or dangerous until it has become familiar, government—state and National—has pressed on in the general welfare; and our reports are full of cases where in instance after instance the exercise of regulation was resisted and yet sustained against attacks asserted to be justified by the Constitution of the United States. The dread of the moment having passed, no one is now heard to say that rights were restrained or their constitutional guaranties impaired."

[3] This is probably true, *e.g.*, of art. I, sec. 9, cl. 4, which provides, *inter alia,* that "No Capitation . . . Tax shall be laid, unless in Proportion to the Census or Enumeration herein before directed to be taken," and of art. I, sec. 9, cl. 5, which provides that "No Tax or Duty shall be laid on Articles exported from any State."

[4] Art. 1, sec. 8, cl. 3.

[5] *Cf.* Radin, *Statutory Interpretation,* 43 Harv. L. Rev. 863 (1930).

[6] The present justices of the Supreme Court of the United States disagree as to what constitutes construction and interpretation, what judicial amendment, of the words of the written Constitution. *Cf.* the majority and minority opinions in Home Building and Loan Association v. Blaisdell, 290 U. S. 398, 54 Sup. Ct. 231 (1934). For the majority, Hughes, C. J., said: "If by the statement that what the Constitution meant at the time of its adoption it means today, it is intended to say that the great clauses of the Constitution must be confined to the interpretation which the framers, with the conditions and outlook of their time, would have placed upon them, the statement carries its own refutation."—290 U. S. 442–443.

[7] A brief review of relevant constitutional history is attempted, *infra,* pp. 407 ff.

[8] It is the possession by American judges of this power to invalidate statutes upon the basis of wholly non-documental constitutional law that differentiates the American institution of judicial review from that of Australia or Canada.

[9] The limits upon judicial statesmanship held by the judges to be created by the words of the impairment clause in art. I, sec. 10, cl. 1, the equal protection clause in Amend-

ment XIV, and the privileges and immunities in art. IV, sec. 2, cl. 1, are so slight that the power of the judges in the construction, interpretation, and application of these clauses approaches very nearly their power under the due process clauses. As to the privileges and immunities clause of art. IV, see note, 18 Calif. L. Rev. 159 (1930); as to the impairment clause, see the opinion of Hughes, C. J., in Home Building and Loan Association v. Blaisdell, 290 U. S. 398, 54 Sup. Ct. 231 (1934).

10 See Dickinson, *Legal Rules: Their Function in the Process of Decision,* 79 U. of Pa. L. Rev. 833 (1931). *Cf.,* for an extreme "realist" view, Frank, *Law and the Modern Mind* (1930).

11 Here, too, the judge, consciously or unconsciously, may usurp the authority which he professes to concede to doctrine and past decisions.

12 The dissenting opinion of Brandeis, J., in Burnet v. Coronado Oil and Gas Co., 285 U. S. 393, 405, 76 L. Ed. 815, 52 Sup. Ct. 433 (1932), states the Court's tradition and practice and lists the cases which have been overruled.

13 This skepticism is perhaps most explicitly stated in Mr. Justice Holmes's dissent in Abrams v. United States, 250 U. S. 616, 630, 63 L. Ed. 1173, 40 Sup. Ct. 17 (1919).

14 Mr. Justice Brandeis's dissenting opinion in Burns Baking Co. v. Bryan, 264 U. S. 504, 517, 68 L. Ed. 813, 44 Sup. Ct. 412 (1924), well illustrates his method. *Cf.* Mr. Justice Stone's dissenting opinion in Ribnik v. McBride, 277 U. S. 350, 359, 72 L. Ed. 913; 48 Sup. Ct. 545 (1928).

15 This is illustrated by holdings that the due process clause of Amendment XIV is violated by state action infringing certain of the rights guaranteed by the first eight Amendments against federal infringement only. See, *e.g.,* Powell v. Alabama, 287 U. S. 45, 77 L. Ed. 158, 53 Sup. Ct. 55 (1932). But see Hurtado v. California, 110 U. S. 516, 28 L. Ed. 232, 4 Sup. Ct. 111, 292 (1884) and Twining v. New Jersey, 211 U. S. 78, 53 L. Ed. 97, 29 Sup. Ct. 14 (1908).

16 *Cf.* the following statement by Hughes, C. J., in Home Building and Loan Association v. Blaisdell, 290 U. S. 398, 442, 54 Sup. Ct. 231, 241 (1934): "It is manifest from this review of our decisions that there has been a growing appreciation of public needs and of the necessity of finding ground for a rational compromise between individual rights and public welfare. The settlement and consequent contraction of the public domain, the pressure of a constantly increasing density of population, the interrelation of the activities of our people and the complexity of our economic interests, have inevitably led to an increased use of the organization of society in order to protect the very bases of individual opportunity. Where, in earlier days, it was thought that only the concerns of individuals or of classes were involved, and that those of the State itself were touched only remotely, it has later been found that the fundamental interests of the State are directly affected...."

17 These generalizations will be supported, in part at least, in subsequent parts of this paper.

18 That the minimum wage decision, Adkins v. Children's Hospital, 261 U. S. 525, 67 L. Ed. 785, 43 Sup. Ct. 394 (1923), is a striking example of this fact is conclusively shown in Powell, *The Judiciality of Minimum-Wage Legislation,* 37 Harv. L. Rev. 545 (1924).

19 Marbury v. Madison, 1 Cranch (U. S.) 137, 2 L. Ed. 60 (1803). For a critical consideration of the reasoning of Marshall, C. J., see Gibson, J., in Eakin v. Raub, 12 S. & R. (Pa.) 330, 345 ff. (1825). *Cf.* Thayer, *The Origin and Scope of the American Doctrine of Constitutional Law,* 7 Harv. L. Rev. 129 (1893), Thayer, *Legal Essays* (1908) 1. That the written Constitution expressly authorizes the judges to declare statutes unconstitutional, see McGovney, Review of Haines: *American Doctrine of Judicial Supremacy,* 21 Calif. L. Rev. 637, 639–41 (1933).

[20] On natural law and natural rights, see Ritchie, *Natural Rights* (1894); Corwin, *The "Higher Law" Background of American Constitutional Law,* 42 Harv. L. Rev. 149, 365 (1928–9); and Haines, *The Revival of Natural Law Concepts* (1930).

[21] See, in general, Becker, *The Declaration of Independence* (1922).

[22] The historical basis of the power of American judges to declare statutes unconstitutional is indicated accurately by the opinion of Mr. Justice Patterson, on circuit, in Vanhorne's Lessee v. Dorrance, 2 Dallas (U. S.) 304, 1 L. Ed. 391 (1795) holding void a Pennsylvania statute. After expounding the theory that the judiciary was coördinate with, not subordinate to, the legislature and referring to a vague clause in the state constitution, he said: "The preservation of property, then, is a primary object of the social compact and, by the . . . constitution of Pennsylvania, was made a fundamental law . . . [An] act divesting one citizen of his freehold, and vesting it in another, without a just compensation . . . is inconsistent with the principles of reason, justice, and moral rectitude; it is incompatible with the comfort, peace, and happiness of mankind; it is contrary to the principles of social alliance in every free government; and, lastly, it is contrary both to the letter and spirit of the constitution. In short, it is what every one would think unreasonable and unjust in his own case."—2 Dallas, 310.

[23] 3 Dallas (U. S.) 386, 1 L. Ed. 648 (1798).

[24] Mr. Justice Chase said: "I cannot subscribe to the omnipotence of a state legislature, or that it is absolute and without control; although its authority should not be expressly restrained by the constitution, or fundamental law of the state. The people of the United States erected their constitutions or forms of government, to establish justice, to promote the general welfare, to secure the blessings of liberty, and to protect their persons and property from violence. The purposes for which men enter into society will determine the nature and terms of the social compact; and as they are the foundation of the legislative power, they will decide what are the proper objects of it. The nature, and ends of legislative power will limit the exercise of it. This fundamental principle flows from the very nature of our free republican governments, that no man should be compelled to do what the laws do not require; nor to refrain from acts which the laws permit. There are acts which the federal, or state legislature cannot do, without exceeding their authority. There are certain vital principles in our free republican governments, which will determine and overrule an apparent and flagrant abuse of legislative power; as to authorize manifest injustice by positive law; or to take away that security for personal liberty, or private property, for the protection whereof the government was established. An act of the legislature (for I cannot call it a law), contrary to the great first principles of the social compact, cannot be considered a rightful exercise of legislative authority. The obligation of a law, in governments established on express compact, and on republican principles, must be determined by the nature of the power on which it is founded."—3 Dallas (U. S.) 387–8.

To which Mr. Justice Iredell answered: "It is true, that some speculative jurists have held, that a legislative act against natural justice must, in itself, be void; but I cannot think that . . . any court of justice would possess a power to declare it so. . . . If any act of congress, or of the legislature of a state, violates . . . constitutional provisions, it is unquestionably void; though, I admit, that as the authority to declare it void is of a delicate and awful nature, the court will never resort to that authority, but in a clear and urgent case. If, on the other hand, the legislature of the Union, or the legislature of any member of the Union, shall pass a law, within the general scope of their constitutional power, the court cannot pronounce it to be void, merely because it is, in their judgment, contrary to the principles of natural justice. The ideas of natural justice are regulated by no fixed standard: the ablest and the purest men have differed upon the subject; and all that the court could properly say, in such an event, would be, that the legislature (possessed of an equal right of opinion) had passed an act which, in the opinion of the judges, was inconsistent with the abstract principles of natural justice."—3 Dallas (U. S.) 398–9.

[25] 6 Cranch (U. S.) 87, 3 L. Ed. 162 (1810).

[26] He held that a grant was a contract and that the clause (art. I, sec. 10, cl. 1: "No State shall . . . pass any . . . Law impairing the Obligation of Contracts") covered not only contracts between individuals but also contracts between a state and an individual. Why the clause forbade the state to exercise against an innocent purchaser with whom it had not contracted a right to rescind which it surely did not prevent the state from exercising against the fraudulent grantee, the opinion does not make clear.

[27] 6 Cranch (U. S.) 135–6, 139 (1810).

[28] 6 Cranch (U. S.) 143 (1810).

[29] The impairment clause was the only possible peg for such views. The *ex post facto* clause (art. I, sec. 10, cl. 1) had been held to apply only to statutes relating to criminal offenses (Calder v. Bull, *supra* note 23). Until the adoption of the Fourteenth Amendment in 1868, the Constitution contained no due process clause applicable to the states.

[30] See Corwin, *A Basic Doctrine of American Constitutional Law,* 12 Mich. L. Rev. 247 (1914).

[31] Wilkinson v. Leland, 2 Pet. (U. S.) 627, 7 L. Ed. 542 (1829).

[32] Ogden v. Saunders, 12 Wheat. (U. S.) 212, 6 L. Ed. 605 (1827). The Court had held before this, in Sturges v. Crowninshield, 4 Wheat. (U. S.) 122, 4 L. Ed. 529 (1819), that the impairment clause did forbid the application of state bankruptcy laws to debts contracted before their enactment.

[33] Barron v. Baltimore, 7 Pet. (U. S.) 243, 8 L. Ed. 672 (1833). This is the leading case on the proposition that the first eight Amendments limit the federal government only, not the states. The Fifth Amendment does forbid such a taking.

[34] Charles River Bridge v. Warren Bridge, 11 Pet. (U. S.) 420, 9 L. Ed. 773 (1837).

[35] Mr. Justice Story's chagrin and determination to resign because "the doctrines and opinions of the 'old Court' were daily losing ground, . . . especially those on great constitutional questions . . . so vital to the country" are expressed by him in a letter to Ezekiel Bacon on April 12, 1845, printed in Story, *Life and Letters of Joseph Story* (1851) 527.

[36] The Fifth Amendment, adopted in 1791, applicable to the federal government only, provides that "No person shall . . . be deprived of life, liberty, or property, without due process of law." The Fourteenth Amendment, adopted in 1868, provides that "No State shall . . . deprive any person of life, liberty, or property, without due process of law."

[37] Note 24 *supra.* Neither Chase, J., nor the later justices have invoked the Ninth Amendment (which reads: "The Enumeration in the Constitution of certain rights, shall not be construed to deny or disparage others retained by the people") although a plausible argument in favor of judicial protection of natural rights might be constructed from it.

[38] *E.g.,* Trustees of the University of North Carolina v. Foy, 1 Murphey (N.C.) 58 (1805).

[39] See Corwin, *The Doctrine of Due Process of Law Before the Civil War,* 24 Harv. L. Rev. 366, 460 (1911).

[40] Bronson, J., in Taylor v. Porter, 4 Hill (N.Y.) 140, 144 (1843).

[41] In Taylor v. Porter, note 40 *supra,* the due process clause was invoked as an alternative ground of decision. In Westervelt v. Gregg, 12 N.Y. 202 (1854) the restrictive interpretation of the state constitution's grant of legislative power was abandoned, the due process clause relied upon as the sole ground of decision.

[42] See Corwin note 39 *supra.*

[43] Story on the Constitution (1833) § 1783. His language is: "... this clause, in effect, affirms the right of trial, according to the process and proceedings of the common law." In all, he devotes thirteen lines of an 1809-page volume to the due process clause.

[44] The two cases are Den dem. Murray v. The Hoboken Land, etc., Co., 18 How. (U. S.) 272, 15 L. Ed. 372 (1855) and Dred Scott v. Sandford, 19 How. (U. S.) 393, 15 L. Ed. 691 (1857). The former held that the Fifth Amendment due process clause did not prevent seizure of property of a federal tax collector, and sale thereof to pay a sum found by the United States auditor to be due the United States, without a judicial proceeding or hearing of any kind, on the ground that there was historical warrant for such a summary procedure in such a case. In the Dred Scott Case, Taney, C. J., voting to hold void the Missouri Compromise, referred briefly to the due process clause as a ground of decision in addition to those he developed at length (19 How. 450). Only two justices concurred in the opinion of Taney, C. J. Curtis, J., dissenting, insisted that such a construction of the due process clause would not "bear examination" (19 How. 626). The other justices did not mention the due process clause. No federal statute was invalidated by the Court on the basis of the Fifth Amendment due process clause until, in 1908, Adair v. United States, 208 U. S. 161, 52 L. Ed. 436, 28 Sup. Ct. 277, was decided. *Cf.,* however, Dred Scott v. Sanford, *supra,* and the first Legal Tender Case, *infra,* text and note 48, in both of which the clause was cited as a makeweight.

[45] See Flack, *The Adoption of the Fourteenth Amendment* (1908), and Kendrick, *The Journal of the Joint Committee of Fifteen on Reconstruction* (1914). Kendrick relies upon assertions made by a member of the committee (Conklin) in 1882 as counsel in the argument of San Mateo County v. Southern Pacific Co., 116 U. S. 138, 29 L. Ed. 589, 6 Sup. Ct. 317 (1885), that the due process clause was intended to protect individuals and corporations against oppressive state legislation.

[46] See Lerner, *The Supreme Court and American Capitalism,* 42 Yale L. Jour. 668 (1933).

[47] See Nelles, Review of Swisher: *Stephen J. Field—Craftsman of the Law* (1930), 40 Yale L. Jour. 998 (1931). In general, see Corwin, *The Supreme Court and the Fourteenth Amendment,* 7 Mich. L. Rev. 643 (1909); Corwin, *Social Planning under the Constitution—A Study in Perspectives,* 26 American Political Science Review 7 (1932).

[48] Hepburn v. Griswold, 8 Wall. (U. S.) 603, 19 L. Ed. 513 (1870).

[49] 8 Wall. (U. S.) 637–8 (1870).

[50] Legal Tender Cases, 12 Wall. (U. S.) 457, 20 L. Ed. 287 (1870). Mr. Justice Field's claim of power in the judges to invalidate laws upon extra-constitutional bases occurs at p. 670.

Allegations that the overruling of the first Legal Tender Case was the result of a "packing" of the Court are discussed and doubted in Hughes, *The Supreme Court of the United States* (1928) 51 ff.

[51] 20 Wall. (U. S.) 655, 22 L. Ed. 455 (1874). Clifford, J., dissenting, protested that "Errors of indiscretion which the legislature may commit in the exercise of the power it possesses cannot be corrected by the courts, for the reason that the courts cannot adjudge an act of the legislature void unless it is in violation of the Federal or State constitution."—20 Wall. 668.

[52] 20 Wall. (U. S.) 662–3. In Davidson v. New Orleans, 96 U. S. 97, 24 L. Ed. 616 (1877), Mr. Justice Miller perhaps accounts for the seeming inconsistency of his Hepburn v. Griswold opinion (*supra* text and note 49) and his Loan Association v. Topeka opinion. In refusing, on writ of error to the Supreme Court of Louisiana, to invalidate a drain-

age assessment which he finds not prohibited by the federal Constitution, he says: "It may possibly violate some of those principles of general constitutional law, of which we could take jurisdiction if we were sitting in review of a Circuit Court of the United States, as we were in Loan Association v. Topeka."—96 U. S. 105.

The doctrine of Loan Association v. Topeka has long been subsumed under the due process clause of the Fourteenth Amendment. See McAllister, *Public Purpose in Taxation,* 18 Calif. L. Rev. 137, 241 (1930).

[53] 16 Wall. (U. S.) 36, 21 L. Ed. 394 (1873).

[54] "No State shall make or enforce any law which shall abridge the privileges or immunities of citizens of the United States." The majority, in rendering this clause nugatory by holding it to guarantee only rights already guaranteed by other clauses of the Constitution, probably indulged in judicial nullification. The clause was, it is fairly certain, intended (in connection with the enforcement power granted to Congress by the Fourteenth Amendment) to increase federal legislative power. See Kendrick, note 45 *supra, passim,* and McGovney, *Privileges or Immunities Clause—Fourteenth Amendment,* 4 Iowa L. Bull. 219 (1918).

[55] 16 Wall. (U. S.) 78. Again it is Miller, J., who speaks thus.

[56] 94 U. S. 113, 24 L. Ed. 77 (1877).

[57] Chicago, etc., R. R. Co. v. Iowa, 94 U. S. 155, 24 L. Ed. 94 (1877); Peik v. Chicago, etc. Ry. Co., 94 U. S. 164, 24 L. Ed. 97 (1877); Chicago, etc., R. R. Co. v. Ackley, 94 U. S. 179, 24, L. Ed. 99 (1877); Winona, etc., R. R. Co. v. Blake, 94 U. S. 180, 24 L. Ed. 99 (1877); Stone v. Wisconsin, 94 U. S. 181, 24 L. Ed. 102 (1877).

[58] 169 U. S. 466, 42 L. Ed. 819, 18 Sup. Ct. 418 (1898).

[59] Occasional questionings do occur in the opinions of Mr. Justice Holmes and Mr. Justice Brandeis.

In Whitney v. California, 274 U. S. 357, 373, 71 L. Ed. 1095, 47 Sup. Ct. 641 (1927) the latter said: "Despite arguments to the contrary which had seemed to me persuasive, it is settled that the due process clause of the Fourteenth Amendment applies to matters of substantive law as well as to matters of procedure." *Cf.* the view of Mr. Justice Story, note 43 *supra.*

In Baldwin v. Missouri, 281 U. S. 586, 595, 74 L. Ed. 1056, 50 Sup. Ct. 436 (1930), Mr. Justice Holmes, dissenting, said: "As the decisions now stand, I can see hardly any limit but the sky to the invalidating of [the constitutional rights of the States] if they happen to strike a majority of this Court as for any reason undesirable. I cannot believe that the [Fourteenth] Amendment was intended to give us *carte blanche* to embody our economic or moral beliefs in its prohibitions. Yet I can think of no narrower reason that seems to me to justify the present and the earlier decisions to which I have referred. Of course the words 'due process of law,' if taken in their literal meaning, have no application to this case; and while it is too late to deny that they have been given a much more extended and artificial signification, still we ought to remember the great caution shown by the Constitution in limiting the power of the States, and should be slow to construe the clause in the Fourteenth Amendment as committing to the Court, with no guide but the Court's own discretion, the validity of whatever laws the States may pass."

[60] See Field, J., dissenting, in Munn v. Illinois, 94 U. S. 113, 145, 24 L. Ed. 77 (1877).

[61] White, C. J., in Brushaber v. Union Pacific Railroad Co., 240 U. S. 1, 24, 60 L. Ed. 493, 36 Sup. Ct. 236 (1916). Federal tax statutes have since been held invalid because in violation of the due process clause of the Fifth Amendment in Heiner v. Donnan, 285 U. S. 312, 76 L. Ed. 722, 52 Sup. Ct. 358 (1932), and other cases.

[62] It is used but once by Roberts, J., in Nebbia v. New York, 54 Sup. Ct. 505 (1934).

[63] See note 15 *supra*. This, of course, is also true as to doctrine pronounced by the judges in interpreting the words of the written Constitution.

[64] *E.g.*, the right to jury trial in the federal courts and the other rights guaranteed by the first eight amendments. *Cf.* art. I, sec. 9.

[65] A possible contention that the calling in of gold violates the provision of Amendment V that "private property [shall not] be taken for public use, without just compensation" is considered *infra* note 71.

[66] Loan Association v. Topeka, 20 Wall. (U. S.) 655, 22 L. Ed. 455 (1874).

[67] They are collected in McAllister, *Public Purpose in Taxation*, 18 Calif. L. Rev. 137, 241 (1930).

[68] Frothingham v. Mellon, 262 U. S. 447, 486, 67 L. Ed. 1078, 43 Sup. Ct. 597 (1923).

[69] Massachusetts v. Mellon, 262 U. S. 447, 67 L. Ed. 1078, 43 Sup. Ct. 597 (1923).

[70] For analysis of the question and discussion of the cases, see Brewster, *Is the Processing Tax Unconstitutional*, 19 A. B. A. J. 419 (1933).

[71] The impairment clause (art. I, sec. 10, cl. 1), of course, has no application to federal governmental action. If it did apply, existing doctrine would make validity depend upon the statesmanship of the judges. Hughes, C. J., said in Home Building and Loan Association v. Blaisdell, 290 U. S. 398, 437, 54 Sup. Ct. 231, 239 (1934) that "The economic interests of the State may justify the exercise of its continuing and dominant protective power notwithstanding interference with contracts."

It will perhaps be contended that the gold coin called in is being "taken for public use" within the Fifth Amendment and that "just compensation" is not being made. There is no relevant past decision or doctrine. Decision either way is within the limits on judicial statesmanship fixed by the words of the clause in the document. See, in general, note, 47 Harv. L. Rev. 479 (1934); United States v. Campbell, 5. F. Supp. 156 (1933) and note thereon, 34 Col. L. Rev. 166 (1934); Nebolsine, *The Gold Clause in Private Contracts*, 42 Yale L. Jour. 1051 (1933); Post and Willard, *The Power of Congress to Nullify Gold Clauses*, 46 Harv. L. Rev. 1225 (1933); Eder, *A Forgotten Section of the Fourteenth Amendment*, 19 Corn. L. Quar. 1 (1933).

[72] See the collection of cases upholding regulatory statutes in Nebbia v. New York, 291 U. S. 502, 525 ff., 54 Sup. Ct. 505, 511 ff. (1934).

[73] As to working conditions, citation of authority seems unnecessary in view of the multitude of statutes of unquestioned validity relating to the safety, health, and comfort of workers. *Cf.* Knoxville Iron Co. v. Harbison, 183 U. S. 13, 46 L. Ed. 55, 22 Sup. Ct. 1 (1901), upholding statute regulating the issuance of store orders for wages.

As to child labor, see Sturges & Burn v. Beauchamp, 231 U. S. 320, 58 L. Ed. 245, 34 Sup. Ct. 60 (1913).

As to hours of work, see Bunting v. Oregon, 243 U. S. 426, 61 L. Ed. 830, 37 Sup. Ct. 435 (1917). Radice v. New York, 264 U. S. 292, 68 L. Ed. 690, 44 Sup. Ct. 325 (1924), upheld the prohibition of night work by women.

[74] Adair v. United States, 208 U. S. 161, 52 L. Ed. 436, 28 Sup. Ct. 277 (1908); Coppage v. Kansas, 236 U. S. 1, 59 L. Ed. 441, 35 Sup. Ct. 240 (1915).

[75] Texas & New Orleans R. Co. v. Brotherhood, 281 U. S. 548, 74 L. Ed. 1034, 50 Sup. Ct. 427 (1930).

[76] Adkins v. Children's Hospital, 261 U.S. 525, 67 L. Ed. 785, 43 Sup. Ct. 394 (1923).

[77] See The Supreme Court and Minimum Wage Legislation: Comment by the Legal Profession on the District of Columbia Case (1925).

[78] On the last-mentioned prohibition, see Terborgh, *Price Control Devices in N. R. A. Codes* (1934).

[79] In dissenting opinions, Mr. Justice Stone had pointed this out and had suggested a meaningful test. Tyson v. Banton, 273 U. S. 418, 447, 71 L. Ed. 718, 47 Sup. Ct. 426 (1927); Ribnik v. McBride, 277 U. S. 350, 359, 72 L. Ed. 913, 48 Sup. Ct. 545 (1928). See McAllister, *Lord Hale and Business Affected with a Public Interest*, 43 Harv. L. Rev. 759 (1930); Hamilton, *Affectation with Public Interest*, 39 Yale L. Jour. 1089 (1930).

[80] Nebbia v. New York, 291 U. S. 502, 54 Sup. Ct. 505 (1934).

[81] 291 U. S. 536, 54 Sup. Ct. 515–516. Such a holding was called for in Carpenter, *The Constitutionality of the National Industry Recovery Act*, 7 S. Calif. L. Rev. 125, 141 (1934).

[82] 285 U. S. 262, 76 L. Ed. 747, 52 Sup. Ct. 371 (1932).

[83] Because its bearing is so wide, a long quotation from Mr. Justice Roberts' opinion seems justified. I omit his citation of cases.

"... there can be no doubt that upon proper occasion and by appropriate measures the state may regulate a business in any of its aspects, including the prices to be charged for the products or commodities it sells.

"So far as the requirement of due process is concerned, and in the absence of other constitutional restriction, a state is free to adopt whatever economic policy may reasonably be deemed to promote public welfare, and to enforce that policy by legislation adapted to its purpose. The courts are without authority either to declare such policy, or, when it is declared by the legislative arm, to override it. If the laws passed are seen to have a reasonable relation to a proper legislative purpose, and are neither arbitrary nor discriminatory, the requirements of due process are satisfied, and judicial determination to that effect renders a court *functus officio*. 'Whether the free operation of the normal laws of competition is a wise and wholesome rule for trade and commerce is an economic question which this court need not consider or determine.' Northern Securities Co. v. United States, 193 U. S. 197, 337–8. And it is equally clear that if the legislative policy be to curb unrestrained and harmful competition by measures which are not arbitrary or discriminatory it does not lie with the courts to determine that the rule is unwise. With the wisdom of the policy adopted, with the adequacy or practicability of the law enacted to forward it, the courts are both incompetent and unauthorized to deal....

"The law-making bodies have in the past endeavored to promote free competition by laws aimed at trusts and monopolies. The consequent interference with private property and freedom of contract has not availed with the courts to set these enactments aside as denying due process. Where the public interest was deemed to require the fixing of minimum prices, that expedient has been sustained. If the law-making body within its sphere of government concludes that the conditions or practices in an industry make unrestricted competition an inadequate safeguard of the consumer's interests, produce waste harmful to the public, threaten ultimately to cut off the supply of a commodity needed by the public, or portend the destruction of the industry itself, appropriate statutes passed in an honest effort to correct the threatened consequences may not be set aside because the regulation adopted fixes prices reasonably deemed by the legislature to be fair to those engaged in the industry and to the consuming public. And this is especially so where, as here, the economic maladjustment is one of price, which threatens harm to the producer at one end of the series and the consumer at the other. The Constitution does not secure to anyone liberty to conduct his business in such fashion as to inflict injury upon the public at large, or upon any substantial group of the people. Price control, like any other form of regulation, is unconstitutional only if arbitrary, discriminatory, or demonstrably irrelevant to the policy the Legislature is free to adopt, and hence an unnecessary and unwarranted interference with individual liberty...." 291 U. S. 537–539, 54 Sup. Ct. 516–517.

[84] Questions of sufficiency of notice and hearing before administrative action is taken and of the extent of judicial review of administrative determinations involve doctrines referable to art. III as well as to the due process clause. Here, as elsewhere, neither document nor existing doctrines or past decisions limit greatly the statesmanship of the judges. See Fuchs, *The Constitutionality of the Recovery Program,* 19 St. Louis L. Rev. 1, 18 ff. (1933); note, 43 Yale L. Jour. 599 (1934).

[85] The President empowered to lower tariff rates, Field v. Clark, 143 U. S. 649, 36 L. Ed. 294, 12 Sup. Ct. 495 (1892). Secretary of Treasury, to define and exclude impure tea, Buttfield v. Stranahan, 192 U. S. 470, 48 L. Ed. 525, 24 Sup. Ct. 349 (1904). Secretary of War, to order removal of obstructing bridges, Union Bridge Co. v. United States, 204 U. S. 364, 51 L. Ed. 523, 27 Sup. Ct. 367 (1907). Secretary of Agriculture, to prescribe regulations (violations of which to be criminal offenses) for use of national forests, United States v. Grimaud, 220 U. S. 506, 55 L. Ed. 563, 31 Sup. Ct. 480 (1911). Interstate Commerce Commission, to specify accounting methods required to be followed by carriers, I. C. C. v. Goodrich Transit Co., 224 U. S. 194, 56 L. Ed. 729, 32 Sup. Ct. 436 (1912). President, to change tariff rates, J. W. Hampton, Jr., & Co. v. United States, 276 U. S. 394, 72 L. Ed. 624, 48 Sup. Ct. 348 (1928). There are other cases. See comment, 31 Mich. L. Rev. 786 (1933).

[86] See, reviewing several recent studies, Carr, *Delegated Legislation in England as Seen from Abroad,* 16 Journal Comparative Legislation and International Law 96 (1934).

[87] *Addresses on Citizenship and Government* (1916). Quoted by Frankfurter and Davison, *Cases on Administrative Law* (1932) 15.

[88] Corwin, *The Spending Power of Congress,* 36 Harv. L. Rev. 548 (1923).

[89] See Notes 68 and 69 *supra.*

[90] There is, of course, no clause conferring upon Congress power to legislate to promote the general welfare. Congress may levy taxes and spend the funds thus raised to promote the general welfare, art. I, sec. 8, cl. 1. See Corwin, note 88 *supra.* The Preamble, which states that the general welfare is one of the objects to promote which the Constitution was established, is not a grant of power. See p. 425 *infra.*

[91] See *e.g.,* East Ohio Gas Co. v. Tax Commissioners of Ohio, 283 U. S. 465, 471 f., 75 L. Ed. 1171, 51 Sup. Ct. 499 (1931), where Pennsylvania Gas Co. v. Public Service Commission, 252 U. S. 23, 64 L. Ed. 434, 40 Sup. Ct. 279 (1920) is thus treated.

[92] The Court frequently upholds an application of a federal statute without deciding which alternative basis of Congressional power is present. See *e.g.,* Local 167, International Brotherhood of Teamsters v. United States, 291 U. S. 293, 54 Sup. Ct. 396 (1934).

[93] The Safety Appliance Act applies validly to intrastate trains on tracks over which interstate trains run. Southern Railway v. United States, 222 U. S. 20, 56 L. Ed. 72, 32 Sup. Ct. 2 (1911). Intrastate rates may be ordered raised if so low that interstate commerce is burdened or discriminated against. Railroad Commission v. Chicago, B. & Q. Ry., 257 U. S. 563, 66 L. Ed. 371, 42 Sup. Ct. 232 (1922). *Cf.* such an application of the Sherman Act (26 Stat. 209, 1890) as that in Swift & Co. v. United States, 196 U. S. 375, 49 L. Ed. 518, 25 Sup. Ct. 276 (1905) with that held invalid in The Sugar Trust Case, 156 U. S. 1, 39 L. Ed. 325, 15 Sup. Ct. 249 (1895).

[94] See *e.g.,* Stafford v. Wallace, 258 U. S. 495, 66 L. Ed. 735, 42 Sup. Ct. 397 (1922). See Ribble, *The "Current of Commerce,"* 18 Minn. L. Rev. 296, 312 ff. (1934).

[95] See *e.g.,* United States v. New York Central Railroad Co., 272 U. S. 457, 464, 71 L. Ed. 350, 47 Sup. Ct. 130 (1926).

[96] Hammer v. Dagenhart, 247 U. S. 251, 62 L. Ed. 1101, 38 Sup. Ct. 529 (1918); Bailey v. Drexel Furniture Co., 259 U. S. 20, 66 L. Ed. 817, 42 Sup. Ct. 449 (1922).

See also Hill v. Wallace, 259 U. S. 44, 66 L. Ed. 822, 42 Sup. Ct. 453 (1922) invalidating regulation under the taxing power of sales of grain for future delivery. Similar regulation, under the commerce clause, was later upheld. Board of Trade v. Olsen, 262 U. S. 1, 67 L. Ed. 839, 43 Sup. Ct. 470 (1923).

[97] As to the taxing power, see McCray v. United States, 195 U. S. 27, 49 L. Ed. 78, 24 Sup. Ct. 769 (1904), upholding a prohibitory tax on yellow oleomargarine, and United States v. Doremus, 249 U. S. 86, 63 L. Ed. 493, 39 Sup. Ct. 214 (1919), upholding a tax intended to eliminate the general sale of narcotic drugs.

As to power under the commerce clause, see The Lottery Case, 188 U. S. 321, 47 L. Ed. 492, 23 Sup. Ct. 321 (1903), upholding the barring of lottery tickets from interstate commerce; Hipolite Egg Co. v. United States, 220 U. S. 45, 55 L. Ed. 364, 31 Sup. Ct. 364 (1911) upholding the barring of impure foods and drugs; and other cases discussed in Corwin, *Congress's Power to Prohibit Commerce,* 18 Corn. L. Quar. 477 (1933).

See, in general, Powell, *Child Labor, Congress, and the Constitution,* 1 N. Car. L. Rev. 61 (1922), and Maggs, *Congressional Power to Control Cotton and Tobacco Production,* 1 Law and Contemporary Problems, 376 (1934).

[98] See articles by Powell and Corwin cited in note 97 *supra.*

[99] The considerations upon which depends the wisdom of the recovery legislation's expansion of federal authority, its delegations of legislative power, and its extensions of governmental regulation—the non-documentary, non-doctrinal, non-decisional considerations upon which, therefore, the judges should base their decisions as to its constitutionality—are admirably stated and developed by John Dickinson in his paper, *Political Aspects of the New Deal,* 28 Am. Pol. Sci. Rev. 197 (1934).

SPECIFIC PERFORMANCE OF CONTRACTS TO DELIVER SPECIFIC OR ASCERTAINED GOODS UNDER THE ENGLISH SALE OF GOODS ACT AND THE AMERICAN SALES ACT

BY WILLIAM E. MASTERSON

THIS PAPER is, briefly, a study of the interpretation and application by the courts of those provisions of the English Sale of Goods Act and the American Sales Act which confer upon courts jurisdiction to decree specific performance of contracts to sell goods, and especially of the effect of these provisions as interpreted by the courts upon the existing law. Such a study necessarily involves a comparison of the decisions in which counsel have relied upon these provisions in suits for specific performance with the decisions in similar cases before the Acts became law. A brief historical sketch will be helpful as an introduction.

From early times courts of chancery in certain cases enforced one's right to the delivery of a specific chattel even if the right did not arise from a contract; as where a chattel was wrongfully withheld and the party asking for the enforcement of the right could not be adequately compensated by damages. If the chattel could be replaced, the defendant was required to pay its value, but if it was "unique," the court would require him to deliver or return it.[1] This was an advance beyond the remedy at law in such cases; this remedy was *detinue,* but the defendant had the option of returning the chattel or paying its value. This option was taken away, however, by the Common Law Procedure Act, 1854,[2] by which the law courts were given even wider powers than the courts of chancery had in these cases: the court or judge was given power "... if they or he see fit so to do, upon the Application of the Plaintiff in any Action for the Detention of any Chattel, to order that Execution shall issue for the Return of the Chattel detained, without giving the Defendant the Option of retaining such Chattel upon paying the Value assessed...." This section was repealed by the Statute Law Revision and Civil Procedure Act, 1883,[3] for, as the Preamble recites, its subject-matter is provided for in the Supreme Court Judicature Act, 1873.[4] The remedy given by both the law and the equity courts when one's chattel was wrongfully withheld is not to be confused, however, with that given by courts of chancery in the enforcement of one's rights to the delivery of a chattel when the right arose from a contract, though the ground of relief was the same in both cases. Such a contract was specifically enforceable if the complaining party could show that the defendant's breach of the agreement by non-delivery of the goods contracted for could not be adequately compensated by damages at law. In 1856, however, the courts of law were given this power, so long wielded by courts of equity, to order the delivery of goods when there was a contract for their delivery. The Mercantile Law Amendment Act, 1856,[5] provided that, "In all Actions and Suits in any of the Superior Courts of Common Law at *Westminster* or *Dublin,* or in any Court of Record in *England, Wales,* or *Ireland,* for Breach of Contract to deliver specific Goods for a Price in Money, on the Application of the Plaintiff," the court or judge "at their or his Discretion . . . shall have Power to order Execution to issue for the Delivery . . . of the said Goods, without giving the Defendant the Option of retaining the same upon paying the Damages assessed; . . ." No decision has been found in which this power given to the law courts was exercised by them before the law's repeal. This Act was repealed in 1893 by the Sale of Goods Act,[6] but the section just quoted was superseded by § 52 of the repealing Act. Since § 52 of this Act and the corresponding section of the American Sales Act form the subject of this paper, they are quoted here in full. Section 52 of the English Act reads:

> In any action for breach of contract to deliver specific or ascertained goods the court may, if it thinks fit, on the application of the plaintiff, by its judgment or decree direct that the contract shall be performed specifically, without giving the defendant the option of retaining the goods on payment of damages. The judgment or decree may be unconditional, or upon such terms and conditions as to damages, payment of the price, and otherwise, as to the court may seem just, and the application by the plaintiff may be made at any time before judgment or decree.[7]

It should be noted that the Act of 1893 covers "specific or ascertained goods," while the earlier law covers only "specific goods," and that the former gives the court the power at its "discretion," while the latter, "if it thinks fit."

The American Uniform Sales Act was recommended by the commissioners on Uniform State Laws in 1906 for enactment by the legislatures of the several states. It was enacted into law in 1907 by the legislatures of Arizona and Connecticut, and it has since become law in some thirty states and two territories.[8] Section 68 of this Act follows § 52 of the English Act, and was, indeed, taken from it, with slight changes. The section reads:

> Where the seller has broken a contract to deliver specific or ascertained goods, a court having the powers of a court of equity may, if it thinks fit, on the application of the buyer, by its judgment or decree, direct that the contract shall be performed specifically, without giving the seller the option of retaining the goods on payment of damages. The judgment or decree may be unconditional, or upon such terms and conditions as to damages, payment of the price and otherwise, as to the court may seem just.[9]

As just noted, even apart from these statutes courts of equity have long granted specific performance of contracts to sell goods where damages at law were found to be an inadequate remedy, if, of course, there were no other factors present which made this remedy impossible, or impracticable; as where, in certain situations, long continued supervision by the court would be required for the contract's enforcement.[10] If such damages were found to be adequate, however, this remedy was denied. There is noticeable in recent times an ever growing disposition on the part of the courts to enlarge upon the number of cases in which damages are considered inadequate.

In starting with the general rule of equity just stated, at once the question arises: Have the English Sale of Goods Act and the American Sales Act had the effect of making innovations upon that rule, so that the courts in applying them may grant specific performance of certain contracts which would not have been specifically enforced under the rule stated without the aid of these Acts, or are such Acts simply declaratory of the preëxisting rule, so that courts will now decree specific performance only of contracts where that remedy was available before? Under the provisions of the sections quoted, a court may direct that the contract shall be performed specifically "if it thinks fit." Before these statutes were passed, a court could not, strictly speaking, give this remedy whenever it *thought fit:* it only did so when damages at law were not an adequate remedy. In determining, therefore, whether the statutes are intended to work innovations upon the preexisting rule or whether they are really restatements of it, it is necessary to determine whether the clause "if it thinks fit," is to be interpreted to mean "if damages are inadequate" (in which event the statutes are restatements); or whether that clause should be interpreted literally and held to mean that specific performance may be directed in the uncontrolled discretion of the court, irrespective of whether damages are inadequate; or, if indeed damages must still be found to be inadequate, whether the number of cases in which this inadequacy may be found is enlarged (in which event the statutes materially change the existing law). As will be seen, the decisions interpreting the statutes are not uniform.

The courts have been called upon to consider two other questions that arise in connection with these statutes: (1) What are "specific or ascertained goods"? (2) What is meant by a "contract to deliver"? These three problems are studied here in the following order and under the following headings:

I. The Sale of Goods Act and the Sales Act as effecting innovations upon the existing law.

Section 1. Cases in which specific performance has been granted in reliance upon these Acts, but in which this remedy would have been granted under the existing law without the aid of the Acts.

Section 2. Cases in which specific performance has been granted with the aid of the Acts, but would not have been granted under the existing law.

Section 3. Cases holding that the Acts make no innovation upon the existing law, and which deny specific performance under the Acts where it would not have been granted under the existing law.

II. What are "specific or ascertained goods"?

Section 1. Contracts to deliver a specific object or future goods.

Section 2. Contracts to sell a part of a parcel of goods.

III. What is meant by a "contract to deliver"? Will specific performance be granted if the property in the goods passes by the contract?

The English Act has been in force now for some forty years, and the American Act for from two to twenty-six years in the several states and territories in which it has been passed; yet there have been surprisingly few decisions under the two sections studied here. Many cases involving specific performance of contracts for the sale of goods have been before the courts in these years, but in very few of them is there even a reference to these statutory provisions. This seems difficult to understand. It means, perhaps, that counsel have either overlooked these provisions altogether, or, being aware of them, have interpreted them as simply restating the preëxisting rule rather than liberalizing it, and have thus felt that they gave no aid.

I. The Sale of Goods Act and the Sales Act as Effecting Innovations upon the Preëxisting Law.

Section 1. *Cases in which specific performance has been granted in reliance upon these Acts, but in which this remedy would have been granted under the preëxisting law without the aid of the Acts.*

The courts have based their decisions upon the provisions of the Sale of Goods Act and the Sales Act in decreeing specific performance in several cases in which damages at law were found to be inadequate, and in which that remedy would therefore doubtless have been granted without the aid of these provisions. Where, in a particular case, a court of equity would decree specific performance without the aid of the statute, *a fortiori* it would do so with its aid. Three cases are of special interest in this connection; the first involves the sale of a ship, the second, the sale of the steel scrap to be accumulated at defendant's factory over a period of five years, and the third, an assignment of land contracts and mortgages.

Behnke v. Bede Shipping Co., Ltd.[11]—In this case German shipowners sued for and were granted specific performance of a contract to buy a ship from its English owner. The vessel was of such kind as to satisfy the German regulations and to enable the German buyers to put her on the German register at once, so that the lower court found that the ship was of "peculiar and practically unique value to the plaintiff," and that damages at law would therefore not be adequate. The Court of King's Bench decreed specific performance: it held that a ship is "goods," "a specific chattel," within the meaning of § 52 of the Sale of Goods Act,[12] to which it referred as giving it discretion, if it thought fit, to give the relief prayed for.[13] Since the court found that damages would be inadequate, it would have decreed specific performance of the contract without the aid of § 52. Indeed, long before the passage of the Act ships had been considered as a special kind of property, and contracts for their sale had generally been specifically enforced in equity. For example, in 1852, in the well-known case of *Claringbould v. Curtis,*[14] an English court decreed specific performance of a contract to sell a barge for £40, and it does not appear that damages would not have been adequate for any reason, apart from the fact that the subject of the contract was a barge.[15]

Eastern Rolling Mill Co. v. Michlovitz.[16]—In this case, the Supreme Court of Maryland, in reliance upon § 68 of the American Act, decreed specific performance of a contract which it would doubtless have specifically enforced without the aid of the section, since damages at law were found to be inadequate. In this case, plaintiff purchased of defendant its entire accumulation of steel scrap from its factory, under contracts which were to run for five years. Prices were to be fixed at the beginning of every quarter for the next succeeding three months by reference to quotations appearing in a named publication at the beginning of such quarter. The amount of scrap produced varied daily. After the contract had been performed for three quarters, the defendant refused to go on with it. The court of appeals affirmed the chancellor's decree of specific performance. It said, "... the equitable remedy of specific performance is indicated by the facts and circumstances; and would seem to be authorized by section 89 of Article 83 of the Maryland Code [§ 68 of the Sales Act]." The court referred to § 246, art. 16, of the Maryland Code,[17] which, it held, had no application here, since the proof showed that defendant had property from which plaintiff might recover damages and costs, and added that therefore, apart from § 68, "the court, as a general rule, will refuse to decree specific performance in respect of chattels because damages are a sufficient remedy." It stated the exception to this rule, however, based on the inadequacy of the remedy at law, and held that plaintiff was entitled to equitable relief because damages at law would have been inadequate.

This same court had granted specific performance of similar contracts before the Sales Act was passed. In 1884, in *Equitable Gas Light Co., etc. v. Baltimore Coal Tar, etc., Co.,*[18] it specifically enforced a contract to sell "all the coal tar that might be produced at the defendant's gas works at Baltimore, for and during a term of five years," on the ground that damages would not be adequate since the profits would be speculative.[19] Thus, even though the court seemingly relies upon § 68 of the Act in the *Eastern Rolling Mill Co.* case, it would seem from the earlier case that it would have given equitable relief in the former case apart from the Act.[20]

Krause v. Hoffman.[21]—In this case, the Supreme Court of Michigan decreed specific performance of a contract to assign "land contracts and mortgages in the sum of forty thousand . . . dollars" belonging to an estate. It first stated the general equitable rule in respect to specific performance and its exceptions, and added that there can be "no question as to the power of the trial court, sitting as a court of chancery, or of this court on appeal, to require the defendants to specifically perform their contract," citing 3 Compiled Laws of Michigan (1915), § 11899, § 68 of the Sales Act, and this is true even though the contract did not specifically enumerate the securities to be assigned. "The relief should be granted or refused in the exercise of a sound judicial discretion. . . . The exercise of such a discretion under the facts here disclosed entitles plaintiff to the relief prayed for."

Courts of equity have never hesitated to grant specific performance of contracts for assignment of debts and contracts, on the ground that damages at law are inadequate, so that the court would have decreed specific performance in this case without the aid of the statute.[22]

Diamond Lumber Company v. Anderson.[23]—This was a Michigan case, in which the lower court said, by way of dictum, that under the Compiled Laws of Michigan (1915), § 11899 (§ 68 of the Sales Act), it had full jurisdiction of the subject-matter of a suit for specific performance of a contract for the sale of a tract of timber near plaintiff's mill, consisting of some three million feet of logs. The court held, however, that it was not necessary to determine whether it would give this remedy, since the bill was dismissed for the reason that the plaintiff had broken the contract and the defendant was excused from performance altogether. The Supreme Court did not disturb the findings of fact on this point, and affirmed the decree of the lower court. It refused to assess damages, because this could be done on the law side of the court. If the plaintiff could have proved the facts alleged by it (among which was inadequacy of damages, concerning which, however, both courts expressed some doubt), and if it had not breached the contract itself, the court would have had jurisdiction to decree specific performance under either § 68, as the lower court said, or apart from this section under the preëxisting rule.[24]

Since in the first three cases discussed—the *Behnke, Eastern Rolling Mill Co.,* and *Krause* cases—specific performance would doubtless have been granted without the aid of the statutes, they are of no assistance in determining what contracts, if any, the courts deciding them would specifically enforce in reliance upon the statutes, that they would not so enforce without the statutes. In other words, these cases give no aid in determining whether the English and American Acts make any innovation upon the preëxisting law. At least, these courts attach some meaning to these statutes and are impressed with their existence.

Section 2. *Cases in which specific performance has been granted with the aid of the Acts, but would not have been granted under the preëxisting law.*

In one English decision the court decreed specific performance in reliance upon § 52 of the English Act, even though it said that damages at law would be adequate; and in several American cases the courts relied upon § 68 of the American Act in decreeing specific performance when there was nothing to show that damages at law would have been inadequate.

James Jones & Sons, Ltd. v. Earl of Tankerville.[25]—In this case, the English Court of Chancery held that, where defendant's refusal to permit plaintiffs to proceed with the performance of a contract to sell growing timber was accompanied by violence, it would decree specific performance even though damages at law would afford an adequate remedy. In this case plaintiffs, in October, 1907, purchased of defendant, for a lump sum of £1565, some timber growing on certain estates. Plaintiffs were to have the right to enter upon the estates, cut the timber and saw it up thereon, and, for that purpose, to erect sawmills, and to remove the timber. Defendant was to give free exit to the hard roads and free sites for the mills. Plaintiffs erected a sawmill and began to cut timber, saw it up, and remove it, all in accordance with the terms of the contract. In February, 1908, a similar contract was entered into, whereby plaintiffs were to pay £4310 for further timber on the same estate; they entered, erected sawmills and machinery, and proceeded to fell timber and saw it up and carry it away. In September, 1908, defendant repudiated the contracts and demanded that cutting should cease; and on October 27, 1908, he forcibly ousted plaintiffs from the estates and wrecked their mills and buildings and stacks of timber. Plaintiffs sued for an injunction restraining defendant from preventing the execution of the contract and for damages. The defendant contended that the plaintiffs' claim for an injunction was equivalent to a claim for specific performance and that the court would not grant specific performance of such contracts, but would leave plaintiffs to their remedy by way of damages only. The court, however, granted the remedy sought. It noted that it had jurisdiction under § 52 of the Sale of Goods Act to grant the injunction, and that, though it of course possessed discretion to award damages if it thought fit, there was every reason in this case for not exercising this discretion: with respect to plaintiffs' timber already cut, their sawmills, machinery, and their other properties on defendant's land, their rights at law under the contract not only had been infringed, but also had been deliberately disregarded with every circumstance of violence and indignity; and even if the court thought that damages would be an adequate remedy, upon which the court makes no finding, it felt it incumbent to assert the authority of the law by refusing to allow the defendant to retain the benefits he had attempted to gain by his high-handed action. The court rests its decision solely upon this reasoning.

There is nothing "unique" about *growing trees.* Contracts for their sale are not specifically enforced in equity unless damages at law for their breach are inadequate or so uncertain and unascertainable that specific performance is indispensable to justice. For example, in *Paddock v. Davenport*[26] the Supreme Court of North Carolina refused to grant this remedy in a suit on a contract to sell to plaintiff, at a certain price, all the trees on defendant's land which plaintiff might select and mark, since it was not shown that the trees had any peculiar value to plaintiff, that the breach of the contract could not be compensated for in damages, or that other trees could not be purchased. And in *Emerzian v. Asato*[27] the District Court of Appeal, Third District of California, refused specifically to enforce a contract to "put, cultivate and care for" orange trees, since plaintiff could have gone into the open market and purchased similar trees.[28] The equitable remedy only is given in contracts for the sale of timber, as in other contracts, if for any reason damages are inadequate, or are inadequate because of their uncertainty or speculative character.[29] Therefore, it cannot be said that specific performance was granted in the *Earl of Tankerville* case because the contract was for the sale of trees. Whether or not damages would have been adequate in this case is of course a question of fact, upon which no finding was made. Indeed, such a finding was unnecessary, since it was held that plaintiff was entitled to the equitable relief asked for, even if the court had thought that damages would have been adequate.[30]

The principal case may be contrasted with another English case, *Fothergill v. Rowland,*[31] decided in 1873, in which a court of equity refused to grant an injunction to restrain the defendant from selling a colliery and the coal got from No. 3 seam, which the plaintiff had contracted to buy for five years at £6 per ton, because the contract was for the sale of ordinary chattels, which could be purchased elsewhere at an advanced price, and the damages were ascertainable. Since it was a contract the specific performance of which would have been denied, the injunction was not granted.[32] The defendant's refusal to go on with the contract in this case was not accompanied by violence or indignity. In this case, the ascertainment of damages would have been more difficult than in the *Earl of Tankerville* case, since, in the former, it could not have been determined how much coal would have been taken from No. 3 seam, and therefore the price to be paid could not have been determined; while in the principal case, a lump sum price was agreed upon. The court, in the *Earl of Tankerville* case, gave specific performance in reliance upon § 52 of the English Act, while in the *Fothergill* case—in which the ascertainment of damages would have been more difficult than in the former case—it refused this remedy without its aid. It would therefore seem that defendant's conduct led the court to see fit to grant specific performance, in reliance upon § 52, in a case in which this remedy would have been denied previous to the enactment of the Act in 1893.

Hughbanks v. Browning.[33]—In this case the Ohio Court of Appeal affirmed the judgment below requiring the defendant to deliver a specific, ascertained crop of tobacco, which he had sold to the plaintiff at a specified price. It declined to entertain the defense that because of injury by storm the tobacco would not meet the terms of the contract in respect to its condition. These are the only facts given in the case. There was nothing to show that the tobacco was of any peculiar value to the plaintiff or that damages would not, for any other reason, have been adequate. The court says of the Uniform Sales Act that it was passed for the purpose of "codifying and declaring in statutory form the common law as it then existed in this and other states, and also to modify and extend it where necessary or proper." It states the common law governing specific enforcement and simply adds:

> Interesting and instructive briefs have been filed by both sides upon the history and state of the law on this question, but for the purposes of this case it seems unnecessary for the court to enter upon any discussion, and it is sufficient to merely say that the language of this section of the law [§ 68 of the Sales Act, § 8448 of the Ohio General Code], as we now find it, clearly gives to the trial court the power to decree an enforcement of the sale, where the purchaser demands that sort of relief and the court finds it to be equitable and proper.

It quotes with approval the observations of Story that courts of equity

> might proceed much farther and might insist upon decreeing a specific performance of all *bona fide* contracts, . . . upon the principles of natural justice, . . . for it is against conscience that a party should have a right of election whether he should perform his covenant or only pay damages for the breach of it. But on the other hand there is no reasonable objection to allowing the other party who is injured by the breach to have an election either to take damages at law or to have a specific performance in equity, the remedies being concurrent but not co-extensive with each other.[34]

Michigan Sugar Co. v. Falkenhagen.[35]—In this case, the Supreme Court of Michigan, also, gave § 68 of the American Act a broad interpretation, and held that it gave a court of equity jurisdiction to decree specific performance of a contract to sell beets to be raised on a certain twenty acres of land, when there was no showing that damages would not have been adequate. The plaintiff was a manufacturer of sugar from beets, and contracts for beets to be raised by farmers were made months before planting. Such a contract was made in this case, by which the seller was to raise the crop, the buyer to furnish the seed and labor. The title to the crop was to remain in the seller "from the time when the same begins to grow." The seller was to deliver the crops to the buyer as and when directed at the seller's factory or on cars at designated receiving stations of the buyer. When the beets were nearly ready for delivery, the seller was about to deliver those grown on five of the twenty acres to another company, under a previous contract; and the buyer sued for specific performance and to enjoin this delivery. In the circuit court the bill was dismissed, and the delivery of the crops from the five acres to the other company was made. On a rehearing, it appearing that this delivery had been made to the other company and the rest to the buyer, the plaintiff, the court dismissed the bill, as it thought the case was a moot one. On appeal, plaintiff insisted that the court was in error in dismissing the bill, both at the hearing and the rehearing, and asked for a determination of its rights because of the great importance to it of knowing how far such a contract holds a crop of beets and binds the grower to make delivery. The Supreme Court noted that under § 68 of the Act (Compiled Laws of Michigan [1915], § 11899), a court of equity had jurisdiction, of course, to decree specific performance or award damages, and with reference to the application of that section to the contract before it, said:

Under the contract the beets to be raised were sold to plaintiff, and defendant was obligated to make delivery. Under such circumstances the court of equity has jurisdiction to decree specific performance [citing §§ 68 and 76 of the Sales Act].... The subject matter of this suit has passed beyond the reach of injunctive process and of specific performance, but if defendant should have been enjoined and specific performance decreed, then the court should have entertained jurisdiction, and, if through error the injunction was dissolved by the decree at the first hearing, the suit should be retained for the assessment of damages.

It was not shown that damages at law would have been inadequate; yet the court was willing to grant specific performance, and since this was impossible, it retained jurisdiction to assess damages.

Contracts for the sale of crops furnish no exception to the general rule, so that, apart from the statute, the courts insist upon finding inadequacy of damages at law before they will grant specific enforcement of such contracts. As will be shown presently, one court has refused equitable relief of such a contract, even under § 68 of the Sales Act, as damages were found to be adequate. In *Curtice Bros. Co. v. Catts,*[36] the New Jersey Court of Chancery enforced a contract to sell the entire product of certain land planted in tomatoes, only because the complainant, who had contracts for them for his canning factory, could not procure, at any price, other tomatoes of the quality needed in the open market during the six-weeks canning season, to ensure the successful operation of the plant, which would have remained idle except to whatever extent an uncertain general market might by chance have supplied the need.[37] The court added that it was therefore more than a question of the complainant's being compelled to purchase tomatoes at a higher price, and that if they could have been purchased in the open market without serious interference with the economic arrangement of the plant, "a court of equity would hesitate to assume to interfere."[38] The factors which induced the court to give specific relief in this case do not appear in the *Hughbanks* and *Michigan Sugar Co.* cases.

Thus, in the *Hughbanks* and *Earl of Tankerville* cases, the English and the Ohio courts decreed specific performance, and in the *Michigan Sugar Co.* case, the Supreme Court of Michigan would have done so had the subject-matter of the suit not passed beyond the reach of specific performance, all in reliance upon the statutes, where this remedy would not have been granted without the aid of such statutes. This generalization, it is admitted, must be made with caution, for the granting of specific performance is, within certain limits, in the discretion of the court, so that the action that the courts might have taken in these three cases without the aid of the statute, cannot be definitely known; but it has been shown already that, from the bare facts as gathered from the opinions, the courts in granting this relief in these three cases have gone further than courts of equity have gone in similar cases when unaided by the statutes. They thus interpret the statutes as something more than restatements, and as making innovations upon the existing law. In the *Earl of Tankerville* case, there is no finding on the question of whether damages would have afforded an adequate remedy; but the court relied upon § 52 of the English Act, and held that plaintiff was entitled to the equitable remedy, even if it thought damages were adequate. In the *Hughbanks* case, specific performance was granted when there was nothing to show that damages at law would not have been adequate and nothing therefore to induce the court to grant this remedy without the aid of § 68 of the American Act. The same observations may be made with reference to the *Michigan Sugar Co.* case. Equitable relief was granted in the English case because of the violence of defendant's conduct in interfering with plaintiff's performance of the contract. In the *Hughbanks* case, the court did not give the facts which, in its opinion, justified the decree: it was content to observe that, under § 68 of the Act, it had power to grant specific performance when the court "finds it to be equitable and proper," but it did not give reasons why it found this remedy "equitable and proper" in the case before it. In the *Michigan Sugar Co.* case, the court simply recited the terms of the contract and held that it had jurisdiction under § 68 to decree its specific enforcement.

In these three decisions, the courts thus gave the statutes a very broad and liberal interpretation and *thought fit* to grant specific performance without finding that damages at law were inadequate, and in two of them, at least, they did so without setting forth any facts which, in their opinion, justify the remedy, and without announcing any rule or principle by which they were or would be guided in the application of § 68. It would in fact be impossible for a court to lay down such a rule (if, indeed, it take the view that the section changes the preëxisting law on the subject), for it may grant equitable relief whenever it "thinks fit"; and it would necessarily have to look at all the facts and circumstances of each case arising to see if it thinks fit.

Section 3. *Cases holding that the Acts make no innovation upon the existing law, and which deny specific performance where it would not have been granted under the existing law.*

In two American cases a more restricted view of the statute has been taken than in the three cases just considered, and in one of them it was announced that the remedy of specific performance would not be given where it did not exist before the statute was passed.

Outten Grain Co. v. Grace.[39]—In this case, decided by the Illinois Court of Appeal, the contract was for the sale of growing corn of no peculiar value to plaintiff, to be delivered on husking day. The purchase price was paid when the contract was made. There was no evidence that the seller was insolvent. The bill alleged that he was about to sell or deliver the corn to a third party; and the relief prayed for was the delivery of the specific corn sold and, in default of the delivery of a part of it, payment of damages occasioned by the breach of the contract, and the delivery of the rest, and that the third party, if he had received any of it, be required to pay the buyer the value thereof. A demurrer, general and special, was overruled. The buyer contended that § 71, c. 121a, Cahill's Rev. Stat. (§ 68 of the Sales Act) applies, that it is "a legislative relaxation of the old rule against equitable aid by specific performance in sales of personal property in cases like that now presented." On appeal, the bill was dismissed. The court held that the Act did not give the remedy of specific performance where it did not exist before the Act, and it refused this remedy because the case presented no ground for equitable relief, since money damages were adequate and the corn was of no peculiar value to the plaintiff—the test which it applied. The court said that the Sales Act was to make uniform the laws of the states adopting it and added that it is

> a codification of the law concerning the sale of goods.... What is now stated in terse form in a code was formerly found in standard treatises stating the law of remedies under contracts of sales under varying conditions of fact.... The section of the Act relied on makes no change in the application of the remedy by specific performance from what it was before. It does not give the remedy where it did not exist before.[40]

Toles v. Duplex Power Co.[41]—The Supreme Court of Michigan in this case followed the existing rule applicable to contracts for the sale of corporate stock and refused to decree specific performance of a contract to sell one thousand shares of defendant corporation at $10 per share, it being alleged that the stock had advanced in value to $20 per share, and it appearing that the purchase was made as a purely commercial speculation.

> In every case [the court said] where specific performance of a contract is sought in a court of equity the primary question is whether the exercise of the power of the chancery court is demanded to subserve the ends of justice, and where there is an adequate remedy at law to recover damages for breach of the contract equity will not interfere. Manifestly plaintiff's anticipated enjoyment of this contract is confined to the enhanced value of the stock of defendant, resulting from the manipulation of which he received advanced information, which money damages adequately compass. While by our statute (3 Comp. Laws [1915], § 11899; § 68 of the Sales Act) a court with equity powers may, if it sees fit, decree specific performance of a contract for delivery of ascertained goods, yet the recognized field for equity interference to enforce specific performance of contracts is limited to matters relating to real estate.

It was added that specific performance is not generally decreed when the contract is for the sale of personal property, and that the exception to this rule, namely, where the measure of damages in a court of law will not afford adequate compensation, does not apply here, since it is not shown that the stock has no ascertainable market value, that it could not be obtained except from defendant (the purchase not involving a controlling interest in the corporation), or that there was "some uncommon and appealing equitable consideration" which would move the court to assume jurisdiction. Since the measure of damages was as readily ascertainable in an action at law as in chancery, plaintiff had an adequate remedy at law.[42]

The court, in the *Toles* case, simply follows the existing rule of equity relating to contracts for the sale of corporate stock: if the stock is easily obtainable on the market, even though at a higher price, specific performance will be denied;[43] while, if it is not easily obtainable, or if its value is uncertain, or if the plaintiff wishes the stock for the purpose of securing control of the corporation, or "if a substantial harm that cannot be accurately measured will be suffered... because of deprivation of voting power or otherwise,"[44] the remedy will be granted.[45] A court of equity would not have given specific performance of the contract in the *Toles* case apart from the Sales Act, and the court did not see fit to grant this remedy under the Act. It did not say explicitly, however, that the statute was simply a restatement of the existing rule that damages must be inadequate, but it refused specific performance seemingly because the case did not present an exception to the rule. The court does not say that it will give specific performance under the Act only when it would do so apart from the Act, even if there is an implication to that effect in the case. In fact, the Supreme Court of Michigan, which decided the *Toles* case, expressed its willingness to grant specific performance in the *Michigan Sugar Co.* case, in reliance upon § 68, without a showing that damages at law would not be adequate.

It may well be that specific performance should not have been granted in the *Outten Grain Co.* and *Toles* cases. No special reason appears for disagreeing with the decisions. It must be borne in mind, of course, that the courts were speaking with special reference to the particular contracts before them. It is believed, however, that the broad language used in the *Outten Grain Co.* case in saying that the statute is nothing more than a codifying statute, and perhaps an implication to that effect in the *Toles* case, are unfortunate.[46] This view of the statute may be said to illustrate the tendency of some courts to treat legal concepts as worked out by traditional case law, as "fundamental conceptions of legal science," to construe statutes by "classical common law"—a "Naturrecht"—and, therefore, to avoid all statutory interpretations that would work "innovations upon this common law," and to "assume, so far as possible, that statutes were meant to declare and reassert its principles."[47] It is true that the rule existing before the passage of the Sales Act, as worked out by the cases, was that specific performance would not be granted if damages at law were adequate; but there is no basis for assuming that the Sales Act was intended to make no innovation upon that rule. No such limitation is placed upon the court, expressly or by implication, as is found in the old rule. Under the statutory provisions, the equitable remedy may be granted whenever the court *thinks fit;* and the court might easily *think fit* in certain cases, whether or not damages at law are adequate. If it be argued that the court under the preëxisting rule could grant or refuse specific performance in its "discretion" and that this is tantamount to allowing this relief only "if it thinks fit," the answer is that the court did not have uncontrolled discretion under that rule, but that the rule became hardened, and specific performance was granted only when damages at law were inadequate, so that, under that rule, a court of equity was not free to grant the relief whenever it *thought fit,* as it may do under the statute.[48] In the *Earl of Tankerville, Hughbanks,* and *Michigan Sugar Co.* cases, the courts proceed upon the theory that the statutes give them wider equitable powers than they had before the enactment of these statutes.[49] Professor Williston, the author of the American Act, observes that both the English and American statutes "afford a clear warrant for an extension of previously existing rules,"[50] and that they will "perhaps dispose courts to enlarge somewhat the number of cases where specific performance is allowed."[51] Indeed, without the aid of these statutes the recent dispostion of the courts has been to extend this remedy,[52] and the statutes were no doubt intended to aid this disposition. If the old requirement of inadequacy of damages is still insisted upon, the statutes, to say the least, might be interpreted to be an advance beyond the existing rule as authorizing courts to enlarge upon the number of cases in which damages may be found to be inadequate. It seems difficult to justify the extreme view taken by the court in the *Outten Grain Co.* case.

The contribution made by the cases to the solution of the problem of whether the Sale of Goods Act and the Sales Act have made innovations upon the preëxisting law, may be summarized as follows:

1. Some of the cases which relied upon the statute would have been decided as they were without the aid of the statute. *A fortiori,* they would have been so decided with the aid of the statute. They therefore contribute little, if anything, to the solution of the problem.

2. The courts have granted specific performance in reliance upon the statute in several cases in which that remedy would not have been granted under the preëxisting law. These cases do not and could not lay down a rule of interpretation of the statute—a rule by which one could predict when a given contract would be specifically enforced in reliance upon the statute, but which would not be enforced under the preëxisting law. Such a rule would indeed defeat the purpose of the statutes, which were unquestionably intended to release the courts from the rule that had grown up in equity, thus leaving them free to

consider the particular facts of each case and to deal with it on its merits, and to enable them to give the equitable remedy in cases in which they may see fit to do so (if they find it "equitable and proper," is the language used in the *Hughbanks* case) irrespective of the adequacy or inadequacy of damages; or, if indeed inadequacy of damages must still be found, irrespective of whether the courts have before found inadequacy of damages in like cases.

3. The courts did not see fit to decree specific performance in some of the cases, and on the bare facts presented in the opinions there is no basis for disagreeing with the disposition of these cases. It is hoped, however, that the broad language to the effect that the statutes make no innovations upon the preëxisting rule, to which objection has already been made, will not influence courts in the future interpretation of the statutes.

There is of course the further possibility that the statute might be invoked for the purpose of decreeing specific performance of contracts that would not be specifically enforced under the preëxisting law, even though damages are found to be inadequate, because of the existence of what have been considered practical difficulties in the way of enforcing the decrees. This question has not been raised in any of the cases. It may well be that the courts, by a liberal interpretation of the statute, will find some of the difficulties less real than they have seemed to be under the fixed rule of the common law.

There remain to be considered two other problems which have arisen in connection with § 68 of the Sales Act and § 52 of the Sale of Goods Act: What are "specific or ascertained goods"? Will specific performance be granted whether or not the property in the goods passes by the contract?

II. What Are "Specific or Ascertained Goods"?

What are "specific or ascertained goods"? This question presents one of the difficult problems connected with the interpretation of the English and American Acts. Neither Act defines "ascertained"; but both define "specific goods," the former as "goods identified and agreed upon at the time a contract of sale is made,"[58] and the latter as "goods identified and agreed upon at the time a contract to sell or a sale is made."[54] There is no essential difference between the two provisions, since the English Act defines a "contract of sale" as a sale whereby the seller "transfers or agrees to transfer the property in the goods."[55] But neither Act defines what constitutes identification. A distinction must be drawn between the sale of a specific object in existence or future goods specifically described, on the one hand, and the sale of a portion of a larger lot, on the other.

Section 1. *Contracts to deliver a specific object or future goods.*

A contract to deliver a definite object is, of course, a contract to deliver "specific or ascertained" goods. This is illustrated by the *Behnke* case, in which a contract to deliver a specified ship was specifically enforced. Also, in the *Earl of Tankerville* case it was held that timber growing on a certain tract of land was "goods" and a contract for its sale specifically enforceable under § 52 of the English Act. In the *Hughbanks* and *Michigan Sugar Co.* cases, it was held that § 68 of the American Act gave jurisdiction to grant specific performance of contracts for the sale of a specific crop of tobacco and beets to be raised.[56] In *Eastern Rolling Mill Company v. Michlovitz,* the Supreme Court of Maryland held that a contract to run for five years, for the entire accumulation of "scrap" from defendant's factory of sheet steel, was a contract for "specific" and "ascertained" goods as these terms are used in the Sales Act. In *Krause v. Hoffman* the Supreme Court of Michigan enforced a contract to assign land contracts and mortgages belonging to an estate, even though the ones to be assigned were not specifically enumerated, but their selection would have to be made.

Section 2. *Contracts to sell a part of a parcel of goods.*

A more difficult question is presented when the contract is for the sale of a part of a specified, or an unascertained, lot or parcel. Is this a contract for the sale of "specific or ascertained goods"? Several recent English cases have answered this question in the negative. No American cases in point have squarely considered it. The leading English case is *In re Wait.*[57]

In re Wait.—In this case, Wait purchased one thousand tons of wheat to be shipped from America. The contract was thus for the future shipment of grain not at the time ascertained. The next day, Wait sold five hundred of the one thousand tons to persons called here the "sub-purchasers," who paid the purchase price. The thousand tons were later shipped, but before their arrival, Wait gave notice of suspension of payment and was adjudicated bankrupt. The trustee refused to deliver the five hundred tons to the sub-purchasers, who thereupon issued a notice of motion in the appropriate county court, asking that the trustee be directed specifically to perform the contract by delivering five hundred tons out of the one thousand tons, of which five hundred and thirty tons were still left. Alternately, they asked for an order for repayment of the purchase price, or, alternately, for a declaration that they had a beneficial interest in the parcel of one thousand tons to the extent of five hundred tons, and a charge upon the wheat and the bill of lading, which had been issued to Wait, to secure the repayment of the purchase price. The Court of Appeal dismissed the motion below for specific performance, on the ground that, at the date of the contract, the goods were not specific or ascertained, since there was "no ascertainment or identification of the five hundred tons out of the cargo in bulk," no identification of the thing, " 'the very thing,' for the goods were not appropriated nor their individuality ascertained."[58] Atkin, L. J., observed that while § 62 defines "specific goods," the Act nowhere defines the words "or ascertained," and that it is not easy to discover the reason for adding these words. He assumed that "ascertained" probably means "identified in accordance with the agreement after the time a contract of sale is made."[59] It was held, also, that there was no equitable assignment of the five hundred tons, because, in order to create such an assignment, the obligation must be to deliver a particular chattel, not to deliver any chattel.[60] Sargant, L. J., delivered a strong dissenting opinion. The wheat, he argued, had been definitely ascertained under the contract and invoice as one-half the particular parcel of one thousand tons placed on board the vessel and covered by the bill of lading,[61] and therefore the contract amounted to an equitable assignment enforceable against the parcel; and as the "specific performance" dealt with in § 52 of the Act includes the enforcement of an equitable assignment, or lien, this case is covered by that section, and the respondents were entitled to have five hundred tons (or the proceeds thereof) of the five hundred and thirty remaining tons made over to them.[62]

Likewise, the sale of ten bales of Hessian bags out of a particular parcel of forty-five bales is not a contract for the sale of specific or ascertained goods, and therefore specific performance of the contract will not be decreed under § 52.[63]

These two cases settle the law of England for the present, so that a contract for the sale of an unascertained portion of a larger quantity of goods is not specifically enforceable under § 52 of the Act.[64]

The Michigan case — *Krause v. Hoffman* — already considered, should be contrasted with these English decisions: it enforced a contract to assign land contracts and mortgages belonging to an estate, even though the contract did not designate what contracts or mortgages were assigned. Whether or not the subject-matter of the contract was "specific or ascertained" was a point that was not raised.

III. What is Meant by a "Contract to Deliver"? Will Specific Performance be Granted if the Property in the Goods Passes by the Contract?

If the property has not passed, there is no difficulty: specific performance will be decreed. The doubt, if there is one, arises when the property has passed, so that replevin or detinue would lie. Should specific performance be allowed in addition under the Sales Acts? This question has not been squarely raised in the English cases. In the *Behnke* case, there was a contract to buy a ship, which was specifically enforced under § 52, but the question of title did not arise. In the *Earl of Tankerville* case, the court enforced what it referred to as a contract of sale of timber growing on a certain tract of land, and stated that § 52 "seems to confer on the Court a statutory power of enforcing . . . specific performance of a contract for the sale of ascertained goods, whether or not the property has passed by the contract." It is admitted in *In re Wait* and in *Thames Sack & Bag Co. Ltd. v. Knowles & Co., Ltd.* that the property in the goods had not passed. When the former case was before the Divisional Court in Bankruptcy,[65] Astbury, J., expressed the opinion that specific performance becomes important only if the property has not passed, and that if the property has passed, this remedy is not necessary. On appeal, however, Hanworth, M. R., disagreed with this view, and held that § 52 applies in all cases in which the goods are specified or ascertained.

Turning to the American decisions, we note that, in the *Michigan Sugar Co.* case title to the crops sold did not pass at the time the contract was made, but the point in respect to title was not discussed by the court. In the *Diamond Lumber Company* case, the lower court said, *obiter dictum,* that it had jurisdiction, under § 68, of the subject-matter of a contract for the sale of a tract of timber when it appeared that title probably did not pass at the time of the contract. In the *Eastern Rolling Mill Co.* case, the contract, which was specifically enforced, was for the accumulation over a period of five years of the scrap of defendant's steel factory: the title to the scrap could not have passed in this case at the time of the contract.[66] In the *Hughbanks* case, it is simply stated that a crop of tobacco had been sold to the plaintiff, and no reference is made to the title. In the *Krause* case, title could not have passed.

The expression, "contract to deliver," appears in both English and American Acts. The choice of this expression is unfortunate. It certainly does not mean a contract of bailment or of carriage: it contemplates, of course, a consensual agreement by which property passes at the time of the agreement or by which it is to be transferred in the future, or both. It is, no doubt, used in a broad sense in both Acts, and Hanworth's opinion that it includes a sale or an agreement to sell is believed to be the correct one. It is true that if the property passes by the contract, the buyer may maintain any action allowed by law to the owner of goods that have been converted or withheld,[67] and this would of course include actions of replevin and trover; this is why it is sometimes said that there is no occasion for specific performance. But the answer is that these remedies do not afford as adequate a remedy as specific performance does, and the statutes under consideration are designed to liberalize the rule governing this remedy in order that complete justice may be done in the particular case. It may well be that the availability of these legal remedies should be considered by the court in deciding whether the case is one for equitable relief, but it should not be a sufficient reason alone for denying specific performance, especially under the very broad and liberal terms of the statutes.[68]

NOTES TO MASTERSON ESSAY

[1] 27 Halsbury, *The Laws of England* (1913) 4, 12; *In re* Wait [1927] 1 Ch. 606, 616; Chalmers, *Sale of Goods Act, 1893* (ed. 9; 1925) 125.

[2] 17 & 18 Vict. c.125 § 78.

[3] 46 & 47 Vict. c. 49 § 3.

[4] 36 & 37 Vict. c. 66. See especially §§ 16, 18, and 24.

[5] 19 & 20 Vict. c. 97 § 2.

[6] 56 & 57 Vict. c. 71.

[7] "The provisions of this section," it is added, "shall be deemed to be supplementary to, and not in derogation of, the right of specific implement in Scotland." "In Scotland specific performance, or, as it is called, specific implement, is an ordinary and not an extraordinary remedy, and it can be demanded as of right wherever it is practicable."—Chalmers, *loc. cit.* "... in Scotland ... the party aggrieved ... cannot be compelled to resort to the alternative of an action of damages unless implement is shewn to be impossible, in which case, loco facti imprestabilis subit damnum et interesse."—Lord Watson in Stewart v. Kennedy (1890) 15 A. C. 75, 102.

See § 62 of the Act for definitions of certain terms used in § 52. Such definitions as have any bearing on the problems considered in this article will be considered in their appropriate places.

[8] For a list of such states and territories, see Williston and McCurdy, *A Selection of Cases on the Law of Sales* (1932) 1027.

[9] See § 76 of the Act for definitions of certain terms used in § 68. Such definitions as have any bearing on the problems discussed in this article will be considered in their appropriate places. For changes in this section made by the legislatures of Connecticut and Pennsylvania, see Cook, *Cases on Equity* (ed. 2; 1932) 522. For the law of Louisiana, see La. Civ. Code (1870) §§ 2458, 2551, 1799, 2046, 2482, 2485. On the question of the right of the vendor to specific performance, see (1929) 4 Tulane L. Rev. 92 and 147.

The sections of the English and American Acts quoted allow specific performance to the buyer only, and they must not be confused with § 63 of the latter and § 49 of the former, which permit an action by the seller for the price when the property has passed by the contract, when the seller has tendered the goods, and the buyer has refused to receive them.

[10] See Pomeroy, *A Treatise on the Specific Performance of Contracts* (ed. 3, by Pomeroy and Mann; 1926) § 8; 2 Williston, *The Law Governing Sales of Goods at Common Law and under the Uniform Sales Act* (ed. 2; 1924) §§ 1507–1510; Walsh, *A Treatise on Equity* (1930) § 58, for statements of this rule.

[11] [1927] 1 K. B. 649.

[12] The court referred to § 62 (1), which declares that " 'goods' include all chattels personal other than things in action and money, and in Scotland all corporeal movables except money. The term includes emblements, industrial growing crops, and things attached to or forming part of the land which are agreed to be severed before sale or under the contract of sale." There is a similar provision in § 76 of the American Act.

[13] The court refused to deny the remedy sought, moreover, simply because, before completion of payment of the balance of the purchase price, the buyer was to have the option of inspecting the vessel afloat and of requiring the seller to place her in dry dock

for inspection and repair of certain damages if any were found. It held that the direction of the performance of this part of the contract would not place the court in the position of decreeing the performance of work and services, since the seller would only be required to give appropriate orders to a dry-dock owner, if necessary, and since repairs may not be found necessary. See *Law of Contracts Restatement* (Am. L. Inst. 1932) § 371, illustration 3.

[14] (1852) 21 L. J. Ch. 541.

[15] The defendant alleged that he had previously sold the barge to W. S. The court said that its decree could not affect W. S.'s interest since he was not a party to the suit, but ordered that "the plaintiff is entitled to a decree for specific performance of the contract, with costs, and I must refer it to the Master to settle the bill of sale in case the parties differ" (*ibid.* 542). See *Law of Contracts Restatement* (Am. L. Inst. 1932) § 368, with respect to the protection of rights of third parties, which are superior to those of plaintiffs.

In Menier v. Donald (1917) 98 Misc. Rep. 684, 685, 165 N. Y. Supp. 50, 51, the New York Supreme Court was asked to decree specific performance of a contract for the sale of a steamship. The court observed that, "there is authority, both in this country and in England, for the proposition that a ship is a special kind of personal property, which in itself may justify a court of equity in decreeing specific performance." But it added that even if this were not so, the allegations of the complaint "as to the special and peculiar value of this ship to the plaintiff and the difficulty of replacing it or determining its value and his damages under present conditions are amply sufficient to sustain the complaint against demurrer." The Sales Act was not referred to in this case. See also Hurd v. Groch (N. J., 1898) 51 Atl. 278; Hart v. Herwig (1873) 42 L. J. Ch. 457; 3 Williston, *The Law of Contracts* (1920) § 2520; Pomeroy, *op. cit.* § 49; *Law of Contracts Restatement* (Am. L. Inst. 1932) § 361.

[16] (1929) 157 Md. 51, 145 Atl. 378.

[17] This section reads: "No court shall refuse to specifically enforce a contract on the mere ground that the party seeking its enforcement has an adequate remedy in damages, unless the party resisting its specific enforcement shall show to the court's satisfaction that he has property from which such damages may be made, or shall give bond, with approved security, in a penalty to be fixed by the court, to perform the contract or pay all such costs and damages as may, in any court of competent jurisdiction, be adjudged against him for breach or non-performance of such contract." For a Maryland case interpreting this statute, see Baltimore Process Co. v. My-Coca Co. (1924) 144 Md. 439, 125 Atl. 179.

[18] (1884) 63 Md. 285.

[19] To the same effect, see Gottschalk v. Stein (1888) 69 Md. 51, 13 Atl. 625. *Cf.*, however, Clarke v. Borough Asphalt Co. (1916) 93 Misc. 662, 157 N. Y. Supp. 581 (Sales Act not cited).

[20] So far as affirmative relief is concerned, such as was prayed for in the two Maryland cases discussed in the text, equity ordinarily will not decree specific performance of a contract "where the duty to be enforced is continuous and reaches over a long period of time, requiring constant supervision by the court," a contract, for example, which entitles the complainant to "have the first call on the vaudeville acts or performances which it shall or may book in the City of San Francisco . . . , for a term of ten years" (Pantages v. Grauman, 191 Fed. 317, 320, 323 [C. C. A. 9th, 1911]). See also Dominion Coal Co., Ltd. v. Dominion Iron and Steel Co., Ltd. (1909) A. C. 293. But when the inadequacy of damages is great, and the difficulties of supervision not great [granting that this difficulty ordinarily stands in the way of a decree for specific performance (see Walsh, *op. cit.* § 65, however)], specific performance will be decreed, and the tendency is to give this

remedy. In these two Maryland cases the inadequacy of damages seems so great and the difficulties of supervision by the court so negligible that specific performance is properly given, in the one case without the aid of the statute, and *a fortiori,* in the other, with its aid. Specific performance was granted by the Supreme Court of Massachusetts without the aid of a statute, in a case somewhat similar to the Maryland cases. In this case—Adams v. Messinger (1888) 147 Mass. 185, 17 N. E. 491—the contract was to make and supply certain patented injectors, the making of which required no particular skill, and which could be made simply by reference to the patents. The two Maryland cases discussed in the text did not even require the manufacture of the goods contracted for, but only the delivery to plaintiff in the one case, of the scrap from defendant's factory, which needed only to be bundled, and in the other, of the tar produced at defendant's gas works.

For cases involving contracts which would have required constant supervision by the court and which were therefore not specifically enforced, see Ross v. Union Pacific Ry. Co. (1863) 4 Woolw. 26, Fed. Cas. No. 12080, and Texas and Pacific Ry. Co. v. Marshall (1890) 136 U. S. 393, 10 Sup. Ct. 846, 34 L. Ed. 385. *Contra* are Joy v. St. Louis (1891) 138 U. S. 1, 11 Sup. Ct. 243, 34 L. Ed. 843; Union Pacific Ry. Co. v. Chicago, Rock Island and Pacific Ry. Co. (1896) 163 U. S. 564, 16 Sup. Ct. 1173, 41 L. Ed. 265; Taylor v. Fla. East Coast Ry. Co. (1907) 54 Fla. 635, 45 So. 574. For suits on contracts to operate mines and quarries, see Rutland Marble Co. v. Ripley (1870) 10 Wall 339, 19 L. Ed. 955; Clarno v. Grayson (1896) 30 Ore. 111, 46 Pac. 426; and Wharton v. Stoutenburgh (1882) 35 N. J. Eq. 266. On this subject generally see 3 Williston, *The Law of Contracts* §§ 1423, 1432; Walsh, *op. cit.* §§ 61, 65; Pomeroy, *op. cit.* §§ 15, 23; *Law of Contracts Restatement* (Am. L. Inst. 1932) §§ 359, 360, 361, and 371.

[21] (1927) 239 Mich. 348, 214 N. W. 146.

[22] O'Donnell v. Chamberlain (1906) 36 Col. 395, 91 Pac. 39; Tuttle v. Moore (1870) 16 Minn. 112; Gottschalk v. Stein (1888) 69 Md. 51, 13 Atl. 625; Scarborough v. Scotten (1888) 69 Md. 137, 14 Atl. 704; Wright v. Bell (1818) 5 Price 325; Cutting v. Dana (1874) 25 N. J. Eq. 265; Walsh, *op. cit.* 313; Pomeroy, *op. cit.* § 20; 3 Williston, *op. cit., supra* note 20 § 2521.

[23] (1921) 216 Mich. 71, 184 N. W. 597.

[24] On the court's refusal to assess damages when specific performance is not given, see Milkman v. Ordway (1870) 106 Mass. 232, and Banaghan v. Malaney (1908) 200 Mass. 46, 85 N. E. 839.

[25] (1909) 2 Ch. 440.

[26] (1890) 107 N. C. 710, 12 S. E. 464.

[27] (1913) 23 Calif. App. 251, 137 Pac. 1072.

[28] See also Bomer Bros. v. Canaday (1901) 79 Miss. 222, 30 So. 638.

[29] Stuart v. Pennis (1895) 91 Va. 688, 22 S. E. 509; St. Regis Paper Co. v. Santa Clara Lumber Co. (1903) 173 N. Y. 149, 65 N. E. 697; Buxton v. Lister and Cooper (1746) 3 Atl. 383; Diamond Lumber Co. v. Anderson, p. 445 *supra.*

[30] One might well speculate in respect to the adequacy of damages in this case, since the performance of the contract in the nature of things would have extended over a considerable period of time. Compare this case with the Stuart and Buxton cases cited in the previous note, in which specific performance was allowed, and the language of the court in the St. Regis Paper Co. case, cited in the same note.

[31] (1873) L. R. 17 Eq. 132, 43 L. J. Ch. 252.

[32] *Cf.* Peale v. Marian Coal Co., 190 Fed. 376 (Cir. Ct. N. D. Pa., 1911) (1913) 204 Fed. 161.

[33] (1917) 9 Ohio App. 114 (C. C. A. 3d).

[34] 2 Story, *Equity Jurisprudence* (ed. 13; 1886) § 717a. See *ibid.* (ed. 14) § 994.

[35] (1928) 243 Mich. 698, 220 N. W. 760.

[36] (1907) 72 N. J. Eq. 831, 66 Atl. 935.

[37] See also White Marble Lime Co. v. Consolidated Lumber Co. (1919) 205 Mich. 634, 172 N. W. 603.

[38] See also Bower v. Bowser (1907) 49 Ore. 182, 88 Pac. 1104; Buxton v. Lister, note 29 *supra* (dictum).

[39] (1925) 239 Ill. App. 284. This case is noted in (1927) 25 Mich. L. Rev. 558.

[40] *Ibid.* at 387. This is the view of Lord Hanworth, M. R. (dictum), in *In re* Wait (1927) 1 Ch. 606.

[41] (1918) 202 Mich. 224, 168 N. W. 495.

[42] In Cohen v. Rocke [1927] 1 K. B. 169, which was an action in detinue rather than specific performance, the court refused to require the delivery of ordinary Hepplewhite chairs of no "special features," which plaintiff had bought of defendant at an auction sale for the purpose of reselling them at a profit. By Order XLVIII, r. 1, the court had power to direct that execution should issue for the delivery of goods without giving the defendant the option of retaining the property upon payment of the value. In an action for detinue, the practice is stated as follows in Whiteleys v. Hilt [1918] 2 K. B. 808, 819: "The power vested in the court to order the delivery up of a particular chattel is discretionary, and ought not to be exercised where the chattel is an ordinary article of commerce and of no special value or interest, and not alleged to be of any special value to the plaintiff, and damages would fully compensate." The court said, by way of dictum, that an action of detinue "rests upon a footing which fully accords with § 52 of the Sale of Goods Act," and the goods in this case being of no special value or interest, there is no ground for any special order for delivery, and plaintiff is limited to damages. The court notes that § 52 is not consistent with an absolute right of plaintiff to an order for compulsory delivery under a detinue judgment in such a case as this one.

[43] This has been the equitable rule from early times. See, for example, Cudd v. Rutter (1719) 1 P. W. 570, and Cappur v. Harris (1723) Bunb. 135.

[44] *Law of Contracts Restatement* (Am. L. Inst. 1932) § 361, illustration No. 2.

[45] For citation of many authorities, see 3 Williston, *op. cit., supra* note 20 § 1419; Pomeroy, *op. cit.* §§ 17, 18, 19; 2 Williston, *The Law Governing Sales . . . Act* (ed. 2) § 602; Walsh, *op. cit.* 312.

[46] Since the passage of the Sales Act in the several states, there have been many suits to enforce specific performance of contracts for the sale of goods. In very few of the cases, however, has the Act been even referred to. The courts simply dispose of the cases by the application of the old rule that inadequacy of damages must be shown before equity will give relief. It by no means follows, however, that these courts would have adhered strictly to this rule, or have used the language of the cases that arose before the Sales Act was passed, had their attention been directed to the Act.

[47] For a discussion of this tendency, see Pound, *The Scope and Purpose of Sociological Jurisprudence* (1911) 24 Harv. L. Rev. 591, 601.

[48] Pomeroy, *op. cit.* §§ 36, 37, 38.

[49] See Radin, *The Law of Sales in California and the Uniform Sales Act* (1920) 9 Calif. L. Rev. 27, 37, for a discussion of § 68 of the American Act.

[50] 3 Williston, *op. cit., supra* note 20, 2525, note 37, citing the Earl of Tankerville case. See also Vold, *Handbook on the Law of Sales* (1931) 493.

[51] 2 Williston, *The Law Governing Sales . . . op. cit.* § 601.

[52] 3 Williston, *op. cit., supra* note 20, §§ 1418, 1419; Curtice Bros. Co. v. Catts (1907) 72 N. J. Eq. 831, 66 Atl. 933, 936; Hughbanks v. Browning (1917) 9 Ohio App. 114, (1927) 25 Mich. L. Rev. 546; Walsh, *op. cit.* 300, 301; *Law of Contracts Restatement* (Am. L. Inst. 1932) § 358, at p. 635.

[53] Sec. 62.

[54] Sec. 76.

[55] Sec. 1.

[56] See note 12 *supra.*

[57] (1926) Ch. 962; (1927) 1 Ch. 606.

[58] The county court judge had held that the five hundred tons were not "specific" or "ascertained" goods within the authorities and that he could not decree specific performance. He ordered the trustee to repay the purchase price, however, on the theory that it was in the nature of a trust fund earmarked for a specific purpose and that, in any event, it would be unconscionable of the trustee, as an officer of the court, to keep both the wheat and the purchase money. The Divisional Court in Bankruptcy, on appeal, applied §§ 52 and 62 of the Sale of Goods Act, and ordered specific performance. It held that § 52 applies, since the goods were "specific," as they were a "specified portion of a future specified shipment."

[59] For discussions of the meanings of "specific" and "ascertained," and the distinction, if any, between the two, as applied to goods, see: Benjamin (Kennedy, ed.), *Treatise on the Law of Sales of Personal Property* (ed. 7; 1931) 1026; 25 Halsbury, *The Laws of England* (1913) 121 note (c), 174 note (r); (1926) 70 Sol. J. 1014; (1927) 43 L. Q. Rev. 293; Chalmers, *The Sale of Goods Act, 1893* (ed. 9; 1925) 125. Some writers, including Benjamin who says that the meaning of the words, "or ascertained," is not clear, and Halsbury, are of the opinion that they mean, made "specific" after the formation of the contract, and that it is not necessary to make them synonymous with "specific" as "specific goods" are defined in the Act, § 62 (1). There is a dictum to this effect by Atkin, L. J., in *In re* Wait [1927] 1 Ch. 606, 630. Benjamin says that the effect of the ruling in Thames Sack and Bag Co. v. Knowles [see note 63 *infra*] bears out this interpretation. Halsbury says that it is "conceived that the term 'specific' includes the unascertained product of what is specific, and is not confined to actually existing goods, so that Howell v. Coupland [see note 64 *infra*] . . . is still law." This is the holding in the Eastern Rolling Mill Co. case. Chalmers, who originally drafted the Act, simply refers to Thames Sack and Bag Co. v. Knowles & Co. for a discussion of what "ascertained" means, and to the Earl of Tankerville case as authority for the proposition that § 52 applies whether the property in the goods has passed or not.

[60] See also Wood v. Corrigan (1928) 28 S. R. N. S. Wales 492, 502 (Australia). There was much discussion in *In re* Wait by the Justices of the case of Hoare v. Dresser (1859) 7 H. L. Cas. 290. In that case, an English merchant had ordered some timber of a Swedish seller. The timber was shipped, and the bill of lading sent to the seller's London agent, who was to deliver it up to the buyer upon the latter's acceptance of a bill of exchange in payment of the purchase price. It was held that, though the contract was at first general, it was made specific by the subsequent shipping, and that, when the timber was laden on the ship, the buyer had an equitable title to the property, while the legal title was in the consignee named in the bill of lading. This case seems to have little bearing on the question involved in *In re* Wait. It simply presents the usual situation of the seller's shipping goods, on an order of the buyer, under a bill of lading which reserves the legal, or security, title in himself or agent. The question of whether there is

a specifically enforceable lien against a parcel of goods when a part of them has been sold is not presented. However, Lord Cranworth uttered some strong dicta in support of the lien theory urged in *In re* Wait: he said that, when there is an engagement to satisfy a contract out of a particular thing, such as to appropriate a part of a larger cargo, equity will give the purchaser a lien upon the larger cargo, in order to enable him to satisfy himself of the smaller demand.

For a criticism of both grounds of the decision in *In re* Wait, see (1927) 43 L. Q. Rev. 293. The writer seems to place much emphasis upon the dicta of Lord Cranworth in Hoare v. Dresser, just referred to, to which, he says, the case of *In re* Wait is "clean contrary."

[61] See (1926) 70 Sol. J. 1014.

[62] All parties admitted that the property to the five hundred tons did not pass. Under the English law, when there is a contract to sell a specified portion of a mass of fungible goods, such as so many tons of oil from a tank containing a large quantity, or bushels of wheat from a larger parcel, the buyer does not become owner as tenant in common with the seller. See, for example, Laurie and Moorewood v. Dundin & Sons [1926] 1 K. B. 223; Snell v. Heighton (1883) 1 Cab. and Ell. 95; White v. Wilks (1813) 5 Taunt. 176; Austen v. Craven (1812) 4 Taunt. 644. For a similar Scottish decision, see Thomas Hayman & Son v. Thomson M'Lintock [1907] (Sess. Cas.) 936. *Cf.*, however, Wait v. Midland Bank (1926) 31 Com. Cas. 172; Gillett v. Hill (1834) 2 C. & M. 530, and Knights v. Whiffen (1870) L. R. 5 Q. B. 660; Sterns, Ltd. v. Vickers, Ltd. [1923] 1 K. B. 78; Inglis v. Stock (1885) 10 App. Cas. 263. The rule in many American states is *contra.* See, for example, Kimberly v. Patchin (1859) 19 N. Y. 330; Newhall v. Langdon (1883) 39 Ohio St. 87; Watts v. Hendry (1869) 13 Fla. 523.

[63] Thames Sack & Bag Co. v. Knowles & Co., Ltd. (1918) 88 L. J. (K. B.) 585.

[64] Several interesting cases have considered the question of what constitutes "specific" goods or things in other connections. For example, it was held in Howell v. Coupland (1874) L. R. 9 Q. B. 462, that, under the rule, when there is a contract with reference to a particular thing or a portion of a particular thing, and the thing cannot be delivered owing to its perishing without the seller's fault, its delivery is excused; the sale of two hundred tons of potatoes to be grown on a specified place of the seller's, which was sufficient to grow more than two hundred tons in an average year, was a contract for the delivery at a future time of a specific thing, "so far as this, that it is for the delivery of a portion of a specific thing." The court said that this contract was like a contract for the purchase of ten or one hundred tons of a cargo of goods out of a particular ship to arrive, which must be so many tons out of the bulk on board the ship. In Mullins v. Smith (1860) 1 Dr. and Sm. 204, 210, the court in discussing the question of what constitutes "specific" legacies, in contradistinction to "general and demonstrative" legacies, observes that, "A stock legacy payable out of the Stock of the same denomination is specific. . . ." See also Kirby v. Potter (1799) 4 Vesey 748, 750. But Atkin, L. J., observes, in discussing Howell v. Coupland in *In re* Wait, that cases like Howell v. Coupland arising before 1893 do not involve the question of whether the goods are "specific" or "ascertained" for the purpose of decreeing specific performance under § 52 of the Act. He adds that the cases before the passage of the Act in 1893 are not of much value in determining this question, for the court is bound by the language of the Act. Sargant, L. J., in his dissenting opinion in *In re* Wait, however, cites this case in support of his position that the goods contracted for in that case were "specific" and that the contract was therefore especially enforceable under § 52 of the Code. This raises the whole question of whether goods may be "specific or ascertained" for one purpose but not for another under the Act. For the view of Sir Mackenzie Chalmers, the draftsman of the Sale of Goods Act, see his treatise, *The Sale of Goods Act, 1893* (1922) 125. His view is in accord with the

rule announced in Howell v. Coupland, that, when there is a sale from a larger quantity, the goods may not be specific for the purpose of passing title, yet they may be specific for the purpose of relieving the seller from liability if they are destroyed. But the learned writer ventures no opinion on the question of whether they are specific or ascertained for the purpose of specific performance of the contract under § 52 of the Act.

Since "specific goods" are defined in § 62 (1) of the English Act and § 76 of the American Act, as "goods identified and agreed upon" at the time the contract is made, goods which are "specific" for one purpose are "specific" for all purposes under these Acts. It is therefore only a question in each case of whether the goods are "identified and agreed upon" in that case, and courts may not, of course, agree upon what constitutes identification.

[65] [1926] Ch. 962, 973.

[66] Sales Act, §§ 1, 5, 76.

[67] *Ibid.* § 66.

[68] *Law of Contracts Restatement* (Am. L. Inst. 1932) 637.

THE CRIMINAL ACT*

BY JUSTIN MILLER

ONE OF THE MOST IMPORTANT ELEMENTS of a crime is the act. In definitions of crime the greatest emphasis is placed upon the act and, although it is a well-known maxim that every crime requires a union of act and intent, in fact many crimes, especially the less serious ones, require merely the commission of the prohibited act.[1] This has been generally recognized in connection with a large group of minor offenses which have been designated by-laws, misdemeanors, acts *mala prohibita,* and violations of police regulations. The recent tendency of the law has been to extend this idea considerably and to establish criminal liability based upon prohibited acts, regardless of the presence or absence of a mental condition which even remotely resembles the general criminal intent of the common law. Conspicuous among recent examples of this tendency is the new federal law making criminal the possession of gold. The crime is complete even though the defendant does nothing more than to continue to possess gold which he had previously placed in a safe-deposit box or other place of safe-keeping.[2] In view of the present interest in the subject and the scattered text discussions of this important element of crime, it seems well worth while to analyze the concept of act in the criminal law as has been done in the following pages.

The common meaning of the word act is "that which is done or doing, a performance, a deed, a movement" as distinguished from remaining at rest.[3] In the criminal law it is impossible to give an inclusive definition of the word in a short space because—as is also true, in lesser degree, of intent—its character varies with each crime. Thus in homicide cases, the act is the killing of a human being;[4] in larceny, it is the taking and carrying away of personal property;[5] in arson, it is the burning of a house;[6] in rape, it is the having of sexual intercourse.[7] In each of these situations the act is quite different, yet there are certain similarities among all of them. In each crime named above the

* From *Miller on Criminal Law,* copyrighted by West Publishing Company, 1934.

act is physical—that is to say, muscular; in each crime it is active as distinguished from passive, and in each it affects the person or property of another. As applied to a great many crimes the act could be defined in terms of these similarities, viz., as a physical or muscular movement; active as distinguished from passive; affecting the person or property of another.[8] Unfortunately such a definition would be incomplete and in many instances it would be inaccurate.

It has long been recognized that in respect of some crimes[9] a mere omission to act may be sufficient. Examples of this sort are to be found in failure to perform an official duty imposed by law;[10] and in failure to move a train from a street crossing after the lapse of a certain length of time.[11] In each of these examples there is no physical, muscular movement at all; indeed it is because of the very absence of such a movement that a crime results.

In some classes of crimes, criminal liability may result from passive participation in a transaction in which the affirmative muscular activity that occurs is that of an accomplice, for example, the passive participant in adultery or sodomy.[12] One may be a guilty participant in a crime, even though entirely unconscious from an anesthetic administered prior to its commission, as in abortion or in an operation performed to prevent the calling of a person for military service.[13]

A person may be guilty of crime when his act has no effect upon the person or property of another, as when he commits suicide;[14] possesses counterfeiting tools,[15] or burglars' tools;[16] manufactures intoxicating liquor;[17] or belongs to a prohibited organization or society.[18] In perhaps the most important group of crimes, those against the government itself, as for example, treason, sedition, and the violation of tax and revenue laws, the persons or property of others is not affected, except in the most remote way.

Some crimes occur upon the happening of very simple, single muscular acts, such as the striking of another, in an assault,[19] or the stepping on the land of another, in a trespass.[20] Other crimes require the happening of acts which are complex and difficult of definition and of proof; such as the "possession" of goods, or "membership" in a society, or the "seduction" of a woman. Again, some crimes require for their commission a series of two or more acts; for example, the taking and the carrying away of personal property, in larceny; the breaking and the entering in burglary.

The criminal liability of a defendant may depend upon the results of his act, which occur after his own physical activity has completely ceased. Thus, if *A* strikes *B* in the eye with his fist and no injury results, he may be guilty of a simple assault or battery;[21] if his blow destroys *B's* eye, he may be guilty of mayhem;[22] if, within a year and a day, *B* dies as a result of *A's* blow, the latter may be guilty of murder, and this is true even though in the meantime *B* may have been subjected to an operation or exposed to disease,[23] under conditions over which *A* has no control whatsoever. In each of these acts it is said that the striking or the destruction of the eye, or the killing of a human being, is *A's* act. Considerable difficulty sometimes results from such use of the word, when it is attempted to work out a concurrence of intent with act.[24] *A's* intent to kill may have long since given way to overwhelming remorse, when *B's* death finally occurs. Difficult problems of jurisdiction also arise, where, for example, *A*, standing in one state, fires a gun which discharges a bullet which strikes *B* in a second state and *B* dies within a year and a day in a third state. In some of the states the law says that the act occurred where the gun was fired;[25] in others, where the impact of the bullet occurred with *B's* body.[26] In some states statutes have been passed declaring that *A* is liable if the act was either commenced or completed in the state.[27]

Because of the great variety of acts which constitute the various crimes, there are many circumstances which affect the criminality of such acts. The absence of the relationship of man and wife may make of a particular act the crime of rape, where had such a relationship existed there would have been no crime.[28] The existence of the relationship of uncle and niece may cause a similar act to be the crime of incest and may invalidate a marriage, where, if such relationship had not existed, the marriage would have been a proper marital union.[29] So the absence of consent of the owner of goods may make their taking and carrying away a crime, where, had his consent been given, it would have been a normal business transaction.[30] The fact that certain goods have been stolen may make their possessor a criminal, where if they had not been stolen he would be guiltless, even though he thought they were stolen.[31] An act otherwise lawful may become unlawful, because of knowledge of the defendant that such act constitutes an aiding and abetting of an unlawful act, subsequently to be performed; as where the defendant sold liquor, knowing that the buyer intended to resell it in violation of the law.[32] The absence of fear upon the part of a person who gives his goods to one who approaches him on the street may prevent the taker from being a robber, even though the latter thinks that he is a robber.[33] Similarly, the presence or absence of justification or excuse in many forms may determine whether particular acts constitute particular crimes.[34] In respect to some acts these situations raise the question of criminal intent. In respect to many others criminal intent is not involved at all, but solely the question of the sufficiency or insufficiency of the act, depending upon states of mind of persons other than the defendant[35] and upon other circumstances beyond his control.

In order to hold him criminally liable, it must be established that the defendant committed the prohibited act. This does not necessarily mean, however, that he must himself personally have performed the physical movement which constituted the act, or himself personally have omitted to perform an act required of him. Thus one may be guilty of first degree murder though he be a helpless, bedridden cripple, if he procure another, who is an innocent agent, to perform the act.[36] Again, a conspirator may be guilty of crime although he be absent from the scene of its commission and not a participant therein.[37] Some causal connection must be worked out, however, between the defendant and the injury which constitutes the alleged crime. This brings us to the important subject of causation.

Much has been written concerning the tort liability of defendants for the results of their acts. It has been said that the problem is much more simple in criminal law.[38] As a matter of fact, it is equally difficult, equally important, and by no means so thoroughly considered in the cases and texts.[39] Most frequently the question will be found discussed in judicial opinions involving homicides;[40] however, it is of great importance in other types of crimes as well.[41] Generally speaking, it may be said that a defendant is liable criminally for acts which do not require specific intent,[42] if his act or omission was the proximate cause of the death, or burning, or other injury which is alleged to constitute the crime;[43] or, expressed in other terms, if the injury was a natural and probable consequence of his act.[44] Difficulty arises in the attempts to define and apply these terms, because the terms represent more or less intangible concepts and because there is undoubtedly a conflict in the minds of the judges concerning the policies which should control their application.[45] "It is generally agreed that results intended by the actor are proximate if they, in fact, take place."[46] Under such circumstances, distance in time or space between defendant's act and the accomplished result are comparatively immaterial. This is well illustrated by the case in which the defendant in California sent a box of poisoned candy to a person in Delaware, who ate the candy and died.[47] The real difficulty arises in respect to acts in which the results were not intended or perhaps not even imagined by the actor and proximity or remoteness between the act and the result must be worked out in other terms than space or time. From one angle, inquiry may be made, whether, at the time of acting or failing to act, in view of existing circumstances and in the light of any existing duty upon the part of the defendant, he, as a reasonable man, should have foreseen the injury would probably result from his act or omission, as a natural and probable consequence.[48] From another angle, inquiry may be made, whether the result which has happened was in fact a natural and logical result of defendant's act or omission. The discussions in the cases usually do not reveal which point of view is being used, and one suspects that, even when the foresight of the defendant is being discussed, the advantage of knowing what has actually happened is put into the balance against him. Presumably, the question which should be determined in order to establish defendant's guilt may be answered in either of two ways. On the one hand, if we are primarily concerned with defendant's individual liability, because of a freely willed action on his part, we will be interested in knowing what a reasonable man in like circumstances would have thought or done. If, on the other hand, we are primarily concerned with the injury which has occurred to society and are interested in the defendant, chiefly as a matter of fixing responsibility, then it becomes less important to know what a reasonable man might have thought, in advance of the act, and more important to know whether the result was a natural and logical consequence, and defendant's act a direct and efficient, or legal and sufficient cause.[49] As we shall see, the second point of view has predominated, especially in cases of negligence and unintended consequences, even though the rules of causation which are applied speak in terms of foreseeable results.

We have seen that a person may be guilty of crime when the act which constitutes it is done in his behalf by someone acting for him, either as an innocent agent or as a confederate in crime. In these crimes the act is so closely connected with the injury that no question of remoteness arises. The problem, then, is rather to establish such a relationship between the person who actually commits the act and the defendant, as to make him liable therefor. Where the defendant has directly procured the act to be done the causal relationship is easily established; as where a defendant was held guilty of kidnapping for procuring a sailor to be drugged with liquor and taken aboard a ship.[50] Where such a relationship does not exist, it is more difficult to work out a causal connection. In a Michigan case it was held that, where a husband at the request of an ailing wife placed poison within her reach, and she swallowed it and thereafter died, her death was the result of his act;[51] even though there was no evidence that the death resulted from his procurement. In that case the defendant's act in itself was not unlawful and by itself was in no way calculated to produce death. Generally, in such cases it is held that there is no liability.[52]

Where the defendant's act, either of procurement or directly toward the commission of the prohibited act, is aided or interrupted by a concurrent or subsequent act of another, several difficult questions of causation arise. One point upon which the cases agree is, that defendant's act need not be the sole cause of the injury, provided that it be a proximate cause actually contributing thereto.[53] Thus, although a person has been mortally wounded by another, a third person who afterwards inflicts a second mortal wound commits a homicide though he merely hastens a death which is bound to happen without his interference, or contributes to the operating causes of death when it occurs.[54] If two persons, acting together, each inflicts a wound which of itself would be sufficient to cause death, each is liable for the homicide.[55] As a matter of fact, under such circumstances both would be liable although only one of the wounds caused death, because of the liability arising out of joint participation in a common criminal enterprise.[56] If two persons, each acting independently of the other, concurrently inflict mortal wounds upon a third person, both are guilty of homicide;[57] and a similar result follows where neither wound alone is sufficient to cause death, but both operating together are sufficient.[58]

Where the defendant's act, although not sufficient by itself to cause the crime, nevertheless causes an intervening force to operate, or, as it is sometimes said, sets in motion a chain of circumstances which produce the unlawful result, the defendant is held liable therefor.[59] This is true even though the result might have been prevented if the injured person, or others for him, had acted with sufficient promptness or had used proper skill. Thus it has been held that where injury not by itself mortal was inflicted by the accused, the neglect or refusal of the injured person to take proper care of himself after the injury did not excuse the accused,[60] nor did his refusal to submit to an operation by which he could have been cured.[61] Nor is it a defense to show that the deceased might have recovered had he been treated according to the most approved surgical methods,[62] or as a reasonably prudent doctor would have treated the case;[63] or even by showing that the treatment was unskillful,[64] or improper,[65] or erroneous;[66] or that the deceased might have survived the shock of the wound alone, but did not survive the additional shock of the operation which was assumed to have been made necessary thereby.[67] If, however, it can be clearly shown that death was caused, not by the wound or other injury inflicted by the defendant, but solely by the misconduct of the deceased or by grossly erroneous treatment, then the defendant is not liable.[68] The misconduct or gross mistreatment are not regarded as acts dependent upon defendant's act, and consequently break the chain of causation.

Where, as a result of defendant's act, the person injured is unable to care for himself and dies from loss of blood or other similar cause, which might have been prevented had medical aid been promptly obtained, the defendant is liable.[69] A similar result has been reached in cases in which the defendant's act caused the deceased to lose consciousness or become unable to help himself and by reason thereof placed him in a position in which he suffered from further injury, and death resulted.[70] Again, where defendant's act in procuring a building to be burned, by blowing it up with dynamite, created a dangerous situation, of which the injured persons had no knowledge; as a result of which, after being safely out of the building, they returned thereinto and were burned to death; it was held that the conduct of the victims did not break the chain of causation, and defendant was held liable.[71] A closely related situation is revealed in an Indiana case in which the defendant raped a girl and she, while suffering from the shock thereof and "distracted with the pain and shame so inflicted upon her," went to a drug store, bought poison, returned to the hotel room which she had been occupying with the defendant, swallowed the poison and died, as a result thereof, several days later.[72] The defendant was found guilty of murder in the second degree. The same result was reached in a California case in which the deceased, suffering from a gunshot wound, cut his own throat to end his suffering.[73]

If a wound causes a disease and death results therefrom, the wound is the cause of death in the eyes of the law, and the act of the person who inflicted the wound is the proximate cause thereof.[74] The same is true where death results from the combined effect of a wound, so inflicted, and of a disease produced by or contributed to by the wound,[75] but it is otherwise if the disease is not connected with the wound in the relation of cause and effect.[76]

If a person inflicts an injury upon another and death results from such injury combined with a preëxisting weakness upon the part of the injured person, such as heart disease, or delirium tremens, or even of another injury, previously inflicted, such preëxisting weakness effects no break in the chain of causation, even though the person killed was likely, or even sure, to die in the near future.[77]

Where the act or acts which intervene after the happening of the defendant's act, are committed by persons acting independently of the defendant, there is much uncertainty in the cases concerning whether or not the defendant's act can still be considered proximate. Some of the cases say that it cannot, even though from the facts it is possible, at least, that defendant's act is still contributing to the final result,[78] and would have alone resulted in death, except for the intervention of the new mortal wound.[79] The theory upon which these cases are decided seems to be that the second injury, being independent of the first, is the sole proximate cause of death. In a North Carolina case the court says: "If one man inflicts a mortal wound, of which the victim is languishing, and then a second kills the deceased by an independent act, we cannot imagine how the first can be said to have killed him, without involving the absurdity of saying that the deceased was killed twice."[80] Of course the absurdity is that the judge can speak of a "mortal wound" previously inflicted, and in the same breath of another person killing the deceased "by an independent act." If, in fact, the first wound was a mortal wound, then it would seem that it must have been contributing to the death at the time of its occurrence. There is no difficulty or absurdity involved in finding that the acts of both persons contributed to the death and that both are guilty thereof, even though they were not acting in concert. The better reasoned cases so hold.[81] Of course if the death or other injury is attributable entirely to the independent intervening act, defendant's act neither contributing to the result nor creating an active risk of danger which is acted upon by the independent intervenor, then the causal connection is broken and defendant's act is not the proximate cause.[82]

If the defendant, while engaged in an unlawful act, produces consequences beyond his expectations or contemplation, he may be guilty of the crime encompassed in the unintended consequences.[83] This situation frequently occurs in the homicide cases.[84] Some courts have insisted that there can be no criminal liability in such cases unless there is actually a causal connection between defendant's unlawful act and the injury;[85] others take the position that the general security requires a holding of such reckless persons, and policy forbids a close inquiry into proximate cause or probable consequences in such cases; as, for example, where a drunken driver runs down a person and kills him.[86] Where defendant's unlawful act produces a retaliatory or defensive act by a second person, which act accidentally injures a third person, the cases are not in accord in respect to defendant's liability.[87] The same considerations of policy would go into the balance here, and it would seem to be a proper question for a jury to decide, upon general instructions of proximate cause.

If defendant's act is a direct and efficient cause, then the fact that it was negligently done is immaterial, except so far as the question of criminal intent is involved.[88] If, as a result of negligence, an act which defendant intended to do produces consequences which were not within his contemplation, or if a negligent omission of duty produces similar consequences, he may be liable nevertheless.[89] If, however, the injury would have happened regardless of the coincidence of defendant's negligent act, then he should not be held therefor.[90]

If defendant's act is accidental, then it is immaterial whether it was a proximate cause of the injury or not. Under circumstances in which a reasonable man could not have avoided the injurious happening, and in which the law does not require an absolute standard of perfection, there is no criminal liability regardless of proximity.[91] Under other circumstances, as we have seen, even a lack of knowledge of the happening of the event, coupled with an entire absence of intent, is not sufficient to excuse the defendant.[92]

In a few cases the question has arisen whether, if a person, by engaging in a lawful act, such as speaking at a public meeting, causes others to commit unlawful acts, such as breaches of the peace in protest at the speaker's remarks, his act is the proximate cause of the breach of the peace. Generally, it is held that if the defendant's act is actually lawful, and without unlawful intent, he is not liable,[93] although there has been a decision to the contrary.[94]

One of the important rules of evidence in criminal cases is that which requires proof of the *corpus delicti*.[95] Literally defined this term means "the body of the offense," or "the substance of crime."[96] In popular language it is used to describe the visible evidence of the crime, such as the dead body of a murdered person. Properly used, however, it is applicable to any crime and relates particularly to the act element of criminality; that is, that a certain prohibited act has been committed or result accomplished and that it was committed or accomplished by a criminal human agency.[97] The *corpus delicti* having been established, it then becomes the duty of the state to prove further that the accused was the human agent who committed the act or procured it to be committed. Of course the evidence of the *corpus delicti* and of defendant's agency are sometimes so inextricably mixed that it is impossible to separate them in the introduction of such evidence.[98] Examples of facts constituting the *corpus delicti* in particular cases are given in the note.[99]

In conclusion it is well to recur to the maxim, that every crime requires a union of act and intent, and to emphasize the fact that, however close that union may be, intent and act are separable concepts. Confusion has been introduced into the subject by some writers who have sought to define act in terms of "willed" or "voluntary" muscular activity or movement.[100] Such definitions do not properly define the word. Although the defendant's mental condition is of great importance in particular cases and though it does undoubtedly often change the effect of his muscular activity, even to the extent of giving it a criminal character where it would otherwise have none; nevertheless, it effects such changes, because it constitutes intent or because it proves the existence of criminal intent, and is not in any proper sense a part of the act itself.

NOTES TO MILLER ESSAY

[1] "In the exercise of the police power for the protection of the public, the performance of a specific act may constitute the crime regardless of either knowledge or intent, both of which are immaterial on the question of guilt. For the effective protection of the public the burden is placed upon the individual of ascertaining at his peril whether his act is prohibited by criminal statute. The law in that regard has most frequently arisen in police regulations of the liquor traffic, but it has been applied in precisely the same way in other cases coming within the same rule and reason, such as a sale of imitation butter, a sale of milk below a prescribed quality, the obstruction of public highway by a railroad corporation for longer than a specified time, the admission of a minor to a pool room, driving an unregistered automobile, killing for sale an animal under a designated age, carriage by an express company for transportation beyond the state line of fish or game, and in prosecutions for bigamy. . . . The section does not infringe upon the bill of rights or the fourteenth amendment to the constitution of the United States."—Cartwright, J., in People v. Fernow (1919) 286 Ill. 627, 630, 122 N. E. 155, 157. See cases collected in Note (1919) 4 Am. L. Rev. 1538, and (1926) 24 Mich. L. Rev. 304.

[2] See Section 2, Title I of H. R. 1491 (73d Cong.) and Title 12 U. S. C. A. (1933) c. 3, § 248 (n), executive order No. 6102.

[3] Webster's New International Dictionary.

[4] Rex v. Brain (1834) 6 Car. & P. 349; People v. Ah Fat (1874) 48 Cal. 61.

[5] State v. Fenn (1874) 41 Conn. 590; State v. Ledford (1872) 67 N. C. 60.

[6] Woolsey v. State (1891) 30 Tex. Cr. App. 346, 17 S. W. 546; Reg. v. Russell (1842) Car. & M. 541.

[7] Taylor v. State, 111 Ind. 279, (1887) 12 N. E. 400; Davis v. State (1875) 42 Tex. 226.

[8] Such a definition would include: homicide, larceny, arson, rape, mayhem, assault and battery, kidnapping, abduction, burglary, robbery, forgery, libel. But what of perjury, treason, compounding of a felony, riot, misconduct in office, illegal voting, blasphemy, etc.?

[9] 4 Bl. Comm. 5.

[10] Rex v. Fell, 1 Ld. Raym. 424, 2 Hawk, P. C. 198; Reg. v. Hughes (1857) Dears & B. 248, 7 Cox Cr. Cas. 301.

[11] Com. v. N. Y., New Haven & Hartford R. R. Co. (1873) 112 Mass. 412. See cases collected Dec. Dig. Railroads, 246.

[12] Com. v. Reardon (1850) 6 Cush. (Mass.) 78; Reg. v. Jellyman (1838) 8 Car. & P. 604.

[13] See State v. Carey (1904) 76 Conn. 342, 345, 56 Atl. 632, 633; Com. v. Follansbee (1892) 155 Mass. 274, 29 N. E. 471.

[14] Larremore, *Suicide and the Law* (1904) 17 Harv. L. Rev. 331; Com. v. Mink (1877) 123 Mass. 422, 25 Am. Rep. 109; State v. Levelle (1891) 34 S. C. 120, 13 S. E. 319, 27 Am. St. Rep. 799.

[15] Reg. v. Roberts (1855) Dears Cr. Cas. 539, 7 Cox Cr. Cas. 39; Baender v. Barnett (1921) 255 U. S. 224, 41 Sup. Ct. 271.

[16] Com. v. Johnson (1908) 199 Mass. 55, 85 N. E. 188; People v. Jefferson (1910) 161 Mich. 621, 126 N. W. 829; State v. Boliski (1914) 156 Wis. 78, 145 N. W. 368, 50 L. R. A. (n.s.) 825.

[17] Cases collected Dec. Dig., Intoxicating Liquors, 137.

[18] Whitney v. People (1927) 274 U. S. 357, 47 Sup. Ct. 641.

[19] People v. Yslas (1865) 27 Cal. 630; State v. Davis (1840) 23 N. C. 125.

[20] State v. Fisher (1891) 109 N. C. 817, 13 S. E. 878.

[21] Com. v. McKie (1854) 1 Gray (Mass.) 61.

[22] Chick v. State (1846) 7 Humph. (Tenn.) 161.

[23] State v. Hambright (1892) 111 N. C. 707, 16 S. E. 411; People v. Kane (1915) 213 N. Y. 260, 107 N. E. 655, L. R. A., F. 607; see opinion Bigelow, C. J., in Com. v. Hackett (1861) 2 Allen (Mass.) 136, 142.

[24] The difficulty is especially apparent under the concept of "act" advanced by Salmond in his book on *Jurisprudence* (ed. 4) 326, 327. He regards the consequences of an act as factors of the act—part of the act itself. See also Beale, *Recovery for Consequences of an Act* (1896) 9 Harv. L. Rev. 82, 84; and Cook, *Act, Intention and Motive in the Criminal Law* (1917) 26 Yale L. J. 645, 650–652.

[25] See People v. Botkin (1901) 132 Cal. 231, 64 Pac. 286, 84 Am. St. Rep. 39, a case in which the defendant sent poisoned candy from California to one in Delaware who died from eating the candy. This decision, however, was based upon a statute giving to California jurisdiction over an offense, any part of which was committed in the state. In the absence of such a statute, the California court would not have jurisdiction. See State v. Caldwell (1894) 115 N. C. 794, 80 S. E. 523; Rex v. Coombes (1785) 1 Leach 388; United States v. Davis (1837) 2 Sumner 482, Fed. Cases, No. 14,932.

[26] See State v. Chapin (1856) 17 Ark. 561, 65 Am. Dec. 452; Simpson v. State (1893) 92 Ga. 41, 17 S. E. 984, 44 Am. St. Rep. 75 (he is considered to accompany his bullet); and notes 79–84, Wharton, *Criminal Law* 339.

[27] See Stat. 2 and 3 Edw. VI c. 24; Mikell, *Criminal Procedure* 3a. For the rule before such statutes, see Wharton, *op. cit.* 340; State v. Carter (1859) 27 N. J. L. 499. See also People v. Gill (1856) 6 Cal. 637; Tyler v. People (1860) 8 Mich. 320, which held that the mere fact that death occurred in a state did not give such state jurisdiction over the offense. See statement of Brewer, J., in State v. Bowen (1876) 16 Kan. 475, 479.

[28] See State v. Dowell (1890) 106 N. C. 722, 11 S. E. 525.

[29] Baker v. State (1857) 30 Ala. 521.

[30] Mitchum v. State (1871) 45 Ala. 29; Rex v. Tideswell (1905) 2 K. B. 273.

[31] People v. Jaffe (1906) 185 N. Y. 497, 78 N. E. 169, 9 L. R. A. (n.s.) 263.

[32] Cook v. Stockwell, 113 L. T. R. 246 (K. B.), (1916) 29 Harv. L. Rev. 453.

[33] Jones v. Com. (1903) 115 Ky. 592, 74 S. W. 263; Fanning v. State (1880) 66 Ga. 167.

[34] State v. Benham (1867) 23 Iowa 154, 92 Am. Dec. 417; Pinder v. State (1891) 27 Fla. 370, 8 So. 837.

[35] The "sufficiency" of the act is the primary consideration in cases involving death by fright. See People v. Studer (1922) 59 Cal. App. 547, 211 Pac. 233; *Ex parte* Heigho (1910) 18 Idaho 566, 110 Pac. 1029, 32 L. R. A. (n.s.) 877, Ann. Cas. 1912, A 138, and see note (1908) 16 L. R. A. (n.s.) 327. *Cf.* Gipe v. State, 165 Ind. 433 (1905) 75 N. E. 881, 112 Am. St. Rep. 238, 1 L. R. A. (n.s.) 419.

[36] Collins v State (1870) 50 Tenn. (3 Heisk.) 14.

[37] People v. Mather (1830) 4 Wend. (N. Y.) 229, 21 Am. Dec. 122.

[38] Green, *Rationale of Proximate Cause* 58, 62.

[39] See (1932) 81 U. of Pa. L. Rev. 189. Variation in amount of proof required in civil and criminal cases has nothing to do with application of rules of causation.

[40] Com. v. Costley (1875) 118 Mass. 1; State v. Hambright (1892) 111 N. C. 707, 16 S. E. 411.

[41] Rex v. De Marny (1907) 1 K. B. 388; Rex v. Gill, 1 Stra. 190. Battery (druggist gave croton oil), State v. Monroe (1897) 121 N. C. 677, 28 S. E. 547; State v. Agnew (1932) 202 N. C. 755, 164 S. E. 578; (Note 1923) 1 N. C. L. Rev. 235.

[42] State v. Moore (1841) 12 N. H. 42 (burglary); Carter v. State (1890) 28 Tex. App. 355, 13 S. W. 147.

[43] Setting fire to one building in order to burn an adjoining one, Grimes v. State (1879) 63 Ala. 166; Combs v. Com. (1892) 14 Ky. L. Rep. 283, 20 S. W. 221; Hennessey v. People (1861) 21 How. Pr. (N. Y.) 239; Homicide, State v. Campbell (1910) 82 Conn. 671, 74 A. 927, 135 Am. St. Rep. 293; Dunville v. State (1919) 188 Ind. 373, 123 N. E. 689.

[44] Professor Beale states the question in these terms: "... when is one responsible for the operation (*a*) of an active force which he has created; (*b*) of an active force which acts upon a passive force which he created; or upon a passive force which he was legally bound to change."—*The Proximate Consequences of an Act* (1920) 33 Harv. L. Rev. 633, 641.

[45] Modern writers are frankly appreciative of the difficulty of establishing any definite rules of causation. Some of them insist that "proximate cause" and "reasonable man" are as close to certainty as we should approach, leaving it to the jury to balance the considerations of policy which may appear in each case.—Morgan (1928) 41 Harv. L. Rev. 939; Edgerton, *Legal Cause* (1924) 72 U. of Pa. L. Rev. 211. See also Edgerton, *op. cit.* at 349 note 136, for Bohlen's consideration of the corresponding problem in tort cases.

[46] McLaughlin, *Proximate Cause* (1925) 39 Harv. L. Rev. 149, 151, citing: Smith, *Legal Cause in Actions of Tort* (1911) 25 Harv. L. Rev. 104, 228; Edgerton, *Legal Cause* (1924) 72 U. of Pa. L. Rev. 211, 358; Terry, *Proximate Consequences in the Law of Torts* (1914) 28 Harv. L. Rev. 10, 17. But see Carpenter, *Workable Rules for Determining Proximate Cause* (1932) 20 Calif. L. Rev. 229, 513.

[47] People v. Botkin (1901) 132 Cal. 231, 64 P. 286.

[48] Hendrickson v. Com. (1887) 85 Ky. 281, 3 S. W. 166; People v. Fowler (1918) 178 Cal. 657, 174 P. 892.

[49] Warner v. State (1922) 104 Ohio St. 38, 135 N. E. 249. For a definition of proximate cause, see Beale, *The Proximate Consequences of an Act* (1920) 33 Harv. L. Rev. 633, 643; Edgerton, *Legal Cause* (1924) 72 U. of Pa. L. Rev. 211.

[50] Hadden v. People (1862) 25 N. Y. 373. The procuring of women for purposes of prostitution has been itself defined as the crime of pandering.—Com. v. Lavery (1915) 247 Pa. 139, 93 A. 276; Younger v. State (1923) 160 Ark. 557, 255 S. W. 294; People v. Torres (1924) 193 Cal. 730, 227 P. 177.

[51] People v. Roberts (1920) 211 Mich. 187, 178 N. W. 690 (1921) 1 Wis. L. Rev. 123.

[52] Burnett v. People (1903) 204 Ill. 208, 68 N. E. 505; Sanders v. State (1908) 54 Tex. Cr. Rep. 101, 112 S. W. 68, 22 L. R. A. (n.s.) 243.

[53] State v. Wilson (1905) 114 La. 398, 38 So. 397. Talley v. State (1912) 174 Ala. 101, 57 So. 445.

[54] Hopkins v. Com. (1904) 117 Ky. 941, 80 S. W. 156; Duque v. State (1909) 56 Tex. Cr. Rep. 214, 119 S. W. 687; Talley v. State (1912) 174 Ala. 101, 57 So. 445; Reg. v. Plummer (1844) 1 Car. & K. 600; People v. Ah Fat (1874) 48 Cal. 61; if accused shot deceased in necessary self-defense, and then shot him again as he was fleeing, both

wounds being mortal, it was held that if the second shot was fired when it was not necessary for defendant to further defend himself, and it contributed in any degree to the death of the deceased, defendant was guilty of felonious homicide.—Caughron v. State (1911) 99 Ark. 462, 139 S. W. 315. See also Bennett v. Com. (1912) 150 Ky. 604, 150 S. W. 806.

55 People v. Rudecki (1923) 309 Ill. 125, 140 N. E. 832, 6 Ill. L. Q. 90. But in the absence of such a common design, one participant in a fight who was without fault could not be held liable for the accidental killing of a bystander by a stray bullet.—State v. Oxendine (1924) 187 N. C. 658, 122 S. E. 568, (Note 1924) 24 Col. L. Rev. 801.

56 State v. Darling (1909) 216 Mo. 450, 115 S. W. 1002, 23 L. R. A. (n.s.) 272, 57 U. of Pa. L. Rev. 635; State v. Finley (1896) 118 N. C. 1161, 24 S. E. 495.

57 Wilson v. State (Tex. Cr. App.) (1893) 24 S. W. 409; Talley v. State (1912) 174 Ala. 101, 57 So. 445.

58 Henderson v. State (1913) 11 Ala. App. 37, 65 So. 721. See Wilson v. State (1893) (Tex. Cr. App.), 24 S. W. 409. Defendant is responsible if results of his act "contribute materially" to death of deceased.

59 Rex v. DeMarny (1907) 1 K. B. 388. Defendant, publisher of a newspaper, published an advertisement of obscene literature as a result of which a sale took place. Defendant was held liable.—People v. Lewis (1899) 124 Cal. 551, 57 P. 470, 45 L. R. A. 783. Deceased cut his throat after being shot by defendant.—Thornton v. State (1899) 107 Ga. 683, 33 S. E. 673. Deceased killed by falling in ravine, while running from defendant's assault.

60 State v. Lane (1900) 158 Mo. 572, 59 S. W. 965; State v. Morphy (1871) 33 Iowa 270, 11 Am. Rep. 122, where, by the use of intoxicating liquors, the deceased materially lessened his chances of recovery; Rowles v. State (1877) 58 Ala. 335, where deceased walked to a wagon and rode over a rough country road a distance of twelve miles; State v. Baker (1854) 46 N. C. 267, where deceased walked seven or eight miles and drank whiskey; Stanton's case, 2 Rogers City Hall Recorder 164 (N. Y.), broken skull followed by trepanning operation, deceased, in delirium from blow, tore open wound and died. But *cf.* State v. Angelina (1913) 73 W. Va. 146, 80 S. E. 141.

61 Franklin v. State (1899) 41 Tex. Cr. R. 21, 51 S. W. 951; People v. Nunes (1920) 47 Cal. App. 346, 190 P. 486 (mayhem—loss of eye).

62 State v. Edgerton (1896) 100 Iowa 63, 69 N. W. 280.

63 State v. Gabriella (1913) 163 Iowa 297, 144 N. W. 9.

64 Thomas v. State (1903) 139 Ala. 80, 36 So. 734; State v. Bantley (1877) 44 Conn. 537, 26 Am. Rep. 486; Clark v. Com. (1893) 90 Va. 360, 18 S. E. 440 (though the unskillful treatment aggravated the wound); People v. Townsend (1921) 214 Mich. 267, 183 N. W. 177, 16 A. L. R. 902.

65 Bailey v. State (1927) 22 Ala. App. 185, 113 So. 830; where deceased might have recovered with the exercise of more prudence and with better nursing; State v. Pell (1909) 140 Iowa 655, 119 N. W. 154; State v. Lane (1900) 158 Mo. 572, 59 S. W. 965; Downing v. State (1901) 114 Ga. 30, 39 S. E. 927; Hopkins v. United States (1894) 4 App. D. C. 430; Com. v. Eisenhower (1897) 181 Pa. St. 470, 37 A. 521.

66 People v. Kane (1915) 213 N. Y. 260, 107 N. E. 655, L. R. A. 1915 F, 607, Ann. Cas. 1916 C, 685; Hamblin v. State (1908) 81 Neb. 148, 115 N. W. 850, 16 Ann. Cas. 569; Johnson v. State (1912) 64 Fla. 321, 59 So. 894; Sharp v. State (1888) 51 Ark. 147, 10 S. W. 228, 14 Am. St. Rep. 27.

67 People v. Williams (1915) 27 Cal. App. 297, 149 P. 768. See also McCoy v. Com. (1912) 149 Ky. 447, 149 S. W. 903.

[68] Parsons v. State (1852) 21 Ala. 300; Quinn v. State (1914) 106 Miss. 844, 64 So. 738; Noble v. State (1908) 54 Tex. Cr. R. 436, 113 S. W. 281, 22 L. R. A. (n.s.) 841. See also State v. Morphy, 33 Iowa 270, 11 Am. Rep. 122; Bush v. Com. (1880) 78 Ky. 268, the attending physician communicated scarlet fever to the deceased.

[69] Mason v. State (1923) 94 Tex. Cr. R. 532, 251 S. W. 1065; Rigsby v. State (1910) 174 Ind. 284, 91 N. E. 925. Nor does such a fact even reduce the offense from murder to aggravated assault.—Embrey v. State (1923) 94 Tex. Cr. R. 591, 251 S. W. 1062.

[70] People v. Fowler (1918) 178 Cal. 657, 174 P. 892, where a train robber forced the engineer to occupy a position in which it was likely that he would be shot by a passenger resisting the robbery, and he was so shot, it was held that the robber's act was the cause of the resulting death.—Taylor v. State (1900) 41 Tex. Cr. R. 564, 55 S. W. 961. See Beale, *The Proximate Consequences of an Act* (1920) 33 Harv. L. Rev. 633. It has been held that where an independent, intervening force is interposed it may prevent criminal liability even under the circumstances described in the text. For example, when one, in a quarrel, knocked his opponent down, whereupon a bystander kicked the latter, so as to cause death, it was said that the accused was not guilty of such death jointly with the bystander, unless he had reason to expect or induced his interference.—People v. Elder (1894) 100 Mich. 515, 59 N. W. 237.

[71] State v. Leopold (1929) 110 Conn. 55, 147 A. 118, (1930) 25 Ill. L. Rev. 208.

[72] Stephenson v. State (Ind.) (1932) 179 N. E. 633, 45 Harv. L. Rev. 1261, 81 U. of Pa. L. Rev. 189; (1933) 31 Mich. L. Rev. 659, (1932) 23 J. Crim. L. & Crim. 649. In its opinion in this case the court said: "We, therefore, conclude that the evidence was sufficient and justified the jury in finding that appellant by his acts and conduct rendered the deceased distracted and mentally irresponsible, and that such was the natural and probable consequence of such unlawful and criminal treatment, . . ."

[73] People v. Lewis (1899) 124 Cal. 551, 57 P. 470, 45 L. R. A. 783. In this case it appeared that both wounds contributed to his death. See also Travelers' Ins. Co. of Hartford v. Melick, 65 Fed. 178 (C. C. A. 8th, 1894).

[74] Bishop v. State (1905) 73 Ark. 568, 84 S. W. 707; Denman v. State (1883) 15 Neb. 138, 17 N. W. 347; Powell v. State (1882) 13 Tex. Cr. App. 244; Burnett v. State (1884) 14 Lea (Tenn.) 439 (where death resulted from pneumonia; question for jury whether assault contributed to pneumonia); People v. Townsend (1921) 214 Mich. 267, 183 N. W. 177, 16 A. L. R. 902; State v. Harmon (1915) 92 A. 853, 5 Boyce (Del.) 296; Lochamy v. State (1921) 152 Ga. 235, 109 S. E. 497. Defendant liable where gunshot wound produced miscarriage, followed by bloodpoisoning and death.—People v. Kane (1915) 213 N. Y. 260, 107 S. E. 655 (Note 1916) 1 Corn. L. Q. 181, (1915) 15 Col. L. Rev. 547.

[75] Cunningham v. People (1902) 195 Ill. 550, 63 N. E. 517; Griffin v. State (1899) 40 Tex. Cr. Rep. 312, 50 S. W. 366, 76 Am. St. Rep. 718; Dumas v. State (1909) 159 Ala. 42, 49 So. 224, 133 Am. St. Rep. 17; Hollywood v. State (1911) 19 Wyo. 493, 122 P. 588, Ann. Cas. 1913 E, 218 (1912).

[76] Livingston v. Com. (1857) 14 Grat. (Va.) 592; Bush v. Com. (1880) 78 Ky. 268; Quinn v. State (1914) 106 Miss. 844, 64 So. 738.

[77] 1 Hale, P. C. 428; Reg. v. Haines (1847) 2 Car. & K. 368; Com. v. Fox (1856) 7 Gray (Mass.) 585; State v. Morea (1841) 2 Ala. 275; People v. Lanagan (1889) 81 Cal. 142, 22 P. 482; Smith v. State (1888) 50 Ark. 545, 8 S. W. 941; State v. O'Brien (1890) 81 Iowa 88, 46 N. W. 752. Although the first shot was in self-defense, if the second was not excusable, and contributed to or accelerated death, defendant was guilty of homicide.—Rogers v. State (1894) 60 Ark. 76, 29 S. W. 894, 31 L. R. A. 465, 46 Am. St. Rep. 154. See also *Ex parte* Heigho (1910) 18 Idaho 566, 110 P. 1029; Wells v. State

(Ga.) (1933) 167 S. E. 709; United States v. Freeman, 4 Mason (U. S.) 505, Fed. Cas., No. 15,162 (Cir. Ct. D. Mass. 1827); Cunningham v. People (1902) 195 Ill. 550, 63 N. E. 517; Hopkins v. Com. (1904) 117 Ky. 941, 80 S. W. 156.

78 State v. Wood (1881) 53 Vt. 560; Walker v. State (1902) 116 Ga. 537, 42 S. E. 787. See, in general, the fact situations of cases cited in subsequent notes under this section.

79 State v. Scates (1858) 50 N. C. 420; State v. Angelina (1913) 73 W. Va. 146, 80 S. E. 141, 51 L. R. A. (n.s.) 877; State v. Wood (1881) 53 Vt. 560; Walker v. State (1902) 116 Ga. 537, 42 S. E. 787, (1903) 16 Harv. L. Rev. 374.

80 State v. Scates (1858) 50 N. C. 420, 423.

81 State v. Snider (1918) 81 W. Va. 522, 94 S. E. 981, limiting State v. Angelina, *supra;* Com. v. Costley (1875) 118 Mass. 1, 26; People v. Lewis (1899) 124 Cal. 551, 57 P. 470, 45 L. R. A. 783. See Beale, *op. cit.* note 49 *supra,* 633, 639; Green, *Are There Dependable Rules of Causation?* (1929) 77 U. of Pa. L. Rev. 601, 610; Edgerton, *Legal Cause* (1924) 72 U. of Pa. L. Rev. 343, 346; McLaughlin, *Proximate Cause* (1925) 39 Harv. L. Rev. 149, 153.

82 Bush v. Com. (1880) 78 Ky. 268; Noble v. State (1908) 54 Tex. Cr. R. 436, 113 S. W. 281, 22 L. R. A. (n.s.) 841. See Phegley v. State (1925) 113 Neb. 138, 202 N. W. 419.

83 State v. Skidmore (1882) 87 N. C. 509. Held not an error to refuse to charge that if ear of injured person was separated while between defendant's teeth, by the violence of those who pulled him away, the defendant was not guilty of mayhem.—Bowers v. State (1888) 24 Tex. App. 542, 7 S. W. 247, 5 Am. St. Rep. 901. Defendant kicked D's arm while D's thumb was in E's mouth; as a result a portion of D's thumb was torn off. Held a question for the jury whether defendant was guilty of mayhem.

84 Mayes v. People (1883) 106 Ill. 306, 46 Am. Rep. 698; Pool v. State (1891) 87 Ga. 526, 13 S. E. 556.

85 People v. Barnes (1914) 182 Mich. 148, 400 N. W. 179; Dunville v. State (1919) 188 Ind. 373, 123 N. E. 689; Jackson v. State (1920) 101 Ohio St. 152, 127 N. E. 870; *cf.* Stecher v. People, for use of Morton (1905) 217 Ill. 348, 75 N. E. 501, where defendant saloon keeper was held liable in civil damages for having proximately caused the death of deceased. The defendant had sold liquor to a third person who shot and killed deceased.

86 Keller v. State (1927) 155 Tenn. 633, 299 S. W. 803, (1928) 41 Harv. L. Rev. 669, where it is said: "But the present problem cannot be treated as a mere question of causation without sacrificing the interest of the general security in deterring conduct of an extremely perilous nature. Since driving while intoxicated is of this character and the unlawful conduct of the accused was the factual cause of an injury which the statute sought to prevent, the accused may well be held liable in a criminal prosecution. *Cf.* Anderson v. State (1922) 18 Ala. App. 429, 93 So. 68. This position would not necessitate a conviction in cases in which the unlawful act was not dangerous to life, or in which the injury occasioned is not within the purview of the statute. State v. Horton, 139 N. C. 588. . . . Nor would a conviction be justified in cases in which the injury would not have occurred but for the willful act of the deceased, or the interference of a stranger."

87 Keaton v. State (1900) 41 Tex. Cr. R. 621, 57 S. W. 1125. Liability, Taylor v. State (1900) 41 Tex. Cr. R. 564, (1900) 55 S. W. 961; no liability, Com. v. Campbell (1863) 7 Allen (Mass.) 541; Butler v. People (1888) 125 Ill. 641, 18 N. E. 338; Com. v. Moore (1905) 121 Ky. 97, 88 S. W. 1085.

[88] People v. Fuller (1823) 2 Parker Cr. R. (N. Y.) 16; Curtis v. State (1897) 118 Ala. 125, 24 So. 111.

[89] Reg. v. Haines (1847) 2 Car. & K. 368.

[90] Queen v. Dalloway (1847) 2 Cox Cr. Cas. 273.

[91] U. S. v. Meagher, 37 Fed. 875 (Cir. Ct. W. D. Tex. 1888), State v. Benham (1867) 23 Iowa 154.

[92] Com. v. Marsh (1844) 7 Metc. (Mass.) 472; Dotson v. State (1878) 62 Ala. 141.

[93] Beatty v. Gilbanks (1882) 9 Q. B. D. 308.

[94] Wise v. Dunning [1902] 1 K. B. 167 (1902) 15 Harv. L. Rev. 492. Upon the subject of causation, considered comparatively from the point of view of German and Anglo-American authorities, see Hirschberg, *The Proximate Cause in the Legal Doctrine of the United States and Germany* (1929) 2 So. Calif. L. Rev. 207. For an intensive examination of the subject, primarily from the point of view of tort liability, see Carpenter, *Workable Rules for Determining Proximate Cause* (1932) 20 Calif. L. Rev. 229; Smith, *Legal Cause in Actions of Tort* (1911) 25 Harv. L. Rev. 103.

[95] United States v. Searcey, 26 Fed. 435 (Dis. Ct. W. D. No. Cas. 1885); Sanders v. State (1910) 167 Ala. 85, 52 So. 417.

[96] People v. Palmer (1888) 109 N. Y. 110, 113, 16 N. E. 529; State v. Knapp (1904) 70 Ohio St. 380, 393, 71 N. E. 705; State v. Millmeier (1897) 102 Iowa 692, 72 N. W. 275.

[97] People v. Dick (1869) 37 Cal. 277, 281; People v. Jones (1898) 123 Cal. 65; 55 P. 698; State v. Millmeier (1897) 102 Iowa 692, 72 N. W. 275; People v. Ranney (1908) 153 Mich. 293, 116 N. W. 999; Spears v. State (1908) 92 Miss. 613, 46 So. 166; State v. Pienick (1907) 46 Wash. 522, 90 P. 645; People v. Palmer (1898) 109 N. Y. 110, 16 N. E. 529; People v. Bennett (1872) 49 N. Y. 137, 143.

[98] State v. Kesner (1905) 72 Kan. 87, 82 P. 720; People v. Tollefson (1906) 145 Mich. 444, 108 N. W. 751.

[99] Arson, State v. Millmeier (1897) 102 Iowa 692, 72 N. W. 275; Rape, State v. Johnson (1909) 85 S. C. 265, 67 S. E. 453; State v. McCord (1911) 237 Mo. 242, 140 S. W. 885; Bryan v. State (1921) 90 Tex. Cr. R. 175, 234 S. W. 83; Robbery, People v. Strider (1929) 96 Cal. A. 632, 274 P. 601; State v. Henry (1929) 168 La. 855, 123 So. 597; State v. Depriest (1921) 288 Mo. 459, 232 S. W. 83.

[100] Cook, *Act, Intention and Motive in the Criminal Law* (1917) 26 Yale L. J. 645, 651.

INSTRUCTING THE JURY UPON PRESUMPTIONS AND BURDEN OF PROOF

BY EDMUND M. MORGAN

"BEHOLD, ALL IS VANITY and vexation of spirit. That which is crooked cannot be made straight." These words of the ancient realist might well furnish the text for any discourse upon charges to the jury in by far the greater number of American courts. No extended experience at the bar or upon the trial bench is required to produce a vivid realization that only in the exceptional case is the jury decisively influenced by the judge's instructions. More rarely still is its determination based upon the allocation of the burden of persuasion. Even the judges seem to be perplexed about presumptions. One ought, therefore, to have a particularly keen sense of futility in attempting to discuss the proper content of instructions dealing with presumptions and burden of proof.[1] Yet the books are full of cases in which the appellate courts purport to make the decision turn upon the charge to the jury; judges, trial and appellate, continue to insist that accurate instructions do perform the function of enabling the jury to make accurate application of the law to the facts disclosed by the evidence; and there are some uncertainties in the expression of the judicial doctrines concerning burden of proof and presumptions which seem to be capable of clarification. Consequently there may be some slight excuse for another attempt to suggest a practical and understandable solution of some of the problems with which the trial judge and the jury are compelled to deal in almost every litigated case.

So far as the phrase "burden of proof" is used to describe the burden which rests upon a party to produce evidence sufficient for the avoidance of a directed verdict, there is no need of saying anything about it to the jury, except perhaps where a presumption comes into operation. But where the phrase indicates the burden of persuading the jury, an instruction cannot be avoided. Under the decisions there are three groups of issues, each requiring its own formula. On some issues the proponent must satisfy the jury beyond reasonable doubt that his proposition of fact is true; on others he must establish it "by clear and convincing" or "by clear, satisfactory and convincing evidence"; on still others he need prove it only "by a preponderance of the evidence."[2] Where a presumption is involved, the problem may become more complicated, for the authorities exhibit a wide variety of views concerning its effect. Each of the following opinions has some express judicial sanction. (1) A presumption puts upon the opponent the burden of producing evidence which would justify a reasonable jury in finding against the presumed fact; only this and nothing more.[3] (2) It places upon the opponent the burden of persuading the jury to believe so much of the evidence against the presumed fact as would justify a reasonable jury in finding against the presumed fact. The effect upon the mind of the particular jury in respect to the existence or nonexistence of the presumed fact is immaterial.[4] (3) It places upon the opponent the burden of persuading the jury not to disbelieve so much of the evidence against the presumption as to leave the remainder insufficient to justify a reasonable jury in finding against the presumed fact. In other words, the presumption will lose all efficacy even though the jury positively believes none of such evidence, positively discredits a part of it, and is unable to determine whether to believe or disbelieve the remainder, provided only that such remainder is of the requisite quantity and quality to justify a reasonable jury in finding the nonexistence of the presumed fact. Here, again, the effect of the evidence upon the opinion of the particular jury in respect to the existence of the presumed fact is immaterial.[5] (4) It puts upon the opponent the burden of persuading the jury that the existence of the presumed fact is so doubtful that the jury cannot determine whether it exists. Beginning with the assumption that the presumed fact does exist, the jury must by the evidence be put in such a state of mind that they cannot say whether it exists or not.[6] (5) It puts upon the opponent the burden of persuading the jury that the presumed fact does not exist.[7] (6) In addition to one of the foregoing, the jury must also consider the presumption as evidence or with the evidence in its process of determining whether or not the presumed fact exists.[8] (7) Each of these six views assumes that a presumption compels the trier upon the establishment of a given fact to assume the existence of another fact. The term is sometimes used to express the idea that the trier will be permitted to deduce from the existence of a particular fact the existence of another, even though ordinary human experience as revealed in judicial experience might not justify such a deduction.[9] (8) Finally, the term is employed with the adjective "conclusive" to denote a positive rule of law, either substantive or procedural, which no evidence to the contrary can overthrow.[10] So far as a presumption affects the activities of the jury in their consideration or decision of issues, it is essential that they be advised of its influence in intelligible language.

It may be well to begin by conceding that a lawsuit is merely a proceeding for the orderly settlement of a dispute and lacks many of the characteristics of an investigation for the ascertainment of truth. Even in the field of the exact sciences it is difficult, if not impossible, to get beyond a working hypothesis; and in judicial inquiries in respect to past events, concerning which there is a dispute, it is idle to hope to discover more than the preponderance of probabilities. That preponderance may be so very heavy as to produce in the mind of the trier a conviction strong enough to make him willing to act upon it as indubitable. It may be heavy enough to create an opinion upon which the trier feels himself abundantly justified in acting although he is willing to concede that he entertains a reasonable doubt against it. Or it may have only such weight as to convince him that, although his deduction is open to considerable doubt, on the whole it is more probably true than not. Of course it is not necessary to explain to the jury the impossibility of acquiring absolutely accurate knowledge concerning any fact of history. Judges and juries have for centuries gone upon the assumption that they find the facts as bases for declarations of the legal relations arising therefrom. And for all practical purposes men do and must act upon what appears to them to be the preponderance of probability.

I

Where proof beyond reasonable doubt is required, the charge should not be difficult to frame. Thus, in a criminal prosecution, when it is once determined what propositions of fact the prosecution has the burden of establishing, the jury may be instructed that they must acquit unless they are convinced beyond a reasonable doubt that each of such propositions is true. It is coming to be recognized that all attempts to define reasonable doubt by paraphrase or circumlocution tend only to obfuscate rather than clarify the concept.[11] Yet convictions are still being set aside because of refusals to charge in the high-sounding but meaningless phraseology of the *Webster* case.[12] This is the sort of conduct by courts of last resort which makes of the request to charge, a trap for the unwary trial judge. Where the judge specifies the particular facts to be proved by the State and then in plain language tells the jury that the State does not satisfy its burden of proving these facts unless the evidence convinces them beyond reasonable doubt of the existence of each of these facts, there is no danger that the average juror will fail to understand. If he is intelligent enough to sit upon a jury, he is intelligent enough to comprehend so simple an instruction. Where a court conceives itself to be helplessly bound by precedent to insist upon the repetition of incomprehensible formulae, the only relief lies in legislation.[13]

The trial judge may have more trouble in making his meaning clear where the law prescribes proof by a preponderance of the evidence or by clear, satisfactory, and convincing evidence. To be sure, he usually merely charges the jury that the party having the burden of proof upon a given proposition must convince them that it is true by evidence having the prescribed characteristics. For example, in a negligence case, he instructs that the plaintiff must satisfy the jury, or must establish, by a preponderance of the evidence, that the defendant was negligent and that his negligence was the proximate cause of the plaintiff's injury. He also explains that the preponderance of evidence does not signify the greater number of witnesses or the larger volume of testimony but denotes, rather, evidence of greater convincing force. But he goes no farther. He does not attempt to describe the state of mind of the jurors which the evidence must create, as he does in criminal cases. All his emphasis is upon the means which call forth the state of mind. When is the juror to be "satisfied," or when is he to find that the plaintiff has "established" that the defendant was negligent?

Is the plaintiff to prevail if he has produced a preponderance of the evidence? Where he introduces evidence sufficient to justify, but not to require, a verdict that the defendant was negligent, and the defendant rests without offering any evidence, it is too clear for argument that the plaintiff has produced a preponderance of the evidence. He has presented more witnesses, he has introduced the heavier mass of testimony, and his evidence is of greater convincing power than no evidence at all, for by hypothesis it would support a finding of negligence. Yet the jury may properly find for the defendant. There is therefore a wide difference between producing a preponderance of the evidence and satisfying the burden of persuasion. And there may be a real danger that the jury will fail to appreciate this distinction unless it is pointed out to them.

An exaggerated fear of this danger may be responsible for the Wisconsin rule. That rule requires the trial judge to tell the jury explicitly that in order to entitle the party having the burden of persuasion

> to a finding in his favor, his evidence must not only be of greater convincing power, but it must be such as to convince the jury of the truth of his contention. This idea, in some definite and certain form, must be given to the jury or the instruction will be incomplete and erroneous.[14]

Such an instruction makes it perfectly clear that something more than the production of a preponderance of the evidence is necessary to sustain the burden of persuasion. But does it convey to the jury an accurate idea of the state of mind required to warrant a verdict or finding? Just as there is a difference between furnishing a preponderance of the evidence and satisfying the burden of persuasion, so there is a difference between convincing a juror that a proposition is true and convincing him that it is more probably true than not. Suppose that a jury should return a special verdict, saying, "We are convinced that it is more probable than not that the defendant was negligent, but we cannot say that we are convinced that the defendant was negligent." Would the Wisconsin court rule that the plaintiff must fail? Does it mean by its charge merely to insist that the jury shall be convinced of defendant's negligence and that the conviction shall be based on nothing less or other than a preponderance of the evidence? How can any juror be convinced by evidence which he does not regard as having greater convincing power than that opposed to it? Why, then, should the court bother about the preponderance of the evidence or go to the trouble of explaining its meaning? Why not merely tell the jury that, to find for plaintiff, it must be convinced of defendant's negligence by the evidence and that it is not allowed to base its verdict or finding upon anything else? What distinction can there be between the requirement for an ordinary issue like that of negligence and that for an issue which is said to call for proof by clear, satisfactory, and convincing evidence? How can a juror really be convinced by evidence which in his judgment is not clear, satisfactory, and convincing; and what but his judgment is the determinant of the existence of these qualities? Indeed, it may be argued that if a juror is convinced of the truth of a proposition he cannot be more than convinced, and that to require such conviction is to put all issues in both civil and criminal cases in the same category. But granting that in the ordinary usage of words there may properly be said to be degrees of conviction or persuasion, the difficulty remains that neither the wording approved by the Wisconsin court nor that used in the ordinary instruction in civil cases attempts to describe the requisite degree, but emphasizes only the quantity and quality of the evidence necessary to create the conviction. Certainly it is implicit in most of the pertinent decisions in which it is not expressly so stated, that the court is intending to prescribe a different measure of persuasion for the different classes of issues.

Upon this special verdict the plaintiff would prevail in Connecticut.[15] And so he should; moreover, the instruction to the jury should be phrased to convey that idea. While it is both unnecessary and inadvisable to explain to the jury the impossibility of obtaining in a judicial proceeding accurate knowledge of past events concerning which there is a dispute, it does not follow that it is unnecessary or unwise to instruct them in civil actions that their findings may be based upon a preponderance of probabilities. The truth is that they can be based upon nothing else. Then why not say so in language that will convey the idea clearly to the ordinary mind? By phrasing the charge in terms of probability, the pertinent distinctions can be made easily understandable. If the trial judge tells the jury that the burden is upon a party to prove a specified fact by a preponderance of the evidence, he should explain that this means only that they must find that the fact does not exist unless the evidence convinces them that its existence is more probable than its nonexistence. Indeed, there is no need for him to talk of burden of proof or of preponderance of evidence. He may well confine his instruction on this matter to a specification of the disputed propositions of fact and a direction specifying which party must fail on each proposition unless the jury is convinced by the evidence that the truth of that proposition is more probable than its falsity. In like manner, if he charges that the burden is upon a party to prove a proposition by clear and convincing evidence, or by clear, satisfactory, and convincing evidence, he should interpret this by saying that it requires the jury to be convinced not only that the truth of this proposition is more probable than its falsity, but also that its truth is much more probable than its falsity, though it is not necessary that the preponderance of probability of its truth shall be so great as to dissipate all reasonable doubt. Here too it is entirely unnecessary to use the orthodox phraseology, though it can do no harm if elucidated. As to issues which must be proved beyond reasonable doubt, there is no necessity for abandoning the familiar formula, though there could be no rational objection to charging, instead, that the preponderance of probability must be so great as to banish all reasonable doubts. There is of course an objection to innovations in procedural rules which work reasonably well; but the ambiguities which the Wisconsin courts have discovered in the orthodox phraseology and those which their remedy in turn creates are sufficient both to justify and to demand a rephrasing which will convey a clear and distinct idea to the ordinary mind.

II

To what extent will the interposition of a presumption complicate the problem? There seems to be no doubt that a presumption does not come into existence until the fact or group of facts upon which it is based has been established for the purposes of the particular lawsuit. Given *A* as a fact or group of facts, a presumption arises that *B* is a fact. In any case *A* alone may be in dispute, or *A* may be established and *B* alone be contested, or both *A* and *B* may be in issue. Thus, if *A* is the unexplained absence for seven years of *X*, and *B* is the death of *X*, the evidence may be directed solely to the period of *X's* absence and have no bearing upon his life or death after the date of his disappearance. Or unexplained absence for the requisite period may be established and the conflict in testimony may be limited to the identity of a person shown to have been alive after the expiration of the period. Or the evidence may be such as to justify a finding either way both upon the period of *X's* unexplained absence and upon his being alive at the commencement of the action.

If the only controversy concerns the existence of *A,* the presumption will not make the task of charging the jury appreciably heavier. The eight possible effects of a presumption reduce themselves to two. It makes no difference whether the presumption be irrebuttable or whether it merely puts upon the opponent the burden of producing evidence of a prescribed quantity and quality, or whether it requires such evidence to have a specified influence upon the mind of the jury. In all these possibilities, the only question for the jury will be the existence of *A.* Once they find *A,* they must find *B,* for there is no evidence against *B.* If the effect of a presumption is only to authorize the trier to find the presumed fact, then the jury ought to be advised that, if they find *A,* they will be justified in finding *B.* The only question is whether such an instruction will amount to an unwarranted comment upon the weight or credibility of the evidence. The rule which forbids such comment has never been thought to prevent the trial judge from laying down for the jury general rules of law to guide them in their evaluation of the evidence. For example, it is proper to instruct them concerning their power to disregard certain testimony of witnesses whom they believe to have given wilfully false evidence upon a material issue.[16] So here, if ordinary human experience would not justify a jury in drawing the inference *B* from *A,* but the courts have ascribed to *A* an artificial quality which makes it proper for the jury to do so, then the court in so instructing is merely expounding an applicable rule of law to enable the jury to appreciate its legal power. Of course, if the presumption does not operate to create an artificial effect in *A,* and is used to describe a deduction which ordinary human experience would warrant any person in drawing from *A,* there is no reason for the judge to say anything about *A* which he would not say concerning any similar group of facts in any case.

Suppose, however, that *A* is established, and the contest is over the existence of *B.* This means that the presumption is not irrebuttable and that the evidence is such that a trier might reasonably find either the existence or the nonexistence of *B*. If the effect of the presumption is solely to require the introduction of evidence sufficient to justify a jury in finding the nonexistence of *B*, there is no need to mention it. Such evidence has been introduced and the presumption has ceased to have any effect whatsoever in the case. Of course, *A* is still in the case as one of the facts to be considered by the jury, but it is to be given its inherently logical value and no more. That value may be nil. If so, and if there is no other evidence of *B*, the judge must direct the jury to find that *B* does not exist. If *A* has some probative force, it does not require treatment different from that required by any other similar item of evidence.

If a presumption operates to fix the burden of persuasion, it will make no more difficult either the judge's task in framing the charge or the jury's duty of applying it. If the party against whom the presumption works already has the burden of persuasion that the presumed fact does not exist, the charge will be entirely unaffected by the presumption. Thus, if the plaintiff in ejectment is claiming as tenant for the life of *X* and the defendant is holding as remainderman, the plaintiff begins with the burden of showing *X* alive; and if the defendant establishes the unexplained absence of *X* for seven years, the plaintiff's burden of persuasion is not thereby affected, that is to say, if the minds of the jury are by the evidence left in equilibrium on the question of *X's* continued existence, they must find for the defendant. If, however, the action is upon a policy of life insurance upon the life of *X*, the plaintiff begins with the burden of persuading the jury that *X* is dead. His establishment of *X's* unexplained absence has the effect of fixing upon the defendant the burden of persuading the jury that *X* is alive. Still the phraseology of the judge's charge will be precisely the same as if there had been no presumption in the case, save only that the word "defendant" will be substituted for the word "plaintiff." Obviously this change will not make harder or easier the work of the judge in composing the instruction or that of the jury in applying it.

If the establishment of *A* puts upon the opponent the burden of meeting or balancing the presumption without affecting the burden of persuasion, it may be a little less easy for the judge to put the matter clearly before the jury. Yet the difficulty is not serious. If the opponent already has the burden of persuasion, then there will be no occasion to mention the presumption. If, in our ejectment case, the establishment of *X's* absence by defendant did no more than require plaintiff to make the jury unable to determine whether *X* was dead, this would be less than the burden with which plaintiff began and would necessarily be comprehended within it. Consequently, to say anything to the jury about the presumption would be both unnecessary and uselessly confusing. If the burden of persuasion rests originally upon the party in whose favor the presumption operates, it will still remain there. But it will be necessary to advise the jury of the precise effect of the establishment of *A*. It can be done in comparatively simple language which anyone having sufficient intelligence to serve as a juryman should readily understand. For example, in a jurisdiction which accepts the Connecticut-California doctrine, the charge might be phrased as follows: "Since *A* is established, you must begin with the assumption that *B* exists. But that assumption may be destroyed by evidence. If from all the evidence you find either that the nonexistence of *B* is more probable than its existence or that the nonexistence of *B* is as probable as its existence, you will find that *B* does not exist; otherwise, you will find that *B* does exist." This clearly places upon the party against whom the presumption operates the burden of putting the jury in such state of mind that each juryman is unable to determine the truth or falsity of the proposition, that the existence of *B* is more probable than its nonexistence. In a jurisdiction adopting the Wisconsin view, the charge would be somewhat as follows: "Since *A* is established, you must begin with the assumption that *B* exists. But that assumption may be destroyed by evidence. If from all the evidence you find that *B* does not exist or that you are unable to determine whether *B* exists or not, you must render a verdict that *B* does not exist; otherwise your verdict must be that *B* does exist." This again is merely requiring the party against whom the presumption operates to put the jury in such a state of mind that they cannot determine the truth or falsity of the proposition that *B* exists.[17]

If any power other than one of the three just discussed is accorded a presumption, greater difficulties are encountered. If the establishment of *A* requires the party asserting the nonexistence of *B* to produce evidence thereof which will justify a jury in so finding and further to induce the jury to believe enough of it to support a verdict, or to induce the jury not positively to disbelieve so much of it as to leave the balance insufficient to support a verdict, the only case in which the charge will be simple will be one in which, in order to rebut the presumption, the jury would have to believe, or at least to fail to discredit, all the evidence against *B*. If it be assumed that the evidence tending to show the nonexistence of *B* is just enough to carry the issue to the jury, or, if more, is such that the jury must react toward it as a unit and cannot separate it into parts, then the judge may easily frame the charge by instructing the jury that, if they credit such evidence or cannot determine whether to credit it or not, they must find that *B* does not exist, but if they disbelieve any part of such evidence, then they must find that *B* does exist. But where the evidence tending to show the nonexistence of *B* consists of numerous items, and each of numerous combinations of the separate items would of itself be sufficient to take the issue to the jury, then two courses are open. The trial judge may either require the jury to answer a special question in respect to the existence of each fact which, by itself or in combination with any others that might be found from the evidence, would justify a reasonable jury in finding against the presumed fact. When he has these answers, he can easily determine whether the presumption has or has not been dissipated. If the existence or nonexistence of the presumed fact is decisive of the lawsuit, then this plan will be workable. If the judge takes only these answers without a general verdict, his only question will be in respect to the conclusion of law which should follow from the facts found. If he permits the jury to find a general verdict as well, no real difficulty is encountered, for, by hypothesis, the answers to the interrogatories are controlling and a judgment, notwithstanding any unwarranted general verdict, will be entered thereon. If, however, the existence of the presumed fact will be helpful but not decisive, either all the issues must be submitted as special interrogatories, or the judge will be unable to charge upon the general verdict without first knowing the jury's answer to the interrogatories. It is conceivable that the judge might take an interlocutory verdict by way of answer to the special questions, but such a procedure is unusual and would doubtless prove very cumbersome. The alternative is for the judge to determine each and every combination of evidential facts which the jury might find from the evidence and from which a reasonable jury would be justified in finding against the presumed fact, and instruct the jury that, if they believe any such combination to exist, they must find against the presumed fact. If the evidence is complicated and there are numerous combinations of fact that the jury might find therefrom, some of which would and others of which would not warrant a reasonable jury in finding against the presumed fact, the task of both judge and jury may be virtually impossible of satisfactory and intelligent performance. First, the judge must have in mind all the testimony so as to determine all the possible combinations of facts capable of being found. He would be in a much worse position than a demurrant to evidence under the strict common law, who had to specify all possible deductions that a jury might reasonably make against him from the evidence, but who did not have to itemize the possible combinations of fact which would justify such deductions. The practical obstructions to a competent compliance with these requirements caused the demurrer to evidence to give way to the motion for a directed verdict. Again, judicial experience with charges in cases of malicious prosecution where the fact situations are complicated, and in cases involving the construction of oral contracts where the evidence is conflicting or uncertain, has made manifest the difficulty if not the impracticability of framing adequate instructions with numerous hypotheses. And granting that the judge by careful attention to the testimony and with the aid of counsel could discover and explain the pertinent combinations, what jury, charged orally, could understand, remember, and apply them? Even if the charge was written, what jury would examine each hypothesis with the care and attention necessary to an intelligent decision? Except, therefore, in simple cases, it is useless to propose the adoption of a theory which requires so intricate a performance by judge and jury. The same considerations apply to cause the rejection of the doctrine which makes the persistence of the presumption depend upon the failure of the jury positively to discredit various combinations of the items of evidence.

If in attempting to determine the existence or nonexistence of *B* the jury is required to use the presumption as evidence of its existence, or to weigh it with the other evidence, it will not be difficult to construct a charge so advising them. But will this not put upon them an impossible psychological task? How can one weigh a presumption against, or with, or as, evidence? Just what will be the mental process? Is the presumption to be treated as if a witness had testified directly to the presumed fact? Surely it cannot be meant that the presumed fact is to be weighed as evidence, for that would be treating it as a fact, and obviously the most that can be attributed to it is a tendency to establish the fact. Just as certainly it cannot mean that the jury is to treat *A* as evidence of *B*, for if it has any probative value on the existence of *B*, it is already in the case for what it is worth; and offering evidence against *B* doesn't destroy *A* as a fact; it tends only to hinder or destroy the process of drawing the inference *B* from *A*. Is telling the jury that the establishment of *A* raises the presumption that *B* exists, and that the presumption is evidence of *B*, effective to convey any intelligible idea to them? Is it not a conglomeration of words, which will parse as a sentence and appears to say something, but which actually is "full of sound signifying nothing"? Suppose that a jury should ask the judge just what the instruction means; would he not be put to it even to give them an illustration of its application?[18] It seems pretty clear that, if such a doctrine serves the purpose of submitting to the jury a question which would otherwise be for the judge, it accomplishes the result in an unintelligible formula. It may be that it conveys to the jury a vague general notion that more evidence is required to find that *B* does not exist than would normally be required, and that it therefore does no real harm. But most certainly such a practice should never be adopted so long as the charge is conceived to be a device for enabling the jury to act intelligently and accurately in evaluating the evidence. If the charge means what it says, the jury can give the presumption as much or as little weight as it chooses. Obviously, outside of the inherently logical value of *A*, there is no actual probative value in the presumption; and what justification can there be for giving the jury power to attribute as great or as little artificial power to an item of evidence as it deems fit in the particular case? Isn't such a rule without any justification except in those cases in which the jury's emotions would lead them to the result which the court considers socially desirable?

If the effect of the establishment of *A* is merely to make the question of the existence of *B* one for the jury, the first inquiry is whether this gives any artificial quality to *A*. If not, the ruling is merely that *A* has inherent logical value sufficient to justify the inference that *B* exists; and there is no reason for singling it out from the other evidence for special treatment. If, however, the presumption is used as a device for endowing *A* with artificial powers of persuasion, it is necessary to know how long these powers persist. By hypothesis the jury is under no compulsion to draw the inference *B*. If, therefore, they refuse to draw it, there is no occasion to consider the presumption further.[19] But if from *A* alone they would find *B*, it is essential to know what limitations or conditions are attached to their power to do so.

Will the power die when evidence is introduced which would justify a reasonable jury in finding that *B* does not exist? If so, then the jury need be told nothing about the presumption, for it is assumed that such evidence is in the case. *A* will possess no power of persuasion beyond that which ordinary human experience would attribute to it. If it is the only evidence upon which its proponent is relying for a finding of *B*, the court must direct the jury to find against him on that issue; if there is other evidence of facts which in conjunction with *A* would furnish a reasonable basis for a finding of *B*, the issue is submitted like all other issues. The presumption has lived and died without the knowledge of the jury, and without affecting the judge's charge in any way.

May it not be given greater powers of endurance? May it not continue until other evidence in the case convinces the jury that its inference that *B* exists has been overcome or rendered doubtful? If from *A* alone the jury believes that *B* should be found, and if, under the law, that belief is justifiable, why should the jury not be permitted to continue in that belief until other evidence makes the nonexistence of *B* at least as probable as its existence? To adopt this rule would not make the judge's task unduly difficult, although it would not be quite so simple as if the presumption ceased to operate upon the mere introduction of evidence. The charge would simply tell the jury that since

A is established, they may, if they see fit, draw the inference therefrom that *B* exists, and if from *A* alone they would draw that inference, they may continue to assume the existence of *B* unless the entire evidence in the case convinces them that the nonexistence of *B* is at least as probable as its existence, in which event they must find that it does not exist. Of course, it would involve the jury in inextricable confusion to make the continued existence of their power to draw this inference depend upon their believing or failing to believe any one of various combinations of the items of evidence tending to show the nonexistence of *B*. Here, as in the case in which the presumption operates as a compelled assumption, the choice must be among these three views: (1) that which decrees the destruction of the power upon the mere introduction of evidence of the requisite quantity and quality; (2) that which make the power persist until the evidence puts the mind of the jury in equilibrium in respect to the existence of *B*; (3) that which causes the power to continue until the evidence persuades the jury that *B* does not exist. The notion that the presumption, as distinguished from fact *A* itself, is here to be weighed with, against, or as evidence upon the question of the existence of *B*, has never been suggested, and, if thinkable, is obviously impracticable.

Where both *A* and *B* are subjects of dispute under the evidence, such instructions as are given concerning the effect of the pertinent presumption must be conditioned upon a finding of the existence of *A* by the jury. Of course, if it be conceived that the presumption cannot operate in the presence of evidence that would justify a reasonable jury in finding the nonexistence of *B*, the judge's charge will be exactly as if no doctrine of presumptions had ever been judicially recognized. Here as elsewhere, this doctrine is capable of application with a minimum of intellectual effort. Nor is any great mental exertion necessary to apply either the rule that makes the presumption disappear only when the evidence puts the mind of the jury in equilibrium upon the issue of the existence of *B*, or that which attributes to the presumption the function of fixing the burden of persuasion. For example, in an action for injuries alleged to have been suffered by a passenger in a railroad wreck, a court adopting the former rule might well charge: "If you find that the train on which the plaintiff was a passenger was wrecked by derailment, you will find that the defendant was negligent unless the evidence convinces you either that it is more probable that the defendant company used due care than that it was negligent or that it is as probable that the defendant company used due care as that it was negligent." A court which adheres to the latter rule would merely omit the latter alternative. In the application of either rule the practical difficulties of the judge in framing the instruction or of the jury in understanding it seem too slight to make them a considerable, much less a decisive, factor in determining the policy of adopting or rejecting such a rule. Even if the effect of the presumption is merely to justify the jury in finding *B,* the difficulty will not be greatly enhanced: the conditional clause will have to bear the addition, "and this causes you to find the defendant negligent," and the first part of the conclusion will read, "you will adhere to that finding unless." But reasons of practicability will demand the rejection of both of the views which make the continuance or disappearance of the presumption depend upon the jury's finding or inability to find the truth of any one of specified combinations of items of the evidence. Except in the simplest situations, both the trial judge and the jury would be intolerably burdened. To a less degree the same is true of the rule which gives the presumption evidential value. While the judge's task in framing the charge is easy, the obstacles to an intelligent or accurate application of it by the jury are insuperable.

III

Which of the three practicable rules should be adopted? As elsewhere suggested,[20] that must depend upon the purposes to accomplish which presumptions were created. If the same purpose lies behind every presumption, then it seems reasonable to give to all presumptions the same procedural effect and the same powers of legal persistence. If, however, different classes of presumptions are originated as means for reaching different judicial objectives, their powers to survive attacks by evidence should be sufficient to enable them to perform the respective functions for which they were called into being. Why were judge-made presumptions invented?

The irrebuttable presumption is not a procedural device. The language of presumptions is used to clothe in an attractive or acceptable form a positive rule of substantive or procedural law. No evidence will destroy it, though evidence may disclose the facts to be such as to make it inapplicable.

The presumptions which operate to compel the assumption of *B* upon the establishment of *A* owe their existence to judicial demands for instruments (*a*) to furnish an escape from an otherwise inescapable dilemma or to work a purely procedural convenience, (*b*) to require the litigant to whom information concerning the facts is the more easily accessible to make them known, (*c*) to make more likely a finding in accord with the balance of probability, or (*d*) to encourage a finding consonant with the judicial judgment in respect to sound social policy.[21]

Sometimes without the aid of a mandatory assumption a judicial problem would be insoluble. Usually, of course, judicial inability to reach a conclusion leaves the matter in *statu quo,* which means, in the trial court, a decision for the defendant. But where a fund has to be distributed by a court, a failure to make the distribution does not result in a decision for anybody. It simply leaves the problem unsolved, the fund on hand legally usable by no one.[22] Thus, the presumption that a person who has been absent for seven years died immediately upon the expiration of the seventh year has no basis at all in human experience; it does not express a result which is deemed by the judiciary to be socially desirable; it serves only the purpose of purely procedural convenience. It enables the court, in the absence of evidence which would justify a reasonable trier in finding when the absentee died, to dispose of any fund the distribution of which depends upon the exact time of his death. Now suppose that the presumption vanishes upon the mere introduction of evidence which would justify a jury in finding the date of his death. If the jury disbelieves the evidence, or cannot make up its mind whether to believe it or not, the real trier has not been aided at all and the procedural device designed to provide a solution fails of its purpose. If the jury does believe it and is unable to draw the inference, the device, it is true, fails in this particular trial, but the inquiry has been advanced a step, and it does not follow that another jury will be unable to draw the inference. Consequently the device is not rendered entirely useless by the mere utterance of testimony upon the stand. If the presumption stands until the evidence makes the jury uncertain whether the absentee died at the time fixed by the presumption, it is still more effective, for it will dispose of the issue in all except that particular and unusual situation. And if the presumption operates until the evidence actually persuades the jury, it will serve its purpose in all cases except those in which the evidence is such as to convince the jury that the death did not occur at the presumed time although they cannot fix the date upon which it did occur. Such a presumption, then, will utterly fail of its purpose with respect to any issue to be decided by the jury if it vanishes upon the mere introduction of evidence which makes the issue one for the jury; it will best justify its existence if it persists until the evidence persuades the jury that the presumed fact does not exist or at least that its nonexistence is equally as probable as its existence. There is no difficulty in framing or applying an instruction which will enable it to perform this most desirable office. Consequently, one of these two views should be adopted. If the oft repeated formula which prohibits the shifting of the burden of persuasion is thought to have any applicable merit, the presumption should be held to disappear when the evidence puts the mind of the jury in equilibrium in respect to the existence of the presumed fact. If that formula be recognized for what it is really worth—a convenient rule applicable in the absence of a presumption, then the presumption should persist until the jury is persuaded by the evidence that the presumed fact does not exist.

If there be any presumption based solely upon inaccessibility of evidence, the same considerations are applicable. What is wanted is not the mere utterance of sounds or the production of writings in a court room, but sounds or writings which have some significance to the trier of fact.

Some presumptions the courts have created because the evidence which will establish the fact is peculiarly accessible to one of the parties. Thus, where a chattel in good condition is entrusted to a bailee for hire and he redelivers it in bad condition to his bailor, the damage is presumed to have been caused by the bailee's negligence. "The goods are entrusted to him. He has charge and control of them. He determines the manner of keeping them. He is in possession of such evidence as there is as to the circumstances attending the loss."[23] Is it reasonable to permit the presumption to be destroyed by the mere production of testimony which would justify a trier in finding due care but which in fact has no tendency to persuade the particular trier that such care has been used? It is true that in judicial discussions of rules of evidence and procedure the dangers of perjury and the supposed efficacy of legal rules to prevent it are greatly overemphasized. Still, is it not true that a doctrine which allows a party to escape liability by merely producing evidence, regardless of its actual convincing power, is a real incentive to perjury? For example, if in cases like *McIver v. Schwartz*[24] or *Pariso v. Towse*[25] the owner of an automobile can by his bare denial escape the effect of the presumption that it was being operated with his authority or consent by the negligent driver, and thereby escape also liability, in how many such cases will this denial be wanting? In the former case, both the jury and the trial judge seem to have thought the defendant's testimony false, and their conclusion was buttressed by the failure of the defendant to call the driver as a witness; yet the necessary effect of the court's opinion was that this totally worthless testimony prevented the case from going to the jury. In the latter, had the court felt itself free to adopt what it thought the proper doctrine, it would have given the same effect to the testimony of the defendant and the driver, although the jury discredited it, and not without reason. Surely the courts do not raise such a presumption merely for the purpose of making the opponent of the presumption cause words to be uttered; its premise is that the opponent knows the facts; for him to produce what the trier believes to be other than the information he really possesses, in no way fulfills the object of the presumption. It is conceded that practical difficulties prevent the adoption of a rule which makes the duration of the presumption depend upon belief or disbelief of specified items of evidence, and if the choice were between that and a rule which makes it disappear upon the mere introduction of the evidence, the latter might be preferred. But no real practical obstacles have ever been shown to exist to hinder or prevent the adoption of the doctrine which continues the presumption in effect until the evidence puts the mind of the jury in equilibrium in respect to the existence of the presumed fact. The same is true of the rule which attributes to such a presumption the function of fixing the burden of persuasion, although this rule does run counter to the dogma which prohibits a shifting of the burden of persuasion. It is therefore entirely reasonable to insist that, where a presumption is created to compel the disclosure of the facts by the litigant to whom the evidence of them is peculiarly accessible, it should not be destroyed, until the evidence persuades the jury at least that the nonexistence of the presumed fact is as probable as its existence.

Sometimes the presumption has its origin in the judicial opinion that it expresses the balance of probability. Thus, it is presumed that a person found to have met his death by violence did not commit suicide. This is not owing to any supposed difficulty of procuring evidence concerning the facts, which will or may result in the impossibility of an answer to a litigated question. It does not express any result which the court deems socially desirable. The conception behind it may be merely that nonsuicidal death is so usual that in the absence of evidence it must be taken for granted. It will not be enough merely to raise the question in the pleadings. It will be necessary to raise it also in the evidence. But once evidence is produced which makes it a question for the jury, the presumption has fulfilled the object of its being. If so, it ought then to vanish from the case. Since there is no difficulty in the application of such a rule, it should be adopted.

However, a court may well believe that the party who is alleging the happening of an unusual event, an event against the balance of probability, should prove it. Thus, while the plaintiff seeking to recover under a policy of insurance against death by accident normally has the burden of showing accident, it might well be thought reasonable to require the defendant to prove that a death shown to have been caused by violence was suicidal. In a case of this sort, the effect to be given to the presumption should depend upon the court's judgment in respect to the reasons which called for the creation of the presumption. If they be anything more than the idea that, until the query is raised in good faith, the usual will be taken for granted, there is no reason in ruling that the presumption must die with the introduction of the evidence. The reason for putting this burden on the plaintiff in the first place is that it is ordinarily fair to require a person who desires the *status quo* to be changed to show cause therefor. If it is to be changed upon the happening of an accident, he must show the accident; but as soon as he has proved a situation of which accident is the usual concomitant, there is no reason why his opponent should not be required to make it appear that in the particular case the unusual happened. Certainly it is hard to find a justification for not requiring him at least to make a showing which leaves the issue of accident or suicide in equilibrium.

If a policy is strong enough to call a presumption into existence, it is hard to imagine it so weak as to be satisfied by the bare recital of words on the witness stand or the reception in evidence of a writing. And if the judicial desire for the result expressed in the presumption is buttressed either by the demands of procedural convenience or by its accord with the usual balance of probability, it is little short of ridiculous to allow so valuable a presumption to be destroyed by the introduction of evidence without actual persuasive effect. Indeed, the only purpose which the reception of such credible but discredited evidence can ever accomplish is to demonstrate that in the particular case the proposition that the presumed fact exists is legally disputable, and the only situation in which such a purpose can furnish a justification for creating a presumption is one in which the presumption expresses a balance of probability not potent enough to overcome the burden which must normally be borne by the litigant seeking to overcome the inertia of the court.

The presumptions which have the function of authorizing a jury to draw an inference which ordinary judicial experience would deem unjustifiable may owe their creation to a realization that the generalizations which judicial experience would ordinarily condemn have been demonstrated to be warrantable in the pertinent repetitive situations, or to a conviction that the judgment likely to be exercised by a jury in such situations will produce a result which the court deems socially desirable. If the former, the court is merely proclaiming that from the basic fact *A* any trier may reasonably deduce the presumed fact *B*; if the latter, it is giving an artificial effect to an item of evidence in order that a desirable result may be reached. So far as *A* is logically potent to produce the inference *B,* its power should not be destroyed except by evidence which persuades the jury that the inference should not be drawn. So far as *A* is given artificial power to produce that effect for the purpose of attaining a socially desirable objective, its power ought to persist until evidence is produced which has an appreciable influence upon the mind of the trier.

The conclusion then is that most presumptions should, where applicable at all, continue to operate unless and until the evidence persuades the trier at least that the nonexistence of the presumed fact is as probable as its existence. This would not interfere with the accepted dogma prohibiting the shifting of the burden of persuasion. It is suggested that this dogma has not the slightest foundation in reason when applied to situations in which a presumption is involved, and should be entirely disregarded where a question arises in respect to the effect of evidence upon the persistence of a presumption. And in situations in which a presumption owes its origin to an important social policy, it should operate to fix the burden of persuasion.

It doubtless requires a presumption unknown to judicial language to waste so much good white paper in an attempt to propose and expound a plan for making simple, sensible, and workable devices which the courts have been using for generations as if they were simple, sensible, and workable. But, after all, the attempt will pass unnoticed except by the few. Will the passing notice of the few serve to divert the current of judicial decision into less muddy channels? Hardly. "Vanity of vanities, saith the Preacher, vanity of vanities: all is vanity. . . . Then I looked on all the works that my hands had wrought, and on the labor that I had labored to do; and behold, all was vanity and vexation of spirit."

NOTES TO MORGAN ESSAY

[1] No doubt it is easy to overemphasize this truth. It requires no extended search to find cases in which a requested charge has been successfully used by counsel as a trap in which to catch an unwary trial judge, or in which an appellate court has used the giving or failing to give requested instructions as a device to control a trial judge or a jury in situations wherein the appellate court has strong convictions, or in which a trial judge has used the charge as an instrument for exercising a technically forbidden control over the jury. It would, however, require a heavy mass of data to buttress a conclusion that the chief or even the important function of the charge has come to be one of these or a combination of them. There is no procedural rule that cannot be made to serve exactly the same ends. A strong trial judge often imposes his will upon the jury so thoroughly throughout the trial that the instructions become a mere formality. The requests which the opposing counsel submit may be read in such a way as to have no influence. A determined appellate court may upset trial court and jury, without the slightest reference to the instructions, and may uphold what it regards as a just result though the charge be a conglomeration of errors. That the charge may be put to such uses does not indicate that it does not also serve its legitimate purpose of furnishing to the jury a real guide for its task.

On the other hand, there can be little doubt that some appellate courts adopt a totally unrealistic attitude in construing instructions to the jury, and assume that jurors get not only the general impression which the words convey, but also that they make a microscopic examination of each instruction in the light of the strict rules of grammar and rhetoric, with the result that trial judges in self-defence are compelled to formulate charges so complex that no ordinary body of men could hope to understand them. Except in those benighted jurisdictions in which the trial judge is obliged to give instructions in the language requested, if the requested instructions state the law correctly, it ought not to be difficult for the judge to state the applicable rules in plain and simple language. And this is particularly so, it is believed, in respect to charges upon the burden of persuasion. See Farley, *Instructions to Juries—Their Rôle in the Judicial Process* (1932) 42 Yale L. J. 194.

[2] See First Nat. Bank v. Ford (1923) 30 Wyo. 110, 216 Pac. 691; Groom, *Proof of Crime in a Civil Proceeding* (1929) 13 Minn. L. Rev. 556.

[3] Alpine Forwarding Co. v. Pennsylvania R. R. 60 F. (2d) 734 (C. C. A. 2d, 1932); McIver v. Schwartz 50 R. I. 68 (1929) 145 Atl. 101. If *A*, the fact upon which the presumption is based, is established and the proponent rests without putting in evidence which would justify a finding against *B*, the presumed fact, the opponent will have the burden of producing such evidence; if, however, the proponent does introduce such evidence, then the opponent's burden created by the establishment of *A* has been satisfied before he has had need or opportunity to meet it. Thus it might, perhaps, more properly be said that the establishment of *A* puts upon the opponent of the presumption the risk of nonproduction of evidence which would justify a reasonable jury in finding that *B* does not exist. Of course *A* may be established for the particular case by (*a*) the process of Judicial notice, (*b*) by the pleadings, (*c*) by stipulation, (*d*) by evidence which would compel a finding of *A*, or (*e*) by the finding of the jury.

Whenever the phrase, "finding the existence of the presumed fact," or its equivalent is used herein without explanation, it must be understood as a convenient method of describing the required action of the jury in deciding issues of fact. As explained later, this may mean that the jury is convinced that the fact exists, or is convinced that the existence of the fact is more probable than its nonexistence.

[4] See Clark v. Diefendorf 109 Conn. 507, 511, (1929) 147 Atl. 33, 35; Gillett v. Michigan United Traction Co. (1919) 205 Mich. 410, 421, 171 N. W. 536.

[5] See cases cited in note 4 *supra.*

[6] Diller v. Northern California Power Co. 162 Cal. 531, (1912) 123 Pac. 359; Klunk v. Hocking Valley Ry. (1906) 74 Ohio St. 125, 77 N. E. 752.

[7] Page v. Phelps 108 Conn. 572, (1928) 143 Atl. 890; Weber v. Chicago, R. I. & Pac. R. R. (1916) 175 Iowa 358, 151 N. W. 852; Bond v. St. Louis-San Francisco Ry. (1926) 315 Mo. 987, 288 S. W. 777; Holzheimer v. Lit Brothers (1918) 262 Pa. 150, (1918) 105 Atl. 73.

[8] Mutual Life Ins. Co. of New York v. Maddox, 221 Ala. 292, (1930) 128 So. 383; Commonwealth v. Spencer (1912) 212 Mass. 438, 99 N. E. 266; *cf.* Wilson v. Grace (1930) 273 Mass. 146, 153, 173 N. E. 524.

[9] See Thayer, *Preliminary Treatise on Evidence* (1898) 340, 351; Legis. (1928) 28 Col. L. Rev. 489.

[10] See the statutory presumption in Heiner v. Donnan (1932) 285 U. S. 312, 52 Sup. Ct. 358; compare that in Brooks v. Blount [1923] 1 K. B. 257.

[11] See Sherwood, J., in State v. Robinson, 117 Mo. 649, 661, (1893) 23 S. W. 1066, 1072; State v. Sykes (1913) 148 Mo. 708, 713, 154 S. W. 1130, 1133; People v. Ahrling (1917) 279 Ill. 70, 85, 216 N. E. 764, 771.

[12] Commonwealth v. Webster, 5 Cush. 295 (Mass. 1850). As examples of reversals for refusal to define reasonable doubt, see Schencks v. United States, 2 Fed. (2d) 185 (App. D. C. 1924); Nanfito v. United States, 20 F. (2d) 376 (C. C. A. 8th, 1927); Davis v. State (1903) 46 Fla. 137, 35 So. 76.

A similar remark would be justified concerning charges in respect to the presumption of innocence. See particularly Commonwealth v. Madeiros (1926) 255 Mass. 304, 151 N. E. 297, for the disastrous results of the laudable effort of Judge Lummus to inject common sense into the Massachusetts practice.

[13] See *e.g.*, a safe if not very acceptable method of protecting the trial judge, Cal. Pen. Code (1931) §§ 1096, 1096a. See the vigorous dissenting opinion of Mr. Chief Justice Wheeler in Kotler v. Lally (1930) 112 Conn. 86, 151 Atl. 433, for the expression of a healthful judicial attitude toward procedural questions.

[14] Anderson v. Chicago Brass Co. (1906) 127 Wis. 273, 106 N. W. 1077. See also Pullman Palace Car Co. v. Adams (1898) 120 Ala. 581, 599, 24 So. 921, 929; Dunbar v. McGill (1887) 64 Mich. 676, 31 N. W. 578; Brown v. Atlanta & Charlotte Air Line Ry. (1882) 19 S. C. 39.

[15] Sullivan v. Nesbit (1922) 97 Conn. 474, 117 Atl. 502; see also in *accord:* Hoyt v. Danbury (1897) 69 Conn. 341, 37 Atl. 1051; Murphy v. Waterhouse (1896) 113 Cal. 467, 45 Pac. 866; Livanovitch v. Livanovitch (1925) 99 Vt. 327, 131 Atl. 799.

[16] See Chicago & Alton R. R. v. Kelly (1904) 210 Ill. 449, 71 N. E. 355. See generally, cases collected in Sunderland, *Cases on Trial and Appellate Practice* (1924) 504–21.

[17] It may be objected that an instruction in the suggested phraseology requires a finding that *B* exists where some of the jurors are persuaded of its existence and others are persuaded of its nonexistence. If this be so, it can readily be corrected by a specific direction that where such a disagreement exists in respect to any material issue, the jury shall not return a verdict for either party.

[18] See *e.g.*, the dilemma into which the Alabama Supreme Court was forced by coun-

sel in Mutual Life Ins. Co. of New York v. Maddox, 221 Ala. 292, (1930) 128 So. 383. And just how could the Massachusetts court harmonize the pronouncements in the cases in note 8 *supra?*

[19] This seems to be what Mr. Chief Justice Wheeler had in mind in Schiesel v. Poli Realty Co. (1928) 108 Conn. 115, 120, 122, 142 Atl. 812, 813–814: "Experience has demonstrated that when certain facts are proven, ordinarily a certain inference follows, and that in the absence of their explanation or rebuttal, reliance may be placed upon the probative strength of the inference, and from it a presumption of law attaching to it certain legal consequences will arise. The presumption is neither the fact nor the inference, but, as Thayer says, 'the legal consequences of it.' . . . The presumption stands or falls with the inference. . . . The legal consequence of such inference when drawn would cast upon the defendant the duty of explaining or rebutting this inference."

[20] Bohlen, *The Effect of Rebuttable Presumptions of Law upon the Burden of Proof* (1920) 68 U. of Pa. L. Rev. 307, reprinted in Bohlen, *Studies in the Law of Torts* (1926) 636; Morgan, *Some Observations Concerning Presumptions* (1931) 44 Harv. L. Rev. 906.

[21] See Bohlen, *supra* note 20. Thayer, *Preliminary Treatise on Evidence* (1898) 313–521.

[22] Montgomery v. Bevans, 1 Sawy. 653, Fed. No. 9735, at p. 633 (C. C. D. Cal. 1871); *In re* Rhodes (1887) 36 Ch. D. 586; *cf. In re* Aldersey [1905] 2 Ch. 181.

[23] Dibell, J., in Rustad v. Great Northern Ry. (1913) 122 Minn. 453, 142 N. W. 727, holding that the burden was upon the bailee for hire to persuade the jury that the bailee had used due care in keeping the bailed goods, which had been destroyed. In such a situation, as Professor Bohlen has pointed out, there are two distinct questions: (1) What was defendant's conduct? (2) Did such conduct constitute due care or negligence? Wherever such a situation exists, Professor Bohlen would attribute to such a presumption the effect of putting upon the opponent of the presumption the burden of persuading the trier of fact upon the first question only. The burden in respect to the second question would be entirely unaffected by the presumption. This view finds some support in O'Day v. Amodeo, 170 Atl. 486 (Conn. 1934). It may be objected that in a complicated case it would encounter the same difficulties as the view which makes the duration of the presumption depend upon the belief or disbelief by the jury of specified items of evidence.

[24] 50 R. I. 68, (1929) 145 Atl. 101.

[25] 45 F. (2d) 962 (C. C. A. 2d, 1930), (1931) 44 Harv. L. Rev. 861.

MORE ABOUT THE NATURE OF LAW

BY ROSCOE POUND

FROM THE BEGINNING the question, What is law?—the problem of the nature of law—has been a battle ground of jurisprudence. More than one important book on jurisprudence is wholly occupied with this question. But in recent times there has been a growing impatience with it and disinclination to engage in the kind of argument which it involves. Bluntschli compared it to Pilate's question, "What is truth?"; and many who propound it today, like Pilate, wait not for an answer.

Undoubtedly there are many things in a science of law which ought not to be postponed to continued discussion of the nature of law. Many jurists who pass by on the other side and go on to other questions have been doing a real service. Yet we cannot ignore so fundamental a question. Too much depends upon it in other connections. Moreover, it is not merely academic. In at least five situations it has been raised as a practical question in the ordinary course of litigation in American courts.

In one type of case a state constitution or a state statute having been construed by the highest court of the state and legal transactions having been entered into on the faith of the interpretation, the state court changes its view in later decisions with the effect that the transactions will not be upheld in the state courts. In such cases the federal courts, where otherwise there would be "gross injustice," follow the earlier rather than the later state decisions in respect to what is the law of the state.[1] What the Supreme Court of the United States has since pronounced "unguarded language" in some of these cases[2] went further than the actual decisions, and suggested that the later state decisions amounted to a state law impairing the obligation of contracts. They suggested that the judicial construction, so far as contract rights under it were concerned, was to be considered as much a part of the statute as the text itself, and that a change in the course of judicial decision affecting such contract rights was to be treated the same as an amendment of the statute by an express legislative enactment.[3] The proposition that such a change in the course of decision in the state courts amounts to a "law impairing the obligation of contracts" within Art. I, § 10, of the Federal Constitution, is now repudiated.[4] But the Supreme Court of the United States still holds that "in determining whether a state law has impaired a contract, it must decide for itself whether there was a contract and whether the law as enforced by the state court impairs it."[5] The bearing upon this question of the later view of English and American analytical jurists, that the law is the sum of the rules administered by the courts and that a law is such a rule, is obvious.

In another type of case, federal courts are called on to administer the law of a state and, finding the common law established therein but the rule in respect to some particular point undetermined by the state courts, determine what in their judgment is the rule applicable at common law. After conveyances have been made on the strength of the decision, the question comes up in the state courts, which take a different view. The question being one of a rule of property, state decisions would ordinarily be controlling. But by a divided court it has been held that they would not be followed so as to impair the rights theretofore acquired.[6] The dissenting opinion of Mr. Justice Holmes brings out clearly that the question is one of the nature of law and cites Gray's discussion of that question.[7] Again, where the federal courts are exercising jurisdiction by virtue of diversity of citizenship, and so are administering the law of a state, if that law is not in the form of legislation as to the point in question and that point is one of "general law," those courts exercise an independent judgment of what the law is and do not hold themselves bound by the decisions of the state courts.[8]

Another type of case arises in connection with the unhappy doctrine concerning mistake of law. Where legal transactions are entered into in reliance upon judicial decisions which are afterward overruled, has there been a change of law or did the parties to the transaction act under a mistake of law?[9] Again, a court having held a penal statute unconstitutional, some person acts in contravention of its provisions. The court thereafter changes its view and holds the statute valid. Was there a violation of law in what was done before the last decision? One court has said that to give such a decision retroactive effect would amount in substance to the prohibited *ex post facto* lawmaking.[10]

Some twenty years ago I pointed out two ideas running through definitions of law: one an imperative idea, an idea of a rule laid down by the lawmaking organ of a politically organized society, deriving its force from the authority of the sovereign; and the other a rational or ethical idea, an idea of a rule of right and justice deriving its authority from its intrinsic reasonableness or conformity to ideals of right and merely recognized, not made, by the sovereign. I suggested that these two ideas corresponded to two elements in a body of authoritative legal materials, one enacted or imperative, the other traditional or habitual, and that, as at some times the growing point of legal systems has been in legislation and at other times in juristic writing or judicial decision, definitions of law have fluctuated between these two ideas according to the prevailing form of law for the time being.[11] Something of the diversity of view concerning the nature of law is to be explained in this way. But there are two other sources of difficulty. One is that we use the term "law" to mean more than one thing and then discuss the nature of law as if we were talking of one thing instead of three. The other is that, even if we use "law" in the narrower sense given to the term by the English analytical jurisprudence of the nineteenth century, it is possible to look at it from more than one standpoint and the resulting picture will be very different according to the one chosen.

Our English word "law" (and the corresponding words in the languages of Continental Europe are open to the same observation) is used in juristic writing in any one of at least three senses, and at times in all three.

Historically, the oldest and longest continued use in juristic writing is to mean the aggregate of laws, the whole body of legal precepts which obtain in a given politically organized society. But in a wider phase of this sense it may mean the body of authoritative grounds of or guides to judicial and administrative action established or recognized in such a society, including precepts, technique, and received ideals. Anglo-American usage until recently ignored administrative action in this connection. The first recognition seems to have been by

Sir Frederick Pollock in 1896.[12] Today, I suppose, we should put judicial decision and administrative determination on much the same plane. Hence, according to the view we entertain of the nature of a legal precept, we may speak of law in this sense as the body of received or established materials on which judical and administrative determinations proceed or ought to proceed. In this sense jurists speak of "systems of law" and of "justice according to law." Usually also we use the word in this sense when we speak of "comparative law."

In the latter part of the nineteenth century and in the present century the influence of Jhering and the rise of sociological and social philosophical jurisprudence led to a functional attitude toward the problems of jurisprudence, so that jurists began to think of a process or an activity instead of a state or condition.[13] But the body of authoritative materials of decision and official action is not a process. It is a body of materials for the guidance of a process. Hence jurists turned from debates on the nature of law to consider the nature of the legal order. From the time of Kant there had been those who defined law in terms of the legal order; and in much that is said and written about "law" today it has that sense. We may say, then, that in a second sense the term is used to mean the legal order (*ordre juridique, Rechtsordnung*). It is used to mean the régime of ordering human activities and adjusting human relations through the systematic application of the force of politically organized society. Here again, however, there is a wider idea. The legal order is a specialized phase of social control. It is from one standpoint a régime of ordering conduct through social pressure backed by the force of the political organization. If we go back a bit in legal history we come to régimes of social pressure without such backing. To unify the phenomena of developed societies with those of the more primitive social orders, historical jurists use "law" to mean the whole régime of social control.[14] The word "law" is used in the sense of the legal order when we speak of "respect for law" or of "the end of law." Most of what is called philosophy of law is a philosophical consideration of the legal order. Also in recent years the science of law has come to be quite as much a science of the legal order as one of the authoritative materials of decision.

A further consequence of the functional attitude toward the problems of jurisprudence is to be seen in increased attention to the phenomena of the actual administration of justice as contrasted with exclusive attention to the authoritative materials for guidance of judicial action. Accordingly, many who write of "law" mean what Mr. Justice Cardozo has taught us to call the "judicial process." Today we must consider along with this what may be called the "administrative process." We must look into the process of determining controversies and adjusting relations whether it goes on judicially or in administration. In this connection we may refer to these processes as they are actually carried on, or as we hold they ought to go on. Those who approach jurisprudence from a psychological standpoint commonly think of law in terms of the judicial process or of both the judicial and the administrative process as phases of one type of governmental activity. The term "law" is used in this sense in much of the neo-realist writing of today and in such pronouncements as that of Professor Llewellyn, that he includes under "law" all that is done officially.[15]

Not infrequently, also, "law" is used to include all three of the foregoing meanings. This is so notably in discussions of the relation of "law and morals." Much of that discussion has been vitiated by the multiplicity of meanings of the terms used. Commonly we consider under that head the relation of morals or morality or both to the body of received or authoritative materials for guidance of judicial or administrative action, or to the legal order, or to the judicial and administrative processes, or any two or all three of them. Similarly, when we speak of the "science of law" we may mean an organized body of knowledge concerning the authoritative materials of judicial and administrative determinations, as did the analytical jurists in the last century. In recent times, however, we are more likely to mean a body of knowledge or investigation in which the legal order, the authoritative materials for guidance of judges and officials, and the judicial and administrative processes are all taken into account as somehow making up one subject.[16]

But the three meanings of the term "law" are not the only source of difficulty in discussions of the "nature of law." If we restrict the term to the authoritative materials for the guidance of judicial and administrative action, it is possible to look at those materials from more than one standpoint, and the answer to the question, What is law?, will depend much upon the standpoint from which it is asked. If it is asked from the standpoint of the judge who has a case before him for decision and of the administrative official who is called upon to take some course of action, the significant thing seems to be a body of authoritative grounds of decision or of administrative determination. If it is asked from the standpoint of the citizen who would walk in the straight path of social conduct and wishes it charted for him, the significant thing seems to be a body of authoritative rules of or guides to conduct. If it is asked from the standpoint of the counselor at law who would advise a client in respect to what he may do or not do safely, or how he may act with assurance that courts and administrative officials will back him and further his quest for desired results, there seems to be a body of threats or of predictions of results attaching to particular states of fact. If it is asked from the standpoint of the teacher, who is called on to put in the order of reason the materials recognized or established as the basis of decision, or at hand for the counselor, or provided for the guidance of the citizen, he may find it hard to say that one of these aspects, as things are today, is more significant than another and yet be puzzled to find the more inclusive order which will enable him to fit his theory to all these points of view.[17]

I. LAW AS AN AGGREGATE OF LAWS

1. *A Law as a Rule of Conduct.*—If we look into the definitions of law from the middle ages to the present, we shall find that until the end of the eighteenth century it was assumed that law was an aggregate of laws and that a law was a rule of conduct for the individual. Bentham's proposition that "law or the law . . . is an abstract term which . . . can mean neither more nor less than the sum total of a number of individual laws taken together"[18] obtained down to Kant. Law was thought to be defined by defining a law, as has been the view of the analytical jurists to this day; and the majority of jurists of all schools have continued in the traditional course. Discussions of the nature of law have been confined to the nature of a law. Also, the point of view of the individual subject to the rule has been the traditional starting point. A law or rule of law was a rule of conduct; but whether an authorita-

tive guide or a command, depended on whether the approach was ethical or political.

Medieval formulas followed those of autiquity, and the latter were Greek or based on Greek originals. Hence, they speak from an undifferentiated or little differentiated social control and conceive of an ethical precept backed by politically organized force, deriving its authority originally from its intrinsic quality but immediately from recognition or establishment by politically organized society. Thus, Thomas Aquinas:

> A law is a rule or measure of acts. . . . Now the rule and measure of human acts is reason. . . .
>
> A law is . . . an ordinance of reason for the common good emanating from him who has the care of the community and promulgated.[19]

There has been a long succession of formulas in this line. For example:

> The proper signification of *ius* is one, namely, when *ius* is used to mean an enactment directing on behalf of the government those things which are right.[20]
>
> A rule of civil conduct, prescribed by the supreme power in a state, commanding what is right and prohibiting what is wrong.[21]
>
> The rule or standard governing as a whole the conditions for the orderly attainment of whatever is good, or assures good for the individual or society, so far as those conditions depend on voluntary action.[22]
>
> Law *(droit)* is the aggregate of precepts or laws *(lois)* governing the conduct of man toward his fellows, the observance of which it is possible, and at the same time just and useful, to assure by way of external coercion.[23]

In another type of definition of law as an aggregate of rules of conduct, the ethical element alone is considered. The rule is thought of as having an intrinsic moral force which alone is significant. Thus:

> A rule of moral actions obliging to that which is right.[24]
>
> A rule to which men are obliged to make their moral actions conformable.[25]

Such definitions, one need not say, are from the standpoint of natural law. They conceive of the legal rule of conduct as declaratory of a precept of morals from which it gets its significance and validity. Reason may take the place of morals in such a conception of law. The legal rule of conduct may be thought of as founded on and declaratory of reason, deriving its significance and validity from its intrinsic reasonableness. For example:

> The rule of law *(la loi)* in general is human reason.[26]

A political conception of the rule of conduct omits all ethical or rational element and sees the authority of a politically organized society as the significant feature. The rule is conceived of as deriving its validity and authority from establishment or recognition and enforcement by the state or some of its organs.

We may begin with Hobbes, whose formula is in transition from the ethical to the political, making the ethical quality a consequence of the guinea stamp of the state instead of holding that establishment by the state is a recognition or declaration of ethical content. He says:

> Civil law is to every subject those rules which the commonwealth hath commanded him . . . to make use of for the distinction of right and wrong: that is to say, of what is contrary and not contrary to the rule.[27]

In the age of absolute governments, on the pattern of the *ancien régime* in France, this type of formula, with all reference to the ethical omitted, becomes usual. Thus:

> A law *(lex)* is an enactment by which a superior obliges one subject to him to direct his actions according to the command of the former.[28]
>
> A rule prescribed by the sovereign of a society to his subjects.[29]

Rousseau having defined law as "the expression of the general will,"[30] the political formula is sometimes put in terms of the will of the state or of some form of declaration expressing its will. Thus:

> The will of the state concerning the civic conduct of those under its authority.[31]
>
> A rule agreed upon by the people regulating the rights and duties of persons.[32]

A variant of this Rousseauist formula, in which the idea of a rule of conduct disappears and in which, according to the practice of some realists today, law is made to cover everything that is done officially, is given by Laurent:

> One may say with Portalis, that a law *(la loi)* is a solemn declaration of the will of the sovereign upon an object of common interest.[33]

But the main current of definition of law in France in the nineteenth century, and a strong current even today, puts the matter in terms of a rule of conduct prescribed by the supreme political authority. French juristic thinking had begun to run along these lines in the eighteenth century because of the modes of political thought in a time of absolute government. Also France reduced the whole of her law to legislative form early in the last century. After the code of 1804 it appeared on the surface that *droit* was an aggregate of *lois* and that a *loi* proceeded from the lawmaking organ of the state. For a long time every other element and every other aspect was obscured by the form of French law.

Some examples of French formulas from this standpoint are:

> The civil law is, therefore, a rule of conduct upon a subject of common interest prescribed to all citizens by their lawful sovereign. It is the solemn declaration of the legislative power, by which it commands, under certain penalties or subject to certain rewards, what each citizen ought to do or not to do or to permit for the common good of society.[34]
>
> A law *(loi)* is a rule established by the authority which, according to the political constitution, has the power of commanding, or prohibiting, or of permitting throughout the state. A law truly and properly so-called, therefore, . . . is a rule sanctioned by the public power, a rule civilly and juridically obligatory. Law *(droit)* is the result, or better, the aggregate or totality of these rules.[35]
>
> What is law *(droit)*? It is the aggregate, or rather the resultant, of the dispositions of the laws *(lois)* to which man is subjected, with the power of following or of violating them. . . . Now these laws *(lois)* are rules of conduct established by a competent authority.[36]
>
> Obligatory rules of conduct, general and permanent, established for men by the temporal sovereign.[37]
>
> The *ensemble* of precepts, rules, or laws which govern human activity in society, the observance whereof is sanctioned in case of need by social constraint, otherwise called public force.[38]

Although the foregoing formulas are drawn primarily from the standpoint of the citizen, and regard law as an aggregate of laws which are rules of conduct proceeding from politically organized society, those of Toullier, Marcadé, and Colin and Capitant suggest the idea of a rule of law as a threat of official action, which has had much currency in the present century. Also those of Demolombe and of Demante have some suggestion of defining law in terms of the legal order.

English analytical formulas down to 1890 run along the same line. For example:

> Of the laws or rules set by men to men, some are established by *political* superiors, sovereign and subject: by persons exercising supreme and subordinate government in independent nations or independent political societies. The aggregate of the rules thus established, or some aggregate forming a portion of that aggregate, is the appropriate matter of jurisprudence, general or particular. To the aggregate of the rules thus established, or to some aggregate forming a portion of that aggregate, the term law, as used simply and strictly, is exclusively applied.[39]
>
> A command proceeding from the supreme political authority of a state and addressed to the persons who are the subjects of that authority.[40]
>
> A general rule of external human action enforced by a sovereign political authority.[41]
>
> Rules of conduct defined by the state as those which it will enforce, for the enforcement of which it employs a uniform constraint.[42]

And, from another starting point, Jhering brings us to much the same result, defining law as

> The sum of the rules of constraint which obtain in a state.[43]

It differs in its taking account of the historical position and so including precepts recognized by the state with those established or enacted by the state.

It is not so easy to determine the standpoint from which the metaphysical and metaphysical-historical formulas proceed in the nineteenth century. Both philosophy and history led to thinking in terms of the individual man rather than of the citizen. Also the idea of rules of conduct is not so clear as in the analytical formulas, because freedom rather than constraint is the central idea. The legal order was thought of in terms of securing liberties rather than in terms of enforcing duties. Yet on the whole we get idealist-philosophical versions of the definition of law as an aggregate of rules of conduct,[44] or, at the end of the century, historical-sociological versions extending the idea of law to include all social control.[45]

After Binding[46] the rule comes more and more to be thought of, not as constraining conduct but as pointing out what it ought to be. Formulas from this standpoint may be normative-analytical, as, for example:

The purpose of all law is a determinate external behavior of men toward men. The means of attaining this purpose, wherein alone the law consists, are norms or imperatives.[47]

A rule expressing the relations of human conduct conceived as subject to realization by state force.[48]

The norms of a customarily followed, comprehensive, and permanent supreme power.[49]

Or they may be normative-sociological, such as:

The limitations imposed upon the free activity of each in the interest of the general peace are expressed in the form of rules of conduct which every man ought to observe in his relations with his fellows. These rules, these precepts to be observed by men in their relations with one another, constitute the law.[50]

Finally, the neo-scholastic jurists revive the old recognition of an ethical element in the rule of conduct with a suggestion both of the historical and of the sociological modes of approach. Thus:

The *ensemble* of the rules to which the external conduct of man in his relations with his fellows is subjected, and which, under the inspiration of the natural idea of justice, in a given state of the collective consciousness of humanity, appearing susceptible of a social sanction where coercion is required, are or tend to be provided with such a sanction and thenceforth take the form of categorical injunctions governing particular wills for the purpose of assuring order in society.[51]

2. *A Law as a Rule of Decision.*—Continental jurists with their eyes fixed chiefly on the legislative organ of the state, which was treated as the significant factor in the Roman tradition as it came from Justinian's law books, thought of enacted or recognized rules of conduct. English and American lawyers, however, because of the part played by judicial decision in the Anglo-American system, as the English analytical formula developed, came to think not of rules of conduct but of rules of decision, or of rules which could be seen as rules of conduct because they were rules of decision. They came to define a law from the standpoint of the judge rather than from the standpoint of the citizen. This tendency seems to have begun with Dicey:

The Law of every country . . . consists of all the principles, rules, or maxims enforced by the courts of that country as being supported by the authority of the state.[52]

It is the prevailing English type. Thus:

The sum of the rules administered by courts of justice.[53]

The rules recognized and acted on in courts of justice.[54]

The rules and principles recognized and applied by the state's authorities, judicative and executive.[55]

Also it has been given currency in this country by Professor Gray:

The law or laws of a society are the rules in accordance with which the courts of that society determine cases, and by which, therefore, the members of that society are to govern themselves; and the circumstance which distinguishes these rules from other rules for conduct, and which makes them the law, is the fact that courts do act upon them.[56]

A recent formula including both the judicial and the administrative enforcement of rules of conduct takes account also of the ethical side of law and even suggests the ideal element. But, defining law in terms of laws, necessarily it leaves the ideal element outside the law:

A rule of conduct, administered by those organs of a political society which it has ordained for that purpose, and imposed in the first instance at the will of the dominating political authority in that society in pursuance of the conception of justice which is held by that dominating authority or by those to whom it has committed the task of making such rules.[57]

3. *A Law as a Threat of Official Action.*—Bentham's utilitarian theory of legislation and his insistence upon sanction as a necessary element in a law leads to a different view of the nature of a law, when looked at from the traditional standpoint of the citizen. The citizen may seek to know what he ought to do and put that question to the body of authoritative legal materials, or he may seek to know what he may do safely and what not, and the law may be thought of as warning him of the consequences of his doing or not doing certain things by a threat that legal consequences of official action will follow. The transition to this standpoint may be seen in a thoroughly Benthamist English formula:

A law is a command; that is to say, it is the signification by a lawgiver to a person obnoxious to evil of the lawgiver's wish that such person should do or forbear to do some act, with an intimation of an evil that will be inflicted in case the wish be disregarded.[58]

Such is perhaps the prevailing standpoint on the Continent today:

Law is the legitimate order given to a human subject, individual or collective, bound to execute to the profit of another subject (entitled to claim from him the execution thereof) that an external fact be followed by another external fact, in default thereof by a third, and so on, with prescribed application of physical constraint to certain links in this chain.[59]

The delimitation of what men and groups of men are at liberty to do or not to do without incurring a condemnation, an execution, or some particular putting in play of force.[60]

Kelsen combines this idea of a threat with a normative-analytical idea.[61]

4. *A Law as a Prediction of Official Action.*—With the development of a complex industrial society involving long-term coöperative enterprises to which large numbers devote their means and their energies, the function of advising in respect to safe courses of conduct becomes the most exacting and lucrative of the lawyer's activities, and law begins to be defined from a new standpoint. More and more the best minds in the profession are engaged, not in the forum nor in drawing up elaborate printed arguments for presentation to the courts, but in advising the leaders of business and industry what they may do without incurring too much risk of official interference or legally enforced liability, and what courses they should take to insure that what they desire to bring about will have the backing of public authorities. Mr. Justice Holmes, in an epoch-making address, in which he led American students of the science of law out of the nineteenth-century analytical and historical jurisprudence toward the methods and ideas which obtain today, noted this shifting of the significance among professional activities and suggested a conception of law from the standpoint of the counselor. He said:

The reason why people will pay lawyers to argue for them or to advise them, is that in societies like ours the command of the public force is intrusted to the judges in certain cases, and the whole power of the state will be put forth, if necessary, to carry out their judgments and decrees. People want to know under what circumstances and how far they will run the risk of coming against what is so much stronger than themselves, and hence it becomes a business to find out when this danger is to be feared. The object of our study, then, is prediction, the prediction of the incidence of public force through the instrumentality of the courts.[62]

Mr. Justice Holmes was addressing law teachers and law students and was putting to them, as the subject of study, the art of the lawyer's craft. One might say he was putting the counseling process as, from the lawyer's standpoint, the object of study of the materials upon which the counselor's predictions are based, and the judicial and administrative processes which it is the counselor's task to foresee. This is brought out clearly as the address proceeds; as, for example, when he says:

For the most important and pretty nearly the whole meaning of every new effort of legal thought is to make these prophecies more precise and to generalize them into a thoroughly connected system.

From this standpoint, then, he says:

The prophecies of what courts will do in fact, and nothing more pretentious, are what I mean by the law.[63]

Mr. Justice Cardozo has pointed out that, using law in the second sense, a law is a basis of prediction rather than a prediction. He says:

A principle or rule of conduct so established as to justify a prediction with reasonable certainty that it will be enforced by the courts if its authority is challenged, is, then, for the purposes of our study, a principle or rule of law.[64]

A notable book has been written on this aspect of law.[65] But the most valuable achievement of thinking of law from the standpoint of the counselor's function has been in leading writers of the present generation, to challenge the idea of law as an aggregate of laws and of taking a law to be a rule.[66] The study of law from cases, as Bingham pointed out long ago,[67] could not fail to make us conscious that behind the judicial and administrative processes there is something more than rules. Recent American juristic writing is much taken up with the question, What is significant in all that goes to make up that something more? One answer lays stress upon the unauthoritative elements in the judicial process and would define a law in terms of everything that enters into the counseling process.[68] Another, with which we are not directly concerned here, would question the proposition that law is an aggregate of laws and, without admitting everything of which the counselor must take account within the category of law, recognize received technique and received ideals as no less part of the law than received precepts and find the precept element a complex category involving rules, principles, conceptions, and standards.[69] Perhaps here also the difference lies in the starting point. One may concede that the counseling process is something of which the science of law must take account, as well as the judicial process and the administrative process, and may concede the service that the juristic realists do in directing our attention to this, without finding it necessary to define law in terms of that process.

Some formulas, more or less from the standpoint of the counseling process, are:

> Law, then, as to any given situation, is either (*a*) actual law, i.e., a past decision as to that situation, or (*b*) probable law, i.e., a guess as to a future decision.[70]
>
> From the point of view of the practical work of the lawyer, law may fairly be said to be past decisions (as to past events which have been judged) and predictions as to future decisions.[71]

5. *A Law as an Authoritative Pattern of What Ought to Be.*—In Kelsen's normative theory, which has a large following today, law, in the second sense (for in other discussions he uses "law" in the sense of the legal order), is a body of authoritative patterns of what ought to be—of what conduct ought to be and of what decisions and official action ought to be. A law is a norm. Thus laws may be looked upon from different standpoints as guides to conduct, as guides to decision, as threats of legal consequences, or as grounds of prediction of official action. The advantage of a theory which unites these points of view is obvious.[72]

II. LAW AS THE LEGAL ORDER

KANT BEGAN a wholly different type of formula by thinking of law not as an aggregate of laws but as the condition in which conflicting human wills were reconciled in action by a general principle of freedom and its corollaries. He said:

> [Law is] the sum of the circumstances according to which the will of one may be reconciled with the will of another according to a common rule of freedom.[73]

Another well-known definition in terms of the legal order conceived as of a state or condition, is:

> The organic whole of the external conditions of life measured by reason.[74]

Later formulas have been put in terms of the legal order thought of as a process rather than as a condition.[75] Thus:

Law is a peaceable ordering of the external relations of men and their relations to each other.[76]

Law is the ordering of the relations of life guaranteed by the general will.[77]

Law is the ordering *(Ordnung)* based upon autonomous government in a state of civilization.[78]

In the present, with its political storms which have shaken the consciousness-of-right of men and of peoples, in a time of confusion which looks upon law sometimes as sheer force, sometimes only as ideal powerlessness, we must call mankind back to a consciousness that law is neither the one nor the other, but rather might in the service of the idea of society, external coercion as the basis of freedom, form of the national community life, in which alone the individual may be free and may strive to fulfill in his person the idea of humanity.[79]

Kohler, indeed, expressly defines the legal order as such and assumes that no further definition of law is required:

The legal order is an adjustment through coercion of the relations of human life arising in a social manner from the social nature of man.[80]

Kelsen uses "law" in this sense in his theory of the unity of law, that is, the unity of the legal order.[81]

III. LAW AS RULES OF CONDUCT AND LEGAL ORDER

EIGHTEENTH-CENTURY philosophical jurisprudence defined law in terms of moral rules of conduct declared by the state. Following Kant, nineteenth-century metaphysical jurisprudence defined law in terms of the legal order. Lorimer, a follower of Krause but thoroughly imbued with the ideas of the classical natural law, sought to combine the two. He says:

The recognition of the law of nature by special enactments and its vindication in special circumstances and relations.[82]

Perhaps the last half of the formula is more appropriate to the judicial and administrative processes than to the legal order, although from the whole context the latter is evidently what the author had in mind. This is the only formula which seeks to bring together the three meanings of law, and in some degree it succeeds in doing so. But it is vitiated for the purposes of today by its natural-law cast.

IV. LAW IN TERMS OF CANONS OF VALUE

SINCE JHERING we have come to recognize the valuing of interests as the fundamental task of the legal order and the finding of a measure of value as the fundamental problem of jurisprudence. From the standpoint of social philosophy, the significant feature of the body of authoritative materials is that it provides authoritative valuings of competing or conflicting human claims. A recent formula brings this out:

A system of canons of valuation of social relations.[83]

V. LAW IN TERMS OF THE JUDICIAL PROCESS

IN A SENSE, definition of law in terms of the judicial process goes back to the classical Roman jurists. Ulpian (third century A.D.) quoting Celsus (end of the first or beginning of the second century A.D.) says:

Law *(ius)* is the art of what is right and equitable.[84]

On this basis, a medieval writer seeks to distinguish law from *a* law:

Ius is the art of what is right and equitable. *Lex* is *ius* enacted by wise princes.[85]

Obviously the art is not enacted. *Ius* in the second sentence is used in the ethical sense. It means "that which is right." We have here a formula seeking to unite the idea of law as the judicial process and of law as a body of rules of moral conduct given efficacy by the state.

Of late the neo-realists have taken up this idea of law. Thus:

From the point of view of the judge, the law may fairly be said to be the judging process or the power to pass judgment.[86]

Llewellyn includes also the administrative process:

This doing of something about disputes, this doing of it reasonably, is the business of the law. And the people who have the doing in charge, whether they be judges or sheriffs or clerks or jailers or lawyers, are officials of the law. *What these officials do about disputes* is, to my mind, the law itself.[87]

Thus there is no such thing as "justice according to law."[88] Is it not better, following Mr. Justice Cardozo, to distinguish the process from the body of authoritative materials by which the process is or ought to be guided; in which the grounds of the result reached by the process are found? We may recognize the importance of the judicial process for the student of jurisprudence and yet not make of it the whole subject of the science of law nor add another to the manifold meanings of the term "law."

CONCLUSION

CAN WE DRAW any conclusions from this survey of definitions of law? The past sought simplicity by rejecting every standpoint but one, which alone it conceived to be significant. Beginning with Kant, another standpoint than the one traditional from the middle ages began to be urged, but that, too, was taken to give the only significant aspect. In the present century, new standpoints have attracted attention. Instead of the standpoint of the citizen or of the individual man at the crisis of decision in respect to his conduct, the standpoint of the judge, the standpoint of the counselor, and the standpoint of the jurist[89] have been urged. To look at the subject-matter of jurisprudence from these several standpoints is a great gain. Unhappily, those who have explored their possibilities have tended to insist, as of old, that there was but one significant approach. Having shown the significance of a new approach they have assumed the exclusion of the significance of any other. But a characteristic of recent thought is to see the complex rather than the simple; to seek knowledge by taking account of as much as possible, rather than by eliminating as much as possible. Is there, then, some more inclusive order which will unify these several standpoints and the conceptions of law derived from them? I take it we must say Yes and No. So far as law in the second sense is concerned, we may find, on the one hand, a common idea in a conception of law as a body of authoritative materials for the guidance of judicial and administrative action, in which, therefore, the individual may find guides to conduct, the bad man to whom Mr. Justice Holmes refers for his criterion[90] may find restraining threats, the counselor may find reasonably assured grounds of prediction, and the jurist may find an assured basis for logical development of doctrines and systems. On the other hand, to unify law in the second sense with law in the first and third senses, making the third include the administrative process and the counseling process—and why not also the juristic process?—is more difficult. Grant that they all are proper subjects of a science of jurisprudence. Are they all therefore to be called law, making an aggregate where we cannot make a unity? The practical result is that each is made to mean law with resulting unnecessary confusion and bickering over which is the one significant meaning. The gain in recent discussion is in bringing home to us that jurisprudence "must be more than an organizing and systematizing of a body of legal precepts."[91] Put in chronological order of their development, the subjects of jurisprudence are the administration of justice, the legal order, and law in the second of the three senses.[92] If we cannot tie up the three in one word, we may yet see them as parts of a study of a specialized form of social control through the orderly and systematic application of the force of politically organized society.

NOTES TO POUND ESSAY

[1] Rowan v. Runnels, 5 How. 134, 139; Gelpcke v. Dubuque, 1 Wall. 175; Butz v. Muscatine, 8 Wall. 575; Douglass v. Pike County, 101 U. S. 677; Anderson v. Santa Anna, 116 U. S. 356; German Savings Bank v. Franklin County, 128 U. S. 526; Los Angeles v. Los Angeles City Waterworks Co., 177 U. S. 558.

[2] Taft, C. J., in Tidal Oil Co. v. Flanagan, 263 U. S. 444, 454.

[3] Insurance Co. v. Debolt, 16 How. 415; Gelpcke v. Dubuque, 1 Wall. 175; Butz v. Muscatine, 8 Wall. 573, 583; Douglass v. Pike County, 101 U. S. 677, 686–87. See also Hackett v. Maxey, 134 Ind. 162, 190–92.

[4] Tidal Oil Co. v. Flanagan, 263 U. S. 444.

[5] *Ibid.* 453, citing as examples, Jefferson Branch Bank v. Skelly, 1 Black 436, 443; Bridge Proprietors v. Hoboken Co., 1 Wall. 116, 145; Wright v. Nagle, 101 U. S. 791, 793; McGahey v. Virginia, 135 U. S. 662, 667.

[6] Kuhn v. Fairmont Coal Co., 215 U. S. 349.

[7] *Ibid.* 370–371, citing Gray, *Nature and Sources of the Law* §§ 535–550. See Schofield, *Swift v. Tyson, Uniformity of Judge-Made Law in State and Federal Courts* (1909) 4 Ill. L. Rev. 533.

[8] Swift v. Tyson, 16 Pet. 1, 18; Salem Trust Co. v. Manufacturers' Finance Co., 264 U. S. 182, 191–192. See Green, *Law as Precedent, Prophecy and Principle; State Decisions in Federal Courts* (1924) 19 Ill. L. Rev. 217.

[9] Kenyon v. Welty, 20 Cal. 637; Harris v. Jex, 55 N. Y. 421.

[10] State v. Longino, 109 Miss. 125, 133–134.

[11] Pound, *Theories of Law* (1913) 22 Yale L. J. 114.

[12] Pollock, *First Book of Jurisprudence* 17.

[13] Kohler, *Einführung in die Rechtswissenschaft* (1902) § 1.

[14] *E.g.*, 2 Vinogradoff, *Historical Jurisprudence* c. 2.

[15] *The Bramble Bush* (1930) 3.

[16] I have discussed these meanings of law in a paper presented to the International Academy of Comparative Law, to be published in its *Acta,* the substance of which appeared in a paper, *A Comparison of Ideals of Law* (1933) 47 Harv. L. Rev. 1. But the subject is introduced there for other ends and I purpose to develop it further in this paper with reference to definitions of law.

[17] I have discussed these standpoints and their relation to the nature of law in a report to the International Congress of Comparative Law, *Hierarchy of Sources and Forms in Different Systems of Law,* published also in (1933) 7 Tulane L. Rev. 475. One might add another standpoint, namely, that of the legislator. "For those who have only to obey, law is what the sovereign commands. For the sovereign, in the throes of deciding what he ought to command, this view of law is singularly empty of light and leading."—Hocking, *Present Status of the Philosophy of Law and of Rights,* Preface.

[18] Bentham, *Principles of Morals and Legislation* (ed. 1879; Oxford) 324.

[19] Thomas Aquinas, *Summa Theologica,* 1, 2, q. 90, arts. 1, 4.

[20] 1 Donellus, *De iure civile* (1589) 3, § 2.

[21] 1 Bl. Comm. (1765) 44.

[22] 1 Ahrens (trans. by Pollock), *Rechtsphilosophische Einleitung* in 1 Holtzendorff, *Encyklopädie der Rechtswissenschaft* (ed. 1; 1871) 3, 38.

[23] Baudry-Lacantinerie, *Précis de droit civil* (éd. 13; 1922) i, § 1.

[24] Grotius, *De iure belli ac pacis* (1625) i, 1, 9, § 1.

[25] 1 Rutherforth, *Institutes of Natural Law* (1754) 1 § 1.

[26] Montesquieu, *L'esprit des lois* (1748) i, 3.

[27] Hobbes, *Leviathan* (1651) c. 26.

[28] Pufendorf, *Elementa jurisprudentiae universalis* (1672) def. 13.

[29] 1 Burlamaqui, *Principes de droit naturel* (1747) 8, 2.

[30] Rousseau, *Contrat Social* (1762) ii, 6.

[31] Woodrow Wilson, *The State* (1898) § 1415.

[32] Andrews, *American Law* (1900) § 72.

[33] 1 Laurent, *Principes du droit civil français* (1878) § 2.

[34] 1 Toullier, *Droit civil français* (1808) § 14.

[35] 1 Demolombe, *Cours de Code Napoléon* (1845) § 2.

[36] 1 Marcadé, *Explication du Code Napoléon* (5 ed.; 1859) § 1.

[37] Vareilles-Sommières, *Principes fondamentaux de droit* (1889) 12.

[38] 1 Colin et Capitant, *Droit civil français* (ed. 1; 1914) 1.

[39] Austin, *The Province of Jurisprudence Determined* (1832) 2.

[40] Amos, *Science of Law* (1874) 48.

[41] Holland, *Jurisprudence* (1880) c. 3.

[42] 1 Anson, *Law and Custom of the Constitution* (1886) 8. Note that this also suggests the idea of a law as a threat.

[43] 1 Jhering, *Der Zweck im Recht* (1887) 320.

[44] "Man stands in the midst of the external world, and the most important element in his environment is contact with those who are like him in their nature and destiny. If free beings are to co-exist in such a condition of contact, furthering rather than hindering each other in their development, invisible boundaries must be recognized within which the existence and activity of each individual gains a secure free opportunity. The rules whereby such boundaries are determined and through them this free opportunity is secured are the law."—1 Savigny, *System des heutigen römischen Rechts* (1840) § 52.

"The recognition of the just freedom which manifests itself in persons, in their exertions of will and in their influence upon objects."—1 Puchta, *Cursus der Institutionen* (1841) § 6.

"The expression of the idea of right involved in the relation of two or more human beings."—Miller, *Philosophy of Law* (1884) 9.

[45] "The sum of the rules which fix the relations of men living in society—or at least of the rules which are sanctioned by the society—imposed upon the individual by a social constraint."—Brissaud, *Manuel d'histoire du droit français* (1898) 3.

"The rule of conduct to which a society gives effect in respect to the behavior of its subjects toward others and toward itself and in respect to the forms of its activity."—Merkel in Holtzendorff, *Encyklopädie der Rechtswissenschaft* (ed. 5; 1890) 5.

[46] *"Recht ist nur der erklärte Rechtswille einer Rechtsquelle"* (1 Binding, *Die Normen und ihre Uebertretung* [ed. 1; 1872] 68). This epigrammatic formula is quite untranslatable. The idea is that law (note that he is defining *a* law, and so presupposes that law

is an aggregate of laws) is the declared will as to what is right on the part of a source of law in the sense of an authoritative law-making organ.

[47] 1 Bierling, *Juristische Prinzipienlehre* (1894) § 3.

[48] 2 Wigmore, *Cases on Torts* (1911) App. A, § 3.

[49] Somló, *Juristische Grundlehre* (1917) 105.

[50] May, *Introduction à la science du droit* (éd. 2; 1925) 5.

[51] *Science et technique en droit privé positif* (1914) 51.

[52] *Private International Law as a Branch of the Law of England* (1890) 6 L. Q. Rev. 3.

[53] Pollock and Maitland, *History of English Law* (ed. 1; 1895) Introduction, p. xxv. Compare: "The sum of the rules of justice administered in a state and by its authority."—Pollock, *First Book of Jurisprudence* (1896) 17. This formula is evidently of the same type, but it is a pioneer formula in Anglo-American science of law in recognizing the administrative as well as the judicial process. Also its recognition of an ethical element is noteworthy.

[54] Salmond, *Jurisprudence* (1902) § 5.

[55] 1 Clark, *Roman Private Law: Jurisprudence* (1914) 75. Note the recognition of the administrative process here also.

[56] Gray, *Definitions and Questions in Jurisprudence* (1892) 6 Harv. L. Rev. 24.

[57] Keeton, *The Elementary Principles of Jurisprudence* (1930) 38.

[58] Poste, *Gaius* (1871) 2.

[59] 1 Roguin, *La science juridique pure* (1923) 122.

[60] Lévy-Ullmann, *La définition du droit* (1917) 165.

[61] See Kelsen: *Hauptprobleme der Staatsrechtslehre* (1911); *Das Problem der Souveränität* (1920; ed. 2, 1929) 94; *Allgemeine Staatslehre* (1925); *Aperçu d'une théorie générale de l'état* (1926) 43 Rev. de Droit Public 562, 571–578. See also Voegelin, *Kelsen's Pure Theory of Law* (1926) 42 Pol. Sci. Q. 268.

[62] Holmes, *The Path of the Law* (1897) 10 Harv. L. Rev. 457.

[63] *Ibid.* 460–461.

[64] Cardozo, *The Growth of the Law* (1924) 52.

[65] Jahrreiss, *Berechenbarkeit und Recht* (1927).

[66] See particularly Bingham, *What is the Law?* (1913) 11 Mich. L. Rev. 1.

[67] Bingham, *Legal Philosophy and the Law* (1914) 9 Ill. L. Rev. 98, 109.

[68] Frank, *Law and the Modern Mind* (1930) c. 5 and app. 2.

[69] I have discussed this matter repeatedly. See *Juristic Science and the Law* (1918) 31 Harv. L. Rev. 1047, 1060–63; *Theory of Judicial Decision* (1923) 36 *id.* 641, 643–53; *The Administrative Application of Legal Standards* (1919) 44 A. B. A. Rep. 443, 454–458; *The Supreme Court and Minimum Wage Legislation*, "Introduction," compiled by the National Consumers' League (1925); *The Ideal Element in American Judicial Decision* (1931) 45 Harv. L. Rev. 136; *Hierarchy of Sources and Forms in Different Systems of Law* (1933) 7 Tulane L. Rev. 475, 477–86.

[70] Frank, *op. cit. supra* note 68, p. 49. Note that the first part of this formula presupposes that a prior decision on the same facts will be followed, which is not necessarily so in the Continental judicial process, nor even in the Anglo-American, especially in some of our newer states. Also as to the last part, one might inquire whether a statute in plain language covering the exact case is not quite as likely to be followed, even in the absence of any decision. Predicting the course of the judicial process is not so completely a matter

of guess as is assumed. But allowance must be made for the fervor which has gone along with every new movement in jurisprudence.

[71] *Ibid.* 274, note. Note that this formula is avowedly from the standpoint of the counselor. It should be added that in the next sentence Mr. Frank defines the law "from the point of view of the judge" in terms of the judicial process.

[72] See note 61 *supra.*

[73] Kant, *Metaphysiche Anfangsgründe der Rechtslehre* (1797) 27.

[74] Krause, *Abriss des Systemes der Philosophie des Rechtes* (1828) 209.

[75] I have discussed this in *Interpretations of Legal History* (1923) 151–153.

[76] Gareis, *Enzyklopädie der Rechtswissenschaft* (1887) § 5.

[77] 1 Dernburg, *Das bürgerliche Recht des deutschen Reichs und Preussens* (1903) § 16.

[78] 3 Berolzheimer, *System der Rechts- und Wirthschaftsphilosophie* (1906) § 17.

[79] Binder, *Philosophie des Rechts* (1925) 1063. There is here less of the process idea, but it is hardly from the standpoint of a condition as with Kant and Krause.

[80] Kohler, *Einführung in die Rechtswissenschaft* (1902) § 1.

[81] As to Kelsen's theory of law, see an excellent discussion by Lauterpacht in *Modern Theories of Law* 105–138.—For Kelsen's writings, see *supra* note 61.

[82] Lorimer, *Institutes of Law* (1880) 9.

[83] Perassi, *Introduzione alle scienze giuridiche* (1922) 23.

[84] Dig. i, l, 1, pr.

[85] *Libellus de uerbis legalibus* 1, appended to *Petri Exceptiones Legum Romanorum* [eleventh century].—Fitting, *Juristische Schriften des früheren Mittelalters* 181.

[86] Frank, *Law and the Modern Mind* (1930) 274 note. Is this true, or is it rather that from the counselor's standpoint significant things are the judicial process and the judicial power of judging? Does not the judge's standpoint make the second sense of law, the body of authoritative guides to decision, the significant thing?

[87] Llewellyn, *The Bramble Bush* (1930) 3.

[88] Sir Frederick Pollock's phrase, *First Book of Jurisprudence* (1896) pt. I, c. 2.

[89] Wurzel, *Das juristische Denken* (1904).

[90] Holmes, *The Path of the Law* (1897) 10 Harv. L. Rev. 457, 459, 461.

[91] See Pound, *Interpretations of Legal History* (1923) 153.

[92] *Ibid.*

A JUSTER JUSTICE, A MORE LAWFUL LAW

BY MAX RADIN

MY TITLE IS A QUOTATION. It is the only extant line of an epic poem which I wrote a long while ago when I was twenty-two or twenty-three years old. And to assuage any possible pang of regret over the loss of the rest of the poem, I hasten to add that this one line was much the best in it.

What the rest of the poem was about I no longer remember in detail, but of course I remember the general tenor. I was very much disturbed over a discovery that I had made, quite for myself, but which, I am told, I was not really the first to make, viz., that in the ordinary processes of legal adjustment, whatever lip-service is rendered to the idea of justice, no real account is taken of justice, but a great deal of account is taken of particular words in statutes, particular words in documents, particular phrases in previous decisions. It seemed a step in advance when, instead of attending to particular words, we examined ideas, analogies, differences, when we discriminated between apparent identities, when we investigated the historical basis of statutes and decisions. And the whole process seemed almost to verge on humanity, when we took into actual consideration the personal motives that swayed lawgiver or court.

What puzzled and disturbed young men prone to write epics about justice or about any other subject, was the fact that while the law not infrequently touched the fringes of humanity, it did not even then really come to grips with justice, although from time to time, a little shamefacedly, courts admitted that justice was what they dimly had in mind, and although on occasions a legislature placed at the head of legislation a preamble concerning the eternal and unquestioned validity of justice as the end of law. But if legal personages rarely set themselves consciously and deliberately to the task of discovering and applying justice, it may well be said that they were just as much at sea about what they consciously and deliberately did set about doing. They loved to think of themselves—they still do—as impersonal logical contrivances, something like adding machines, or these intricate lace-machines that are our wonder and amazement. You adjust a cog here, a cog there, you push up one lever, pull down another, and there is the result in the form of a judgment, quite complete and desperately accurate. If you have pushed the right lever, the resultant total cannot be wrong. The answer was in the machine when it was constructed, immutably, eternally. It was there from the foundation of the universe, when the morning stars sang together and all the sons of God shouted for joy. The judge found it by taking the specific situation, putting it into the machine, pushing the lever of this principle and that rule, and handing you the decision.

That is the way judges like to think of their operations, as the inevitable and, we should say, unescapably tautologous result of logical processes. Of course, when they are self-critical, and above all when they are criticized by others, they are aware that the adding-machine theory of justice does not even remotely correspond with the facts and that what really happens is a wholly different thing. And not only is the final result very different from what legal persons usually think it is, but it is also evident that the means used to obtain it do not in the least resemble pulling levers and pushing buttons. From what has already been said, it must be evident that the methods in use in law, if they include determining what words mean, what historical background a specific statement had, how terms have changed in purport and content in the course of centuries, how personality and temperament have stamped utterances with a peculiar form and a special significance,—that these methods are the methods of philology and that lawyers and judges, to an extent they would probably be appalled to discover, are neither more nor less than philologers.

I may say at once that they compensate for this situation by being bad philologers. When they look up a word in a dictionary—and they often do—they are as likely as not to select a poor dictionary. When they cite a historical event to explain a statement, it is often uncritically derived from a source of dubious authority. When they depend on etymology it is apt to be a false etymology. This last is just as likely to happen to unvarnished philologers and should not be used in disparagement of lawyers. Nothing in the various etymologies found in legal sources can quite equal the curious performances in the great theologians or in that splendid old philologer, Marcus Terentius Varro—not to speak of the Renaissance humanists. But on the whole, it must be confessed that although a very great deal of legal activity is unmistakable philology, it is not so well done by lawyers as it is by professional philologers.

Lawyers would be far better off if, when they acted as philologers, they adopted the methods which such persons actually use. They would make the discovery we have all made. Philologers deal with words in all their possible aspects and relations. It is popularly supposed that they come thereby to set too high a value on words. The contrary is the fact. They may love words but they do not venerate them, nor very much respect them. And above all, they are not afraid of them. Now, no one is really more afraid of a word than a lawyer, unless it is an exact scientist. Both have a dread of what may be contained in the few syllables of the words they use, which is only equaled by some tribes of primitive men. If lawyers had the experience of philological training, they would know these words for what they are, and would not hang desperately on a wretched explosion of breath when their task required them to do even justice between man and man.

That brings me back to my title. The word "justice," too, is a word. It has not merely inspired epics—no longer extant; it has also been defined by philosophers, logicians, politicians, lawyers—defined over and over again. It had to be defined because it has been declared on the highest authority that it is the foundation not only of civil society, but of the entire universe. It would seem to be important to know how to recognize a thing so fundamental and at the same time so homely and common that it is appealed to at every turn by all persons of all classes.

We can be quite sure that the earliest ideas of justice were not the product of definition and that before there were logicians, politicians, philosophers, or even lawyers—if so backward a society can be imagined—there were men who cried for justice, and got it. Or at any rate they got what they and their contemporaries were willing to call justice. And it is curious that justice, when it is finally formulated by logicians, philosophers, and lawyers, after centuries of thought and under the stimulus of lofty moral ideals, turns out to be precisely what these earliest claimants demanded and got. Justice, said the Stoics, among others, is a distributive virtue, it gives to every man his due. *Suum cuique*. And it will be noted that the ancient formulation says, "Every man his *own*." That is precisely what the claimant before the rude tribunals of early society demanded—"his own." What is a man's own depends on circumstances, mostly historical. But this ancient doctrine says that, if it is his own, he must get it or be allowed to take it. That is justice.

Evidently, if that is justice, the result of justice is not always pleasant. It may involve cruelty and exploitation. It may require enslavement of man by man. It is perfectly consistent with a complete repudiation of the Kantian formula of justice, which asserts that no man may be merely the means to another man's end. This justice may indeed be distributive, but it is hard to call it a virtue when the distribution is so very unequal that it gives all to one man and nothing to his fellow, and harder still to understand how so evil a consequence can flow from what is the fundament of society and the linchpin of the universe.

In other words, justice, in this its proper sense, the demand by a man for his own and no more than his own, is not based on a moral foundation at all. It is δίκη; it "points out" where the thing lies that may be claimed. It exercises no moral censure over the claim. (*Iu-dex, iu-dicis* has the same root in its second syllable.) And the fact that it can result so disastrously for many persons—while still retaining its name of justice—was one of the first things that men noted and bitterly resented.

We should today be inclined to say that this justice is not justice at all, but injustice. But that is the very thing trained philologers should avoid, even if lawyers and historians do not avoid it. The word "justice" which we use did not always have either the meaning or the color we give to it, and those who cried out most bitterly over the justice meted out to them, did not deny that it was justice. They asked for something better than justice.

A moral censorship of justice is a difficult thing to apply. If morals cannot be philologically divorced from *mores*, we cannot morally deny that what in accordance with existing *mores* a man has—which may be a slave, a harem, or a knout—he may claim, however little the fact might be relished by those who do not have these things. And to identify morals with good mores, *boni mores,* may merely imply that justice, in the sense of *suum cuique,* is a bad practice, without requiring us to change our definition of justice.

There is another censorship that might be applied to *suum cuique.* The earliest basis of what was a man's own, was custom. A man had what from time immemorial it was supposed he had. It was a purely historical matter to discover what it was. But for those who had a scheme of the universe, like Socrates, Plato, and Aristotle, such an agglutination of accidents could not constitute what belonged to a man. Each man had a place in an ideal state, each man was required to adjust himself to the general regulative *nomos.* And what was his own, was only what his function required him to have or what he needed in order to carry out the final cause of his being. The censure was one of logic. Justice was only justice for a particular person if, all the relations of that person being considered, he was permitted to use all the means necessary to make those relations effective.

To Plato, this was all that there was to the matter. Justice was a form of perfection. It was less the foundation of the universe than it was its framework. But Aristotle was aware that when justice was done, there might still be something left to do. The regulative force in the community, the *nomos,* operated by general application. Here and there, there were gaps—νόμος ἐλλείπει—and these gaps must be filled. By what? Not by δικαιοσύνη—not by justice. That had got both a special and a general meaning in Aristotle, and both of them depended on *nomos.*

Aristotle filled the gap with what he called ἐπιείκεια—usually translated by "equity." He tells us what this ἐπιείκεια is. It is ἐπανόρθωμα νόμου ᾗ ἐλλείπει διὰ τὸ καθόλου—a straightening out of the law in those places where it fails because of its general character. If we wish to make ἐπανόρθωμα quite literal, we might say, where the law buckles because of its great length.

If we knew nothing about the word ἐπιείκεια except its use here, we should have particular difficulty with this definition. Just what does he mean by the law failing? Our own notion about such matters is that a general rule may prove unjust because it might be cruel and oppressive in a particular situation, but Aristotle does not equate justice with the absence of oppression. If—as most persons do in such instances—he has a criminal case in mind, it is conceivable that a generally arranged punishment might be too severe, but it is equally conceivable that it might be too light. A creditor might with justice demand all his debtor's property, which is undoubtedly hard on the debtor; but he might by law be forced to take less than the compensation of his injury, which is too easy on the debtor. The straightening-out process might work in either direction. The buckling of the line of the law might be above or below.

But ἐπιείκεια is not a ἅπαξ λεγόμενον. The adjective ἐπιεικής is an extremely common word. It is common in Homer and, in certain phrases like ὡς ἐπιεικές, it is reduced to a half-automatic expletive. It means "as is meet, fitting, proper" in any particular case. An ἐπιεικής τύμβος was a mound of the right size. The ἐπιεικὴς ἀμοιβή demanded by Helios against the Greeks is adequate requital for his lost oxen. Alcinous knows that it is ἐπιεικές to give presents to his guest. Hera confesses that it is ἐπιεικές for Zeus, and not for her, to determine the fate of the Trojans.

This is something like the Aristotelian ἐπιείκεια, which, if it does not quite make the crooked straight, may be said at least to iron out the wrinkles of the law. But it is not, after all, quite like it. The word is of transparent etymology and it means essentially something that is expected, that is likely to happen because it has happened. To Homeric gentlemen, as to English gentlemen, that was ἐπιεικές which nice people like themselves did. The foundation of ἐπιεικές was identical with that of δίκαιον; it was an accumulation of historical facts. The Aristotelian ἐπιείκεια, on the contrary, was a logical concept. When it eked out a general rule in a particular situation which the general rule seemed to exclude, it did so because the situation came within the purpose or the harmony of the rule. If I may repeat a common Greek pun on the words νόμος, "the law," and νόμος, "the tune," ἐπιείκεια was an overtone of the tonic sounded in the law.

The Aristotelian ἐπιείκεια is therefore not determined by custom or historical fact. It is, as I have said, a logical concept, sufficiently abstracted from the accidents of time and space to be as much entitled to the epithet of eternal as law itself. If law—the νόμος—embodies justice, this new thing will make that justice juster, the law more lawful, because in more nearly complete accord with the right sense of the word "law" or "justice."

A nice, hard, logical scheme is one that doubtless gives a logician or philosopher the same sort of thrill that a mystic gets when he has a beatific vision. But it is highly likely that the merely logical defects of a scheme of law or justice would not have been burning questions in the minds of people most concerned. A harsh creditor bitterly pursuing a forfeiture nominated in the bond, the creditor for whom Shylock is the permanent literary type, may denounce a refusal of his cruel demand as a denial of justice, as an eternal blot on laws which should form a perfect Aristotelian symmetry of deduction from the fundamental principle of *pacta sunt servanda*. But he is not seeking to improve justice. It is quite good enough for him as it is. It is the persecuted debtor who fears, not that he will be denied justice, but that he will get it. Justice is precisely what he does not want.

Now, what he asks is not an eking out of the ellipsis of law by something that will make the law conform to itself and be a more complete representation of what law should be. No, he asks for ἐπιείκεια, but he does not mean to throw himself on the mercy of a Homeric gentleman. What a feudal lord might think quite fitting for an ἐπιεικής to do or say, might still be intolerably harsh for one with no pretensions to ἐπιείκεια to bear.

What the person crushed by justice—by the very universality of the law—asks for, is an exception in his favor, the exception that proves the rule, it may be, in the proper sense of that much abused phrase—but better really without reference to any rule. He wants human sympathy, benignity, kindness from his judge. He asks it not as justice, but as something better than justice, and he has little doubt that in this demand he is supported by the great mass of the majority—as indeed, he almost always is.

It is quite true that even the arrogant exploiter of his rights might sometimes feel that the ordinary justice, well enough in its generalizing way, does not fit the particular character of his demand, not because it is too harsh but because it is too lenient. An English squire might accept the law of trespass for a general rule, but demand the death penalty for certain types of poachers. There is, besides, a popular sentiment that demands something better than justice, even when that better thing is far more severe and cruel than what justice accords. The man who kills his wife's paramour, or the woman who kills her betrayer, are apt enough to appeal specifically to a "higher law" than justice, something that is juster than the official justice. The most popular of American ballads, the moving tale of Frankie and Johnny, and the infallible mirror of popular concepts presented to us in the cinema, make clear that this higher and crueler law accords with popular judgment as fully as does the demand for human sympathy on the part of an unfortunate and hard-pressed debtor. This is likely enough to happen when official justice has outdistanced, as it often has, the mores of the community. It will be noticed that ordinarily the demand for exceptional humanity or inhumanity takes no effective means to accommodate the official law to the justice expressed in the mores. If there is an ellipsis in the *nomos,* the hundred-headed Demos, being no Aristotle, has no intention of filling it permanently with ἐπιείκεια or anything else.

Does the Greek notion of higher justice in the form of ἐπιείκεια dwell on the equity of humanity or on that of inhumanity? The Greeks certainly knew what sympathy was. Philologists might prove it by the very word itself. Did they esteem it enough to make it the corrective of justice?

To lament for the misfortunes of another is at least one way of showing that you feel with him, that you have compassion for him, "compassion" being, as we may recollect, merely the literal Latin rendering of sympathy. And in Homer there is a striking incident which is one of the significant passages in the epic:

> ὣς ἔφατο κλαίουσ' ἐπὶ δὲ στενάχοντο γυναῖκες
> Πάτροκλον πρόφασιν σφῶν δ' αὐτων κήδε' ἑκάστη.*

("Thus spake Briseis, wailing; And the women lamented with her, in semblance for Patroklos, but each for her own woe.") Sympathy which is limited to those situations in which we can feel ourselves suffering with the person pitied, is that a real compassion? It will be of little help

* *Iliad,* XIX. 301–302.

when it is asked of men whose proud strength cannot contemplate that they will ever need sympathy for themselves. It is a weakness in Menelaus that he is about to spare a fallen foe and it is the boast of Andromache that her great husband showed no pity in the field.

The Homeric ἐπιεκεῖς—even the most chivalrous of them—were not, as heroes, compassionate men. Our high estimation of Hector is based in part on his tendency to human sympathy; but it may well be that this tendency was a mark whereby to Homer's mind he fell short of ἐπιεικής. That was the attitude of Homeric Greeks; the later literature has a different tone.

Homer never ceased to be for the Greeks the greatest of all poets; but they soon repudiated his morals and perhaps even sooner his manners. The idea that an ἐπιεικής was a perfect gentleman persisted. As we have seen, it was the practical equivalent of the Platonic καλοκάγαθός, but the conduct that marked the ἐπιεικής underwent a decided change. Not only did compassion cease to be culpable weakness, but it became—even if but moderately practiced—a virtue. A great spirit did not harbor malice and a really lofty soul did not exact all that was due. The result was that the overwhelming suggestion of ἐπιείκεια in later Greek was just this meaning of compassion, of sympathy, in the particular sense of foregoing what in justice one might demand. The contrast is well made by Gorgias in an epideictic oration on the fallen heroes of Athens. Against "harsh justice" he sets "gentle ἐπιείκεια"; against the precise application of nomos, he puts uprightness, or better, the straight path to the purpose of the law—something, that is to say, of the logical concept later worked out by Aristotle, but with the assumption that the end of the law is humanity.

It is this idea which made headway, both in popular speech and in learned discourse. In ordinary Greek, ἐπιείκεια became almost unqualifiedly the virtue which we have in mind when we say "kindness" or "clemency," of which the *hesed* of the Old Testament, the χάρις of St. Paul, are extreme and one might say—a Greek would certainly say—exaggerated forms. When Romans learned Greek, they translated ἐπιείκεια by *clementia,* so that the two were equated throughout almost the entire course of later Greek literature. The *clementia* which Caesar made his ostentatiously characteristic virtue, is represented on a coin in his honor by ἐπιείκεια αὐτοῦ. The word is frequently on Plutarch's lips and always in this sense. When, in Byzantine and medieval times, bilingual glossaries are made, ἐπιείκεια, both in that form and in what may be called the rubbed form, ἐπικεία, is almost uniformly glossed by words like *clementia, mansuetudo, modestia,* and the adjective by *clemens, mitis, modestus.* It became so common a word in ordinary speech that the adverb, ἐπιεικῶς, was used as an ordinary intensive, the equivalent of *admodum,* or as an affirmation, much as "fine" may be used in English.

This corresponds well enough with popular feeling, which usually is inclined to show compassion rather than vindictiveness toward a person caught in the toils of the law. It received of course a great impulse in Christian Europe through the generally accepted ethical ideal that mercy was better than justice, but it contradicted the logical notion that if justice was really what was at the foundation of civil society—if not of the universe—it was no light thing to remove this foundation stone for another, however pleasant and alluring the other seemed to be.

We find accordingly that ἐπιείκεια is not universally accorded the position of something superior to justice, once the sense of "clemency," "mercy," "kindness," was firmly attached to it. If we posit justice, it is supposed that we take justice in its perfect form. Once we have agreed upon its perfect form, there can be no gap, no ellipsis, nothing for ἐπιείκεια to fill or to straighten out. And the Stoics, who had the courage of their pedantry, said so unqualifiedly. The perfect sage was just. It was his greatest quality. But he was not kind, clement, merciful, gentle. He was not ἐπιεικής in the popular sense. It is unmistakably so stated. He could not make exceptions in perfection without lessening its perfection, without becoming less than a sage, and therefore not a sage at all. For this famous Stoic paradox is a sublimated form of that recent discovery of neurologists and biologists, the "all or nothing" reaction, which is a marked human characteristic in many relationships.

In other words, what happened to the ἐπιείκεια which was a righting of justice was that it was absorbed in the concept of justice itself, and what happened to the ἐπιείκεια which was a corruption of justice by compassion was that it was rejected as unworthy of a tough-minded sage. Whether this was a workable scheme in practice is another matter altogether.

We have seen that when the Romans first heard the term ἐπιείκεια, they translated it by *clementia, misericordia,* an idea which we have been falsely taught to think foreign to the Roman character. Nothing is farther from the truth; but it is true that when the Romans struggled through to a conception of a higher type of justice, they did not base it on a demand for kindliness or compassion.

Whatever "justice" is in philosophic or logical contemplation, as a word it is derived from *ius*. And although the final definition of *ius* by an eminent jurist of the first century A.D. is still the loftiest conception that has been reached of the term, *ius* was not understood in a lofty sense by the peasants and herdsmen who first made a city on the Tiber hills. *Ius* was something a man had, something he owned, *meum ius, tuum ius;* and the idea of ownership was even more emphatic than it had been in ancient Greece. Such words imply indeed not merely ownership, and as such exclusion, but they further seem to imply in Rome more than elsewhere a differentiation of *iura*. My right was not merely different from yours because it was mine and not yours; it ordinarily was different in content.

This may have arisen from a special fact of Roman history. It is likely enough that from the beginning the city was a conglomerate. Or if not from the beginning, very soon groups of residents were distinguished by the possession of different complexes of *iura*. We may say that the essence of *ius* was its inequality. So far from men being equal before the law, what a man insisted on, when he demanded *ius,* was ordinarily something which other men could not ask.

Thus very early in Roman history it was realized that something better must be provided—or, rather, that the possessors of lesser and poorer *iura* would not be permanently satisfied with their inferior possession. When they made their demand articulate, it took a special form. They did not appeal to the Homeric ἐπιείκεια, the sense of propriety which prevented a gentleman from abusing his privileged position, nor the humanitarian ἐπιείκεια which was an act of charity. They asked for *bonum et aequum*.

I think we shall be well advised if we divorce these words in their original setting from any moral tone. *Bonum* was not moral good and *aequum* was not fairness or equity in the sense in which we understand it. It is likely that *bonum* meant a "good" in the sense in which the neuter plural *bona* is used in Latin, and that *aequum* meant equal in the sense of non-discriminating. *Bonum* was an economic notion and *aequum* a quantitative one. The force of the doublette therefore may well have been that of demanding an equalization of the benefits secured by the interference of the magistrate, and of expressing resentment against *ius* which was claimed as an exclusive privilege of the claimant—a privilege which under like circumstance he would not accord to the defendant.

This phrase *bonum et aequum* was stereotyped in the time of Plautus and must at that time have had a long history in ethics as in law. Almost as early, the word *aequitas* is used alone for a concept that is indistinguishable from the more primitive phrase, a semantic development easy enough to understand. Its oldest occurrence is doubtless the dialectic form, in the dedication from Volci, *Aecetiae pocolom*. However, it is likely that the Aequitia to whom this cup was sacred was not the moral nor the legal *equity,* but "Equality" in its political sense—the equality which was the goal toward which the members of the Latin league, the Tuscan league, or any other confederation, strove. It was the characteristic of most of these confederations that treaties which bound these members to each other were dissimilar. The most desirable treaty was that which gave a state a formal equality with the dominant member, the *aequum foedus,* an equality which was usually rather honorific than substantial. Just as temples were raised to Concordia at Rome by men who sought to make permanent the peace between the classes, so at Volci and at Praeneste there was a shrine to Aequitas, "Equality," in the sense of the equal rights of the federated states. It is intelligible enough that at Praeneste, which fought so stubbornly to maintain its individuality in the Latin league, Equality should be conspicuously honored as a goddess.

But *aequitas* and *bonum et aequum* took on a different aspect when *ius* was to be granted or refused by a magistrate. It may well be that the basis was again political. Long before a foreign praetor was established at Rome, resident allies and foreigners must have claimed before a Roman magistrate the right to be treated as peers of their hosts in those cases in which they had an *aequum foedus*. It might almost be said that the *ius* of such persons was to a reciprocal equality of advantage with Roman *aequum et bonum,* so that the words became a characteristically Roman paraphrase for the equitable maxim found in all parts of the world and most familiar to us as the "Golden Rule."

Between this quantitative and economic stage of the concept and its moral and legal development, the step was less sharp and decided than we might suppose. The demand for equality among states in a federation was not a logical one. It did not flow from the nature of things or the nature of the state. If a developed theory of sovereignty had existed and taken the unfortunate dialectical form which it assumed in Hobbes and Austin, it would have been possible to say that, as a universal, all forms of sovereignty were equivalent. But no such claim as that was ever made for these peasant states and no such idea of sovereignty was ever entertained by their citizens. The states were concededly unequal in power, wealth, importance, strength—in everything that in ancient eyes made a state. For the weaker to demand an equality with the stronger could be based only on the moral element. It might well have been the compact which the states made in entering into the federation. And perhaps there was a dimly felt notion that a certain minimum of *iura* was a fundamental condition of state existence.

These ideas were transferred, it seems, from the political field into the legal one without anyone being aware that a transfer had taken place, since the distinction between law and politics did not exist, or at any rate did not come into conscious reflection. It seemed an elementary right therefore—in the sense of *bonum et aequum*—to resist the constantly repeated demand of powerful and important groups for a privileged position in the law and to create a minimum of rights which every citizen—or litigant—might have.

Evidently it was more necessary to have recourse to *bonum et aequum* in the foreign praetor's court after 246 B.C. than in the ordinary jurisdiction, since the claim to equity was itself something that had first to be made out and was easier to establish in a court which like that of the peregrine praetor was not compelled to take an accumulation of established proprietary rights into account. But it is certainly not true that *aequitas* was a creation of the foreign praetor's court or that there was no occasion for its application in the specifically Roman courts.

There was first of all the fact that new *iura* were constantly being created and, as the state increased in complexity, were consciously created by the action of the magistrates. That these needed a moral basis is evident enough, and that the most obvious one was the reciprocal give and take implied in the Roman *aequitas* may be accepted. There was also an application of an idea like the Homeric *ἐπιείκεια*, in which it was declared that equity would take into account general public sentiment or traditional customs. It was certainly because it was improper and therefore inequitable, that the praetor declined to permit father and son to sue each other. Perhaps a moral test—in this rude sense of morality—determined whether a praetor might refuse to entertain an action—*denegare actionem*—although the formal right to it was unquestioned.

But that element which stains the logic of the law with a faint touch of red—the quality of compassion—did not fail to enter the Roman system. The law offered to some persons, hard pressed to fulfill their legal obligations, certain definite *beneficia,* which we translate by "privileges," though clearly, as their name implies, they were acts of kindness or indulgence.

The most characteristic of these *beneficia* is the one which in much later times—in late Renaissance times, in fact—was called the "benefit of competence." In some special circumstances—by no means in all—a creditor could not take all his debtor had. He must leave him what was necessary for the debtor's subsistence. It corresponded somewhat to our exemption laws. Evidently such a *beneficium* was a softening of the rigor of the law. At one time all that a debtor had belonged to his creditor—including the debtor himself, or at least his working power—and in a measure this continued where a *beneficium competentiae* did not exist. But where it did exist, the creditor was compelled to stop far short of such an extreme; he could not take even all that was seizable.

Such a benefit has nothing to do with *aequitas* in the sense of an equality of advantage, but it is very much like that phase of Greek justice which was a foregoing of a full claim, an ἐλάττωσις δικαίων. It was an act of clemency, of kindness, like the pardon of a condemned felon, depending on no claim of right, but on mere humanity.

Now, as a matter of fact, we do not find that *aequitas* is equated with *clementia* or *mansuetudo*, or even combined with these qualities into doublettes. But the function which Aristotle declared ἐπιείκεια to perform, that of straightening out the law and filling its ellipses, *aequitas* quite clearly accepts as its proper business. The range of circumstances in which a man may claim the letter of his bond became more and more restricted, and this process was accelerated as magistrates came to depend more and more on the carefully prepared discussions of jurisconsults who had received a grounding in philosophic ethics. *Bonum et aequum* was not merely a check on the law; it became its purpose. If *ius* did not result in *bonum et aequum*, its right to be called *ius* might be challenged. Equity was the perfect form of law and there was no good reason why one should be satisfied with anything less.

We can see here the result of Stoic analysis. The difference between *ius* in the older sense when equity was needed to correct it, and *ius* in the newer, which was merely an instrument of equity, was the difference we have already noted in the Greek development of our idea. The older *ius* was a piece of property which the owner might wrest from anyone who disputed it, whatever the consequences. The newer *ius* had been absorbed by equity. It was still a man's own, but it did not become his own unless it could be applied against him as well as for him and unless it corresponded to a general sense of moral fitness.

The essential fact is, however, that this newer *ius* also professed generality of application. The *bonum et aequum* at which it aimed was not an act of clemency; it was not merely a modification of an older and harsher legal rule; it was the substitution of one rule by a better one, but still by a rule, not by an exception to a rule. If a Stoic sage could not properly be ἐπιεικής without in some degree forfeiting his wisdom, there seemed no reason why a just and equitable judge might not continue to be just and equitable, even when he refused clemency. Unless the humanitarian notion which had given rise to the need of equity could be generalized, unless the conditions could be determined within which and by reason of which charity and kindliness were regularly to be applied, this encroachment on *ius* would have to remain an arbitrary interference prompted by an emotional wave of compassion or by expediency. It would not be equity.

It is this doctrine which was taken up by the Church fathers, and it finds, as we might expect, an especially full formulation in St. Augustine. Equity is the goal at which human justice aims, the perfect archetype of which human justice is an imperfect and turbid image.

The goal will be attained only in divine justice. Indeed it is unqualifiedly asserted that God is *Aequitas*. But obviously this divine justice is not the popular and Stoic notion of ἐπιείκεια, of clemency. We need hardly be told that, in St. Augustine's concept of it, God's justice is not sentimental benignity. It is perfect because it gives unfailingly and to the uttermost scruple of a grain, *suum cuique;* it is equitable because it is always the same and is no respecter of persons. But it is harsh and by human standards cruel, because of the very precision of its adjustment of deserts to punishment and because of its very equality of application. This logical carrying out of justice into its equitable perfection, rules out the equity of ἐπιείκεια in the sense in which both Romans and Greeks had come to understand it.

There was also a theological difficulty. God was *Aequitas* because justice was one of his attributes. But mercy was also one of his attributes. This fact, so far from blurring the two concepts into one, kept them all the more firmly apart. Nothing was more heretical than a confusion of divine aspects, even if they were aspects of the same essence.

The church fathers were of course familiar with *clementia*—ἐπιείκεια, and very insistent indeed that this divine virtue should be exemplified in the practice of Christians. In the divine pattern, where virtues reached their fullest expression, justice which condemned all men in Adam's fall was completely reconcilable with clemency which freed men from the consequences of Adam's fall. The fact that not all men were in fact freed, but only the non-sinning members of the church, in no way derogated from the perfection of the virtue of clemency. Equality of application was not a part of that virtue, although it was a part of the virtue of justice. We have therefore the paradox that the "equity" which became later a common translation of ἐπιείκεια is not a characteristic at all of ἐπιείκεια in an even more common sense of the word.

It may be said that in a sense, just as the Stoic sage could not consistently be compassionate, because by definition he must be just, so the perfect Christian could not show clemency, if by that is meant that he might disregard a failure of obligation. Every sin, even when absolution had been obtained, must be purged by appropriate penalties in this world or in the next, and in this respect there could be no exception or remission of any kind. As between man and man, of course, forgiveness of debts, remission of punishment, was common and laudable, since actual debts involved property, and punishment implied laws, and both property and laws were established by human convention and had no real roots in nature. Human justice, which depended on property and laws, was not really justice at all, but a device to mitigate the rapacity which Adam's fall had made endemic among men—therefore a purely practical device. And justice was not impaired when a claim was foregone because the claim was itself a mild example of rapacity.

The earlier Middle Ages rested their conception of justice on the patristic development of Biblical doctrines, but did so in an atmosphere thoroughly saturated with the eclectic philosophic notions of the late Roman Empire. In the current philosophy a mysticized theosophy had taken the place of metaphysics, and it was against this theosophy—which flaunted the badge of Platonism—that Christian theology directed its chief attack. On the side of ethics, a broadened and slightly vulgarized Stoicism had given to accepted morals their color and had, as we know, formulated principles which could be taken over into Christianity without the change of more than a few words. Our materials for the period just after the break-up of imperial authority in the West are extremely inadequate, and terms like "justice" and "equity" are vague and undefined concepts in the literature, both lay and secular, of the time. The tribal customs, mostly of Germanic origin, had no theory of law and certainly no concept of either a perfected or a perfectible justice.

Administrative officials found themselves in the position of the ancient Mediterranean magistrates of more than ten centuries earlier, compelled to grant or deny *ius* claimed as a self-justifying privilege. For Christians, indeed, the development of the *episcopalis audientia* into unmistakable courts had kept alive the doctrine that a claim needed more than its proved existence to be just, and fragments of the work of Justinian, in which so much ado was after all made about justice, had never been completely dispersed.

When the great revival of intellectual and political activity in the eleventh century rediscovered and, in a sense, republished the legislation of Justinian, there was given in bulk a mass of doctrine about justice which seemed to settle and solidify even the theological aspects of the problem. Not only was the enormously authoritative formulation of justice in the Corpus Juris in full accordance with patristic teaching; there were also similarities in phraseology which plainly resulted from the common Stoic groundwork of both legal and ecclesiastic morality. That similarity, we may remember, was based on the notion that a perfect justice included equity and therefore could not yield its perfection to the demands of a special case.

But what Christianity had derived from the divine virtue of compassion, the Roman law had itself derived from the mere operation of human feeling. While the main philosophic influence on the Roman law was Stoic, it was not an undiluted or rigidly logical Stoicism. In the Stoic Cosmopolis, the city of Zeus, there was neither slave nor free, neither Greek nor barbarian, neither man nor woman. There was also no ἐπιείκεια, which, we can readily believe, would have little application to conditions in that fortunate, but I fear priggish community. But outside of the Cosmopolis, in the common or garden *civitas,* the distinctions of status took on a fundamental importance, and the established and enforced inequalities based on an imperfect justice, needed, by way of compensation, a surrender to such irrational factors as compassion and humanity.

So clemency, which was the characteristic virtue of the founder of the Empire, became almost a characteristic title of his successors. The later emperors refer to themselves as *Clementia Nostra.* Pope John addresses Justinian as *Clementia Vestra.* And the special point of the honorific allocution is what His Majesty is pleased to consider an exceptional favor on his part.

Further, the terms *benigna interpretatio, humanitas, inhumanum,* occur frequently in the later texts of the Code and Digest. They show that, however directly law pointed to equity in principle and even in practice, the result often presupposed an inflexibility that human nature could not furnish. By logic many men would be slaves, who should in humanity be free, and the law, disregarding even equity, made them free. It was *durum et inhumanum* to take an angry father too precisely at his word, and the law therefore would not do so. Many similar examples occur. The result, of course, is disastrous to the symmetry of the system, whether of equity or of justice, but it satisfies a quite asymmetrical emotional impulse.

The rediscovery of Roman law was followed after a little more than a century by the rediscovery of Aristotle, and in an extraordinarily short time the authority of Thomas Aquinas had made Aristotelian terms and theories familiar to every educated man. There were few books so widely read and annotated as the *Nicomachean Ethics,* in which Aristotle's theory of ἐπιείκεια is most fully developed, and the term made an immediate impression. It could not be translated as *aequitas* nor as *clementia,* which had already been so fully utilized in different associations. The only recourse was to transliterate it. It accordingly makes its appearance as *epieicheia,* generally shortened to *epichia,* and as "epiky" the word makes a brave but unsuccessful attempt to enter the English language on its own. It appears in the Oxford Dictionary, which is not quite a complete naturalization. But, English or Latinized Greek, it had a romantic charm for scholastic philosophers and canon lawyers, even if the ordinary civilian could not be expected to take seriously a word that could not be found in the entire Corpus.

Just what the medieval Aristotelians thought *epichia* meant is not altogether clear. Apparently it served to indicate the defects of justice, but it did not, like the Roman *aequitas,* give justice a new goal to climb to, nor, like the popular ἐπιείκεια, sacrifice consistency to a stirring of compassion. Indeed, there is less talk of *clementia, humanum, benevolentia,* in the *Secunda Secundae* of Thomas and in the voluminous elucidations of Thomas, than there is in the decisions on the same subject in the Digest. The reason is doubtless not that Roman administrators were more humane men than Dominican and Jesuit casuists, but that these latter treated *clementia* and its associated virtues as wholly apart from the virtue of justice, and effected by different agencies.

What justice as a word popularly meant in the Middle Ages and still means to a great many persons, is unfortunately all too clear. I remember seeing in a suburb of Paris, in an exquisite spot with a view of the Seine, a bronze plaque with the legend: "Here formerly stood the Justice of the Counts of Croissy." In many other connections we find that when men said "the Justice," they meant the gallows. It was a hard period in human history and was rendered a bit harder by a religious philosophy that made easy the acceptance of harsh reprisals as justice, since all harshness and all excesses would be so quickly and completely rectified in a world beyond human life. In this life justice required that the hand-having or back-bearing thief be incontinently hanged and that feudal lords who cruelly and capriciously used their right of *fossa et furca,* their corvées, their mill-rights and their aids, be held to be strictly and properly justified in their injustice.

Indeed, even the term "equity" retained enough of its assumed etymology to justify what was little more than a law of talion. As one sowed, so must one reap. He who would not keep the peace, might properly and equitably be removed from the peace. One can only note that in this revised form, the law of talion contrasted unfavorably with the ancient Mediterranean codes in Leviticus and in the Twelve Tables, where talion was confined to a sharply limited group of injuries with respect to which ancient and primitive religious concepts were still active. So in medieval Europe, a wrong done could be balanced only by suffering what was roughly regarded as the equivalent.

The Romans had worked out the notion of equity through procedure. Whatever it was that was claimed, its justice was measured by the extent to which it could be equally applied to all who claimed it, *paribus in causis paria iura.* When all men were Roman citizens, as when all men were Stoic sages, or Christian brethren, this form of equity had in it the seeds of perfect justice. But obviously medieval society could hardly operate with an idea that was contradicted by almost every element in its structure. It may well be said that it would be difficult to find two men in medieval society whose status in all respects was exactly the same. Parity—complete parity—of rights, was very nearly excluded, and when the notion of parity took a particular form in the *iudicium parium,* it was a characteristically medieval form; it was the idea that equality was a relative and limited privilege, something which withdrew a man from the generality of his fellows and enabled him to claim a treatment which others dared not demand.

Evidently a movement toward equality would, as in the early Roman law, have been a movement toward equity. Most of the rights claimed in medieval law were special privileges incapable of generalization. But that was not the path by which the law broadened. It must be remembered that reforms or revolutions are rarely carried out by subterranean movements that begin at the very bottom of the social structure. More often than not they are the result of a disturbance in the layer just below the top. So liberty and equality—especially the latter—have been the watchwords of a class which challenged the superiority of the governing class, because it was just below it. No medieval class, however, could have failed to be aware that equality was a dangerous weapon. Everything they had was based upon rights which could be asserted only as an exclusive privilege, as a proclamation of inequality. The demand for a better thing than justice took a different path. As has been said, no one had any illusion about the character and quality of the ordinary justice. It was harsh, it was inflexible, it was irrational; and those who suffered, as they felt, undeservedly under it, had only one recourse—to throw themselves at the feet of the men that administered this justice, and ask that it be not administered, that an exception be made. They asked for grace, for mercy, for compassion.

In most European countries, the Enlightenment of the seventeenth and eighteenth centuries had the curious effect of reëstablishing in one form the authority which was challenged in another. What was objectionable in law was its irrational character and this irrationality was more apparent in that part of the law which had grown up by custom than in the part which, since the twelfth century, had dominated the thinking of European lawyers, that is, the Corpus Juris. To appeal to reason as to a better law was merely to appeal from the wilderness of feudal customs or from the Roman law swallowed whole, to the Roman law rearranged, reorganized, rationalized. The proponents of natural law—as a better law than existing systems—had little quarrel with what they believed to be the principles of the best law hitherto developed, the Roman law. They quarreled a great deal with the way in which that law was received and applied. Domat in France was one of many who proposed to reorganize it and undertook single-handed to do so. But it was not till the following century, the century of Burlamaqui, Montesquieu, and Beccaria, and above all, of Rousseau, that the appeal to rationality became tinged with a special interest in humanity. Laws were reasonable when they conduced to human happiness and not otherwise. The privileges of groups, classes, and corporations were not in themselves valuable ends.

In England the search for a better justice was not based on the irrationality of existing law. When the effect of the Enlightenment reached England, that happy country was found to be in possession of something that could be described, not as a system, but certainly as a method, a way, of what once had been ἐπιείκεια. It had begun long before the Enlightenment, and shortly after the king's courts were established in the twelfth and thirteenth centuries. It had developed out of the fact that the king's council through the king's chancellor could not close its ears to petitions for mercy, addressed to it by persons for whom the king's justice was difficult, remote, or hard.

The influences that made the chancery a formal court cannot be examined here. The important thing for our present purposes is what was sought there. In the other courts a claim of right was made, a privilege asserted, an attack repelled, a remedy demanded. The royal writ by which a suit was initiated was a peremptory order, "Let right be done." But that is not the way one approached the chancery. "To the Most Reverend Fader in God, John Archbishop of Caunterbury, Chancelor of England; mekely besechith your good and gracious lordshyp your continuell orator Sebastian Giglis"—in this way does one Master Giglis in 1492 appear before the court of chancery; and he concludes his humble petition with the words, "This at the reverence of God and and in the way of charitie." It is not because his claim is of a kind that entitled him to the relief he demands, but because of the special circumstances and because of what Robert Welby had done to him, that he meekly besought Archbishop Morton. Even at the present time a bill in equity in the United States federal courts ends properly with the words: "And your orator will ever pray *etc.*," the words "*etc.*" standing for this appeal to the reverence of God and the way of charity on which the petition is in theory based.

The petition which I have cited is part of an elaborate case in the year 1492, but long before that year this type of petition had become part of a regular procedure. There were principles established and precedents known. However, the essential character of the petition was still the fact that it addressed itself to a clemency which at discretion might be exercised or denied.

Indeed, it was not till the beginning of the nineteenth century under the grim Eldon that the chancery can be said to have become completely assimilated to the other courts, so that the terms "prayer," "petition," and "humble beseeching" became mere formulas. Vestiges, however, of the earlier fact still are found in chancery practice, in the wide range of discretion which is permitted to the judges of this court and its successors. But in all courts the demand is now that "right be done," and the discretion, so far from being an act of clemency, is circumscribed within narrow limits and is in no sense an example of arbitrary power, even of power to do kindness.

It may well be that the legitimate survival of this phase of chancery procedure is in the petition for pardon of a condemned felon. In the words of Coke, a pardon is a "work of mercy whereby the King forgiveth any crime, offense, punishment, execution, right, title, debt or duty." In earlier days, petition to the king's council for such purposes did not differ in language or in substance from the petitions addressed to the council's representative, the chancellor. They were both dependent upon "grace." The word "grace" is used in both. The term "clemency" is almost a technical word for the power to grant these pardons, just as *gracier* is a technical word for the same thing in French. And the clemency is a veritable ἐπιείκεια. It is an exception in a special situation based on conditions of which no generalization is attempted, and indeed of which the special character is that it cannot very well be generalized.

The curious fact, however, of the English development of the idea of ἐπιείκεια is that the chancellor at a relatively early time had begun to call the relief which he granted to the humble petition of his poor orators, by the name of "equity"; that is, by a name which, if its proper sense was taken, was not an act of mercy but the reshaping of justice.

It is not a new word in the history of English law. The oldest of English law books, that usually ascribed to Henry II's justiciar, Ranulph Glanvil, used it in the sense of "justice" in referring to the ordinary process of a then undifferentiated royal court: *Super hoc ultimo casu in curia domini regis de consilio curiae et ex aequitate consideratum est.* If equity is a flexible justice, one that is constantly reshaping itself into a fuller and finer example of its essence, such a type of flexible justice the Norman and Angevin kings of England declared was available in their curia, and they used for it the term which in their canon and civil law sources was peculiarly adapted to it, a word in fact that was little more than a synonym of justice. It must be remembered that *aequitas* in the sense of human justice was crowding out *iustitia* among men clerically trained, since *iustus* and *iustitia* had a marked theological flavor, being used of men justified in Christ.

The early common law courts which boasted of giving a writ for any demand certainly administered what they, as well as canonists and civilians, would have called equity. But toward the end of the thirteenth century this power of giving writs became restricted and courts could no longer profess that the law they announced was still flexible enough to follow the path of equity, even when the path was clear.

It was under such circumstances that direct application, made to the council and chancellor for a relief that the law did not give, could put itself on a little stronger basis than a mere clamor for an act of grace. The words used were still those of a humble suppliant who sought a personal and special favor. The situation, however, was not always personal. It was one which could easily be generalized and which, in the earlier stages, would have justified a demand for an equitable expansion or delimitation of a legal rule. The king's courts proper had given up their power to transform law into equity. And the idea of equity thus abandoned by its proper parents could therefore be absorbed by the newer and more malleable jurisdiction of the chancellor.

As a matter of fact, the chancellor, nearly always a great churchman, was at first inclined to speak of his action as determined by "conscience," which was a word of definite theological connotations. Indeed, the term "conscience" remained with the chancellor permanently, long after he ceased to be a churchman and even after John Selden had sneered at its inadequacy. But although conscience is obviously a personal affair, it was impossible for a churchman before the thirteenth century to be ignorant of the patristic and civilian doctrine of *aequitas,* and after the thirteenth century it was equally impossible for him to be unaware that there was such a thing as ἐπιείκεια (*epichia*) and that on the authority of Thomas piled up on that of Aristotle, *epichia* did something for justice—something very similar to what for centuries Roman equity had done to law—but did it a little externally.

In this way, the ἐπιείκεια which in prevailing Greek usage had been equated with *clementia,* became, among the post-Thomist canonists and theologians, equated with *aequitas,* and gave to the English ecclesiastical chancellors an opportunity to base their jurisdiction upon principles that could be formulated into rules which were as unmistakably rules as those of law. But they never quite forgot that what was asked of them was not the enforcement of a rule however sound, but an act of charity, in the non-Aristotelian sense.

So, in a book which was written long before the final battle was fought between chancery and the king's courts, in the *Dialogue of Doctor and Student,* composed by Christopher St. Germain in 1502 or thereabouts, equity is described in these words:

> Equity is a right wiseness that considereth all the particular circumstances of the deed, the which also is tempered with the sweetness of mercy. And such an equity must always be observed in every law of man, and in every general rule thereof: and that knew he well that said thus: Laws covet to be ruled by equity.

St. Germain is speaking for a highly sophisticated doctor who knows a chancery that is fully developed and is beginning to claim a power of direct interference with the ordinary law-courts, and evidently he has not far to look to find a scholastically authoritative formulation of equity which would go far to substantiate the claims of the chancery. But he inserts the word "mercy," which pulls the formulation to pieces, since not merely in Shakespeare but also in theology the essence of mercy is that it deals with specific situations and not with typical ones. St. Germain cannot help inserting it, since he has first-hand acquaintance with chancery and knows what is expressly asked there. As a matter of fact, when he later makes specific comparison between chancery law and the common law, he is apt to say "in conscience" rather than "in equity," as later lawyers did.

Equity was still a eulogistic term and not yet technical. Since it was eulogistic, it could be used effectively as a weapon of controversy when the chancery was seeking to become, by virtue of its personal association with the king, a tribunal that dominated all the courts, that set the crooked straight and filled up the gaps, much as Aristotle's and Thomas' *epichia* did, but not quite as Roman *aequitas* did and certainly not as an exercise of individual and casual benevolence. The term "equity" still carried both religious and philosophic warranties. But during the sixteenth century both warranties lost their authority in England and the rapid growth of a self-confident nationalism made it possible for the common law not only to admit the absence of both equity and conscience in its judgments, but even to boast of it. The law of the king's courts could dispense with either *aequitas* or ἐπιείκεια, so long as it was English. Being English became in that period a more desirable quality than either the perfection of justice or the sweetness of compassion.

It will be seen from what has just been said, that English equity had a characteristic development. It began as a real ἐπιείκεια, a reservation of the power in the king's council to make exceptions in the name of mercy and compassion. The chancery extended and regularized its jurisdiction, rationalized and organized it or part of it, and proceeded as though Roman *aequitas* and Greek ἐπιείκεια were the same. We might say that the process was characteristically English, both because it would not bear a logical analysis and because the concepts were worked out not by men meditating on theological subtleties, but by rival organs of royal administration.

When equity in England regained its prestige, in the eighteenth century, it leaned heavily on the natural law which was the most striking intellectual phase of the Enlightenment. Evidently, this equity could only be *aequitas,* not *ἐπιείκεια*. It was a formulation of fundamental truths in grand principles and not a mere stirring of nerve centers.

Being principles, they were capable of all the logical arrangements, subsumptions, qualifications, and distinctions that are imposed on propositions sought to be forced into a system; and unless the systematization has some end outside of its inherent beauty and consistency, it will narrow into a technique to be put by the side of other techniques. That is what happened to English equity between Hardwicke in the eighteenth and Eldon in the nineteenth century. Though Hardwicke was a humane man and Eldon was not, the equity of the eighteenth century lent itself easily to the mechanization that Eldon succeeded in putting into it, and if the common law itself had not begun to become humanized under the impact of political, intellectual, and economic revolutions, equity in England would have lost even an external resemblance to the *ἐπιείκεια* in which it was born, and the *aequitas* whereby it sought to grow to maturity.

If law or justice really were what philosophers have said, something that proceeded from right reason and had as its goal human happiness, there would be validity enough in the popular theory that our difficulties are caused by wicked men who do unlawful and unjust things in the name of law and justice. But we are philologers enough to know that the difficulties are in the words themselves, that law has its roots in historic systems of society, so that the perfection of law can be little else than the perfection of that system. In any system, formulation has its inevitable dangers. To do even and equal justice between man and man is good, and yet it may well be a cold and cruel portion to many other men by reason of its very equality and evenness. *Bonum et aequum* raised to its loftiest pitch leaves gaps which *ἐπιείκεια* must fill—but it must be a human *ἐπιείκεια,* not a logical concept.

It is, as I have suggested, not a novel discovery that there is a juster justice than Justice and a more lawful law than Law. Twenty-six centuries ago, the word of Yahweh came to Micah the Morasthite, in the days of Jotham, Ahaz, and Hezekiah, kings of Judah, and caused him to utter the splendid verse: "He hath shewed thee, O man, what is good; and what doth Yahweh desire of thee but to do justice and love mercy and walk humbly with thy God?" Micah's contemporaries knew that justice (*mishpat*) could be made ideally straight by equity (*yashar*) but also that even this unswerving straightness and evenness was too difficult a path for the feeble feet of men. There must be added "loving-kindness" (*hesed*), the quality that appears in our text as "mercy," and which a Corinthian congregation once heard preached to them as "charity."

And if prophetic and apostolic company is a little awesome for us to keep, perhaps we might refer to a casual dictum of my Lord St. Albans, sometime chancellor of England, whose moral growth did not quite keep pace with his intellectual development. "Laws," he said, "are likened to the grape, that being too much pressed yields a hard and unwholesome wine." A generation that looks forward to a little freer enjoyment of pressed grapes than has hitherto obtained, will doubtless heed the warning in respect of the symbol. Perhaps with a freer attitude toward the history of words, they will remember that the warning applies even more to the thing symbolized.

THE LAW AND MORALS OF PRIMITIVE TRADE*

BY FRANK I. SCHECHTER

I. INTRODUCTION

THE HISTORY OF MORALS has, in the past, been written almost exclusively as the history of the relations of the sexes, of the taming of man's blood lust, and of the development of personal and social benevolence.[1] Strangely enough, although, as is seemingly self-evident, business is "the main interest in the waking life of most people,"[2] the data of ethics are still gathered from man's sleeping, day-dreaming, or combative hours rather than from the grim realities of the economic struggle. It is in that struggle that "the collision between self and others" is most marked; it is there that the actual deliberation in the choice between just and unjust, between fair and unfair, which Aristotle posited as essential for the existence of virtue,[3] must necessarily occur with far greater clarity and regularity than in any other phases of man's moral experience.

This neglect of so fertile a field for the observation of moral practice and ethical theory is particularly to be noted in those sources of inquiry which should be most helpful and fundamental—in the economic life of primitive man. The failure to utilize primitive economic life for this purpose is probably owing to the fantastic and paradoxical figure, or, as Frazer terms it,[4] the "dismal fiction," of primitive economic man, from which anthropologists and economists have but recently freed themselves—the figure of an irrational but intuitively wise child, careless but hard of heart, naïve but egotistic, shortsightedly greedy yet improvident, without ability to plan for the future.[5] Writers on primitive law, likewise, have apparently absorbed this confusion of thought concerning the economic rationality of primitive man; while evidently regarding the law of property and family developed by savage peoples

* This essay will be included in a projected work by the present writer on the history of trade morals and control. For another phase of the subject dealing with so-called "Oriental" trade morals, see the writer's *A Study in Comparative Trade Morals and Control* in *Virginia Law Review*, XIX, 1933, pp. 794–845.

as of profound importance for comparative jurisprudence, they are, on the whole, prone to discount, if not altogether to ignore, the significance of primitive commercial custom, at any rate until its crystallization in its very advanced stage as "market law."[6] The student of primitive law as well as of morals will, however, find distinctly interesting material in the development of primitive commercial custom, provided, of course, that his quest be unhampered by either the romanticism of a Rousseau on the one hand, or by a sense of civilized superiority, on the other. It should be remembered that the methods of primitive trade have frequently been reported, not merely by ignorant or unsympathetic though possibly disinterested observers, but more often by disgruntled competitors and customers.[7] "I know," said Akaitcho, a Copper Indian chief, to the surgeon of the John Franklin polar expedition, "you write down every occurrence in your books; but probably you have only noticed the bad things we have said and done, and have omitted to mention the good."[8] To notice both the good and the bad, to observe the development of canons of fair dealing and the customary devices for the promotion of fair, and the control of unfair, dealing among primitive peoples will be the endeavor of this present paper.

That primitive peoples formulate certain standards of fair trade and that they ponder upon the discrepancies between these standards and actual practice, is evident from their numerous proverbs on this theme.[9] The corroding effect of the pursuit of gain is thus described by the Maori as "a certain lure to decoy a man, that his heart shall not ponder, and he be caught as a fish of the ocean."[10] The Ashanti of the Gold Coast find that "Money is sharper than a sword,"[11] and that "A Chief's weights are not the same as a poor man's weights."[12] To the Ewe of West Africa, "Cowries are men"—the equivalent of our "Money makes the man."[13] The Nandi of East Africa say that "if a man wishes to make a bargain, he will cheat his own sister,"[14] while in the Punjab the native goldsmith "will," it is thought, "steal a scrap of his mother's nose-ring."[15] The Wolofs of Senegambia believe that "The born merchant goes not to the other world";[16] "Nobody buys yams in the ground" is their version of *caveat emptor*.[17] The Yoruba of West Africa warn a man about to buy a female slave: "You find a hen in the market and hasten to buy her. Had she been worth keeping, her owner would not have sold her."[18] "No snuff-seller," they also say, "likes to own that she sells bad tobacco, but all profess to sell tobacco as sweet as honey."[19] Of the unsuccessful extortioner, the Ba-Ila of Rhodesia say: "The rat tried his teeth on the iron"; of false assurances: "You shave me with a blunt razor"; of suspicious solicitude for an intended victim: "He has the kindness of a witch."[20]

II. GIFT EXCHANGE

THE QUESTION whether Adam Smith was correct in finding among primitive peoples a "natural propensity to barter," [21] or whether "economic rationality was learned and barter was a part of it,"[22] though interesting, can only be suggested by the general nature of our inquiry; nor, in our quest, shall we attempt to go back to the time described by Thucydides, when "there was no mercantile traffic and the people did not mingle with each other without fear, either on land or by sea, and they each tilled their own land only enough to obtain a livelihood from it, having no surplus of wealth, and not planting orchards. . . ."[23] Without entering the perilous waters of controversy in respect of the "stages" or "phases" or "planes" or "periods" through which primitive economic life is variously thought to pass,[24] we shall commence our study at "a state of affairs" for which Malinowski has conveniently coined the term, "tribal economy"—"a state of affairs where production, exchange and consumption are socially organized and regulated by custom, and where a special system of traditional economic values governs their activities and spurs them on to efforts."[25] In discussing this phase of trade morals and control, it should be remembered that the "traditional . . . values" of "tribal economy" are not only those based on utility, but also those subtle display or "prestige" values which play so important a rôle in primitive economic life.[26] We commence our study when trade still means *any* exchange, within or outside the tribe, of goods, or services, irrespective of the sort of value of the goods or services exchanged.[27] This "tribal economy" is characterized by various forms of gift exchange,[28] the customary basis of which—equivalence or reciprocity[29]—is of fundamental interest to the student of trade morals. Of Homeric gift exchange "we remember," recently writes Professor Radin, "how Glaucus and Diomede exchanged shields in the *Iliad* and how Diomede ruefully discovered that he had given gold for brass, a hundred-oxen shield for a nine-oxen one. It was a sort of overreaching to get more than you gave, and evidently if we get only what we give, that is not a good way to make a profit out of the transaction."[30] The significant point in Homeric gift exchange, however, is not so much that good morals as well as good business sense imply a fair exchange, but that custom already *prescribes* such reciprocity. As long as the donor of gifts lives, he is entitled to return gifts: death alone cancels the debt. "And these gifts," says Laertes to Odysseus, "countless gifts, thou didst bestow in vain. For if thou hadst found that man yet living in the land of Ithaca, he would have sent thee on thy way with good return of thy presents, and with all hospitality, *as is due to the man who begins the kindness.*"[31]

The sociological and psychological bases of gift exchange cannot be considered here; all that is important to note in our present study is that tribal economic life is dominated by this principle or duty of give and take, of equivalence.[32] "Although the savages," wrote Father Le Jeune, of the Algonquins in 1663, "will give you something for a 'thank you' (this is a word they have learned from the French), you must make them some return for another 'thank you,' otherwise you will be looked upon as ungrateful . . . ; they do not know what it is to give without receiving."[33] This reciprocity is everywhere a cardinal principle of primitive trade morals, of trade custom. Among the Dénés of the Canadian Northwest, if you express admiration for an object,

> forthwith it passes into your hands and becomes your property. But you are always expected to return at least its equivalent in goods. . . . In case the beneficiary of these "bounties" should forget to return the compliment, he is soon reminded of his obligations through the intervention of a third person. Unless desirous of provoking a dispute, the creditor will never accost the debtor bent on mentioning such a subject. If the object offered the former through the obliging friend be not agreeable, it is mercilessly declined until something of a value at least commensurate with that of the original transaction is brought forward.[34]

Of the Carnelos Indians of Ecuador, a traveler there writes:

> Numbers of Indians presented themselves with their families . . . to bring us their offerings of plantains, *yuca,* and *chicha,* in expectation of

return, or, as they term it, as an "invitation" to us to give them knives, needles, thread and cotton cloth, with ornaments in the shape of beads and small looking-glasses.[35]

In the island of Rotuma (northeast of Fiji),

if a man, say, wants a pig for a feast, he goes to another who has plenty and asks him for one. He cannot well refuse, but in his turn is entitled to ask for something at some future time.[36]

Among the Maori of New Zealand, gift exchange was equally common and the theme of much folklore: of him whose generous gift was unreciprocated, the Maori saying was, "Glad heart went away, Bitter mind remained." There was, in Maori legend, a man named Tokoahu,

who was continually traveling from place to place, getting presents made to him, for which he gave no return. . . . His friends used to go on waiting, waiting, waiting, expecting something but in vain. At last one man grew so incensed at Tokoahu's failure to disburse anything in return that he laid a curse upon him, from the effects of which the covetous fellow died.[37]

III. COLLECTIVE OR CEREMONIAL EXCHANGES

The same principle of a regulated mutuality in the exchange of gifts emerges with striking clarity in the institution of the collective or communal ceremonial feast or exchange, so characteristic of "tribal economy."[38] The ceremonial feast or exchange represents not merely a benevolent or vainglorious rivalry or reciprocation in hospitality or generosity, not merely a picturesque, communal gorging and bragging contest, as the wholesale consumption and distribution of goods, or even occasionally the wanton destruction of goods, would imply. On the contrary: this communal ceremonial is often combined with some social or religious function, such as the celebration of a birth, the giving of a name, the attainment of puberty, the raising of a house, and with marriage or mortuary rites. Found, in various forms, in places as far apart as British Vancouver and the South Sea Islands, it is, moreover, from the economic standpoint, far less irrational and naïve than the "hundred-thousand-dollar wedding" or the "fifty-thousand-dollar dance," with accounts of which the press so frequently regales the so-called civilized world.[39] With the complicated technique of the ceremonial feast or exchange we cannot deal here, but the legal and moral implications of the economic mechanism involved have a definite bearing upon our present inquiry.

Closest at hand, among the Indians of northwestern America, is the potlatch, a system of ceremonial feasts or exchanges. Through the potlatch may be acquired the prestige incidental to the lavish distribution and ostentatious destruction of property, while at the same time a long-term investment is made in that there is the expectation of still more lavish reciprocity in an ultimate return of the property so distributed.[40] The potlatch marks every important event from birth to death. "Formerly," writes Professor Boas, to whom we are much indebted for our knowledge of the potlatch system, "feats of bravery counted as well as distribution of property, but now-a-days [1897], as the Indians say, 'rivals fight with property only'."[41] Stripped, however, of its competitive significance, of its colorful and ceremonial feasting and boasting, and of its graphic terminology, the economic and legal essence of the potlatch can be boiled down, as it has been by Boas, to

> contracting of debts on the one hand and the paying of debts on the other. It must be clearly understood [he says], that an Indian who invites all his friends and neighbours to a great potlatch, and apparently squanders all the accumulated results of long years of labour, has two things in his mind, which we cannot but acknowledge as wise and worthy of praise. His first object is to pay his debts. This is done publicly and with much ceremony, as a matter of record. His second object is to invest the fruits of his labour so that the greatest benefit will accrue from them for himself as well as for his children. The recipients of gifts at this festival receive these as loans, which they utilise in their present undertakings, but after the lapse of several years they must repay them with interest to the giver or to his heir. Thus the potlatch comes to be considered by the Indians as a means of insuring the well-being of their children if they should be left orphans while still young. It is, we might say, their life insurance.[42]

The giver of the potlatch has at stake not only his own reputation but also that of the family group or tribe.[43] From them, from his friends, or even from the very persons to whom the potlatch will be given,[44] he borrows that which is to be distributed at the potlatch, and whatever is thus loaned to him must ultimately be repaid with interest, sometimes running as high as 100 per cent. Or, if he desires to "finance" the enterprise with his own means instead of borrowing from others, he will lend out his own property at interest, to be repaid in time for his use of it at the potlatch. The person to whom a "gift" is offered at a potlatch cannot refuse it,[45] and automatically becomes obligated to repay the gift with interest later on. If the recipient of a present should die, his heirs become bound to return it; if the giver of the potlatch should die, the debts due him will be collected by his heirs.[46] The amount of interest with which debts must be paid is prescribed by custom. The unit of value in all such transactions is the single blanket. The double blanket is valued at three single blankets.

These blankets [says Boas] form the means of exchange of the Indians, and everything is paid for in blankets or in objects the value of which is measured by blankets. When a native has to pay debts and has not a sufficient number of blankets, he borrows them from his friends and has to pay the folowing rates of interest: For a period of a few months, for 5 borrowed blankets 6 must be returned; for a period of six months, for 5 borrowed blankets 7 must be returned; for a period of twelve months or longer, for 5 borrowed blankets 10 must be returned. When a person has a poor credit, he may pawn his name for a year. Then the name must not be used during that period, and for 30 blankets which he has borrowed he must pay 100 in order to redeem his name.... [For his final naming-ceremony a boy] will borrow blankets from the other members of the tribe, who all assist him. He must repay them after a year, or later, with 100 per cent interest. Thus he may have gathered 100 blankets. In June, the time set for this act, the boy will distribute these blankets among his own tribe, giving proportionately to every member of the tribe, but a few more to the chief. When after this time any member of the tribe distributes blankets, the boy receives treble the amount he has given. The people make it a point to repay him inside of a month. Thus he owns 300 blankets, of which, however, he must repay 200 after the lapse of a year. He loans the blankets out among his friends, and thus at the close of the year he may possess about 400 blankets.[47]

Debts must be repaid according to a certain definite procedure. Said the speaker for a great Kwakiutl chief, who came to pay a marriage debt:

My chief here has come and walks the road made by his grandfather for him to follow. I came to pay the marriage debt in this way, which is not new, which we were made to go by our ancestors, all the tribes. Now I come, and we go the road made by my grandfather, ... who was an expert at paying marriage debts....[48]

The potlatch system has, then, distinct legal and ethical implications. On the one hand, there is the seemingly consistently usurious rate of interest for loans.[49] On the other, it is equally apparent how scrupulous a forbearance by creditors and a fulfillment of obligations by debtors[50] were essential to the effective operation of the system.

> The economic system of the Indians of British Columbia [says Boas] is largely based on credit, just as much as that of civilized countries. . . . This economic system has developed to such an extent that the capital possessed by all the individuals of the tribe combined exceeds many times the actual amount of cash that exists: that is to say, the conditions are quite analogous to those prevailing in our community: if we want to call in all our outstanding debts, it is found that there is not by any means money enough in existence to pay them, and the result of an attempt of all the creditors to call in their loans results in disastrous panic, from which it takes the community a long time to recover.[51]

Apart from the necessity for the preservation of the credit structure, the fulfillment of potlatch obligations was a matter of serious social concern. Failure to give, and in turn accept, and, finally, to reciprocate a potlatch, and slackness or meanness in observing any of the duties incidental to the potlatch system were disciplined as grave breaches of faith and treated with the contempt and ridicule that were so effective a deterrent of unfair dealing in primitive society.[52] When a Tsimshian chief failed to uphold the glory of his tribe at a potlatch, his people sang: "You shall be the last one among all the chiefs, because you were not able to throw away coppers as the high chief has done."[53]

Throughout the Southern Hemisphere, among both Melanesian and Polynesian peoples, are to be found many such examples of collective ceremonial feasts or exchanges based upon the principle of equivalence. Thus, in the isolated island of Rossel, the extreme southeasterly outpost of the Louisiade group in Eastern New Guinea, while the ostentatious display of wealth so characteristic of the potlatch system is absent,[54] certain other features of the ceremonial feast or exchange, and particularly the elaborate credit and currency system, strongly suggest the potlatch. The purchase of important or of expensive property, such as houses, land, big-fish nets, pigs, dogs, and men (for eating purposes), or a wife, is a collective transaction, accompanied by much ceremonial.[55] In the purchase of a pig, for example, "there are," says Armstrong, who visited the island in 1921, "complex social factors determining who shall have a pig to sell, and who shall be in a position to buy. . . ."[56] If *A* agrees to buy a pig from *B*, a feast is held in the village of B. The pig is cut up in a ritual way, divided into portions, and distributed according to custom, while *B*, who receives the money for the pig from *A*, must distribute the greater part of the purchase price among relatives, those who have helped him fatten the pig, and so on.[57] *A* pays for the pig in shell money unique to Rossel Island, the outstanding features of which are that

of each grade of the tokens in use there is a virtually unchanging stock that has come down to the present generation from time immemorial, and that, into the grading of the tokens—their value-relationships to one another—there enters the novel principle of a time-element or interest-element, in place of the more familiar principle of simple proportionality.[58]

Thus, if, as is extremely probable, *A* has not the exact coin of the particular value of the pig, he must borrow such a coin, even though he has money of a higher value in his possession at the moment.

He may have Nos. 11 and 13, but not No. 12 which he requires at the moment. He cannot get change as a rule, for No. 13 is not a simple product of any lower value. He therefore borrows the required value, and if possible he takes the opportunity of lending what he has.[59] This peculiar system [says Armstrong], makes possible the existence of a profession very much like that of a London bill-broker, working with different material. The members of this profession on Rossel render an important service by transferring the possession of coins, *i.e.*, by borrowing from one who does not want a particular coin, and lending to another who does. Their profit is made by increasing the time unit for their debtors and decreasing it for their creditors, and by keeping their capital on loan as far as possible; in other words, by borrowing at a lower rate of interest and discounting at a higher.[60]

To the northwest of Rossel Island lie the Trobriand Islands, where is to be found the *kula*, a form of extensive intertribal exchange, the complicated economic mechanism of which "implies a high degree of mutual trust and commercial honour."[61] The *kula*, writes Malinowski, who observed and minutely recorded its operation,

is carried on by communities inhabiting a wide ring of islands, which form a closed circuit. . . . Along this route, articles of two kinds, and these two kinds only, are constantly travelling in opposite directions. In the direction of the hands of a clock, moves constantly one of these kinds—long necklaces of red shell. . . . In the opposite direction moves the other kind—bracelets of white shell. . . . Each of these articles, as it travels in its own direction on the closed circuit, meets on its way articles of the other class, and is constantly being exchanged for them. Every movement of the *kula* articles, every detail of the transactions is fixed and regulated by a set of traditional rules and conventions, and some acts of the *kula* are accompanied by an elaborate magical ritual and public ceremonies.[62]

The *kula,* it should be noted, is not carried on promiscuously, but only by partners belonging to various tribes.[63]

Like the coppers of the potlatch system,[64] the arm-shells and necklaces of the *kula* are "objects of parade" rather than of utility,[65] and they must be exchanged for arm-shells and necklaces of equal prestige value, without, however, any unseemly bargaining or coercion or any open calculation of this equivalence—behavior which would appear highly indecorous to the Trobriander. But while "the decorum of the *kula* transaction is strictly kept, and highly valued,"[66] as in all the other collective exchanges we have studied, there are effective forces at work compelling fair exchange or equivalence in the *kula.* The custom and ethics of the *kula* prescribe not only equivalence in exchange but also a scrupulous observance of the customary time limits for such exchange.

A man who is in the *kula* never keeps any article for longer than, say, a year or two. Even this exposes him to the reproach of being niggardly, and certain districts have the bad reputation of being "slow" and "hard" in the *kula.* On the other hand, each man has an enormous number of articles passing through his hands during his life time, of which he enjoys a temporary possession, and which he keeps in trust for a time. This possession hardly ever makes him use the articles, and he remains under the obligation soon again to hand them on to one of his partners.[67]

Equivalence or *noblesse oblige* may be the criterion of fair dealing in the *kula:* its actual and spontaneous attainment, however, among the Trobriand islanders, as among ourselves, is a problem of social control. "Right through their ceremonial give and take, there runs the crude and fundamental dissatisfaction with the value received,"[68] and when that dissatisfaction reaches a certain point, recriminations and abuse, although indirectly conveyed,[69] and the censure of public opinion applied in *kula* legends and popular sayings,[70] will confront the offender. Finally, magic is of course a potent element in success in the *kula:* to punish him who has been tardy or niggardly in his return, black magic is invoked, while to ensure success in *kula* there are "numerous rites and spells, all of which act directly on the mind [*manola*] of one's partner, and make him soft, unsteady in mind, and eager to give *kula* gifts."[71]

The so-called *solevu* ("Great Presentation") of the Fijians is a similar formal presentation of property by one clan or sept to another: a tribe, for example,

> that owned salt-pans such as those at Nandi Bay wanted mats. . . . The *solevu* took place, both donors and recipients preserving a very accurate remembrance of the value of the present. After some months, or even years, Yasawa, having plaited a store of mats equivalent to their estimate of the value of the salt, would propose to return the *solevu,* and the score would be wiped off. If they seemed to hang fire, deft hints would be conveyed to them by the gossip-mongers, that they were fast becoming a by-word on the Nandi coast. If their offering fell short of the value due from them the formal gratitude of their entertainers would lose nothing of its correctness at the time. The speeches would be as complimentary as usual, the hand-clapping as hearty, but none the less would they be made to hang their heads with shame when they had returned to their own island, and heard from the gossip-mongers some of the caustic epigrams current in Nandi at their expense. . . .[72]

Among the Maori of New Zealand, those invited to a *hakari,* or intertribal feast,[73] were expected to make a present to their hosts. "When accepting such an invitation, it is not meet that you should attend with empty hands, to go thereto with a bare forehead, as the Maori puts it. Take some offering with you, a calabash of preserved rats for example. . . ."[74] Furthermore, guests at such a feast were under "a stringent obligation" to reciprocate by a return feast as speedily and lavishly as possible.[75] Such was the fear of dishonor for failure to reciprocate a *hakari,* that tribes unable to gather food for a return feast would, instead, even cede their precious lands to their former hosts, "a practice which illustrates the depth of the impulse to give compensation for obligations incurred—for land was the most prized possession of the Maori."[76]

IV. SALES AND MARKETS

THE PRIMITIVE LAW OF SALE develops, as we shall see, to an extraordinarily minute degree, in the custom of the primitive market. But even prior to the establishment of the recognized security for buyer and seller meeting vis-à-vis and the advanced technique of sale implied in "the peace of the market," we find, usually existing between two peoples the one of a lower and the other of a higher cultural level,[77] the curious and ancient institution known as "silent trade"—the exchange of goods at a certain fixed point or depot without any communication between the parties. Intermingled as it is with fear and hope, "silent trade" is thus one of the earliest forms of "gentleman's agreement." According to Herodotus, the Carthaginians, in their dealings with African peoples beyond the Pillars of Hercules, upon their arrival

> forthwith . . . unlade their wares, and having transposed them after an orderly fashion along the beach, leave them, and returning aboard their ships, raise a great smoke. The natives, when they see the smoke come down to the shore, and, laying out to view so much gold as they think the worth of the wares, withdraw to a distance. The Carthaginians upon this come ashore and look. If they think the gold enough, they take it and go their way; but if it does not seem to them sufficient, they go aboard ship once more and wait patiently. Then the others approach and add to their gold till the Carthaginians are content. Neither party deals unfairly by the other.[78]

The Chukchee of Siberia have, today, a similar legend of "silent trade" —this time with America:

> On the other side of the sea, in a large forest, live "the invisible ones." When they come to trade, one can see only the fox and beaver skins which they carry in their hands, and it seems as if the peltries move of themselves. They come to meet our traders on the border of the forest, and shout, "Let us trade!" The traders take a bundle of tobacco and fling it far away. "Tobacco, tobacco," rings through the forest, but nobody is seen. After a while a bag filled with fox or beaver skins is flung from the forest. For one bundle of tobacco they will give a bagful of white fox-skins.[79]

"Silent trade," however, is not merely legendary; among the primitive peoples of modern times it is still a common method of exchange. For example, Christians in the Lowlands of Northern Luzon recently told Vanoverbergh

> that the custom of secret barter prevailed among the Negritos; they said it

was their custom, when they went to the Negrito country for commercial purposes, to go to the brink of the forest and there to deposit the products they wanted to sell, clothes, rice, &c., as it was impossible to approach the Negritos on account of their timidity. The Negritos would come at night, place alongside whatever they had for sale, beeswax, rattan, &c., and set apart the things they desired in exchange. Then the Christians would go, take the Negritos' products, if they wanted them, and leave their own wares; else they would take these back and leave the Negritos' property untouched.[80]

Particularly interesting is the "silent trade" recently noted among the pygmies of the Congo, who, at any rate theoretically, neither see nor hear each other in the course of this trade. Of these, writes Torday in 1925,

Their only occupation is hunting and their habitations follow the game. To obtain vegetable food or iron (required for their arrows, or knives or spear-heads) they use the most primitive form of barter known: an animal they have killed is deposited at night near the entrance of a village; next night they come to fetch the price, which they expect to find in the same place where they have put their game. No villager would dare to take some of the meat without paying its full value; for, unseen by him, he is watched by the little men, and should he defraud them he is sure to be found dead a few days later with a tiny poisoned arrow in his side.[81]

This poisoned arrow of the lurking pygmy points the way to the proper evaluation of "silent trade" as a matter of primitive trade morals and control. The deposit of goods at a fixed point is made, as we have said, with mingled fear and hope; "self-interest is the guarantee of good faith."

In its simplest forms [writes Grierson], this practice does little to improve the mutual relations of the parties to it, for it leaves them as it found them, enemies. They, indeed, keep faith with one another; but, in so doing, they are actuated, not by any feeling of amity, but wholly and solely by the wish to serve their own interests. Still, if the practice itself do not improve these relations, it makes improvement possible; for it implies the view that an enemy, although he is an enemy, can be dealt with otherwise than by violence.[82]

Apart from "silent trade," and when men have ceased to fear to trade directly in each other's presence, germs of the primitive law of sale are to be found both within and outside "the peace of the market."[83] As in more advanced stages of civilization, among primitive peoples certain ceremonial or formal acts, publicly performed, are calculated to ensure the good faith and regularity, and also even to guarantee the fairness or equity of the transaction of sale. Early observers of the Iroquois Indians were much struck by the fact that

no written contract could have been more binding, nor sworn oath more solemn, than the strings of wampum given to each other by parties concerned in a transaction, as a witness and record of what had passed between them. The law held equally good in intercourse between different clans or gentes, villages, and tribes. "For all these peoples," the *Jesuit Relations* say, "have no voice except it be accompanied by presents; these serve as contracts, and as public proofs which are handed down to posterity and attest what has been done in any matter."[84]

Among the Baganda of Central Africa an ancient custom requires that

no one is allowed to sell or purchase anything of value, such as a woman, cattle, or goat, unless some one is present who will act as a witness and receive payment for his services. The percentage on the sale of a woman is a goat which has had a kid; on a slave, a he-goat; on a full-grown nanny goat, 5 shells . . . ; on an old shield, on which percentage had already been paid, 20 shells; and on an old spear, 10 shells. All articles had to pay a percentage. The custom prevented theft.[85]

Among the Bavili of Loango the seller must "bless" the transaction in the presence of witnesses.

He lifts his hands to his armpits, and then throws them towards the buyer, and breathes or blows over the thing sold. This is . . . equivalent to saying "God bless thee."[86]

Among the Palaungs of the hills of Burma,

when, in trading men make agreements to buy or sell at a certain price, they sometimes call in a professional scribe, who writes the agreement [in Burmese or Shan], which a passer-by is asked to read aloud. . . . If the persons buying and selling cannot read, they burn the agreement (after it has been read to them) on a large flat stone, then carefully taking the charred pieces of paper they beat them into powder and sprinkle them on water in a bowl. The water is then stirred with a spear or a sword, or with the barrel of a gun, and the persons say, "May I die by spear (or sword, or gun) if I do not keep this agreement!" Then they each drink half of the water. A few drops may be poured out on the ground, so that the earth also is a witness to the transaction.[87]

Not only were the rights of the contracting parties (as well as of the community) carefully safeguarded by such formalities as those just noted, but frequently we even find a right of rescission given to the unwary or unfortunate buyer or seller, after the transaction has been formally closed. Thus, among the Eskimo, "if a man repented of a bargain, he had a right to retract it."[88] In the Philippines, Ifugao law requires that,

> if a rice field after passing into the hands of a purchaser, is subject to an unusual number of slides in the terrace or is . . . washed away by a freshet, the purchaser may at any time within the year following the purchase, relinquish the field and demand the return of his purchase price. This is on the ground that the seller may have put a curse on the field when it left his hands, or that, at least, he did not relinquish his hold on its welfare and fertility. In Kalinga, if a water buffalo, horse, or ox die within the year following the sale, the purchaser may demand the return of the purchase price.[89]

Among the Nabaloi, also of the Philippines, a person selling an animal not owned by him, or one known to him to be sick, but not so known to the buyer, must refund the price, while, irrespective of defects,

> title is not vested in the buyer until payment in full has been made. At any time before payment has been completed, the vendor, after returning what he has received, has the right to demand the return of the thing sold.[90]

African law and custom[91] are rich in similar devices for ensuring fair and willing bargains. Among the Mandingos of Gambia and the Yarriba on the Niger, the purchaser may rescind the agreement until the expiration of the day on which it was made, while the law of certain other African tribes permits the purchaser to return goods within three days after his discovery of latent defects and also awards him damages.[92] The Ainamwanga and Awiwa tribes of North-Eastern Rhodesia go even farther in the protection of the buyer: "thus, if a cow is handed over and dies within a year without bearing a calf, the buyer dries the meat and takes it to the seller, who is bound to supply him with another cow without further charge."[93] In the native law of Natal, cattle or other stock are guaranteed by the seller to be free from latent disease for fourteen days from the day of sale; *any* article sold or bartered is taken as guaranteed by the seller to be free from latent flaws or defects unless the seller has especially contracted with the buyer that this presumption of law is abrogated.[94]

Among the Thonga of Portuguese East Africa, the purchaser of an ox that dies from a disease not discovered but already existing at the date of purchase can ask for another in its place, but must bring the skin of the dead ox with him and one hoe inside it for the meat he has eaten,[95] while among the Chagga of Kilimanjaro,

> when two agree on the sale of an animal, the purchaser will generally stipulate a period in which to prove if it is sound before the transaction is final. But if for any reason he wishes to revise the price before payment is made, the seller has a claim to a small fee; provided this is paid, he cannot insist on the transaction being completed on the original terms, and if they cannot agree, the purchaser may give back the animal.[96]

Among the Bavili of Loango

> when it is proposed to cancel a contract the contracting parties buy *malafu* (palm wine) in equal quantities, but deposited in one bottle or other vessel, and then in the presence of witnesses drink and agree to cancel the compact. But in the case of one of the parties refusing to annul the contract, the matter is taken before two or three chiefs or princes and talked out. In the event of the dispute arising out of inequality of service rendered, the division of profits is rearranged, or the contract declared then and there null and void.[97]

But apart from the law governing and the ceremonial recordation of the making and cancellation of agreements, the religious sanction or protection of the primitive market threatened speedy retribution to the unfair trader.[98] Andrew Battell, in his *Strange Adventures* on the African Gold Coast at the end of the sixteenth century, reported that at Loango "in the *banza* . . . or chief city, the chief idol is named *Chekoke*. Every day they have there a market, and the *Chekoke* is brought forth by the *Ganga,* or priest, to keep good rule, and is set in the market place. . . ."[99] In the twentieth century the markets of the Birilsa and Kassena tribes of the Northern Gold Coast are likewise described as

> being under the direct control of an Earth-god. Violations of his wishes were punishable religiously—sometimes a community would be, so to speak, ex-communicated from all intercourse in the markets, and all other communities saw to it that the order of the market *tindada* [the High Priest of the local Earth-god] was obeyed.[100]

In Morocco, Westermarck found that there are still traces of at least theoretical domination of various occupations and trades by saintly patrons.[101] In Samoa, also, "each particular trade or employment had its well-known God."[102]

The primitive market is a most interesting field for the observation of trade morals, reflecting, as it does, the commercial ingenuity as well as the ethical standards of natives who have already passed the gift-exchange stage.[103] The Abbé Proyart, describing trade conditions on the African Gold Coast in the eighteenth century, was much impressed with the fair dealing at the market he observed there, reporting that "No fraud is known in the market; a mother sends thither a child six years old, convinced that they will not deceive him. It is not necessary to understand the language in order to buy, no one ever cheapens or bargains. . . ."[104] Similarly, as recently as 1920, an English missionary to the Loyalty Group of Islands in New Caledonia lauded the honesty of the natives when dealing with each other at the market:

> *A.*, a member of the fishing village, would walk with a stately tread across the intervening space to the yam stalls, and selecting a yam would gravely inquire the price. Then *B.*, after looking at it fixedly for a minute or two, as though mentally calculating its weight and quality, would reply, "Oh, just give me as much fish as you think it is worth" and the bargain was closed. When *B.* went to buy fish, the same formula was observed; and in this manner business flourished until the sun sank low in the horizon, which was the time agreed upon for closing the market. It frequently happened that neither side had sold out all its produce, and as no one could be so mean as to carry his unsold wares home again, each party handed over all that was left as a present to the other party.[105]

However, usually primitive market conditions are not quite so idyllic: with the growth of commerce, the primitive market requires and develops its own machinery for promulgating and enforcing the canons of fair trade. The Baütschi of the Sudan have market police and judges to control the quality of produce, to prevent the adulteration of milk, and to adjust disputes;[106] at the market of Wydah in Guinea, an official went the rounds with four armed servants, listening to the complaints of buyer and seller, giving summary judgments, and then and there selling thieves and disturbers of the peace into slavery;[107] in the lower Congo, market law may be enforced thus: "the culprit is either buried to his neck in a hole, in the centre of the market-place, and his skull crushed by a heavy stone; or he is beaten to death with sticks, and his body subsequently lashed to a pole, which is erected alongside a native path."[108] The market women of the Chagga of Kilimanjaro do their own police work; watered milk is poured on the ground and the calabashes containing it are smashed; sometimes they even surround the seller and make her drink it.[109] Among the Kadayans, hill-men in Borneo, a commercial rather than a warlike race, "a meeting of their chiefs takes place, they settle the price of rice, and none of their followers will swerve from it."[110]

Among the Ibos of Southern Nigeria, where trade in the markets is mainly confined to women, is found an official known as the "market queen," who has most remarkable disciplinary powers over market practices. Sometimes alone, and occasionally assisted by a women's council, of which she is the head, she fixes prices; she punishes the women of her town who may attend a market at some other town; she prevents the sending of produce to other markets; she sets the rate of cowrie (shell money) exchange; she decrees what articles are to be sold in the market and what is taboo, and otherwise controls market conditions. Those violating her orders in this respect are, in certain communities, subject to fine or confiscation of their goods.[111] Similar discipline was maintained in the markets and fairs on the river banks in the Sandwich Islands. There traders examined articles of barter on a rock in the middle of the Wairiku River, in the presence of certain market officials, who stood on each side of the rock and arbitrated any disputes that arose, their remuneration being received from the different parties to the transaction.[112] In the Bukana Pig-Market in New Guinea a bit of root is burned and the ashes are secretly and symbolically sprinkled over the market site "so that they may impart their coolness to the foot of a buyer who should be fired with anger."[113] The result of violating market custom has been graphically portrayed by the explorer Stanley, who, writing from the Congo in 1881, relates:

> On the 25th of June a curious incident occurred at the market of Manyanga, which was held every week. A man bought a goat, and, contrary to custom, attempted to resell it the same day in the same market, which was considered such an outrage upon custom that the public indignation was

aroused, to be vented upon the goat and a couple of pigs. These animals were cut to pieces and distributed round the market-place, and not until a general smash-up of gourds of palm-wine had taken place was the public anger sufficiently allayed.[114]

V. LOANS AND BAILMENTS

THE EXTENSION OF CREDIT in goods or currency, which we have already found to be the basis of the potlatch and other collective ceremonial enterprises, is likewise a most important element in the more individualistic economic activities of primitive peoples, among whom default in the repayment of loans and the return of bailments is considered to be exceedingly reprehensible, and dealt with accordingly.[115] Two basic principles of primitive law contribute most effectively to the protection of creditor or bailor. In the first place, even in individual transactions, the responsibility for repayment or return does not remain individual: it falls not only upon the debtor or bailee, but also upon his entire family or upon even a wider social group or circle.[116] In Ashanti, for example, there once existed a custom of

> the creditor seizing any person in any way connected with the debtor, or even sometimes a complete stranger to all concerned. The kindred of the person thus made prisoner came down upon the debtor's family and compelled them to pay the debt, plus a sum equivalent to 3s. 6d. to compensate the person seized in order that he might "wash his soul."[117]

Among certain of the Ibo in Nigeria the creditor can seize objects of value equal to the debt from any person in the quarter of the town where the debtor resides—which gives him scope of an average of about four thousand persons from whom to collect.[118]

Coincident with the principle of joint or group responsibility is the absence in primitive law of any statute of limitations. This theory that "a debt never rots"[119]—as the Ashanti legal maxim goes—is based not so much, as has been suggested, on the superabundance of time attributed to primitive man or on his leisurely way of asserting his grievances,[120] as upon the deep-seated belief in the sanctity of an obligation, and a repugnance, shared by more advanced systems of jurisprudence,[121] to the extinguishment of a claim except by its fulfillment. Claims may be enforced in favor of and against even the third or fourth generation;[122] the mere fact that the debtor dies leaving more debts than the value of his estate does not enable the heir to renounce the inheritance.[123]

With these principles in mind, we may examine a few of the devices for preserving and enforcing the rights of the primitive individual borrower and lender, of bailor and bailee. Among the Melanesians of New Guinea, payments of shell money are essential at many stages of ceremonial and social progress; if not owned, it must be borrowed, and thus arises a most complete and interesting credit system.

> The rate of interest [says Codrington], is cent. per cent. without regard to time. . . . A debt is not only contracted by borrowing, but a rich man upon occasion imposes a loan, which his friend for his own credit is bound to accept, and to discharge with a double return. The pressure put on a debtor who does not pay when payment is demanded is admirably effective. All the men of the creditor's place come and sit, bringing their wives with them, in the debtor's premises; the debtor lights his fire and cooks food for them; if the payment is not forth-coming, they stay over night, go home next morning, and after a while repeat the visit. The debtor's neighbours and friends pity him and help him with goods and money, till he scrapes enough together to pay the debt.

The lender's equity in the money loaned is, it should be noted, carefully protected: "if a man borrows money and lends that again to another, he is said . . . to treat him unfairly; if a man uses money he has borrowed of one man to satisfy another creditor, he is said to divert the payment into another course."[124] In Melanesian commercial transactions, likewise, and especially in the sale of canoes, credit plays an important rôle. A first instalment will be paid "cash down," as, for example, "two white man's axes, two big knives, two looking-glasses, a string . . . of beads and one pound of tobacco," or again "six pairs of arm-shells and one spiral boar's tusk." The seller was, in both transactions, observed by Seligmann to be quite confident that ultimately the balance of a "fair price" would be paid.[125] In the Torres Straits, Haddon found an equally elaborate credit system for the purchase of canoes. He

> particularly inquired whether cheating occurred, and pointed out the difficulty there would be in redress. The continuance of the custom proved that dishonesty was very rare. There was a good chance for cheating to be discovered, as friends of the creditor would be sure to inform. Should partial

or entire repudiation of debt take place, the supply of canoes would cease, and then (said his informant) "how we get fish, or turtle, or dugong, we hungry all the time, that no good," and furthermore there would be a fight.... Payment was usually made annually until the canoe was a little broken; generally three instalments were paid. When a piece came off the canoe, it was forwarded together with the final payment as a proof of the statement as to the condition of the canoe.[126]

Among the Negro peoples of Africa, many of whom have an especially keen feeling for justice,[127] or at any rate a particularly strong relish for litigation and an accordingly highly developed jurisprudence,[128] the interests and rights of both creditor and debtor are carefully safeguarded. In Southern Nigeria interest ranges, among the Edo, from none to a friend to 40 per cent to a stranger; "a creditor who dies, will tell his son. If a debtor dies far from home, his creditors take his body to his family and claim the money."[129] The Ibo law of debtor and creditor is particularly diversified: the rate of interest ranges up to 50 per cent; collection may be enforced by seizure of person or property, through the action of the medicine men, whom the debtor was bound to compensate for their services to his creditor, through the action of the dreaded secret societies,[130] or through sending a slave to sleep in the debtor's house until the debt was paid and the slave himself fed and ritually purified.[131] The Yoruba sometimes used a leper to collect in this way—doubtless effectively.[132] Again, if an Ibo man "takes charge of a goat and it bears a kid, he sends notice to the owner in five months and tells him to take it; the second one goes to the owner, the third to the bailee, after that they take alternately. If the goat dies, the body must be carried to the owner...."[133] Among the Boloki of the Congo,

in their business transactions credit is frequently given, and for such credit no interest is expected. To recover a debt a creditor first duns the debtor until he is tired, then he breaks the pots and saucepans and anything he finds outside the debtor's house and finishes by telling him that on a certain day he will call again for the money. If the debtor then fails to pay, the creditor will collect a few of his friends and together they will go and lie in ambush near the farms until a wife of the debtor comes along, when they will pounce upon her and take her to their town. The woman will kick, struggle and scream for the sake of appearances; but she knows that she will be lightly tied and well treated.[134]

To the Hottentots of South-West Africa,

the payment of debts . . . is an obligation of honour. If a man is unable to satisfy his creditors, a trustee is appointed to take over and divide his assets among them. He is allowed to keep a few goats and cows, whose milk he may use for the maintenance of himself and his family, but he may not slaughter these animals, for he is regarded as holding them in trust for the creditors.[135]

A man staying at a Kafir kraal as a guest

holds the owner of the kraal responsible for all theft of his possessions under his roof. Long credit is given for the payment of debt, and when a man cannot pay, his relations have to help him; his debts descend to his son after death.[136]

Among the natives of Sena, in Portuguese East Africa, contracting debts or sales on credit are made in the presence of witnesses—belonging usually to the families of the parties—and a token *(chimbarese)* is given by the debtor or buyer as a token of the amount owed.[137] Among the A-Kamba of British East Africa, if the debtor refuses to pay, the lender complains to the elders, and they go to the debtor and threaten him with the *Kithito* ordeal—the oath on the sacred horn of the ox or the antelope.[138]

Similar machinery for permitting and protecting credits and bailments is to be found in various other primitive societies. Writing in 1688, Cogolludo, the historian of the Mayas, says that

in sales and contracts they had neither writings to oblige them to keep their word nor promissory notes with which to give satisfaction, but still the contract remained valid provided only that the parties drank together publicly before witnesses. This was particularly in the sale of slaves or of cacao-lands, and even today (it is said) they use it still among themselves in the sale of horses and cattle. The debtor never denied the debt, even though he could not pay at once; but all was made certain by the debtor's confessing his debts, for the wife, children and relatives of the debtor would pay the debt after his death. . . .[139]

Among the Omaha Indians of the nineteenth century, Dorsey could find no example of a refusal to return a borrowed article. "If the use of the thing had impaired its value, the borrower always returned another article of the same kind, which had to be in as good condition as the former when it was borrowed."[140] In Central India "the unconverted Bhils are held to be tolerably reliable. When they borrow money or stock for cultivation, they seldom abscond from their creditors,"[141] while "such is the simplicity and honesty of character" of the wild forest Gonds, "that, when they have agreed to a *jama* (assessment of revenue for land), they will pay it though they sell their children to do so, and will also pay it at the precise time they agreed to."[142] Among the Lhote Nagas of the hill country in Assam "the rate of interest on loans varies according to the nature of the thing lent. That on money is usually 50 per cent simple interest, running for two years only. The interest on rice is four baskets a year for every six baskets borrowed. The interest has to be paid year by year till the principal has been returned." Every rich man there keeps a basket holding about 30 lb.—the standard measure for rice that is loaned. "When the rice is repaid, it is measured out in the same basket as that in which it was measured when lent. Should it be necessary to make a new basket the creditor calls his debtors together and compares it with the old one in their presence."[143]

In the Nicobar Islands, in the absence of writing, tally sticks are used to record debts. "When the debt was fully paid," says a recent observer, "the tally-stick was to be thrown away; and nothing but a sense of honesty prevented a Nicobarese man from throwing away his stick at any time and repudiating his debts."[144] Among the Ostyaks of Siberia tallys are similarly honored:

> It was also said that a promise made operates even after the death of him who made it, the son voluntarily paying his father's debts; and that frequently families have discharged the engagements of deceased members after several generations, on the production of incontestable proofs. Among these may be reckoned certain notches cut in wood, which, without having the value of written characters, are adopted by, and descend in some families, as ciphers, representing names. It has happened, that marks of this kind found on the woodwork of a yurt, were deemed sufficient proof of the building having been pledged for debt, and that the claimant, relying on this evidence alone, obtained possession.[145]

VI. PARTNERSHIP AND AGENCY

THE GERMS of the fiduciary obligations implied in partnership or agency, previously noted in ceremonial collective transactions, are also to be found in various other aspects of primitive trade. Occasionally, indeed, agency is the *only* or principal method of trade used. Thus, Father Veniaminoff, who went to Alaska in 1824, reports as a "custom ... of great age" that

> the Aleuts never transact with each other personally, but always through a third person, who is called a *Tayanak*.... Whoever wishes to sell anything sends it by his agent.... The agent, in coming into the house, says, "Here is the tayak" (salable object), without mentioning the owner. The buyer looks at the object, asks what is wanted in return, keeps the article, and sends as much as he likes of the article required in return. The agent takes this to the seller, and if he is satisfied the bargain is concluded; if not, he proposes a new exchange, or an additional quantity of tobacco or other ware, to boot. If the buyer does not agree he returns the article, and some one else makes an offer. They never bid over one another, and, however long the barter may last, the buyer and seller never know each other's names.[146]

Similarly in the Solomon Islands,

> when a Melanesian is buying or selling anything it never does to assume that the person who is proffering the yams or whatever may be for sale, or is inquiring about the price of a thing, or whether one has such and such a thing, is the actual buyer or seller, or himself wants the article. Someone standing by has been commissioned to act....[147]

Among the Ifugao of the Philippines "no transaction of importance of any sort between persons of different families is consummated without the intervention of a middle-man or go-between," who is the principal witness to the transaction. These go-betweens "are responsible to both parties ... for the correct rendering of tenders, offers, and payments. Their word binds only themselves, however—not their principals."[148]

In primitive commerce the partnership or agency relationship may be very simple, as for example in the Torres Straits folk tale of "Greedy Gwoba," who was commissioned by the men of Wakait to go to Argau to barter their *biiu* (a slimy paste of mangrove sprouts) for turtle meat. Caught eating—instead of selling—some of the *biiu* and also the turtle meat received for the rest of the *biiu,* Gwoba was promptly killed by his principals, the Wakait men. "Very good job you kill him," was the comment of the community.[149] As economic life grows in complexity, the technique of agency becomes accordingly more complicated. Thus, in the canoe traffic of the Torres Straits mentioned above,[150] the canoe was usually not purchased directly from the seller but through several intermediaries, who

were paid for their services [says Haddon], by "charging on," the amount depending upon individual cupidity, or they might be recompensed for their trouble by presents from the purchaser. There would appear to be considerable opportunities for cheating, but this was guarded against by the vigilance of the intermediary traders, who were themselves looked after by the Daudai men. If cheating occurred, the supply of canoes would cease, thus putting a stop to all fishing and commercial operations. In addition there would be war and the canoe confiscated.[151]

Among the Melanesians on their trading voyages is found a

reciprocal agency: each head of a family [at Dobu] has an agent . . . in the places visited, whose duty it is to look out for good *bagi* [shell disk ornaments]. Return visits are paid to Dobu to secure *moari* . . . shell armlets. The people to the south have . . . agents at Dobu.[152]

Similarly among the Chilkat of Alaska

each man traded with a special man (of another tribe) year after year, and would trade with no one else until he had offered his wares to him and he had got what he wanted. This right to trade with a particular man seems to be an inheritable right.[153]

Among the Bavili of the Congo the responsibilities devolving upon both principal and agent are defined with precision.

A man [says Dennett], may commission another to carry on trade for him. He gives him exact instructions, paying him half the profits, but exacts from him or his family any loss incurred. The sender is responsible to the family for any evil that may overtake the one sent provided that it cannot be shown that the evil was the consequence of his own folly. A man on leaving the country may commission his friend to act for him, but the service requested must be mentioned to the man commissioned in the presence of witnesses, and he may only act for him in that particular instance or on that occasion. No procuration to act generally for another is ever given. A present is given to one so acting for another where no profit can be expected. The act or service accomplished and the profits shared or present given, ends the commission.[154]

Perhaps, however, the most curious, and, at the same time, practical precautions to be found among primitive peoples to ensure the fidelity of agents are to be found among the Australian tribes on the lower Murray, who barter with those living on the coast:

When a man has a child born to him, he preserves its umbilical cord, by tying it up in the middle of a bunch of feathers. This is called *kalduke*. He then gives this to the father of a child or children who belong to another tribe, and those children are thenceforth *ngia-ngiampe* to the child from whome the *kalduke* was procured, and that child is *ngia-ngiampe* to them. From that time none of the children to whom the *kalduke* was given may speak to their *ngia-ngiampe,* or even touch or go near him; neither must he speak to them. . . . When two individuals who are in this position with respect to each other have arrived at adult age, they become the agents through which their respective tribes carry on barter. . . . The estrangement of the *ngia-ngiampes* seem to answer two purposes: it gives security to the tribes that there will be no collusion between their agents for their own private advantage, and also compels the two always to conduct the business through third parties.[155]

VII. COMPETITIVE MAGIC

IN PRIMITIVE TRADE, as in all other phases of savage economic life, whether canoe-building, mining, cowherding, the dairy industry, agriculture, fishing, whale-catching, hunting, etc.,[156] magic is a potent factor and it should not be overlooked here. Of course, barter is less hazardous and uncertain in its course, and less directly dependent upon the inexplicable forces of nature or upon the mysteries of technological processes than are many other of these economic activities. In this degree, to the savage mind the intercession of magical influences is perhaps somewhat less imperative in primitive trade than in other economic fields.[157] However, trade journeys are themselves often perilous and may be liable to interruption from man, beast, and the elements, as well as from the interposition of some magic agency already invoked by a wide-awake competitor.[158] Furthermore, irrespective of these perils, and arising from the eternal desire for a good bargain, that is, to obtain something for nothing, which we have seen is as omnipresent in the savage as in the civilized breast, there is always the advisability of having fate working affirmatively on one's own side and against the other party of the prospective transaction. Accordingly, in order to bolster up his own acumen and resourcefulness in bargaining while ensuring stupidity or shortsightedness in his customer, to obtain high prices for his sales and low prices for his purchases, to protect and make desirable his own products while blighting his competitor's wares and preventing their safe transportation and profitable sale, the primitive trader prefaces and accompanies his transactions by all sorts of magic, defensive and offensive, benevolent and maleficent, invoked by a variety of charms, countercharms, fetishes, incantations, and ceremonies.

In order that he may dispose of his stock promptly after his arrival in the market, the Junkun trader of the Sudan distils and inhales a mixture of black tubas, white onions, red kola nuts, and resin: "the intention being that as resin catches everything, black, white or red, so the trader will capture trade."[159] Among the Ba-ila of Northern Rhodesia, before starting on his expedition, the trader thus exhorts his medicine or talisman:

> "May you help me to buy slaves, guns, cattle, blankets, whatever I want." Having done this he thinks, "I shall return having made good bargains. . . ." Just as the . . . hawk swoops down on its prey and rarely, if ever, misses, so this *musamo* (talisman) will enable the trader to carry off good bargains.[160]

In Andjra, Morocco, Westermarck found that

> if anybody wants to sell one of his animals or something else, he collects the earth from seven different ant-hills on the roadside, and, after mingling it, strews it on the animal or object he offers for sale; the result will be that people gather round it like ants, for the purpose of buying it.[161]

Among the natives of Mailu in British New Guinea, Malinowski found that

> a man—usually the chief of a sub-clan—used to make a charm and pronounce a spell . . . in order that the expedition should be successful and that they should sell the arm-shells in a lucrative manner and bring back many pigs. . . .[162]

In the New Guinea pig market,

> the seller makes use of a charm so that he may get the highest possible price; the buyer does the same, in order to make a good impression with the things he offers in exchange, and to get the fattest pig that he can.[163]

In Surinam, the Dutch traveler de Goeje states,

> when making a purchase the buyer will put some turalla, a vegetable talisman, between his lips to prevent the seller over-reaching him.[164]

Among the wild bush-tribes of tropical Africa, there are idols known as *Sansa,* whose functions are described by a recent traveler, Claridge, as "the business genii. The images are a sort of board of trade which exists to promote its own trade and ruin that of everyone else." The efficacy of these *Sansa* is remarkable.

We once [relates Claridge], quite accidently proved the effectiveness of a charm against extortion. An article we stood greatly in need of was made unobtainable by the excessive price the Negro charged for it. . . . Upon his second visit to us he found us examining an image called *Sansa.* Putting the figure under our arm, the particular business position of the fetish, we wheeled round and renewed the bargaining at once. The native was taken by complete surprise. What could he do? He had left his own *Sansa* in the house. He was theoretically helpless. Without the least hesitation, cavil, or fear, he laughingly accepted the market price for what he was selling, much to his own glee and to the mirth of his colleagues at the way he had been outwitted.[165]

Magic is likewise found useful in the enforcement of contracts and the collection of debts. The Thonga creditor makes a ritual offering in order to make a debtor receptive to the idea of payment of his debt.[166] On the Ogowe River in equatorial Africa the skull of someone expressly killed for the purpose is regarded as an especially effective fetish: there, as recently as 1913, "an elderly man was killed in a canoe. The murderer . . . committed the crime in order to secure a fetish by means of which he hoped to ensure the fulfilment of their contracts by people who owed him goods and money."[167] Among the Bantu in Kikiyu, if a debtor repudiates his contract to repay, the creditor goes to the elders and demands that both be given "the ordeal of the bead." "Now the bead," says Hobley,

must be of a particular kind, which has been handed down from past ages and is evidently believed to be of magical value. . . . On the appointed day the creditor and debtor meet the elders; the latter sit in a circle and the former sit on the ground in the middle and facing each other. Each takes a piece of fine grass and places it inside the aperture in the bead and swears, as the case may be, that he lent a cow, or that he borrowed a cow, and that if he testifies falsely may he be eaten by the bead (*i.e.,* falsely destroyed). . . . Perjury is believed to result in the death of the perjurer, and furthermore, serious harm, even death, to his near relatives.[168]

VIII. THE PRIMITIVE TRADER IN ACTION

HOWEVER, in spite of all the standards set up by primitive custom and the controlling influences of primitive society that we have noted above—in spite of all this social pressure of "Market Gods," "Market Queens," ridicule, physical coercion, and the forces of magic, primitive man, in his own limited fashion, apparently exhibits, in his commercial methods, precisely the same tendency to depart from these standards of fair trade and manifests the same necessity for constant surveillance and external control which characterize his more civilized fellow-trader. Like the latter, he, too, in his dealings with other primitive peoples must be watched and disciplined, lest he use short weights and measures, adulterate his goods, puff them unconscionably, gouge his customers for extortionate profits, cheat his partners or principals, break his contracts, and harass his debtors. A few illustrations, offered with reservations in respect to the credibility of the evidence as suggested at the outset of this paper, must suffice. The Kwakiutl Indian berry-vendor, for example, mixes impure salalberries with elderberries, "so that they will show up better."[169] The fish-seller of the Marshall Islands (Oceania) attempts to palm off poor and undersized fish;[170] the Dusun tobacco seller in North Borneo wraps tobacco "outside a core of grass or other make-weight";[171] the Fan-man of West Africa "knows exactly how much rubbish you could incorporate in a ball of India rubber";[172] the Hausa of Northern Nigeria dare not pay for a horse or a slave without several days of trial and minute inspection;[173] in equatorial French Congo, where the length of cloth or metal wire is measured between the tips of the fingers of outstretched arms, the seller tries "to make his arms shorter, while the buyer attempts to spread his out as widely as possible. Sometimes they ask for assitance from a dwarf and a giant repectively in their endeavours to cheat one another more thoroughly";[174] among the Baganda of Uganda, likewise, where cloth is bought "by the cubit, *i.e.,* from the tip of the second finger to the elbow joint, the purchaser would bring a friend with a long arm to measure the goods. . . .";[175] in Guiana "the Indian knights of the road" tell their unsophisticated customers "that the glass beads which they are selling them grow on bushes which they themselves plant";[176] in the Nicobar Islands ambergris is adulterated with vegetable resins;[177] among the Angami of North-East India coins of nominal value were whitened with quicksilver and passed off on the innocent Semas as rupees; also powdered charcoal was sold as gunpowder;[178] the Patharis of Central India counterfeit gold by heating brass in resin;[179] the Mawatta of Western New Guinea palm off on the unsophisticated bushmen "old tools, knives, axes, old print dresses, in fact all the rubbish they could find no use for themselves..." in exchange for tons of fine yams.[180]

The methods of the primitive trader as a middleman or broker, likewise often require the closest scrutiny. The preying by native American-Indian traders upon the ignorance of remotely situated tribes was notorious. "In Alaska," says Father Morice,

> the opportunity to make large profits was great. They improved it without remorse. Thus the easternmost Dénés sold with a profit of a thousand per cent. to their inland congeners, the Dog-Ribs and the Yellow-Knives, hatchets for which they had themselves paid one beaver or lynx skin, or again three common marten skins.... For a small brass kettle of two pounds or two pounds and a half weight, they exacted as much as sixty martens or the value of twenty beaver skins; and if the vessels were in good order, they had the cheek to demand even more....[181]

In the development of native trade in Africa and elsewhere, we find similar conditions. In 1519, in Portuguese South Africa, "the smallest profit on anything [brought on a vessel from India] was four hundred per cent. and ... on some things it rose to two thousand eight hundred per cent."[182] At the end of the following century Jean Barbot complained that

> those crafty [native] factors [will cheat the native merchants] to their faces, either in concert with the super-cargo, or by amusing them with some flam, whilst another broker or Black, who is in the secret, cuts off some part of the linen and stuff he has bought for them, or alters the weights of what is weighable or mixes liquores with water.[183]

The explorer Stanley, describing the market at *Ujiji* in 1876, noted that "the Wajiji, who are sharp, clever traders, ... have raised their prices on some things a hundred per cent. over what they were when I was in Ujiji last."[184] Among the Ba-Mbala, according to Torday and Joyce, "middle-men are not paid, but make their own profit by cheating both sides."[185] Similarly, Papuan fishdealers in New Guinea, who barter their fish for vegetables and fruit, were observed (1880) to "get for one fish as many bananas as they gave for two the day before."[186] Later a highly trustworthy German observer significantly contrasts the seeming helplessness of the primitive Papuan, when confronted by European trading methods, with his commercial ingenuity among his own people:

There is an enormous difference when Papuans barter amongst themselves. One must also see what clever and crafty merchants even the most primitive Papuans in the wildest mountain forests are. They know, for instance, that the smaller the quantity is that they offer, the higher they can raise their prices. When they have a large supply of any article in stock, they will never bring everything all at once; they will hide their supply, and only gradually bring it out, piece by piece. For instance, two people will never offer the same article at the same time, and when they wish to sell something, they do not offer it but only show it, so to say, flirt with it; and these are not Coast Papuans, that have perhaps been spoiled by the intercourse with the Malay and the European, but tribes who probably never saw a European, before they met me.[187]

It would take us too far afield to discuss here at any length the effect of the commercial impact of a more civilized upon a primitive people. The classic illustration of such trade is, of course, that of the Spanish crew of Columbus, whom he was compelled to forbid to offer in exchange for gold "broken crockery and scraps of broken glass, and ends of straps. . . ."[188] Perhaps the whole matter was very neatly summed up by Robert Louis Stevenson's friend, old Tembinok, the royal trader of the South Seas, who classified captains and super-cargoes with whom he had done business under three heads: "He cheat a litty"—"He cheat aplenty"—and "I think he cheat too much." "For the first two classes," says Stevenson, "he expressed perfect toleration; sometimes, but not always, for the third."[189] But primitive man himself is often equipped, or at any rate soon learns, to hold his own and even to outplay his more civilized fellow-trader.[190] Finally the two may join hands in a common enterprise, as when "the sophisticated savage" works with the European trader to palm off all sorts of "primitive" relics on the "unsophisticated globe-trotter."[191] Indeed, at Birkenfeld, an outlying province of Oldenburg, Germany, a special and highly respectable factory was maintained in response to commissions sent from England, for the making of green-stone or New Zealand jade, and imitation Maori weapons and ornaments to be sent to New Zealand for sale there by the natives at high prices to the eager and gullible representatives of Ethnographical Museums![192]

CONCLUSION

In the foregoing survey of the morals and control of primitive trade, we have endeavored to follow the injunction of Akaitcho, "to mention the good" as well as "to notice the bad." In primitive collective or communal activity we have noted, as the basis of fair dealing, the notion of equivalence which, translated into medieval economic doctrine, would be that of the just price. We have found highly developed systems of credit, as in the potlatch, the Rossel Island currency, and the *kula,* which could not operate successfully without a great deal of good faith being exercised by all parties concerned. In addition to the fundamental idea of equivalence, we have also found an emphasis on the necessity for a scrupulous observance of the time element in the repayment of gifts or loans, as well as, particularly in the potlatch and *kula,* the emergence of a trustee or partnership relationship. In individual, as distinguished from collective or communal trade, we have noted various devices for the making and recording of fair bargains, for the rescission of improvident ones, and, as finally crystallized in market law, for the prevention of adulteration, short weights and measures, and other forms of overreaching and unfair trade generally. We have thus seen primitive man, on the one hand, developing, enunciating, extolling, and seeking to enforce certain principles of fair trade, and, on the other hand, frequently restless and resentful at the application of these principles to his particular case, with the consequent recurring necessity for coercing him into compliance through all the agencies at the command of primitive society—expostulation, gossip, ridicule, magic, violence, and even exile. This picture may not square with the "absolute respect for custom," the "blind unquestioning obedience," the "spontaneous" or "automatic conformity" with a "group morality" frequently imputed to primitive man.[193] But, with mere variations in technique and proportion, it faithfully foreshadows the conduct and necessary restraints of man in his more sophisticated, or, as we would say, in his "civilized" economic life. In this picture, likewise, primitive trade practice and regulation, both before and when these are dignified as market custom, assume their proper significance in legal history, as making substantial contributions to one of the most ancient and at the same time virile branches of jurisprudence, the history of commercial law.

BIBLIOGRAPHY

ADAM, L. G. *Potlatch* in *Festschrift für Eduard Seiler* (Stuttgart, 1922).

ALEXANDER, B. *From the Niger to the Nile* (London, 1908).

ALLIER, R., trans. by ROTHWELL, F. *The Mind of the Savage* (London, 1929).

ANDERSEN, J. C. *Maori Life in Ao-tea* (Wellington, New Zealand, 1907).

ARMSTRONG, W. E. *Rossel Island* (Cambridge, 1928).

—— *Rossel Island Money* (1924) 34 *The Economic Journal* (London).

BALL, V. *Jungle Life in India* (London, 1880).

BARBOT, J. *Description of the Coasts of North and South Guinea* in Churchill, A., *A Collection of Voyages and Travels,* Vol. V (London, 1732). 6 vols.

BARTON, R. F. *Ifugao Law* (1922) 15 *University of California Publications in American Archaeology and Ethnology,* No. 1.

BASDEN, G. T. *Among the Ibos of Nigeria* (London, 1921).

BATTELL, ANDREW. *See* RAVENSTEIN, J. A.

BATUTA, IBN, trans. by GIBB, H. A. R. *Travels in Asia and Africa* (London, 1929).

BEAVER, W. N. *Unexplored New Guinea* (ed. 2; London, 1920).

BENEDICT, R. *The Guardian Spirit in North America* in *American Anthropological Association Memoirs,* No. 29 (Lancaster, Pennsylvania, 1923).

BEST, E. *Maori Magic* (1902) 34 *Transactions of the New Zealand Institute* (Wellington, New Zealand).

—— *The Maori* (1924) 5 *Memoirs of the Polynesian Society* (Wellington, New Zealand). 2 vols.

BLAIR, E. J., and ROBERTSON, J. A., eds. *The Philippine Islands, 1493–1803* (Cleveland, 1903–1909), II.

BOAS, F. *Contributions to the Ethnology of the Kwakiutl* (New York, 1925).

—— *Ethnology of the Kwakiutl* in *Thirty-fifth Annual Report of the United States Bureau of Ethnology,* 1913–1914, Parts 1 and 2 (Washington, 1921).

—— *Kwakiutl Tales* (New York, 1910).

—— *Tsimshian Mythology* in *Thirty-first Annual Report of the United States Bureau of Ethnology,* 1901–1910 (Washington, 1916).

—— *Report on the North-Western Tribes of Canada* (1888) 59; (1891) 61; (1898) 68 *Report of the British Association for the Advancement of Science* (London, 1889, 1892, 1899).

—— *The Social Organization and the Secret Societies of the Kwakiutl Indians* (Washington, 1895).

—— *What the Negro Has Done in Africa* (1903) 5 *The Ethical Record* (New York).

BOGORAS, W. *The Chukchee* in *Jesup North Pacific Expedition* VII (1904–1909).

BOVILL, E. W. *The Silent Trade of Wangara* (1929) 29 *Journal of the African Society* (London).

BRINKMANN, C. *Economic Incentives* in *Encyclopedia of the Social Sciences* (New York, 1931) V.

BROWN, A. R. *The Andaman Islanders* (Cambridge, 1922).

BROWN, G. *Melanesians and Polynesians* (London, 1910).

BROWNE, E. *A Journey to Dar-Für* in Pinkerton, J., *A General Collection of the Best and Most Interesting Voyages and Travels in All Parts of the World* XV (London, 1814). 17 vols. (1808–1814).

BÜCHER, K., trans. by WICKETT, S. M. *Industrial Revolution* (New York, 1901).

BUCKLAND, W. W. *Manual of Roman Private Law* (Cambridge, 1925).

—— *Text-Book of Roman Law* (Cambridge, 1921).

BURROWS, G. *On the Natives of the Upper Welle District of the Belgian Congo* (1889) 1 n.s. *Journal of the Royal Anthropological Institute* (London) 35 ff.
BURTON, R. F. *Wit and Wisdom from West Africa* (London, 1865).
BUTT-THOMPSON, F. W. *West African Secret Societies* (London, 1929).
CAIRNS, H. *Law and Anthropology*, 31 *Columbia Law Review*. Reprinted in *The Making of Man* (V. F. Calverton, ed.; New York, 1931).
CALISSE, C., trans. by REGISTER, L. R. *History of Italian Law* (Boston, 1928).
CALVERTON, V. F., ed. *The Making of Man* (New York, 1931).
CAPELLO, H., and IVENS, R., trans. by ELWES, A. *From Benguella to the Territory of Yacca* (London, 1882) I and II.
CARDINALL, A. W. *The Natives of the Northern Territories of the Gold Coast* (London, n.d.).
CHALMERS, J. *Pioneer Life and Work in New Guinea* (London, 1895).
CHAMPLAIN, SIEUR DE. *Voyages of Sieur de Champlain*, 1604–1610, in *Hakluyt Society Publications*, No. XXIII, ser. 1, trans. by Wilmere, A.
CHURCHILL, A. *Collection of Voyages* (London, 1732). 6 vols.
CLARIDGE, G. C. *Wild Brush Tribes of Tropical Africa* (London, 1922).
CODRINGTON, R. H. *The Melanesians* (Oxford, 1891).
COGOLLUDO. *See* MEANS, P. A.
COLENSO, W. *Maori Races of New Zealand* (1875) 1 *Transactions of the New Zealand Institute* (Wellington, New Zealand).
COXHEAD, J. C. C. *The Native Tribes of North-Eastern Rhodesia* (1914) *Occasional Papers, Royal Anthropological Institute of Great Britain and Ireland* (London) No. 5.
CRAWLEY, E. *The Mystic Rose* (ed. 2; London, 1927) I.
CROOKE, W. *Natives of Northern India* (London, 1907).
CUREAU, A. L., trans. by ANDREWS, E. *Savage Man in Central Africa* (London, 1915).
DALL, W. H. *Alaska and Its Resources* (Boston, 1870).
DANQUAH, J. B. *Akan Laws and Customs* (London, 1928).
DAVY, G. *La Foi jurée* (Paris, 1922).
DEANE, W. *Fijian Society* (London, 1921).
DENNETT, R. E. *At the Back of the Black Man's Mind* (London, 1906).
—— *Laws and Customs of the Fjort Bavili Family, Kingdom of Loango* (1901–1902) 1 *Journal of the African Society* (London) 272 ff.
DEWEY, J., and TUFTS, J. *Ethics* (New York, 1908).
DONNE, T. E. *The Maori, Past and Present* (London, 1927).
DORSEY, J. O. *Omaha Sociology* in *Third Annual Report of the Bureau of American Ethnology*, 1884 (Washington).
DU BOIS, C. A. *Tolowa Notes* in *American Anthropologist*, n.s., Vol. 34 (Menasha, Wisconsin, 1932).
DUNDAS, C. C. F. *Kilimanjaro and Its People* (London, 1924).
EDGE-PARTINGTON, J. *Note on Forged Ethnographical Specimens from the Pacific Islands* in *Man* Vol. I (1901) No. 56.
—— *Note on Forged Ethnographical Specimens from the Pacific Islands* in *Man* Vol. V (1901) No. 41.
—— *Maori Forgeries* in *Man* Vol. IX (1909) No. 31.
—— *Maori Forgeries* in *Man* Vol. X (1910) No. 31.
EDGE-PARTINGTON, J. and SMITH. *Forgeries of New Zealand Stone Implements* in *Man* Vol. I (1901) No. 92.
ELLIS, A. B. *The Ewe-Speaking Peoples on the Slave Coast of West Africa* (London, 1890).
—— *The Yoruba-Speaking Peoples* (London, 1894).

Ellis, W. *Polynesian Researches* (new ed.; London) IV.
Erdland, P. A. *Die Marshall-Insulaner* (Münster, 1914).
Erman, A. *Travels in Siberia* (London, 1848) I.
Evans, I. H. N. *Studies in Religion, Folklore and Custom in British North Borneo and the Malay Peninsula* (Cambridge, 1923).
Farabee, W. C. *The Central Caribs* (1924) 10 *Anthropological Publications of the University of Pennsylvania* (Philadelphia).
Firth, R. *Primitive Economics of the New Zealand Maori* (New York, 1929).
—— *Proverbs in Native Life* (1926) 37 *Folk-Lore* (London).
Franklin, John. *Journey to the Shores of the Polar Sea* (London, 1823).
Frazer, Sir J. G. *Man, God and Immortality* (London, 1927).
—— Preface to Malinowski, *Argonauts of the Western Pacific* (London, 1922).
—— *Psyche's Task* (London, 1909).
—— *Spirits of the Corn* (London, 1912) I.
—— *The Golden Bough* (ed. 3; London, 1915) I.
Frobenius, L., trans. by Blind, R. *The Voice of Africa* (London) I and II.
Gardiner, J. S. *The Natives of Rotuma* (1897–1898) 27 *Journal of the Royal Anthropological Institute of Great Britain and Ireland* (London).
Gatschet, A. S. *The Karankwa Indians* (1891) 1 *Papers of the Peabody Museum of American Archaeology and Ethnology* (Cambridge) No. 2.
Glotz, G. *Le Travail dans la Grèce ancienne,* trans. by Dobie, M. R., as *Ancient Greece at Work* (New York, 1926).
Goddard, P. E. *Indians of the Northwest Coast* (New York, 1924).
Godden, G. M. *Naga and Other Frontier Tribes of North-East India* (1897-1898) 27 *Journal of the Anthropological Institute* (London).
Goldenweiser, A. A. *Early Civilizations* (New York, 1926).
Gouldsbury, C., and Sheane, H. *The Great Plateau of Northern Rhodesia* (London, 1911).
Gras, W. S. B. *Anthropology and Economics* in *The Social Sciences* (ed. by W. F. Ogburn and A. Goldenweiser; Boston, 1927).
—— *Introduction to Economic History* (New York, 1922).
—— Review of Hoyt, E. E., *Primitive Trade* (1927) 42 *Political Science Quarterly.*
—— *The Silent Trade* (Edinburgh, 1903).
Gunther, E. *Further Analysis of the First Salmon Ceremony* (1928) 2 *University of Washington Publications in Anthropology* (Seattle).
Gutmann, B. *Das Recht der Dschagga* (Munich, 1926).
Haddon, A. C. (1904) 5 and 6 *Reports of the Cambridge Anthropological Expedition to Torres Straits* (Cambridge).
Hadfield, E. *Among the Natives of the Loyalty Group* (London, 1920).
Handy, E. S. C. *Polynesian Religion* (Honolulu, 1927).
Hartland, E. S. *Primitive Law* (London, 1924).
Heckwelder, J. G. E. *History of the Indian Natives, 1771* (1876) 12 *Memoirs of the Pennsylvania Historical Society* (Philadelphia).
Herodotus, trans. by Rawlinson, G. *The History of Herodotus,* II, 4 vols.
Hill-Tout, C. *British North America* (London) I.
Hilton-Simpson, M. W. *Land and Peoples of the Kasai* (London, 1911).
Hobhouse, L. T. *Morals in Evolution* (ed. 4; New York, 1924).
Hobley, C. W. *Bantu Beliefs and Magic* (London, 1922).
—— *Ethnology of the A-Kamba* (Cambridge, 1910).
Hogbin, H. I. *Law and Order in Polynesia* (New York, 1934).
—— *Sorcery at Ongtong, Java* in *American Anthropologist,* n.s., Vol. 34 (Menasha, Wisconsin, 1932).

HOLDSWORTH, W. S. *History of English Law* (Boston, 1924) IV.
HOLLIS, A. C. *The Nandi* (Oxford, 1909) No. 41.
HOMER, trans. by BUTCHER and LANG. *The Odyssey.*
HOWITT, A. W. *The Natives of South-East Australia* (London, 1905).
HOYT, E. E. *Primitive Trade* (London, 1926).
HUVELIN, P. *Essai historique sur le droit des marches et des foires* (Paris, 1897).
ISHMAEL, G. C. *Old Customs of the Baganda* (1910) 10 *Man* (London).
IVENS, W. G. *Melanesians of the South-East Solomon Islands* (London, 1927).
JANE, C., ed. *Select Documents Illustrating the Four Voyages of Columbus, Hakluyt Society Publications,* ser. 2, LXV (London, 1930).
JENNESS, D., and BALLANTYNE, A. *The Northern d'Entrecasteaux* (Oxford, 1920).
JOCHELSON, W. *The Yukaghir* in *Jesup North Pacific Expedition* IX (New York, 1926).
JOHNSTON, H., ed. *George Grenfell and the Congo* (London, 1908) I and II.
JUNOD, H. A. *The Life of a South African Tribe* (ed. 2; London).
KEASBEY, L. M. *Prestige Value* (1903) 17 *Quarterly Journal of Economics.*
KENTON, E. *The Indians of North America* (New York, 1927).
KIDD, D. *The Essential Kafir* (London, 1904).
KINGSLEY, M. H. *Travels in West Africa* (London, 1900).
—— *West African Studies* (ed. 2; London, 1901).
KNORRINGA, H. *Emporos, Data on Trade and Trader in Greek Literature from Homer to Aristotle* (Amsterdam, 1926).
KOCOUREK, A., and WIGMORE, J. H. *Primitive and Ancient Legal Institutions* (Boston, 1915).
KOEHNE, C. *Markt-, Kaufmanns- und Handelsrecht in primitiven Kulturverhältnissen* (1895) *Zeitschrift für die vergleichende Rechtswissenschaft* (Stuttgart) Vol. XI, 196 ff. Translated in part in KOCOUREK, A., and WIGMORE, J. H., *Primitive and Ancient Legal Institutions* (Boston, 1915) 420–434.
KROPOTKIN, P. R., trans. by FRIEDLAND, L. S. *Ethics, Origin and Development* (New York, 1926).
LANCASTER, SIR JAMES. *Voyages of Sir James Lancaster* in *Hakluyt Society Publications,* No. LVI, ser. 1, ed. by CLEMENT R. MARKHAM.
LANDTMANN, G. *The Folk-Tales of the Kiwai Papuans* (1917) 47 *Acta Societatis Scientiarum Fennicae* (Helsingfors), No. 467A.
LASCH, R. *Das Marktwesen auf den primitiven Kultur-Stufen* (1906) 9 *Zeitschrift für Socialwissenschaft* (Berlin).
LAWES, W. G. *Notes on New Guinea* (1880) 2 n.s. *Proceedings of the Royal Geographical Society* (London).
LECKY, W. E. H. *History of European Morals* (ed. 3; New York, 1924).
LE JEUNE, C. *Jesuit Relations* (1663) V. Reprinted in Kenton, E., *The Indians of North America* (New York, 1927) I.
LEROY, O. *Essai d'introduction critique à l'étude de l'économie primitive* (Paris, 1925).
LEVY-BRUHL, L., trans. by CLARE, L. A. *Primitive Mentality* (London, 1923).
LING-ROTH, H. *Note on the Occurrence of Forgeries in the Pacific* in *Man,* Vol. I (1901), No. 93.
LIPPMANN, WALTER. *A Preface to Morals* (New York, 1929).
LOEB, E. M. *Tribal Initiations and Secret Societies* (1929) 25 *University of California Publications in American Archaeology and Ethnology,* No. 3.
LOPES, M. M. *Usages and Customs of the Natives of Sena* (1906–1907) 6 *Journal of the African Society* (London) 350 ff.
LOWIE, R. H. *Anthropology and Law* in *The Social Sciences* (ed. by W. F. Ogburn and A. Goldenweiser; Boston, 1927).
—— *Primitive Religion* (New York, 1924).

Lowie, R. H. (*Continued*). *Primitive Society* (New York, 1925).
—— *Incorporeal Property in Primitive Society* (1928) 37 *Yale Law Journal* 551.
McClennan. *Studies in Ancient History* (London, 1896).
Maine, H. *Early History of Institutions* (London, 1875).
—— *Village Communities* (New York, 1876).
Malinowski, B. *Argonauts of the Western Pacific* (London, 1922).
—— *Crime and Custom in Savage Society* (London, 1926).
—— *Economic Aspect of the Intichiuma Ceremonies* in *Festschrift für Tillagnad Edward Westermarck* (Helsingfors, 1911).
—— *Marriage* in *The Encyclopaedia Britannica* (ed. 14; 1929).
—— *Primitive Psychology* (New York, 1926).
—— *The Natives of Mailu* (1915) 39 *Transactions of the Royal Society of Southern Australia.*
—— *The Primitive Economics of the Trobriand Islanders* (1921) 31 *The Economic Journal* (London).
Man, E. H. *On the Original Inhabitants of the Andaman Islands* (1893) 12 *Journal of the Royal Anthropological Institute* (London).
Mauss, M. *Essai sur le don* (1923–1924) 1 n.s. *L'Année Sociologique* (Paris, 1925).
Mayer, Fr. *Zulu Proverbs* (1912) 7 *Anthropos* (Vienna).
Mead, Margaret. *Growing Up in New Guinea* (New York, 1930).
—— *The Changing Culture of an Indian Tribe* (New York, 1932).
Mead, M. *More Comprehensive Field Methods* in *American Anthropologist,* n.s., Vol. 35 (Menasha, Wisconsin, 1933).
Means, P. A. *History of the Spanish Conquest of Yucatan* (1917) 7 *Papers of the Peabody Museum of Archaeology and Ethnology* (Cambridge, Massachusetts). Quoted by Cogolludo.
Meek, C. F. *A Sudanese Kingdom* (London, 1931).
Mendaña de Neira, A. *The Discovery of the Solomon Islands* in *Hakluyt Society Publications,* ser. 2, VII and VIII (London, 1901) trans. by Lord Amherst.
Mills, J. P. *The Lhota Nagas* (London, 1922).
Milne, L. *The House of an Eastern Clan* (Oxford, 1924).
Moret, A., and Davy, G. *From Tribe to Empire* (New York, 1926).
Morice, A. G. *The Great Déné Race* (1910) 5 *Anthropos* (Vienna) 643 ff.
Moss, C. R. *Nabaloi Law and Ritual* (1922) 15 *University of California Publications in American Archaeology and Ethnology,* No. 3.
Moszkowski, M. *Vom Wirtschaftsleben der primitiven Völker* (Jena, 1911).
Müller-Lyer, F., trans. by Lake, E. C., and Lake, H. A. *The History of Social Development* (New York, 1921).
Neuhauss, R. *Deutsch Neu-Guinea* (Berlin, 1911) I.
Osgood, C. *Tanaina Culture* in *American Anthropologist,* n.s., Vol. 35 (Menasha, Wisconsin, 1933).
Ostermann, L. *The Navajo Indians of New Mexiko and Arizona* (1908) 3 *Anthropos* (Vienna) 857 ff.
Page, E. D. *Trade Morals* (New Haven, 1914).
Parsons, E. C., ed. *American Indian Life* (New York, 1922).
Polack, J. S. *Manners and Customs of the New Zealanders* (London, 1840) II.
Post, A. H. *Afrikanische Jurisprudenz* (Oldenburg, 1887) II.
—— *Grundriss der ethnologischen Jurisprudenz* (Oldenburg, 1894–1895).
Pound, R. *Law and Morals* (Chapel Hill, North Carolina, 1924).
Powdermaker, H. *Feasts in New Ireland* in *American Anthropologist,* n.s., Vol. 34 (Menasha, Wisconsin, 1932).

PROYART, ABBÉ L. B. *History of Loango,* trans. in PINKERTON, J., *A General Collection of . . . Voyages and Travels,* XVI (London, 1808–1814). 17 vols.
RADIN, M. *The Lawful Pursuit of Gain* (Boston, 1931).
RADIN, P. *Primitive Man as Philosopher* (New York, 1927).
—— *The Story of the American Indian* (New York, 1927).
RATTRAY, R. S. *Ashanti* (Oxford, 1923).
—— *Ashanti Law and Constitution* (Oxford, 1929).
—— *Ashanti Proverbs* (Oxford, 1916).
—— *Hausa Folk-Lore, Customs, Proverbs, Etc., Collected and Transliterated with English Translation and Notes* (Oxford, 1913). 2 vols.
RATZEL, F., trans. by BUTLER, A. J. T. *The History of Mankind* (London, 1898) II and III. 3 vols.
RAVENSTEIN, J. A., ed. *The Strange Adventures of Andrew Battell, Hakluyt Society Publications,* ser. 2, VI (London, 1901).
RILEY, H. T. *Memorials of London* (London, 1867).
RINK, H. *Tales and Traditions of the Eskimo* (London, 1875).
RIVERS, W. H. R. *History of Melanesian Society* (Cambridge, 1914) I and II.
—— *Psychology and Ethnology* (London, 1926).
—— *The Todas* (London, 1906).
ROBERTS, H. H. *Karuk First Salmon Ceremony* in *American Anthropologist,* n.s., Vol. 34 (Menasha, Wisconsin, 1932).
ROSCOE, J. *The Baganda* (London, 1911).
—— *The Soul of Central Africa* (London, 1922).
ROTH, H. L. *The Natives of Sarawak and British North Borneo* (London, 1896) II.
ROTH, W. E. *Additional Studies of the Arts, Crafts and Customs of the Guiana Indians* (1929) Bull. 91, *Bureau of American Ethnology* (Washington).
—— *Arts and Crafts of Guinea Indians* in (1924) *Thirty-eighth Annual Report of the Bureau of American Ethnology 1916–1917* (Washington).
ROWLEY, H. *The Story of the Universities' Mission to Central Africa* (ed. 2; London, 1867).
RUSDEN, G. W. *History of New Zealand* (London, 1883) I.
RUSSELL, R. V. *The Tribes and Castes of the Central Provinces of India* (London, 1916) II, III, IV.
ST. JOHN, S. *Life in the Forests of the Far East* (ed. 2; London, 1863) II.
SAPIR, E. *Sayach' Apis, a Nootka Trader* in *American Indian Life* (E. C. Parsons, ed.; New York, 1922).
SARBAH, J. M. *Fanti Customary Laws* (ed. 2; London, 1904).
SCHAPERA, I. *The Khoisan Peoples of South Africa* (London, 1930).
SCHECHTER, F. I. *Oriental Trade Morals* in *Virginia Law Review,* Vol. XIX (Charlottesville, Virginia, 1933).
SCHURTZ, H. *Alterklassen und Männerbunde* (Berlin, 1902; London, 1910) Part 1.
SCHWEITZER, A., trans. by CAMPION, C. T. *On the Edge of the Primeval Forest* (London, 1922).
SELIGMANN, C. G. *The Melanesians of British New Guinea* (Cambridge, 1910).
SIMSON, A. *Travels in the Wilds of Ecuador* (London, 1886).
SMITH, ADAM. *The Wealth of Nations* (Everyman ed.; New York, 1914).
SMITH, E. W., and DALE, A. M. *The Ila-Speaking Peoples of Northern Rhodesia* (London, 1920) I and II.
SMITH, S. P. *Incidents in the History of Horehore Pa* (1906) 15 *Journal of the Polynesian Society* (Wellington, New Zealand).
SMYTH, R. B. *The Aborigines of Victoria* (London, 1878) I.
SOHM, R., trans. by LEDLIE, J. R. *The Institutes* (ed. 3; Oxford, 1907).

SOMLO, F. *Der Güterverkehr in der Urgesellschaft* (1909) 1 *Travaux de l'Institut de Sociologie, Notes et Mémoirs,* fasc. 8 (Brussels). Trans. in part in KOCOUREK, A., and WIGMORE, J. H., *Primitive and Ancient Legal Institutions* (Boston, 1915).

SPECK, F. G. *Ethical Attributes of The Labrador Indians* in *American Anthropologist,* n.s., Vol. 35 (Menasha, Wisconsin, 1933).

SPENCER, B. *Wanderings in Wild Australia* (London, 1928) I.

SPENCER, HERBERT. *Principles of Ethics* (New York, 1898).

—— *The Morals of Trade,* and *Railway Morals* in *Essays: Moral, Political and Aesthetic* (New York, 1883).

STANLEY, H. M. *The Congo and the Founding of Its Free State* (New York, 1885) I.

—— *Through the Dark Continent* (New York, 1878) II.

STEVENSON, R. L. *In the South Seas* (London, 1924).

STITES, S. H. *Economics of the Iroquois* (1905) 1 *Bryn Mawr Collection of Monographs,* No. 3.

SWANTON, J. R. *Haida Songs* (1912) 3 *Publications of the American Ethnological Society* (Leyden).

—— *Social Conditions, Beliefs, and Linguistic Relationship of the Tlingit Indians* in *Twenty-sixth Annual Report of the Bureau of American Ethnology* 1904–1905 (Washington).

—— *The Tlingit Indians* in *Twenty-sixth Annual Report of the Bureau of American Ethnology* (Washington, 1908).

TALBOT, P. A. *The Peoples of Southern Nigeria* (Oxford) III and IV.

TATE, H. R. *Native Law of the Southern Gikuyu* (1909–1910) 9 *Journal of the African Society* (London).

THEAL, G. M. *History of Africa South of the Zambezi* (ed. 3; London, 1916) I.

THOMAS, N. W. *Edo-Speaking Peoples of Nigeria* (London, 1910) Part 1.

—— *Ibo-Speaking Peoples of Nigeria* (London, 1913–1914) Parts 1 and 4.

—— *The Market in African Law and Custom* (1908) 9 n.s. *Journal of the Society of Comparative Legislation* (London) 90 ff.

—— *Sierra Leone, Timne and Other Tribes* (London, 1916) Part 1.

THOMSON, A. S. *The Story of New Zealand* (London, 1859) I.

THOMSON, B. W. *The Fijians* (London, 1908).

THURNWALD, R. *Banaro Society* (1916) 3 *Memoirs of the American Anthropological Association.*

—— *Economics in Primitive Communities* (Oxford, 1932).

TORDAY, E. *Camp and Trail in Savage Africa* (Philadelphia, 1913).

—— *On the Trail of the Bushongo* (Philadelphia, 1925).

TORDAY, E., and JOYCE, T. A. *Notes on the Ethnography of the Ba-Mbala* (1905) 7 n.s. *Journal of the Royal Anthropological Institute* (London) 398 ff.

TREMAINE, A. J. N. *Hausa Superstitions and Customs* (ed. 2; London, 1913).

VANOVERBERGH, M. *Negritos of the Northern Luzon* (1925) 20 *Anthropos* (Vienna).

VON FALLATI. *Keime des Völkerrechts bei wilden und halbwilden Stämmen* (1850) 6 *Zeitschrift für die gesammte Staatswissenschaft* (Tübingen) 151 ff.

WALLIS, W. D. *Ethical Aspect of Chilkat Culture* (1918) 29 *American Journal of Psychology* (Albany) 66 ff.

WARD, H. *Ethnographical Notes Relating to the Congo Tribes* (1894–1895) 24 *Journal of the Royal Anthropological Institute* (London) 285 ff.

WEEKS, J. H. *Among the Congo Cannibals* (London, 1913).

—— *Among the Primitive Bakongo* (London, 1914).

—— *Congo Life and Folk-Lore* (London, 1911).

WESTERMARCK, EDWARD. *History of Human Marriage* (ed. 5; London, 1921).

—— *Ritual and Belief in Morocco* (London) I and II.

WESTERMARCK, EDWARD (*Continued*). *The Origin and Development of the Moral Ideas* (ed. 2; London, 1926).
—— *Wit and Wisdom in Morocco* (London, 1930).
WHITFIELD, G. M. *South African Native Law* (Cape Town, 1929).
WHITEHEAD, G. *In the Nicobar Islands* (London, 1924).
WILLIAMS, F. E. *Orokaiva Society* (London, 1930).
WISSLER, C. *Societies of the Plains Indians* (1916) 11 *Anthropology Papers of the American Museum of Natural History* (New York).
—— *The Social Life of the Blackfoot Indians* (1911) 7 *Anthropology Papers of the American Museum of Natural History* (New York).
WOOD, H. G. *Limitation of Actions* (ed. 4; Albany) I.
WOOD, W. *New-England's Prospect* (London, 1634); (1865) 1 *Prince Society Publications* (Boston).

NOTES TO SCHECHTER ESSAY

[1] In Westermarck's monumental *The Origin and Development of the Moral Ideas,* chapters 30 and 31 present some material under the heading of "Truth and Good Faith," but it is only incidental and of a very general nature, consisting mainly of an accumulation of dicta concerning the honesty of this tribe or the dishonesty of that tribe in trade or otherwise. Chapter 36 deals with the moral duty of industry in contradistinction to idleness. Hobhouse, *Morals in Evolution,* and Lecky, *History of European Morals,* practically ignore any specific inquiry in this field, in which, nevertheless, Herbert Spencer showed considerable interest. See his *Principles of Ethics,* also his essays on "The Morals of Trade" and "Railway Morals."

[2] Lippmann, *Preface to Morals,* p. 88. Mr. Lippmann's classification of business as one of the "lost provinces" of religion is based on a very questionable assumption, which the present writer hopes to discuss elsewhere.

Page (*Trade Morals,* pp. vi–vii) likewise points out that "business acts . . . may make three-fourths of civilized life." Unfortunately what might have been a valuable starting point on this subject is rendered so obscure by Page's unwieldy and artificial terminology, often ill adapted from Sumner's *Folkways,* that frequently not even his four pages (xii–xv) of "definitions" give any clue to his argument.

[3] Dewey and Tufts, *Ethics,* p. 12.

[4] Frazer, Preface (p. x) to Malinowski, *Argonauts of the Western Pacific.*

[5] Of the enormous literature on this whole subject of primitive economic life and rationality, see particularly Bücher, *Industrial Evolution,* chapters 1 and 2, and criticisms of his theories in Moszkowski, *Vom Wirtschaftsleben der primitiven Völker;* Leroy, *Essai . . . de l'Economie Primitive;* Malinowski, not only throughout his *Argonauts . . . ,* but also in his *Economic Aspects . . . Intichiuma Ceremonies,* and *Primitive Economics . . . Trobriand Islanders,* p. 1; Hoyt, *Primitive Trade;* Firth, *Primitive Economics . . . New Zealand Maori;* Brinkmann, *Economic Incentives,* pp. 330–332. Perhaps Malinowski seems to go unduly to the other extreme when he speaks of the "constant economic undertow to all public and private activities—this materialistic streak which runs through all their doings" (*Trobriand Islanders,* p. 8). But see Mead's recent account of the Manus of the Admiralty Islands, northeast of New Guinea, an "untouched" and "essentially a primitive society," to whom, she says, "trade is the most important thing in life; trade with far-away islands, trade with the land people, trade with the next village, trade with his relatives-in-law, trade with his relatives. His house roof is stacked with pots, his shelves piled with grass skirts, his boxes filled with dogs' teeth. The spirit of his ancestor presides over his wealth and chastises him if he fails to use it wisely and well. When he speaks of his wife he mentions the size of the betrothal payment which was made for her, when he quarrels with his neighbours he boasts of the number of large exchanges he has made for her. When he speaks of his sister he says, 'I give her sago and she gives me bead-work'; when he speaks of his dead father he mentions the huge burial payment he made for him. When he angers the spirit of a neighbour's house he atones in pigs and oil, or boxes and axes. The whole of life, his most intimate relation to people, his conception of places, his evaluation for his guarding spirits, all fall under the head of *kawas,* 'exchange' " (*Growing Up In New Guinea,* p. 81). See also the remarkable incantation for the prosperity of a youth, *ibid.,* pp. 200–201. *Cf.* Weeks, *Among Congo Cannibals,* p. 143; and *infra* note 41, for similar glimpses of the economic education of primitive children. *Cf.* Mead's plea for a broadening of the traditional inquiries of field ethnologists in "more comprehensive field methods" in *American Anthropologist,* n.s., XXXV, 1.

[6] Post (*Grundriss . . . Jurisprudenz,* II, 684–685), considers this branch as quite outside the field of ethnological jurisprudence. Koehne (*Markt-, Kaufmanns- und Handelsrecht* . . . pp. 196 ff., trans., in part, Kocourek and Wigmore, pp. 420–434) holds "Silent Trade" to be "of no significance for jurisprudence" and deals almost exclusively with "market law." Hartland *(Primitive Law)* gives less than two pages (115–116) to barter —in which he actually does not discuss barter but currency—and tucked away in a chapter on "Procedure" is some information (pp. 181 ff.) concerning the primitive debtor and creditor. Lowie *(Anthropology and Law)* ignores primitive commercial law, but his highly interesting studies in the law of incorporeal property in primitive society ([1928] 37 Yale L. J. 551, and *Primitive Society,* pp. 235 ff.) are a most valuable contribution to the history of the law of patent, copyright, and unfair competition. See also R. Benedict, "The Guardian Spirit in North America," *American Anthropological Association Memoirs,* No. 29, pp. 77–78. Somlo (*Der Güterverkehr in der Urgesellschaft,* trans. Kocourek and Wigmore, pp. 439 ff.) correcly points out the overemphasis that has been placed on the juristic form of primitive transactions, and stresses the importance from the legal standpoint of seemingly naïve and elementary economic life. Malinowski, in particular, has developed this thought and has put primitive economic custom in its proper relation to primitive commercial law. See not only his works cited *supra* note 4, but especially his *Crime and Custom in Savage Society. Cf.* H. I. Hogbin, *Law and Order in Polynesia,* p. 77; Cairns, *Law and Anthropology,* pp. 37–38. For "market law" as a later development of primitive commercial law, see pp. 14–22.

[7] "It is certainly a difficult task to sketch the moral qualities of a nation, of which a few tribes or bands only were known to the white people, and under circumstances which make us doubt the veracity of the informants. Indeed who would be inclined to believe what one man says about another, whom he is constantly trying to rob & kill, & who is on that account cruelly punished by him from time to time?" (Gatschet, *The Karankwa Indians,* p. 64). "The disposition of early explorers and missionaries is to describe the races with whom they came in contact as living in a state of savage anarchy, the motive of travellers being to excuse their own rapacity and cruelty; and of missionaries to vindicate their iconoclasm and to magnify their courage and self-sacrifice. 'Nothing,' says McClennan *(Studies in Ancient History),* 'is more common in these old narratives than to find the peoples who were being sacrificed to European cupidity described as living in a purely animal state, without government, laws, or religion, and yet the student will sometimes be able to spell out from these very narratives themselves that the peoples so described were intensely religious, and that they dwelt under the constant pressure of a rigid body of customary law, and what we would call a highly developed system of constitutional government?"—Thompson, B. W., *The Fijians,* p. 387.

[8] Franklin, *Journey . . . Polar Sea,* p. 475.

[9] Proverbs are not merely highly informative as to primitive trade practices but are in themselves a potent factor in social control, "a means of enforcement of social conduct." "The maxim, being of its very nature a summary or crystallization of a piece of communal wisdom, represented in itself a long popular judgement." See Firth, *Proverbs . . .,* pp. 258–259; also Westermarck, *Wit and Wisdom in Morocco,* p. 63; Weeks, . . . *Primitive Bakongo,* p. 79.

[10] Andersen, *Maori Life in Ao-tea,* p. 288.

[11] Rattray, *Ashanti Proverbs,* p. 162.

[12] Rattray, *Ashanti,* p. 304.

[13] Ellis, A. B., *The Ewe-Speaking Peoples . . .,* p. 260, No. 32.

[14] Hollis, *The Nandi,* No. 41.

[15] Crooke, *Natives of Northern India,* p. 131.

[16] Burton, *Wit and Wisdom from West Africa,* p. 8, No. 23.

[17] *Ibid.,* p. 166, No. 175. The Ashanti likewise warn that "when two wise men are dividing up a yam between them, one turns a piece over and puts it down (for the other), but the other again turns it over and exposes the other side" (Rattray, *Proverbs,* p. 155, No. 599). The Solomon Islanders even have a proverb concerning the cornering of the yam market: " 'Barter like Paru hoi i'e,' which is founded on the story of a Port Adam woman of that time, who got in first at the fish market with a load of shell fish and secured all the taro and yams of the buyers. As she paddled away canoes arrived bringing fish."—Ivens, *Melanesians . . . ,* p. 403.

[18] Ellis, A. B., *The Yoruba-Speaking Peoples,* p. 228, No. 135.

[19] *Ibid.,* p. 230, No. 147. No Yoruba trader acknowledges that he has sold all his goods. "When asked, he will only say, 'Trade is a little better.' "—*Ibid.,* pp. 236–237.

[20] Smith, E. W., and Dale, *The Ila-Speaking Peoples . . . Rhodesia,* II, 319, 323. The Zulu say that "Cunning men do not deal with each other."—Mayer, *Zulu Proverbs,* p. 257, No. 4.

[21] Adam Smith, *The Wealth of Nations,* I, 12.

[22] Hoyt, p. 135. *Cf.* Bücher, p. 88.

[23] Thucydides, I, 2 ff.

[24] For various aspects of this controversy see Bücher and his critics, *supra* note 5; see also Müller-Lyer, *Social Development;* Gras, *Introduction to Economic History,* and *Anthropology and Economics,* p. 24; also Gras's review of Hoyt, *Primitive Trade* ([1927] 42 *Pol. Sci. Q.* 314); Thurnwald, *Economics in Primitive Communities,* pp. xi–xii.

[25] See Malinowski, . . . *Trobriand Islanders,* p. 15.

[26] For example, in both the potlatch and the *kula* transactions discussed hereafter (pp. 573 ff.) the property involved has no utility value: on the contrary, potlatch entails a wanton destruction of property, while many *kula* arm-shells are too small or too large and shell strings too cumbersome to be worn. In the Trobriand Islands, furthermore, yams are accumulated merely for display in special yam-houses until they decay; fish—even when rotten—likewise have a display value (see Malinowski, *Argonauts,* pp. 168–169, 187). *Cf.* Keasbey, *Prestige Value,* p. 456; Stites, *Economics . . . Iroquois,* pp. 66–68; Firth, *Primitive Economics . . . ,* pp. 386 ff.

[27] Malinowski, *Argonauts,* p. 84.

[28] Firth (*Primitive Economics . . . ,* pp. 14–15, 418) insists that gift-exchange is not a mere transition between pure gift and barter, but "an integral institution, standing in direct relation to a complex set of ideas and emotional attitudes, and quite in equilibrium with the other structural elements of the social life." As will be seen later, in our study of such ceremonial gift-exchanges as the Indian potlatch, the Trobriand *kula,* and Fijian *solevu,* actual barter may exist side by side or in connection with gift-exchange. *Cf.* Somlo, trans., p. 439.

[29] I cannot discuss here the interesting problem of the relation of the bride-price, of marriage by purchase, and of the mutual exchange of women to the principle of mutuality in gift-exchange. See Westermarck, . . . *Human Marriage,* II, chapter 22; Thurnwald, *Banaro Society;* and Malinowski, *Marriage.*

[30] Radin, M., *The Lawful Pursuit of Gain,* p. 5.

[31] *The Odyssey,* XXIV, 283; *cf.* Gotz, G., *Le Travail dans la Grèce ancienne* (tr. as *Ancient Greece at Work*), pp. 54–55; H. Knorringa, *Emporos* (Amsterdam, 1926), p. 4.

[32] See Mauss, *Essai sur le Don,* p. 30; Malinowski, *Crime and Custom . . . ,* chapters 3, 4, 8, 9; Thurnwald, *Banaro Society,* also *Economics in Primitive Communities,* p. xi; he

there regards "the absence of any desire to make profits either from production or exchange" as "a characteristic feature of primitive economics." *Cf.* Mead, *The Changing Culture . . .*, p. 32.

[33] Le Jeune, *Jesuit Relations*, V, 179, reprinted in Kenton, *The Indians of North America*, I, 87. *Cf. Voyages of Sieur de Champlain*, II, 110–111: "In this place [Saco, Maine, in September, 1605] Sieur de Pontrincourt secured a prisoner that Onemechin had, to whom Messamouët [a chief] made presents of kettles, hatchets, knifes and other things. Onemechin reciprocated the same with Indian corn, squashes and Brazilian beans; which was not very satisfactory to Messamouët, who went away very ill-disposed towards them for not properly recognizing his presents, and with the intention of making war upon them in a short time. For these nations give only in exchange for something in return, except to those who have done them a special service, as by assisting them in their wars." Care should be taken to distinguish between this principle of equivalence in gift-exchange and the generous aid freely given to fellow-Indians in distress. Thus, see the Moravian missionary, Heckwelder, . . . *Indian Natives*, p. 120: "The Indians are not only just, they are also in many respects a generous people, and cannot see the sick and the aged suffer for want of clothing. To such they will give a blanket, a shirt, a pair of legging, mocksens, &c. Otherwise, when they make presents it is done with a view to receive an equivalent in return, and the receiver is given to understand what that ought to be. In making presents to strangers, they are content with some trifle in token of remembrance; but when they give anything to a trader, they at least expect double the value in return, saying that he can afford to do it, since he had cheated them so often."

[34] Morice, *The Great Déné Race*, p. 643.

[35] Simson, *Travels . . . Ecuador*, p. 99.

[36] Gardiner, *The Natives of Rotuma*, pp. 408–409. *Cf* Rowley, . . . *Universities' Mission to Central Africa*, pp. 162–163; Capello and Ivens, *From Benguella to . . . Yacca*, I, 116; Hilton-Simpson, *Land . . . Kasai*, p. 174; Chalmers, *Pioneer Life . . . New Guinea*, pp. 90, 108; H. Powdermaker, in *American Anthropologist*, n.s., XXXIV, 243.

[37] Firth, *Proverbs . . .*, pp. 250–251. *Cf.* Rusden, *New Zealand*, I, 14; Polack, *Manners . . . New Zealanders*, II, 157–158. Firth, *Primitive Economics . . .*, *s.v.* "gift-exchange" and "gift"; Colenso, *Maori Races*, I, 354–355.

[38] See, generally, Mauss, p. 30, containing much valuable material on reciprocal communal feasts and gifts; Malinowski, *Crime and Custom . . .*, chapters 4, 8, 9.

[39] *Cf.* Goldenweiser, *Early Civilization*, p. 61, note 2: "Strange as these ideas may appear to the modern mind, they are not by any means foreign to our socio-economic life. While the economic distinctions current to our society are unknown among these Indian tribes, the 'conspicuous waste' (to speak with Mr. Veblen) attendant upon expenditure of property among our rich, presents a close parallel to the potlatch psychology of the Haida and Tlingit."

[40] For descriptions of the potlatch system see the following works by Boas: *Social Organization . . . Kwakiutl Indians*, pp. 341 ff.; *Ethnology . . . Kwakiutl Indians*, Index, *s.v.* "Potlatch"; *Tsimshian Mythology*, pp. 511, 537 ff., and other references to Boas hereafter; Swanton, *Social Conditions . . . Tlingit Indians*, pp. 434 ff.; Radin, P., . . . *American Indian*, chapter 14; Sapir, *Nootka Trader*, p. 297. For analyses of the sociological, ethical, and legal significance of the potlatch, see Mauss, p. 30; Davy, *La Foi Jurée*, chapter 3; Moret and Davy, *From Tribe to Empire*, pp. 90 ff.; Adam, *Potlatch*, p. 27.

[41] Boas, *Social Organization . . .*, p. 343.

In his very cradle the Indian child of the Northwest is lulled to sleep with songs promising him wealth or gloating upon the worldly acumen of his grandsires or family (Swanton, *Haida Songs*, pp. 47–52). The names of the chiefs are in themselves significant:

"Giving-Wealth"; "Whose-Body-Is-All-Wealth"; "Wealthiest"; "Wealth-Coming-Up"; "About-Whose-Property-People-Talk"; "Throwing-Away-Property"; "Satiating"; "Envy"; "Too-Much"; "From-Whom-Presents-Are-Expected"; "Property-Giver-Of-The-World." See Boas, *Kwakiutl Tales,* pp. 255, 323, 415; Radin, P., ... *American Indian,* p. 323. Among the Tolowa Indians of California "sometimes people go crazy wishing so hard to be rich."—C. A. Du Bois, "Tolowa Notes," *American Anthropologist,* n.s., XXXIV, 256.

42 Boas, *Tribes of Canada* (1898) 68 *Report* 681–682. Of course the economic aspect of the potlatch system can be overdone. "Potlatch is an extremely complex institution, at once ritual, legal, economic and social" (Moret and Davy, p. 90). It is, however, necessary to limit ourselves here to the phase concerned with the exchange of goods—though fully recognizing that "men exchange goods only to exchange titles and acquire rank."—*Loc. cit.*

The climax of a great potlatch is the destruction or presentation to a rival chief of a "copper"—intrinsically, a worthless and useless metal plate, but symbolic of the tremendous wealth in blankets with which it has been purchased. Each transfer of the copper enhances its value and endows it with a new name. The copper named "All-Other-Coppers-Are-Ashamed-To-Look-At-It" was worth 7500 blankets, that named "Making-The-House-Empty-Of-Blankets" only 5000 blankets (Boas, *Social Organization* ... Kwakiutl ..., p. 344). *Cf.* Boas, *Kwakiutl Tales,* pp. 91, 93: "... Then Wā'xwid invited [people] in, and he gave a potlatch, and then he sold his copper Found. Causing Destitution was named "Found," and then the copper had two names. It was called Causing-Destitution because there was nothing that was not paid for it. It made the houses empty. Twenty canoes was its price; and twenty slaves was its price; and also ten coppers tied to the end was its price; and twenty lynx-skins, and twenty marmot-skins, and twenty sewed blankets, was its price; and twenty mink blankets was its price; and one hundred boards was its price; and forty wide planks was its price; and twenty boxes of dried berries added to it, and twenty boxes of clover, and also ten boxes of hemlock-bark, was its price; and forty boxes of grease was its price; and one hundred painted boxes was its price; and two hundred mats was its price; and dried salmon not to be counted was its price; and two hundred cedar blankets was its price; and two hundred dishes was its price. That was the amount of its price. And that was given away by Wā'xwid to the tribes."

The purchase of a high-priced copper is based on credit machinery of the type already described. "When the buyer is ready," says Boas, "he gives to the owner of the copper blankets about one-sixth of the total value of the copper. This is called 'making a pillow' for the copper ...; or 'making a feather bed' ... or 'the harpoon line at which game is hanging' ..., meaning that in the same manner the copper is attached to the long line of blankets; or 'taken in the hand, in order to lift the copper.' ... The owner of the copper loans these blankets out, and when he has called them in again, he repays the total amount received, with 100 per cent interest, to the purchaser. On the following day the tribes assemble for the sale of the copper. The prescribed proceeding is as follows: The buyer offers first the lowest prices at which the copper was sold. The owner declares that he is satisfied, but his friends demand by degrees higher and higher prices, according to all the previous sales of the copper. On the following day all the blankets which have been paid for the copper must be distributed by the owner among his own tribe, paying to them his old debts first, and, if the amount is sufficient, giving new presents. This is called 'doing a great thing.' "—Boas, *Social Organization ... Kwakiutl ...,* p. 346.

43 Said a Kwakiutl chief to his family group: "You will give me this property for the potlatch ... for it will not be in my name. It will be in your name, and you will become famous among the tribes, when it is said that you have given your property for a pot-

latch, that I may invite the tribes."—Boas, *Ethnology . . . Kwakiutl,* p. 341, quoted by Mauss, p. 39, note 2.

44 See Boas, *Tribes of Canada* (1888) 59 *Report* 834–835.

45 See Goddard, *Indians . . . Northwest Coast,* p. 133; Hill-Tout, *British North America,* I, 155.

46 See Boas, *Tribes of Canada* (1891) 61 *Report* 415.

47 Boas, *Social Organization . . . Kwakiutl . . . ,* pp. 341–342.

48 Boas, . . . *Ethnology . . . Kwakiutl,* pp. 349, 351.

49 Mauss, p. 108; Davy, p. 217.

50 Adam, p. 43, says that the obligation to repay potlatch loans is not merely a customary ("sittliche") but a legal obligation ("eine Rechtspflicht").

51 Boas, *Social Organization . . . Kwakiutl . . . ,* pp. 681–683.

52 See Mauss, pp. 100–110; Davy, pp. 238–239. Throughout this study we shall find ridicule as a potent factor in the prevention of unfair trade. For the primitive fear of ridicule, generally, the effectiveness of ridicule as a sanction or agency of social control, and the technique of "formal ridicule," see Hartland, *Primitive Law,* pp. 161 ff.; Radin, P., *Primitive Man as Philosopher,* pp. 50–51; Williams, *Orokaiva Society,* pp. 308–309, 329; Rattray, *Ashanti Law . . . ,* p. 372; Wissler, . . . *Blackfoot Indians,* p. 24.

53 Boas, *Tsimshian Mythology,* p. 386. Another chief, who at a potlatch has been able to cast only a wooden "copper" on the water to match a rival's real and expensive copper, "was wandering about in the country to hide somewhere, because . . . he was ashamed that his wooden copper . . . was floating on the water" in front of his enemy's camp (*ibid.,* p. 364). "A common man" of the Kwakiutl "never gave a potlatch and never gave a feast, and therefore he was called 'clay-face,' as they call those who never gave a feast to their tribe."—Boas, . . . *Ethnology . . . Kwakiutl,* p. 93. Among the Tlingit Indians of Alaska insufficiency of food at a potlatch feast might result in the guests' taking three or four "high names" away from their hosts by way of retaliation.—Swanton, *The Tlingit Indians,* 26 Ann. Rep., Bureau of Am. Ethnology, p. 435.

54 Armstrong, *Rossel Island Money,* p. 429: "Indeed it is considered 'bad form' to make any display of one's wealth. . . ."

55 Armstrong, *Rossel Island,* p. 87.

56 *Ibid.,* p. 82.

57 *Ibid.,* p. 81, 88.

58 Armstrong, *Rossel Island Money,* p. 423; see also his *Rossel Island,* pp. 59 ff.

59 *Ibid.,* p. 64.

60 *Ibid.,* p. 66. "In practice, a form of magic is employed, by means of which these brokers, and others who are not members of this profession, claim to act on the minds of their debtors, making them repay within the customary time, while the minds of their creditors are affected in the reverse way."—*Loc cit.*

61 Malinowski, *Argonauts . . . ,* pp. 86–87.

62 *Ibid.* 81.

63 These tribes may differ in language, culture, and even race, and may even be at war with one another while the partners are friendly.—*Ibid.,* pp. 85, 275 ff.

64 For analogies between *kula* and potlatch, see Mauss, pp. 65 ff.

65 "Indeed . . . by far the greater number of the arm-shells, easily ninety per cent, are of too small a size to be worn even by young boys and girls. A few are so big and valuable that they should not be worn at all, except once in a decade by a very important man

on a very festive day. Though all the shell-strings can be worn, some of them are again considered too valuable, and are cumbersome for frequent use, and would be worn on very exceptional occasions only" (Malinowski, *Argonauts,* p. 88). "The prestige-value, rather than utility-value of these objects has, it would seem, led to a deprecation of the *economic* significance of the *kula* system by Hoyt (pp. 129–130); she sees economic activity only in the secondary trade carried on in connection with the *kula.* However, this trade is not carried on with *kula* partners, but with strangers, and is not the trade of prestige-values and solicitary gifts of the *kula* itself."—Malinowski, *Argonauts,* pp. 362–364.

66 "The natives sharply distinguish it (*i.e., kula*) from barter, which they practise extensively, of which they have a clear idea, and for which they have a settled term—in Kiriwinian: *gimwali.* Often, when criticising an incorrect, too hasty, or indecorous procedure of *kula,* they wil say: 'He conducts his *kula* as if it were *gimwali*'."—Malinowski, *Argonauts,* p. 96, also pp. 95, 97–98, 352 ff.

However, while in the actual exchange of *kula* valuables (arm-shells and necklaces) decorum bans any form of barter, curiously enough, the competitive inducement of a receptive frame of mind leading up to such exchange, through the offer of "solicitary gifts," is a fundamental part of *kula* mechanism. "If I, an inhabitant of Sinaketa, happen to be in possession of a pair of arm-shells more than usually good, the fame of it spreads, for it must be remembered that each one of the first-class arm-shells and necklaces has a personal name and a history of its own, and as they circulate around the big ring of the *kula,* they are all well known, and their appearance in a given district always creates a sensation. Now, all my partners—whether from overseas or from within the district—compete for the favour of receiving this particular article of mine, and those who are especially keen try to obtain it by giving me *pokala* (offerings) and *kaributu* (solicitary gifts). The former (*pokala*) consist as a rule of pigs, especially fine bananas, and yams of taro; the latter (*kaributu*) are of greater value: the valuable, large axe-blades (called *beku*), or lime spoons of whale bone are given" (*ibid.,* 98–99; 354–355). The ethics and custom governing the acceptance of solicitary gifts are as clearly crystallized as those relating to the *kula* valuables themselves; acceptance of such gifts obligates the recipient to exchange the coveted arm-shell or necklace with the donor; furthermore there must be equivalence in the return of certain of the gifts themselves.—*Ibid.,* 354.

67 *Ibid.,* p. 94; also p. 360.

68 *Ibid.,* p. 353.

69 *Ibid.,* p. 359. Mead (*The Changing Culture . . . ,* pp. 42–43) has similarly remarked concerning the amenities of gift-exchange among a certain Indian tribe: "But the charming assumption that no returns were made, that all gave freely out of the kindness of their hearts and the nobility of their minds, removed all atmosphere of bicker and barter from the stately public proceedings and added greatly to their dignity. Private comments might be made; it might be whispered that such and such a family were so close that they never helped out their own kin and if they did give anything away . . . But these are private remarks and the attitudes which give rise to them are permitted no sort of institutional expression."

70 Malinowski, *Argonauts,* pp. 99, 309, 322–324, 360. For the disciplinary effect of popular sayings see *supra* p. 566.

71 *Ibid.,* p. 102, 356–361.

72 Thomson, B. W., *The Fijians,* p. 281. *Cf.* Deane, *Fijian Society,* p. 119.

73 For a description of these feasts and their economic and social importance see Best, *The Maori,* I, 379 ff.; Firth, *Primitive Economics . . . ,* chapter 9.

Like the "coppers" presented or destroyed at the Indian potlatches, the most famous of these *hakari* acquired names that became part of Maori history. Firth (pp. 318–320) collates some interesting data on the amount of food consumed at noted *hakari* in 1873, *e.g.*, 6 large albatrosses, 19 calabashes of shark oil, several tons of fish, 20,000 dried eels, a great quantity of pigs, and baskets of potatoes almost without number.

[74] Best, *The Maori*, I, 381.

[75] Firth, *Primitive Economics . . .*, p. 327. *Cf.* Best, *Maori Magic*, p. 93: "When the food was cooked he . . . put the food in baskets, . . . and presented the food to the people of Ngati-pukenga and Ngai-te-rangi. . . . Then those people thought as to what return they could make of this present of food." "Taunts of illiberality were cast upon tribes not following the custom."—Thomson, A. S., . . . *New Zealand*, I, 90. *Cf.* H. Powdermaker, "Feasts in New Ireland," *American Anthropologist*, n.s., XXXIV, 237.

[76] Firth, *Primitive Economics . . .*, p. 328. Thus one chief, Te Angiangi, his people, having exhausted their food supply, gave "vast areas . . . at the present time (1906) worth millions."—Smith, S. P., *History of Horehore Pa*, pp. 87–88.

For similar collective food- or gift-exchanges in the Andaman Islands, see Brown, A. R., *The Andaman Islanders*, pp. 42, 83; Man, . . . *Original Inhabitants . . . Andaman Islands*, pp. 340, 392. In Ongtong, Java, Hogbin saw an exchange "at which two taro puddings each almost four feet square were presented. The return gift included sixteen thousand coconuts and ten baskets of dried fish."—*Law and Order in Polynesia*, p. 98.

[77] Grierson, *The Silent Trade*, p. 63; Brit. Assoc. Adv. Sci., *Notes and Queries on Anthropology* (ed. 5), p. 138. While I have stated that "silent trade" precedes the "peace of the market," this does not mean that "silent trade" precedes barter itself without a fixed and regulated rendezvous: on this point and on the whole controversy as to the origin and development of "silent trade" and its relation to barter, with which I cannot deal here, see Grierson's treatise just cited; Lasch, *Das Marktwesen . . . Kultur-Stufen*, pp. 621 ff.; Bovill, *The Silent Trade of Wangara;* Hoyt, pp. 115, 116, 133–135; Somlo, trans., pp. 442–446. "Silent Trade" has been regarded as a development from robbery (Müller-Lyer, pp. 159–160), but Firth (*Primitive Economics . . .*, pp. 14–15) criticizes this evolutionary treatment. *Cf.* Hoyt, p. 135.

[78] Herodotus II, 196 (trans. Rawlinson). The famous medieval Arabian traveler Ibn Batuta thus describes "silent trade" in "the Land of Darkness" (probably Northern Siberia): "each traveler arriving 'at the Darkness' leaves the goods he has brought there and they retire to their usual camping-ground. Next day they go back to seek for their goods, and find, opposite them, skins of sable, minever and ermine. If the merchant is satisfied with the exchange, he takes them, but if not, he leaves them. The inhabitants then add more skins, but sometimes they take away their goods and leave the merchants'. This is their method of commerce. Those who go there do not know whom they are trading with or whether they be jinn or men, for they never see anyone."—Ibn Batuta, *Travels in Asia and Africa*, p. 151.

[79] Bogoras, *The Chukchee*, p. 54.

[80] Vanoverbergh, *Negritos . . . Northern Luzon*, p. 421.

[81] Torday, . . . *Trail of the Bushongo*, pp. 57–58. Burrows, in the nineteenth century, gives even more detailed an account of pygmy "silent trade": "As a rule," he says, "the pygmies settle near a village of some big chief, where they are sure to find extensive banana plantations. Though the pygmies grow no food stuffs whatever on their own account, they are very fond of the long unripe banana. Mr. Pygmy's method of obtaining this delicacy is simple, if original. On his return from a day's hunting, small pieces of meat are carefully wrapped up in grass or leaves and the pygmy betakes himself to the nearest banana plantation. There he selects the bunch of bananas he requires, shins up the trees and cuts them down, affixing one of the small packages of meat to the tree-trunk

with a little wooden skewer—by way of payment. In this manner he satisfied his conscience, and declares that he has not stolen the bananas, but only bought them. He becomes angry at the merest suggestion of theft. This custom is recognized universally by the tribes among whom he lives. . . ."—Burrows, *On the Natives . . . Belgian Congo,* p. 39. See also Johnston (ed.), *George Grenfell and the Congo,* II, 789; Moszkowski, *Vom Wirstschaftsleben der primitiven Völker,* pp. 12–13.

[82] Grierson, *Silent Trade,* pp. 66, 87.

[83] For "the peace of the market" and for market law among primitive peoples generally, see Huvelin, *Essai Historique sur le Droit des Marches et des Foires,* chapter 13; Grierson, *Silent Trade,* secs. 30–35; Thomas, *The Market in African Law and Custom,* p. 90; Lasch, *Das Marktwesen . . . ,* pp. 619, 700, 764; Schurtz, *Das afrikanische Gewerbe,* chapter 5; Koehne, *Markt-, Kaufmanns- und Handelsrecht . . . ,* p. 196, trans., p. 420; Gutmann, *Das Recht der Dschagga,* pp. 425 ff., 466 ff.; von Fallati, *Keime des Völkerrechts bei wilden und halbwilden Stämmen,* pp. 216 ff.; Maine, *Village Communities,* pp. 193–194.

[84] Stites, *Economics . . . Iroquois,* p. 154.

[85] Ishmael, *Old Customs . . . Baganda,* No. 19. Among the Songos and Kiokos of the Congo "to buy even a small article, you must go to the market; people avoid trading elsewhere. If a man says to another, 'Sell me this hen' or 'that fruit,' the answer as a rule will be 'Come to the market-place'."—Ratzel, *History of Mankind,* II, 376. See also Thomas, *The Market . . . ,* p. 94, note 3.

[86] Dennett, *Laws and Customs . . . Vavili Family,* p. 272.

[87] Milne, *The House of an Eastern Clan,* p. 216. See also the formalities in contracting or enforcing payment of a loan, *infra* pp. 584–585.

[88] Rink, *Tales . . . Eskimo,* p. 29.

[89] Barton, *Ifugao Law,* pp. 49–50.

[90] Moss, *Nabaloi Law and Ritual,* p. 255 and note 214.

[91] In dealing with "primitive" African commercial law it must always be remembered that the term "primitive" is, as thus applied, even more obviously relative and perhaps delusive than with respect to many other "primitive" peoples. "It may happen," says an authority on the African races, "that we shall have to revise entirely our view of the Black races, and regard those who now exist as the decadent representatives of an almost forgotten era rather than as the embryonic possibilities of an era yet to come." (Quoted opposite the title-page to Dennett, *At the Back of the Black Man's Mind.* See *e.g.,* Frobenius, *The Voice of Africa,* I, 14–15, for the ancient commerce of the cannibal Bassonge along whose wonderful trade routes iron was carried through the heart of the so-called "impenetrable forests of the Congo"; he also points out (*ibid.,* II, 357–359) that when Islam "crept its way through the back doors of Soudanese palaces in the comfortable slippers of inner African commercial life," which "was already thousands of years old," the Mohammedan merchants (about 1,000 A.D.) found "great cities" and "roads splendidly built for traffic." For ancient African native trade monopolies see Johnston (ed.) *George Grenfell . . . Congo,* I, 395; Ratzel, *History of Mankind,* III, 121–122. *Cf.* Rivers, *Psychology and Ethnology,* p. 159.

[92] Post, *Afrikanische Jurisprudenz,* II, 181–182. Among the Fanti, *caveat emptor* is expressed in the proverb "Nobody buys the footprints of a bullock." There is an implied warranty of title in the seller and where the title is found to be defective, the purchase price must be returned and all expenses waived by the purchaser must be repaid. In view of the binding force of obligations upon the heirs of the obligor in primitive law, it is peculiar that in this transaction the purchaser discovering a defect in title after the death

of the seller has no remedy against his heirs, for, it is held, he should have specially contracted with the seller for a good title and should have included the seller's heirs in the agreement.—See Sarbah, *Fanti Customary Laws*, pp. 93, 95.

[93] Coxhead, *The Native Tribes ... Rhodesia*, p. 57.

[94] Whitfield, *South African Native Law*, pp. 399–400.

[95] Junod, *The Life of a South African Tribe*, I, 439.

[96] Dundas, *Kilimanjaro and Its People*, p. 299.

[97] Dennett, *Laws and Customs ... Basili Family*, p. 272.

[98] For the "peace of the market" see *supra* note 83.

[99] *The Strange Adventures of Andrew Battell* (Ravenstein, ed.), pp. 79–80. "Theft in the market was dealt with as a rule on very different lines from ordinary theft. In other parts of Africa the death penalty is often inflicted on the spot. In Southern Nigeria a milder rule prevails, and beyond refund, sometimes of double the value of the stolen object, a market thief at Awka suffers nothing except abuse and the throwing of dust on him. ... At Nibo they laugh and shout at the man, but there is no penalty beyond replacing the stolen object. At Ugwoba a woman is fined 5s. by the women of her own quarter. At Mbwaku people would keep their eye upon a market thief, for he is a man who steals from the alose (demi-god), which is found in every market-place. In some respects the laws as to the stealing of plants, and sometimes even of fowls and goats, differed considerably from the ordinary laws of theft. At Agolo, for example, a man who stole *okwa* (bread-fruit) seeds would be abused, a man who stole palm nuts or coconuts would be dealt with in the same way until he paid the fine. At Nofia a man who stole *okwa* was fined one big pot; if he stole corn the woman who owned it would shout and take the man to the chief; the fine of 5s. would be divided among all the women. At Ugwoba a man who stole *okwa* would only be laughed at; a woman would be fined 5s., which went to the women of her quarter."—Thomas, *Ibo-Speaking Peoples ...*, pt. 7, pp. 119–120. See also by the same author, *Edo-Speaking Peoples ...*, pt. 1, pp. 106–107: "In all this part of the country theft in the market, which in some parts of Africa is severely punished, is regarded as a trivial offence, because detection is so easy"; also his article, *The Market ...*, at pp. 100–101.

[100] Cardinall, *The Natives ... Northern Territories ... Gold Coast*, p. 54, also p. 96. For Aje, the God of Trade, among the 600 Yoruba (Gold Coast) Gods, see Dennett, *... Black Man's Mind*, p. 245.

[101] Westermarck, *Ritual and Belief in Morocco*, I, 179–181.

[102] Brown, G., *Melanesians and Polynesians*, p. 306.

[103] Hoyt, pp. 118 ff. Among the tribes of Southern Nigeria and the Wajagga of East Africa, markets are so common an institution that the days of the week are named after them. See Talbot, *The Peoples of Southern Nigeria*, III, 872–873; Thomas, *The Market ...*, p. 94.

[104] Proyart, *History of Loango ...*, p. 587.

[105] Hadfield, *Among the Natives ... Loyalty Group*, p. 220.

[106] Koehne, trans., p. 433.

[107] Von Fallati, p. 217. See also Thomas, *The Market ...*, p. 102. For other forms of market police see Lasch, pp. 772–774; Schurtz, *Das ... Gewerbe*, pp. 120–121.

[108] Ward, *Ethnographical Notes ... Congo Tribes*, p. 290.

[109] See Gutmann, pp. 428–429, 693. Similarly, in 1364, the Mayor and Aldermen of London decreed "that the said John Penrose shall drink a draught of the same wine

which he had sold to the common people; and the remainder of such wine shall then be poured on the head of the same John."—Riley, *Memorials of London*, p. 318.

[110] St. John, *Life in the Forest . . . Far East*, II, 295.

[111] See Thomas, *The Ibo-Speaking Peoples . . .*, pt. 4, pp. 7, 187–190; Basden, . . . *Ibos of Nigeria*, pp. 194–195; Talbot, IV, 904. At Maidugari, the largest market of Bornu, Nigeria, where women do not appear to be the principal traders, there is a "market king," to whom the merchants and the buyers submit their disputes for settlement. For their own protection, the women also choose a "market queen," through whom all transactions with the women's stalls, at the market, are carried on. See Alexander, *From the Niger to the Nile*, I, 268. The "market queen" appears to be paid voluntarily a percentage of the produce sold at the market.

[112] Ellis, W., *Polynesian Researches*, IV, 326.

[113] Lowie, *Primitive Religion*, p. 56.

[114] Stanley, *The Congo and . . . Its Free State*, I, 281.

[115] To the Manus of New Guinea "their hatred of debt, their uneasiness beneath undischarged economic obligations is painful." Mead, . . . *New Guinea*, pp. 9, 307–308. Among the Ifugao of the Philippines, "while a debt is a sacred thing" and non-payment is "disgraceful," "the non-collection is still more disgraceful, for the presumption is that a man who does not collect from his creditors [*sic*] cannot do so."—Barton, p. 56. See also Westermarck, *Origin and Development . . .*, II, 83, 705; Dennett, . . . *Black Man's Mind*, p. 367; Vanoverburgh, *Negritos . . .*, p. 432.

[116] See Rattray, *Ashanti Law . . .*, pp. 369–370, 403; Thomas, *Ibo-Speaking Peoples . . .*, pt. 4, p. 161; Talbot, *The Peoples of Southern Nigeria*, III, 632, 650, 657; Ellis, A. B., *The Ewe-Speaking Peoples . . .*, p. 209; Danquah, *Akan Laws and Customs*, p. 184; Torday, . . . *in Savage Africa*, pp. 93, 133; Barton, p. 14; Lowie, *Primitive Society*, pp. 399–400.

[117] Rattray, *Ashanti Law . . .*, p. 370. See also Talbot, III, 661. In respect of the spread of legal institutions, it is interesting to note (*ibid.*, p. 370) that the Hindu practice of "sitting *dharna*," *i.e.*, the creditor's sitting before the debtor's door and threatening to starve himself unless paid, prevalent also in parts of West Africa, was not allowed in Ashanti, where a creditor driving a debtor to suicide through excessive importunity would be punished. For "sitting *dharna*" in West Africa see Sarbah, chapter 9; Kingsley, *West African Studies*, p. 372; for "sitting *dharna*" in India and generally, see Maine, *Early History of Institutions*, pp. 40, 297 ff.; Westermarck, *Origin and Development . . .*, II, 245.

[118] Thomas, *Ibo-Speaking Peoples . . .*, pt. 4, p. 161. Among the Thongas of Portuguese East Africa "the headman is more or less responsible for all the claims lodged against his subordinates" (Junod, I, 332). Among the Bavili of West Africa "in the event of a time for the repayment of a debt having been fixed, the creditor asks for payment, and if this is put off or refused he has the right to arrest anyone belonging to the debtor's family. This person is held until the matter has been publicly settled by palavar in the courts of law, when, the debt being paid, the prisoner is set at liberty. The person thus arrested is not necessarily of the same family as the debtor, but he should be of a family in the same princedom or province, that is some one living not very far from the debtor. This captive receives payment from the debtor quite apart from the creditor, but as the result of the judgment of the same palaver. And this is the only form of security for the payment of a debt which the native law provides for."—Dennett, . . . *Black Man's Mind*, p. 67.

[119] Rattay, *Ashanti Law . . .*, p. 371.

[120] Hartland, p. 169.

[121] Less than a century ago we find a judge of the Supreme Court of the United States writing: "It is not pretended that the defendant has a defence to the merits. He relies solely upon the technical plea of the statute. Although this is a legal defence, it is not a conscientious one, and is not favored in law (Mac Lean, in Reed & Mix v. Clark (1844) 3 Mac Lean U. S. Cir. Ct. Rep. 480. For the change in judicial attitude toward statutes of limitations, now esteemed as "statutes of repose" and not regarded as merely technical, but "substantial and meritorious" defenses see cases collated in United States v. Oregon Lumber Co. (1922) 260 U. S. 299 at 299–300; Bell v. Morrison (1828) 26 U. S. 351 at 359–360; and Judge Mac Lean himself in M'Clung v. Silliman (1830) 28 U. S. 270 at 278–279; *cf.* Pound, *Law and Morals,* p. 3, note 6. For the history of statutes of limitation in Anglo-American law see Wood, *Limitation of Actions,* I, secs. 2 ff.; Holdsworth, *History of English Law,* II, 533. For a similar late development (5th century A.D.) of the limitation of actions in Roman law see Buckland, . . . *Roman Law,* pp. 683–684, also his . . . *Roman Private Law,* pp. 341, 367; Sohm, *The Institutes,* p. 283. *Cf.* Calisse, . . . *Italian Law,* pp. 773–774.

[122] Hartland, pp. 169–170; Thomas, *Ibo-Speaking Peoples . . . ,* pt. 4, p. 164; Tate, *Native Law of the Southern Gikuyu,* p. 245; Moss, p. 257, note 215.

It should be noted, however, that while theoretically the claim may not be barred by any statute of limitations, at the same time many primitive systems of law require such claims to be admitted formally on the deathbed of the debtor or proved by prescribed procedure within a certain time after the debtor's death. Thus, among the A-Kamba of British East-Africa, "when an old man is on the point of death he will collect his sons and tell them to walk around his *shambas* (cultivated field) and take note of the shrubs he planted on the various parts of the boundaries, and he will also enumerate any debts that are owing to him. The sons will then ask him to mention any witnesses who could testify to the planting of the boundaries or to the matter of the debts, these persons will, if they are available, be called up and reminded of the fact in the old man's presence, and after that, in any dispute with regard to the estate of the deceased, their evidence would settle the matter" (Hobley, *Ethnology . . . A-Kamba,* p. 83). Similarly among the Thongas of Portuguese East Africa, the dying man calls together all his relations and after uttering his last wishes, "reminds them of his debts, those he owes and those which are owing to him" (Junod, I, 134). Among the Bavili of the Congo, "When about to bury the deceased, the inheritor plants a sword in the ground, before the assembled guests, and asks if there is anything more to be paid by him on behalf of the deceased. Any creditor then goes up to the sword and placing his hand upon it declares that the deceased owes him money or goods, and that he will give particulars of the debt later on. These are considered as proved. Any creditor claiming his money after that must bring his witnesses and be prepared to substantiate the debt" (Dennett, . . . *Black Man's Mind,* pp. 46–47). Among the Chagga of Kilimanjaro, "four days after the father's death it is announced that all persons having claims against him must come to the village to declare them. In theory no claim can be admitted if it is not claimed on this day, and if in practice this is not strictly adhered to, failure to appear on the appointed days will at least go against the claimant if later he sues for recovery" (Dundas, p. 308). Among the Ibo of Southern Nigeria, if any creditor not named by the debtor presented himself after the death of the debtor, he had to swear to the debt before the *alose* or demigod.—Thomas, *Ibo-Speaking Peoples . . . ,* pt. 4, pp. 164–165.

[123] See Thomas, *Ibo-Speaking Peoples . . . ,* pt. 7, p. 121; *ibid.,* pt. 4, p. 165; Dennett, . . . *Black Man's Mind,* pp. 46–47.

[124] Codrington, *The Melanesians,* pp. 326, 327; see also Seligmann, *The Melanesians of British New Guinea,* p. 95; Rivers, . . . *Melanesian Society,* I, 60, 169.

[125] Seligmann, p. 534. "Everywhere there seems to be a strong sense of commercial morality, indeed it is difficult to see how the extensive trading operations—elsewhere alluded to—could persist without this. Credit is freely given, and payments are often by instalments. Partnerships formally entered into as such, do not seem to exist, and a man who is buying a canoe will borrow from his neighbours in order to pay for it, and although it may be a long time before he can pay them back he is regarded as the owner of that canoe, not as a part owner."—*Ibid.*, p. 573.

[126] Haddon, *Reports . . . Cambridge Anthropological Expedition to Torres Straits,* V, 276, 296. *Cf.* Jenness and Ballantyne, *The Northern d'Entrecasteaux,* p. 207: "In trading with one another the natives readily give away food and other things on credit. Once when we had run out of tobacco we engaged a native to carry the camera and its outfit two or three miles, promising him a stick of tobacco on the following day. We never saw him again for a month; then when we asked why he had not come earlier to receive his tobacco, he merely replied that he had not needed it before, and knew he could always obtain it whenever he wished. He would have acted the same with a fellow native, for with these people a promise is far more binding than many a legal contract is with us."

[127] On the Negro's "unspoilt sense of justice" see Schweitzer, . . . *Primeval Forest,* pp. 74–76; Junod, I, 436; Kidd, *The Essential Kafir,* p. 286. Colonial administrators are rather fond of attributing the African's sense of justice to British influence. *E.g.,* Gouldsbury and Sheane, *The Great Plateau of Northern Rhodesia,* p. 78; Lugard, *The Dual Mandate in British Tropical Africa,* p. 5. See, however, *supra* note 91.

[128] See Boas, *What the Negro Has Done in Africa,* p. 106; Lowie, *Primitive Society,* p. 418; Junod, I, 436. In Ashanti there appears to have developed the same official attitude toward litigation in the native tribunals that marked the struggle for jurisdiction in the history of English law. "Councillors, instead of regarding a dearth of lawsuits as a blessing, came to look upon empty courts as a misfortune. Prayers were offered to the gods to send cases, and a chief in whose time court fees dropped to a minimum was likely to be regarded not wholly with favour" (Rattray, *Ashanti Law . . . ,* pp. 369, 370, 403); *cf.* Smith, E. W., and Dale, I, 360: "The Ba-ila are a litigious people, and extremely rapacious. Some of the cases brought before the chiefs, and even before the European magistrate, are extraordinary. The acme, we think, was reached in a claim brought by a man against another whose cock had committed adultery with his hen; he gravely claimed damages amounting to the value of a cow. In the event they were persuaded that the ends of justice would be met by killing and eating the cock." For the overcrowding of the legal profession in the superimposed native courts and the disintegrating influence of those courts on native law enforcement see Meek, *A Sudanese Kingdom,* p. 350; Lugard, p. 544.

[129] Thomas, *Edo-Speaking Peoples . . . ,* pt. 1, p. 99.

[130] Among the Ibo at Awka the members of the secret society "might order the farm, farm trees, and so on to be seized and announce their decision by beating drums. The property was vested in them and worked for the benefit of the creditor until the debtor asked for a meeting and agreed to sell part of his own property" (*ibid.,* p. 121). *Cf.* Talbot, III, 660, 664, 674. For the influence and various spheres of governance exercised by primitive secret societies generally, see Lowie, *Primitive Society.* Index, *s.v.* "Societies, Secret"; Butt-Thompson, *West African Secret Societies;* Schurtz, *Alterklassen und Männerbunde,* pt. 1; Kingsley, pp. 448 ff.; Frobenius, I, 160 ff.; Wissler, *Societies . . . Plains Indians;* Loeb, *Tribal Initiations . . . Societies,* pp. 249 ff.; Rivers, . . . *Melanesian Society,* II, chap. 24.

[131] Thomas, *Ibo-Speaking Peoples . . . ,* pt. 1, pp. 121–133; *ibid.,* pt. 4, pp. 161–164. See also the same author's report on *Sierra Leone, Timne and Other Tribes,* pt. 1, pp. 81, 169–171.

[132] Talbot, III, 635.

[133] Thomas, *Ibo-Speaking Peoples . . .*, pt. 1, pp. 122–123. Among the Bavili of West Africa "a man may lease his cattle to another under the following recognized conditions: first increase goes to the owner; of the second the caretaker takes a female; of the third a male; the fourth goes to the owner" (Dennett, . . . *Black Man's Mind*, p. 49). *Cf.*, for the Chagga laws, Dundas, p. 299.

[134] Weeks, . . . *Congo Cannibals*, pp. 114–115, 195. This form of temporary and often voluntary "attachment" should be distinguished from the pawning by the debtor of himself or a member of his family to secure payment of his debt, for which see Rattray, *Ashanti Law . . .*, pp. 47–55; Thomas, *Ibo-Speaking Peoples*, pt. 4, pp. 166 ff.; Talbot, III, 623, 633, 697–698

[135] Schapera, *The Khoisan Peoples of South Africa*, p. 319.

[136] Kidd, *The Essential Kafir*, p. 357.

[137] Lopes, *Usages and Customs . . . Natives of Sena*, p. 359.

[138] Hobley, *Ethnology . . . A-Kamba*, p. 81. See *infra*, pp. 592–593.

[139] Quoted in Means, . . . *Spanish Conquest of Yucatan*, p. 13.

[140] Dorsey, *Omaha Sociology*, p. 367. The Navajo of Arizona and New Mexico, though he may delight in over-reaching the white man, if entrusted with money or property and put on his honor, "will honestly guard and deliver either according to instructions. He seems to see no wrong in stealing that for which another is responsible, in fact, seems to look at it in the light of a cute clever trick; but entrust the same thing to him, shift the responsibility for it upon his shoulders, and he will be strictly honest" (Ostermann, *The Navajo Indians . . .*, p. 865). Farabee (*The Central Caribs*, p. 383), a recent traveler among the Central Caribs of South America, records (1924) that "at the first village we encountered, eight days after leaving the Waiwais, where a number of Parukutus are taking up their abode, there was one family living with some Mapidians, an old man, his wife, and one son. They had very little about them of any value, nothing to exchange. The man had one fish hook only, but fortunately for him now he had several years before sold a dog to one of the party travelling with us. It was the first time they had met since the transaction and our boy immediately discharged his debts by giving the old man some fish hooks, beads and trinkets he had received from us."

[141] Russell, *Tribes and Castes . . . India*, II, 293.

[142] *Ibid.*, III, 119.

[143] Mills, *The Lhota Nagas*, pp. 45, 399. Contrast with this very fair procedure, the oppressive rate of interest for loans of salt among these people—100 per cent compound interest (*ibid.*, p. 45).

[144] Whitehead, . . . *Nicobar Islands*, p. 81: "I have only once heard of this having been done, where the offender was a good lady of Malacca. The Nicobarese now call that village Palire, which means 'their own lies'—I suppose the lies of the traders though occasionally, as in this case, the lies of the Nicobarese. On the other hand, the Nicobarese are very careless, and the stick of ten gets lost, and they go on paying long after the debt has been liquidated."

[145] Erman, *Travels in Siberia*, I, 492. *Cf.* Jochelson, *The Yukaghir*, p. 433: "The aim of the hunter is to obtain as large a number of trade articles as possible, with no thought of the future. The more debts a man has, the richer he is regarded. A Yukaghir proverb says that every newborn boy appears in the world as a rich man, *i.e.*, loaded with debts; when he attains manhood he must pay the debts of his father or even his grandfather. It is a matter of honor to pay the father's debts, and to be trusted by merchants."

[146] Dall, *Alaska and Its Resources,* p. 394. Grierson, *Silent Trade,* p. 67, points out that this agency subsists only as a survival of the time—long past—when the parties may have been enemies.

[147] Ivens, *Melanesians . . . Solomon Islands,* p. 17.

[148] Barton, pp. 57–59.

[149] See Haddon, *Cambridge . . . Expedition . . .,* V, 98–99. *Cf.* the tale of Agiwai's misappropriation of the axe in Landtmann, *The Folk-Tales . . . Kiwai Papuans,* p. 515. *Cf.*, for so-called "hunting partners" among the Tanaina, C. Osgood, "Tanaina Culture," *American Anthropologist,* n.s., 35, p. 710.

[150] *Supra* p. 24.

[151] Haddon, V, 269.

[152] Seligmann, p. 539.

[153] Wallis, *Ethical Aspects of Chilkat Culture,* p. 76.

[154] Dennett, . . . *Black Man's Mind,* p. 50.

[155] Smyth, *The Aborigines of Victoria,* I, 181–182. This relationship may perhaps be explained in terms of taboo. See Grierson, *Silent Trade,* p. 61, note 1; Crawley, *The Mystic Rose,* I, 287. As to the honesty of the Australian aboriginal agent, however, *cf.* Spencer, B., *Wanderings in Wild Australia,* I, 159: "Whatever may be the faults of the Australian aborigine, he is, in his native state, perfectly honest and trustworthy in regard to matters of trading. A native will hand over his bag of *Pituri,* a narcotic plant, to another man, who acts as intermediary, with most perfect confidence that, sooner or later, he will receive its full worth in kind." For a reciprocal relation see also the custom among the Dieri of South-East Australia called "Yutchin" in Howitt, *The Natives . . . Australia,* pp. 713–714.

Among the natives of German New Guinea, boys are sent to other tribes to learn their languages so as ultimately to become interpreters there. See Neuhauss, *Deutsch Neu Guinea,* I, 366, somewhat inaccurately translated in Hoyt, p. 130.

[156] From the vast literature on "economic magic," see, as typical of these various aspects: Frazer, *The Golden Bough,* I, 85 ff., 108 ff., 136 ff., his *Spirit of the Corn,* I, chapter 3, and his *Psyche's Task,* chapter 3; Haddon, VI, No. 13; Rivers, *The Todas,* chapters 3, 4, 8, 9; Roscoe, *The Soul of Central Africa,* pp. 86, 158, 163; Hobley, *Bantu Beliefs and Magic,* pp. 166–176; Westermarck, *Ritual and Belief in Morocco,* II, chapter 16; Handy, *Polynesian Religion,* pp. 282 ff.; Malinowski, *Argonauts,* chapters 5, 6, 17; Firth, *Primitive Economics . . .,* Index, *s.v.* "Magic"; Gunther, . . . *First Salmon Ceremony.*

[157] See Malinowski, *Primitive Psychology,* pp. 79–82; Brit. Assoc. Adv. Sci., *Notes and Queries on Anthropology* (ed. 5) p. 175; Levy-Bruhl, *Primitive Mentality,* pp. 308–309.

[158] See Allier, *The Mind . . . Savage,* pp. 54–55.

[159] Meek, *A Sudanese Kingdom,* p. 304.

[160] Smith and Dale, *The Ila-Speaking Peoples . . .,* I, 262–263. *Cf.* Weeks, pp. 203–205: "When a caravan of native traders is ready to start for the white man's trading factory, they call a luck-giving medicine-man. The medicine-man of this particular cult has a luck-giving bag of charms, containing pieces of leopard's skin, hyaena's skin, lion's skin, and, in fact, a piece of the skin of every strong animal he could procure, and also some albino's hair. . . . This medicine-man is supposed to have the power of making his customers to be specially favoured by women, slaves, and also by his family and friends, and very fortunate in trading. . . . This medicine-man can not only impart good luck to his

clients, but, if paid, he can remove good luck from his client's enemies, and overwhelm them with misfortune; he has only to tap on the image, and hold it up and down three times and hang it outside his house, and away its spirit will fly to ruin the person against whom it has been invoked." See also Weeks, *Congo Life and Folk-Lore*, pp. 231–233.

[161] Westermarck, *Ritual ... Morocco*, I, 593.

[162] Malinowski, *The Natives of Mailu*, p. 627.

[163] Levy-Bruhl, pp. 309–310. Magic is also invoked "to avert the premature death of the pigs selected for the market." See Lowie, *Primitive Religion*, p. 56.

[164] See Roth, W. E., *Arts and Crafts of Guinea Indians*, sec. 822

[165] Claridge, *Wild Bush Tribes of Tropical Africa*, pp. 122, 129–130; see also H. I. Hogbin, "Sorcery at Ongtong, Java," *American Anthropologist*, n.s., XXXIV, 441.

[166] Junod, II, 392.

[167] Schweitzer, p. 51.

[168] Hobley, *Bantu ... Magic*, pp. 241–242. See *supra* p. 583.

[169] Boas, *Ethnology ... Kwakiutl*, pt. F, p. 269.

[170] Erdland, *Die Marshall-Insulaner*, p. 47. "Wenn die Insulaner auch kein Latein verstehen so denken sie doch: *prima charitas sibi*."—*Loc. cit.*

[171] Evans, *Studies in Religion, Folklore and Custom in British North Borneo ...*, p. 132. For similar adulteration of gutta percha by the natives of North Borneo, see Roth, H. L., *The Natives of Sarawak and British North Borneo*, II, 232.

[172] Kingsley, *Travels in West Africa*, p. 256.

[173] Rattray, *Hausa Folk-Lore*, II, 226, 228. According to Tremaine, *Hausa Superstitions and Customs*, pp. 47–50, the Hausa evidently have a profound respect for astuteness in trade and in the evasion of debts.

[174] Cureau, *Savage Man in Central Africa*, pp. 253–254.

[175] Roscoe, *The Baganda*, p. 453.

[176] Roth, W. E., sec. 822; see also his *Additional Studies*, sec. 822.

[177] Ball, *Jungle Life in India*, p. 201

[178] Godden, *Naga ... Tribes of North-East India*, p. 42.

[179] Russell, IV, pp. 356–357.

[180] Beaver, *Unexplored New Guinea*, p. 108.

[181] Morice, pp. 646–647. According to Wood, W., *New-Englands Prospect*, chapter 3, the Pequod Indians of the seventeenth century who, it was contemptuously said by other tribes "seek rather to grow rich by industrie, than famous by deeds of Chevalry," returned from their trading journeys to the English "loaded with English commodities, of which they make a double profit, by selling them to more remote Indians, who are ignorant at what cheape rates they obtain them ..., so making their neighbour's ignorance their enrichment."

[182] Theal, ... *Africa South of the Zambesi*, I, 221.

[183] Barbot, pp. 259–260. Barbot saw (p. 259) "many of our Europeans making no scruple to weigh the gold by a heavier weight than they aught," while, on the other hand, he noticed several of the native factors, "who, either to make the parcel of gold answer, or exceed, would slily blow upon the scale it was in; others making a show, as if they added more gold, would take it up between their nails, which ... are very long and the tops of their fingers."

[184] Stanley, *Through the Dark Continent*, II, 2. See also (pp. 121–123) his description of the market-place at Nyangwe: "And how like any other market-place it was! with its

noise and murmer of human voices. The same rivalry in extolling their wares, the eager quick action, the emphatic gesture, the inquisitive look, the facial expressions of scorn and triumph, anxiety, joy, plausibility, were all there. I discovered, too, the surprising fact that aborigines of Manyema possessed just the same inordinate ideas in respect to their wares as London, Paris, and New York shop-keepers." *Cf.* Capello and Ivens, II, 17–18: "It is really curious to observe the eagerness with which the negro will seek to do a little business. A cloth or handkerchief purchased but a moment before, will be readily exchanged if he see the most trifling profit can be made by the barter. In our own encampment we have had opportunities of observing within the short space of twenty-four hours a yard of red baize pass into the hands of six succesive owners." See also Browne, *A Journey to Dar Für,* p. 153; Hilton-Simpson, p. 110.

185 Torday and Joyce, . . . *Ethnography of the Ba-Mbala,* p. 408.

186 Lawes, p. 611.

187 Moszkowski, p. 15.

188 Jane (ed.), . . . *Four Voyages of Columbus,* I, 8.

189 Stevenson, *In the South Seas,* p. 281. For complaints relating to the "insatiable greed," "competitive selfishness," and "deliberate cheating" of European traders in the extreme north, see F. G. Speck, "Ethical Attributes of The Labrador Indians," *American Anthropologist,* n.s., XXXV, 559, 562.

190 When, for instance, in 1565, the Spanish expedition to the Philippines under Legazpi landed at the Ladrones Islands to barter for rice and cocoanut oil, "the trading was all done from the canoes, for the natives would not enter the vessels. They cheated much, passing up packages filled mainly with sand, or grass, and rocks, with perhaps a little rice on top to hide the deceit; the cocoa-nut oil was found to be mixed with water." Furthermore, the Spanish governor was compelled to beg the Moro chief not to befuddle his crew with palm-wine which was found to be "better than that of Castilla." See Blair and Robertson (eds.), *The Philippine Islands, 1493–1803,* II, 110, 137, 198–199. For similar early deceptions by natives of European traders see Mendaña de Neira, . . . *Solomon Islands,* II, 349–350; also *The Voyages of Sir James Lancaster, Kt., to the East Indies,* p. 68.

191 Edge-Partington, article in (1905) 5 *Man,* No. 41.

192 Edge-Partington, articles in (1909) 9 *Man,* No. 31, and (1910) 10 *Man,* No. 31. For similar instances of forgeries of native relics see Donne, *The Maori, Past and Present,* pp. 150–151; Ling-Roth (1901) 1 *Man,* No. 93; Edge-Partington (1901) 1 *Man,* Nos. 56 and 92.

193 *E.g.,* Frazer, *Man, God and Immortality,* p. 232; Lowie, *Primitive Society,* p. 398; Williams, *Orokaiva Society,* pp. 309, 315; Seligmann, p. 565; Best, *The Maori,* I, 356–358; Kropotkin, p. 77. For criticisms of these views see Malinowski, *Crime and Custom . . . ,* pp. 41–43; Firth, *Proverbs . . . ,* pp. 259–260; Radin, P., *Primitive Man . . . ,* pp. 36 ff.; H. I. Hogbin, *Law and Order in Polynesia,* p. 83.

THE BUSINESS RELATIONS OF PATRON AND FREEDMAN IN CLASSICAL ROMAN LAW

BY A. ARTHUR SCHILLER

RECENT YEARS have seen an increasing number of studies upon the commercial law of Rome.[1] Its comparative neglect during preceding centuries is undoubtedly due to the fact that the legal system of the late Republic and early Empire, the classical epoch of Roman law, like the Anglo-American and in contrast to the modern Continental, knew no such concept as "commercial law."[2] The particular incidents of business law must be extracted from the spheres of the law of persons, property, obligations, etc. The law of partnership is found in obligations, bankruptcy in the law of succession, agency in great part in procedural law. Strange to say, a great mass of the material is hidden in the law of persons; a phase of commercial law in which the author is interested at the present time, the law of business organizations in classical Rome, is an example of this.[3]

Business corporations were practically nonexistent; partnership was a well recognized but not the most common type of commercial organization. By far the greater number of business enterprises were based upon the principal and agent relation—this in the modern sense of the concept, for the Romans had no law of agency.[4] A further point to note is that the family, in its widest sense, figures prominently in this respect. The Roman *pater familias,* socially and often legally prevented from engaging in commercial enterprises,[5] placed his sons in control of trading companies, employed his slaves in business transactions of all types, and utilized his freedmen in commercial and industrial organizations. It was only in postclassical times, with the incursion of the state into the commercial field, that the family ceased to be the major type of business organization.[6]

In this article, honoring my former teacher and a scholar interested from his earliest days in Roman law, the attempt is made to picture summarily but one small sector of this topic. Under what circumstances might a patron and his freedman have business dealings with each other and with third persons? What situations, dependent upon the parties' familial or personal connections, may also be of commercial significance? These and other points are presented in this survey, which is intended to cover every possible business relation between patron and freedman, but leaves the detailed discussion of such relations to a future date. Necessarily omitted herein are the relations in which the employment of such terms as *institor* and *procurator* without further identification leaves open the question whether a friend, child, slave, or freedman of the principal is concerned.[7]

The status relation of patron and freedman.[8]—Manumission did not completely destroy the ties that had bound the freedman to his former master.[9] The patron has been compared to a father; in fact, the freedman has no other legally recognized father.[10] If the freed person was a minor the patron became the guardian, an ancient legal principle deriving from juristic interpretation of the Twelve Tables.[11] Under certain conditions the patron could bring the freedman back into the immediate family, *i. e.*, by adrogation; none but the patron could adrogate his freedman.[12] It is not at all strange, therefore, that a great number of freedmen, whether it was the majority or not cannot be determined, after their manumission continued to live with the patron and were in some degree subject to his power.[13] Often this would be to the advantage of the freedman; the patron could be liable for certain torts committed by the freedman,[14] but more replete with commercial implications was the rule that the patron could not bring an action for theft against a freedman residing with him, inasmuch as his house-power was deemed sufficient to recover the property stolen and punish the guilty freedman.[15]

One of the normal principal and agent relationships in classical Roman law was that of patron and freedman. Besides the innumerable designations of freedmen as institors or procurators,[16] the sources sometimes state specifically that the freedman was, *e.g.*, over-sea agent, attorney.[17] The freedman is found carrying on the same enterprises as when he was a slave,[18] and often appears as the administrator of the business affairs of the minor children or daughter of the patron.[19] Some few activities deserve specific mention. A freedman who, believing himself to be a slave, acts in the interests of his patron, may or may not recover for any expenses that he incurs thereby, the actual holding being disputed by modern scholars.[20] Where a third person, on the strength of a written power of attorney, lends money to a freedman-agent, the patron is liable for its return, even though it has not been spent in his behalf.[21] The stipulation of a freedman-agent that money loaned is to be repaid to his principal, together with interest, is invalid so far as the capital is concerned, but if the person to whom the interest is to be paid is not specifically mentioned, it is construed to be the freedman, and the latter must thereupon transfer it to the patron.[22] Where a freedman has been appointed to handle his patron's banking business, and gives a note to a slave of a depositor, there is normally no right to enforce the note against the freedman.[23] Another occurrence of deposit seems to present the opposite holding, if the depositor is urged by the patron to place with his freedman instead of himself.[24] Finally, a freedman directs his banker to pay money over to his patron; the banker, without doing so, later delivers to the freedman a statement which purports to cancel any previous orders the freedman has made; and the cancellation is held invalid.[25] These examples well illustrate the complicated transactions in which patron, freedman, and third person may be involved and direct attention to the necessity of the reëxamination of commercial obligations from the point of view of the persons involved rather than from the legal aspect of the contract.

The close tie existing between patron and freedman is shown by the donations or bequests of *peculium* to the latter, thereby enabling him to set himself up in business.[26] The patron may make an outright gift, which, however, he can recover in the event of the freedman's ingratitude,[27] or he may pay the whole or part of the purchase price of property destined for the freedman.[28] Legacies by patrons to their freedmen are numerous, often of land or houses with restrictions upon alienation,[29] one passage clearly indicating a desire on the part of the testator to preserve the family name.[30] Bequests, providing that the freedman need not account to the heirs,[31] or granting annuities provided he handles the business of the patron's daughter,[32] or a gift of everything the freedman has "in credits, movable property, or money,"[33] clearly show the intention of the patron to continue a business which during his life had been administered by the freedman (or slave manumitted by the will) in his behalf.

The patron thus could be as liberal as he liked with the freedman, but there were certain limitations upon the duties that could be exacted from the freedman as part of the *ius patronatus.* In the first place, certain classes of freedmen were wholly or in part freed from patronate duties. The slave manumitted directly by the will of the owner, *libertus orcinus,* has actually no patron.[34] If a slave is granted manumission by means of *fideicommissum,* he is considered the freedman of the *fideicommissarius,* but the latter's rights are less extensive than those of the normal patron.[35] A similar situation existed in respect of slaves whose freedom was purchased "with their own money."[36] We can but mention that, on the one hand, there was a gradual extension by imperial constitutions of freedom from patronate duties,[37] and, on the other hand, that certain inferior groups of manumitted slaves were subject to increased liabilities.[38]

Even in respect of normal freedom there were bounds to what the patron could exact. If a patron granted freedom to a slave only after an agreement *(societas)* had been made between them leading to the unwarranted exploitation of the freedman, such agreement was in classical times *ipso iure* void.[39] In addition, if something was to be exacted from the freedman which served to make the grant of freedom oppressive, the *praetor* would not permit the patron to sue because of the freedman's nonperformance, or he would grant to the freedman the *exceptio onerandae libertatis causa.*[40] If the patron wished to exact what the former slave, if he had been free, would have been compelled to hand over as the profits from the master's business, the *exceptio* could not be raised,[41] nor if the promise had been made to a creditor of the patron, or by a debtor of the freedman to the patron, though here the freedman is granted a *condictio* against the patron.[42]

As might be expected, there are numerous restraints upon the activities of the freedman in respect to his patron, that are significant within the sphere of their commercial relations. A freedman could not summon his patron to trial without the *praetor's* permission,[43] and a violation of this rule entitled the patron to an *actio in factum* against the freedman.[44] The freedman could not bring an infamous or criminal action at all,[45] nor seek an interdict *unde vi* or *quod vi,*[46] or raise an *exceptio doli, vis,* or *metus causa* against the patron.[47] Even where suit was permitted the patron could introduce any surety,[48] need not swear for vexatiousness,[49] and could only be condemned for as much as he could pay.[50] But the freedman also had certain rights. He was entitled to a *praeiudicium* to determine the status of the litigating parties,[51] and generally the rules set forth above did not apply to any but the individual patron and freedman.[52]

The patron's right to one-half the inheritance of his freedman who died possessed of 100,000 *sesterces* or more and did not have two sons, is not connected immediately with the commercial relations of patron and freedman;[53] yet it had some effect in that it prevented the freedman from alienating his property in order to defraud his patron.[54] Under certain circumstances the patron was deprived of his share in the inheritance.[55] Another duty that lay upon the freedman and that would, in some degree, affect his pecuniary acquisitions, was the support of the patron if the latter was in need.[56] The patron, however, must prove to the official in charge of the proceedings that he had no other means of support,[57] and, in such a situation, the freedman was obligated to the extent of his means, whether he owed other obligations or not.[58] More pertinent to the topic here considered is the accusation of ingratitude (*accusatio ingratus*) by a patron against a freedman.[59] The accusation was granted for a number of causes,[60] though not all violations of the *obsequium* made the freedman liable.[61] It was only available where the manumission was voluntary;[62] the punishment inflicted varied,[63] and the most severe, namely, revocation into slavery, was rarely imposed.[64]

We have seen that the freedman, as compared to other free men, sometimes derived advantage from his position, sometimes was at a disadvantage, but that in any event the status relation of freedman and patron played a significant part in the daily life and therefore in the commercial life of both freedman and patron. We turn now to a survey of an obligation peculiar to the patron and freedman, and normally entered into by these persons, which, in some degree, regulated their business relations, namely, the *operae libertorum.*

Operae libertorum.—In addition to the interrelation of patron and freedman dependent upon the status of the parties, it seems to have been the common practice for the slave to swear, before his manumission, that he would perform a specified number of days' labor for his master after his manumission.[65] This so-called *operae libertorum* ranged from a few days' labor to services extending over a considerable period of time; in fact, one passage in the Digest states "as many *operae* as the patron shall decide."[66] In the time of Justinian the work that the freedman was to perform as *operae* was of two kinds, *officiales* and *fabriles*.[67] The former were those within the *officium*, or duties for which there was a natural obligation on the part of the freedman to perform, such as accompanying the patron about the city or on his travels, taking care of his house, and performing various domestic duties.[68] If, however, the freedman had become skilled in a trade before or after manumission, he might offer such commercial activities as *operae;* these were termed *fabriles*.[69] Juristic distinctions accompanied the factual one, notably the hereditability or nonhereditability of *operae* by an *heres extraneus* of the patron.[70] Until recently, scholars had assumed that a similar classification existed in classical times.[71] Mitteis has shown,[72] however, that *operae* of freedman were not so classified with resultant legal distinctions.[73] Just what classification existed remains a matter of dispute. Mitteis held that *operae* of freedmen (*officiales*) were contrasted with the *operae* of free employees, arising out of the contract *locatio conductio operarum;* Biondi[74] says that the distinction was between *operae* performed and those to be performed. Further discussion of this highly complicated question is out of place here.[75] The sources, juristic as well as literary and inscriptional, indicate that the *operae* might range from the lowliest domestic duties to highly complicated commercial operations.[76]

Inasmuch as the promise of a slave was not binding after his manumission, the slave was required to utter an oath to perform *operae*.[77] The religious obligation herein necessitated a renewed promise after manumission by means of another oath or a stipulation.[78] A further step was necessary before the promised *operae* were due; the patron must indicate the time when they were to be performed.[79] If the time fixed passed without performance, the *operae* became *praeteritae*,[80] and the patron now had a cause of action, the so-called *iudicium operarum.*[81] The nature and origin of this action is a matter of some dispute. Segrè holds it to be a praetorian action based on the praetorian nature of the services promised by oath;[82] Biondi differentiates between the praetorian *iudicium operarum* and the civil *actio ex stipulatu* for *incerta.*[83] But the greater number of scholars hold it to be a civil action, which is recognized by the *praetor* in his edict.[84] Krüger points out that he does so in order to indicate the particular cases in which the action is to be denied.[85] It is to be noted that money could not be exacted instead of *operae,*[86] yet the condemnation in the *iudicium operarum* is a money condemnation, and fixed at the value of the services imposed.[87]

It now remains to point out such commercial factors as may be found in the *operae libertorum. Operae* are not due at all if freedom is acquired by fideicommissary manumission[88] or by purchase of freedom *suis nummis,*[89] nor does an adopting father or husband acquire them;[90] in the great number of examples it will be noted that there is a definite separation from the person with whom the freedman may previously have had business relations.[91] The direct descendants of the patron, however, even an emancipated son, succeed to *operae,* whereas an *heres extraneus* does not.[92] There are some interesting examples with reference to copatrons.[93] In one example copatrons seem to have severed relations and departed to different places, yet seek to have the *operae* due each performed at the same time.[94] In another we find that the freedman can satisfy copatrons at one time.[95]

Variants from the normal *operae* may have commercial significance; for example, to attend the patron rather than offer him business or professional competition.[96] Similarly, the fact that *operae* can only be exacted when the freedman has been given sufficient time to earn money to support himself has a commercial slant;[97] if this is not done the patron must support the freedman during the period of the services.[98] Only *operae* which are in accord with the age, rank, health, requirements, and mode of life of the freedman (or of the patron) are to be performed;[99] the rank of the freedman or the nature of the occasion might affect the business relations of the two parties, though this is not expressly mentioned.[100] So also may commercial activities be concerned in the voluntary release of *operae* by the patron.[101]

When a third party enters into the picture, however, the business element presses to the foreground. Perhaps the simplest example is the hiring out of the *operae* by the patron.[102] This was considered nothing more than the exaction of *operae* if the patron himself could not profit from the particular services the freedman was able to render.[103] But if the patron could use the *operae* and preferred to hire them out, then he receives a price for them, which is in violation of the *lex Aelia Sentia,*[104] as the obligation of the freedman to hand over money to the patron is invalid.[105] The stipulation addressed to the freedman might even be phrased to include possible performance to a third person (*solutionis causa adiectus*).[106] Such a stipulation was undoubtedly valid;[107] the only question was whether the freedman pursued a trade which made such *operae* available and whether they could be performed without injury to his rank, health, and so forth.[108] The performance to a third party might be in satisfaction of a debt of the patron to the third-person creditor.[109] In such a circumstance the freedman could not avail himself of the exemption from *operae* by reason of the *lex Papia,*[110] nor could he raise the *exceptio onerandae libertatis causa* against the creditor.[111] There is no way of determining the frequency of the hiring or assigning of *operae,* but it seems likely that the patron would rather pay off a debt by utilizing *operae* than money, and would hire out the skilled labor of the freedman to his best advantage, if that were possible.[112]

A conclusion to this article is unwarranted. All the possible groups of sources presented above, supplemented with nonlegal materials, must be examined at length, before we can picture even this small portion of commercial law. If the attention of the reader has been directed to the vast field virtually unsurveyed from the point of view here involved, the purpose of this survey will have been accomplished.

NOTES TO SCHILLER ESSAY

[1] Periodicals cited in abbreviated form are: AG = Archivio Giuridico "Filippo Serafini"; Ann. Pal. = Annali del Seminario Giuridico della R. Università di Palermo; Bull. = Bullettino dell'Istituto di Diritto Romano; Jher. Jahr. = Jherings Jahrbücher für die Dogmatik des bürgerlichen Rechts; RH = Revue historique de droit français et étranger (Quatrième série); SZ = Zeitschrift der Savigny-Stiftung für Rechtsgeschichte, romanistische Abteilung; Tijd. = Tijdschrift voor Rechtsgeschiedenis. All other works are given in full the first time cited; the usual abbreviations for the Latin sources are employed.

[2] Huvelin, *Études d'histoire du droit commercial romain* (1929), pp. 77 ff.; Schiller, (1930) 30 Col. L. Rev. 845 n. 75.

[3] Through the offices of the Council for Research in the Social Sciences at Columbia University, the author is being ably assisted by Mr. Elvin Vl. Abelès in his research in this field.

[4] Buckland, *The Roman Law of Slavery* (1908), pp. 702 ff., points out that it is difficult to believe that the Romans had any theory of representation, and certainly not one held in any particular modern legal system.

[5] Cicero, De officiis i. 150–51, presents admirably the prejudice against business: "Equally contemptible is the business of the retail dealer.... The work of the mechanic is also degrading; there is nothing noble about a workshop.... Business on a small scale is despicable; but if it is extensive and imports commodities in large quantities from all the world and distributes them honestly, it is not so very discreditable.... But of all sources of wealth farming is the best, the most agreeable, the most profitable, the most noble."—Gardiner's translation.

[6] Huvelin, *Etudes ... droit commercial,* pp. 68 ff.

[7] For a general discussion of these relations see Mitteis, *Die Lehre von der Stellvertretung nach römischem Recht* (1885); Costa, *Le azioni exercitoria e institoria nel diritto romano* (1891); Le Bras, *L'évolution générale du procurateur en droit privé romain des origines au IIIe siècle* (1922); and specifically on the actions involved, Lenel, *Das Edictum perpetuum* (ed. 3; 1927), pp. 258 ff.

[8] On patronate law generally see Leist, *Das römische Patronatrecht,* 2 vols. [Glück's *Pandektencommentar,* Serie der Bücher 37/38] (1879); Karlowa, *Römische Rechtsgeschichte,* II (1901), 142 ff., 1118 ff.; Bonfante, *Corso di diritto romano,* I (1925), 172 ff. and VI (1930), 112 ff.

[9] Virtually all the relations between patron and freedman discussed in the following pages are, from the Roman point of view, incorporated within the concept of obsequium, which signifies the respect, fealty, loyalty, and allegiance due to one's superior from the modern point of view. *E.g.,* D. 37.15.9: Liberto et filio semper honesta et sancta persona patris ac patroni videri debet.

[10] Festus, *De verb. sign., s.v. patronus.* On the names of freedmen see Duff, *Freedmen in the Early Roman Empire* (1928), pp. 52 ff.; Lemonnier, *Etude historique sur la condition privée des affranchis* (1887), pp. 167 ff., 304 ff.

[11] G. 1.165; D. 26.4.1.3 *i.f.;* 26.4.3; see Buckland, *A Text-Book of Roman Law* (ed. 2; 1932), pp. 145 f.

[12] D. 1.7.15.3; C. 8.47.3; see Leist, *Patronatrecht,* II, 6 ff.

[13] Instanced in D. 7.8.2.1; 18.6.19 pr.; 21.1.17.15. But there is no obligation to do so,

C. 6.3.12, and see Partsch, SZ, XXVIII (1907), 434; *cf.* generally Leist, *Patronatrecht*, I, 545 ff.

[14] D. 9.3.5.1, granting an action for injuring a passer-by or property by things thrown out of a house against both the libertus and patronus but not cumulatively, see Levy, *Die Konkurrenz der Aktionen und Personen im klassischen römischen Recht*, I (1918), 328 ff. Possibly also with reference to res suspensae, *arg.* D. 9.3.5.10, but *cf.* 9.3.5.12 which would seem to be contra; the substitution by Arangio-Ruiz, Bull., XXV (1912), 162 n., of ⟨in factum⟩ for [ad exemplum huius actionis] in the latter passage would support my view.

[15] D. 47.2.90; *cf.* 48.19.11.1, where Solazzi, AG, XCIV (1925), 80 f., considers [nam-*fin.*] *a gloss.* D. 47.2.17.2 may be contra—Karlowa, *Röm. Rechtsgesch.*, II, 143 n. 6.

[16] *Supra* note 7.

[17] Traveling agent in D. 34.1.19; 34.2.4; 40.9.10, but this part is interpolated according to Schulz, SZ, XLVIII (1928), 250, and Arangio-Ruiz, *Studi in onore di P. Bonfante*, I (1930), 515. Attorney, *arg.* D. 3.1.1.11 and C. 2.6.2, but *cf.* Taubenschlag, *Mélanges de droit romain dédiés à Georges Cornil*, II (1926), 500. Generally on freedmen as agents see Duff, *Freedmen*, pp. 91 ff.

[18] D. 14.3.19.1; 26.7.58 pr.; *cf.* Costa, *Azioni exercitoria*, pp. 43 f.

[19] D. 26.7.58 pr.; 35.1.101.4: . . quamdiu res patroni filiae gesserit; C. 2.18.5; 5.37.4; 5.43.1. Generally on guardianship by freedmen, see Leist, *Patronatrecht*, II, 189 ff.

[20] D. 3.5.5.7 (Ulp. 10 ad ed.). Si quis quasi servus meus negotium meum gesserit, cum esset vel libertus vel ingenuus, dabitur negotiorum gestorum actio. The case is fully discussed by Partsch, *Studien zur Negotiorum Gestio* I [Sitz. d. Heidelberger Akad. d. Wiss., phil.-hist. Kl., (1913), Abh. 12], 95 ff., where the insertion of ⟨utilis⟩ by Cujas and Krüger is noted, with which Partsch agrees. Riccobono, *Ann. Pal.*, III/IV (1917), 679 ff., in a long discussion, substitutes ⟨non tenetur mihi negotiorum gestorum actione⟩ for [dabitur-*fin.*], and Beseler, SZ, XLIV (1924), 382, is in accord, reading ⟨non⟩ dabitur, both thereby holding that the classical jurists denied recovery to the bona fide serviens. Is it possible that we can distinguish between the libertus and the ingenuus?

[21] D. 3.5.30 pr. (Papin. 2 resp.). Liberto vel amico mandavit pecuniam accipere mutuam: cuius litteras creditor secutus contraxit et fideiussor intervenit: etiamsi pecunia non sit in rem eius versa, tamen dabitur in eum negotiorum gestorum actio creditori vel fideiussori, scilicet ad exemplum institoriae actionis. Schlossmann, in a long article, Jher. Jahr., XXVIII (1889), 287–343, believes that Papinian wrote that an actio ad exemplum institoriae actionis was granted the creditor and the surety, while Albertario, *L'actio quasi institoria* (1913), p. 29, denying the action, and Bonfante, *Istituzioni di diritto romano* (ed. 8; 1925), p. 395 n. 1, hold that the quasi institoria is entirely Justinian, *contra:* Solazzi, Bull., XXIII (1911), 153 ff. at pp. 168 ff., where he notes [creditori vel]. Partsch, *Aus nachgelassenen und kleineren verstreuten Schriften* [Freiburger Rechtsgeschichtliche Abhandlungen, I (1931)], 97 ff., sees the owner liable to the creditor by the a° negot. gest., to the surety by the utilis a° negot. gest. ad exemplum institoriae, accord Krüger, Digest, *ad h. l.* Further, see Pacchioni, trans. of Savigny, *Le Obbligazioni*, II (1915), 423–469, and Rabel, *Ein Ruhmesblatt Papinians, Festschrift für Ernst Zitelmann* (1913).

[22] D. 45.1.126.2 (Paul 3 quaest.). This is perhaps one of the most suspected passages of the Digest. Paul holds that a loan made in another's name would have been valid, but a stipulation for it is invalid. He further holds—Vassalli, Bull., XXVII (1914), 248 n. 2: [superest-*fin.*] is unwarranted—that if the loan and stipulation are simultaneous there is no action, supplying ⟨sed magis est, ne possit⟩ after petere possit, so Mommsen and Beseler, *Beiträge zur Kritik der römischen Rechtsquellen*, III (1913), 147—for there is but one obligation. What follows is in the main interpolated: Siber, *Naturalis obligatio*

[Leipziger rechtswissenschaftliche Studien, XI (1926)], 2 f., sees plane-obligatione as genuine, but contra Perozzi, *Istituzioni di diritto romano* (ed. 2; 1928), II, 33, n. 3; Beseler, *loc. cit.;* Vážný, *Studi . . . Bonfante,* IV, 134; and others. Beseler, SZ, XLV (1925), 484: [non eodem-ideoque] and [stipulatio-cedere], saying "Stipulationen kann man nicht zedieren!" seems too radical to me, though [neque-videri] of Beseler, *Beiträge,* III, 147, may be correct. For interpolations at the close of the passage see Eisele, SZ, X (1889), 321; Riccobono, SZ, XXXV (1914), 260, and XLIII (1922), 276, 352; Beseler, *loc. cit.,* and Tijd., X (1930), 188; Scherillo, *Studi . . . Bonfante,* IV, 212. The law involved is handled by Segrè, *Studi giuridici in onore di Vincenzo Simoncelli* (1917), pp. 333 ff.

23 D. 14.3.20 (Scaev. 5 dig.). Kübler, SZ, XXIX (1908), 210, says that the principal would have been liable to an a° institoria if the freedman was an institor, the usual circumstance. Costa, *Azioni exercitoria,* p. 44 n. 24, and Lenel, *Palingenesia iuris civilis* (1889), II, col. 221 n. 2, point out that the compilators inserted [Lucius Titius] and [Gaio Seio]. Beseler, SZ, XLV (1925), 453, substitutes ⟨non posse⟩ for [nec iure-*fin.*].

24 D. 16.3.1.14 (Ulp. 30 ad ed.). See the discussion of Bortolucci, Bull., XXVII (1914), 150 ff. The observed interpolations do not relate to the libertus unless Perozzi, *Istituti,* II, 306, n. 2: [sed si-non video] be correct, but *cf.* Rabel, *Studi . . . Bonfante,* IV, 283 f. and 284 n. 7. For the other interpolations see *Index Interpolationum,* I (1929), col. 268 f.

25 D. 2.14.47.1 (Scaev. 1 dig.). The holding depends upon the construction of the epistula.

26 On the favors conferred by patrons on freedmen generally, see Leist, *Patronatrecht,* I, 554 ff. Peculium, see D. 33.8 *passim;* 46.3.62; C. 7.23.1; Vat. Fr. 261. The whole question of the peculium is better discussed in connection with the servus and filius.

27 C. 8.55.1 pr., 1, 3.

28 D. 17.1.12.8 (Ulp. 31 ad ed.) . . . si patronus praedium quod emerat, pro quo pretii bessem exsolverat, iusserit liberto suo tradi, ut ille residuum pretii redderet, . . .

29 With restraints upon alienation: D. 31.77.27; 31.77.28; 31.88.6; 31.88.14; 32.38.5; 33.1.18 pr. Other legacies: 33.1.10.3; 34.1.19; fideicommissum: 30.108.15. Of two freedmen in partnership, one is made heres, the other left a legacy, D. 17.2.71.1.

30 D. 35.1.108 (Scaev. 19 dig.). Libertis omnibus legavit domum et haec verba adiecit: "ut in ea habitent liberti, ne de nomine exeat et ut ad unum, qui novissimus exstiterit, perveniat: . . ."

31 D. 34.3.31.1 (Scaev. 3 resp.). Inter cetera liberto ita legavit: "et si quid me vivo gessit, rationes ab eo exigi veto." . . . Though the heirs might get possession of the account books and such sums as properly belonged to the estate, the freedman was entitled to the remainder.

32 D. 35.1.101.4 (Papin. 8 resp.). Fideicommissa menstrua et annua sub ea condicione liberto relicta "quamdiu res patroni filiae gesserit". . .

33 D. 39.5.35 pr. (Scaev. 31 dig.). Ad eum, quem manumiserat, epistulam misit in haec verba: "Titius Sticho liberto suo salutem. Cum te manumiserim, peculium quoque tuum omne, quidquid habes tam in nominibus quam in rebus moventibus sive in numerato, me tibi concedere . . . notum tibi facio.". . .

34 References in Bonfante, *Corso,* I, 177 n. 15; Loreti-Lorini, Bull., XXXIV (1925), 29 ff., portrays at length the privileged condition of the libertus orcinus and demonstrates that his position as a libertus familiae under the quasi-patronage of the son of the testator is a post-classical development, pp. 42 ff., 47 ff.

35 Loreti-Lorini, Bull., XXXIV (1925), 32 f.; Leist, *Patronatrecht,* I, 437 ff. If the

fideicommissarius failed to carry out the trust he lost all patronal rights, *cf.* Buckland, *Text-Book,* p. 84, and Bonfante, *Corso,* I, 178 n. 2.

[36] See Seuffert, *Festschrift für die juristische Fakultät in Giessen* (1907), pp. 13 ff.

[37] Summarized in Buckland, *Text-Book,* p. 90 and Bonfante, *Corso,* I, 172 f. The condition of the imperial freedman is wholly outside the private business relations of patronus and libertus; *cf.* Duff, *Freedmen,* chap. 8 and Appendix III.

[38] Notably the Latini Iuniani, upon whom there is a voluminous literature, referred to, in part, by Jörs, *Geschichte und System des römischen Privatrechts* [Enzyklopädie der Rechts- und Staatswissenschaft, hgg. von Kohlrausch, Kaskel, Spiethoff, II/III (1927)], p. 49 n. 7.

[39] D. 38.1.36 (Ulp. 11 ad l. Iul. et Pap.). Labeo ait libertatis causa societatem inter libertum et patronum factam ipso iure nihil valere palam esse. *Cf.* also D. 44.5.1.7. The statement of Servius in D. 38.2.1 pr., and the edict of the praetor Rutilius, D. 38.2.1.1, seem to indicate that the agreement earlier gave rise to an action, at least sometimes, when the freedman violated his duty of obsequium. *Cf.* Schmidt, *Das Pflichttheilsrecht des Patronus und des Parens Manumissor* (1868), pp. 8 ff., particularly p. 9 n. 22; Pernice, SZ, III (1882), 101 ff.; Leist, *Patronatrecht,* II, 292 ff.; Karlowa, *Röm. Rechtsgesch.,* II, 1118 ff. The a° societatis was replaced by bonorum possessio contra tabulas under later praetors, D. 38.2.1.2, see *infra.*

[40] Defined: D. 44.5.1.5–6; lies to the surety or attorney of the freedman, D. 44.5.1.8, with [procurator] for ⟨cognitor⟩, Frese, *Studi ... Bonfante,* IV, 418 n. 81; and to the successors of freedmen and against the heirs of patrons, D. 44.5.1.12. *Cf.* generally Leist and Karlowa, *loc. cit.* note 39 *supra.*

[41] D. 44.5.1.4, *cf.* Vážný, *Studi ... Bonfante,* IV, 169.

[42] D. 44.5.1.10–11 (Ulp. 76 ad ed.). These two passages are fully discussed by Duquesne, *Mélanges P. F. Girard* (1912), I, 404 ff., as an analogy to a condictio in donationes ultra modum legis Cinciae. Appleton, RH, X (1931), 443 f., however, denies the classical existence of such a condictio and regards [verumtamen-fecit] and [sed-repetet] as interpolated. If Duquesne be correct, as the author is inclined to believe, we have here further complicated business transactions involving patron, freedman, and third party.

[43] Provided for in the edict, D. 2.4.4.1: Praetor ait: "parentem, patronum patronam, liberos parentes patroni patronae in ius sine permissu meo ne quis vocet." This is commented upon in D. 2.4.10.12. *Cf.* generally Lenel, *Edictum,* pp. 68 ff.; further note G. 4.183; C. 6.6.4.1. A petition (libellus) to the emperor is held not to be a summons, D. 2.4.15 ([vel praesidi] is clearly interpolated).

[44] D. 44.7.25.1 *i.f.;* G. 4.46; *cf.* Lenel, *loc. cit.,* note 43 *supra.* Also corporal punishment, D. 2.4.25 ([vel-vel] is interpolated), and the emperor denies a rescript to one who has so acted, C. 2.2.2.

[45] Infamous: D. 37.15.5.1; C. 6.6.1. Specifically mentioned are the a° de dolo, D. 4.3.11.1; 37.15.2 pr.; the a° iniuriarum, 37.15.2 pr.; the a° servi corrupti, 37.15.6; the a° calumniae, 37.14.1. Criminal: D. 1.2.1.10; 37.14.1; 37.14.5 pr.; 48.2.8 *i.f.* In addition the freedman must have been severely handicapped by the inability to bring the penal a° in factum intimated by the neque si of D. 37.15.5 pr., *cf.* Lenel, *Edictum,* p. 109.

[46] D. 37.15.2.1; 37.15.7.2.

[47] D. 37.15.7.2.

[48] D. 2.8.2.2. *i.f.,* where [fideiussor-causa] replaces ⟨vindex⟩. This was part of the edict *re* summons, *cf.* Lenel, *op. cit.,* pp. 65 ff.

[49] D. 37.15.7.3.

[50] D. 37.15.7.1: Et in quantum facere possunt, damnantur; 42.1.16–17: Sunt qui in id quod facere possunt conveniuntur, . . .

[51] *I.e.* a preliminary examination, D. 40.14.6; the person who alleges he is patron is always plaintiff. See generally on this praeiudicium, Leist, *Patronatrecht*, II, 149 ff.

[52] The heirs of the freedman all have causes of action against the patron of the deceased, D. 37.15.8; the exceptions available to a patron do not lie to his surety, D. 44.1.7 pr., though Beseler, *Studi . . . Bonfante*, II, 61, holds this all interpolated. Respect is not due persons intervening for patrons, D. 37.15.7.5: Honor autem his personis habebitur ipsis, non etiam interventoribus eorum: et si forte ipsi pro alii interveniant, honor habebitur. If this last means the prohibition of a suit by the freedman, it would seem that he was greatly restricted in enforcing his rights.

[53] The various stages of the iura in bonis are depicted in G. 3.39–53. The significant praetorian bonorum possessio contra tabulas, granted to the patron in classical times, grew out of the earlier a° societatis, D. 38.2.1 and *supra* note 39, and was greatly affected by the lex Papia Poppaea of Augustus; see generally D. 38.2: de bonis libertorum. Among the numerous works consult Leist, *Patronatrecht*, II, 318–557.

[54] Generally D. 38.5: si quid in fraudem patroni factum sit; Frag. de formula Fabiana. *Cf.* also D. 37.14.16 pr. In the secondary literature see, besides Leist, Lenel, *Edictum*, pp. 352 ff.

[55] D. 25.3.6 pr.; 37. 14.5.1; 37.14.9.1; 37.14.10; 38.1.32.

[56] Leist, *Patronatrecht*, II, 14 ff.

[57] D. 1.12.1.2; 25.3.5.19; 25.3.9. The freedman, however, is entitled to a praeiudicium, D. 25.3.5.18.

[58] P. 2.32; D. 38.1.41; *cf.* generally de Francisci, *Studi Sassaresi*, ser. 2, I (1921), abstracted in SZ, XLV (1925), 570. Note, in passing, that a condition in appointing a person to civil law testamentary dispositions (*cf.* Lenel, *Edictum*, p. 362) which read "si parentibus suis patronove alimenta non praestiterit" was held invalid, D. 28.7.9.

[59] See generally Leist, *Patronatrecht*, I, 384 ff.; Duff, *Freedman*, pp. 40 ff.

[60] D. 1.12.1.10; 25.3.6.1; 37.14.1; C. 6.6.4 pr.

[61] C. 6.3.12.

[62] D. 37.15.3; C. 6.3.2; 6.3.8; 6.7.1.

[63] References cited *supra* note 60, and D. 1.16.9.3; 2.4.25 ([vel-vel] a post-classical addition); 37.14.7.1; C. 8.55.1 pr.-1.

[64] Sources cited and a long discussion by de Francisci, *Mélanges . . . Cornil*, I, 295–323.

[65] Buckland, *Text-Book*, p. 89: "An opera is a day's work, conceived of as a definite unit of value, a dandum, not a faciendum." *Cf.* Thélohan, *Etudes d'histoire juridique offertes à P. F. Girard*, I (1912), 355 ff. The references to imposition of operae are collected by Gradenwitz, SZ, XXIII (1902), 338.

[66] D. 38.1.30 pr. (Cels. 12 dig.). Si libertus ita iuraverit dare se, quot operas patronus arbitratus sit, non aliter ratum fore arbitrium patroni, quam si aequum arbitratus sit. . . . Cf. also D. 37.14.6.1: Stipulatus est centum operas . . .; 38.1.15.1: . . . si communis libertus patronis duobus operas mille daturum se iuraverit. . . .

[67] Significant passages presenting this distinction are D. 12.6.26.12 (Ulp. 26 ad ed.); 38.1.6 (Ulp. 26 ad Sab.); 38.1.9.1 (Ulp. 34 ad Sab.); 38.1.23.1 (Iul. 22 dig.); 38.1.24 (Iul. 52 dig.).

[68] See generally Leist, *Patronatrecht*, II, 220 ff., who cites 38.1.26; 38.1.38.1; 38.1.45; 38.1.49. Note D. 38.1.1 (Paul sing. de var. lect.) Operae sunt diurnum officium.

[69] D. 38.1.38.1 (Callist. 3 ed. mon.). Si tamen libertus artificium exerceat, eius quo-

que operas patrono praestare debebit, etsi post manumissionem id didicerit. . . .; D. 38.1.16 pr. (Paul 40 ad ed.) Eius artificii, quod post manumissionem didicerit libertus, operas debebit praestare, ...

[70] D. 38.1.6 (Ulp. 26 ad Sab.). Fabriles operae ceteraeque, quae quasi in pecuniae praestatione consistunt, ad heredem transeunt, officiales vero non transeunt; 29.2.20.2; C. 6.3.6.

[71] Notably Leist, *Patronatrecht,* II, 220 ff.; Karlowa, *Röm. Rechtsgesch.*, II, 144 ff. *Cf.* also the non-legal commentaries, *e.g.*, Duff, *Freedmen,* pp. 44 ff., but note the doubt raised by Lemonnier, *Affranchis,* pp. 123 ff.

[72] *Operae officiales und operae fabriles,* SZ, XXIII (1902), 143–158.

[73] Summarized: The distinction of freedman's operae into officiales and fabriles is found only in Ulpian (see his passages cited *supra* note 67), while Julian (D. 38.1.23 pr.; 38.1.24) holds that fabriles are outside the sphere of operae libertorum. The resultant legal effects that fabriles are owed at once and officiales only when indicated by the patron, and that fabriles must be certa species operarum, can thus be explained. D. 38.1.22.1 (Gai. 14 ad ed. prov.) removes the distinction with respect to succession of operae, since 38.1.16, which appears contra: Fabriles operae . . . ad heredem transeunt, officiales vero non transeunt, originally dealt with the effect of adrogation. Mitteis concludes that services of freedmen are never fabriles; whether they will be industrial cannot be foretold. Professional services known as artificiales are only a type of officiales, *cf.* synonymous usage of operae and officium in D. 12.6.26.12 and 38.1.22 pr.

[74] *Iudicium operarum.* Annali della facoltà di giuresprudenza dell'Università di Perugia, XXVIII (1914), 55–76, especially pp. 66 ff., summarized: patronate and hereditas are distinctly independent of one another [*cf.* now Rabel's survey of Bonfante, SZ, L (1930), 311 ff.]; thus the right to succeed to operae was not governed by rules of succession. Classical law differentiates operae praeteritae and operae futurae, 38.1.3 pr. (Pomp. 6 ad Sab.): Operas stipulatus ante peractum diem operam eius diei petere non potest, and D. 38.1.13.2 (Ulp. 38 ad ed.): Iudicium de operis tunc locum habet, cum operae praeterierint . . . , and the former pass to the heres extraneus. With Justinian the operae futurae also pass. So for classical law we reconstruct D. 38.1.6: [Fabriles] ⟨Praeteritae⟩ operae [ceteraeque], quae quasi in pecuniae praestatione consistunt, ad heredem transeunt, [officiales] ⟨futurae⟩ vero non transeunt; and D. 38.1.9.1: Sed [officiales] quidem futurae . . . [cum constitit] ⟨et liberis eius⟩: [fabriles] ⟨praeteritae⟩ [autem aliaeve] eius generis sunt, ut [a quocumque] cuicumque solvi possint. [sane-*fin.*].

[75] Albertario, Atti della R. Accademia delle scienze di Torino, XLIX (1913/14), 728 ff., holds that operae of freedmen whether praeteritae or not, do not pass to the heres extraneus and thus reconstructs D. 38.1.6: Fabriles (operae outside of patronate) operae ad heredem transeunt, officiales (all the operae of freedman) vero non transeunt; and in D. 38.1.9.1 he holds only [quidem futurae] and [aliaeve] interpolated. This he bases on the complete differentiation of patronate and hereditas, *cf.* his earlier article in Il Filangieri, XXXV (1910), 707 ff. In accord with Mitteis, Biondi, or Albertario are Dessserteaux, *Etudes sur la formation historique de la capitis deminutio,* II (1919), 290 ff.; Bonfante, *Corso,* VI, 115 ff.; Buckland, *Text-Book,* pp. 89 n. 10, 316 n. 2.

[76] *Cf.* generally Lemonnier, *Affranchis,* pp. 266 ff.; Duff, *Freedmen,* chap. 6.

[77] G. Epit. 2.9.4: Item et alio casu, uno loquente et sine interrogatione alii promittente, contrahitur obligatio, id est, si libertus patrono aut donum aut munus aut operas se daturum esse iuravit. In qua re supradicti liberti non tam verborum solemnitate, quam iniurandi religione tenentur. Sed nulla altera persona hoc ordine obligari potest. *Cf.* D. 40.4.36.

[78] D. 40.12.44 pr. (Venul. 7 action.) . . . ideo autem solet iusiurandum a servis exigere,

ut hi religione adstricti, posteaquam suae potestatis esse coepissent, iurandi necessitatem haberent, dummodo in continenti, cum manumissus est, aut iuret aut promittat. On the oath *cf.* D. 38.1.7 pr.-1, 3; 46.4.13 pr. which states that the oath may be extinguished by acceptilatio, *cf.* Biondi, *Iudicium operarum,* p. 57 n. 5. The stipulation for operae is a genus obligation and divisible, D. 45.1.54.1. A stipulation for operae to be tendered the slave of the patron is invalid, D. 38.1.10 pr.; 45.3.38; further instances of stipulation: 37.14.6.1; 38.1.22 pr.; 38.1.24; 38.1.39 pr.-1.

[79] D. 45.1.73 pr.: . . . item si operas a liberto quis stipulatus sit, non ante dies earum cedit, quam indictae fuerint nec sint praestitae; and *cf.* D. 38.1.13.2; 38.1.23.1; 38.1.24. See Siber, SZ, XXIX (1908), 62 f., and Pernice, SZ, V (1884), 21 n. 4. G. 4.162: <Si> igitur restitutorium vel exhibitorium interdictum redditur, . . . aut exhibeatur libertus cui patronus operas indicere vellet, . . . , reveals how the indication might be made; on this exhibitory interdict see Demelius, *Die Exhibitionspflicht* (1872), pp. 243 ff., and Berger, SZ, XXXVI (1914), 202.

[80] D. 38.1.3 pr. (*supra* note 74). Performance defined: 38.1.3.1; 38.1.22 pr. Place of performance: 38.1.20.1; 38.1.21; 38.1.23.1; 38.1.24.

[81] Consult generally, Demelius, *Schiedseid und Beweiseid im römischen Civilprozesse* (1887), pp. 40 ff.; Segrè, *Studi Senesi,* XXIII (1906), 313 ff.; Biondi, *Iudicium operarum;* Krüger, SZ, XXXVII (1916), 280 ff.; Lenel, *Edictum,* §140.

[82] *Loc cit.* When the stipulatio was analogized to the oath, he holds, the civil action was extended to cases of operae promised by oath. The serious objection to Segrè's theory, the acceptilatio of iusiurandum, D. 46.4.13 pr., he dismisses as an interpolation, substituting <non> for [verius est], but see Biondi, *op. cit.,* p. 57 n. 5.

[83] *Op. cit.,* note 74 *supra,* especially pp. 72 ff. He says there is no evidence of civil origin, while D. 38.1.2.1 indicates praetorian; so also the use of "iudicium dare," references p. 72 n. 1. Inasmuch as iusiurandum was the earliest it was within the praetor's jurisdiction as a sacral matter. The iudicium operarum had advantages over the a° ex stipulatu in that it permitted iusiurandum in iure and, possibly, a penal sponsio. The fact that the intentio and condemnatio of the iudicium were certa also explains its preference over an action born of any stipulatio.

[84] Lenel, *loc cit.;* and authorities cited by Biondi, *op. cit.,* p. 61.

[85] *Loc. cit.,* note 81 *supra.* Among these cases are those of a freedman who has two sons in his potestas, a freedwoman over fifty years of age, and a freedwoman marrying with the consent of her patron.

[86] This is clearly stated in C. 6.3.7 pr. (224 A.D.): Nec patronis pro operis mercedem accipere licet, . . . ; *cf.* also C. 6.3.1: . . . ut pro operis aliquid praestetur, licet pretium non possit, . . . It may also be inferred from D. 38.1.25 pr. (Iul. 65 dig.): Patronus, qui operas liberti sui locat, non statim intellegendus est mercedem ab eo capere: [sed-*fin.*]; so Beseler, *Beiträge,* II (1911), 55. *Cf.* also D. 38.1.25.1 *i.f.,* 4. See, however, D. 40.9.32.1–2, and discussion by Deschamps, *Mélanges Gerardin,* pp. 169 ff.

[87] 'Services or money payment' is often found in the stipulations for operae, D. 37.14.6.1: Stipulatus est centum operas aut in singulas aureos quinos dari: . . . (held valid); 38.1.39 pr.: . . . 'si decem dierum operas non dederis, viginti nummos dare spondes?' . . . The following paragraph, 38.1.39.1, holds that the condemnation may be for more than 20, but the reason given seems absurd; Beseler, SZ, XLV (1925), 477, considers the whole of it, as well as the end of 38.1.39 pr., interpolated. Condemnation at value of operae: D. 38.1.26.1 *i.f.;* 45.1.54.1 *i.f.,* if not interpolated, Beseler, SZ, XLV (1925), 484.

[88] D. 38.1.7.4; 38.1.13.1; 38.2.29 pr.; C. 6.3.5. See note 35 *supra.*

[89] D. 38.1.13 pr.-1; C. 6.3.3; 6.3.8. *Cf.* C. 6.3.3 (manumissionis causa traditus), and see note 36 *supra.*

[90] G. 3.83: (the adoptive father or husband acquires all rights) exceptis his quae per capitis deminutionem pereunt, quales sunt usufructus, operarum obligatio ⟨libertinorum⟩ quae per iusiurandum contracta est . . . ; *cf.* Desserteaux, *Capitis Deminutio,* II, 289 ff.

[91] In the fideicommissary case the quasi-patron had had nothing to do with the freedman; are the operae due to an adopted person or spouse lost because these persons are now incapable of free business activity, *cf.* Desserteaux's explanation of the fiction which resulted in the loss of operae futurae only.

[92] D. 37.14.9 pr. (Modest. 9 reg.). Filii hereditate paterna se abstinentus ius, quod in libertis habent paternis, non amittunt: idem et in emancipato. Succession to heres extraneus is post-classical, see *supra* notes 73 ff.

[93] D. 38.1.4 [*cf.* Albertario, Atti . . . Torino, XLIX (1914), 738 f.]; 38.1.8 pr. [*cf.* Beseler, SZ, XLVI (1926), 97]; 38.1.15.1 *i.f.;* 38.1.23.1; 38.1.49; 38.1.51; 45.1.54.1.

[94] D. 38.1.23.1 (Iul. 22 dig.).

[95] D. 38.1.49 (Gai. sing. de casibus) Duorum libertus potest aliquo casu singulis diversas operas uno tempore in solidum edere, veluti si librarius sit et alii patrono librorum scribendorum operas edat, alter vero peregre cum suis proficiscens operas custodiae domus ei indixerit. . . .

[96] D. 38.1.26 pr. (Alf. Var. 7 dig.). Medicus libertus, quod putaret, si liberti sui medicinam non facerent, multo plures imperantes sibi habiturum, postulabat, ut sequerentur se neque opus facerent: id ius est nec ne? respondit ius esse, ... Full discussion of this and the related passages, D. 37.14.2; 37.14.18; 37.15.11; 38.1.25, in a projected article by the author.

[97] D. 38.1.19 (Gai. 14 ad ed. prov.) aut certe ita exigendae sunt ab eo operae, ut his quoque diebus, quibus operas edat, satis tempus ad quaestum faciendum, unde ali possit, habeat:. Also D. 38.1.20 pr. [*cf.* Beseler, SZ, XLV (1925), 450]; 38.1.33. Besides, time to take care of his physical needs, 38.1.22.2.

[98] D. 38.1.18; 38.1.50.1.

[99] D. 38.1.16.1 (Paul 40 ad ed.). Tales patrono operae dantur, quales ex aetate dignitate valetudine necessitate proposito ceterisque eius generis in utraque persona aestimari debent:; 38.1.16 pr.; 38.1.17; all interpolated according to Beseler, *Subsiciva* (1930), p. 12. *Cf.* also statement in D. 12.6.26.12: . . . nam plerumque robor hominis, aetas temporis opportunitasque naturalis mutat causam operarum, . . . but interpolated according to Trampedach, Benigni and others, see *Index Interpolationum,* I, col. 184.

[100] Suppose the freedman had entered the imperial service.

[101] Not in the statutory exemption cases, *e.g.,* D. 38.1.37.5; C. 6.3.7.1; but note D. 38.1.37.4. Business relations may enter into the acceptilatio of D. 46.4.13 pr. and the peculiar 38.1.41 [*cf.* de Francisci, abstracted in SZ, XLV (1925), 570].

[102] *E.g.,* D. 33.2.3; 38.1.25 pr.-4; C. 6.3.4.

[103] D. 38.1.25.1 (Iul. 65 dig.). Nam si quis pantomimum vel archimimum libertum habeat et eius mediocris patrimonii sit, ut non aliter operis eius uti possit quam locaverit eas, exigere magis operas quam mercedem capere existimandus est.

[104] D. 38.1.25.3: Sed qui operis liberti sui uti potest et locando pretium earum consequi mallet, is existimandus est mercedem ex operis liberti sui capere. *Cf.* Mitteis, SZ, XXIII (1902), 154 n. 1.

[105] D. 40.9.32.1–2; *cf.* Leist, *Patronatrecht,* II, 233 ff.

[106] D. 38.1.10.1: . . . 'patrono aut Lucio Titio' . . . ; 38.1.23 pr.: . . . quare sicut . . .quis potest sibi aut Titio stipulari, . . . [*cf.* Mitteis, SZ, XXIII (1902), 149 n. 1].

[107] Mitteis, SZ, XXIII (1902), 153 ff., on D. 38.1.10.1–38.1.12. The limitation of such a stipulation to operae fabriles, Karlowa, *Röm. Rechtsgesch.*, p. 147, is, in view of the present theory *re* officiales and fabriles, untenable.

[108] D. 38.1.38 pr.-1 (Callist. 3 ed. monit.).

[109] D. 12.6.26.12, greatly interpolated, but at least: . . . sed si delegatus [? sit a patrono] ⟨an teneatur alii exhibere⟩ [officiales] operas . . . ; 38.1.37.4 and 44.5.1.10 (see notes *infra*).

[110] D. 38.1.37.4 (Paul 2 ad l. Iul. et Pap.). Sed si creditori suo libertum patronus delegaverit, non potest idem dici: solutionis enim vicem continet haec delegatio. potest tamen . . . Pringsheim, SZ, L (1930), 365, and Rabel, *Grundzüge des römischen Privatrechts* [Enzykopädie der Rechtswissenschaft, hgg. Holtzendorff, Kohler (ed. 7; 1915), I], p. 488 n. 3, hold [potest tamen-*fin.*] interpolated, but the first part of the text is genuine, Erman, SZ, XXV (1904), 469.

[111] D. 44.5.1.10 (Ulp. 76 ad ed.). Quod si patronus libertum suum delegaverit creditori, an adversus creditorem, cui delegatus promisit libertatis causa onerandae, exceptione ista uti possit, videamus . . . creditorem quidem minime esse submovendum exceptione, . . . See *supra* note 42.

[112] A complete examination of all available material upon the freedman in commercial life would be necessary to an attempt to decide this question. Lemonnier, *Affranchis,* pp. 251–284, and Duff, *Freedmen,* pp. 89–128, summarize the material but not from this point of view.

THE SCIENTIFIC RÔLE OF CONSIDERATION IN CONTRACT

BY JOHN H. WIGMORE

I. INTRODUCTION

"Alas, poor Consideration!—I knew him, Horatio. A fellow of infinite scope, of most excellent obscurity and tenuity. He hath borne a heavy contract on his back a thousand times. And now, how abhorred in our imagination is he!—Where be your quid pro quo *now? your subtleties? your technicalities? your definitions that were wont to set judges and jurists in a quandary? Not one now! Quite chapfallen!"*

THUS MIGHT SOME FUTURE JURIST soliloquize as he turned back the pages of contract law and perused the various law review articles that would consign Consideration to the grave as an outworn osseous relic of a once lively element of Contract.

There lies before me, as I write, a single page of manuscript, in my own handwriting, containing a memorandum of (what I once thought —and still deem, for that matter) an important juristic discovery, namely, the close relation of Contract, Deceit, and Estoppel, and its practical consequences for the function of Consideration. That manuscript is worn and musty. It bears no date. A calligraphic expert—like the author of *Court Hand in the 14th Century*—could probably date it, by comparison with specimens of my hand from various years. But its date may be guessed as not later than 1896 or 1898; for I then still had a dream of writing a book on what used to be called "Analytic Jurisprudence."

However, as Contract was not my field, I laid aside this manuscript, with its juristic discovery. Nobody else then took any interest in the subject.

But after a time there arose, in the legal world, signs of grumbling against the vapid technicalities of Consideration. Some of the older jurists had already dared to question publicly its value,[1] and a new generation of jurists, emboldened by the candor of these skeptics, from time to time said other things in disparagement thereof.[2] A juristic revolution was seen to be fomenting. Then the great treatise of Williston took notice, conservatively, of the issue.[3] Finally, when the American Law Institute's Restatement of Contract came to be "in gremio legis," it was actually proposed by more than one jurist to abolish (or at least to shelve) poor old Consideration, as only a cluttering useless survival.[4]

Meanwhile, I became restive; for no one had invoked, to help save the soul of Consideration, this relation which lay unpublished in my manuscript. Still, as I noted the progress of the controversy, I said to myself, like the old woman in Mother Goose, "Lawk-a-massy on me, This is none of I!" And so I kept out of the zone of operations.

Now, however, that the opportunity is offered to do my small part in paying a merited tribute to the eminent scholar and friend in whose honor this volume is assembled, I am moved at last to promulgate my theory. Whether it finds acceptance by the juristic public or is rejected as an artificial fantasy, it is at least an attempt to throw new and original light on the problem and to help toward its solution.

Perhaps one reason why the present theory has not yet been advanced is that hitherto all discussions of the usefulness of Consideration have concentrated themselves upon Contract and its direct varieties. My theory, however, is reached by a survey of Contract in relation to its cousin species, Deceit and Estoppel.[5] I propose to show that Contract and Deceit and Estoppel are three species of one genus. The general function of that genus is to define the conditions upon which one person's *assertion* of fact, made to another person, will charge the former legally. And the three species represent three different type-situations in which (experience shows) the conditions should be different, in order to secure the just incidence of the respective obligations.

Let me say at the outset that the practical consequence of this discovery of the triple juristic relationship would be to salvage consideration from the scrap heap. And it is this practical consequence which makes the juristic inquiry well worth while.

Before coming to the point of expounding the discovery itself, as a climax, I shall have to set forth an analysis of the accepted rules of law applicable to the three obligations above named, as the premises for the conclusion. Therefore I must ask you to bear with me and follow patiently this preliminary analysis.

In using the term "estoppel," one is of course aware of its kaleidoscopic varieties. One reads of estoppel by conduct, by deed, by laches, by misrepresentation, by negligence, by silence, and so on. There is also an estoppel by judgment and by verdict; these, however, obviously involve procedure. The first-named varieties have certain aspects in common. But these aspects are not always interpreted by the same rules in all courts. The institution seems to be flexible. At any rate, in what follows here, the reader will concede that there is at least *some* authority for the rules of law here assumed. And, as will be seen, the analysis here does not depend on the validity of any one of the dubitable rules assumed: it would explain the situation equally well if the rule were the opposite.

But, first of all, be good enough to look at this chart, showing the elements of (Informal) Contract, Deceit, and Estoppel. Do not try to criticize it, or even to understand it, at this stage. Merely glance through it, so that my later references to it will be readily apprehended.

I now proceed, first, to analyze the elements of the three obligations, and then to point out the practical significance of their relation.

II. EXPOSITION: ANALYSIS OF CONTRACT–DECEIT–ESTOPPEL

A FEW ABSTRACT TERMS must be used, for ready reference. Contract, Deceit, and Estoppel are each *bi-factoral;* that is, their obligations are formed by two acts—one by each of the two parties. The act of the obligor is termed the primary act; the act of the obligee, the secondary act. And between the primary and the secondary acts is a *relation.* Thus there are three elements common to each obligation.

The primary act of all three is an *assertion of fact.* Thus: "My land boundary runs from this tree stump to the west bank of the river." This assertion may serve typically as the primary act of any one of the three obligations.

The secondary act of all three is some act involving *detriment suffered* or *benefit conferred* by the obligee. Thus: The obligee pays money or gives a note or builds a garage at a certain place. Any one of these acts may be typical for all three obligations.

KEY TO CHART I

I. Primary act: Assertion of fact by Obligor	*a.* Time-content of the Assertion	1. Past or 2. Present or 3. Future } Fact
	b. Obligor's Mental State as to Fact	or 1. Knowledge of Falsity of Fact or 2. Reckless as to Fact or 3. No knowledge nor recklessness
	c. Obligor's Control as to Fact	1. Fact of existing property or duty within Control or 2. Not in Control
	d. Obligor's Expression	1. Active or 2. Passive
II. Relation of III to I	Done in reliance	
III. Secondary act: Detriment incurred or benefit done by obligee	Range as to Obligor's Intention	1. Specified by obligor or 2. Not specified though intended or 3. Neither
IV. Measure of breach	See A, 1, 2, 3 C, 1, 2 See B, 12, 13, 14	1. Making good the content asserted or equivalent or 2. Restoration of the loss suffered

CHART I

COMPARATIVE SCHEME OF ELEMENTS OF CONTRACT, DECEIT, AND ESTOPPEL

See opposite page for key to letters and figures at left of chart.

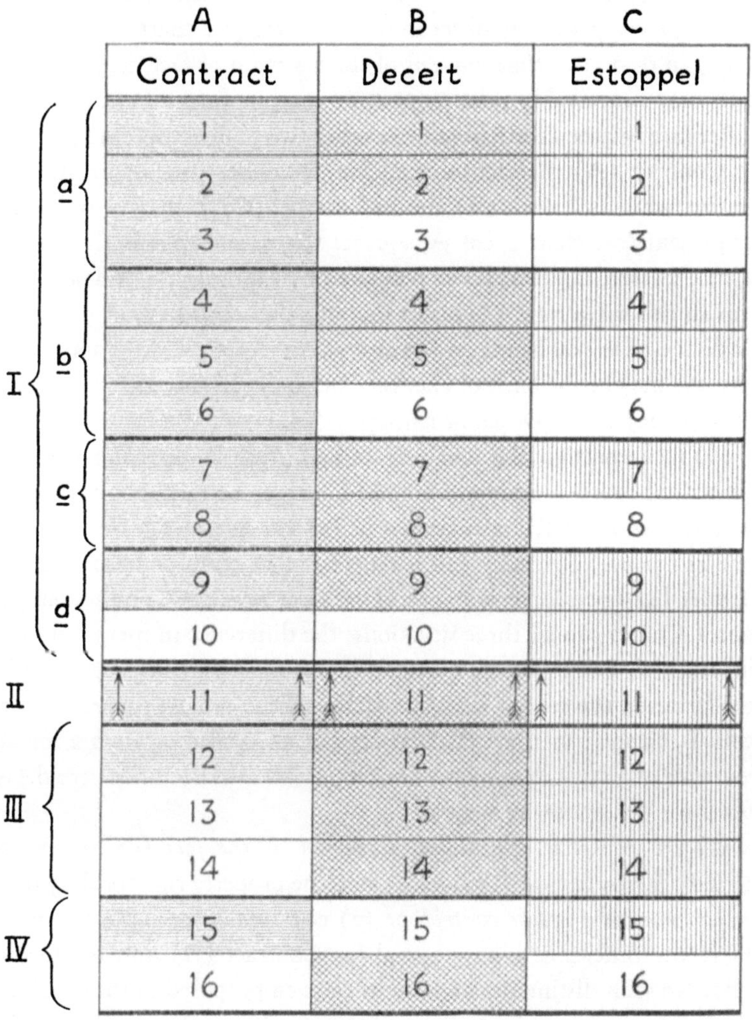

The relation in all three consists in the doing of the secondary act *in reliance upon the primary act.* This also is typical of all three (see chart 1, col. 1).

Let us now examine more closely the specific differences among the three obligations in respect to each of these three elements.

The *primary act* may differ in four respects (see chart 1, col. 3):

(*a*) In respect to *time content* of the assertion of fact, for the assertion may conceivably refer to past, present, or future fact. Here the difference between the first and the other two obligations emerges; for in Contract (A) the fact asserted may be either past, or present, or future, while in Deceit (B) and in Estoppel (C), it may be only past or present (see chart 1, col. A, squares 1, 2, 3, and cols. B, C, squares 1, 2). "I assert that this horse was sired by Lightning"; "I assert that this ship is seaworthy"; "I assert that one thousand kegs of nails will be delivered to you by me on January 1 next"; of these three assertions, any one may be the basis of Contract, but only the first and the second may be the basis of Deceit or Estoppel.

(*b*) In respect to the *obligor's mental state* in asserting the fact (which of course turns out not to be a fact, or no dispute over breach would have arisen), it may be that he (1) *has knowledge* of its falsity, or (2) has *no* knowledge but is *reckless* of its truth or falsity, or (3) *neither* has *knowledge nor* is *reckless.* Now here the Contract obligation (A) arises in all three situations; the difference in mental state is immaterial. But in Deceit (B) and in Estoppel (C), it arises only in the first and the second situations (see chart 1, col. A, squares 1, 2, 3, cols. B, C, squares 1, 2). (Courts are not all agreed on item 2 for all varieties of Estoppel, nor even for Deceit; but we need not here delay for these differences of view.)

(*c*) In respect to the *obligor's control of the fact* (or matter asserted), it may be that it concerns (1) some property right or duty over which the obligor *has control,* or (2) over which he has *no control.* Here the difference is immaterial for Contract (A) and for Deceit (B). No such distinction has ever been even proposed in these obligations (see chart 1, cols. A, B, squares 7, 8). But in Estoppel (C), the distinction is vital: it is *the* characteristic of Estoppel; for the obligation is here recognized only when it can be given effect by transferring a right or duty; that is, by ascribing to the obligee a right which either the obligor formerly had or by refusing to ascribe to the obligee a duty (to the obligor) which he formerly had.

The first form is of course quite common. The books are full of examples; a recent one will suffice. The plaintiff owned water rights of more than 36 inches of water, in a stream where defendant also had rights; but after a transaction in which 36 inches was stated as the limit of the plaintiff's rights, and in which defendant had exercised rights to the excess of 36 inches and had made improvements on the faith of plaintiff's acquiescence, the defendant was held entitled to that excess; that is, a virtual transfer of the right from plaintiff to defendant.[6] The situation of boundary lines being built upon is also a frequent example.

For the second form, take this recent example: Plaintiff let R manage certain oil properties; R sold oil to defendant, and defendant paid the price to R as the seller; but in these transactions plaintiff was aware that R was acting as the owner and was so believed to be by defendant; therefore defendant was now declared not liable to pay plaintiff;[7] that is, the court refused to ascribe to the defendant the duty legally existing for the defendant to the plaintiff.

In all these situations (mortgages, liens, land boundaries, etc.) the law of Estoppel reaches the result by the expression "the party is *estopped* from *asserting* (or denying)" that the facts would create his right or his opponent's duty. This of course is simply a fiction. What is the reality? The reality is that the party has asserted (or allowed someone else to assert) a fact, and so the law now obliges him to *make good that fact,* by attaching the legal consequences that would issue from it. Hence, the obligation is *limited* to that class of assertions of fact which can be made good by judicial fiat; that is, by merely taking away the party's right which he has against the opponent and handing it to the opponent, or by negating the duty which the opponent has to him. For example, the plaintiff endorses stock certificates in blank to M, who is a faithless fellow; M fills them in and sells them to defendant, B, who is ignorant of the fraud; the plaintiff, now suing to prevent their transfer on the corporate books, is estopped; thus the obligation is performed by a simple transfer of the title on the books.[8]

In other words, this obligation is limited to facts (of right or duty) *within the plaintiff's control.* Perhaps some better phrase could be devised; but the idea is plain. The odd thing is that though this characteristic runs through all the varieties of Estoppel, the jurists seem not to have generalized it.

The contrast here with Contract (A) and Deceit (B) is also plain. In Contract, the obligor's assertion may be that, for example, someone else's ship will arrive at a port by January 1. In Deceit, the obligor's assertion may be that he owns land acreage or stock shares which he does not own but M does, and if the obligee is thus deceived he may obtain compensation for his loss, but the obligor is not "estopped," because merely estopping him from denying his title would not avail to transfer M's title to the obligee. In contrast, Estoppel is limited to assertions which can be *made good* by merely placing the obligee in the position *with reference to the obligor* where he would be if the assertion had been true. This omits from Estoppel a vast area of assertions which are included in Contract and Deceit.

(*d*) As to the *obligor's form of expression,* it may be (1) active, or (2) passive. Here the breadth of the several obligations reverses itself, relatively. For Contract (A) and Deceit (B), there must be *active* expression; for Estoppel (*C*) *passive* expression also suffices. A common—almost the typical—situation in Estoppel is that of the party who stands by, silently and knowingly, while the obligee builds or pays or otherwise changes his position on the faith of certain supposed facts. In Contract and Deceit, on the contrary, the assertion must be some expression by action.

The contract "implied in fact" is not a disproof of the foregoing distinction. Such a contract must rest on some active utterance, though the utterance may not use explicit words of promise. For example, if A asks B to come and repair A's garage, though saying nothing about payment, the request contains an implied promise to pay. In other words, Contract both express and implied is based on action, not on passive silence; but Estoppel may be based on silence.

So much for the *primary act.* Let us now take up the secondary act (III) and follow it with a discussion of the relation (II) between these two acts, primary and secondary.

III. The *secondary act* may be different in only one respect (but that respect is of the greatest consequence of all), namely, in respect to *range of the obligor's intention.* The range of the secondary act in respect to the obligor's intention may be (1) *specified* by the obligee, or (2) *not* specified though *intended,* or (3) *neither* specified nor intended, but a *probable consequence.*

At this point comes the greatest cleavage between Contract (A) and Deceit (B) and Estoppel (C)—greatest, that is, in practical effects. The obligor's assertion in Contract will never bind him unless the secondary act done by the obligee is an act *specified beforehand* by the obligor as a condition, at the time of making the assertion. This specification by the obligor is *the* characteristic of Consideration.[9] The obligee, by doing precisely that act, and not otherwise, can hold the obligor to the assertion.

In Deceit (B) and Estoppel (C) however, *any act,* done by the obligee, involving loss, may bind the obligor (see chart 1, cols. A, B, C, squares 12, 13, 14). Note the great practical difference. The obligor in Contract on the one hand, may rest in peace, go about his business, and arrange his other affairs, knowing that nothing but the act expressly specified and limited by him can bind him. In Deceit and Estoppel, on the other hand, the range of the secondary act is limitless; the obligee may build a house, buy shares, sell land, make commitments, insure his property, take a journey, or perhaps even go skating—any act at all (if done in reasonable reliance, see "II" below) that involves a loss will suffice to bind the obligor.

Two discriminations must here be kept in mind: In Deceit, the present condition is often disguised by discussions concerning whether the secondary act is a reasonable consequence. This, however, is because the second of our three elements, the relation between I and III, that is, Reliance, requires that the secondary act be such a one as a reasonable man would have performed in reliance on the primary act.

In Estoppel, moreover, it may be necessary to omit the item (3) above, namely, an act which is a probable consequence but neither specified nor intended by the obligor. This item suffices to hold him in Deceit, but not in Estoppel, at least not in all courts and in all varieties of Estoppel.

II. Now, coming to the *relation between I and III,* the primary act and the secondary act, we find that it is identical for all three forms of obligation, Contract, Deceit, and Obligation; the secondary act must be done *in reliance upon* the primary act.

As to Contract (A), this is usually simple enough, for the secondary act is specified beforehand, and when the obligee does it knowingly he does it in reliance. There are occasional doubtful situations—as where he performs the secondary act precisely as specified, but without knowing of the obligor's primary act containing the specification; for example, when the finder of a lost article returns it without having heard of the loser's offer of reward. But such borderline examples merely illustrate more clearly the idea of reliance as implied and essential.

As to Deceit (B), there are various detailed rules of thumb; but they all can be reduced to the general idea that the secondary act—the loss suffered—must have been done in reliance as a reasonable man upon the primary assertion of fact. This general idea is sometimes enforced by rules of thumb apparently limiting the primary act; for example, the vendor of a horse asserts that it is worth $2000 and that it was sired by Kentucky Giant; he would be liable in Deceit for the latter statement, but not for the former. This, however, is because a reasonable man as vendee would rely upon the latter but not on the former assertion; the judicial opinions make very clear that such rulings rest upon the reliance idea, that is, the same idea as in Contract.

As to Estoppel (C), the principle of reliance is exemplified in much the same way as in Deceit.

IV. It remains to notice the differences among the three obligations that affect the *measure of the breach of the obligation* (see chart 1, cols. A, B, C, squares 15, 16).

In Contract (A), the obligor is held to *make good* the *content of the assertion;* or if that is impracticable, to give an equivalent. Specific performance illustrates this.

In Estoppel (C), the same measure is used, *making good* the fact asserted. However, owing to the limited class of assertions—that is, affecting rights or duties within the obligor's control—the requirement to make good the assertion can always be satisfied directly; there is no need of resorting to an equivalent in the way of "damages" so-called.

In Deceit (B), however (see chart 1, col. B, square 16), that measure of the breach would not be feasible or equitable. The obligee is often entitled, in fairness, to a higher measure. He is here entitled to the *reparation of his loss* incurred in reliance, and this may often be greater than the content of the assertion, or that content may not be exactly measurable.

For example, the vendor sells for $2000 a horse asserted to be sired by Kentucky Giant; the assertion is knowingly false; and the horse actually is worth only $100; so that the vendee has lost $1900. Now if the measure of making good the fact asserted were used, the value of a horse sired by Kentucky Giant might be only $1500; to hold the obligor to that sum only would be to leave the vendee with a net loss of $400. Instead of that, let him be simply repaid his actual loss, namely, $1900. In Deceit it is more equitable to adopt this measure than the other.

Again, suppose the promoter of African mining shares asserts falsely that the mine is located next to a mine with shares now selling at $50; the buyer pays $50 a share; the mine proves empty. If here the measure of making good the fact asserted were used, how could the vendee say what the actual share value would have been, had the mine been located as represented? The influence of that location on value would be purely speculative; to fix a value is not feasible. So the measure of the vendee's loss is for him the feasible measure.

Such are the differences among the three obligations in respect to the measure of breach.

III. THE CONCLUSION

And now it remains to point the conclusion. (But before studying the conclusion, the reader is requested to glance once more at chart 1, and note the relation of the gaps in it.)

The conclusion is this: That each of these three obligations represents what is *fair and practical* for *three different types of situation* of the parties; and that the variances in the conditions of the three obligations represent the concrete differences of rule that are *appropriate to the different types* of situation.

This is illustrated most strikingly by the secondary act, in the difference between Contract and Deceit. A typical business situation covered by Contract is this: A cotton-goods manufacturer, in a sale of first-quality sheeting, promises (1) that the cotton came from Egypt, (2) that his factory has a capacity of 5000 yards a day, and (3) that the sheeting will be delivered by March 1—facts past, present, and future. He specifies in his offer the exact secondary act which alone will clinch his promise, namely, the price (or a promise of it) of $2.00 a yard. He now knows that nothing can bind him to make good his promise other than the very thing that he specifies as consideration. He then builds up his entire commercial enterprise on that footing. He knows where he stands. Nothing done by anyone else can bind him except the very thing—out of a million things—that he himself chooses. This is the vital need of economic transactions—certainty and accuracy in the liabilities account. These it is that Contract supplies.

The Deceiver, however, who has falsified in his assertions, is equitably not entitled to any such protecting limitation. He should bear whatever loss has been induced by his falsity. The range of acts involving that loss should therefore be unlimited. We do not care to protect him, for he is a falsifier. His attitude has not been the normal sound one of economic transactions. Therefore we need not seek to limit the secondary act—the only thing that we will do is to limit the primary act to assertions of fact past or present (see chart 1, col. B, square 3). The reason for this is simply that the conception of known falsity—the basis of Deceit—is tangibly and readily applicable to past and present fact. But for future fact it becomes too difficult to distinguish it from mere over-optimistic expectation. It is no longer a conception practically applicable.

Take, again, the contrast between Contract and Estoppel. The vital difference here again is the range of the secondary act over any sort of act. But the parties' economic situation here is of a type different from that of Deceit. We are here concerned with a situation in which the obligee has *not yet suffered loss,* but he has so changed his position that he *will* suffer loss unless we can do something to preserve him from it. What can we do? Well, if his situation is such that we can save him by simply *legalizing his "status quo,"* that is a simple thing to do.

What would be such a typical situation? It would be a situation in which the obligee had changed his position in reliance on (*a*) an assertion of a past or present fact (p. 645; see chart 1, col. C, squares 1, 2), (*c*) involving the existence of a right (or nonexistence of a duty) of the obligee, which right or duty now actually is in the obligor's control (p. 645; squares C, 7, 8); so that all the law needs to do is (square C, 15) to declare that the fact asserted *is* a fact, and thus to force the obligor to make good his assertion and to legalize the obligee's situation. And as to (*b*) the mental state of the obligor (p. 646), we shall go no farther than to do this for those obligors who knew the assertion to be false, or were reckless in assertion (squares C, 4, 5), but we shall readily bind such persons even when they were only passive (squares C, 9, 10).

Thus the typical situation of which Estoppel takes care is morally, economically, and legally different from that of Contract and of Deceit.

Enough of these details, though they might be pursued further.

To go back to our beginning theme—the salvage of Consideration. The foregoing analysis of the relation of Contract to Deceit and Estoppel demonstrates—does it not?—that Consideration has a distinctive, vital, and permanent function in the formation of a contract. The essential thing in Consideration is not the precise concrete nature of the act in itself—whether it be a barleycorn, or a tree falling, or a thousand-dollar treasury note. All criticisms of Consideration as a petty technicality, because any (apparently) trifling act may serve to satisfy it, are dwelling on an immaterial aspect of it. The essential point is that Consideration is *something specified in advance by the obligor,* and thus limited to that specified thing. And this essence is made clear by the Contract with Deceit and Estoppel, where the obligor becomes bound by any secondary act, *unspecified* by him, and ranging over a million possible acts. So, to abolish Consideration would be to throw the range for Contract as wide open as it is for Deceit and Estoppel, and thus to abolish the distinction between them.

To sum up: These three obligations represent three typical situations, roughly but widely distinct from one another and requiring different conditions for fixing the obligation. And in the course of judicial experience the law has fumblingly worked out three sets of conditions, or terms, which fairly meet the needs of the three situations. These three sets of terms expand and contract at the various points, and thus take care of the appropriate differences.

To close, I offer chart 2, which will serve to show the singular yet felicitous contrasts among the three obligations. This second chart is simply the first one turned on end. It displays, from another angle, the elements at which each of the three serves as a complement of the others.

KEY TO CHART 2

I. Primary act: Assertion of Fact by Obligor

(*a*) Time-content of Fact	1. Past	2. Present	3. Future
(*b*) Obligor's Mental State	4. Knowledge (of falsity)	5. Reckless (true or false)	6. Neither
(*c*) Obligor's Control over Fact	7. Within control	8. Not within control	
(*d*) Obligor's Expression	9. Active	10. Passive	

II. Relation of III to I: Done in Reliance

III. Secondary act: Act of Detriment (to Obligee) or Benefit (to Obligor)

11. Whether intended by Obligor	12. Specified	13. Intended though not specified	14. Neither
IV. Measure of Breach of Obligation	15. Making good asserted content	16. Restoring detriment	

What is now wanted is that someone should compose a treatise, assembling these three obligations as species of a single genus. By so doing, the logic of these large contrasting principles could be employed to straighten out the inconsistencies of detail which now are found so noticeably in the decisions on Estoppel, and to give scientific unity to the whole conception of—let us call them—Assertory Obligations, or Obligative Assertions.

CHART 2

Complementary Use of the Common Concepts in Contract, Deceit, and Estoppel

See opposite page for key to letters and figures at left of chart.

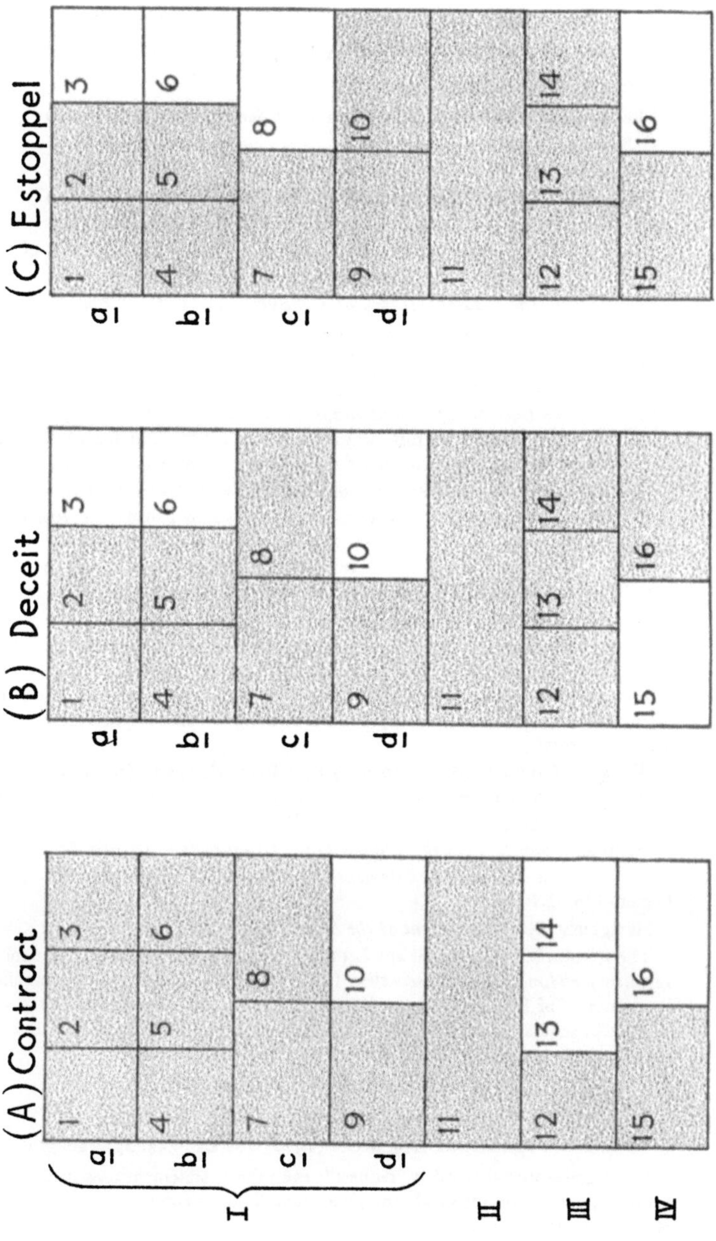

NOTES TO WIGMORE ESSAY

[1] Markby, Pollock, Salmond, Jenks.

[2] Ballantine, *Is the Doctrine of Consideration Senseless and Illogical?* (1913) 11 Mich. L. Rev. 427.

Cohen, *The Basis of Contract* (1932) 46 Harv. L. Rev. 553.

Lorenzen, *Causa and Consideration in the Law of Contracts* (1919) 28 Yale L. J. 621, 646.

Willis, *What Is Consideration in Anglo-American Law?* (1924) 62 U. of Pa. L. Rev. 245, 395.

Holdsworth, *The Modern History of Consideration* (1922) 2 Boston U. L. Rev. 87, 207.

Pound, *Consideration in Equity* (1919) 13 Ill. L. Rev. 667, 691.

[3] *Contracts* (ed. 2; 1920) § 100.

[4] Ashley, *The Doctrine of Consideration* (1913) 26 Harv. L. Rev. 436; "a technicality existing simply because of its historical importance; . . . the time has come for . . . a brief statute stating in accurate terms that the doctrine of Consideration is abolished."

Willis, *Consideration in the Anglo-American Law of Contracts* (1932) 8 Ind. L. Rev. 93; "[if by a certain ruling Consideration would be abolished] the writer would still advocate it."

Whittier, *The Restatement of Contracts and Consideration* (1930) 18 Calif. L. Rev. 611; "the law of Consideration needs reform; it needs a fundamental restatement; it needs to be modernized."

[5] There have indeed been some perceptions that Estoppel has some sort of cousinship to Contract, but no attempt to analyze that relationship appears to have been made. The occasional references to a "promissory estoppel" have concerned promises of a future event (*i.e.*, not an orthodox estoppel) held binding without requiring a consideration of the correct sort:

Williston, *Contracts* (ed. 2; 1920) § 139; Page, *Contracts* (ed. 2; 1920) § 524; DeVault, *Promissory Estoppel* (1931) 6 Ind. L. J. 564; Laidlaw, *Consideration and Promissory Estoppel* (1932) 5 Lincoln L. Rev. No. 2, p. 1.

Humble, *Promissory Estoppel in the Law of Contracts* (1929) 63 Am. L. Rev. 33.

Winfield, *The American Restatement of the Law of Contracts* (1929) 11 J. Soc. Comp. Leg. and Int. Law 186.

Havighurst, *The Restatement of the Law of Contracts* (1933) 27 Ill. L. Rev. 916, 920.

The relation between Deceit and Estoppel has been pointed out by Professor Williston, *Liability for Honest Misrepresentation* (1911) 24 Harv. L. Rev. 415: "it is difficult to see how the law of Estoppel and the [law of Deceit in the] doctrine of Derry v. Peck can be kept in separate compartments when law and equity are fused, etc." But that article did not touch upon the analogy of Contract and Consideration.

[6] LaLuz C. D. Co. v. Alamogordo (1929) 34 N. M. 127, 279 Pac. 72.

[7] Dobbins v. Texas Co. (1929) 136 Okl. 40, 275 Pac. 643.

[8] Powers v. Pacific Diesel Engine Co. (1929) 206 Cal. 334, 274 Pac. 512.

[9] The conventional word is "request"; even the Restatement uses it. But of course an actual request is not universal, nor even usual. What is conventionally termed "request" is actually a specification.

THE AMERICAN LAW INSTITUTE

BY HESSEL E. YNTEMA

THE AMERICAN LAW INSTITUTE was formed in 1923 under the laws of the District of Columbia "to promote the clarification and simplification of the law and its better adaptation to social needs, to secure the better administration of justice, and to encourage and carry on scholarly and scientific work." The salient position which the Institute has occupied in the scientific study of the law of the United States during the decade in which it has been in existence justifies belief that a brief account of the situation with which it was designed to deal and of its activities may be of more than local interest. From this point of view, items which deserve attention are the background and purposes of the Institute, its organization and mode of operation, and the results thus far achieved.

I

In point of immediate conception, the American Law Institute originated in ideas fostered by the Association of American Law Schools, an association, which, since its establishment in 1900, has played an increasingly significant part in the advancement of legal education in the United States. At the annual meeting in 1914, in a notable address as president of the Association, the late Wesley N. Hohfeld, of Yale, drew attention to the opportunity of the great universities, through the establishment of liberal schools of jurisprudence, to "contribute toward the fundamental, conservative and permanent betterment of our legal institutions."[1] At the same meeting, a paper was read by Professor Joseph H. Beale, of Harvard, who has been prominently identified with the work of the American Law Institute since its inception, in which the maladjustment of law to modern conditions was remarked and the necessity "for the law schools to take the lead in this modern work of bringing the law into close relation with the needs of contemporary life" was emphasized.[2]

Owing to the war, substantial progress in the discussion of these proposals was delayed until 1921, when a "Committee on the Establishment of a Juristic Center" was authorized by the Association of American Law Schools to invite representatives of the other branches of the legal profession to coöperate in creating a "permanent organization for the improvement of the law."[3] Consequently, in May, 1922, a distinguished group of American judges, lawyers, and law teachers organized for the purpose indicated by its somewhat formidable title, "Committee on the Establishment of a Permanent Organization for the Improvement of the Law." This body, having elected Mr. Elihu Root, the recognized leader of the American bar, as its chairman and obtained a grant from the Carnegie Corporation to defray preliminary expenses, embodied the conclusions of its discussions, extending over several months, in a carefully prepared report, analyzing the chief defects in the law of the United States and proposing an appropriate organization of scholarly and professional effort to remedy them. On the basis of this report, at a meeting in Washington, February 23, 1923, composed of leading members of the federal and state judiciaries and representatives of the bar associations and law schools, as well as specially invited members of the profession, the American Law Institute was established.[4]

II

In Professor Beale's paper, to which allusion has above been made, a restudy of the law, looking to its readjustment and reform, was contemplated from two points of view. On the one hand, it was pointed out that the law was being and must be examined "objectively to learn its social purpose and to see how far that purpose is being accomplished." On the other hand, specific emphasis was laid upon the claims of "the subjective study" of the law, on the ground that it is "as necessary a preliminary to any lasting reform as study of the other sort."[5] This latter type of study, it was explained, is based upon the conception of the common law as—

> Surely a philosophical system, a body of scientific principle which has been adopted in each of the common law jurisdictions in this country, as the basis of its law. Courts of each jurisdiction, in attempting to apply this general body of principles in its own jurisdiction, have sometimes miscon-

ceived it and misstated it, and this misstatement is apt to lead to a local peculiarity in the particular common law of the jurisdiction in question. But the general scientific law remains unchanged in spite of these errors; the same throughout all common law jurisdictions. This is the science which we teach, and this is the science which requires systematic statement in order that progress and reform may be possible.[6]

The historical significance of this point of view is not touched by recent criticism impugning its validity.[7] Until recently at least, the familiar conception of the common law as a general body of scientific principle has been thought satisfactorily to express three fundamental aspects of American jurisprudence. In the first place, it has been accepted as a more or less tacit, but nevertheless essential, premise of the system of *stare decisis* in the United States, justifying the adaptation by the courts of prior decisions and statutes in response to social needs and the successful assertion of the doctrine of judicial supremacy.[8] Furthermore, the conception has not merely been thought progressive, but it responds to the need of uniformity in the laws of the United States; the theory of "a transcendental body of law outside of any particular state but obligatory within it unless and until changed by statute,"[9] is a reflection of the slow but inexorable trend toward the creation of a common national law, by which the inconveniences of local diversities can be mitigated. And, in the third place, it has, until the past decade, been undisputed as a scientific conception; it is the principle of the intensive, "inductive" study of judicial decisions, which has inspired the outstanding achievements of historical and analytical jurisprudence in the United States since the introduction of the case method of legal instruction and research. These achievements are perhaps of most immediate importance in the present connection; as Mr. Justice Holmes foresaw in 1886, they would need to be consummated by the restatement of the law.[10]

The conception, like the prophecy, is fulfilled in the work undertaken by the American Law Institute. Although empowered by its articles to make objective surveys of the operation of law, the Institute has thus far devoted its efforts to the "subjective study" or, as it has come to be termed, the "restatement" of the law.[11] In the report which led to the establishment of the Institute, mentioned above, the considerations which assured the adoption of this policy are thus summarized:

> Our examination of the causes of the present uncertainty of the law shows conclusively the need of a restatement of the law that will have an authority much greater than that now accorded to any existing encyclopedia or treatise. We are convinced therefore that the specific work which any organization created by the legal profession to improve the law should undertake on its formation is the production of such a "Restatement of the Law."[12]

As this statement suggests, the "Restatement" looks to uniformity in the laws of the United States. The prime object is to formulate the common "body of scientific principle" underlying the provisions of the various legal systems in this country. The task has been undertaken, not specifically on the ground suggested by the remark attributed to Gladstone, "that you should first get a comprehensive account of what the law is before you commence amending it,"[13] but rather as the principal reform immediately required by what were conceived to be the chief defects in the law of the United States—its uncertainty and complexity.

This view of the function of the Institute, it will be observed, has the effect of bringing a powerful practical argument to the support of prevailing theory as to the common law, without proposing serious change in the legal system itself. To the extent that foreknowledge of the judicial process is attainable through formulation of legal principle, it could scarcely be gainsaid that a denial of certainty as to legal rights, a matter of particular concern in the conduct of affairs, correspondingly aggravates the occasions, costs, and delays of litigation. "Miserable," said Lord Coke, "is the slavery of that people among whom the law is either unsettled or unknown."[14] "The same causes have produced the same results," Lord Halsbury has more recently remarked, "and in every country it has been found that the system of providing for each necessity as it arises, without reference to any principle which governs the whole, has over and over again produced confusion and contradiction."[15] Irrespective of the extent to which a subjective restatement of the law may serve to eliminate "the admitted uncertainty and difficulty in law and its administration,"[16] the objective sought thereby—simplicity and uniformity in the formulated principles of law—represents a universal need felt in any legal system subject to change in doctrine or legislation.

Conditions will necessarily affect the degree in which this need is felt. During the controversy over the proposal to enact a civil code in the state of New York, James C. Carter, a leader of the New York bar, in a paper approved by the Association of the Bar of the City of New York, expressed the opinion that the lack of system in the common law, which had been urged by John Austin and others as an argument for its codification, constituted a defect, which was, "in a practical point of view, of but a moderate degree of importance."[17] In 1884, this was disputed ground, but since then the complexity of the law of the United States has been so aggravated by the operation of various factors as to explain both the emphasis laid in 1923 upon the "restatement of the law" as the chief reform justifying the formation of the American Law Institute and also the approving interest which the legal profession has evinced in its work. Brief reference may be made to the more obvious of these factors, the sheer multiplication of precedents and statutes emanating from forty-nine separate legal systems and the difficulties occasioned by "the fecundity of our case law"[18] in the operation of the system of *stare decisis*.

III

The mushroom growth of the *elephantini libri* of the law is the original difficulty. To attest its dimensions, it is enough to cite but a few august witnesses. In 1810, Judge Swift, considering the few reports of decisions in the United States, expressed "a hope, that the period is not distant, when the American Common Law will be found in American authorities."[19] Only eleven years later, in 1821, there being then some one hundred and fifty volumes of reports of American jurisprudence, Mr. Justice Story, in an oft-cited address to the Suffolk Bar, remarking upon the "almost incredible rapidity" with which the mass of the law was accumulating, saw no remedy adequate "to avert the fearful calamity, which threatens us, of being buried alive, not in the catacombs, but in the labyrinths of the law," save "a gradual digest under legislative authority of those portions of our jurisprudence, which under the forming hand of the judiciary shall from time to time acquire scientific accuracy."[20] To like effect are contemporary statements: in 1823, Nathan Dane indicated that "The evil to be feared in our country is, that so many sovereign legislatures, and so many Supreme courts, will produce too much law, and in too great a variety; so much and so various, that any general revision will become impracticable,"[21] while in 1826 Chancellor Kent termed the increasing number of periodical law reports and treatises a "grievance" and suggested that a digest to remedy "the evils resulting from an indigestible heap of laws, and legal authorities," would be "an immense public blessing."[22]

The growth of what was a grievance in the eyes of Chancellor Kent to the proportions of the calamity anticipated by Mr. Justice Story, is too large a tale to be here even delineated. It is appropriate, however, to allude briefly to the interest exhibited a half-century later by the bar associations, which were then being organized, in the problem created by the mass of the law. In 1873, a committee of the then newly formed Association of the Bar of the City of New York, apparently inspired by the establishment of the Council of Law Reporting in England in 1865, subjected the system of law reporting in New York State to critical examination. From the report of this committee it appeared that from 1307 to 1872 there were published in England 1,036 volumes of reports, while in the United States, in one-seventh of the time, *i.e.*, within approximately eighty years prior to 1872, over 2,000 volumes of reports of judicial decisions had been published. Upon these latter reports, the committee thus reflected: "If anything could draw the spirit of the great commentator [Judge Story] back to the earth, it might well be a wish to retract his opinion as to the ability of the reporters; and if anything were needed to keep it away, the 2,000 volumes of our decisions might have this effect."[23] In 1883, ten years later, the number of American law reports having meanwhile increased by a thousand volumes, John M. Shirley directed the attention of the American Bar Association, organized in 1878, to the "multiplicity of reports" that "crowd upon us like the pests of Egypt."[24] In the annual address to the Association of the following year, Judge John F. Dillon referred in some detail to the condition as urgent, and a committee, of which Mr. David Dudley Field was chairman, was appointed to consider whether the delay and uncertainty in judicial administration could be lessened. In 1885, an extensive report was submitted by this committee, attributing the uncertainty in the administration of justice in large part to the character and volume of the statutes and reports and recommending, among other things, that "The law itself should be reduced, as far as possible, to the form of a statute." This resolution was adopted by the Association in slightly modified form in 1886.[25] It was a Fabian victory. In 1923, upon the establishment of the American Law Institute, Mr. Elihu Root remarked that "for many years we have been talking in The American Bar Association and in many State Bar Associations about the increasing complexity and confusion of the substantive law which is applied in all our states and in the Federal courts. We have been talking about it. We have had committees appointed but nothing has been done."[26]

In another and intimately related direction, it should be noticed parenthetically, this discussion in the bar associations ripened more rapidly. As early as 1823, Nathan Dane had remarked that the "inundation of books, made in different States and nations, will increase, until we can shake off our local notions," and had suggested that the true course was "to make our laws more uniform and national," for which only "a general efficient plan" was wanted.[27] A half-century later, when the bar associations appeared, the growth of local legislation had accentuated the obvious need for such a plan. Accordingly, the first projects of the American Bar Association, which was organized in 1878 to promote, among other things, "uniformity of legislation throughout the Union," looked to this end.[28] Three years later, an interstate code commission, the possibilities of which had been suggested twenty years before, was advocated in a paper to the Alabama Bar Association.[29] In 1888, the ephemeral National Bar Association, composed of delegates from state and local bar associations, was organized, chiefly it would seem, to "promote the unification, so far as practicable, of the laws of the various states which relate to matters in which the people of the United States have common interest."[30] Meanwhile, suggestions were being made in various quarters, urging conventions of delegates, representing the several states, to draft uniform laws for adoption by their legislatures.[31] In 1890, these suggestions took effect in a New York statute, providing for the appointment of three commissioners to promote uniformity of legislation in the United States and, thereafter, in similar acts, which were passed in the remaining fifty-two jurisdictions by 1912.[32] The national conference of state commissioners of uniform laws first met in 1892 and in its forty years of existence has drafted some seventy acts, of which fifty-three were on the approved list in 1933. Of these acts, two, the Negotiable Instruments Act and the Warehouse Receipts Act, have achieved approximate uniformity in their subject-matter, while three other acts have been adopted in over half the jurisdictions in the country.[33]

However, it was apparent within a generation that this effort to secure uniformity in the enactment and interpretation of legislation was attended by difficulty and uncertainty. The great majority of proposed uniform acts failed of enactment in more than a few jurisdictions,[34] while the few that obtained with something like generality had by 1914 suggested a problem of assuring uniformity in the decisions under the uniform acts.[35] No more did the expansion of federal legislation in the fields of bankruptcy and interstate commerce secure simplicity in the law of the United States. As Mr. Justice Stone, then dean of the Columbia University Law School, remarked in 1915:

> It would be difficult to imagine what would have been the reflections of Story and Kent if they had foreseen that the law reports in the United States in 1915 would have reached a total of about 9,000 volumes and that there would have been a corresponding increase in the volume of statute law. Not only has the last century witnessed an enormous increase in the mass of legal literature of all classes, but the substance of law itself has increased more rapidly than in any other like period. The greater part of the law of corporations, public service companies, interstate commerce, life and accident insurance, bankruptcy, constitutional rights under the Fourteenth Amendment, not to mention other branches of modern law, were unknown to Kent and Story.[36]

That the situation was manifestly aggravating, is indicated by the remarks of Mr. Elihu Root, in presenting the report which led to the establishment of the American Law Institute, with which this testimony may be concluded:

> The great number of books, the enormous amount of litigation, the struggles of the courts to avoid too strict an application of the rule of *stare*

decisis, the fact that the law had become so vast and complicated that the conditions of ordinary practice and ordinary judicial duty made it impossible to make adequate examinations—all these had tended to create a situation where the law was becoming guesswork.

You will find in the paper which has been distributed the statement that a count made in 1917 showed 175,000 pages of reported decisions in the United States, as against 7,000 in Great Britain. Three years before that I had a count made in the Library of Congress, the result of which I have often stated. It showed that during the five years preceding 1914 over 62,000 statutes had been passed and included in the printed volumes of laws in the United States, and that during the same five years over 65,000 decisions of courts of last resort had been delivered and included in the printed volumes of reports. And still it goes on.[37]

IV

The expense and complexity of so great a volume of formal legal materials are obvious, as well as the practical difficulty of defining the law in the mass of authority.[38] As John Bassett Moore has remarked, in commenting upon the indiscriminate and "turgid stream of judicial decisions" reported in the United States, there are effects, more subtle and, if possible, more serious:

> This system is supported by the Bar, with mingled feelings of gratitude and despair; for the Bar is conscious of the fact that, while it is in a sense served by the system, it is also enslaved and debauched by it. The very multiplicity of cases, and the consequent impossibility of dealing with them scientifically, reduces practitioners to a reliance upon particular decisions rather than upon general principles; and this in turn augments the tendency, long ago abnormally developed, to pay undue respect to mere cases as authority. How often do counsel produce with an air of triumph the latest decision, rendered perhaps in some far-off jurisdiction by a judge whose opinions derive their weight solely from his official position![39]

Beneath this situation which cries for relief, however, there are certain conditions which complicate the problem with which the American Law Institute has sought to deal. The first is the awkward dilemma between desires for local autonomy and for uniformity in law, created by the federal distribution of judicial power in the United States, a dilemma which the so-called uniform acts have thus far not effectively solved and which is accentuated by the rapidly shifting views as to the proper scope of federal legislation.[40]

A more basic condition of the simplification of law results from progress in science and art, changes in the technical equipment and standards of civilization, and shifts in social *mores*. In a generation when economic and cultural change is a commonplace, the problem of formulating law can scarcely be regarded as merely static or retrospective.[41] Indeed, the effect of the most important development in American juristic thinking in recent years, sociological jurisprudence, has been to emphasize this consideration in order to avoid serious maladjustment in the legal system.[42]

A third limitation inheres in the judicial process itself. As finely put by Mr. Justice Cardozo, "We reach the land of mystery when constitution and statute are silent, and the judge must look to the common law for the rule that fits the case."[43] Without entering upon the vexed question as to the degree in which the law can be clarified by codification, it is admitted, whether by extreme proponents of codification, such as Bentham, who believe that the "vast hot-bed of uncertainty" which is jurisprudential law, can and should be codified,[44] or by those, like James C. Carter, who share the conviction that, in the ordinary relations of life, "unwritten law offers a means by which justice may be better attained, though it must sometimes happen at the sacrifice of certainty,"[45] that a system of *stare decisis,* such as prevails in the United States, will necessarily in some measure defy prior formulation.

If there were any doubts as to the complexity of the problem with which the American Law Institute is engaged, they would be dispelled by a comparative glance at the experience, under less difficult conditions, of other legal systems. For instance, to allude to the system which has been most intimately related to the laws of the United States, it will be recalled that, as long ago as 1616, shortly after a mere "fifteen books or treatises, and as many Volumes of the Reports, besides the Abridgments," were enumerated as the "right profitable" books of the English common laws,[46] Bacon proposed to compile and amend the system of English law, upon the ground that "Certain it is that our laws, as they now stand, are subject to great uncertainties, and variety of opinion, delays, and evasions."[47] It was left for later generations in part to realize these proposals, but meanwhile the Reports, which Coke had just published "for the common good . . . in quieting and establishing of the possessions of many in these general cases, wherein there hath been such variety of opinions,"[48] served as a restatement of the common law. As Coke's chief rival admitted, had it not been for the Reports, "the law by this time had been almost like a ship without a ballast; for that the cases of modern experience are fled from those that are adjudged and ruled in former times."[49]

It would be highly presumptuous to endeavor to sketch in this connection, even in grossest outline, the history of all that has been done and written since Bacon's time to clarify and restate the law of England; to refer, for example, to the abridgments, the commentaries and the texts, to notice Blackstone's influence or Bentham's critique of the common law and his simple passion for codification, to suggest the rôle played by the monumental series of statutes which resulted from the reform movement initiated by Lord Brougham in 1825,[50] or even to cite, as more immediately in point, Lord Westbury's elaborate project for a digest of the entire law, a project which, it will be recalled, came to an ineffectual public end in 1870[51] but was later partially realized, through private initiative, in Lord Halsbury's *Laws of England*.[52] These are aspects of a story, sufficiently familiar to suggest that, even in a legal system relatively simpler than that of the United States and yet closely akin, a system of laws largely stated in judicial precedents,[53] but these chiefly of a single jurisdiction, the doubts expressed by both Coke and Bacon as to the propriety of codifying the common law[54] have found a degree of justification in the difficulties which have been experienced in reaching toward an end which is by no means achieved.[55]

V

A *corpus juris communis* of English laws, states Sir Matthew Hale in the well-known preface to Rolle's *Abridgment,* "is a work of time, and requires many industrious and judicious hands and heads to assist in it."[56] In the organization of the American Law Institute, these requirements were recognized, and, although the ten years originally contemplated for the restatement of the law have proved insufficient, this is to be attributed to the inherent difficulties of the task, rather than to lack of resources. As the distinguished president of the Institute has remarked:

Organized under the most favorable auspices, with the coöperation of the leaders of the profession on the bench and at the bar; equipped with ample funds for its purpose; the Institute only can fail in the accomplishment of its undertaking, if the scholarship of the American bar shall prove inadequate to the work.[57]

And, it may be added, the expert services of leading scholars and lawyers have been available for the work of the Institute, in no small part, at modest expense.[58] Furthermore, the support of the bar associations and of the American bar generally has been enlisted more promptly than could have been anticipated, while the favorable publicity which the Institute has received has been calculated to assure the sympathetic reception of the restatements of the law by the courts. It may be of interest to allude to certain of the details before noticing the essential matter, the restatements themselves.

In the first place, the organization of the Institute is well conceived to secure the interested suggestions of the profession, a matter of some importance in view of the plan to issue the restatements of the law upon the authority of the Institute and without legislative sanction. There is a membership of over seven hundred, including a select and distinguished representation of the judiciary, the law schools, and the bar throughout the country, and annual meetings are held at Washington to consider the drafts of proposed restatements of the law. Also, since 1928, in conjunction with the appointment of an adviser on professional and public relations,[59] as the work has progressed, the state bar associations in a large number of the states have been actively interested in preparing local annotations of the restatements of the law. Beyond this, the organization is simple and the personnel eminent. Mr. Elihu Root, as honorary president; Mr. George W. Wickersham, as president; Mr. George Welwood Murray, as treasurer; and Mr. William Draper Lewis, as director, have acted as officers of the Institute from its inception. These officers are annually elected, and the affairs of the Institute are managed by a council, originally of twenty-one members, now of thirty-three, who are chosen at the annual meetings in three classes for overlapping terms of nine years each. In no small degree, the prestige which the Institute has enjoyed, is attributable to the distinguished membership of the council, who share the primary responsibility for the publications authorized,[60] as well as to the reputation of the scholars who have assumed the burden of preparing the actual restatements of the law.[61]

In a second respect, the Institute has been no less fortunate. Very considerable funds have been provided for its purposes, which funds are materially supplemented by the generous coöperation of the law schools in providing the essential personnel from their staffs, thus obviating the expense of a large independent establishment. The details of the original financing have been related as follows:

> Largely through the advocacy of Mr. Root, the Carnegie Corporation had contributed $25,000 to cover the expenses of conducting the preliminary inquiry and of securing the services of those who united in the report on the establishment of a permanent organization, including the expenses of the Washington meeting. Shortly after its corporate organization, the Institute laid its plans before the Carnegie Corporation and solicited its aid in carrying its plans into effect. Again with Mr. Root's potent aid, the Corporation appropriated to the use of the American Law Institute for its general purposes the sum of $1,075,000, to be paid at substantially the rate of $100,000 a year over a period of 11 years.[62]

In 1927, the annual payments by the Corporation were increased to $140,000 a year, thus exhausting the original gift in October, 1931.[63] Since then, payments have been made at the rate of $155,000 a year, the arrangement last announced expiring in 1934.[64] In addition to these funds, sums totaling $147,000 were provided by the Laura Spelman Rockefeller Memorial to enable the Institute to undertake the model code of criminal procedure.[65]

In the third place, the scope and progress of the Restatement of the Law, necessarily reflecting upon the funds which will be required for its completion, deserve notice. In general, it has been proposed that the Restatement should cover, not all, but the more important branches of the common, as distinguished from the statutory, law of the United States. At the outset, on the assumption that it would not prejudice any classification of the law to be ultimately adopted,[66] four subjects—contracts, conflict of laws, torts, and agency—were approved for restatement. Since 1923, three other subjects, exclusive of the model code of criminal procedure which was undertaken in 1925, have been added—business associations in 1925, property in 1926, and trusts in 1927.[67]

Tentatively, nine additional subjects have been listed as suitable for restatement, viz., bailments, bills and notes, insurance, persons, public utilities, quasi contracts, sales of chattels, sales of land, and security, the last comprising mortgages, pledges, suretyship, and guaranty.[68] On this basis, it was estimated by the director in 1930 that "there would be twenty-two volumes of from 500 to 700 pages each in the first Restatement of the Law as thus tentatively conceived; that the final volumes would appear in 1941"; and that the total cost would be $1,500,000 in addition to the $1,100,000 originally granted.[69] For reasons which will be appreciated, progress in so large a task has necessarily been expensive and slow. Thus far, the restatements of two subjects have been completed. The Restatement of the Law of Contracts was published in two volumes in 1932; the Restatement of the Law of Agency, also in two volumes, in 1933.[70] In addition, the model Code of Criminal Procedure was published in pamphlet form in 1930. The remaining subjects in process of restatement are in various stages of progress.[71]

A fourth aspect of the work of the Institute is the extensive employment of coöperative methods of research. The complexity of the problems presented by restatement of the law and the need of comprehensive accuracy, have made it desirable to ensure the participation, not merely of leading scholars in the respective subjects, but also of active leaders of the profession, both on the bench and at the bar. The procedure which has been developed is thus outlined by Dean Goodrich, who has been intimately connected with the work of the Institute in the past five years:

> The work of restatement is entrusted to a lawyer called the Reporter.... [The Reporters] begin this work with the Institute as experts in their respective branches of the law. They are provided with assistants who help in the examination of all relevant material, reports of cases, legal essays, and text-books in the particular branch of the law.
>
> The Reporter, having made a tentative outline of his subject, reëxamines the source material of a subdivision of it and makes a draft of what he considers to be the correct rules of law therein. When in form and substance it appears satisfactory to him, he submits it to a group of Advisers. They are men also chosen for knowledge and experience in that particular field of law; some from the practice, some from the bench, some from the law

schools. The Director, the Reporter and the Advisers, having studied the material, meet and talk it over.... Generally three, sometimes four, such meetings on the same material are required to prepare it satisfactorily for submission to the Council. In the Council the tentative Restatement is again examined and again discussed. Finally it is submitted to the membership of the Institute for discussion at its annual meeting. Here, too, it is only tentative, still open to criticism. Many such suggestions are received and many improvements are made.[72]

The object of "this heroic process" is to produce "a carefully prepared, sound and accurate statement of the common law"; substantially, it is a development of the methods successfully employed by the national conference of state commissioners in the preparation of uniform laws.[73]

It remains to characterize the restatements themselves. As explained by the director in 1924, the original conception was that the publications of the Institute should consist of: (*a*) restatements of the law; (*b*) accompanying treatises.[74] In conformity with conclusions tentatively prescribed in 1923, the restatements contain "Principles of law, Comment and Illustrations." The Principles are "direct and positive statements of law," printed in black letter in separate paragraphs numbered consecutively in each topic. The Comment is confined to "direct statements of law explaining the conditions under which a Principle operates in such manner as to facilitate its correct application," and explanations of the reasons for such statements or for the Principle. The Illustrations are "formal statements of cases," actual or hypothetical, introduced to fix upon the mind the operation of the Principle when it is thought to be helpful by the Reporter, but without any citations to the reports.[75] The restatements of the law have been developed in the form originally contemplated, but the plan to supplement them by treatises, providing an analysis and citation of authorities, has apparently been given up, for the time being at least, presumably on account of the difficulties and expense involved in their preparation.[76] In part, the state annotations and the private treatises published by the reporters will supply the deficiency.[77]

Earlier in this discussion it was suggested that the American Law Institute sprang from the juxtaposition of two chief influences—the academic theory that the common law is a body of scientific principle and the very practical demand of the bar for greater simplicity and uniformity in the enormous mass of the sources of American law. These same influences explain the character of the Restatement of the Law. Hence, the selection of the so-called unwritten common law of the United States for restatement, as being "the body of scientific principle" which is conceived to underlie both precedents and statutes. Hence, too, the elision from the restatements of all historical or argumentative matter, as well as the discussion of authorities, on the ground that the objective sought—uniformity in judicial decision—will not be promoted by intimation of the possibility of change or uncertainty in the common law; the Restatement is a systematic definition of "the law as it is," as ascertained by subjective investigation.[78] Hence, most characteristically, the style of the restatement is "ex cathedra"; it speaks with the authority, not of a legislature, but of the Institute as "a most representative part of the Bar."[79] The adoption of this basis for the promulgation of the Restatement of the Law is attributable to three considerations. *Imprimis,* it escapes the curse which Mr. Justice Cardozo prognosticated would be upon a project of Codification.[80] Also, it obviates the difficulties and delays which have been experienced in securing uniform legislation in a number of states. And it eschews the ephemeral implications attached to mere enactment. As the president of the American Bar Association in 1923, Mr. John W. Davis, somewhat drily remarked at the organization meeting of the Institute: "None of us here, I fancy, certainly none of us who are familiar with Congress or the forty-eight legislatures of our States, anticipate that this labor shall be committed to their charge."[81] In fine, the Restatement of the Law is the product of the circumstances which attended its conception—the aspirations toward simplicity and uniformity in the laws of the United States, the long dispute over codification, and the conviction that the situation could be cured only by scientific definition of the common law.

It will be of interest to those familiar with English law books to note the resemblance of the Restatement of the Law to a certain type of legal text, of which Dicey's *Conflict of Laws* is easily *primus inter impares.* A distinction, however, is noteworthy; in the restatements, no authorities are discussed or even cited, and, in consequence, as Chief

Justice Hughes has observed, "differences have yielded to a statement which leaves no trace."[82] The Restatement speaks, not to the student, but primarily to the judge engaged in the actual decision of a case; it is put forth as "a statement of the common law of America which will be the *prima facie* basis on which judicial action shall rest."[83] In short, it is a Code without benefit of legislation or, to employ the equivocal terms of the resolution adopted by the American Bar Association in 1886, a reduction of the law itself, "so far as its substantive principles are settled, to the form of a statute."[84]

VI

It is somewhat premature, and this is scarcely an occasion, to venture a critique of the work of the American Law Institute. Two points, however, may serve to suggest a perspective. The first is that, as the president of the Institute has observed more than once, it has assumed "a comparatively modest rôle in the work of improving our modern law and its administration."[85] It is no reflection upon the rôle to indicate what it does not include. Thus, apart from the single and important contribution of a model code of criminal procedure, the Institute has not been concerned with the acute and vital problems of the administration of justice in the United States, civil or criminal. It has excluded from its purview those fields of law which have been typically regulated by legislation, albeit in some such fields the need of clarity and uniformity is perhaps as imperative as in any of the branches of the so-called unwritten law.[86] Again, the character of the restatement of the law has largely precluded effective consideration of the philosophical theories and social necessities, expressed in the historical development of legal doctrine, which are relevant in ascertaining the value, if not even the meaning, of such doctrine. Moreover, there is no evidence that serious effort has been made to take advantage of foreign experience, past or present—a limitation doubtless justified by requirements of time and cost but more probably inspired by the provincial preoccupations of American legal scholarship during the past half-century; as Dean Falconbridge has observed, the pursuit of an exclusive nationalism is not quite satisfactory in a subject such as the conflict of laws, with which our Canadian neighbors and others are properly concerned.[87] To these limitations, by which the scope of the Restatement of the Law was circumscribed at the outset, must be added certain departures from the original design. Emphasis upon simplicity and generality of principle has involved an "abandonment of particulars"[88] in two essentials. In the first place, the initial purpose to improve as well as clarify the law was obviated at an early stage; no objective examination of the operation of legal rules, in cases where such inquiry might be indicated, has been undertaken with a view to stating the law as it ought to be rather than as it is.[89] In the second place, the preparation of treatises has been indefinitely postponed; consequently, save so far as such may eventually be provided by the state annotations, there is to be no comprehensive exposition of the sources of existing law to verify its formulation.[90] The fact is that the American Law Institute has restricted its activities to a limited and somewhat theoretical part in a larger scene, and that, fortunately, the importance of its work, as well as of the various types of investigation which it does not encompass, is being more fully understood.

The second point to be referred to is that the extrinsic influence of the American Law Institute has been by no means defined by its limited rôle. The Restatement of the Law could suffer no more ignominious fate than to be received in a pool of silence. But, fortunately, the activities of the Institute have thus far stimulated, rather than settled, the examination of legal problems. The proposed restatement of the conflict of laws, for instance, has incited inquiry as to the doctrines in that difficult and important field of law, the issue of which is not yet defined.[91] The same has been true, though perhaps in lesser degree, of other subjects, such as contracts and trusts.[92] In addition to the critique of theories and specific propositions presented in the several restatements, various more general suggestions, pertinent and impertinent, have been made, viz., that the active research of the Institute is too largely dominated by law professors; that the high cost of restating the law has drawn effort and money which could more profitably have been expended in other directions; that the results are meager and slow; that the form adopted for the restatement of the law is a barren and uninforming "straight jacket" of black letter principles and abstract theory; that the publication of the restatements without treatises defeats their chief value for professional purposes in view of the importance of the precedents; that there is no adequate criticism of the restatements after they are completed by the original drafters; that the mode of research and form of presentation are not aptly calculated to secure simplicity and certainty in the law, much less to improve its substance; that, in fine, the objective sought—clarity and uniformity in the law of the United States—is a consideration of doubtful relative importance under contemporary conditions.[93] It is not necessary to ascertain how far these and like criticisms are justified, to remark that they are a healthy symptom. In addition to such discussion, an extensive expository literature on various aspects of the individual restatements is appearing, and the decisions in particular states, pertinent thereto, are being studied with a care and on a scale not hitherto envisaged.[94] By these alone, the work of the Institute is being abundantly justified.

"For bringing of the common laws into a better method," my Lord Coke has observed, "I doubt much of the fruit of that labor. This I know, that abridgments in many professions have greatly profited the authors themselves; but as they are used, have brought no small prejudice to others."[95] It should not be too disconcerting to discover that the profits indirectly taken from the activities of the American Law Institute are of more consequence than its intended achievements. The assistance given in their private legal studies to the individual scholars who participate in the work of restatement, the stimulus to the examination of many salient legal problems by others, not to mention the intellectual mobilization of the different branches of the legal profession in a common enterprise, are, presently and prospectively, of major importance. Whether, in addition, the Restatement of the Law will attain the finality to which the founders of the Institute have highly aspired; whether it will be received as, or pave the way to, a national civil code in the near future; whether the technique of subjective formulation employed is a key to master the mystery of the judicial process, or, by such means, the law can be adequately adapted to contemporary needs; whether simplicity and uniformity, vainly sought these hundred years in the laws of the country, will thus descend upon their provisions; whether, at the least, the enormous flood of legal literature will in consequence be somewhat abated—this all is for the future to disclose. The doubts which the writer shares with others on questions such as these do not discount one whit the present need of a more precise statement of the rules of law, the validity of the objectives thereby sought by the American Law Institute, and the value of the results which may be expected to flow, however incidentally, from its accomplishments. A more scientific definition of the common law cannot fail to promote the march of critical analysis and the adjustment of the legal system to modern conditions. To abbreviate the inspiring remarks of Chief Justice Hughes, of the Supreme Court of the United States, at the last annual meeting of the Institute: "We must not lose sight of the great objective. The quest of certainty may be endless, and the goal may be unattainable, but progress is practicable. The Restatement, focusing attention on definite propositions, cannot fail to facilitate discussion and improvement."[96]

NOTES TO YNTEMA ESSAY

[1] Hohfeld, *A Vital School of Jurisprudence and Law* (1914) 14 Ass'n of Am. L. Schools, Proc. 76, 137. As suggested in note 26 below, the proposal was anticipated by prior developments in the American Bar Association and, in particular, by the plan for an American Academy of Jurisprudence, which was projected in 1913 by James DeWitt Andrews, for purposes quite similar to those later undertaken by the American Law Institute.

[2] Beale, *The Necessity for a Study of Legal System, ibid.* 31, 35.

[3] (1921) 21 *ibid.* 115.

[4] The report of the organizing committee is printed in (1923) Am. L. Inst. Proc., Part I. (Unless specifically indicated, references below are to the pagination in this report and not to the proceedings themselves, which are separately paged as Part II.)

For brief general accounts of the American Law Institute, see Root, *The Origin of the Restatement of the Law* 4 Docket (Jan. 1933) 3575; Corbin, *The Restatement of the Common Law by the American Law Institute* (1929) 15 Iowa L. Rev. 19.

[5] *Op. cit. supra* note 2, p. 39.

[6] *Ibid.* 38.

[7] The question of the validity of the classical conception of the common law as a general "body of scientific principle" is more or less directly involved in much of the critical literature relating to the nature of law and of legal science, which has appeared in the United States during the past decade. This literature is far too extensive to permit an estimate of its effect upon the status of the classical theory in the present connection. Interested readers will find a useful bibliography of a substantial portion of this literature in Llewellyn, *Some Realism about Realism—responding to Dean Pound* (1931) 44 Harv. L. Rev. 1222, 1257–1259. A brief résumé of the more obvious difficulties in the classical theory is given in the writer's article, *The Implications of Legal Science* (1933) 10 N. Y. U. L. Rev. 279, 295–297.

[8] The emphasis upon the conception of the common law as a body of scientific principle, prevalent during the nineteenth century, was in part directed against the mechanical use of precedents in decision. Thus, in an address at the opening of the Law Department of the University of Michigan in 1859, Justice James V. Campbell stated:

"Any system of law which does not approve itself by its applicability to all the ordinary concerns of life, is defective. But if precedents were not based upon general principles, there could be no such thing as a legal system. . . . The Law exists in as complete a form as human foresight could make it, and is as dependent on general principles as any human science. Like all other sciences, it is capable of enlargement and extension, but, like them, its growth should be by harmonious increase, and not by added excrescences. And no one can assume to have attained any progress in the knowledge of this science, until he has learned to recognize its living and eternal principles, and learned also to apply them to the exigencies of human life."—*On the Study of Law* (Ann Arbor, 1859) pp. 34, 35.

Similar ideas will be found more elaborately expressed in the series of articles, *Nature and Method of Legal Studies,* published by John Livingston in (1851) 3 U. S. L. Mag. 379–395, 491–518, and especially at 510 ff. Citations to like effect could be multiplied; without endeavoring to canvass the historical prevalence of the conception, it may be noted in passing that James C. Carter's opposition to the civil code advocated in New

York by David Dudley Field, was principally based upon the need of flexibility in dealing with the rules to be applied to ordinary relationships of business and private life.—Carter, *The Proposed Codification of Our Common Law* (New York, 1884) at pp. 13 ff.

It will also be recalled that in *The Common Law* (Boston, 1881) at pp. 35, 36, Holmes stresses the fact that:

"Every important principle which is developed by litigation is in fact and at bottom the result of more or less definitely understood views of public policy; most generally, to be sure, under our practice and traditions, the unconscious result of instinctive preferences and inarticulate convictions, but none the less traceable to views of public policy in the last analysis. And as the law is administered by able and experienced men, who know too much to sacrifice good sense to a syllogism, it will be found that, when ancient rules maintain themselves in the way that has been and will be shown in this book, new reasons more fitted to the time have been found for them, and that they gradually receive a new content, and at last a new form, from the grounds to which they have been transplanted."

[9] Mr. Justice Holmes *in* Black and White Taxicab & Transfer Co. v. Brown and Yellow Taxicab & Transfer Co. (1927) 276 U. S. 518, 533.

[10] "The law has got to be stated over again; and I venture to say that in fifty years we shall have it in a form of which no man could have dreamed fifty years ago. And now I venture to add my hope and my belief, that, when the day comes which I predict, the Professors of the Harvard Law School will be found to have had a hand in the change not less important than that which Story had in determining the form of the text-books of the last half-century."—Holmes, *Collected Legal Papers* (New York, 1920) 42.

This remarkable prediction was made in 1886, just forty-five years before the establishment of the American Law Institute.

[11] It should be added that, in addition to the "restatement" of various branches of the common law, as indicated below (see note 67), the American Law Institute has sponsored a model code of criminal procedure, which differs from the restatements in that it is designed for consideration and enactment by the legislatures of the several states. This code, which was drafted by Dean Mikell and Professor Keedy, of the University of Pennsylvania, with the assistance of a group of advisers, was undertaken in 1925 and completed in 1930. See also note 65 below.

[12] *Op. cit. supra* note 4, p. 13.

[13] 1 Halsbury's *Laws of England* (1907) ccix.

[14] Quoted in Bentham, 5 *Works* (Bowring, 1843) 236.

[15] *Op. cit. supra* note 13, p. ccviii.

[16] In *The Proposed Codification of Our Common Law* (New York, 1884) at p. 114, it is remarked by James C. Carter:

"The candid inquirer, after such a study, will find that a large, perhaps the largest, part of the admitted uncertainty and difficulty in our law and its administration, proceeds from causes quite beyond human control. The interpretation of laws, written or unwritten, must forever depend upon human *opinion;* and uncertainty, variety, and conflict are, and must be, inseparable attendants upon this condition. The evils thus resulting have afflicted every form of society from the beginning of time. They cannot be avoided. The utmost that can be done is to keep them within the narrowest possible range."

[17] *Ibid.* at p. 72.

[18] "Our law stands indicted for uncertainty, and the names of weighty witnesses are endorsed upon the bill. If we seek for causes, there are many. Eight or more were enumerated by the American Law Institute at its organization meeting, adopting the report

of a committee. There was the lack of agreement on the fundamental principles of the common law; lack of precision in the use of legal terms; conflicting and badly drawn statutory provisions; attempted distinction between cases where the facts present no distinction in the legal principles applicable; the great volume of recorded decisions; ignorance of judges and lawyers; the number and nature of novel legal questions. Of all these causes, the weightiest, I fancy, is the multiplication of decisions. The fecundity of our case law would make Malthus stand aghast."—Cardozo, *The Growth of The Law* (New Haven, 1924) 3–4.

[19] Swift, *A Digest of the Law of Evidence* (Hartford, 1810) ix.

[20] Story, *Address to the Suffolk Bar, September 4, 1821* (1829) 1 Am. Jurist 1, 31.

[21] 1 Dane, *A General Abridgment and Digest of American Law* (Boston, 1823) xiv.

[22] 1 Kent, *Commentaries on American Law* (ed. 1; New York, 1826) 442.

[23] *Report of the Committee on Law Reporting to the Association of the Bar of the City of New York* (New York, 1873) 6.

[24] In this paper, *The Future of Our Profession*, Mr. Shirley stated:

"We have a multiplicity of reports, and they crowd upon us like the pests of Egypt.

"A century ago there was not a single volume of reported cases published in the United States. Ninety years ago there were but two small volumes. To-day we have at least 3,100 volumes. They are increasing at the rate of about 100 volumes annually.... At this rate, with its natural acceleration, how shall we stand a century or even fifty years hence? But this is not all. Our courts constantly turn to the reports of the mother country and her dependencies. These number about 2,400, and are rapidly increasing.... Few things are more absurd to any good lawyer or judge than the idea that, with a mass of other work pressing upon him, he can read, much less understand, two or three volumes of reports a week."—(1883) 6 A. B. A. Rep. 195, 209–210.

[25] In 1884, the annual address to the American Bar Association was given by Judge John F. Dillon, to the theme, *American Institutions and Laws*. In this address, the problems arising from the condition of the laws and precedents were pointedly emphasized:

"The statutes," it was pointed out, "are frequently fragmentary, 'cross and intricate,' superimposed one upon another. Case-law has to be sought in almost numberless reports and often among conflicting decisions. *Our law is thus fairly open to the three-fold criticism of want of certainty, want of publicity, and want of convenience.* Its existing condition urgently calls for some remedy, if any practicable and expedient remedy exists."—(1884) 7 A. B. A. Rep. 203, 226–227.

The committee referred to was appointed in 1884 (*ibid.* 75), and the report submitted to the Association in 1885 constitutes an exhaustive and extremely suggestive study of the delay and uncertainty in the administration of justice. The report is printed in (1885) 8 *ibid.* 323–449. Discussion thereof, *ibid.* 42–62, 67–84. The subject of the codification of the laws was referred back to the committee (*ibid.* 84), which submitted a second exhaustive report in 1886 ([1886] 9 *ibid.* 325–502). The discussion of this report (*ibid.* 11–74), disclosed the existing variety of views as to the extent to which codification of the laws of the United States was deemed possible or desirable and resulted in the passage of the following resolution, the vote being 58 to 41:

"The law itself should be reduced, so far as its substantive principles are settled, to the form of a statute."—(1886) 9 *ibid.* 74.

An account of these proceedings in the Association and of the problems created by the mass of the law, is given in the work by Judge Dillon, who was a member of these committees, *The Laws and Jurisprudence of England and America* (Boston, 1895) 242–292. See especially pp. 244–255.

[26] Root, Address at organization meeting of the American Law Institute (1923) 1 Am. L. Inst. Proc., Part II, at p. 48.

Mention should be made of two committees of the American Bar Association, which were appointed to consider various aspects of the problems of the simplification of the law. The first was the committee on the classification and restatement of the law, as it was eventually termed, which was originally appointed in 1888 ([1888] 11 A. B. A. Rep. 19, 22) in response to a letter from Mr. Henry T. Terry, suggesting the need of a scientific arrangement of American law ([1889] 12 *ibid.* 327–338). This committee submitted extensive reports in 1891 ([1891] 14 *ibid.* 379–408), and in 1902 ([1902] 25 *ibid.* 425–475), and was apparently discontinued after 1907. In 1917, the committee was reinstated, presumably as a result of the suggestions in Mr. Root's annual address to the Association at the previous annual meeting ([1916] 41 *ibid.* 355, 364–366). In 1919, the committee recommended that "plans for a general conference of scholars and jurists to consider the subject" of classification and restatement of the law be submitted to the executive committee of the Association ([1919] 44 *ibid.* 261). In 1920, at the instance of the committee, of which Mr. James DeWitt Andrews was then chairman, the Association passed a resolution authorizing such steps to be taken "as may be deemed necessary and expedient to co-operate with any body which has for its purpose the carrying on of the proposed work of classification and restatement of law" ([1920] 45 *ibid.* 84). The plan which the committee had in mind was that the Association should coöperate with the tentative American Academy of Jurisprudence, which had been projected in 1913 (see [1920] 6 A. B. A. J. 426; Andrews, *Jurisprudence* [New York, 1913] 1), and it is contemplated that:

"The proposed restatement must be looked at as a task to be undertaken after the classification has been agreed upon; that is, after the analytical and synthetical work of discovering the order and relationship of the elementary concepts of the law....

"When this step has been taken the work of restatement consists in filling in of the framework or outline produced by the classification with the details which constitute the actual law of each and every of the several subjects outlined in the classification" ([1920] 6 A. B. A. J. 420, 423). In 1921, the executive committee of the Association resolved in principle that the Association should coöperate with the so-called Academy of Jurisprudence, subject to reference of specific plans to the Association ([1921] 46 A. B. A. Rep. 482). In 1922, the special committee presented to the Association a plan to have the work proposed undertaken by a publishing company to be organized for the purpose and to be financed by subscriptions of $800 ([1922] 47 *ibid.* 391) but, at the suggestion of the executive committee of the Association, this plan was not endorsed, presumably, as Mr. Andrews suggested, on account of activities of the committee sponsored by the Association of American Law Schools (*ibid.* 82–95). In consequence of this action, the committee on classification apparently became defunct, its last report being made in 1924 ([1924] 49 *ibid.* 39), and the plans proposed having been superseded by the establishment of the American Law Institute.

It should be added that, in 1924, a preliminary report on the classification of the law was submitted to the council of the American Law Institute by Dean Pound. This report will be found in (1924) 2 Am. L. Inst. Proc. 379–425.

The second committee of the Association deserving notice in this connection, is the committee on law reporting and digesting, which was appointed in 1894 ([1894] 17 A. B. A. Rep. 72), at the suggestion of Mr. J. Newton Fiero, by whom the matter had been brought to the attention of the New York State Bar Association in 1891 (Fiero, *Can the Present System of Reporting the Decisions of the Courts of This State Be Substantially Improved, and If So, By What Method?* [1891] 14 N. Y. State B. A. Rep. 173–178; see also [1892] 15 *ibid.* 100; [1893] 16 *ibid.* 51. This discussion in the New York

State Bar Association led to the provision for a miscellaneous reporter, appointed by the governor (*Laws of New York* [1892] c. 598). In 1895, the committee appointed by the American Bar Association made an extensive report, advocating improved and more uniform law reports ([1895] 18 A. B. A. Rep. 343–366). Thereafter, the committee made annual reports until 1919, when it was apparently discontinued in consequence of the adoption of a motion that an association of law reporters be formed.—[1919] 44 *ibid.* 30.

27 "This inundation of books, made in different States and nations, will increase, until we can shake off more of our local notions. Our true course is plain, that is, by degrees to make our laws more uniform and national, especially where there is nothing to make them otherwise, but local feelings and prejudices. We have in the common and federal law, the materials of national uniformity in numerous cases. We have a national judiciary, promoting this uniformity; and we have lawyers, learned, industrious, and able, to second this judiciary. We only want a general efficient plan, supported with zeal, energy, and national feelings."—Dane, *op. cit. supra* note 21, p. xv.

28 See Article I of the constitution of the American Bar Association ([1878] 1 A. B. A. Rep. 30). At the first meeting of the Association in 1878, the committee on commercial law was instructed to report at the next annual session upon the law in the several states, "touching the form and requisites of negotiable or commercial paper," and to furnish suggestions "as to the propriety and expediency of action on the part of the Association, looking toward further uniformity in the law on that subject." At the same time, the committee on jurisprudence and law reform was instructed to report similarly on the law as to the authentication of instruments conveying land and the requisites with respect to the execution of wills (*ibid.* 26–27), and in 1879 on the laws as to marriage and divorce, the common purpose of both committees being to secure uniformity in the legislation on these subjects ([1879] 2 *ibid.* 18). In 1882, the latter committee reported two proposed uniform acts, dealing with acknowledgments and fraudulent divorces; upon the instruction of the Association these acts were recommended to the legislatures of the various States for adoption and with some success ([1882] 5 *ibid.* 283–308; [1883] 6 *ibid.* 38–39). In 1886, the committee in a report considered the law as to settlement of estates without recommending uniform legislation ([1886] 9 *ibid.* 294–311). See also (1888) 11 *ibid.* 47–58, 307–321, for the committee's proposed act as to foreign marriages.

The committee on commercial law failed to report as instructed in 1878, but, in 1887, in pursuance of a reference at the previous session ([1886] 9 *ibid.* 79, 505–509), the committee submitted an extensive report, examining the powers of Congress under the Interstate Commerce clause and recommending the enactment by Congress of three proposed bills looking to uniformity in legislation, a bill to establish a uniform system of bankruptcy, a bill to regulate the collection of interstate debts, and a bill to codify the law relating to bills of exchange of an interstate character ([1887] 10 *ibid.* 332–395). In 1889, the Association authorized the committee to present the matter to Congress ([1889] 12 *ibid.* 23–35). It may be noted in passing that the first two of these measures were provided for in the act to establish a uniform system of bankruptcy, enacted by Congress in 1898, and now in force, while the third is covered by the uniform negotiable instruments law, approved by the conference of commissioners on uniform state laws (1896) and since adopted by all jurisdictions in the United States.

29 Taylor, *Inter-State Code Commission* (1881) 1 Ala. State B. A. Rep. 210. The conception of an interstate code commission had been suggested in detail in an article presumably written by John Livingston and published in 1851 (*National Jurisprudence* [1851] 3 U. S. L. Mag. 125, 133).

A committee on correspondence of the Alabama Association, it may be noted, interested itself in 1886 and 1887 in advocating uniform state legislation, including especially the enactment of the English Bills of Exchange Act, by circular letters to other bar associations ([1894] 17 Ala. State B. A. Rep. 145–148; [1888] 9 Ohio State B. A. Rep. 31–33). In 1881, an earlier committee took up, with other bar associations, the possibility of some organization to work for uniform laws [1926] 19 Vt. B. A. Proc. 138, Statement by Mr. George B. Young; [1881] 1 Ala. State B. A. Rep. 177).

[80] See (1888) Ohio State B. A. Rep. 32–38, 77–95; (1889) 10 *ibid.* 166–169 (annual address by J. J. Moore); (1888) 22 Am. L. Rev. 271, 614, 767, 929; (1890) 24 *ibid.* 126. At the meeting of the National Bar Association in 1889, three uniform acts were approved for recommendation to the state legislatures (*ibid.*, and see [1890] 11 Ohio State B. A. Rep. 22–25, 55–84). This association apparently died from inanition after the meeting in 1892, when the national conference of commissioners on uniform state laws first met. See also (1888) 11 A. B. A. Rep. 23–26.

[81] See the suggestion of L. B. McFarland, as president of the Tennessee Bar Association ([1889] 23 Am. L. Rev. 819), to the effect suggested, and its adoption by the American Bar Association ([1889] 12 A. B. A. Rep. 50–51). For an analogous proposal by Governor Hill of New York, see (1889) 23 Am. L. Rev. 121.

[82] *Laws of New York* (1890) c. 205. For the discussion and approval of this development by the American Bar Association, see (1890) 13 A. B. A. Rep. 29–30, 48–52, 336–337; (1891) 14 *ibid.* 51–53, 365–375. See also Snyder, *The Problem of Uniform Legislation in the United States* (1892) 15 *ibid.* 287, 289: Jones, *Uniformity of Laws through National and Interstate Codification* (1894) 6 Va. State B. A. Rep. 157, 167–169; Young, *Uniform State Laws* (1926) 19 Vt. B. A. Proc. 137–154; National Conference of Commissioners on Uniform State Laws, *Handbook* (1933; Washington) 465–467.

[83] For a report of the proceedings at the first conference, at which seven states were represented, see (1893) 16 N. J. L. J. 10–16.

Lists of the acts which have been drafted and approved by the conference, and by the jurisdictions in which they have been adopted are given in the 1933 *Handbook* of the conference cited in the previous note, pp. 503–518. The five acts, which have been adopted in a majority of jurisdictions, are: the negotiable instruments act, approved in 1896 and adopted in all fifty-three jurisdictions; the warehouse receipts act, approved in 1906 and adopted in forty-eight jurisdictions, the sales act, approved in 1906 and adopted in thirty-four jurisdictions; the bills of lading act, approved in 1909 and adopted in twenty-nine jurisdictions; the veterans' guardianship act, approved in 1928 and adopted in thirty-three jurisdictions. Of the remaining forty-eight acts on the approved list in 1933, twelve had been adopted in more than fifteen jurisdictions. The foregoing figures are as given in the 1933 *Handbook*.

[84] See the remarks to the conference in 1927 by Mr. Gilbert H. Montague.—National Conference of Commissioners on Uniform State Laws, *Handbook* (1927) 270–305.

[85] See the remarks of Charles T. Terry in his address as president of the conference in 1914, *ibid.* (1914) 106, 127 ff.; Hargest, *Keeping the Uniform State Laws Uniform* (1927) 76 U. of Pa. L. Rev. 178–184.

[86] (1915) 15 Ass'n of Am. L. Schools, Proc. at p. 84.

[87] Root, Address at organization meeting of the American Law Institute (1923) 1 Am. L. Inst. Proc., Part II at p. 48.

[88] "To hope that such a mass of precedent can be penetrated even with the aid of digests and glossators or that there could be extracted from it any harmonious and workable legal doctrine is to disregard the teachings of experience and to indulge, Micawber-like, in the illusion that something, we know not what, will turn up to remedy the growing difficulties of our situation."—Stone, *Some Aspects of the Problem of Law Simplification* (1923) 23 Col. L. Rev. 318, 319.

[39] *The Passion for Uniformity* in *International Law and Some Current Illusions* (New York, 1924) 316 at pp. 331 ff.

[40] *Ibid.* 336.

[41] For the position taken by the American Law Institute with respect to this aspect of the problem, see (1923) 1 Am. L. Inst. Proc. p. 14 and the discussion below, particularly notes 78 and 89 *infra.*

[42] Thus, in the epoch-making paper, *The Need of a Sociological Jurisprudence,* published in 1907, Dean Pound declared:

"It is sometimes assumed that law must needs aim at a different kind of justice from what is commonly understood and regarded by the community. But this cannot be. Law is a means, not an end. Such a divergence cannot endure unless the law is in the hands of a progressive and enlightened caste whose conceptions are in advance of the public and whose leadership is bringing popular thought to a higher level. When, instead, law is in the hands of a highly cautious and conservative profession, whose thought on such matters lags behind, the divergence provokes irritation at law and disregard of its mandates."—(1907) 19 Green Bag 607, 612.

The problem is that of securing a proper balance between certainty and flexibility in the application of the rules of law to specific cases. In a subsequent article, Dean Pound has suggested that such a balance, appropriate to American conditions, can in some degree be secured by a combination of summary procedure and strict, but scientific, rules of law. "If in the final result," he states, "the relations of the parties have been adjusted in strict accordance with the rules of substantive law, an oriental directness of procedure can hurt no one."—*Enforcement of Law* (1908) 20 *ibid.* 401, 408.

[43] Cardozo, *The Nature of the Judicial Process* (New Haven, 1925) 18–19.

[44] See for example, Bentham, *Rationale of Judicial Evidence,* Book VIII, c. 24, in 7 *Works* (Bowring, 1843) 309–311. The point of view is epitomized as follows:

"Jurisprudential law—the imaginary law extracted by each man for himself out of a mass of jurisprudence—is a vast hot-bed of uncertainty. By statute law, in proportion as it extends, keeping clear of entanglement with jurisprudential law, that most poisonous of all weeds is extirpated."—*Ibid.* 310. See also the comment in Bentham's tract, *Truth v. Ashhurst,* in 5 *Works,* 230, 235.

A more restrained and classical exposition of the pro-codification argument is to be found in Austin, *Lectures on Jurisprudence* (ed. 5; London, 1885) 620–681. See also Amos, *An English Code, Its Difficulties and the Modes of Overcoming Them* (London, 1873). For the views of Field, see his *Speeches, Arguments, and Miscellaneous Papers* (ed. Sprague; New York, 1884) I, 219–383 *passim.*

[45] Carter, *op. cit. supra* note 8, p. 14. *Cf. ibid.* 20, and his address, *Provinces of the Written and Unwritten Law* (1889) 2 Va. State B. A. Rep. 95–137. It should be remarked that James C. Carter regarded a good digest of the law, as contrasted with a code, as a work that would be "of priceless value."—*Ibid.* 125.

[46] "Atque quindecim invenies sive libros sive tractatus, totidemque etiam (praeter compendia) relationum justa volumina de communi nostro jure scripta."—3 Coke's Reports (ed. 1826), Preface, at p. viii.

[47] 6 Spedding, *The Letters and the Life of Francis Bacon* (London, 1872) 64, where Bacon's Proposition, etc., touching the compiling and amendment of the Laws of England, is reproduced (pp. 61–71). And see 5 *ibid.* 84–86. For Bacon's more detailed analysis of the problems involved in the uncertainty of law, see the aphorisms appended to the *De Augmentis Scientiarum,* in 1 Spedding, *The Works of Francis Bacon* (London, 1870) 814–827.

[48] 1 Coke's Reports (ed. 1926), Preface, at p. xxix.

[49] 6 Spedding, *Letters and Life of Francis Bacon* 65.

[50] See Pollock, *A First Book of Jurisprudence* (ed. 6, London, 1929) 361 *et seq.* for a brief summary.

[51] For Lord Westbury's project and the commissions appointed in 1866 and 1870, see Dillon, *op. cit. supra* note 25, pp. 276–280. See also the article by Wickersham, who has been, since its establishment, president of the American Law Institute, *The American Law Institute and the Projected Restatement of the Common Law in America* (1927) 43 L. Q. Rev. 449, 451 ff.

[52] See 1 Halsbury's *Laws of England* (London, 1907) at p. ccxvi.

[53] For a discussion of the extent to which English law, despite the extent to which it has been covered by statutes, is still fundamentally judge-made, see Dicey, *Law & Public Opinion in England during the Nineteenth Century* (London, 1914) 486 ff.

[54] In the Preface (p. x) to the fourth part of the Reports, after giving a qualified approval to the scheme to consolidate and amend the penal statutes, Coke states: "Quod vero ad reductionem Juris Communis in commodiorem Methodum attinet, de illius laboris fructu plurimum dubito; illud scio, quod compendiae in multis quidem scientiis authoribus ipsis profuerunt, verum aliis (praesertim ut nunc usurpantur) non mediocriter obfuerunt." For translation as given by the translator, see *infra,* at note 95

Bacon states in the Proposition referred to above in note 47:

"In all sciences, they are soundest that keep close to particulars; and sure I am there are more doubts that rise upon our statutes, which are a text law, than upon the common law, which is no text law. But howsoever that question be determined, I dare not advise to cast the law into a new mould. The work which I propound tendeth to proyning and grafting the law, and not to ploughing up and planting it again; for such a remove I should hold indeed for a perilous innovation."—*Op. cit.* 67.

[55] In the work referred to in note 50 *supra,* reference is made to the more important of the acts, relating especially to public law and to commercial law, in which codification has proved relatively successful (pp. 364 ff.).

[56] "It were to be wished that some compleat *Corpus Juris Communis* were extracted out of the many Books of our *English* laws, for the publick use, and for the contracting of the Laws into a narrower compass and method, at least for ordinary study. But this is a work of time, and requires many industrious and judicious Hands and Heads to assist in it."—Rolle's *Abridgment* (London, 1668), at the fifth page of the preface. (Reprinted in 1 *Collectanea Juridica* [London, 1791] at p. 263, 272).

See also the anecdote in Burnet, *Life and Death of Sir Matthew Hale* (London, 1682) at p. 73:

"Upon this hint, some pressed him [Hale] to Compile a Body of the English Law; it could hardly ever be done by a Man who knew it better, and would with more Judgment and industry have put it into Method; But he said, *"As it was a Great and Noble Design, which would be of vast Advantage to the Nation; so it was too much for a private Man to undertake: It was not be entered upon, but by the Command of a Prince, and with the Communicated Endeavours of some of the most Eminent of the Profession."*

[57] (1924) 2 Am. L. Inst. Proc. at p. 21 (address of President Wickersham).

[58] Thus, in the year 1927, out of a total expenditure of approximately $130,000 disbursed toward the work of the Institute (exclusive of the items connected with the model code of criminal procedure), $15,000 more or less was expended in the form of *honoraria* to the thirty or forty legal advisers who assisted the reporters in the seven fields of law being restated. This expenditure was supplemented by about $8,500 for

legal assistants, while the salaries paid to the reporters (six), totaled $29,000. For further details of the budgets of the Institute for 1927 and 1928, see the director's report to the council in December, 1927, and the condensed reports of the treasurer ([1928] 6 Am. L. Inst. Proc. 128 ff., 299–300; [1929] 7 *ibid.* 31). Owing to a change in publication policy in 1928, the details of budgets for years subsequent to 1928 have not been printed. The latest of the very condensed reports by the treasurer is for 1931 ([1932] 10 *ibid.* 36).

59 For the appointment of Dean Herbert F. Goodrich to this office, see (1928) 6 *ibid.* 150 (December 14, 1927).

60 For example, two of the present justices of the Supreme Court of the United States have been, and two other justices of the same Court, are at present members of the council. Various others have held high offices. According to the information available, the present council of thirty-three members is composed as follows: twenty lawyers in active practice; eleven judges; two from the schools of law. Of the eleven judges, six are from the federal courts and five from the state judiciaries. The membership of the council as last published appears in (1932) 10 Am. L. Inst. Proc. 345. For its methods of work, see (1927) 5 *ibid.* 125–127.

61 The four reporters originally selected have thus been characterized by the president of the Institute, Mr. George W. Wickersham (*op. cit. supra* note 51, p. 462):

"Professor Samuel Williston, of Harvard University, is perhaps the best known and most highly esteemed law teacher in the country, and the best author of a standard work on contracts. He was retained to act as reporter in preparing a restatement on the law of contracts. Scarcely less highly considered is Professor Joseph H. Beale, of the same University. He was retained to act as reporter in preparing a restatement of the conflict of laws. Professor Francis H. Bohlen, of the University of Pennsylvania (later of Harvard), is one of the younger law teachers who has established a high reputation in dealing with the law of torts. He was retained to prepare a restatement of that subject. Professor Floyd R. Mechem, of the Law School of Chicago University, is the author of a standard work on the law of agency. He was accordingly retained to prepare the restatement on that subject." See also note 67 below.

62 Wickersham, *op. cit. supra* note 51, p. 461.

63 *Loc. cit.* See also the statement by President Wickersham in his annual address as president of the Institute in 1927 ([1927] 5 Am. L. Inst. Proc. 109), and the statement of the director, Mr. Lewis.—*Ibid.* 119 ff.

64 *Address of President Wickersham* (1933) 19 A. B. A. J. 327. Since this was written a subsequent arrangement, involving a further gift of $638,000, has been announced (1934) 20 *ibid.* 335 ff.

65 See the statement by the director in 1928 ([1928] 6 Am. L. Inst. Proc. 295–296; and also his statement in 1931 ([1931] 9 *ibid.* 61). As the statement last cited indicates, $30,000 of the total sum was appropriated to assist the state bar associations in their study of the model code of criminal procedure with a view to facilitating its adoption by the state legislatures.

66 As indicated above in note 26, the original plan of the committee of the American Bar Association on the classification and restatement of the law, was, as suggested in its report of 1920, to give priority to the proper classification of the law and, when that was determined, to restate the law by filling in "the framework or outline produced by the classification."

The reasons for the abandonment of this plan by the American Law Institute are thus indicated in the report which led to its establishment:

"It is not merely that such classification and terminology would necessarily take many years to prepare, though that in itself is a serious objection to this method of proceeding, because it would so far postpone any practical results as to make the establishment of the Institute improbable. The fundamental objection is that a complete and satisfactory classification and terminology can more certainly be produced as the result of actual experience in the work of restating the different subjects."—(1923) 1 Am. L. Inst. Proc. at p. 46.

At an early stage, however, Dean Roscoe Pound, of Harvard University, was designated as special adviser on this problem (*ibid.* Part III 41), and his preliminary report, submitted in February, 1924 ([1924] 2 *ibid.* 379–425), confirmed the policy which had been adopted. As he stated with reference to this report:

"Classification must flow from a deep study of the common law and not the statement of the common law flow from any classification, and, more especially, from any so-called universal classification which has grown up for the purpose of a radically different legal system" (*ibid.* 58–60). See also *ibid.* 28–30, 253; (1925) 3 *ibid.* 124 ff. See also Pound, *Classification of Law* (1924) 37 Harv. L. Rev. 933–969; *Classification of Law* ([1924] 5 Ann. L. School Rev. 269–278), and the discussion of this address (*ibid.* 321–323); and also the references in note 26 above.

[67] The reporters for the several restatements undertaken are as follows: *Contracts*, Professor Samuel Williston, of Harvard; *Conflict of Laws*, Professor Joseph H. Beale, of Harvard; *Torts*, Professor Francis H. Bohlen, of the University of Pennsylvania; *Agency*, Professor Floyd R. Mechem, of the University of Chicago and, after his death in December, 1928, Professor Warren A. Seavey, of Harvard; *Business Associations*, Mr. William Draper Lewis, director of the Institute, formerly of the University of Pennsylvania; *Property*, Professor (now Dean) Harry A. Bigelow, of the University of Chicago, succeeded upon his resignation in 1929 by Professor Richard B. Powell, of Columbia; *Trusts*, Professor Austin W. Scott, of Harvard. Since this was written, the following additional appointments of reporters have been announced: *Rights in Land*, Dean Everett Fraser, of the University of Minnesota; *Constructive Trusts*, Professor Austin W. Scott, of Harvard; *Quasi Contracts*, Professor Warren A. Seavey, of Harvard; *Sales of Land*, Professor Samuel Williston, of Harvard.

[68] (1930) 8 Am. L. Inst. Proc. 50 ff.

[69] *Op. cit.* at p. 52. See also the director's comment in 1931, (1931) 9 *ibid.* 55.

[70] These have been published by the American Law Institute Publishers, an association of the American Law Institute, the West Publishing Company, and the Lawyers' Coöperative Publishing Company.

[71] A recent account of the progress which has been made is given in the summary of the director's report at the annual meeting of the Institute in May, 1933.—(1933) 19 A. B. A. J. 320 ff. And see the more recent statement of the director, (1934) 20 *ibid.* 336 ff.

[72] Goodrich, *The Work of the American Law Institute, in Progress of the Law* (March, 1928) 136 Ann. Am. Acad. Pol. and Soc. Sci. 10, 12.

[73] See the remarks in the report which led to the establishment of the Institute.—(1923) 1 Am. L. Inst. Proc. 48 ff.

[74] (1924) 2 *ibid.* 34, 44–45, and see the discussion in the report referred to in the preceding note at pp. 19 ff. As there proposed, at p. 19:

"The chief characteristic of the form of presentation should be the separation by typographical or other device of the statement of the principles of law from the analysis of the legal problems involved, the statement of the present condition of the law and the reasons in support of the principles as stated."

And also, at p. 22:

"The work should contain a complete citation of authorities, decisions, treatises and articles. The legal profession will never have confidence in the result unless those responsible for the work give this tangible proof of care and thereby also show that they know and have set forth any differences between the law expressed in the statement of principles and that found in the decisions of the courts in each State considered separately. In view of the present great volume of the sources of American law this examination and setting forth of authorities will entail much labor and materially affect the details of the organization necessary to carry on the work."

[75] (1924) 2 *ibid.* 35–36.

[76] In 1925, the council of the Institute resolved that it was not advisable to submit with the tentative drafts of the restatements "complete paralleling treatises repeating everything that is said in the Restatements, with full citations of cases bearing on every statement made" ([1925] 3 *ibid.* 416, 405–410. For further discussion, see [1926] 4 *ibid.* (Appendix) 28–29, 47–50; [1927] 5 *ibid.* 103–107; [1928] 6 *ibid.* 39, 96). In 1928, the council resolved to publish "explanatory notes" in connection with the publication of an official draft of the restatements ([1928] 6 *ibid.* 242), upon the statement of the director that "what is needed are explanatory notes, not in connection with each section, but in connection with those sections selected by the Council in which the Council believe some explanation other than that contained in the Restatements themselves should be made to the profession as to why the rule of law in the section is worded as it is" (*ibid.* 234). At the meeting of the Institute in 1933, President Wickersham stated:

"As time went on, it became increasingly evident that if the publication of the restatements were to await the preparation of treatises to accompany them, another decade would be required for the accomplishment of the task. Accordingly, the Council, on February 25, 1932, approved the recommendation of the Executive Committee that the Restatement of Contracts be published without commentaries, treatises or explanatory notes."—(1933) 19 A. B. A. J. 329.

[77] This is particularly true of the Restatement of the Law of Contracts, since the reporter in this subject, Professor Williston, is also the author of the standard American treatise.

For the proposal to supplement the restatements by state annotations of local decisions and the appointment of Dean Goodrich as adviser on professional and public relations, see (1928) 6 Am. L. Inst. Proc. 41 ff., 122–127, 234–238, 289–295. Information as to the progress made in the preparation of state annotations and also extensive bibliographical notices will be found in the various reports of the adviser (*ibid.* 169–172, 240–242, 303–308; [1929] 7 *ibid.* 55–64; [1930] 8 *ibid.* 57–67; [1931] 9 *ibid.* 64–76; [1932] 10 *ibid.* 52–63; [1933] 19 A. B. A. J. 322–324); (1934) 20 *ibid.* 338 ff.

[78] The expressions defining the policy of the Institute on this essential point, it must be confessed, do not speak *una voce*. According to the original report which led to the establishment of the Institute, "The object of the restatement to be undertaken by the Institute is to improve the law, not merely by clarifying and simplifying it, but also by better adapting it to existing needs. The Institute must not only ascertain what the law is but what it ought to be, bearing in mind that the changes advocated should be confined to those designed to carry out the policies which are generally admitted to be desirable and which do not touch subjects of general public controversy" (1 Am. L. Inst. Proc. 55–56). Accordingly, it was contemplated that an important part of the bureau of research which was originally envisaged, should be to conduct legal surveys as to the operation of specific legal rules.—*Ibid.* 56.

It is apparent, however, that this view was modified early in the development of the process of restatement of the law, perhaps in connection with the formulation of the conclusions as to what the restatements should contain, which, as indicated above in the text, occurred in 1923. See note 75 *supra*. In any event, the question was alluded to in various connections at the annual meeting in 1925, and the very understanding comment of Mr. Justice Cardozo, who presided at the meeting, as well as the expressions of the director and of Professors Williston, Beale, Scott, and Bohlen, who reported to the meeting ([1925] 3 *ibid.* 98–100, 159, 222, 230, 270–273, 282–285), confirm the statement of Mr. W. H. Washington, "this restatement... is to be a concrete restatement concisely made, in different sections, of the common law as it is today in the United States" (*ibid.* 273), a statement which was subsequently quoted with approval by President Wickersham.—[1927] 5 *ibid.* 104.

It needs scarcely be explained that this conception of the restatement as a formulation of "the law as it is" requires rationalization of the precedents and not mere mechanical reliance on the weight of authority. As Professor Beale suggested, "It is undoubtedly true that if we take our law from the decision of the courts alone, we are writing the law of yesterday, and what we ought to do is to write the law of today" ([1925] 3 *ibid.* 233). But, as the director has explained, "We are not reforming the law. We are stating and clarifying the law. Now in that process we find in a large number of cases that with the overwhelming weight, or perhaps the universal weight, of decided cases under situations which are practically identical or are identical with what is stated in the Restatement, there is no problem. But we sometimes have another problem—the problem where the cases are conflicting.... We have always taken the position that we should express what we believe to be the correct American law.... The real issue as I see it before the group is not whether we should make new law.... It was whether as lawyers, if they were now judges sitting on the bench and the case was presented in a court which was not controlled by any one jurisdiction, what would they decide" ([1931] 9 *ibid.* 100–101). And see earlier statements to the same effect by the director ([1924] 2 *ibid.* 49–50; [1925] 3 *ibid.* 270–273; [1927] 5 *ibid.* 193–194). See also the references in note 89 *infra*.

79 See the director's statement ([1928] 6 Am. L. Inst. Proc. 40). For discussion of the basis of the authority of the restatement, see (1923) 1 *ibid.* 23–28 (Part I), 51 (Part II); (1924) 2 Am. L. Inst. Proc. 21, 36–38, 89. And see the penetrating consideration of the problem in the article by Mr. Justice (then Dean) Stone, cited above in note 38, where it is suggested, at p. 335:

"If we may assume that a restatement of the law or a portion of it may be prepared by the cooperative effort of a body of experts in such form and with such content as to commend itself to the profession at large, then it may be asked that it receive legislative recognition and sanction, not as a body of legal rules and doctrine imposed on the courts and litigants as a formal statute or code, but as 'an aid and guide' to the courts in formulating legal rules, with full liberty reserved to them to accept and follow any of the precepts of the restatement when they conflict with precedents but without making such action mandatory."

In the report which led to the establishment of the Institute, this suggestion was referred to as "at least an interesting one," but without committing the Institute thereto.—(1923) 1 Am. L. Inst. Proc. 24.

80 "I think we should elicit little enthusiasm for our Academy if we allowed the impression to go forth that it was about to codify the law. The whole project of Codification has been so long in the arena of controversy, it has aroused such antipathies among those who are hostile to it, and is, perhaps in any event, so far reaching, and, it may be, so visionary, that a curse will be upon us from the outset if we adopt such a project as our

own. Codification may come later. It ought not to be our primary aim, our immediate objective."—Cardozo (1921) Ass'n of Am. L. Schools Proc. 119.

81 Davis, 1 Am. L. Inst. Proc., Part II, p. 112.

82 Hughes, Address to the American Law Institute at the annual meeting in 1933, (1933) 19 A. B. A. J. 326.

83 Root, Address at the organization meeting of the American Law Institute, *op. cit. supra* note 81, at p. 51.

84 See note 25 *supra.*

85 Wickersham (1928) 6 Am. L. Inst. Proc. 282. See also (1926) 4 *ibid.* (Appendix) 32; (1929) 7 *ibid.* 36; (1930) 8 *ibid.* 39; *op. cit. supra* note 82, p. 337.

86 See the director's statement. (1924) 2 Am. L. Inst. Proc.

"We are not, indeed, as so many newspaper editors assume we are when they hear of our work, revising the state law of the United States, or of any of the States. Neither are we engaged in the work of the Uniform State Law Commissioners: the work of making uniform the statute law throughout the United States. It may be that in any subject the Reporter may believe that a Restatement of the Law should recommend some small incidental statutory change. He and his Advisers have a right to make such a recommendation. If they should do so, it will be first for the Council, and ultimately for a Meeting of the Institute, to determine whether that suggestion is, or is not, acceptable."

87 Falconbridge, *Contract and Conveyance in the Conflict of Laws* (1933) 81 U. of Pa. L. Rev. 661, 663. See also Cook, *The Law Book of the Future* (1923) 21 Mich. L. Rev. 365.

88 In commenting upon the character of the Restatement of the Law, Mr. Justice Cardozo remarked at the annual meeting in 1925 ([1925] 3 Am. L. Inst. Proc. 99):

"It is hard enough, shunning generalities, or putting them forward as merely approximate hypotheses, to declare the rights and wrongs engendered by a concrete situation, definitely envisaged. It is harder still when, abandoning particulars, we must announce in magisterial tones the rationalizing principle in which particulars are enveloped, the co-ordinating rule under which they are subsumed. This is the high emprize on which the scholars of the Institute have ventured."

89 The necessity of restating the law in progressive terms which will put it abreast of the times, a consideration which, as suggested above in the discussion, has been emphasized by sociological jurisprudence, was envisaged and in some measure provided for in the plan, as originally conceived, for the work of the American Law Institute. As indicated above in note 78, the report which led to the establishment of the Institute anticipated the creation of a bureau of research, a chief function of which would be to conduct surveys, particularly on questions relating to the administration of justice and also as to the operation of substantive rules of law, where it was deemed desirable to have such information as a criterion of decisions to be made between conflicting rules in their restatement.—1 Am. L. Inst. Proc. 55–56.

In delineating the nature of the proposed restatement of the law, the report definitely states that its object "should not only be to help make certain much that is now uncertain and to simplify unnecessary complexities, but also to promote those changes which will tend better to adapt the law to the needs of life. The character of the restatement which we have in mind can be best described by saying that it should be at once analytical, critical and constructive."—*Ibid.* 14.

It was, however, quite properly recognized in the report that there is a definite limitation as to the extent to which, in a restatement of the law, the law could appropriately be defined so as to adapt it to the needs of life. "Changes in the law which are, or which would, if proposed, become a matter of general public concern and discussion should not be considered, much less set forth, in any restatement of the law such as we have in mind. Changes which do not fall under the ban of this limitation, and which will carry out more efficiently ends generally accepted as desirable are within the province of the restatement to suggest."—*Ibid.* 15.

Shortly after the organization of the Institute, consideration was given to this part of the plan and, in August, 1923, the council of the Institute resolved that it was sound method to base its choice between conflicting rules upon the practical working of the alternatives. In the same resolution, the executive committee and the director were authorized and directed to take advice as to the questions which should be so investigated and as to the most practical methods for the fact-finding which would be involved. This resolution apparently died a natural death by reference to a subcommittee, and this difficult but essential portion of the original plan was thus inferentially eliminated.—(1924) 2 *ibid.* 115, 130, 138.

For discussions of the policy which was shortly thereafter formulated, implicitly excluding objective research from the program, see the various references cited above in notes 75 and 78. Illuminating discussions as to the basis on which decision should be made between conflicting rules in situations such as would have been covered by the resolution of the council noted above, are to be found in (1925) 3 *ibid.* 368–374; (1927) 5 *ibid.* 193–197; (1931) 9 *ibid.* 86–103, 148–153.

[90] See notes 74, 76, and 77 above. As indicated in note 76, the decision to postpone indefinitely the preparation and publication of treatises has not been made without misgivings and is attributable immediately to the exigencies encountered in the work of restating the law. That, in addition, the decision may have been influenced by a discovery of a difficulty of squaring the existing principles of law, as they have been conceived, with the precedents on precisely those issues most needing clarification, and by a feeling that it would not promote the uniform reception of the restatements to refer them to the confused mass of authority which it is desired to simplify, is perhaps suggested by the remarks of the director:

"If we are engaged in giving to the profession the confusion of the existing law and the reasons for certain solutions, then these Restatements should be expanded and wholly changed into learned monographs of the law. Now as between that monograph idea and what we are actually doing there is, as you will realize, quite an essential difference that we must straddle, and not try to do both at one time. . . . In sitting in on these conferences of experts in the making of these Tentative Drafts I have found it possible, after we used words in the same sense, and not each one in his own peculiar sense, to bring a group of ten learned experts, to a united conclusion in the great majority of cases. The moment we have tried to state what a particular case stands for we find utter impossibility of united opinion. You can get an individual to write a learned monograph or treatise based on a discussion of the cases, and having put the manuscript before a group of men it is almost impossible to agree on how the thing should be stated and how it should be worked out and whether the discussion of this or that point should be full."—(1928) 6 Am. L. Inst. Proc. 40–41.

[91] *E.g.,* Cook, *The Logical and Legal Bases of the Conflict of Laws* (1924) 33 Yale L. J. 457; Lorenzen, *Territoriality, Public Policy, and the Conflict of Laws, ibid.* 736; Yntema, *The Hornbook Method and the Conflict of Laws* (1928) 37 *ibid.* 468; de Sloovere, *The Local Law Theory and Its Implications in the Conflict of Laws* (1928) 41 Harv. L. Rev. 421; Beale, *Negligence, the Conflict of Laws and the American Law Institute* (1928) 51 N. Y. State B. A. Rep. 179; Cavers, *Critique of the Choice-of-Law Problem* (1933) 47 Harv. L. Rev. 173; Heilman, *Judicial Method and Economic Objectives in Conflict of Laws* (1934) 13 Yale L. J. 1082.

[92] *E.g., Contracts:* Oliphant, *Mutuality of Obligations in Bilateral Contracts at Law* (1925) 25 Col. L. Rev. 705; Williston, *The Effect of One Void Promise in a Bilateral Agreement, ibid.* 857; Whittier, *The Restatement of Contracts and Mutual Assent* (1929) 17 Calif. L. Rev. 441; Corbin, *The Restatement of the Common Law by the American Law Institute* (1929) 15 Iowa L. Rev. 19; Whittier, *The Restatement of Contracts—Again* (1930) *ibid.* 278; idem, *The Restatement of Contracts and Consideration* (1930) 18 Calif. L. Rev. 611; Willis, *Restatement of the Law of Contracts of the American Law Institute* (1932) 7 Ind. L. J. 429. See also articles, reviewing the Restatement of the Law of Contracts upon its publication in 1932, by Dean C. E. Clark (1933) 42 Yale L. J. 643; Patterson (1933) 33 Col. L. Rev. 397; Havighurst (1933) 27 Ill. L. Rev. 910; Goble (1933) 21 Calif. L. Rev. 421; and the book review by Sir Frederick Pollock (1933) 47 Harv. L. Rev. 363.

Trusts: Arnold, *The Restatement of the Law of Trusts* (1931) 31 Col. L. Rev. 800; Scott, *The Restatement of the Law of Trusts, ibid.* 1266.

[93] The articles by Dean C. E. Clark, Professors Patterson and Goble, and the review by Sir Frederick Pollock, cited in the previous note, are suggestive, particularly the first, which emphasizes the cost and queries the importance of the work of the Institute. The late William W. Cook, in considering the problem of the statement of American Law, suggested various defects in the plan of the American Law Institute and expressed a preference for a treatise combining its features with those of Lord Halsbury's *Laws of England.—Legal Research* (1927) 13 Am. B. A. J. 281.

The comment of a former president of the American Bar Association, Mr. Henry Upson Sims, is also worth noting:

"The trouble with restatement is that it doesn't get us anywhere. It is essentially merely the getting together of a new encyclopedia of law; and while it may clarify much of the uncertainty which now exists, it would not modify the law to any substantial extent, for that would not be restatement. And, too, it would not be binding in the fullest sense of the term." *The importance of enacting in Alabama more of the uniform state laws as prepared by the national conference* (1923) 46 Ala. State B. Ass'n Proc. 188.

Various of the criticisms noted in the text have been considered by Mr. Wickersham in his annual addresses as president of the Institute. See (1927) 5 Am. L. Inst. Proc. 106 ff.; (1933) 19 A. B. A. J. 328 ff.

[94] See note 77 *supra.*

[95] Coke, *loc. cit. supra* note 54.

[96] "Reason has a way of playing havoc with 'authority.' But allowing full opportunity for the essential processes of reason, we must not lose sight of the great objective. The law is not an end in itself; it does not exist simply for the play of wits. The law governs the relations of men and women in an ordered society. They are entitled, so far as is humanly possible, to know the rules that govern them and to have these rules applied consistently. Clarity and certainty are thus desirable ends, but they cannot be attained even measurably without coöperative effort, in and out of courts, which seeks to develop a coherent jurisprudence. The authority of the Institute is the authority of a coöperative effort of the most intelligent and expert sort. It stands opposed to mere impressionism. The Restatement will foster analysis, rather than replace it. It will promote examination of principles, rather than discourage it. It will tend to diminish the careless use of digests and cyclopaedias. Focusing attention on definite propositions, it cannot fail to facilitate discussions and improvement.

"The quest of certainty may be endless, and the goal may be unattainable, but progress is practicable. The Institute in securing this expert endeavor in the statement of law is the most helpful agency of that progress."—Hughes (1933) 19 A. B. A. J. 326.

A PARTIAL LIST OF THE PUBLISHED WRITINGS

OF

ORRIN KIP McMURRAY

Changing Conceptions of Law.
3 California Law Review 441, 6 California Bar Association Proceedings 34.

Common Carriers of Goods and Warehousemen.
7 The Commercial Laws of the World 480.

Community Property.
5 California Jurisprudence 261.
1930 Supplement to California Jurisprudence, Appendix.

Community Property System in California, Beginnings of, and *The Adoption of the Common Law.*
3 California Law Review 359.

Factors and Other Private Commercial Agents.
7 The Commercial Laws of the World 454.

Field's Work as Lawyer and Judge in California.
5 California Law Review 87.

First Chief Justice of the Supreme Court of California.
17 California Bar Association Proceedings 84.

Foreign Trade and Legal Progress.
Foreign Trade Lecture Course, Lecture No. 40, 1919.

"Historical Sketch of the Supreme Court of California, An."
In Historical and Contemporary Review of Bench and Bar in California 22.

Inter-Citizenship: A Basis for World Peace.
27 Yale Law Journal 299, 1 Washington Law Review 1.

"Legal and Political Development of the Pacific Coast States."
In Nature and Science on the Pacific Coast, 1915.

Legal Aspects of the Japanese Question.
1 Pacific Review 396.

"Liberty of Testation and Some Modern Limitations Thereon."
In Wigmore Celebration Essays (1919) 536; 14 Illinois Law Review, 96.

Place of Research in the American Law School, The, Address of the President of the Association of American Law Schools.
253 Association of American Law Schools Proceedings 20, 5 American Law School Review 631.

Procedural Reform.
7 California Law Review 147

"Sale of Goods."
In 7 The Commercial Laws of the World 346.

Seventy-Five Years of California Jurisprudence.
13 California Law Review 445, 16 California Bar Association Proceedings 68.

Some Defects in Our Legal Education.
National Education Association Proceedings, August 1915.

Some Tendencies in Constitution Making.
2 California Law Review 203.

Unified Courts.
8 California Bar Association Proceedings 25, 1 Journal of the American Judicature Society 119, 63 Ohio Law Bulletin 161.

www.ingramcontent.com/pod-product-compliance
Ingram Content Group UK Ltd.
Pitfield, Milton Keynes, MK11 3LW, UK
UKHW040233290926
15471UKWH00002B/178

9 780520 32